## *Table 2* Right-tail Critical Values for the *t*-distribution

| DF | $\alpha = .05$ | $\alpha = .025$ | $\alpha = .005$ |
|----|------|-------|--------|
| 1 | 6.314 | 12.706 | 63.657 |
| 2 | 2.920 | 4.303 | 9.925 |
| 3 | 2.353 | 3.182 | 5.841 |
| 4 | 2.132 | 2.776 | 4.604 |
| 5 | 2.015 | 2.571 | 4.032 |
| 6 | 1.943 | 2.447 | 3.707 |
| 7 | 1.895 | 2.365 | 3.499 |
| 8 | 1.860 | 2.306 | 3.355 |
| 9 | 1.833 | 2.262 | 3.250 |
| 10 | 1.812 | 2.228 | 3.169 |
| 11 | 1.796 | 2.201 | 3.106 |
| 12 | 1.782 | 2.179 | 3.055 |
| 13 | 1.771 | 2.160 | 3.012 |
| 14 | 1.761 | 2.145 | 2.977 |
| 15 | 1.753 | 2.131 | 2.947 |
| 16 | 1.746 | 2.120 | 2.921 |
| 17 | 1.740 | 2.110 | 2.898 |
| 18 | 1.734 | 2.101 | 2.898 |
| 19 | 1.729 | 2.093 | 2.861 |
| 20 | 1.725 | 2.086 | 2.845 |
| 21 | 1.721 | 2.080 | 2.831 |
| 22 | 1.717 | 2.074 | 2.819 |
| 23 | 1.714 | 2.069 | 2.807 |
| 24 | 1.711 | 2.064 | 2.797 |
| 25 | 1.708 | 2.060 | 2.787 |
| 26 | 1.706 | 2.056 | 2.779 |
| 27 | 1.703 | 2.052 | 2.771 |
| 28 | 1.701 | 2.048 | 2.763 |
| 29 | 1.699 | 2.045 | 2.756 |
| 30 | 1.697 | 2.042 | 2.750 |
| 40 | 1.684 | 2.021 | 2.704 |
| 50 | 1.676 | 2.009 | 2.678 |
| 60 | 1.671 | 2.000 | 2.660 |
| 70 | 1.667 | 1.994 | 2.648 |
| 80 | 1.664 | 1.990 | 2.639 |
| 90 | 1.662 | 1.987 | 2.632 |
| 100 | 1.660 | 1.984 | 2.626 |
| 110 | 1.659 | 1.982 | 2.621 |
| 120 | 1.658 | 1.980 | 2.617 |
| $\infty$ | 1.645 | 1.960 | 2.576 |

*Source:* This table was generated using the SAS® function TINV

# Undergraduate Econometrics

R. Carter Hill
William E. Griffiths
George G. Judge

John Wiley & Sons, Inc.

*New York • Chichester • Weinheim • Toronto • Singapore • Brisbane*

| ACQUISITIONS EDITOR | Whitney Blake |
| MARKETING MANAGER | Wendy Goldner |
| SENIOR PRODUCTION EDITOR | Jeanine Furino |
| SENIOR DESIGNER | Kevin Murphy |
| MANUFACTURING MANAGER | Dorothy Sinclair |
| ILLUSTRATION COORDINATOR | Jaime Perea |

This book was set in Times Roman by Bi-Comp Incorporated and
printed and bound by Hamilton Printing. The cover was printed by Lehigh Press.

ISBN 0-471-13993-9

Printed in the United States of America

10  9  8  7  6

*Carter Hill dedicates this work to his wife, Melissa Waters*

*Bill Griffiths dedicates this work to his parents,
Noel and Evelyn Griffiths*

*George Judge dedicates this work to Heather Judge Price*

# Preface

*Undergraduate Econometrics* is an elementary book, designed for a one-semester or one-quarter introduction to econometrics. It is intended for undergraduate students who have taken introductory courses in economics and elementary statistics, and an introduction to the ideas of calculus. The tools of calculus are referred to but are not used in any important way. Matrix algebra is not used. Students taking the class are likely to be in their 3rd or 4th undergraduate year, majoring in economics, agricultural economics, finance, accounting or marketing. Our earlier book, *Learning and Practicing Econometrics,* has been popular in the advanced-undergraduate and introductory-graduate econometrics markets. However, its size and its use of matrix algebra made it difficult to use in many introductory econometrics courses. *Undergraduate Econometrics* is clearly focused on the undergraduate student in an introductory course, and is designed with the classroom instructor in mind.

Chapters 1-8 of *Undergraduate Econometrics* cover the core material on simple and multiple regression and provide a foundation for the remainder of the book. Chapters 9-17 are devoted to specific topics in Econometrics and, with minor discomfort, can be taught in any order. We suspect that most courses will cover Chapters 1-11 and then, depending on instructor preference, deal with selected topics in the time remaining.

*Undergraduate Econometrics* introduces econometrics to undergraduate students using an intuitive approach that starts with an economic model. The objective of the book is to show students how economic data are used with economic theory to estimate key economic parameters, test economic hypotheses and predict economic outcomes. We make clear how the economic model, statistical assumptions, estimation and inference procedures, and the data are interdependent links in the process of obtaining empirical information. To achieve this goal the book's chapters will i) begin by identifying a particular economic problem, ii) formulate an economic model consistent with the problem, iii) introduce statistical assumptions describing the data generation process, thus defining the econometric model, iv) identify data that are consistent with the econometric model and note the data's characteristics, v) discuss estimation and inference procedures appropriate for the econometric model, vi) present empirical results and discuss their implications for the economic model, vii) suggest other models and situations in which the inference procedures discussed in the chapter might be appropriate.

The book is *not* an econometrics cookbook, nor is it in a theorem-proof format. It emphasizes motivation, understanding and implementation. Motivation is achieved by introducing very simple economic models and asking economic questions that the student can answer. Understanding is aided by lucid description of techniques, clear interpretation and appropriate applications. Learning is reinforced by doing, with worked examples in the text and exercises at the end of each chapter, with asterisks (*) denoting the more difficult exercises. Numerous supplementary exercises are available in the Instructor's Manual. Many of the exercises involve the student using a sample of data and computer software to answer economic questions. Nonessential algebraic material and some relatively advanced concepts are identified by a border in the margin and end (or begin) with Skippy the Kangaroo, to indicate that they can be skipped without loss of continuity.

A comprehensive Instructor's Manual accompanies the book. It contains solutions to all exercises as well as a computer disk containing data (in an ASCII format) and **SAS** and **SHAZAM** programs for numerical exercises, thus relieving the instructor of a substantial burden. The Instructor's manual also contains teaching hints and supplementary illustrations of textbook material. It also contains brief handouts on the **SAS** and **SHAZAM** commands necessary to execute programs on each topic, and to complete the homework assignments. In addition, PowerPoint slides, created by Professor Lawrence C. Marsh, University of Notre Dame, are available for *Undergraduate Econometrics* and are previewed in the Instructor's manual.

For additional information on *Undergraduate Econometrics* visit the College Home Page at the Web site of John Wiley and Sons: *http://www.wiley.com.* Data files, SAS and SHAZAM commands for examples in the text, and other relevant material, can be downloaded from there.

The authors would like to acknowledge the contributions of several reviewers of this book: Dek Terrell, Louisiana State University; Richard Saba, Auburn University; Andrew Allen and Andrew Narwold, University of San Diego. We would also like to thank a number of special individuals who read early chapter drafts, gave comments and provided information on data sources: Melissa Waters, University of Southwestern Louisiana; Doug McMillin, David Johnson, Asli Ogunc, Janet Daniel, and Omer Ozcicek of Louisiana State University; Lee Adkins, Oklahoma State University; and Jim Chalfant, University of California-Davis. We would like to thank Sue Nano for her expert and patient contribution to the preparation of the manuscript and the Instructor's Manual.

R. Carter Hill
William E. Griffiths
George G. Judge

# Contents

**Chapter 1   The Role of Econometrics in Economic Analysis**      1

1.1  The Setting                                                    1
1.2  The Learning Process                                           2
1.3  Some "How Much" Questions                                      3
1.4  The Statistical Model                                          4
1.5  A Sample of Data: The Big Picture                             5
1.6  Statistical Inference                                          7
1.7  A Format for Learning From Economic Data                       8
1.8  Suggestions for Further Reading                                9


**Chapter 2   Some Basic Probability Concepts**                    10

2.1  Experiments, Outcomes, and Random Variables                   10
    2.1.1  Controlled Experiments–Experimental Data            10
    2.1.2  Uncontrolled Experiments–Nonexperimental Data       11
    2.1.3  Discrete and Continuous Random Variables            12
2.2  The Probability Distribution of a Random Variable             13
    2.2.1  Probability Distributions of Discrete Random Variables    13
    2.2.2  The Probability Density Function of a Continuous
           Random Variable                                14
2.3  Expected Values Involving a Single Random Variable            15
    2.3.1  The Rules of Summation                               15
    2.3.2  The Mean of a Random Variable                        17
    2.3.3  Expectation of a Function of a Random Variable       18
    2.3.4  The Variance of a Random Variable                    19
2.4  Using Joint Probability Density Functions                     20
    2.4.1  Marginal Probability Density Functions               22
    2.4.2  Conditional Probability Density Functions            22
    2.4.3  Independent Random Variables                         23
2.5  The Expected Value of a Function of Several Random Variables:
    Covariance and Correlation                                25
    2.5.1  The Mean of a Weighted Sum of Random Variables      28
    2.5.2  The Variance of a Weighted Sum of Random Variables  29
2.6  The Normal Distribution                                       30
2.7  Distributions Related to the Normal Distribution              33
    2.7.1  The Chi-Square Distribution                         33
    2.7.2  The $t$-Distribution                                34
    2.7.3  The $F$-Distribution                                35
2.8  Summing Up                                                    36

2.9  Exercises                                                                37
2.10  References                                                              40


# Part I  The Simple Linear Regression Model                                  41

## Chapter 3  The Simple Linear Regression Model: Specification and Estimation   43

3.1  An Economic Model                                                        43
3.2  An Econometric Model                                                     46
   3.2.1  Introducing the Error Term                                  48
3.3  Estimating the Parameters for the Expenditure Relationship               51
   3.3.1  The Least Squares Principle                                 52
   3.3.2  Estimates for the Food Expenditure Function                 56
   3.3.3  Interpreting the Estimates                                  57
      3.3.3a  Elasticities                                58
      3.3.3b  Prediction                                 58
   3.3.4  Other Economic Models                                      59
3.4  Summing Up                                                               60
3.5  Exercises                                                                61
3.6  References                                                               65

## Chapter 4  Properties of the Least Squares Estimators                       66

4.1  The Least Squares Estimators as Random Variables                         66
4.2  The Sampling Properties of the Least Squares Estimators                  67
   4.2.1  The Expected Values of $b_1$ and $b_2$                      68
   4.2.2  The Variances and Covariance of $b_1$ and $b_2$            71
   4.2.3  Linear Estimators                                          74
4.3  The Gauss-Markov Theorem                                                 74
4.4  The Probability Distributions of the Least Squares Estimators            77
4.5  The Consistency of the Least Squares Estimators                          78
4.6  Estimating the Variance of the Error Term                                78
   4.6.1  Estimating the Variances and Covariances of the Least
      Squares Estimators                              79
   4.6.2  The Estimated Variances and Covariances for the Food
      Expenditure Example                             80
4.7  The Least Squares Predictor                                              81
   4.7.1  Prediction in the Food Expenditure Model                   82
4.8  Summing Up                                                               83
4.9  Exercises                                                                83
4.10  References                                                              86

## Chapter 5  Inference in the Simple Regression Model: Interval Estimation, Hypothesis Testing, and Prediction   87

5.1  Interval Estimation                                                      88
   5.1.1  The Theory                                                 88
   5.1.2  An Illustration                                            92
   5.1.3  The Repeated Sampling Context                              93

5.2 Hypothesis Testing 94
    5.2.1 The Null Hypothesis 95
    5.2.2 The Alternative Hypothesis 95
    5.2.3 The Test Statistic 95
    5.2.4 The Rejection Region 96
    5.2.5 The Food Expenditure Example 97
    5.2.6 Type I and Type II Errors 99
    5.2.7 The *p*-Value of a Hypothesis Test 100
    5.2.8 A More General Null Hypothesis 101
    5.2.9 One-Tailed Tests 101
    5.2.10 A Comment on Stating Null and Alternative Hypotheses 103
    5.2.11 A Relationship Between Hypothesis Testing and
          Interval Estimation 104
5.3 Prediction Intervals 104
    5.3.1 Prediction in the Food Expenditure Model 106
5.4 Summing Up 107
5.5 Exercises 108
5.6 References 110

Chapter 6   The Simple Linear Regression Model:
Reporting the Results and Choosing the Functional Form 111

6.1 The Coefficient of Determination 111
    6.1.1 Correlation Analysis 114
    6.1.2 Correlation Analysis and $R^2$ 115
6.2 Summarizing Regression Results 115
    6.2.1 Computer Output 115
    6.2.2 Reporting the Results of a Regression Analysis 117
    6.2.3 The Effects of Scaling the Data 118
6.3 Choosing a Functional Form 119
    6.3.1 Some Commonly Used Functional Forms 120
    6.3.2 Examples Using Alternative Functional Forms 123
        6.3.2a The Food Expenditure Model 123
        6.3.2b Some Other Economic Models and Functional Forms 124
6.4 Summing Up 126
6.5 Exercises 126
6.6 References 128

Part II   The General Linear Regression Model 129

Chapter 7   The Multiple Regression Model:
Specification and Estimation 131

7.1 Model Specification and the Data 131
    7.1.1 The Economic Model 131
    7.1.2 The Statistical Model 133
        7.1.2a The General Model 135
        7.1.2b The Assumptions of the Model 135
7.2 Estimating the Parameters of the Multiple Regression Model 137
    7.2.1 Least Squares Estimation Procedure 137

7.2.2 Least Squares Estimates Using Hamburger Chain Data ... 139
7.2.3 Estimation of the Error Variance $\sigma^2$ ... 140
7.3 Sampling Properties of the Least Squares Estimator ... 141
   7.3.1 The Variances and Covariances of the Least
      Squares Estimators ... 142
   7.3.2 The Properties of the Least Squares Estimators Assuming
      Normally Distributed Errors ... 144
7.4 Interval Estimation ... 145
7.5 Summing Up ... 146
7.6 Exercises ... 147
7.7 References ... 149

**Chapter 8   The Multiple Regression Model: Hypothesis
Tests and the Use of Nonsample Information** ... 150

8.1 One-Tailed Hypothesis Testing for a Single Coefficient ... 151
8.2 Testing the Significance of a Single Coefficient ... 152
8.3 Measuring Goodness of Fit and Reporting the Regression Results ... 154
   8.3.1 Coefficient of Determination ... 154
   8.3.2 Reporting the Regression Results ... 156
8.4 Testing the Significance of the Model ... 157
   8.4.1 The *F*-Test ... 158
   8.4.2 The *F*-Test for a Single Hypothesis ... 159
   8.4.3 The *F*-Test for the Overall Significance of the Model ... 160
   8.4.4 The Relationship Between Joint and Individual
      Hypothesis Tests ... 162
8.5 An Extended Model ... 163
8.6 Testing Some Economic Hypotheses ... 165
   8.6.1 The Significance of Advertising ... 165
   8.6.2 The Optimal Level of Advertising ... 165
   8.6.3 The Optimal Level of Advertising and Price ... 167
8.7 The Use of Nonsample Information ... 168
8.8 Collinear Economic Variables ... 171
   8.8.1 The Statistical Consequences of Collinearity ... 172
   8.8.2 Identifying and Mitigating Collinearity ... 173
8.9 Prediction ... 174
8.10 Summing Up ... 175
8.11 Exercises ... 176
8.12 References ... 178

**Chapter 9   Extensions of the Multiple Regression Model** ... 179

9.1 Introduction ... 179
9.2 The Use of Intercept Dummy Variables ... 180
9.3 Slope Dummy Variables ... 183
9.4 Some Additional Examples ... 185
9.5 Testing for the Significance of Qualitative Factors ... 188
   9.5.1 Testing for a Single Qualitative Factor ... 188
   9.5.2 Testing Jointly for the Presence of Several Qualitative Effects ... 189
9.6 Testing the Equivalence of Two Regressions Using
   Dummy Variables ... 190

9.7  Interaction Variables                                                          193
    9.7.1  Polynomial Terms in a Regression Model                             193
    9.7.2  Interactions Between Two Continuous Variables                       195
9.8  Dummy Dependent Variables                                                      198
    9.8.1  The Linear Probability Model                                       198
    9.8.2  The Probit Model of Discrete Choice                                 200
    9.8.3  Estimation of the Probit Model                                     201
    9.8.4  Interpretation of the Probit Model                                 202
    9.8.5  An Example                                                         203
    9.8.6  Concluding Remarks About Discrete Choice Models                    205
9.9  Summing Up                                                                     206
9.10  Exercises                                                                     206
9.11  References                                                                    209


## Part III  Violations of Basic Assumptions                                       211


## Chapter 10  Heteroskedasticity                                                   213

10.1  The Nature of Heteroskedasticity                                              213
10.2  The Consequences of Heteroskedasticity for the Least
      Squares Estimator                                                       216
    10.2.1  White's Approximate Estimator for the Variance of the Least
         Squares Estimator                                              218
10.3  Proportional Heteroskedasticity                                              219
10.4  A Sample with a Heteroskedastic Partition                                    222
    10.4.1  Economic and Statistical Model                                    222
    10.4.2  Generalized Least Squares Through Model Transformation             224
    10.4.3  Implementing Generalized Least Squares                             225
10.5  Detecting Heteroskedasticity                                                 226
    10.5.1  Residual Plots                                                     226
    10.5.2  The Goldfeld-Quandt Test                                          227
10.6  A More General Heteroskedastic Error Model                                   229
10.7  Summing Up                                                                   231
10.8  Exercises                                                                    232
10.9  References                                                                   236


## Chapter 11  Autocorrelation                                                     237

11.1  The Nature of the Problem                                                    237
    11.1.1  An Area Response Model for Sugar Cane                             238
        11.1.1a  Least Squares Estimation                                   239
11.2  First-Order Autoregressive Errors                                            240
    11.2.1  Statistical Properties of an AR(1) Error                           241
11.3  Consequences for the Least Squares Estimator                                 242
11.4  Generalized Least Squares Estimation for the AR(1) Model                     244
    11.4.1  A Transformation                                                   245
        11.4.1a  Transforming the First Observation                         246
11.5  Implementing Generalized Least Squares                                       247
    11.5.1  The Sugar Cane Example Revisited                                   248

11.6 Testing for Autocorrelation                                           250
11.7 Prediction with AR(1) Errors                                          253
11.8 Summing Up                                                            255
11.9 Exercises                                                             256
11.10 References                                                           259


# Part IV    Topics in Econometrics                                        261


# Chapter 12    Pooling Time–Series and Cross–Sectional Data               263

12.1 An Economic Model                                                     263
12.2 Seemingly Unrelated Regressions                                       264
    12.2.1 Estimating Separate Equations              265
    12.2.2 Joint Estimation of the Equations          266
    12.2.3 Separate or Joint Estimation               268
12.3 A Dummy Variable Specification                                        269
    12.3.1 The Model                                   270
12.4 An Error Components Model                                             272
12.5 Summing Up                                                            274
12.6 Exercises                                                            275
12.7 References                                                            278


# Chapter 13    Simultaneous Equations Models                              279

13.1 Introduction                                                          279
13.2 A Macroeconomic Model                                                 279
    13.2.1 A Simultaneous Equations Statistical Model 280
    13.2.2 The Reduced Form Equations                  282
    13.2.3 The Failure of Least Squares Estimation in Simultaneous
        Equations Models          283
    13.2.4 Consistent Estimation of the Parameters of the
        Consumption Function      286
13.3 A Supply and Demand Model                                            287
    13.3.1 The Identification Problem                  289
    13.3.2 A Two-Stage Least Squares Estimation Procedure for the
        Supply Equation           290
    13.3.3 The General Two-Stage Least Squares Estimation Procedure   291
    13.3.4 The Properties of the Two-Stage Least Squares Estimator     292
13.4 An Example of Two-Stage Least Squares Estimation                     293
    13.4.1 Identification                              293
    13.4.2 The Reduced Form Equations                  293
13.5 Summing Up                                                           296
13.6 Exercises                                                            297
13.7 References                                                           298


# Chapter 14    Nonlinear Least Squares                                    299

14.1 A Simple Nonlinear Model                                             299
14.2 The CES Production Function                                          301

14.3 An AR(1) Error Model                                              303
   14.3.1 Checking the Dynamic Specification                       304
14.4 Summing Up                                                        305
14.5 Exercises                                                         305
14.6 References                                                        307

**Chapter 15   Distributed Lag Models**                                308

15.1 Introduction                                                      308
15.2 Finite Distributed Lag Models                                     309
   15.2.1 An Economic Model                                        309
   15.2.2 The Statistical Model                                     310
   15.2.3 An Empirical Illustration                                 310
   15.2.4 The Arithmetic Lag                                        312
   15.2.5 Polynomial Distributed Lags                               314
   15.2.6 Selection of the Length of the Finite Lag                 317
15.3 The Geometric Lag                                                 318
15.4 The Koyck Transformation                                          320
   15.4.1 Least Squares Estimation of the Koyck Model              320
   15.4.2 Two-Stage Least Squares Estimation of the Koyck Lag       321
15.5 An Infinite Distributed Lag Based on the Adaptive
   Expectations Hypothesis                                          322
   15.5.1 Adaptive Expectations                                     322
   15.5.2 An Example of the Adaptive Expectations Model             323
15.6 An Infinite Distributed Lag Based on the Partial
   Adjustment Hypothesis                                            325
15.7 Summing Up                                                        326
15.8 Exercises                                                         327
15.9 References                                                        328

**Chapter 16   Time Series Models**                                    330

16.1 Autoregressive Processes                                          330
16.2 Moving Average Processes                                          333
   16.2.1 Autoregressive Moving-Average Processes                  335
16.3 Integrated Nonstationary Processes                                335
16.4 Autoregressive Integrated Moving-Average Models                   337
16.5 Vector Autoregressive (VAR) Models                                337
16.6 Nonstationary Series and Cointegration                            339
   16.6.1 An Error Correction Model                                 340
16.7 Summing Up                                                        342
16.8 Exercises                                                         343
16.9 References                                                        344

**Chapter 17   Economic Data Sources, Guidelines for
Choosing a Research Project, and the Writing of a
Research Report**                                                      346

17.1 Sources and Characteristics of Economic Data                      346
   17.1.1 Nonexperimental Data                                     347
     17.1.1a Data Published in Text Form                         348

17.1.1b Data on Electronic Media                     350
17.1.1c Data Sources on the Internet                 351
17.1.2 Data From Surveys                             351
17.1.3 Controlled Experimental Data                  354
17.1.4 Some Characteristics of Economic Data         355
17.2 Selecting a Topic for an Economics Project      356
17.2.1 Choosing a Topic                              356
17.2.2 Writing an Abstract                           357
17.3 A Format for Writing a Research Report          357
17.4 Exercises                                       358
17.5 References                                      359
Index                                                361

# Chapter *1*

# The Role of Econometrics in Economic Analysis

## *1.1* The Setting

We often hear that this is the information age, and it certainly is true that the economy runs on information. A firm needs information on the best way to produce its products, given limited resources and the current technology; a consumer needs information to make consumption decisions, given a limited budget; and a government needs information on its society and the global community to best formulate a set of laws and regulations, subject to its constitutional restrictions.

If economic actors are to function efficiently, given the restrictions under which they operate, there must be a steady flow of information. But where does this information come from? How do the decision makers involved acquire it? One source of information is provided by economic theory—you have some knowledge of the usefulness of this type of information through your introductory courses in micro- and macroeconomics. Economic theory gives you a basis for identifying important economic variables, an understanding of the allocation of resources and determination of prices within a capitalistic economy, and an appreciation of the interdependent nature of economic variables. If this information is to be useful for decision making, we must know more about the relationships between economic variables, and we must answer questions like the following:

- What is the impact of an increase in the federal budget deficit on the level of interest rates and the rate of inflation?
- Is there a relationship between the level of interest rates and the level of the Dow Jones Industrial Average?
- How do recent mergers and leveraged buyouts of corporations affect the returns to stockholders?
- How does the trade deficit affect the level of employment and the bargaining position of labor unions?
- What is the relationship between the quantity of money, say M-1, and the level of economic activity?
- If the Federal Reserve increases the discount rate, will this cause stagflation?
- How will changes in the tax law affect the distribution of income?
- Does the level of economic well-being have an impact on crime patterns across cities?

- What is the impact of changing the capital gains tax on the level of investment?
- If the rent control law is repealed, what will be the impact on apartment and house prices in Berkeley, California, next year?
- Should I invest in long-term government bonds or short-term treasury bills?
- How much of a financial impact does a "sold out" football game in Louisiana State University's Tiger Stadium, the legendary "Death Valley," have on Baton Rouge's businesses?

Where does information of this type come from? As we noted, economic theory is one source. It helps us identify the important economic variables and develop a theory of choice to guide decision making and action. Another source is the economic data we observe, such as prices, incomes, consumption, and supply levels. These economic outcomes help us *describe* what has happened, but alone they do not answer the types of questions we just asked. The challenge is how to combine economic theory with the information supplied by economic data to estimate the unknowns we need for decision making and choice. This is precisely what this book is about: "How do we learn about the real world from a sample of economic data?"

## *1.2* The Learning Process

If you ask an economist a question, you will probably get the answer, "It all depends." That is because the answer depends on other economic variables and on unknown relationships connecting the economic variables. To express our ideas about relationships between economic variables we use the mathematical concept of a function.

For example, if we think there is a relationship between income $i$ and consumption $c$, we may write

$$c = f(i)$$

which says that the level of consumption is *some* function, $f(i)$, of income.

If we focus on an individual commodity, say the Honda Accord, we might express our conjecture or economic hypothesis as

$$q^d = f(p, p^s, p^c, i)$$

which says that the quantity of Honda Accords demanded, $q^d$, is *some* function $f(p, p^s, p^c, i)$ of the price of Honda Accords $p$, the price of cars that are substitutes $p^s$, the price of items that are complements (like gasoline) $p^c$, and the level of income $i$.

Alternatively, if we were considering the supply of an agricultural commodity such as beef, we might write

$$q^s = f(p, p^c, p^f)$$

where $q^s$ is the quantity supplied, $p$ is the price of beef, $p^c$ is the price of competitive products in production (for example, the price of hogs), and $p^f$ is the price of factors or inputs (for example, the price of corn) used in the production process. Since decision making occurs in a dynamic world, current, past, and future (expected) values of the prices may be relevant in specifying the economic supply response model.

Each of these equations is a general economic model that describes how we visualize the way in which economic variables are interrelated. Economic models of this type guide our economic analysis. However, in this form they are not sufficient for testing hypotheses or predicting economic outcomes.

## *1.3* Some "How Much" Questions

For most economic decision or choice problems, it is not enough to know that certain economic variables are interrelated. We also want to know the direction of relationships and the magnitudes involved. That is, we must be able to answer the *how much* question, or at least say something about the *probability of how much.*

As a case in point, consider the problem faced by the Federal Reserve System. In a period when price increases are beginning to indicate an increase in the inflation rate, the central bank must decide whether to dampen the rate of growth of the economy by raising the interest rate it charges its member banks when they borrow money, or to reduce the supply of money. These actions reduce the supply of loanable funds and increase the interest rates faced by would-be investors, who may be firms seeking funds for capital expansion or individuals who wish to buy consumer durables like automobiles and refrigerators. As the quantity of the durable goods demanded declines, this reduces aggregate demand and slows the rate of inflation. Although these relationships are suggested by economic theory and are reflected in our economic model, the real question faced by the central bankers is, "*How much* do we have to reduce the money supply to reduce the rate of inflation by 1 percent?" The answer will depend on the responsiveness of firms and individuals to increases in the interest rates and to the effects of reduced investment on Gross National Product (GNP). The key elasticities and multipliers, such as those that depend on the marginal propensity to consume, are called **parameters.** The values of economic parameters are unknown and must be estimated using a sample of economic data when formulating economic policies. Errors in the *estimates* of these parameters are of social significance, because *policy makers will take corrective actions based on them, rather than the true values,* and thus they may overcorrect or undercorrect.

As another example, the U.S. Department of Agriculture has a complicated set of policies that are designed to stabilize the prices of farm goods and reduce the risk of farming. One of these policies is to "support" prices of specific goods, like corn, sugar, and milk, by creating a price floor. As you probably learned in your economics classes, the existence of price floors sometimes leads to excess supply in the marketplace. As Department of Agriculture officials ponder their programs, one question they must ask is, "If we raise the support price for milk by 25 cents, how much will the excess supply of milk increase?" To answer the question, the unknown price elasticities of supply and demand for milk must be estimated. Errors in the estimates will affect the cost of the program and the amount of milk that U.S. consumers do not purchase and that must be stored or dumped.

Thus, the economic models that express relationships between economic variables also involve questions concerning the signs and magnitudes of *unknown and unobservable parameters,* such as the price elasticities and multipliers. The next question, then, is how we introduce parameters into an economic model and how we estimate them.

## 1.4  The Statistical Model

The following is a general overview of the components of a statistical model, but some statistical terms might be unfamiliar to you. Be assured that before you are too far into this book, all the terminology will be clearly defined. In a statistical model we must first realize that economic relations are not exact. Economic theory does not claim to be able to predict the specific behavior of any individual or firm, but rather, it describes the *average* or *systematic* behavior of *many* individuals or firms. When studying consumption we will recognize that actual consumption is the sum of this systematic part and a random and unpredictable component, *e,* that we will call a **random error.** Thus, a **statistical model** representing aggregate consumption is

$$c = f(i) + e$$

The random error *e* accounts for the many factors that affect consumption that we have omitted from this simple model, and it also reflects the intrinsic uncertainty in economic activity.

To complete the specification of the statistical model, we must also say something about the form of the algebraic relationship among our economic variables. For example, in your first economics courses, aggregate consumption was depicted as a *linear* function of aggregate income. In that case the systematic part of consumption is

$$f(i) = \beta_1 + \beta_2 i$$

and the corresponding statistical model is

$$c = \beta_1 + \beta_2 i + e$$

The functional form represents a hypothesis about the relationship between the variables. Our interest centers on trying to determine a form that is compatible with economic theory and the data.

Other economic functions, such as demand functions, supply functions, and production functions, also contain both a predictable systematic component and an unobserved and unpredictable random error component, *e.* In a demand relation, preferences might not have been controlled for, an important economic variable may have been omitted, or perhaps human behavior has a random component. In the supply relation for an agricultural commodity, weather might not have been taken into account. In a consumption function, measurements on the wealth variable might not be available. Economic theory describes the systematic part; *e* is the nonsystematic, *random,* error component that we know is present but cannot be observed. *Adding random errors converts our economic model into a statistical model that gives us a basis for statistical inference.* That is, it gives us a basis for estimating unknown parameters and testing hypotheses about them.

## *1.5* A Sample of Data: The Big Picture

One way to acquire information about the unknown parameters of economic relationships is to conduct or observe the outcome of an experiment. The statistical model describes the process by which experimental outcomes, such as prices and outputs, are determined. In an ideal (research) world, an economic model would describe how we might design an experiment that could be used to obtain economic observations or sample information, that then could be used to provide insights about the unknown economic parameters. Repeating the experiment $T$ times would create a sample of $T$ observations.

Let's see if we can bring all this together using a picture that describes a "controlled" experiment and the formulation of an econometric, statistical model that can be used as a basis for estimating unknown parameters and testing hypotheses about them. Suppose we are interested in trying to understand how the quantity of Honda Accord automobiles that consumers purchase is determined. The microeconomic theory of consumer behavior suggests that the quantity purchased ($q^d$) should depend on the price of Honda Accords ($p$), the price of substitutes—perhaps Nissan Maximas—($p^s$), the price of complements like gasoline ($p^c$), and the level of income ($i$).

In an ideal world for research, controlled experiments could be conducted to investigate the relationship between these "explanatory" variables and the "dependent" variable $q^d$. In a controlled experiment, the experimental design team (headed by Einstein in this ideal world) sets the levels of the explanatory variables, runs the experiment, and obtains one observation on the dependent variable. This process is depicted in Figure 1.1, where on the left-hand side Einstein operates a control panel that fixes the price $p$ of Hondas, the price of the substitute $p^s$, the price of

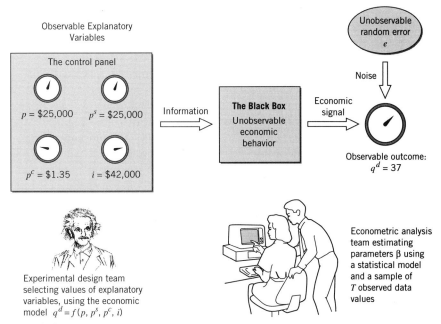

FIGURE *1.1*  A controlled experiment generating data for an econometric study of the demand for Honda Accords

the complement $p^c$, and the level of income $i$ of a population group. Once these controls are set, economic firms and individuals react to this information so as to maximize their well-being. The exact workings of the economic actors are hidden from us in a "black box" into which we can never really see. What we do observe, at the end, is the number of Honda Accords that are purchased. For example, suppose Einstein sets the price and income variables under his control as:

$$p = \text{price of Accords} = \$25{,}000$$
$$p^s = \text{price of Maximas} = \$25{,}000$$
$$p^c = \text{price of gasoline per gallon} = \$1.35$$
$$i = \text{income of individuals in sample} = \$42{,}000$$

At the end of a month we *observe* the number of Honda Accords sold at one dealership to be $q^d = 37$. In our ideal world, Einstein can *repeat* the experiment, changing (or leaving unchanged) any of the price variables or income, and observing the number of Hondas sold. By repeating this process a number of times, a **sample** of economic data is created.

But even in a controlled experiment there is unobservable random error, or *noise,* that enters the observable outcome. Einstein sets the values of the primary explanatory variables that are indicated by economic reasoning, but it is clear that there are "other" substitute and complement goods whose prices are not controlled; there are unobservable factors dictating the level of consumer confidence and willingness to spend; there is the crucial issue (for car buyers Melissa Waters, Marge Judge, and others) of how this year's Accord model "looks" relative to the competition, and so on. These "random" factors are not controlled, but they affect the outcome we observe by blurring the picture or adding noise to the problem. The outcome we observe is the sum of a systematic component that depends on the controlled explanatory variables and this random noise. Consequently, the observable experimental outcome is random too. We never know what we will observe in any trial of the experiment, and thus, the outcome variable, $q^d$, is random. That means that even if we carry out two experiments in a row with the same settings of the explanatory variables the outcomes will be different. If we collect a sample of $T$ observations on $q^d$ by repeating the experiment $T$ times with different settings on the controls each time, and then if we collect another sample of $T$ observations by repeating those same settings, the two samples will be different. Every sample of size $T$ we collect will be different, and the differences are due to *sampling variability,* which is evidence of the presence of the random error $e$.

Econometricians wish to determine the relationship between each of the explanatory variables ($p$, $p^c$, $p^s$, $i$) and the outcome $q^d$ *using* a sample of $T$ observations on values of the explanatory variables and the observed outcomes. Specifically, we want to know (estimate from the data) the effect ($\beta$) of a change in one explanatory variable on the average outcome, or expected sales of Honda Accords. To do this we must combine economic theory, statistics, and computer science, the combination being **econometrics.** An absolutely fascinating part of econometrics and statistics is that if we obtained another sample of $T$ observations using the same process, our *estimates* would change, since the observed outcomes $q^d$ would change. So, from just one sample of data, how are we to know the reliability of any estimate we obtain? The answer to this question is one of the important things that you will learn by reading this book. Most economic data do not come from controlled experiments, however, and in this context we are like astronomers. When the experiments are *uncontrolled,* economists take the role of observers, and economic theory indicates the relevant variables to consider.

In Figure 1.1 we have tried to depict an "ideal" experimental situation. It shows us how economic data would be generated for research purposes if we could arrange it. Of course, most of the time we do not have Einstein, or anyone else, controlling the experiment. Economists and other social scientists work in the hazy world in which data on all variables are "observed," not controlled, and this makes the task of learning about economic parameters all the more difficult. This book provides procedures for using such data to answer questions of economic importance.

We now have the following:

1. An economic model that helps us identify the relevant economic variables and economic parameters and gives us a basis for reaching economic conclusions

2. A statistical model that specifies a sampling process by which the sample data are generated and that identifies the unknown parameters that describe the underlying probability system

3. Observed values of the economic variables

We must determine how to adapt this information to learn enough about the unknown economic parameters to improve decision making and choice.

## *1.6* Statistical Inference

In discussing the role of the economic and statistical models we have focused on the relationships among observable economic variables such as prices, consumption, and investment, and the desire to obtain information about corresponding unknown and unobservable parameters such as elasticities and marginal products. Information about these unknown economic parameters helps us understand the underlying economic relationships and puts us in a position to discriminate among alternative hypotheses about how the world works (theories). It also helps to draw economic policy implications or to predict, and perhaps control, the outcomes of important economic variables. Given these objectives and a collected sample of data, we must devise some procedures for using the information in a sample of economic data for purposes of parameter estimation and inference. By *inference* we mean we want to use the information in a sample of data to "infer" something about the real world. For example, as the price of a commodity increases, how much does the quantity consumed decrease? Does aggregate output increase in a linear or nonlinear way with increases in the quantity of labor? Statistical theory lets us use our sample information to move from the theoretical parameters in the economic and statistical models to their empirical counterparts, and to make probability statements concerning possible outcomes.

It is the complete bag of tools, including economic theory, the economic model, the statistical model, the sample information, and statistical theory, that defines econometrics and that provides a basis for the science of measurement in economics. If we are successful, then we have the possibility of understanding, predicting, and having some control over the economy.

## *1.7* A Format for Learning from Economic Data

Let us see if we can now pull all of these ideas together and see what they mean for the practice of econometrics.

1. It all starts with a problem—a lack of information or uncertainty regarding an outcome, or a question that involves "what if. . . ."

2. Economic theory gives us a way of thinking about the problem: What economic variables are involved, and what is the possible direction of the relationship(s)? How would we make use of new information if we had it—for example, how would we make use of a production function to determine the "best" mix of factors, the optimum level of output, or the demand for an input?

3. This information is then arranged in terms of a working economic model that lists our underlying assumptions. Hypotheses of interest are specified.

4. The working economic model leads to the statistical model that describes the process by which the sample observations are viewed as having been generated, the classification of the variables, and the functional form of the relationship.

5. Sample observations that are consistent with the economic model are generated or, more usually, collected.

6. Given the statistical model and sample observations, an estimation rule is selected or developed that has good statistical properties.

7. Estimates of the unknown parameters are obtained with the help of a statistical software package and a computer; appropriate hypothesis tests are performed.

8. The statistical and economic consequences and the implications of the empirical results are analyzed and evaluated. For example, were all of the right-hand-side explanatory variables relevant? Was the correct functional form used? What economic resource allocation and distribution results are implied, and what are their policy-choice implications?

9. If consistency between the economic and statistical models and the sample data was not achieved, what are the potential trouble spots, and what are the suggestions for future analysis and evaluation? For example, were the data inadequate to support the questions asked, were the variables in the economic model classified correctly and did they appear with the correct leads and lags; should the statistical model have involved nonlinearities in both the variables and the parameters?

This is the format we will follow as we work our way through the chapters ahead, and this is a format that will serve you well in your econometric work as you try to learn from a sample of economic data. It will also be useful in writing up your econometric results and in evaluating the applied econometric work of others.

In Chapter 2 we will review some of the basic concepts of probability that we will need in formulating our statistical-econometric models and in interpreting our results. Then we will turn to the problems of estimation and inference for an observed sample of economic data.

# *1.8* Suggestions for Further Reading

For additional perspective on the scope and methods of econometrics see:

GRIFFITHS, W. E., R. C. HILL, AND G. G. JUDGE (1993). *Learning and Practicing Econometrics.* New York: John Wiley & Sons, Chapter 1.

GUJARATI, DAMODAR N. (1995). *Basic Econometrics. 3d ed.* New York: McGraw-Hill, Chapter 1.

RAMANATHAN, RAMU (1995). *Introductory Econometrics with Applications. 3d ed.,* Fort Worth, TX: Dryden, Chapter 1.

# Chapter 2

# Some Basic
# Probability Concepts

Economic variables are by nature random. We do not know what their values will be until we observe them. Probability is one way of expressing uncertainty about economic events and outcomes. Consequently, in this chapter we review the foundations of probability that we will use throughout the book, as we devise methods for analyzing economic data.

## 2.1 Experiments, Outcomes, and Random Variables

Where do data come from? A large amount of scientific data are obtained by experimentation. In contrast, economics is a social science, where much of the data do not come from a controlled experimental process. Such data are said to be *nonexperimental.* In this section we provide you with a framework that describes the nonexperimental process in economics.

### 2.1.1 CONTROLLED EXPERIMENTS—EXPERIMENTAL DATA

If an agricultural economist wants to study the yield of a certain variety of seed corn, it seems natural to do an experiment in which the corn variety is planted on several plots of land of the same fertility and treated with identical amounts of fertilizer, pesticide, and so on, during the growing season. At the end of the growing season the yield can be measured in a variety of ways. We might measure the number of bushels per acre, the number of ears per stalk, or the moisture content of an ear of corn, just to name a few possibilities.

What we just described is a **controlled experiment,** similar to the one described in Figure 1.1 in Chapter 1. Controlled experiments are characterized by the fact that the conditions surrounding the experiment are under the control of the experimenter. One of the advantages of a controlled experiment is that *it is reproducible and can be repeated by independent researchers as a check on experimental procedures.* A second advantage of controlled experiments is that the experiment can be repeated under different settings for the control variables (the amount of fertilizer, pesticide, water) to see what effect that has on yield.

The experimental *outcome* is characterized by one or more measures of yield. Let $X$ = bushels per plot and $Y$ = number of ears per stalk. These measures are called **random variables.** Their distinguishing characteristic is that their values are not known until *after* the experiment is performed. After the experiment, when we make the measurements, we obtain observed *values* of the random variables, like $x = 100$ bushels and $y = 15$ ears.

One interesting characteristic of outcomes from controlled experiments is that in repeated trials of the same experiment the actual values of the random variables will change from one trial to another. That is, if we planted corn on several identical plots, and grew it under "identical" conditions, the yield of corn from each plot would differ. The reason for the difference is that the conditions are not really *identical* from one trial of an experiment to another. There will be errors in measurement, some factors that are uncontrolled and, the truth is, every seed is a little different. This type of variation in experimental outcomes, which occurs naturally and uncontrollably, is called **sampling variation;** it is a fact of life in all experiments.

---

A **random variable** is a variable whose value is unknown until it is observed. The *value* of a random variable results from an experiment; it is not perfectly predictable.

---

In this chapter random variables are indicated by uppercase letters, such as $X$ or $Y$ or $Z$, and the values that the random variables can take are represented by lower case letters, $x$ or $y$ or $z$. *After this chapter, we will not make this distinction and you will recognize the difference by the context.*

### 2.1.2 UNCONTROLLED EXPERIMENTS—NONEXPERIMENTAL DATA

Economic variables like gross national product (GNP), the prime interest rate, the unemployment rate, the price of ice cream, or the number of bottles of mineral water sold are random variables. We do not know what their values will be until we *observe* them. There is obviously a big difference between the process by which the values of these random variables are obtained and the controlled experimental process used in the previous section to obtain the number of bushels of corn. Socioeconomic random variables have values that are generated by an *uncontrolled* experiment carried out by society and not under the complete control of any one person or group. The values of the macroeconomic variables, such as GNP and the unemployment rate, are affected by changes in factors such as tax rates, government spending, and monetary policy. Even if we could control such factors, we still could not predict with certainty the values that the macroeconomic variables would take.

There are both public and private sources of economic data, and some of these are listed in Chapter 17. Although many data sources exist, for the most part (1) the data are "observed" and not the result of a controlled experiment, and (2) the data may have been collected for purposes other than economic analysis. Thus, the data might not contain observations on variables that a particular investigator wants, or, in the case of survey data, the variables might be based on questions that the investigator may have preferred to ask in a different way. As a result, *one of the challenges of economic research is to obtain data that are consistent with the theoretical variables in the economic model and that are useful in analyzing an economic problem.*

### 2.1.3   DISCRETE AND CONTINUOUS RANDOM VARIABLES

Random variables from controlled or uncontrolled experiments are either **discrete** or **continuous.**

---

> A **discrete random variable** can take only a finite number of values, that can be counted by using the positive integers.

---

Examples of discrete economic variables are the following:

- The number of children in a household: 0, 1, 2, . . .
- The number of shopping trips an individual takes to a particular shopping mall per week: 0, 1, 2, . . .

These economic variables take only a limited number of values, and it makes sense to *count* them in whole numbers. Discrete variables are also commonly used in economics to record qualitative, or nonnumerical, characteristics. In this role they are sometimes called **dummy variables.** For example, if we are studying individual behavior, we might want to record an individual's gender. One way to do this is to let the random variable, *D,* take the value 1 if the person is female and 0 if male. That is, the random variable is defined as

$$D = \begin{cases} 1 \text{ if person is female} \\ 0 \text{ if person is male} \end{cases}$$

Any qualitative characteristic that has two states (e.g., a yes-or-no, or buy-or-not-buy type of variable) can be characterized by a dummy variable like *D.* The actual *values* the dummy variable takes do not matter mathematically, but the choice of the values 0 and 1 is convenient for a variety of reasons.

In contrast to situations in which discrete random variables can be used, there are many times when it is not convenient to think of random variables as having a countable number of possible outcome values or states.

---

> A **continuous random variable** can take *any* real value (not just whole numbers) in at least one interval on the real number line.

---

An example is gross national product. For practical purposes, the GNP variable can take any value in the interval zero to infinity and, thus, is a continuous random variable. Admittedly, the GNP is measured in dollars and *can* be counted in whole dollars, but the value is so large that counting individual dollars serves no purpose. It is more convenient simply to assume that the number can be any real number larger than, or equal to, zero. Other examples of continuous random economic variables are all the usual macroeconomic variables, like money supply, interest rates, the federal deficit, and government spending; microeconomic examples are prices, household income, and expenditures on specific products.

## *2.2* The Probability Distribution of a Random Variable

The values of random variables are not known until an experiment is carried out, and all possible values are not equally likely. We can make **probability** statements about certain values occurring by specifying a **probability distribution** for the random variable. If event $A$ is an outcome of an experiment, then the *probability of A,* which we write as $P(A)$, is the relative frequency with which event $A$ occurs in *many* repeated trials of the experiment. For any event, $0 \leq P(A) \leq 1$, and the total probability of all possible events is one.

In this section we discuss how to make probability statements about discrete and continuous random variables using their probability distributions.

### 2.2.1  PROBABILITY DISTRIBUTIONS OF DISCRETE RANDOM VARIABLES

> When the values of a discrete random variable are listed with their chances of occurring, the resulting table of outcomes is called a **probability function** or a **probability density function.**

The probability density function spreads the total of 1 "unit" of probability over the set of possible values that a random variable can take. Consider a discrete random variable, $X$ = the number of heads obtained in a single flip of a coin. The values that $X$ can take are $x = 0,1$. If the coin is "fair" then the probability of a head occurring is .5. The probability density function, say $f(x)$, for the random variable $X$ is

| Coin Side | $x$ | $f(x)$ |
|-----------|-----|--------|
| tail      | 0   | .5     |
| head      | 1   | .5     |

"The probability that $X$ takes the value 1 is .5" means that the two values 0 and 1 have an equal chance of occurring and, if we flipped a fair coin *a very large number of times,* the value $x = 1$ would occur 50 percent of the time. We can denote this as $P[X = 1] = f(1) = 0.5$, where $P[X = 1]$ is the probability of the event that the random variable $X = 1$.

> For a discrete random variable $X$, the value of the probability density function $f(x)$ is the probability that the random variable $X$ takes the value $x$, $f(x) = P(X = x)$. Therefore, $0 \leq f(x) \leq 1$ and, if $X$ takes $n$ values $x_1, \ldots, x_n$, then $f(x_1) + f(x_2) + \cdots + f(x_n) = 1$.

Sometimes, as the following example illustrates, the probability density function of a discrete random variable can be represented by a mathematical formula.

*Example* **2.1**

Consider the discrete random variable that only takes two values, 1 and 0. The probability of a 1 occurring is $p$ and the probability of a 0 occurring is $1 - p$. An example of this random variable is the number of heads (i.e., whether or not one occurs) on a coin toss with $p = 0.5$. Then, $P[X = x] = f(x) = p^x(1 - p)^{1-x}$, for $x = 0,1$.    ■

### 2.2.2   THE PROBABILITY DENSITY FUNCTION OF A CONTINUOUS RANDOM VARIABLE

> For the continuous random variable $Y$ the probability density function $f(y)$ can be represented by an **equation,** which can be described graphically by a curve. For continuous random variables the *area* under the probability density function corresponds to probability.

For example, the probability density function of a continuous random variable $Y$ might be represented as in Figure 2.1. The total area under a probability density function is 1, and the probability that $Y$ *takes* a value in the interval $[a,b]$, or $P[a \le Y \le b]$, is the area under the probability density function between the values $y = a$ and $y = b$. This is shown in Figure 2.1 by the shaded area.

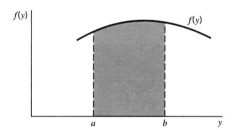

FIGURE **2.1**   Probability as an area under a probability density function

Since a continuous random variable takes an uncountably infinite number of values, the probability of any *one* occurring is zero. That is, $P[Y = a] = P[a \le Y \le a] = 0$.

In calculus, the *integral* of a function defines the area under it, and therefore

$$P[a \le Y \le b] = \int_{y=a}^{b} f(y)dy. \qquad (2.2.1)$$

You will not be asked to find integrals in this book, but if you continue to study statistics and/or econometrics, differential and integral calculus will be important.

Even if you cannot find the probability of an event involving a continuous random variable via integration of the probability density function, you may be able to use geometry to achieve the same objective, as the following example illustrates.

*Example 2.2*

A very useful continuous random variable is the *uniform* random variable. $U$ is a uniform random variable on the interval $[a,b]$ if its probability density function is

$$f(u) = \begin{cases} 1/(b - a) & \text{if} \quad a \le u \le b \\ 0 & \text{otherwise} \end{cases} \qquad (2.2.2)$$

The graph of this probability density function is given in Figure 2.2. Suppose the values of $a$ and $b$ are $a = 0$ and $b = 1$. Then function $f(u)$ is the horizontal line shown in the figure intersecting the vertical axis at height 1. The probability that the random variable $U$ falls between the values 0.1 and 0.3, for example, is the area under the line representing $f(u)$ between the limits .1 and .3. The probability is given by the area of the shaded rectangle in Figure 2.2; $P[.1 \le U \le .3] = length \times width = (1 \times .2) = .2$. ∎

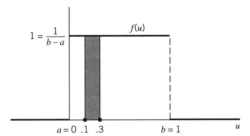

FIGURE **2.2**   Probability density function of a uniform random variable

# *2.3* Expected Values Involving a Single Random Variable

When working with random variables, it is convenient to summarize their probability characteristics using the concept of *mathematical expectation*. These expectations will make use of summation notation.

### 2.3.1   THE RULES OF SUMMATION

Throughout this book we will use *summation signs*, denoted by the Greek symbol $\Sigma$, to shorten algebraic expressions. The following rules apply to the summation operation.

1.   If $X$ takes $n$ values $x_1, \ldots, x_n$ then their sum is

$$\sum_{i=1}^{n} x_i = x_1 + x_2 + \cdots + x_n$$

2.  If $a$ is a constant then

$$\sum_{i=1}^{n} ax_i = a\sum_{i=1}^{n} x_i$$

3.  If $X$ and $Y$ are two variables, then

$$\sum_{i=1}^{n} (x_i + y_i) = \sum_{i=1}^{n} x_i + \sum_{i=1}^{n} y_i$$

4.  If $X$ and $Y$ are two variables, then

$$\sum_{i=1}^{n} (ax_i + by_i) = a\sum_{i=1}^{n} x_i + b\sum_{i=1}^{n} y_i$$

5.  The arithmetic mean (average) of $n$ values of $X$ is

$$\bar{x} = \frac{\sum_{i=1}^{n} x_i}{n} = \frac{x_1 + x_2 + \cdots + x_n}{n}$$

Also,

$$\sum_{i=1}^{n} (x_i - \bar{x}) = 0$$

6.  We often use an abbreviated form of the summation notation. For example, if $f(x)$ is a function of the values of $X$,

$$\sum_{i=1}^{n} f(x_i) = f(x_1) + f(x_2) + \cdots + f(x_n)$$

$$= \sum_{i} f(x_i) \text{ (``Sum over all values of the index } i\text{'')}$$

$$= \sum_{x} f(x) \text{ (``Sum over all possible values of } X\text{'')}$$

7.  Several summation signs can be used in one expression. Suppose the variable $Y$ takes $n$ values and $X$ takes $m$ values, and let $f(x, y) = x + y$. Then the *double summation* of this function is

$$\sum_{i=1}^{m} \sum_{j=1}^{n} f(x_i, y_j) = \sum_{i=1}^{m} \sum_{j=1}^{n} (x_i + y_j)$$

To evaluate such expressions, work from the innermost sum outward. First set $i = 1$ and sum over all values of $j$, and so on. That is,

$$\sum_{i=1}^{m} \sum_{j=1}^{n} f(x_i, y_j) = \sum_{i=1}^{m} [f(x_i, y_1) + f(x_i, y_2) + \cdots + f(x_i, y_n)]$$

The *order* of summation does not matter, so

$$\sum_{i=1}^{m} \sum_{j=1}^{n} f(x_i, y_j) = \sum_{j=1}^{n} \sum_{i=1}^{m} f(x_i, y_j)$$

### 2.3.2 THE MEAN OF A RANDOM VARIABLE

An important characteristic of a random variable is its mathematical expectation or expected value, which is also called the ***mean* of the random variable.**

> The expected value, or **mean,** of a random variable $X$ is the average value of the random variable in an infinite number of repetitions of the experiment (repeated samples); it is denoted $E[X]$.

As an example, let $X$ be the number of heads occurring in the toss of a single, well-balanced coin. The values that $X$ can take are $x = 0, 1$. If this experiment is repeated *a very large number of times,* the average value of $X$ will be 0.5. Note that $E[X] = 0.5$ is *not* the value we expect to obtain on a single toss, since the value 0.5 cannot even occur. It is the *long-run average value we expect after making repeated trials of an experiment.*

Although $E[X]$ is easy to determine intuitively in the example of the coin toss, it will not always be so obvious. The mathematical representation of the expected value of a discrete random variable can be summarized as follows:

> If $X$ is a discrete random variable that can take the values $x_1, x_2, \ldots, x_n$ with probability density values $f(x_1), f(x_2), \ldots, f(x_n)$, the expected value of $X$ is
>
> $$E[X] = x_1 f(x_1) + x_2 f(x_2) + \cdots + x_n f(x_n)$$
>
> $$= \sum_{i=1}^{n} x_i f(x_i) \qquad\qquad (2.3.1)$$
>
> $$= \sum_{x} x f(x)$$

Equation 2.3.1 shows that for a discrete random variable, its mathematical expectation or *mean value* is a *weighted average of the values of the random variable,* with the weights being the probabilities attached to each value.

*Example 2.3*

---

Let us find the expected value of the discrete random variable $X$ with probability density function given by $f(x) = p^x (1 - p)^{1-x}$, for $x = 0,1$. Using Equation 2.3.1 we write

$$E[X] = \sum_x xf(x) = 0f(0) + 1f(1) = 0(1 - p) + 1(p) = p$$ ■

To calculate the expected value of a *continuous* random variable $Y$, we once again "add up" all the values of the random variable weighted by the corresponding values of the probability density function $f(y)$. The only problem now is that we must add up an *infinite* number of weighted values. The way to actually do this is to use integration. Although we do not use integration, we will continually refer to the mean of continuous random variables, as in the following example.

*Example 2.4*

---

In Example 2.2 we considered the uniform random variable $U$. Suppose that the distribution parameters are $a = 0$ and $b = 1$, so that $f(u) = 1/(b - a) = 1$ for $0 \le u \le 1$. The expected value of $U$ is $E[U] = .5$, which is the center of the probability density function $f(u)$ shown in Figure 2.2. *The mean of a random variable is always the "center" of its probability distribution.* In general, the expected value of a uniform random variable is $E[U] = (a + b)/2$. Note that the parameters $a$ and $b$ that define the distribution of the uniform random variable are used to calculate the mean of the uniform random variable. ■

### 2.3.3   EXPECTATION OF A FUNCTION OF A RANDOM VARIABLE

There are several useful rules for calculating expected values of functions of random variables.

---

1. If $X$ is a discrete random variable and $g(X)$ is a function of it, then

$$E[g(X)] = \sum_x g(x)f(x) \qquad (2.3.2a)$$

However, $E[g(X)] \ne g[E(X)]$ in general.

2. If $X$ is a discrete random variable and $g(X) = g_1(X) + g_2(X)$, where $g_1(X)$ and $g_2(X)$ are functions of $X$, then

$$E[g(X)] = \sum_x [g_1(x) + g_2(x)]f(x)$$

$$= \sum_x g_1(x)f(x) + \sum_x g_2(x)f(x) \qquad (2.3.2b)$$

$$= E[g_1(x)] + E[g_2(x)]$$

The expected value of a sum of functions of random variables, or the expected value of a sum of random variables, is always the sum of the expected values.

The idea of how to determine the expected value of a function of a continuous random variable $Y$, say $g(y)$, is exactly the same as in the discrete case. The terms $g(y)$ must be weighted by $f(y)$ and then all those products summed. This operation is carried out via integration, but the interpretation of the result is the same.

Some properties of mathematical expectation work for both discrete and continuous random variables. For the discrete case, these results are shown using equation 2.3.2.

---

1. If $c$ is a constant,

$$E[c] = c \qquad (2.3.3a)$$

2. If $c$ is a constant and $X$ is a random variable, then

$$E[cX] = cE[X] \qquad (2.3.3b)$$

3. If $a$ and $c$ are constants then

$$E[a + cX] = a + cE[X] \qquad (2.3.3c)$$

---

### 2.3.4   THE VARIANCE OF A RANDOM VARIABLE

We define the *variance* of a discrete or continuous random variable $X$, based on the rules in Section 2.3.3, as the expected value of $g(X) = [X - E(X)]^2$. Like the mean, the variance of a random variable is important in characterizing the scale of measurement and the spread of the probability distribution. We give it the symbol $\sigma^2$, or "sigma squared." Algebraically,

---

$$\mathrm{var}(X) = \sigma^2 = E[g(X)] = E[X - E(X)]^2 = E[X^2] - [E(X)]^2 \quad (2.3.4)$$

---

Examining $g(X) = [X - E(X)]^2$, we observe that the variance of a random variable is the *average* squared difference between the random variable $X$ and its mean value $E[X]$. Thus, the variance of a random variable is the weighted average of the squared differences (or distances) between the *values* $x$ of the random variable $X$ and the mean (center of the probability density function) of the random variable. The larger the variance of a random variable, the greater the average squared distance between the values of the random variable and its mean, or the more "spread out" are the values of the random variable.

A useful property of variances is the following.

---

Let $a$ and $c$ be constants, and let $Z = a + cX$. Then $Z$ is a random variable and its variance is

$$\mathrm{var}(a + cX) = E[(a + cX) - E(a + cX)]^2 = c^2 \, \mathrm{var}(X) \qquad (2.3.5)$$

This result says that if you:

1.  Add a constant to a random variable it does not affect its variance, or dispersion. This fact follows, since adding a constant to a random variable *shifts* the location of its probability density function but leaves its shape, and dispersion, unaffected.

2.  Multiply a random variable by a constant, the variance is multiplied by the square of the constant.

The square root of the variance of a random variable is called the **standard deviation;** it is denoted by σ. It, too, measures the spread or dispersion of a distribution, and it has the advantage of being in the same units of measure as the random variable.

## *2.4* Using Joint Probability Density Functions

Frequently we want to make probability statements about more than one random variable at a time. To answer probability questions involving two or more random variables, we must know their *joint probability density function.* For the continuous random variables $X$ and $Y$, we use $f(x,y)$ to represent their joint density function. A typical joint density function might look something like Figure 2.3.

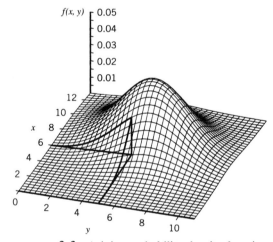

FIGURE *2.3* A joint probability density function

This joint probability density function has the total probability of one unit as the total *volume* under its surface. The probability that the bivariate variable $(X, Y)$ has $x \le 6$ and $y \le 5$, written $P[X \le 6, Y \le 5]$, corresponds to the *volume* under $f(x,y)$ above the rectangle (in the base of the figure) defining the event. If the joint probability density function were known, the probability of the event in question could be calculated by using integral calculus or numerical methods on a computer.

*Example* **2.5**

As an example involving discrete random variables, suppose there is a *population* (not a sample) of 1,000 individuals whom we wish to categorize by their gender (male or female) and political affiliation (Democrat, Republican, or other). Suppose the population breakdown is given in Table 2.1. Given this population of 1,000 persons, consider the experiment of drawing an individual at random. Define two discrete random variables $G$ (gender) and $P$ (political affiliation) as

$$G = \begin{cases} 0 & \text{individual is male} \\ 1 & \text{individual is female} \end{cases}$$

$$P = \begin{cases} 0 & \text{individual is Democrat} \\ 1 & \text{individual is Republican} \\ 2 & \text{individual has other affiliation} \end{cases}$$

*Table* **2.1**   **Population Breakdown by Gender and Political Affiliation**

|  | Male | Female | Political Totals |
|---|---|---|---|
| **Democrat** | 200 | 270 | 470 |
| **Republican** | 300 | 100 | 400 |
| **Other** | 60 | 70 | 130 |
| **Gender totals** | 560 | 440 | 1000 |

Given that the experiment is random, then the *joint* probability distribution of $G$ and $P$ is obtained by dividing the entries of Table 2.1 by 1,000, to obtain the results shown in Table 2.2. Note that the joint probabilities $f(g,p)$ sum to 1.

*Table* **2.2**   **Joint Probability Function $f(g,p)$ of $G$ and $P$**

|  |  | G | | |
|---|---|---|---|---|
|  |  | 0 | 1 | $h(p)$ |
|  | 0 | .20 | .27 | .47 |
| **P** | 1 | .30 | .10 | .40 |
|  | 2 | .06 | .07 | .13 |
|  | $f(g)$ | .56 | .44 | 1.00 |

The joint probability density function is a function of the values $g$ and $p$ and can be used to compute the probabilities of joint events involving the random drawing of individuals from the population. Thus, the probability of drawing a female Republican is .10, or $f(1,1) = .10$.   ■

The idea of a joint probability density function extends to more than two random variables. For example, if $X_1, X_2, \ldots, X_n$ are random variables, then their joint probability density function will be written $f(x_1, x_2, \ldots, x_n)$, and if it is known, it can be used to calculate probabilities involving $X_1, X_2, \ldots, X_n$.

### 2.4.1   MARGINAL PROBABILITY DENSITY FUNCTIONS

Given a joint probability density function, we can obtain the probability distributions of individual random variables.

---

If $X$ and $Y$ are two discrete random variables, then

$$f(x) = \sum_y f(x,y) \text{ for each value } X \text{ can take}$$

$$f(y) = \sum_x f(x,y) \text{ for each value } Y \text{ can take}$$

(2.4.1)

---

Note that the summations in (2.4.1) are over the *other* random variable, the one that we are eliminating from the joint probability density function. This operation is sometimes called "summing out" the unwanted variable in the table of joint probabilities. If the random variables are continuous the same idea works, with integrals replacing the summation sign.

### Example 2.6

As an example we can obtain the probability distributions of $G$ and $P$ introduced in the previous section. From the totals in Table 2.1 we can see that the population contains 560 men and 440 women. Thus, the probability of randomly drawing a male is .56; it is .44 for a female. In Table 2.2 these values are given in the bottom margin in the row labeled $f(g)$, which is the probability density function of $G$ alone, and is sometimes called the *marginal* distribution of $G$, since it is obtained from the joint distribution $f(g,p)$ and is found in the margin of the table. The probability of drawing a male $f(0) = .56$ is found by summing down the first column of the joint probability Table 2.2, corresponding to $g = 0$, over *all* the values of $P$. Similarly, $f(1) = .44$, the probability of randomly choosing a female from the population is found by summing the second column of the joint probability table over all values of $P$. ∎

### 2.4.2   CONDITIONAL PROBABILITY DENSITY FUNCTIONS

Often the chances of an event occurring are *conditional* on the occurrence of another event. For example, a weather forecaster on the morning news might say, "If the cold front reaches here today, then the chances of rain are 80 percent, but otherwise the chance of rain is low." The forecaster is giving the probability of rain *conditioned* by the event that the cold front arrives.

For discrete random variables $X$ and $Y$, conditional probabilities can be calculated from the joint probability density function $f(x,y)$ and the marginal probability density function of the *conditioning* random variable. Specifically, the probability that the random variable $X$ takes the value $x$ *given* that $Y = y$, is written $P[X = x|Y = y]$. This conditional probability is given by the *conditional probability density function* $f(x|y)$:

$$f(x|y) = P[X = x|Y = y] = \frac{f(x,y)}{f(y)} \qquad (2.4.2)$$

---

*Example 2.7*

---

As an example, consider the population of individuals represented by Table 2.1. Suppose we wish to focus on female voters, and ask the question: What is the probability that a randomly selected woman (from this population) is a Republican? Thus, we are asking for the probability that the random variable $P = 1$ given (or conditional upon) that $G = 1$. From Table 2.1 we calculate that the probability of selecting a Republican, given that we sample *only* from the female population, is 0.227 (=100/440). Similarly, the conditional probability of drawing a Democrat from the female population is 0.614, and the conditional probability of drawing an "other political affiliation" from the female population is 0.159.

The complete conditional distribution $f(p|1)$ is:

| $p$ | $f(p|1)$ |
|---|---|
| 0 | $f(1,0)/f(1) = .27/.44 = .614$ |
| 1 | $f(1,1)/f(1) = .10/.44 = .227$ |
| 2 | $f(1,2)/f(1) = .07/.44 = .159$ |

Note that the sum of the conditional probabilities is 1.    ■

---

For discrete random variables the conditional probability density function gives the probabilities of one event conditional on another. If the random variables are continuous, then the conditional probability density function is constructed in the same way but it yields an equation. The equation describes a curve that can be used to calculate probabilities as areas (or volumes) beneath it.

### 2.4.3 INDEPENDENT RANDOM VARIABLES

Making probability statements about more than one random variable is simplified if the random variables involved are unrelated, or *statistically independent* of one another. *Two random variables are statistically independent, or independently distributed, if knowing the value that one will take does not reveal anything about what value the other may take.* A simple example is what happens when two coins are tossed simultaneously. The fact that one coin lands "heads" reveals nothing about the outcome for the other coin. Thus, if the discrete random variable $X$ is the number of heads showing on a toss of the first coin, and $Y$ is the number of heads occurring on the second coin, then $X$ and $Y$ are independent random variables. An example of independent economic variables might be the expenditures on beef by two randomly chosen individuals. An example of dependent economic variables might be the inflation and unemployment rates.

When random variables are statistically independent, their *joint* probability density function factors into the product of their *individual* probability density functions, and vice versa.

---

If $X$ and $Y$ are independent random variables, then

$$f(x,y) = f(x)f(y) \qquad (2.4.3)$$

for each and every pair of values $x$ and $y$. The converse is also true.

---

To consider more than two independent random variables, let $X_1, \ldots, X_n$ be independent random variables with joint probability density function $f(x_1, \ldots, x_n)$ and individual probability density functions $f_1(x_1), f_2(x_2), \ldots, f_n(x_n)$.

---

If $X_1, \ldots, X_n$ are statistically independent, the joint probability density function can be factored and written as

$$f(x_1, x_2, \ldots, x_n) = f_1(x_1) \cdot f_2(x_2) \cdot \cdots \cdot f_n(x_n) \qquad (2.4.4)$$

---

The idea of conditional probability provides a useful way to characterize the statistical independence of two random variables.

---

If $X$ and $Y$ are independent random variables, then the conditional probability density function of $X$, given that $Y = y$, is

$$f(x|y) = \frac{f(x,y)}{f(y)} = \frac{f(x)f(y)}{f(y)} = f(x) \qquad (2.4.5)$$

for each and every pair of values $x$ and $y$. The converse is also true.

---

## Example 2.8

Continuing the voting-gender example, suppose that knowing the gender of an individual from a population tells us *nothing* about the probability that a randomly chosen individual is a Democrat, a Republican, or an Independent. That is, suppose that the conditional probability of a woman or man being Democrat, Republican, or Independent is the same as the unconditional, or marginal, probability; or

$$f(p|g) = h(p) \qquad \text{for } g = 0,1$$

If the conditional probabilities of $P = 0, 1, 2$ given $g = 0, 1$ are all the same as the marginal (unconditional) probabilities for $P$, then knowing gender gives no information about political affiliation, and the two random variables are *statistically independent*. For the population in Table 2.1 this is *not* the case. ∎

## 2.5 The Expected Value of a Function of Several Random Variables: Covariance and Correlation

In economics we are *usually* interested in exploring relationships between economic variables. One question that is frequently asked is: How closely do two price variables move together? An answer to this important question is provided by the **covariance** and **correlation** between these two random variables. The covariance literally indicates the amount of covariation exhibited by the two random variables. As with the mean and variance of single random variables, the covariance is a mathematical expectation.

---

If $X$ and $Y$ are random variables, then their covariance is
$$\text{cov}(X,Y) = E[(X - E[X])(Y - E[Y])] \qquad (2.5.1)$$

---

This expectation is more complicated than the ones we have taken thus far because it involves two random variables. However, there are expressions analogous to equation 2.3.2 that we can use.

---

If $X$ and $Y$ are discrete random variables, $f(x,y)$ is their joint probability density function, and $g(X,Y)$ is a function of them, then
$$E[g(X,Y)] = \sum_x \sum_y g(x,y)f(x,y) \qquad (2.5.2)$$

---

Let $g(X,Y) = (X - E[X])(Y - E[Y])$, then $\text{cov}(X,Y)$ can be obtained using equation 2.5.2.

If $X$ and $Y$ are discrete random variables and $f(x,y)$ is their joint probability density function, then

$$\text{cov}(X,Y) = E[(X - E[X])(Y - E[Y])]$$
$$= \sum_x \sum_y [x - E(X)][y - E(Y)]f(x,y) \qquad (2.5.3)$$

If $X$ and $Y$ are continuous random variables, then the definition of covariance is similar, with integrals replacing the summation signs.

The *sign* of the covariance between two random variables indicates whether their association is positive (direct) or negative (inverse). The covariance between $X$ and $Y$ is the expected, or average, value of the random product $[X - E(X)][Y - E(Y)]$. In Figure 2.4 are plotted typical pairs of randomly drawn values $(x,y)$ of two continuous random variables, $X$ and $Y$. In quadrant I the values $(x,y)$ are greater than their means, $[E(X), E(Y)]$, and thus the product $[x - E(X)][y - E(Y)]$ is positive. In quadrant III the values of the random variables are both less than the mean values, and the product is also positive. In quadrants II and IV the product is negative. Because a greater proportion of values falls in quadrants I and III, *on the average,* the product is positive, and in this case $\text{cov}(X,Y) > 0$. If two random variables have positive covariance then they tend to be positively (or directly) related.

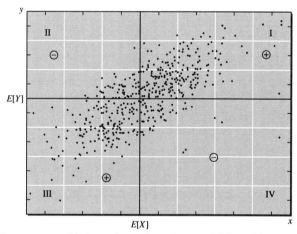

FIGURE 2.4   Data scatter of joint values of random variables with a positive covariance

In Figure 2.5 the greater proportion of values $(x,y)$ falls in quadrants II and IV, where $[x - E(X)][y - E(Y)]$ is negative, and thus, on average, the product is negative and $\text{cov}(X,Y) < 0$. The values of two random variables with negative covariance tend to be negatively (or inversely) related. Zero covariance implies that there is neither positive nor negative association between pairs of values. The magnitude of covariance is difficult to interpret because it depends on the units of measurement of the random variables. The meaning of *covariation* is revealed more clearly if we divide the covariance between $X$ and $Y$ by their respective standard

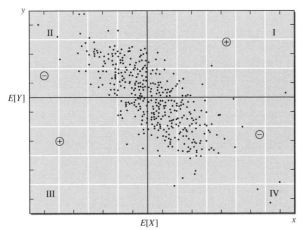

FIGURE **2.5**  Data scatter of joint values of random variables with a negative covariance

deviations. The resulting ratio is defined as the correlation between the random variables $X$ and $Y$ and is often denoted by the Greek letter rho, $\rho$.

---

If $X$ and $Y$ are random variables then their *correlation* is

$$\rho = \frac{\text{cov}(X,Y)}{\sqrt{\text{var}(X)\text{var}(Y)}} \qquad (2.5.4)$$

---

As with the covariance, the correlation $\rho$ between two random variables measures the degree of *linear* association between them. However, unlike the covariance, the correlation must lie between $-1$ and $1$. Thus, the correlation between $X$ and $Y$ is 1 or $-1$ if $X$ is a perfect positive or negative linear function of $Y$. If there is no linear association between $X$ and $Y$, then $\text{cov}(X,Y) = 0$ and $\rho = 0$. For other values of correlation the magnitude of the absolute value $|\rho|$ indicates the "strength" of the association between the values of the random variables. The larger the absolute value $|\rho|$ the more nearly exact the linear association between the values. This is illustrated in Figure 2.6.

A consequence of statistical independence is the following:

---

If $X$ and $Y$ are *independent random variables* then the *covariance* and *correlation* between them are zero. The converse of this relationship is *not* true.

---

Independent random variables $X$ and $Y$ have zero covariance, indicating that there is *no linear association* between them. However, just because the covariance or correlation between two random variables is zero *does not* mean that they are necessarily independent. *Zero covariance means that there is no linear association between the random variables.* Even if $X$ and $Y$ have zero covariance, they might have a nonlinear association, like $X^2 + Y^2 = 1$.

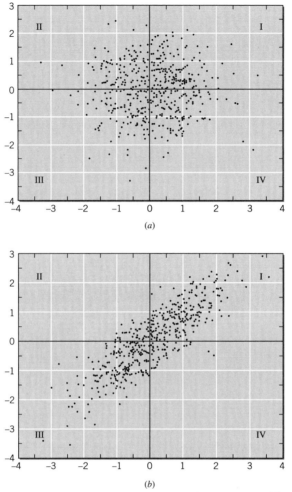

FIGURE **2.6**   Data scatters from joint probability density functions: (*a*) $\rho = 0$; (*b*) $\rho = .3$; (*c*) $\rho = .7$; (*d*) $\rho = .95$

### 2.5.1   THE MEAN OF A WEIGHTED SUM OF RANDOM VARIABLES

In equation 2.5.2 we presented the rule for finding the expected value of a function of two discrete random variables. Let the function $g(X,Y)$ be

$$g(X,Y) = c_1 X + c_2 Y$$

where $c_1$ and $c_2$ are constants. This is called a *weighted* sum. Now use equation 2.5.2 to find the expectation

$$E[c_1 X + c_2 Y] = c_1 E(X) + c_2 E(Y) \qquad (2.5.5)$$

This rule says that the expected value of a weighted sum of two random variables is the weighted sum of their expected values. This rule works for any number of random variables whether they are *discrete or continuous:*

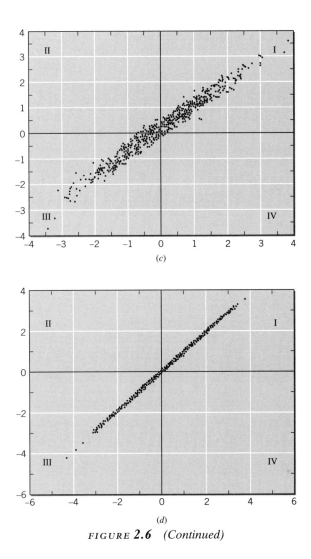

(c)

(d)

FIGURE **2.6**    (Continued)

---

If $X_1, \ldots, X_n$ are random variables and $c_1, \ldots, c_n$ are constants, then

$$E[c_1 X_1 + c_2 X_2 + \cdots + c_n X_n] = c_1 E[X_1] + c_2 E[X_2] + \cdots + c_n E[X_n] \quad (2.5.6)$$

---

Note that if all the $c_i = 1$, then the rule says that the expected value of the sum of a set of random variables is the sum of their expected values. In fact, the rule can be extended to sums of *functions* of random variables. So, we can say, in general, *the expected value of any sum is the sum of the expected values.*

## 2.5.2    THE VARIANCE OF A WEIGHTED SUM OF RANDOM VARIABLES

The following rules of variance are useful. They can be established using equation 2.5.2 and its generalization to $n$ random variables.

1. If $X_1$ and $X_2$ are random variables and $c_1$ and $c_2$ are constants, then

$$\text{var}[c_1X_1 + c_2X_2] = c_1^2 \, \text{var}[X_1] + c_2^2 \, \text{var}[X_2] + 2c_1c_2 \, \text{cov}(X_1, X_2) \quad (2.5.7)$$

2. If $X_1, \ldots, X_n$ are random variables and $c_1, \ldots, c_n$ are constants, then

$$\text{var}[c_1X_1 + c_2X_2 + \cdots + c_nX_n] = c_1^2 \, \text{var}[X_1] + c_2^2 \, \text{var}[X_2] + \cdots +$$
$$c_n^2 \, \text{var}[X_n] + \sum_i \sum_j c_ic_j \, \text{cov}(X_i, X_j) \quad (2.5.8)$$

where the double sum $\Sigma\Sigma_{i\neq j}$ means "take the double sum for all pairs of subscripts except those where $i=j$."

3. If $X_1, \ldots, X_n$ are all *independent* random variables, then the covariance terms are zero and:

$$\text{var}[c_1X_1 + c_2X_2 + \cdots + c_nX_n] = c_1^2 \, \text{var}[X_1] +$$
$$c_2^2 \, \text{var}[X_2] + \cdots + c_n^2 \, \text{var}[X_n] \quad (2.5.9)$$

If $c_1 = c_2 = \cdots = c_n = 1$ we see that, if the random variables are all independent, or if their covariances are zero, the variance of the sum of random variables is the sum of their variances.

## 2.6 The Normal Distribution

In the previous sections we discussed random variables and their probability density functions in a general way. In real economic contexts some *specific* probability density functions have been found to be very useful. The most important is the normal distribution.

If $X$ is a normally distributed random variable with mean $\beta$ and variance $\sigma^2$, symbolized as $X \sim N(\beta, \sigma^2)$, then its probability density function is expressed mathematically as:

$$f(x) = \frac{1}{\sqrt{2\pi\sigma^2}} \exp\left[\frac{-(x - \beta)^2}{2\sigma^2}\right], \qquad -\infty < x < \infty \qquad (2.6.1)$$

where $\exp[a]$ denotes the exponential function $e^a$. The mean $\beta$ and variance $\sigma^2$ are the parameters of this distribution and they determine its location and dispersion. The range of the continuous normal random variable is minus infinity to plus infinity. Pictures of normal probability density functions are given in Figure 2.7 for various values of the mean and variance. The normal probability density function is a symmetric, bell-shaped curve centered at $\beta$, its mean value. Note from Figure 2.7 that normal distributions with the same mean $\beta$ but different variances $\sigma^2$ are more or less spread out about the mean, depending on the magnitude of the variance. For example, the larger the variance, the more disperse and spread out the values. Distributions with the same variance but different means are identical in shape but located at different points along the $x$-axis.

Like all continuous random variables, probabilities involving normal random variables are found as areas under probability density functions. Unfortunately, these areas are not easy to calculate directly unless you have a computer program that will do the work. Alternatively, we can make use of the relation between a

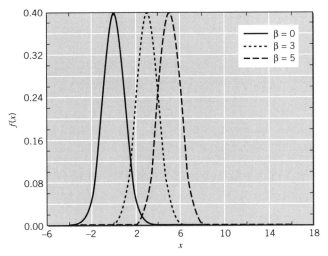

*FIGURE* **2.7**    (*a*) Normal probability density functions: means $\beta$ and variance 1

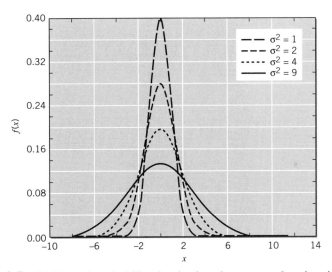

*FIGURE* **2.7**    (*b*) Normal probability density functions: mean 0 and variances $\sigma^2$

normal random variable and its "standardized" equivalent. A **standard normal random variable** is one that has a normal probability density function with mean 0 and variance 1. If $X \sim N(\beta, \sigma^2)$, then

$$Z = \frac{X - \beta}{\sigma} \sim N(0,1)$$

Dividing by the standard deviation $\sigma$ is appropriate, since it has the same units of measure as the random variable $X$. Since $Z = (X/\sigma) - (\beta/\sigma)$, it is easy to use the rules for mean and variance that we have derived to verify that the mean and variance of $Z$ are 0 and 1, respectively.

The standard normal random variable is important for theoretical and practical reasons. Theoretically, the standard normal random variable is important because it is related to a number of other random variables that are central to the study of econometrics. Examples are the chi-square random variable, the $t$ random variable, and the $F$ random variable, all of which are introduced in Section 2.7. Practically, the relationship between the standard normal random variable $Z$ and the normal random variable $X$ is very useful, since any probability statement involving $X$ can be recast as a probability statement involving $Z$; probabilities (areas under the probability density function) for $Z$ are found in Table 1 inside the front cover of this book. Computer programs have various functions that make calculating standard normal probabilities simple and accurate.

To calculate probabilities involving normal random variables, the following rules are useful:

If $X \sim N(\beta, \sigma^2)$ and $a$ is a constant, then

$$P[X \geq a] = P\left[\frac{X - \beta}{\sigma} \geq \frac{a - \beta}{\sigma}\right] = P\left[Z \geq \frac{a - \beta}{\sigma}\right] \qquad (2.6.2)$$

and

If $X \sim N(\beta, \sigma^2)$ and $a$ and $b$ are constants, then

$$P[a \leq X \leq b] = P\left[\frac{a - \beta}{\sigma} \leq \frac{X - \beta}{\sigma} \leq \frac{b - \beta}{\sigma}\right]$$

$$= P\left[\frac{a - \beta}{\sigma} \leq Z \leq \frac{b - \beta}{\sigma}\right] \qquad (2.6.3)$$

For example, if $X \sim N(3, 9)$, then using Table 1

$$P[4 \leq X \leq 6] = P[.33 \leq Z \leq 1] = .3413 - .1293 = .212$$

The standard normal probability density function is depicted in Figure 2.8. On it are marked the positions of one, two, and three standard deviations. From Table 1 inside the front cover of the book we see that 68.2 percent of the probability of a standard normal random variable falls within one standard deviation, on either side, of the mean value (zero), 95.4 percent of the probability falls within two standard deviations, and 99.7 percent of the probability falls within three standard deviations.

An interesting and useful fact about the normal distribution is that a weighted sum of normal random variables has a normal distribution.

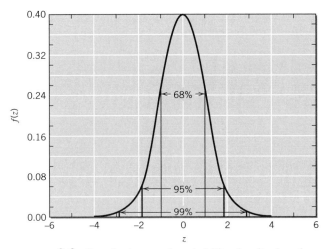

FIGURE **2.8**   Standard normal probability density function

---

If $X_1 \sim N(\beta_1, \sigma_1^2)$, $X_2 \sim N(\beta_2, \sigma_2^2)$, ... , $X_n \sim N(\beta_n, \sigma_n^2)$ and if $c_1, \ldots, c_n$ are constants, then

$$Z = c_1 X_1 + c_2 X_2 + \cdots + c_n X_n \sim N[E(Z), \text{var}(Z)] \qquad (2.6.4)$$

---

Equations 2.5.6 and 2.5.8 can be used to calculate the mean and variance of $Z$ in the usual way. We will use this rule countless times in the remainder of this book.

## *2.7* Distributions Related to the Normal Distribution

Three very important probability distributions are related to the normal distribution: the chi-square distribution, the $t$-distribution and the $F$-distribution. In this section we give a brief description of each of these distributions.

### 2.7.1   THE CHI-SQUARE DISTRIBUTION

Chi-square random variables arise when standard normal, $N(0,1)$, random variables are squared.

---

If $Z_1, Z_2, \ldots, Z_m$ denote $m$ *independent* $N(0,1)$ random variables, then

$$V = Z_1^2 + Z_2^2 + \cdots + Z_m^2 \sim \chi_{(m)}^2 \qquad (2.7.1)$$

---

The notation $V \sim \chi_{(m)}^2$ is read as: the random variable $V$ has a **chi-square distribution** with $m$ *degrees of freedom*. The **degrees of freedom** parameter $m$ indicates the number of *independent* $N(0,1)$ random variables that are squared and summed to form $V$. The value of $m$ determines the entire shape of the chi-square distribution and its mean and variance.

$$E[V] = E[\chi^2_{(m)}] = m$$

$$\text{var}[V] = \text{var}[\chi^2_{(m)}] = 2m$$

(2.7.2)

In Figure 2.9, graphs of the chi-square distribution for various degrees of freedom, $m$, are presented. Since $V$ is formed by squaring and summing $m$ standardized normal $[N(0,1)]$ random variables, the values of $V$ must be nonnegative, $v \geq 0$, and the distribution has a long tail, or is *skewed*, to the right. As the degrees of freedom $m$ gets larger, however, the distribution becomes more symmetric and "bell-shaped." In fact, as $m$ gets large, the chi-square distribution converges to, and essentially becomes, a normal distribution.

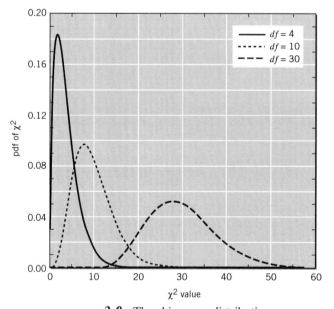

FIGURE **2.9**   The chi-square distribution

Computer programs have functions that calculate probabilities involving chi-square random variables, and their use will be discussed when needed.

### 2.7.2   THE *t*-DISTRIBUTION

A "*t*" random variable (no uppercase) is formed by dividing a standard normal, $Z \sim N(0,1)$, random variable by the square root of an *independent* chi-square random variable, $V \sim \chi^2_{(m)}$, that has been divided by its degrees of freedom, $m$.

If $Z \sim N(0,1)$ and $V \sim \chi^2_{(m)}$, and if $Z$ and $V$ are independent, then

$$t = \frac{Z}{\sqrt{V/m}} \sim t_{(m)} \qquad (2.7.3)$$

The shape of the **$t$-distribution** is completely determined by the degrees of freedom parameter, $m$, and the distribution is symbolized by $t_{(m)}$.

Figure 2.10 shows a graph of the $t$-distribution with $m = 3$ degrees of freedom relative to the $N(0,1)$. Note that the $t$-distribution is less "peaked," and more spread out than the $N(0,1)$. The $t$-distribution is symmetric, with mean $E[t_{(m)}] = 0$ and variance $\text{var}[t_{(m)}] = m/(m - 2)$. As the degrees of freedom parameter $m \to \infty$ the $t_{(m)}$ distribution approaches the standard normal $N(0,1)$.

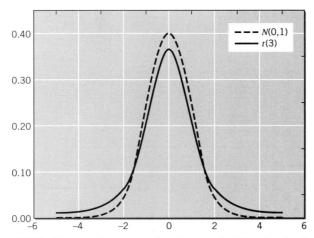

FIGURE **2.10**   The standard normal and $t_{(3)}$ probability density functions

Computer programs have functions that calculate probabilities involving $t$ random variables, and we will introduce their use when needed. Since certain probabilities are widely used, Table 2 inside the front cover of this book contains percentiles of $t$-distributions.

## 2.7.3   THE $F$-DISTRIBUTION

An $F$ random variable is formed by the ratio of two independent chi-square random variables that have been divided by their degrees of freedom.

If $V_1 \sim \chi^2_{(m_1)}$ and $V_2 \sim \chi^2_{(m_2)}$ and if $V_1$ and $V_2$ are independent, then

$$F = \frac{V_1/m_1}{V_2/m_2} \sim F_{(m_1, m_2)} \qquad (2.7.4)$$

The **F-distribution** is said to have $m_1$ *numerator degrees of freedom* and $m_2$ *denominator degrees of freedom.* The values of $m_1$ and $m_2$ determine the shape of the distribution, which in general looks like Figure 2.11. The range of the random variable is $(0,\infty)$ and it has a long tail to the right.

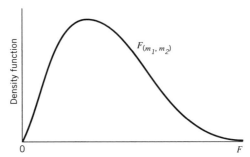

FIGURE **2.11**   The density function of an *F* random variable

Computer programs have functions to calculate probabilities involving *F* random variables, and we will explore their use when they are needed.

## *2.8* Summing Up

In this chapter we have reviewed some probability concepts that we will use repeatedly in the remainder of the book. We hope that as you proceed through the book you will refer to this chapter when your recollection of how to work with probabilities and random variables becomes fuzzy. Some highlights from the chapter are:

1.  Experiments can be controlled or uncontrolled. Economic data are usually nonexperimental. That is, they are created by an uncontrolled experiment.
2.  Random variables have values that are unknown until they are observed.
3.  Random variables can be discrete or continuous.
4.  Discrete random variables have probability density functions that give the probability that the random variable takes a specific value.
5.  Continuous random variables have probability density functions that may be expressed in the form of equations of curves. The probability that the random variable takes a value in an interval is the area under the curve corresponding to the interval.
6.  The expected value of a random variable is its average value in many repeated trials of the underlying experiment. If $X$ is a discrete random variable with probability density function $f(x)$, then $E[X] = \Sigma x f(x)$
7.  The variance of a random variable is the average squared distance between the values of the random variable and its expected value in many repeated trials of the underlying experiment. The variance of a random variable $X$ is $\text{var}(X) = \sigma^2 = E[X - E(X)]^2$.

8. If $g(X)$ is a function of the discrete random variable $X$ with probability density function $f(x)$, then $E[g(X)] = \Sigma g(x)f(x)$

9. If $a$ and $c$ are constants then $\text{var}(a + cX) = c^2 \text{var}(X)$.

10. A joint probability density function $f(x,y)$ is used to make joint probability statements about the random variables $X$ and $Y$.

11. If $X$ and $Y$ are discrete random variables, then the marginal probability density function of $X$ is $f(x) = \Sigma_y f(x,y)$ for each value of $X$.

12. If $X$ and $Y$ are random variables, then the conditional probability density function of $X$ given that $Y=y$ is $f(x|y) = \dfrac{f(x,y)}{f(y)}$

13. If $X$ and $Y$ are independent random variables, then $f(x,y) = f(x)f(y)$. The converse is also true. Furthermore, if $X$ and $Y$ are independent random variables, then $f(x|y) = f(x)$.

14. The covariance between the random variables $X$ and $Y$ measures the linear association between them. It is $\text{cov}(X,Y) = E[(X - E[X])(Y - E[Y])]$.

15. The correlation between the random variables $X$ and $Y$ measures the linear association between them. It is a pure number falling between $-1$ and $1$. It is $\rho = \dfrac{\text{cov}(X,Y)}{\sqrt{\text{var}(X)\ \text{var}(Y)}}$

16. Independent random variables have zero covariance and correlation. The converse is not true.

17. The expected value of a weighted sum of random variables is the sum of the expectations of the individual terms.

18. The variance of a weighted sum of random variables is the sum of the variances, each times the square of the weight, plus twice the covariances of all the random variables times the products of their weights.

19. If $X \sim N(\beta,\sigma^2)$ then $Z = (X - \beta)/\sigma \sim N(0,1)$.

20. If $V \sim \chi^2_{(m)}$, and if $Z$ and $V$ are independent, then $t = Z/\sqrt{V/m} \sim t_{(m)}$.


## 2.9 Exercises

2.1   Define the following terms:
    (a) Sampling error
    (b) Probability density function
    (c) Discrete random variable; continuous random variable
    (d) Mean of a random variable
    (e) Variance of a random variable
    (f) Mathematical expectation
    (g) Covariance and correlation

2.2*  Use equation 2.3.2 to show that equations 2.3.3a, b, and c are true.

2.3   Let $X$ be a discrete random variable with values $x = 0,1,2$ and probabilities $P(X = 0) = .25$, $P(X = 1) = .50$ and $P(X = 2) = .25$ respectively.
    (a) Find $E(X)$.
    (b) Find $E(X^2)$.

(c) Find var($X$).

(d) Find the expected value and variance of $g(X) = 3X + 2$.

2.4   Use the properties of expectations to show that equation 2.3.5 is true.

2.5   Let $X$ be a discrete random variable that is the value shown on a single roll of a fair die.

(a) Represent the probability density function $f(x)$ in tabular form.

(b) What is the probability that $X = 4$? That $X = 4$ or $X = 5$?

(c) What is the expected value of $X$? Explain the meaning of $E(X)$ in this case.

(d) Find the expected value of $X^2$.

(e) Find the variance of $X$.

2.6   Let $X$ be a continuous random variable whose probability density function is

$$f(x) = \begin{cases} 2x & 0 \le x \le 1 \\ 0 & otherwise \end{cases}$$

(a) Sketch the probability density function $f(x)$.

(b) Geometrically calculate the probability that $X$ falls between 0 and $\frac{1}{2}$.

(c) Geometrically calculate the probability that $X$ falls between $\frac{1}{4}$ and $\frac{3}{4}$.

2.7   Suppose $X_1$ and $X_2$ are independent continuous random variables, each of which has the probability density function $f(x)$ in Exercise 2.6. What is their *joint* probability density function $f(x_1, x_2)$?

2.8   The random variables gender ($G$) and political affiliation ($P$) have (hypothetical) joint probability density function $f(g, p)$ in Table 2.2.

(a) Are the random variables $G$ and $P$ independent? If not, why not?

(b) Find the complete conditional distribution $f(p|g=0)$.

2.9   Let the discrete random variable $X$ have probability density function

$$f(x) = p^x(1 - p)^{1-x} \qquad for\ x = 0,1$$

(a) Find the mean and variance of $X$.

(b) Let $X_1, \ldots , X_n$ be independent discrete (0,1) random variables, each with probability density function $f(x)$. The random variable $B = X_1 + X_2 + \cdots + X_n$ has a binomial distribution with parameters $n$ and $p$. The values of $B$ are $b = 0, \ldots , n$ and represent the number of "successes" (i.e., $X_i = 1$) in $n$ independent trials of an experiment, each with probability $p$ of success. Calculate the mean and variance of $B$.

(c) Let $X_1, \ldots , X_n$ be independent discrete (0, 1) random variables with probability density functions $f(x)$. The random variable $B = X_1 + \cdots + X_n$ has a binomial distribution. The random variable $Y = B/n$ is the proportion of successes in $n$ trials of an experiment. Find the mean and variance of $Y$.

2.10   Use a geometric argument to show that the expected value, or mean, of a uniform random variable is $(a + b)/2$.

2.11   The joint probability density function of two discrete random variables $X$ and $Y$ is given by the following table:

$$
\begin{array}{c|ccc}
 & \multicolumn{3}{c}{Y} \\
 & 1 & 3 & 9 \\
\hline
2 & \frac{1}{8} & \frac{1}{24} & \frac{1}{12} \\
X \quad 4 & \frac{1}{4} & \frac{1}{4} & 0 \\
6 & \frac{1}{8} & \frac{1}{24} & \frac{1}{12}
\end{array}
$$

(a) Find the marginal probability density function of $Y$.
(b) Find the conditional probability density function of $Y$ given that $X = 2$.
(c) Find the covariance of $X$ and $Y$.
(d) Are $X$ and $Y$ independent?

2.12   A fair die is rolled two times. Let $X_1$ and $X_2$ denote the number of points showing on the first and second rolls, respectively. Let $U = X_1 + X_2$ and $V = X_1 - X_2$.
(a)  Find the mean and variance of $V$.
(b)  Find the covariance of $U$ and $V$.
(c)* Show that $U$ and $V$ are not independent.

2.13*  Let $X_1$ and $X_2$ be *independent* discrete random variables with joint probability density function $f(x_1,x_2)$. Show that

$$E[X_1 X_2] = E[X_1]E[X_2].$$

2.14   Show that var($X$) can be expressed as $E[X^2] - [E(X)]^2$ using the properties of expected values.

2.15   Use equation 2.5.2 to show that equation 2.5.5 is true.

2.16   Use the properties of expectations and variances to show that if $X \sim N(\beta,\sigma^2)$ then

$$Z = \frac{X - \beta}{\sigma} = \frac{X}{\sigma} - \frac{\beta}{\sigma} \sim N(0,1)$$

2.17   Let $X_1, X_2, \ldots , X_n$ be independent random variables that all have the same probability distribution, with mean $\beta$ and variance $\sigma^2$. Let

$$\overline{X} = \frac{1}{n}\sum_{i=1}^{n}X_i$$

(a) Prove that $E[\overline{X}] = \beta$
(b) Prove that var($\overline{X}$) = $\sigma^2/n$

2.18*  Consider the joint probability density function

$$f(x,y) = (0.6)^x(0.4)^{1-x}(0.3)^y(0.52)^{1-y}2^{xy}$$

where the possible values for $X$ and $Y$ are $x = 0,1$ and $y = 0,1$. Find:
(a) $f(0,0), f(0,1), f(1,0), f(1,1)$
(b) The marginal density functions $f(x)$ and $f(y)$
(c) The conditional density function $f(y|x = 0)$
(d) $E(X)$ and $E(Y)$

(e) $\text{var}(X)$ and $\text{var}(Y)$
(f) $\text{cov}(X,Y)$ and the correlation between $X$ and $Y$
(g) $E(X + Y)$ and $\text{var}(X + Y)$

2.19    Suppose that $Y_1, Y_2, Y_3$ is a sample of observations from a $N(\beta,\sigma^2)$ population but that $Y_1, Y_2,$ and $Y_3$ are *not* independent. In fact suppose

$$\text{cov}(Y_1, Y_2) = \text{cov}(Y_2, Y_3) = \text{cov}(Y_1, Y_3) = .5\sigma^2.$$

Let $\overline{Y} = (Y_1 + Y_2 + Y_3)/3$.
(a) Find $E(\overline{Y})$.
(b) Find $\text{var}(\overline{Y})$.

2.20    The length of life (in years) of a personal computer is approximately normally distributed with mean 2.9 years and variance 1.96 years.
(a) What fraction of computers will fail in the first year?
(b) What fraction of computers will last 4 years or more?
(c) What fraction of computers will last at least 2 years?
(d) What fraction of computers will last more than 2.5 years but less than 4 years?
(e) If the manufacturer adopts a warranty policy in which only 5 percent of the computers have to be replaced, what will be the length of the warranty period?

2.21    Fifteen male economists are in a life raft with a maximum carrying capacity of 2,850 pounds. If the distribution of weights of male economists is normal with a mean of 178 pounds and with a standard deviation of 17 pounds, find
(a) the probability that all the economists weigh less than 189 pounds.
(b) the probability that the raft is overloaded, thus making some economists shark-bait.
(c) What is the maximum number of economists that should enter the raft if the probability of overloading [see part (b)] is not to exceed 0.001? (Can't you just see the economists bidding for the available positions?)

## *2.10* References

The material we have considered in this chapter is presented in many elementary and intermediate statistics texts. An excellent statistics text is Keller, Warrack, and Bartel (1994, Chapters 5 an 6.) Useful resources at an elementary level are Beals (1972, Chapters 1–6), Caniglia (1992, Chapters 1–8) and Mirer (1995, Chapters 8–10.) A slightly more advanced treatment may be found in Griffiths et al. (1993, Chapter 2).

BEALS, R. E. (1972). *Statistics for Economists: An Introduction.* Chicago: Rand McNally & Co.

CANIGLIA, ALAN S. (1992). *Statistics for Economists: An Intuitive Approach.* New York: HarperCollins.

GRIFFITHS, W. E., R. C. HILL AND G. G. JUDGE (1993). *Learning and Practicing Econometrics.* New York: John Wiley and Sons.

KELLER, GERALD, BRIAN WARRACK, AND HENRY BARTEL (1994). *Statistics for Management and Economics, Abbreviated Edition.* Belmont, Calif.: Duxbury Press.

MIRER, THAD W. (1995). *Economic Statistics and Econometrics, Third Edition.* Englewood Cliffs, N.J.: Prentice Hall.

# Part *I*

# The Simple Linear Regression Model

In Chapters 3 through 6, building on some of the basic concepts of probability and the conceptual basis provided by economic theory, we will specify simple economic and statistical models that can be used for the purposes of estimating unknown parameters, carrying through the process of inference and drawing economic conclusions. Specifically, in Chapter 3 we will specify the simple linear regression model, starting from the economic base. The assumptions are thoroughly discussed, and the principle of least squares is introduced and used to estimate the model parameters. Chapter 4 contains a discussion of the properties of the least squares estimation procedures—how they perform in repeated samples. Also, the variance of the error term is estimated and the prediction problem is introduced. Procedures for constructing interval estimates and prediction intervals are presented in Chapter 5. There we also discuss testing hypotheses about economic parameters. How regression results are summarized and presented is the subject of Chapter 6.

# Chapter *3*

# The Simple Linear Regression Model: Specification and Estimation

Economic theory suggests many relationships between economic variables. In microeconomics you considered demand and supply models in which the quantities demanded and supplied of a good depend on its price. You considered "production functions" and "total product curves" that explained the amount of a good produced as a function of the amount of an input, such as labor, that is used. In macroeconomics you specified "investment functions" to explain that the amount of aggregate investment in the economy depends on the interest rate and "consumption functions" that related aggregate consumption to the level of disposable income.

Each of these specifications involves a relationship among economic variables. In this chapter we consider how to use a sample of economic data to learn about such relationships. As economists, we are interested in questions such as: If one variable (e.g., price of a good) changes in a certain way, *by how much* will another variable (e.g., quantity demanded or supplied) change? Also, given that we know the value of one variable, can we *forecast* or *predict* the corresponding value of another? We will answer these questions in this chapter by using a **regression model**. Like all models the regression model is based on assumptions. In this chapter we hope to be very clear about these assumptions, as they are the conditions under which the analysis in subsequent chapters is appropriate.

## *3.1* An Economic Model

In order to develop the ideas of regression models we are going to use a simple, but important, economic example. Suppose that we are interested in studying the relationship between household income and expenditure on food. Consider the "experiment" of randomly selecting households from a particular population. The population might consist of households within a particular city, state, province, or country. For now, suppose that we are only interested in households with a household income of $480 per week, or $24,960 per year. In this experiment we randomly select a number of households from this population and interview them. The characteristic that we are interested in is the household's weekly expenditures on food, so we ask the question, "How much did your household spend on food last week?"

Weekly food expenditure, which we denote as *y,* is a *random variable* because the value is unknown to us until a household is selected and the question is asked and answered.

> **Remark:** In Chapter 2 we distinguished random variables from their values by using uppercase ($Y$) letters for random variables and lowercase ($y$) letters for their values. We will not follow this practice any longer, as it leads to unacceptably complicated notation. We will use $y$ to denote random variables as well as their values, and we will make the interpretation clear in the surrounding text.

The continuous random variable $y$ has a *probability density function, $f(y)$,* that describes the probabilities of obtaining various food expenditure values. Clearly, the amount spent on food will vary from one household to another for a variety of reasons. Some households will be devoted to gourmet food, some will contain teenagers, some will contain senior citizens, some will be vegetarian. All of these factors and many others, including random, impulsive buying, will cause weekly expenditures on food to vary from one household to another, despite the fact that they all have the same income. The probability density function in this case describes how expenditures are "distributed" over the population, and it might look like one of those in Figure 3.1.

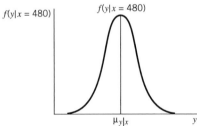

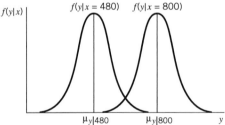

FIGURE **3.1a**  Probability distribution $f(y|x = 480)$ of food expenditure $y$ given income $x = \$480$

FIGURE **3.1b**  Probability distributions of food expenditures $y$ given income $x = \$480$ and $x = \$800$

The probability distribution in Figure 3.1a is actually a conditional probability density function, since it is "conditional" upon household income. If $x$ = weekly household income, then the conditional probability density function is $f(y|x = \$480)$. The *conditional mean,* or *expected value,* of $y$ is $E(y|x = \$480) = \mu_{y|x}$ and is our population's average weekly food expenditure. The *conditional variance* of $y$ is $\text{var}(y|x = \$480) = \sigma^2$, which measures the dispersion of household expenditures $y$ about their mean $\mu_{y|x}$. The parameters $\mu_{y|x}$ and $\sigma^2$, if they were known, would give us some valuable information about the population we are considering. If we knew these parameters, and if we knew that the conditional distribution $f(y|x = \$480)$ was *normal,* $N(\mu_{y|x}, \sigma^2)$, then we could calculate probabilities that $y$ falls in specific intervals using properties of the normal distribution.

As economists, we are usually more interested in studying relationships *between* variables, in this case the relationship between $y$ = weekly food expenditure and $x$ = weekly household income. Economic theory tells us that expenditure on economic goods depends on income. But in your economics classes it was probably not mentioned that expenditure is a *random variable.*

An econometric analysis of the expenditure relationship can provide answers to some important questions, such as: If weekly income goes up by $20, how much will *average* weekly food expenditures rise? Or, could weekly food expenditures *fall* as income rises? How much would we predict the weekly expenditure on food to be for a household with an income of $800 per week? The answers to such questions provide valuable information for decision makers. For example, suppose that we are managers of a supermarket chain and are responsible for long-range planning. If economic forecasters are predicting that local income will increase over the next few years, then we must decide if and how much to expand our facilities to serve our customers. Or, if the chain has one supermarket in a high-income neighborhood and another in a low-income neighborhood, then forecasts of expenditure on food for different income levels give an indication of how large the supermarkets in those areas should be.

In order to investigate the relationship between expenditure and income, we must build an **economic model** and then an **econometric,** or *statistical,* **model** that forms the basis for a quantitative economic analysis. In our food expenditure example, economic theory suggests that *average* weekly household expenditure on food, represented by the conditional mean $E(y|x)$, depends on household income, $x$. If we consider households with different levels of income, we expect the average expenditure on food to change. In Figure 3.1b we show the probability density functions of food expenditure for two different levels of weekly income, $480 and $800. Each density function $f(y|x)$ shows that expenditures will be distributed about the mean value $\mu_{y|x}$, but the mean expenditure by households with higher income is larger than the mean expenditure by lower income households.

In most economics textbooks, consumption or expenditure functions relating consumption to income are depicted as *linear functions,* and we will begin by assuming the same thing. But *remember,* it is just an assumption. Our economic model of household food expenditure, depicted in Figure 3.2, is

$$E(y|x) = \mu_{y|x} = \beta_1 + \beta_2 x. \tag{3.1.1}$$

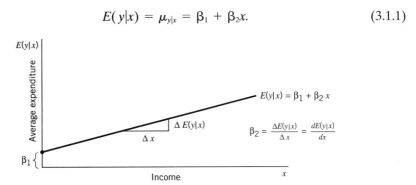

FIGURE **3.2**  The economic model: a linear relationship between average expenditure on food and income

The conditional mean $E(y|x)$ in equation 3.1.1 is called a **simple regression function.** It is called *simple* regression not because it is easy, but because there is only one economic variable on the right-hand side of the equation. The unknown **regression parameters** $\beta_1$ and $\beta_2$ are the intercept and slope of the regression function, respectively. In our food expenditure example, the intercept, $\beta_1$, represents the average weekly household expenditure on food by a household with *no* income, $x = \$0$. The slope $\beta_2$ represents the change in $E(y|x)$ given a \$1 change in weekly income; it could be called the *marginal propensity to spend on food.* Algebraically,

$$\beta_2 = \frac{\Delta E(y|x)}{\Delta x} = \frac{dE(y|x)}{dx} \qquad (3.1.2)$$

where $\Delta$ denotes "change in" and $dE(y|x)/dx$ denotes the "derivative" of $E(y|x)$ with respect to $x$. We will not use derivatives to any great extent in this book, and if you are unfamiliar or rusty with the concept, you can think of $d$ as a "stylized" version of $\Delta$ and go on. We will come back to the interpretation and uses of these parameters later in the chapter.

The economic model (3.1.1) summarizes what theory tells us about the relationship between household income $(x)$ and average household expenditure on food, $E(y|x)$. The parameters of the model, $\beta_1$ and $\beta_2$, are quantities that help characterize economic behavior, and that serve as a basis for making economic decisions. In order to use data, we must now specify an *econometric* or *statistical model* that describes how the data on household income and expenditure are obtained, and that guides the econometric analysis.

## 3.2  An Econometric Model

The model $E(y|x) = \beta_1 + \beta_2 x$ that we specified in Section 3.1 describes economic behavior, but it is an abstraction from reality. If we take a random sample of households with weekly income $x = \$480$, we know the actual expenditure values will be scattered around the average or mean value $E(y|x = 480) = \beta_1 + \beta_2 (480)$, as shown in Figure 3.1. If we were to sample household expenditures at other levels of income, we would expect the sample values to be scattered around their mean value $E(y|x) = \beta_1 + \beta_2 x$. In Figure 3.3 we arrange bell-shaped figures like Figure 3.1, depicting $f(y|x)$, along the regression line for *each* level of income.

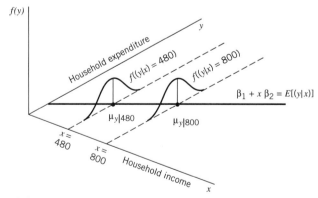

FIGURE **3.3**   The probability density function for $y$ at two levels of income

This figure shows that at each level of income the *average* value of household expenditure is given by the regression function, $E(y|x) = \beta_1 + \beta_2 x$. It also shows that we assume *values* of household expenditure on food will be distributed around the mean value $E(y|x) = \beta_1 + \beta_2 x$ at each level of income. This regression function is the foundation of an econometric model for household food expenditure.

In order to make the econometric model complete, we have to make a few more assumptions. In Figure 3.1a we assumed that the *dispersion* of the values $y$ about their mean is $\text{var}(y|x = \$480) = \sigma^2$. We must make a similar assumption about the dispersion of values at each level of income. The standard assumption is that the dispersion of values $y$ about their mean is the *same for all levels of income, x.* That is, $\text{var}(y|x) = \sigma^2$ for all values of $x$. In Figure 3.1b the probability density functions of food expenditures by households with two different incomes have different means but they have identical variances. This assumption is also illustrated in Figure 3.3, as we have depicted the "spread" of each of the distributions, like Figure 3.1, to be the same.

The constant variance assumption, $\text{var}(y|x) = \sigma^2$ implies that at each level of income $x$ we are *equally* uncertain about how far values of food expenditure, $y$, may fall from their mean value, $E(y|x) = \beta_1 + \beta_2 x$, and the uncertainty does not depend on income *or anything else.* Data satisfying this condition are said to be **homoskedastic.** If this assumption is violated, so that $\text{var}(y|x) \neq \sigma^2$ for all values of income, $x$, the data are said to be **heteroskedastic.**

Next, we have described the sample as *random.* By this we mean that when data are collected, they are statistically independent. If $y_i$ and $y_j$ denote the expenditures of two randomly selected households, then knowing the value of one of these (random) variables tells us *nothing* about what value the other might take. For example, knowing that the Smith household spends $100 from its $480-per-week income on food does not affect how much the next randomly selected household might spend.

Mathematicians spend their lives (we exaggerate slightly) trying to prove the same theorem with weaker and weaker sets of assumptions. This mindset spills over to statisticians and econometricians to some degree. Consequently, econometric models often make an assumption that is weaker than statistical independence, but that is sufficiently strong to prove the things we want to prove in the next few chapters. If $y_i$ and $y_j$ are the expenditures of two randomly selected households, then we will assume that their *covariance* is zero, or $\text{cov}(y_i, y_j) = 0$. This is a weaker assumption than statistical independence (since independence implies zero covariance, but not vice versa); it implies only that there is no systematic *linear* association between $y_i$ and $y_j$. Refer to Chapter 2.5 for a discussion of this difference.

In order to carry out a regression analysis we must make an assumption about the values of the variable $x$. The idea of regression analysis is to measure the effect of changes in one variable, $x$, on another, $y$. In order to do that, $x$ must take several different values, at least two in this case, within the sample of data. If all the observations on $x$ within the sample take the same value, say $x = \$480$, then regression analysis fails. This will be demonstrated in the next section. For now we simply state the additional assumption that $x$ cannot take the same constant value for all observations.

Finally, it is sometimes assumed that the distribution of $y$, $f(y|x)$, is known to be *normal.* The justification for this is the observation that in nature, the "bell-shaped" curve describes many physical phenomenon, ranging from IQs to the length of corn stalks to the birth weights of Australian male children. It is reasonable, sometimes, to assume that an economic variable is normally distributed about its mean. We will say more about this assumption later, but for now we will make it an "optional" assumption, since we do not *need* to make it in many cases, and it is a very *strong* assumption when it is made.

These ideas, taken together, define our econometric model. They are a collection of assumptions that describe the data. To keep things uncluttered in this summary *and henceforth,* we will *not* use the "conditioning" notation $y|x$.

---

**ASSUMPTIONS OF THE SIMPLE LINEAR REGRESSION MODEL—I**

1. The average value of $y$, for each value of $x$, is given by the *linear regression*

$$E(y) = \beta_1 + \beta_2 x$$

2. For each value of $x$, the values of $y$ are distributed about their mean value, following probability distributions that all have the same variance,

$$\text{var}(y) = \sigma^2$$

3. The values of $y$ are all *uncorrelated,* and have zero *covariance,* implying that there is no linear association among them.

$$\text{cov}(y_i, y_j) = 0$$

This assumption can be made stronger by assuming that the values of $y$ are all *statistically independent.*

4. The variable $x$ must take at least two different values, so that $x \neq c$, where $c$ is a constant.

5. (*optional*) The values of $y$ are *normally distributed* about their mean for each value of $x$,

$$y \sim N[(\beta_1 + \beta_2 x), \sigma^2]$$

---

### 3.2.1 INTRODUCING THE ERROR TERM

It is convenient for economists to describe the assumptions of the simple linear regression model in terms of $y$, which in general is called the *dependent* variable in the regression model. However, for statistical purposes it is also useful to characterize the assumptions another way.

The essence of regression analysis is that any observation on the dependent variable $y$ can be decomposed into two parts: a systematic component and a random component. The systematic component of $y$ is its mean $E(y)$, which itself is not random, since it is a mathematical expectation. The random component of $y$ is the difference between $y$ and its mean value $E(y)$. This is called a **random error term,** and it is defined as

$$e = y - E(y) = y - \beta_1 - \beta_2 x \qquad (3.2.1)$$

If we rearrange equation 3.2.1 we obtain the simple linear regression model

$$y = \beta_1 + \beta_2 x + e \qquad (3.2.2)$$

The dependent variable $y$ is explained by a component that varies systematically with the *independent* variable $x$ and by the random error term $e$.

Equation 3.2.1 shows that $y$ and error term $e$ differ only by the constant $E(y)$, and since $y$ is random, so is the error term $e$. Given what we have already assumed about $y$, the *properties* of the random error, $e$, can be derived directly from equation 3.2.1. Since $y$ and $e$ differ only by a constant, $\beta_1 + \beta_2 x$, the probability density functions for $y$ and $e$ are identical except for their location, as shown in Figure 3.4.

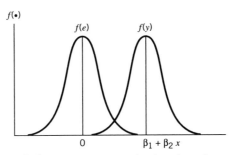

FIGURE **3.4**    Probability density functions for $e$ and $y$

It is customary in econometrics to state the assumptions of the regression model in terms of the random error $e$. They are:

---

**ASSUMPTIONS OF THE SIMPLE LINEAR REGRESSION MODEL—II**

1. The value of $y$, for each value of $x$, is

$$y = \beta_1 + \beta_2 x + e$$

2. The average value of the random error $e$ is

$$E(e) = 0$$

since we assume that

$$E(y) = \beta_1 + \beta_2 x$$

3. The variance of the random error $e$ is

$$\text{var}(e) = \sigma^2 = \text{var}(y)$$

since $y$ and $e$ differ only by a constant, which does not change the variance.

4. The covariance between any pair of random errors, $e_i$ and $e_j$ is

$$\text{cov}(e_i , e_j) = \text{cov}(y_i , y_j) = 0$$

If the values of $y$ are *statistically independent*, then so are the random errors $e$, and vice versa.

5. The variable $x$ must take at least two different values, so that $x \neq c$, where $c$ is a constant.

6. (*optional*) The values of $e$ are *normally distributed* about their mean

$$e \sim N(0,\sigma^2)$$

*if* the values of $y$ are normally distributed, and vice versa.

The random error $e$ and the dependent variable $y$ are both random variables, and the properties of one can be determined from the properties of the other. There is one interesting difference between these random variables, however, and that is that $y$ is "observable" and $e$ is "unobservable." If the regression parameters $\beta_1$ and $\beta_2$ were *known*, then for any value of $y$ we could calculate $e = y - (\beta_1 + \beta_2 x)$. This is illustrated in Figure 3.5.

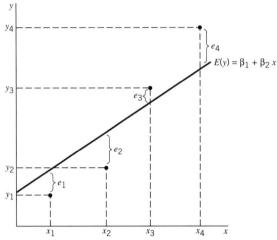

FIGURE **3.5**    The relationship among $y, e$ and the true regression line

Knowing the regression function $E(y|x) = \beta_1 + \beta_2 x$, we could separate $y$ into its fixed and random parts. Unfortunately, since $\beta_1$ and $\beta_2$ *are never known*, it is *impossible* to calculate $e$, and no bets on its true value can ever be collected.

It is useful to think about $e$ in a slightly different way. The random error $e$ represents all factors affecting $y$ other than income. These factors cause individual observations $y$ to differ from the mean value $E(y|x) = \beta_1 + \beta_2 x$. In the food expenditure example, what factors can result in a difference between expenditure $y$ and its mean, $E(y|x)$?

1.  We have included income as the only explanatory variable in this model. *Any **other** economic factors that affect expenditures on food* are "collected" in the error term. Naturally, in any economic model, we want to include all the important and relevant explanatory variables *in* the model, so the error term $e$ is a "storage bin" for unobservable and/or unimportant factors affecting household expenditures on food. As such, it adds noise that masks the relationship between $x$ and $y$, as shown in Figure 1.1.

2.  The error term $e$ captures any approximation error that arises, because the linear functional form we have assumed may be only an approximation to reality.

3.  The error term captures any elements of random behavior that might be present in each individual. Knowledge of all variables that influence an individual's food expenditure *might not* be sufficient to perfectly predict

expenditure. An unpredictable random behavioral component might also be contained in *e*.

## *3.3* Estimating the Parameters for the Expenditure Relationship

The economic and statistical models we developed in the previous section are the basis for using a sample of data to *estimate* the intercept and slope parameters, $\beta_1$ and $\beta_2$. Data on food expenditure from "last week" and weekly income from a random sample of forty households are given in Table 3.1. They are typical of those obtained by conducting a survey in a large city.

We cannot stress strongly enough that in order to use the data in Table 3.1 to estimate the parameters of the food expenditure model *we must assume that the simple linear regression model, and the assumptions that we have stated, describe the sample observations.* That is, the expenditure data in Table 3.1 are observed values of the random variable $y_t$, $t = 1, \ldots, 40$, that satisfy the assumptions:

1.  $y_t = \beta_1 + \beta_2 x_t + e_t$
2.  $E(e_t) = 0 \Leftrightarrow E(y_t) = \beta_1 + \beta_2 x_t$
3.  $\text{var}(e_t) = \sigma^2 = \text{var}(y_t)$                                      (3.3.1)

*Table 3.1*   **Food Expenditure and Income Data**

| Observation $t$ | Food Expenditure $y_t$ | Weekly Income $x_t$ | Observation $t$ | Food Expenditure $y_t$ | Weekly Income $x_t$ |
|---|---|---|---|---|---|
| 1 | 52.25 | 258.30 | 21 | 98.14 | 719.80 |
| 2 | 58.32 | 343.10 | 22 | 123.94 | 720.00 |
| 3 | 81.79 | 425.00 | 23 | 126.31 | 722.30 |
| 4 | 119.90 | 467.50 | 24 | 146.47 | 722.30 |
| 5 | 125.80 | 482.90 | 25 | 115.98 | 734.40 |
| 6 | 100.46 | 487.70 | 26 | 207.23 | 742.50 |
| 7 | 121.51 | 496.50 | 27 | 119.80 | 747.70 |
| 8 | 100.08 | 519.40 | 28 | 151.33 | 763.30 |
| 9 | 127.75 | 543.30 | 29 | 169.51 | 810.20 |
| 10 | 104.94 | 548.70 | 30 | 108.03 | 818.50 |
| 11 | 107.48 | 564.60 | 31 | 168.90 | 825.60 |
| 12 | 98.48 | 588.30 | 32 | 227.11 | 833.30 |
| 13 | 181.21 | 591.30 | 33 | 84.94 | 834.00 |
| 14 | 122.23 | 607.30 | 34 | 98.70 | 918.10 |
| 15 | 129.57 | 611.20 | 35 | 141.06 | 918.10 |
| 16 | 92.84 | 631.00 | 36 | 215.40 | 929.60 |
| 17 | 117.92 | 659.60 | 37 | 112.89 | 951.70 |
| 18 | 82.13 | 664.00 | 38 | 166.25 | 1014.00 |
| 19 | 182.28 | 704.20 | 39 | 115.43 | 1141.30 |
| 20 | 139.13 | 704.80 | 40 | 269.03 | 1154.60 |

4.   $\operatorname{cov}(e_i, e_j) = \operatorname{cov}(y_i, y_j) = 0$
5.   $x_t \neq c$ for every observation
6.   $e_t \sim N(0, \sigma^2) \Leftrightarrow y_t \sim N[(\beta_1 + \beta_2 x_t), \sigma^2]$ *(optional)*

Given this theoretical model for explaining the sample observations on household food expenditure, the problem now is how to use our sample information $y_t$ and $x_t$ to estimate the unknown parameters $\beta_1$ and $\beta_2$ that represent the unknown intercept and slope coefficients for the food expenditure–income relationship. If we represent the 40 data points as $(y_t, x_t)$, $t = 1, \ldots, 40$, and plot them, we obtain the **scatter diagram** in Figure 3.6.

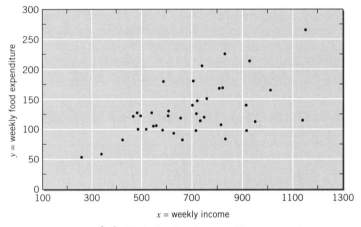

*FIGURE 3.6* Data for food expenditure example

Our problem is to estimate the location of the mean expenditure line $E[y] = \beta_1 + \beta_2 x$. We would expect this line to be somewhere in the middle of all the data points, since it represents *average behavior*. To estimate $\beta_1$ and $\beta_2$ we could simply draw a freehand line through the middle of the data and then measure the slope and intercept with a ruler. The problem with this method is that different people would draw different lines, and the lack of a formal criterion makes it difficult to assess the accuracy of the method. Another method is to draw a line from the smallest income point to the largest income point. This approach does provide a formal rule. However, it might not be a very good rule, because it ignores information on the exact position of the remaining 38 observations. It would be better if we could devise a rule that uses all the information from all the data points.

### 3.3.1  THE LEAST SQUARES PRINCIPLE

To estimate $\beta_1$ and $\beta_2$ we want a rule, or formula, that tells us how to make use of the sample observations. Many rules are possible, but the one that we will use is based on the **least squares principle.** This principle asserts that to fit a line to the data values we should fit the line so that the sum of the squares of the vertical distances from each point to the line is as small as possible. The distances are squared to prevent large positive distances from being canceled by large negative distances. This rule is arbitrary, but very effective, and is simply one way to describe a line that runs through the middle of the data. The intercept and slope of this line, the line that best fits the data using the least squares principle, are $b_1$ and $b_2$, the least squares estimates of $\beta_1$ and $\beta_2$. The fitted line itself is then

$$\hat{y}_t = b_1 + b_2 x_t \qquad (3.3.2)$$

The vertical distances from each point to the fitted line are the *least squares residuals*. They are given by

$$\hat{e}_t = y_t - \hat{y}_t = y_t - b_1 - b_2 x_t \qquad (3.3.3)$$

These residuals are depicted in Figure 3.7a.

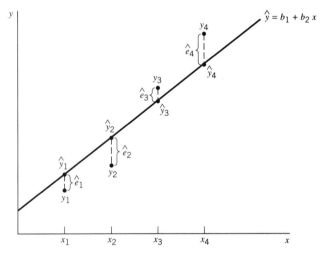

FIGURE **3.7a**    The relationship among $y, \hat{e}$ and the fitted regression line

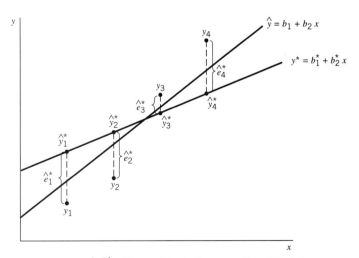

FIGURE **3.7b**    The residuals from another fitted line

Now suppose we fit another line, *any other line,* to the data, say

$$\hat{y}_t^* = b_1^* + b_2^* x_t$$

where $b_1^*$ and $b_2^*$ are any other intercept and slope values. The residuals for this line, $\hat{e}_t^* = y_t - \hat{y}_t^*$, are shown in Figure 3.7b. The *least squares estimates* $b_1$ and $b_2$ have the property that the sum of their squared residuals is *less than* the sum of squared residuals for *any* other line,

$$\Sigma \hat{e}_t^2 = \Sigma(y_t - \hat{y}_t)^2 \le \Sigma \hat{e}_t^{*2} = \Sigma(y_t - \hat{y}_t^*)^2$$

no matter how the other line might be drawn through the data. The *least squares principle* says that the estimates $b_1$ and $b_2$ of $\beta_1$ and $\beta_2$ are the ones to use, since the line using them as intercept and slope fits the data best.

Now the problem is to find $b_1$ and $b_2$ in a convenient way. Given the sample observations on $y$ and $x$, we want to find values for the unknown parameters $\beta_1$ and $\beta_2$ that minimize the "sum of squares" function

$$S(\beta_1, \beta_2) = \sum_{t=1}^{T}(y_t - \beta_1 - \beta_2 x_t)^2 \tag{3.3.4}$$

*Since the points $(y_t, x_t)$ have been observed,* the sum of squares function $S$ is a function of the unknown parameters $\beta_1$ and $\beta_2$. This function, which is a quadratic in terms of the unknown parameters $\beta_1$ and $\beta_2$, is a "bowl-shaped surface" like the one depicted in Figure 3.8. For a two-dimensional illustration see Exercise 3.7.

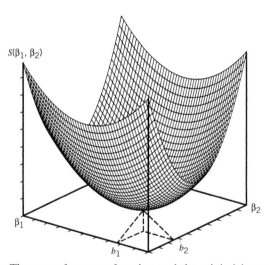

FIGURE **3.8**   The sum of squares function and the minimizing values $b_1$ and $b_2$

Our task is to find, out of all the possible values $\beta_1$ and $\beta_2$, the point $(b_1, b_2)$ at which the sum of squares function $S$ is a minimum. This minimization problem is a common one in calculus, and the minimizing point is at the "bottom of the bowl."

**Remark:** Occasionally there will be algebraic material in this book that can be skipped on the first reading of a chapter, or that can be skipped if you are unfamiliar or uncomfortable with calculus. We will mark these sections with a dark bar in the left-hand margin and we will indicate their end by inserting a small portrait of "Skippy" the kangaroo. The first such section follows. In this section we use calculus to solve the minimization problem of finding the "bottom of the bowl." You can "hop" down to Skippy if you are not comfortable with calculus.

Those of you familiar with calculus and "partial differentiation" can verify that the partial derivatives of $S$ with respect to $\beta_1$ and $\beta_2$ are

$$\frac{\partial S}{\partial \beta_1} = 2T\beta_1 - 2\Sigma y_t + 2\Sigma x_t \beta_2$$

$$\frac{\partial S}{\partial \beta_2} = 2\Sigma x_t^2 \beta_2 - 2\Sigma x_t y_t + 2\Sigma x_t \beta_1$$

(3.3.5)

These derivatives are equations of the slope of the bowl-like surface in the directions of the axes. Intuitively, the "bottom of the bowl" occurs where the slope of the bowl, in the direction of each axis, $\partial S/\partial \beta_1$ and $\partial S/\partial \beta_2$, is zero.

Algebraically, to obtain the point $(b_1, b_2)$ we set the equations 3.3.5 to zero, and replace $\beta_1$ and $\beta_2$ by $b_1$ and $b_2$, respectively, to obtain

$$2(\Sigma y_t - Tb_1 - \Sigma x_t b_2) = 0$$

$$2(\Sigma x_t y_t - \Sigma x_t b_1 - \Sigma x_t^2 b_2) = 0$$

(3.3.6)

Rearranging equation 3.3.6 leads to two equations usually known as the *normal equations*,

$$Tb_1 + \Sigma x_t b_2 = \Sigma y_t \qquad (3.3.7a)$$

$$\Sigma x_t b_1 + \Sigma x_t^2 b_2 = \Sigma x_t y_t \qquad (3.3.7b)$$

These two equations comprise a set of two linear equations in two unknowns $b_1$ and $b_2$. We can find the least squares estimates by solving these two linear equations for $b_1$ and $b_2$. To solve for $b_2$, multiply the first equation, 3.3.7a by $\Sigma x_t$; multiply the second equation, 3.3.7b by $T$; subtract the second equation from the first and then isolate $b_2$ on the left-hand side. To solve for $b_1$, divide both sides of equation 3.3.7a by $T$.

The formulas for the least squares estimates of $\beta_1$ and $\beta_2$ that give the location of the minimum of the sum of squared errors in Figure 3.8 are:

$$b_2 = \frac{T\Sigma x_t y_t - \Sigma x_t \Sigma y_t}{T\Sigma x_t^2 - (\Sigma x_t)^2}$$    (3.3.8a)

$$b_1 = \bar{y} - b_2 \bar{x}$$    (3.3.8b)

where $\bar{y} = \Sigma y_t / T$ and $\bar{x} = \Sigma x_t / T$ are the sample means of the observations on $y$ and $x$.

This formula for $b_2$ reveals why we had to assume that the values of $x_t$ were not the same constant value for all observations. If $x_t = c$ for all observations, then $b_2$ *does not exist,* since the denominator of (3.3.8a) is zero (see Exercise 3.10).

If we plug the sample values $y_t$ and $x_t$ into equations 3.3.8, then we obtain the least squares *estimates* of the intercept and slope parameters $\beta_1$ and $\beta_2$. It is interesting, however, and very important, that the formulas for $b_1$ and $b_2$ in equations 3.3.8 are *perfectly general,* and can be used *no matter what the sample values turn out to be.* This should ring a bell. When the formulas for $b_1$ and $b_2$ are taken to be rules that are used whatever the sample data turn out to be, then $b_1$ and $b_2$ are *random variables.* When actual sample values are substituted into the formulas, we obtain numbers that are the observed *values of random variables.* To distinguish these two cases we call the rules or general formulas for $b_1$ and $b_2$ the **least squares estimators.** We call the numbers obtained when the formulas are used with a particular sample **least squares estimates.**

- Least squares *estimators* are general formulas and are *random variables.*
- Least squares *estimates* are numbers that are the observed *values of random variables.*

The distinction between *estimators* and *estimates* is a fundamental concept that is essential to understand *everything* in the rest of this book. Keep this distinction in mind. This is going to take some concentration, since from now on we do not make any notation difference between these random variables and their values.

### 3.3.2    ESTIMATES FOR THE FOOD EXPENDITURE FUNCTION

We have used the least squares principle to derive equations 3.3.8, which can be used to obtain the least squares estimates for the intercept and slope parameters $\beta_1$ and $\beta_2$. To illustrate the use of these formulas, we will use them to calculate the values of $b_1$ and $b_2$ for the household expenditure data given in Table 3.1. From equation 3.3.8a we have

$$b_2 = \frac{T\Sigma x_t y_t - \Sigma x_t \Sigma y_t}{T\Sigma x_t^2 - (\Sigma x_t)^2} = \frac{(40)(3834936.497) - (27920)(5212.520)}{(40)(21020623.02) - (27920)^2}$$    (3.3.9a)

$$= 0.1283$$

and from equation 3.3.8b

$$b_1 = \bar{y} - b_2 \bar{x} = 130.313 - (0.1282886)(698.0) = 40.7676$$    (3.3.9b)

A convenient way to report the values for $b_1$ and $b_2$ is to write out the *estimated* or *fitted* regression line:

$$\hat{y}_t = 40.7676 + 0.1283x_t \tag{3.3.10}$$

This line is graphed in Figure 3.9. The line's slope is 0.1283 and its intercept, where it crosses the vertical axis, is 40.7676. The least squares fitted line passes through the middle of the data in a very precise way, since one of the characteristics of the fitted line based on the least squares parameter estimates is that it passes through the point defined by the sample means, $(\bar{x}, \bar{y}) = (698.00, 130.31)$. See Exercise 3.3.

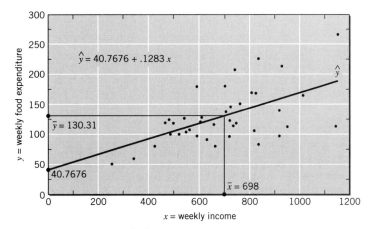

**FIGURE 3.9** The fitted regression line

### 3.3.3 INTERPRETING THE ESTIMATES

Once obtained, the least squares estimates can be interpreted in the context of the economic model under consideration. The value $b_2 = 0.1283$ is an estimate of $\beta_2$, the amount by which weekly expenditure on food increases when weekly income increases by \$1. Thus, we estimate that if income goes up by \$100, weekly expenditure on food will increase by approximately \$12.83. A supermarket chain with information on likely changes in the income and the number of households in an area could estimate that it is likely to sell \$12.83 more per household per week for every \$100 increase in income. This is a very valuable piece of information for long-run planning.

Strictly speaking, the intercept estimate $b_1 = 40.7676$ is an estimate of the weekly amount spent on food for a family with zero income. In most economic models we must be very careful when interpreting the estimated intercept. The problem is that we usually do not have any data points near $x = 0$, which is certainly true for the food expenditure data shown in Figure 3.9. If we have no observations in the region where income is zero, then our estimated relationship may not be a good approximation to reality in that region. So, although our estimated model suggests that a household with zero income will spend \$40.7676 per week on food, it might be risky to take this estimate literally. You should consider this issue in each economic model that you estimate.

### 3.3.3a.  Elasticities

The income elasticity of demand is a useful way to characterize the responsiveness of consumer expenditure to changes in income. From microeconomic principles, the elasticity of any variable $y$ with respect to another variable $x$ is

$$\eta = \frac{\text{percentage change in } y}{\text{percentage change in } x} = \frac{\Delta y/y}{\Delta x/x} = \frac{\Delta y}{\Delta x} \cdot \frac{x}{y} \qquad (3.3.11)$$

In the linear economic model given by equation 3.1.1 we have shown that

$$\beta_2 = \frac{\Delta E(y)}{\Delta x} \qquad (3.3.12)$$

so the elasticity of "average" expenditure with respect to income is

$$\eta = \frac{\Delta E(y)/E(y)}{\Delta x/x} = \frac{\Delta E(y)}{\Delta x} \cdot \frac{x}{E(y)} = \beta_2 \cdot \frac{x}{E(y)} \qquad (3.3.13)$$

To estimate this elasticity we replace $\beta_2$ by $b_2 = 0.1283$. We must also replace "$x$" and "$E(y)$" by something, since in a linear model the elasticity is different on each point upon the regression line. One possibility is to choose a value of $x$ and replace $E(y)$ by its fitted value $\hat{y}_t = 40.7676 + 0.1283x_t$. Another frequently used alternative is to report the elasticity at the "point of the means" $(\bar{x},\bar{y})=(698.00, 130.31)$ since that is a representative point on the regression line.

 If we calculate the income elasticity at the point of the means, we obtain

$$\hat{\eta} = b_2 \cdot \frac{\bar{x}}{\bar{y}} = 0.1283 \times \frac{698.00}{130.31} = 0.687 \qquad (3.3.14)$$

This *estimated* income elasticity takes its usual interpretation. We estimate that a 1 percent change in weekly household income will lead, on average, to approximately a 0.7 percent increase in weekly household expenditure on food when $(x,y) = (\bar{x},\bar{y})$ = (698.00, 130.313). Since the estimated income elasticity is less than one, we would classify food as a "necessity" rather than a "luxury," which is consistent with what we would expect for an "average" household.

### 3.3.3b.  Prediction

Finally, the estimated equation can be used for prediction or forecasting purposes. Suppose that we wanted to predict weekly food expenditure for a household with a weekly income of $750. This prediction is carried out by substituting $x = 750$ into our estimated equation to obtain

$$\hat{y}_t = 40.7676 + 0.1283x_t = 40.7676 + 0.1283(750) = \$136.98 \qquad (3.3.15)$$

We *predict* that a household with a weekly income of $750 will spend $136.98 per week on food.

### 3.3.4  OTHER ECONOMIC MODELS

We have used the household expenditure on food versus income relationship as an example to introduce the ideas of simple regression. The simple regression model can be applied to estimate the parameters of many other economic relationships. Examples include a demand relationship involving price and quantity data for a particular commodity; a production function reflecting the relationship involving the output of a product and the input of a factor; an aggregate consumption function relating aggregate consumption to income; an aggregate investment function representing the level of investment and the rate of interest; a supply function involving data on quantity supplied and the product price; and an environmental relation between gasoline consumption and air quality in San Francisco.

The simple linear regression model is much more flexible than it looks at first glance, because the variables $y$ and $x$ can be *transformations,* involving logarithms, squares, cubes, or reciprocals of the basic economic variables. Thus, the simple linear regression model can be used for *nonlinear relationships between variables.* This somewhat weird terminology results from the fact that the term *linear* in "linear regression" actually means that the *parameters* are not transformed in any way. The model is *linear* in the parameters, and expressions like $\ln(\beta_2)$ are not permitted. To get a feel for a nonlinear model that uses variable transformations, but is linear in the parameters, try Exercise 3.6. Also, we treat this topic more fully in Chapter 6.3. There we discuss details of different functional forms that can be created through various variable transformations.

A word of warning: If $y$ and $x$ are transformed in some way, then the economic interpretation of the parameters can change. A popular transformation in economics is the natural logarithm. Economic models like $\ln(y) = \beta_1 + \beta_2 \ln(x)$ are common. A nice feature of this model, if the assumptions of the regression model hold, is that the parameter $\beta_2$ is the elasticity of $y$ with respect to $x$. This fact is used in Exercise 3.6. The proof relies on calculus; if you are not comfortable with calculus, skip the marked text.

The derivative of $\ln(y)$ with respect to $x$ is

$$\frac{d[\ln(y)]}{dx} = \frac{1}{y} \cdot \frac{dy}{dx}$$

The derivative of $\beta_1 + \beta_2 \ln(x)$ with respect to $x$ is

$$\frac{d[\beta_1 + \beta_2 \ln(x)]}{dx} = \frac{1}{x} \cdot \beta_2$$

Setting these two pieces equal to one another, and solving for $\beta_2$ gives

$$\beta_2 = \frac{dy}{dx} \cdot \frac{x}{y} = \eta \qquad (3.3.16)$$

Look back at equation 3.3.11. There we defined the elasticity of $y$ with respect to $x$. It is defined in terms of finite changes, $\Delta y$ and $\Delta x,$ and is actually an *arc* elasticity. If we replace $\Delta y$ and $\Delta x$ by $dy$ and $dx$, the *point* elasticity is defined. Equation 3.3.16 shows that in an economic model in which $\ln(y)$ and $\ln(x)$ are linearly related, the parameter $\beta_2$ is the point elasticity of $y$ with respect to $x$.

In subsequent chapters we take a very close look at the least squares principle and why and when it is an effective rule to use. Each economic model, and its associated statistical model, must be carefully scrutinized to confirm that the assumptions of the regression model are valid. If they are not valid, then the least squares procedure may *not* be very effective. Checking the assumptions is sometimes a difficult task since economics is not an exact science and because economic data are *not* obtained by a controlled laboratory experiment. Economic data are usually "messy." This is one way "econometrics" differs from "statistics."

## 3.4 Summing Up

In this chapter we have introduced several important concepts and derived the least squares estimators for the simple linear regression model. Important points in the chapter include the following:

1.  Economic theory is useful in identifying economic relationships reflecting individual and aggregate behavior. If $y$ is an economic variable that theory suggests depends on another economic variable $x$, then a linear economic (regression) model can be represented as $E(y|x) = \beta_1 + \beta_2 x$.

2.  A statistical (econometric) model recognizes that, for a variety of reasons, economic data are not going to exactly follow the economic model. In the statistical model a random error $e = y - \beta_1 - \beta_2 x$ accounts for differences between observed values $y$ and their averages $E(y) = \beta_1 + \beta_2 x$.

3.  The parameter $\beta_1$ is the intercept of the regression line and $\beta_2$ is its slope.

4.  The assumptions of the linear statistical regression model, which characterize the relationship between $y$ and $x$, are:
    a.  $y_t = \beta_1 + \beta_2 x_t + e_t$
    b.  $E(e_t) = 0 \Leftrightarrow E(y_t) = \beta_1 + \beta_2 x_t$
    c.  $\text{var}(e_t) = \sigma^2 = \text{var}(y_t)$
    d.  $\text{cov}(e_i, e_j) = \text{cov}(y_i, y_j) = 0$
    e.  $x_t \neq c$
    f.  $e_t \sim N(0,\sigma^2) \Leftrightarrow y_t \sim N[(\beta_1 + \beta_2 x_t), \sigma^2]$ *(optional)*

5.  The least squares principle leads us to estimates of $\beta_1$ and $\beta_2$ that minimize the sum of squared differences (errors) between the actual values of $y$ and their predicted values.

6.  The least squares estimator of $\beta_1$ is $b_1 = \bar{y} - b_2 \bar{x}$.

7.  The least squares estimator of $\beta_2$ is $b_2 = \dfrac{T\Sigma x_t y_t - \Sigma x_t \Sigma y_t}{T\Sigma x_t^2 - (\Sigma x_t)^2}$

8.  For the linear regression model in which the variables are not transformed, the elasticity of the average value of $y$ with respect to $x$ is

$$\eta = \frac{\Delta E(y)/E(y)}{\Delta x/x} = \frac{\Delta E(y)}{\Delta x} \cdot \frac{x}{E(y)} = \beta_2 \cdot \frac{x}{E(y)}$$

9.  For the linear regression model in which the dependent and independent variables are transformed using the natural logarithm, $\ln(y) = \beta_1 + \beta_2 \ln(x) + e$, then the elasticity of $y$ with respect to $x$ is constant for all values of $x$ and is equal to $\beta_2$.

10. An estimated regression model can be used for predicting values of $y$. To predict the value of $y$ that corresponds to a value of $x = x_0$, $\hat{y}_0 = b_1 + b_2 x_0$.

## *3.5* **Exercises**

3.1  Define the following terms:
(a) Economic model
(b) Statistical model
(c) Econometric model
(d) Least squares principle
(e) Least squares estimator
(f) Least squares estimates

3.2  Consider the following five observations on $y_t = \{5, 2, 3, 2, -2\}$ and $x_t = \{3, 2, 1, -1, 0\}$. Do this exercise by hand.
(a) Find $\sum_{t=1}^{5} x_t^2$, $\sum_{t=1}^{5} x_t y_t$, $\sum_{t=1}^{5} x_t$, $\sum_{t=1}^{5} y_t$, $\bar{x}$, $\bar{y}$
(b) Find $b_1$ and $b_2$.
(c) On a graph, plot the data points and sketch the fitted regression line, $\hat{y}_t = b_1 + b_2 x_t$.
(d) Give an interpretation of $b_1$ and $b_2$.
(e) On the sketch in part (c), locate the point of the means, $(\bar{x},\bar{y})$. Does your fitted line pass through that point? If not, go back to the drawing board, literally.

3.3* Algebraically show that the fitted least squares line $\hat{y}_t = b_1 + b_2 x_t$ passes through the point of the means, $(\bar{x},\bar{y})$.

3.4* Algebraically show that the average value of $\hat{y}_t$ equals the sample average of $y$. That is, show that $\bar{\hat{y}} = \bar{y}$, where $\bar{\hat{y}} = \Sigma\hat{y}_t/T$

3.5  Consider the problem of estimating a production function that expresses the relationship between the level of output of a commodity and the level of input of a factor of production. Assume that you have the production data given in Table 3.2.
(a) Assume that the data can be described by the simple linear regression model $y = \beta_1 + \beta_2 x + e$ and that all the assumptions hold. Use the least squares principle to estimate $b_1$ and $b_2$ (use the computer!).
(b) Give an economic interpretation to the estimated parameters.
(c) Use the results of part (a) to plot the estimated production function.

*Table 3.2*    **A Sample of Observations on Poultry Feed Inputs and Meat Outputs**

| Input $x$ | Output $y$ |
|---|---|
| 1 | 0.58 |
| 2 | 1.10 |
| 3 | 1.20 |
| 4 | 1.30 |
| 5 | 1.95 |
| 6 | 2.55 |
| 7 | 2.60 |
| 8 | 2.90 |
| 9 | 3.45 |
| 10 | 3.50 |
| 11 | 3.60 |
| 12 | 4.10 |
| 13 | 4.35 |
| 14 | 4.40 |
| 15 | 4.50 |

(d)  If the cost of feed input is 6 cents per pound, derive the total cost and marginal cost functions.

(e)* Show how to use the total cost function (which relates total cost to output) to obtain estimates of the parameters of the production function connecting feed inputs and poultry meat outputs.

3.6    Assume that Moscow Makkers, a new hamburger outlet in Moscow, is unsure of its pricing policy. Each week the store changes the hamburger price slightly, using various specials. The quantities sold and their corresponding prices are as shown in Table 3.3. Suppose that the demand equation that relates quantity sold ($q_t$) to price ($p_t$) is $\ln(q_t) = \beta_1 + \beta_2 \ln(p_t) + e_t$. Note that this equation can be written in the more familiar form $y_t = \beta_1 + \beta_2 x_t + e_t$ by defining $y_t = \ln(q_t)$ and $x_t = \ln(p_t)$.

*Table 3.3*    **Quantity and Price Data**

| Week | Number Sold ($q_t$) | Price ($p_t$) |
|---|---|---|
| 1 | 892 | 1.23 |
| 2 | 1012 | 1.15 |
| 3 | 1060 | 1.10 |
| 4 | 987 | 1.20 |
| 5 | 680 | 1.35 |
| 6 | 739 | 1.25 |
| 7 | 809 | 1.28 |
| 8 | 1275 | 0.99 |
| 9 | 946 | 1.22 |
| 10 | 874 | 1.25 |
| 11 | 720 | 1.30 |
| 12 | 1096 | 1.05 |

(a) Using your computer software package, find $y_t = \ln(q_t)$ and $x_t = \ln(p_t)$, for $t = 1, 2, \ldots, 12$ and plot them on a graph. "ln" denotes the "natural" logarithm.

(b) Assume that the assumptions of the simple regression model hold for the transformed values $y$ and $x$. Find least squares estimates $b_1$ and $b_2$ of $\beta_1$ and $\beta_2$.

(c) Give an economic interpretation to $b_2$. (Hint: See equation 3.3.16 and the discussion surrounding it.)

(d) Should the Makkers increase or decrease price if they want to increase total receipts?

3.7* Suppose that in a simple linear regression model we know that the intercept $\beta_1$ is equal to zero, that is, $\beta_1 = 0$.

(a) Algebraically, what does the sum of squares function become?

(b) Find a formula for estimating $\beta_2$ by using the least squares principle. This requires the use of calculus.

(c) Use a geometric instead of a calculus approach. Taking the production model in Exercise 3.5 as an example, and the data in Table 3.2, use your software package to plot the sum of squares function from part (a). What is the minimizing value? Is this a least squares estimate?

(d) Repeat this exercise assuming that $\beta_2 = 0$, but that $\beta_1$ is not zero.

3.8 An interesting and useful economic concept is the "learning curve." The idea is related to a phenomenon that occurs in assembly line production, such as in the automobile industry, or any time a task is performed repeatedly. Workers learn from experience and become more efficient in performing their task. This means it takes less time and labor costs to produce the final product. This idea forms the basis for an economic model relating cost per unit at time $t$ $(u_t)$ to the *cumulative* production of a good up to, but not including, time $t$ $(q_t)$. The relationship between the variables is often taken to be

$$u_t = u_1 q_t^a$$

where $u_1$ equals the unit cost of production for the first unit produced, and $a$ equals the elasticity of unit costs with respect to cumulative production (which we expect to be negative) . This nonlinear relationship between the variables is transformed to a linear one by taking logarithms of both sides:

$$\ln(u_t) = \ln(u_1) + a \ln(q_t) = \beta_1 + \beta_2 \ln(q_t)$$

We have "renamed" $\ln(u_1)$ and $a$ so that the model looks more familiar. Ernst Berndt is the author of an excellent book, more advanced than this one, entitled *The Practice of Econometrics: Classic and Contemporary* (Addison and Wesley, 1991). On page 85 of that book Berndt gives the example of learning in the production of a product called titanium dioxide, which is used as a thickener in paint. He provides data on production and unit costs from the DuPont Corporation for the years 1955 to 1970. The data are given in Table 3.4.

(a) Use your computer software to plot a graph of $u$ against $q$, and $\ln(u)$ against $\ln(q)$.

*Table 3.4*   **Learning Curve Data**

| Year | Real Cost | Cumulative Production |
|------|-----------|---------------------|
| 1955 | 24.96350 | 1127.00 |
| 1956 | 25.49296 | 1239.00 |
| 1957 | 25.27027 | 1363.00 |
| 1958 | 25.44460 | 1479.00 |
| 1959 | 25.03401 | 1580.00 |
| 1960 | 24.73404 | 1705.00 |
| 1961 | 23.12746 | 1839.00 |
| 1962 | 21.71053 | 1988.00 |
| 1963 | 21.49410 | 2156.00 |
| 1964 | 21.24352 | 2333.00 |
| 1965 | 20.15113 | 2511.00 |
| 1966 | 20.14652 | 2700.00 |
| 1967 | 20.35928 | 2892.00 |
| 1968 | 18.59649 | 3078.00 |
| 1969 | 16.72316 | 3280.00 |
| 1970 | 16.41631 | 3488.00 |

(b) Obtain the least squares estimates $b_1$ and $b_2$ of $\beta_1$ and $\beta_2$ and give their economic interpretation. Do these numbers make sense?

3.9   The capital asset pricing model (CAPM) is an important model in the field of finance. It explains variations in the rate of return on a security as a function of the rate of return on a portfolio consisting of all publicly traded stocks, which is called the *market* portfolio. Generally, the rate of return on any investment is measured relative to its opportunity cost, which is the return on a risk-free asset. The resulting difference is called the *risk premium,* since it is the reward or punishment for making a risky investment. The CAPM says that the risk premium on security $j$ is *proportional* to the risk premium on the market portfolio. That is

$$r_j - r_f = \beta_j(r_m - r_f)$$

where $r_j$ and $r_f$ are the returns to security $j$ and the risk-free rate, respectively, $r_m$ is the return on the market portfolio, and $\beta_j$ is the $j$'th security's *beta* value. A stock's *beta* is important to investors because it reveals the stock's volatility. It measures the sensitivity of security $j$'s return to variation in the whole stock market. As such, values of *beta* less than one indicate that the stock is "defensive," since its variation is less than the market's. A *beta* greater than one indicates an "aggressive stock." Investors usually want an estimate of a stock's beta before purchasing it. The CAPM model shown above is the "economic model" in this case. The "econometric model" is obtained by including an intercept in the model (even though theory says it should be zero) and an error term,

$$r_j - r_f = \alpha_j + \beta_j(r_m - r_f) + e$$

(a) Explain why this econometric model is a simple regression model like those discussed in this chapter.

(b) Ernst Berndt (1991, p. 42) provides data on the monthly returns of Mobil Oil (MOBIL) for the 10-year period January 1978 to December 1987. In addition, he gives the returns on the market portfolio, MARKET, and the return on a risk-free asset, 30-day U.S. Treasury bills (RKFREE). These data are contained in the file "*capm.dat*" provided by your instructor. The three columns of numbers in this file are MOBIL, MARKET, and RKFREE, respectively. Use these 120 observations to estimate Mobil Oil's *beta*. What do you conclude about the stock of Mobil Oil?

(c) Finance theory says that the intercept parameter $\alpha_j$ should be zero. Does this seem correct, given your estimates?

(d) Estimate the model under the assumption that $\alpha_j = 0$. (Hint: See Exercise 3.7). Does the estimate of the stock's *beta* change much?

3.10 Show that the denominator of equation 3.3.8a is zero if all the values $x_t = c$, $t=1, \ldots, T$, where $c$ is any constant, like $c = 5$. Consequently, if $x_t$ does not take *at least* two values, then the least squares estimate $b_2$ cannot be calculated.

## *3.6* References

BERNDT, ERNST R. (1991). *The Practice of Econometrics: Classic and Contemporary*. Reading, Mass.: Addison-Wesley Publishing Company.

CANIGLIA, ALAN S. (1992). *Statistics for Economists*. New York: HarperCollins, Chapter 9.

GRIFFITHS, W. E., R. C. HILL, AND G. G. JUDGE (1993). *Learning and Practicing Econometrics*. New York: John Wiley & Sons, Inc., Chapter 5.

MIRER, THAD W. (1995). *Economic Statistics and Econometrics, Third Edition*. Englewood Cliffs, N.J.: Prentice Hall, Chapters 5 and 6.

PINDYCK, ROBERT S., AND DANIEL L. RUBINFELD (1991). *Econometric Models and Economic Forecasts, Third Edition*. New York: McGraw-Hill, Chapter 3.

# Chapter 4

# Properties of the Least Squares Estimators

The simple linear regression model that we developed in Chapter 3 is a statistical model that is useful for studying the relationship between economic variables. The example we are using as a basis for discussion relates weekly household expenditure on food to weekly household income. In this example we wish to estimate how changes in income affect expenditure on food. The statistical model summarizes what economic theory says about the relationship, namely, that expenditure on food is a linear function of income; it also makes explicit the fact that when data are collected by sampling, then the household food expenditure data are *random*. At any given level of income, $x$, the actual expenditures we observe will be scattered about $E(y|x)$, the average or *expected value* of expenditure for that income. The assumptions of the simple linear regression model, which we make prior to any data analysis, are summarized by equation 3.3.1, which we repeat here. We will refer frequently to these assumptions by number in this chapter.

---

**ASSUMPTIONS OF THE SIMPLE LINEAR REGRESSION MODEL**

1. $y_t = \beta_1 + \beta_2 x_t + e_t$
2. $E(e_t) = 0 \Leftrightarrow E(y_t) = \beta_1 + \beta_2 x_t$
3. $\text{var}(e_t) = \sigma^2 = \text{var}(y_t)$
4. $\text{cov}(e_i, e_j) = \text{cov}(y_i, y_j) = 0$
5. $x_t \neq c$ for every observation
6. $e_t \sim N(0, \sigma^2) \Leftrightarrow y_t \sim N[(\beta_1 + \beta_2 x_t), \sigma^2]$ *(optional)*

---

## *4.1* The Least Squares Estimators as Random Variables

In Chapter 3 we obtained just one sample of data consisting of observations on income and expenditure for forty households. Using these data we obtained the *least squares estimates* $b_1 = 40.7676$ and $b_2 = .1283$ of the unknown intercept and slope parameters, $\beta_1$ and $\beta_2$, respectively. There are, of course, many other households that could have been chosen. Other samples of forty households would yield *different* values for household food expenditure, $y_t$, $t = 1, \ldots, 40$, even if we carefully selected households with the same incomes as in the initial sample. These samples would lead to different estimates $b_1$ and $b_2$ of the model parameters. Household food expenditures, $y_t$, $t = 1, \ldots, 40$ are random variables, because their values are not known until the sample is collected. Consequently, when viewed as an estimation procedure, $b_1$ and $b_2$ are also random variables, since their values depend on the random variable $y$ whose values are not known until the sample is collected.

To repeat an important passage from Chapter 3, when the formulas for $b_1$ and $b_2$, given in equations 3.3.8, are taken to be rules that are used whatever the sample data turn out to be, then $b_1$ and $b_2$ are *random variables*. In this context we call $b_1$ and $b_2$ the *least squares estimators*. When actual sample values, numbers, are substituted into the formulas, we obtain numbers that are *values of random variables*. In this context, we call $b_1$ and $b_2$ the *least squares estimates*.

---

**REMARK:** In this chapter, based on assumptions 1–6, we investigate the statistical properties of the least squares *estimators,* which are procedures for obtaining estimates of the unknown parameters $\beta_1$ and $\beta_2$ in the simple linear regression model. In this context $b_1$ and $b_2$ are random variables. The properties of the least squares estimation procedures we establish in this chapter do not depend on any particular sample of data, and they can be established "pre-data," that is, *prior to* any data collection or analysis.

After the data are collected, the least squares estimates are calculated numbers, such as $b_2 = .1283$, from the previous chapter. In "post-data" analysis, nonrandom quantities such as this have *no statistical properties.* Their reliability and usefulness are assessed in terms of the properties of the procedures by which they were obtained.

---

We can investigate the properties of the random estimators $b_1$ and $b_2$ and deal with the following important questions:

1. If the least squares estimators $b_1$ and $b_2$ are random variables, then what are their means, variances, covariances, and probability distributions?

2. The least squares principle is only *one* way of using the data to obtain estimates of $\beta_1$ and $\beta_2$. How do the least squares estimators compare with other rules that might be used, and how can we compare alternative estimators? For example, is there another estimator that has a higher probability of producing an estimate that is close to $\beta_2$?

These are two of the questions that we will investigate in Chapter 4.

## *4.2* **The Sampling Properties of the Least Squares Estimators**

The least squares estimators $b_1$ and $b_2$ are random variables and they have probability distributions that we can study prior to the collection of any data. The characteristics of their probability density functions are of great interest to us. If the probability density functions are known, then they can be used to make probability statements about $b_1$ and $b_2$. The means (expected values) and variances of random variables provide information about the location and spread of their probability distributions (see Chapter 2.3). The means and variances of $b_1$ and $b_2$ provide information about the range of values that $b_1$ and $b_2$ are likely to take. Knowing this range is important, because our objective is to obtain estimates that are *close* to the true parameter values. In this section we determine the means and variances of the least squares estimators $b_1$ and $b_2$. Since $b_1$ and $b_2$ are random variables, they may have a covariance, and this we will determine as well. These "pre-data" characteristics of $b_1$ and $b_2$ are called **sampling properties,** because the randomness of the estimators is brought on by sampling from a population.

### 4.2.1   THE EXPECTED VALUES OF $b_1$ AND $b_2$

Given the statistical model described by the assumptions in equation 3.1.1, the least squares *estimator $b_2$* of the slope parameter $\beta_2$, based on a sample of $T$ observations, is

$$b_2 = \frac{T\Sigma x_t y_t - \Sigma x_t \Sigma y_t}{T\Sigma x_t^2 - (\Sigma x_t)^2} \qquad (3.3.8a)$$

The least squares *estimator $b_1$* of the intercept parameter $\beta_1$ is

$$b_1 = \bar{y} - b_2\bar{x} \qquad (3.3.8b)$$

where $\bar{y} = \Sigma y_t / T$ and $\bar{x} = \Sigma x_t / T$ are the sample means of the observations on $y$ and $x$, respectively.

In this section we will determine the expected value of $b_2$. We also give the expected value of $b_1$, but we will not derive it. We begin by rewriting the formula in equation 3.3.8a into the following one that is more convenient for theoretical purposes:

$$b_2 = \beta_2 + \Sigma w_t e_t \qquad (4.2.1)$$

where $w_t$ is a constant (nonrandom) given by

$$w_t = \frac{x_t - \bar{x}}{\Sigma(x_t - \bar{x})^2} \qquad (4.2.2)$$

Equation 4.2.1 is very easy to use, but *not* so easy to obtain. After we present and discuss the expected value of $b_2$, we will look at how equation 4.2.1 is obtained.

Since $w_t$ is a constant, depending only on the values of $x_t$, we can find the expected value of $b_2$ using the fact that the *expected value of a sum is the sum of the expected values* (see Chapter 2.5.1):

$$E(b_2) = E(\beta_2 + \Sigma w_t e_t) = E(\beta_2) + \Sigma E(w_t e_t)$$

$$= \beta_2 + \Sigma w_t E(e_t) = \beta_2 \qquad (4.2.3)$$

since $E(e_t) = 0$. When the expected value of any estimator of a parameter equals the true parameter value, then that estimator is *unbiased*. Since $E(b_2) = \beta_2$, the least squares estimator $b_2$ is an unbiased estimator of $\beta_2$. The intuitive meaning of unbiasedness comes from the repeated sampling interpretation of mathematical expectation. (See Chapter 2.3.2.) If many samples of size $T$ are collected, and the formula 3.3.8a for $b_2$ is used to estimate $\beta_2$, then the average value of the estimates $b_2$ obtained from all those samples will be $\beta_2$, *if the statistical model assumptions are correct.*

However, if the assumptions we have made are *not correct,* then the least squares estimator may not be unbiased. In the second line of equation 4.2.3 note in particular the role of the assumptions 1 and 2. The assumption that $E(e_t) = 0$, for each and every $t$, makes $\Sigma w_t E(e_t) = 0$ and $E(b_2) = \beta_2$. If $E(e_t) \neq 0$, then $E(b_2) \neq \beta_2$. Recall that $e_t$ contains, among other things, factors affecting $y_t$ that are *omitted* from the economic model. If we have omitted anything that is important, then we would expect that $E(e_t) \neq 0$ and $E(b_2) \neq \beta_2$. Thus, having an economic and statistical model that is correctly specified, in the sense that it includes all relevant explanatory variables, is a must in order for the least squares estimators to be unbiased.

The unbiasedness of the estimator $b_2$ is an important sampling property. When sampling repeatedly from a population, the least squares estimator is "correct," on average, and this is one desirable property of an estimator. This statistical property by itself does not mean that $b_2$ is a good estimator of $\beta_2$, but it is part of the story. The unbiasedness property depends on having *many* samples of data from the same population. The fact that $b_2$ is unbiased does not imply *anything* about what might happen in just *one* sample. An individual estimate (number) $b_2$ may be near to, or far from, $\beta_2$. Since $\beta_2$ is *never* known, we will never know, given one sample, whether our estimate is "close" to $\beta_2$ or not. Thus, the estimate $b_2 = .1283$, from the previous chapter, may be close to $\beta_2$ or not. The least squares estimator $b_1$ of $\beta_1$ is also an *unbiased* estimator, and $E(b_1) = \beta_1$.

In the remainder of this section we show that equation 4.2.1 is correct. For now, you may skip over the marked text, down to Skippy, if you choose. We *highly* recommend, however, that you work through this algebra at some point. It will enhance your understanding of the remainder of this chapter, as well as much of the remainder of the book.

**Derivation of Equation 4.2.1:** The first step in the conversion of the formula for $b_2$ into (4.2.1) is to use some tricks involving summation signs. The first useful fact is that

$$\Sigma(x_t - \bar{x})^2 = \Sigma x_t^2 - 2\bar{x}\Sigma x_t + T\bar{x}^2 = \Sigma x_t^2 - 2\bar{x}\left(T\frac{1}{T}\Sigma x_t\right) + T\bar{x}^2$$

$$= \Sigma x_t^2 - 2T\bar{x}^2 + T\bar{x}^2 = \Sigma x_t^2 - T\bar{x}^2 \qquad (4.2.4)$$

$$= \Sigma x_t^2 - \bar{x}\Sigma x_t = \Sigma x_t^2 - \frac{(\Sigma x_t)^2}{T}$$

To obtain this result we have used the fact that $\bar{x} = \Sigma x_t / T$, so $\Sigma x_t = T\bar{x}$.

The second useful fact is similar, and that is

$$\Sigma(x_t - \bar{x})(y_t - \bar{y}) = \Sigma x_t y_t - T\bar{x}\bar{y} = \Sigma x_t y_t - \frac{\Sigma x_t \Sigma y_t}{T} \qquad (4.2.5)$$

This result is proven in a similar manner.

If the numerator and denominator of $b_2$ are divided by $T$, then using equations 4.2.4 and 4.2.5 we can rewrite $b_2$ in *deviation from the mean form* as:

$$b_2 = \frac{\Sigma(x_t - \bar{x})(y_t - \bar{y})}{\Sigma(x_t - \bar{x})^2} \qquad (4.2.6)$$

*This* formula for $b_2$ is one that you should remember, as we will use it time and time again in the next few chapters. Its primary advantage is its theoretical usefulness. For example, it clearly shows that if assumption 5 is violated and $x_t = c$ for every observation, then $b_2 = 0/0$ and is mathematically undefined.

In order to derive equation 4.2.1 we make a further simplification using another property of sums. The sum of any variable about its average is zero; that is,

$$\Sigma(x_t - \bar{x}) = 0 \qquad (4.2.7)$$

Then, the formula for $b_2$ becomes

$$b_2 = \frac{\Sigma(x_t - \bar{x})(y_t - \bar{y})}{\Sigma(x_t - \bar{x})^2} = \frac{\Sigma(x_t - \bar{x})y_t - \bar{y}\Sigma(x_t - \bar{x})}{\Sigma(x_t - \bar{x})^2}$$

$$\qquad (4.2.8a)$$

$$= \frac{\Sigma(x_t - \bar{x})y_t}{\Sigma(x_t - \bar{x})^2} = \Sigma w_t y_t$$

where $w_t$ is the constant given in equation 4.2.2.

*Finally*, we make one more substitution. To obtain equation 4.2.1, replace $y_t$ by $y_t = \beta_1 + \beta_2 x_t + e_t$ and simplify:

$$b_2 = \Sigma w_t y_t = \Sigma w_t(\beta_1 + \beta_2 x_t + e_t) = \beta_1 \Sigma w_t + \beta_2 \Sigma w_t x_t + \Sigma w_t e_t$$

$$\qquad (4.2.8b)$$

$$= \beta_2 + \Sigma w_t e_t$$

using the facts that

$$\Sigma w_t = 0 \ (\text{since } \Sigma(x_t - \bar{x}) = 0) \qquad (4.2.9a)$$

and

$$\Sigma w_t x_t = \frac{\Sigma(x_t - \bar{x})x_t}{\Sigma(x_t - \bar{x})^2} = \frac{\Sigma x_t^2 - \bar{x}\Sigma x_t}{\Sigma(x_t - \bar{x})^2} = \frac{\Sigma x_t^2 - \bar{x}\Sigma x_t}{\Sigma x_t^2 - \bar{x}\Sigma x_t} = 1 \qquad (4.2.9b)$$

where we used (4.2.4) in the next to the last step.

### 4.2.2   THE VARIANCES AND COVARIANCE OF $b_1$ AND $b_2$

Given the expected values, or means, of $b_1$ and $b_2$, we now obtain the variances and covariance of these random *estimators*. Before presenting the expressions for the variances and covariance, let us consider why they are important to know. The variance of the random variable $b_2$ is the average of the squared distances between the values of the random variable and its mean, which we now know is $E(b_2) = \beta_2$. The variance (Chapter 2.3.4) of $b_2$ is defined as

$$\mathrm{var}(b_2) = E[b_2 - E(b_2)]^2$$

It measures the spread of the probability distribution of $b_2$. In Figure 4.1 are graphs of two possible probability distributions of $b_2$, $f_1(b_2)$ and $f_2(b_2)$, that have the same mean value but different variances.

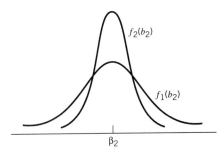

FIGURE **4.1**   Two possible probability density functions for $b_2$

The probability density function $f_2(b_2)$ has a smaller variance than the probability density function $f_1(b_2)$. Given a choice, we are interested in estimator precision and would *prefer* that $b_2$ have the probability distribution $f_2(b_2)$ rather than $f_1(b_2)$. With the distribution $f_2(b_2)$ the probability is more concentrated around the true parameter value $\beta_2$, giving, relative to $f_1(b_2)$, a *higher* probability of getting an estimate that is *close* to $\beta_2$. Remember, getting an estimate close to $\beta_2$ is our objective.

The variance of an estimator measures the *precision* of the estimator in the sense that it tells us how much the estimates produced by that estimator can vary from sample to sample. Consequently, we often refer to the *sampling variance* or **sampling precision** of an estimator. The lower the variance of an estimator, the greater the sampling precision of that estimator. One estimator is *more precise* than another estimator if its sampling variance is less than that of the other estimator.

We will now present and discuss the variances and covariance of $b_1$ and $b_2$. Then we will derive the variance of the least squares estimator $b_2$. *If the regression model assumptions 1–5 are correct* (assumption 6 is not required), then the variances and covariance of $b_1$ and $b_2$ are:

$$\text{var}(b_1) = \sigma^2 \left[ \frac{\Sigma x_t^2}{T\Sigma(x_t - \bar{x})^2} \right]$$

$$\text{var}(b_2) = \frac{\sigma^2}{\Sigma(x_t - \bar{x})^2} \tag{4.2.10}$$

$$\text{cov}(b_1, b_2) = \sigma^2 \left[ \frac{-\bar{x}}{\Sigma(x_t - \bar{x})^2} \right]$$

At the beginning of this section we said that for unbiased estimators, smaller variances are better than larger variances. Let us consider the factors that affect the variances and covariance in equation 4.2.10.

1.  The variance of the random error term, $\sigma^2$, appears in each of the expressions. It reflects, as we discussed in Chapter 3.2, the dispersion of the values $y$ about their mean $E(y)$. The greater the variance $\sigma^2$, the greater is the dispersion, and the greater is the *uncertainty* about where the values of $y$ fall relative to their mean $E(y)$. The information we have about $\beta_1$ and $\beta_2$ is less precise the larger is $\sigma^2$. We saw in Figure 3.3 that this variance is reflected in the spread of the probability distributions $f(y|x)$. The *larger* the variance term $\sigma^2$, the *greater* the uncertainty there is in the statistical model, and the *larger* the variances and covariance of the least squares estimators.

2.  The sum of squares of the values of $x$ about their sample mean, $\Sigma(x_t - \bar{x})^2$, appears in each of the variances and in the covariance. This expression measures how *spread out* about their mean are the sample values of the independent or explanatory variable $x$. The more they are spread out, the larger the sum of squares. The less they are spread out the smaller the sum of squares. The *larger* the sum of squares, $\Sigma(x_t - \bar{x})^2$, the *smaller* the variances of the least squares estimators and the more *precisely* we can estimate the unknown parameters. The intuition behind this is demonstrated in Figure 4.2.

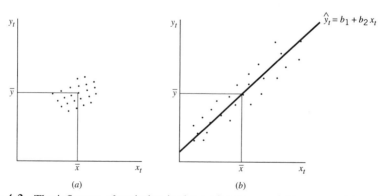

*FIGURE 4.2*   The influence of variation in the explanatory variable on precision of estimation (*a*) Low variation, low precision (*b*) High variation, high precision

On the right, in panel (b), is a data scatter in which the values of $x$ are widely spread out along the $x$-axis. In panel (a) the data are "bunched." Which data scatter would you prefer, given the task of fitting a line by hand? Pretty clearly, the data in panel (b) do a better job of determining where the least squares line must fall, because they are more spread out along the $x$-axis. Also, if $x_t = c$ for all observations, then the variances and the covariance have a zero in the denominator and are mathematically undefined.

3. The larger the sample size $T$, the *smaller* the variances and covariance of the least squares estimators; it is better to have *more* sample data than less. The sample size $T$ appears in each of the variances and covariance because each of the sums consists of $T$ terms. Also, $T$ appears explicitly in var($b_1$). The sum of squares term $\Sigma(x_t - \bar{x})^2$ gets larger and larger as $T$ increases because each of the terms in the sum is positive or zero (being zero if $x$ happens to equal its sample mean value for an observation). Consequently, as $T$ gets larger, both var($b_2$) and cov($b_1,b_2$) get smaller, since the sum of squares appears in their denominator. The sums in the numerator and denominator of var($b_1$) both get larger as $T$ gets larger and offset one another, leaving the $T$ in the denominator as the dominant term, ensuring that var($b_1$) also gets smaller as $T$ gets larger.

4. The term $\Sigma x^2$ appears in var($b_1$). The larger this term is, the larger the variance of the least squares estimator $b_1$. Why is this so? Recall that the intercept parameter $\beta_1$ is the expected value of $y$, given that $x = 0$. The farther our data are from $x = 0$ the more difficult it is to interpret $\beta_1$, as in the food expenditure example, and the more difficult it is to accurately estimate $\beta_1$. The term $\Sigma x^2$ measures the distance of the data from the origin, $x = 0$. If the values of $x$ are near zero, then $\Sigma x^2$ will be small and this will reduce var($b_1$). But if the values of $x$ are large in magnitude, either positive or negative, the term $\Sigma x^2$ will be large and var($b_1$) will be larger.

5. The sample mean of the $x$-values appears in cov($b_1,b_2$). The covariance *increases* the larger in magnitude is the sample mean $\bar{x}$, and the covariance has the *sign* that is opposite that of $\bar{x}$. The reasoning here can be seen from Figure 4.2. In panel (b) the least squares fitted line must pass through the point of the means. Given a fitted line through the data, imagine the effect of increasing the estimated slope, $b_2$. Since the line must pass through the point of the means, the effect must be to *lower* the point where the line hits the vertical axis, implying a *reduced* intercept estimate $b_1$. Thus, when the sample mean is positive, as shown in Figure 4.2, there is a negative covariance between the least squares estimators of the slope and intercept.

The preceding lengthy discussion describes the characteristics of the model and data that affect the least squares variances and the covariance between them.

As an illustration, we will derive the variance of $b_2$. You may, if you choose, skip the marked text for the present. Once again, we urge you to work through this algebra at some point. Only by working through the algebra will you appreciate the important point that the variance formulas are correct only if assumptions 3 and 4 hold.

**Deriving the variance of $b_2$:** The starting point is equation 4.2.1.

$$\text{var}(b_2) = \text{var}(\beta_2 + \Sigma w_t e_t) = \text{var}(\Sigma w_t e_t) \qquad [\text{since } \beta_2 \text{ is a constant}]$$

$$= \Sigma w_t^2 \, \text{var}(e_t) + \sum_{i \neq j} \sum w_i w_j \, \text{cov}(e_i, e_j) \qquad [\text{using equation 2.5.8}]$$

$$= \Sigma w_t^2 \, \text{var}(e_t) \qquad [\text{using cov}(e_i, e_j) = 0]$$

$$= \sigma^2 \Sigma w_t^2 \qquad [\text{using var}(e_t) = \sigma^2]$$

$$= \frac{\sigma^2}{\Sigma(x_t - \bar{x})^2} \tag{4.2.11}$$

The very last step uses the fact that

$$\Sigma w_t^2 = \Sigma \left[ \frac{(x_t - \bar{x})^2}{\{\Sigma(x_t - \bar{x})^2\}^2} \right] = \frac{1}{\Sigma(x_t - \bar{x})^2} \tag{4.2.12}$$

Note carefully that the derivation of the variance expression for $b_2$ depends on assumptions 3 and 4. If the $\text{cov}(e_i, e_j) \neq 0$ then we cannot drop out all those terms in the double summation. If $\text{var}(e_t) \neq \sigma^2$ for all observations then $\sigma^2$ cannot be factored out of the summation. If either of these assumptions fails to hold then $\text{var}(b_2)$ is *something else,* and is not given by equation 4.2.11. The same is true for the variance of $b_1$ and the covariance.

### 4.2.3    LINEAR ESTIMATORS

The least squares estimator $b_2$ is a weighted sum of the observations $y_t$, $b_2 = \Sigma w_t y_t$ [see equation 4.2.8]. In mathematics weighted sums like this are called **linear combinations** of the $y_t$; consequently, statisticians call estimators like $b_2$, that are linear combinations of an observable random variable, **linear estimators.** Putting together what we know so far, we can describe $b_2$ as a *linear, unbiased estimator* of $\beta_2$, with a variance given in equation 4.2.10. Similarly, $b_1$ can be described as a *linear, unbiased estimator* of $\beta_1$, with a variance given in equation 4.2.10.

## *4.3* The Gauss–Markov Theorem

The one and only "theorem" that we will prove in this book is the Gauss–Markov Theorem. The theorem is about the estimators $b_1$ and $b_2$ of the unknown intercept and slope parameters, $\beta_1$ and $\beta_2$. The theorem and proof are about the least squares estimation *procedure,* and thus can be established prior to the collection of any data. We will first state and discuss this famous result, and then prove it.

---

**GAUSS–MARKOV THEOREM:** Under the assumptions 1–5 of the linear regression model, the estimators $b_1$ and $b_2$ have the *smallest variance of all linear and unbiased estimators* of $\beta_1$ and $\beta_2$. They are the **Best Linear Unbiased Estimators (BLUE)** of $\beta_1$ and $\beta_2$.

---

Let us clarify what the Gauss–Markov Theorem does, and does not, say.

1. The estimators $b_1$ and $b_2$ are "best" when compared to *similar* estimators, those that are linear *and* unbiased. The theorem does *not* say that $b_1$ and $b_2$ are the best of all *possible* estimators.

2. The estimators $b_1$ and $b_2$ are best within their class because they have the minimum variance. This definition of "best" goes back to our discussion in Chapter 4.2.2. When comparing two linear and unbiased estimators, we *always* want to use the one with the smaller variance, since that estimation rule gives us the higher probability of obtaining an estimate that is close to the true parameter value.

3. In order for the Gauss–Markov Theorem to hold, assumptions 1–5 must be true. If any of these assumptions are *not* true, then $b_1$ and $b_2$ are *not* the best linear unbiased estimators of $\beta_1$ and $\beta_2$.

4. The Gauss–Markov Theorem does *not* depend on the assumption of normality (assumption 6).

5. The theorem is *not* about the least squares principle. It is about the estimation rules $b_1$ and $b_2$ given in equation 3.3.8. The theorem would hold if we used another principle to come up with these formulas.

6. In the simple linear regression model, if we want to use a linear and unbiased estimator, then we have to do no more searching. The estimators $b_1$ and $b_2$ are the ones to use. This explains why we are studying these estimators (we wouldn't have you study *bad* estimation rules, would we?) and why they are so widely used in research, not only in economics but in all the other social and physical sciences as well.

7. The Gauss–Markov Theorem applies to the least squares estimators. It *does not* apply to the least squares *estimates* from a single sample.

Now the proof. On the *first* reading of the chapter you can skip the marked text.

---

**Proof of the Gauss–Markov Theorem:** We will prove the Gauss–Markov Theorem for the least squares estimator $b_2$ of $\beta_2$. Our goal is to show that in the class of linear and unbiased estimators, the estimator $b_2$ has the smallest variance. Let $b_2^* = \Sigma k_t y_t$ (where the $k_t$ are constants) be any other linear estimator of $\beta_2$. To make comparison to the least squares estimator $b_2$ easier, suppose that $k_t = w_t + c_t$, where $c_t$ is another constant and $w_t$ is given in equation 4.2.2. While this is tricky, it is legal, since for any $k_t$ that someone might choose we can find $c_t$.

Into this new estimator substitute $y_t$ and simplify, using the properties of $w_t$ in equation 4.2.9.

$$b_2^* = \Sigma k_t y_t = \Sigma(w_t + c_t)y_t = \Sigma(w_t + c_t)(\beta_1 + \beta_2 x_t + e_t)$$

$$= \Sigma(w_t + c_t)\beta_1 + \Sigma(w_t + c_t)\beta_2 x_t + \Sigma(w_t + c_t)e_t$$

$$= \beta_1\Sigma w_t + \beta_1\Sigma c_t + \beta_2\Sigma w_t x_t + \beta_2\Sigma c_t x_t + \Sigma(w_t + c_t)e_t \qquad (4.3.1)$$

$$= \beta_1\Sigma c_t + \beta_2 + \beta_2\Sigma c_t x_t + \Sigma(w_t + c_t)e_t$$

since $\Sigma w_t = 0$ and $\Sigma w_t x_t = 1$.

Take the mathematical expectation of the last line in equation 4.3.1, using the properties of expectation (see Chapter 2.5.1) and the assumption that $E(e_t) = 0$:

$$E(b_2^*) = \beta_1\Sigma c_t + \beta_2 + \beta_2\Sigma c_t x_t + \Sigma(w_t + c_t)E(e_t)$$

$$= \beta_1\Sigma c_t + \beta_2 + \beta_2\Sigma c_t x_t \qquad (4.3.2)$$

In order for the linear estimator $b_2^* = \Sigma k_t y_t$ to be unbiased, it must be true that

$$\Sigma c_t = 0 \text{ and } \Sigma c_t x_t = 0 \qquad (4.3.3)$$

These conditions must hold in order for $b_2^* = \Sigma k_t y_t$ to be in the class of *linear* and *unbiased* estimators. So we will assume the conditions (4.3.3) hold and use them to simplify expression 4.3.1:

$$b_2^* = \Sigma k_t y_t = \beta_2 + \Sigma(w_t + c_t)e_t \qquad (4.3.4)$$

We can now find the variance of the linear, unbiased estimator $b_2^*$ following the steps in equation 4.2.11 and using the additional fact that

$$\Sigma c_t w_t = \Sigma\left[\frac{c_t(x_t - \bar{x})}{\Sigma(x_t - \bar{x})^2}\right] = \frac{1}{\Sigma(x_t - \bar{x})^2}\Sigma c_t x_t - \frac{\bar{x}}{\Sigma(x_t - \bar{x})^2}\Sigma c_t = 0$$

Use the properties of variance to obtain:

$$\text{var}(b_2^*) = \text{var}(\beta_2 + \Sigma(w_t + c_t)e_t) = \Sigma(w_t + c_t)^2 \text{ var}(e_t)$$

$$= \sigma^2\Sigma(w_t + c_t)^2 = \sigma^2\Sigma w_t^2 + \sigma^2\Sigma c_t^2$$

$$= \text{var}(b_2) + \sigma^2\Sigma c_t^2 \qquad (4.3.5)$$

$$\geq \text{var}(b_2) \text{ since } \Sigma c_t^2 \geq 0$$

The last line of equation 4.3.5 establishes that, for the family of linear and unbiased estimators $b_2^*$, each of the alternative estimators has variance that is greater than or equal to that of the least squares estimator $b_2$. The *only* time that $\text{var}(b_2^*) = \text{var}(b_2)$ is when all the $c_t = 0$, in which case $b_2^* = b_2$. Thus, *there is no other linear and unbiased estimator of* $\beta_2$ *that is better than* $b_2$, which proves the Gauss–Markov Theorem.

## 4.4 The Probability Distributions of the Least Squares Estimators

The properties of the least squares estimators that we have developed so far do not depend in any way on the normality assumption 6 in equation 3.3.1. If we additionally make this assumption, that the random errors $e_t$ are normally distributed with mean 0 and variance $\sigma^2$, then the probability distributions of the least squares estimators are also normal. This conclusion is obtained in two steps. First, based on assumption 1, if $e_t$ is normal, then so is $y_t$. Second, the least squares estimators are linear estimators, of the form $b_2 = \Sigma w_t y_t$, and weighted sums of normal random variables, using equation 2.6.4, are normally distributed themselves. Consequently, *if* we make the normality assumption, assumption 6 about the error term, then the least squares estimators are normally distributed.

$$b_1 \sim N\left(\beta_1, \frac{\sigma^2 \Sigma x_t^2}{T\Sigma(x_t - \bar{x})^2}\right)$$

$$b_2 \sim N\left(\beta_2, \frac{\sigma^2}{\Sigma(x_t - \bar{x})^2}\right)$$

(4.4.1)

As you will see in Chapter 5, the normality of the least squares estimators is of great importance in many aspects of statistical inference. Note that this is another least squares estimator property that we can establish before the data are drawn, based on the model assumptions.

What if the errors are not normally distributed? Can we say anything about the probability distribution of the least squares estimators? The answer is, sometimes, yes.

If assumptions 1–5 hold, and if the sample size $T$ is *sufficiently large,* then the least squares estimators have a distribution that approximates the normal distributions shown in equation 4.4.1.

The \$64 question is "How large is sufficiently large?" The answer is, there is no specific number. The reason for this vague and unsatisfying answer is that "how large" depends on many factors, such as what the distributions of the random errors look like (are they smooth? symmetric? skewed?) and what the $x_t$ values are like. In the simple regression model, some would say that $T = 30$ is sufficiently large. We, the authors of this book, are somewhat stodgy on this question, and would say that $T = 50$ would be a reasonable number. The bottom line is, however, that these are rules of thumb, and that the meaning of "sufficiently large" will change from problem to problem. Nevertheless, for better or worse, this *large sample,* or *asymptotic,* result is frequently invoked in regression analysis.

## 4.5 The Consistency of the Least Squares Estimators

What are the properties of the least squares estimators if we have a *very large* sample, or when the sample size $T \to \infty$? The answer for the least squares estimators, whether the errors are normal or not, is found in two properties of the least squares estimators that we have already established. First, the least squares estimators are unbiased. Second, the variances of the least squares estimators, given in equation 4.2.10, *converge to zero* as $T \to \infty$. As the sample size gets increasingly large, the probability distributions of the least squares estimators collapse about the true parameters. In Figure 4.3 this is illustrated. As $T \to \infty$ *all* the probability is concentrated about $\beta$. This is a very reassuring result. Its consequence is that as $T \to \infty$ the probability approaches *one* that a least squares estimate $b$ will be *close* to $\beta$, no matter how narrowly you define the term "close." Estimators with this property are called *consistent* estimators, and consistency is a nice large-sample property of the least squares estimators.

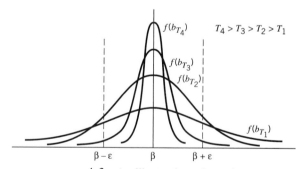

FIGURE 4.3    An illustration of consistency

## 4.6 Estimating the Variance of the Error Term

The variance of the random error term, $\sigma^2$, is the one unknown parameter of the simple linear regression model that remains to be estimated. The variance of the random variable $e_t$ (see Chapter 2.3.4) is

$$\text{var}(e_t) = \sigma^2 = E[e_t - E(e_t)]^2 = E(e_t^2) \qquad (4.6.1)$$

if the assumption $E(e_t) = 0$ is correct. Since the "expectation" is an average value we might consider estimating $\sigma^2$ as the average of the squared errors,

$$\hat{\sigma}^2 = \frac{\Sigma e_t^2}{T} \qquad (4.6.2)$$

The formula in equation 4.6.2 is unfortunately of no use, since the random errors $e_t$ are *unobservable*! However, while the random errors themselves are unknown, we do have an analogue to them, namely, the least squares residuals. Recall that the random errors are

$$e_t = y_t - \beta_1 - \beta_2 x_t$$

and the least squares residuals are obtained by replacing the unknown parameters by their least squares estimators,

$$\hat{e}_t = y_t - b_1 - b_2 x_t$$

It seems reasonable to replace the random errors $e_t$ in equation 4.6.2 by their analogues, the least squares residuals, to obtain

$$\hat{\sigma}^2 = \frac{\Sigma \hat{e}_t^2}{T} \qquad (4.6.3)$$

Unfortunately, the estimator in equation 4.6.3 is a *biased* estimator of $\sigma^2$. Happily, there is a simple modification that produces an unbiased estimator, and that is

$$\hat{\sigma}^2 = \frac{\Sigma \hat{e}_t^2}{T - 2} \qquad (4.6.4)$$

The "2" that is subtracted in the denominator is the number of *regression parameters* ($\beta_1$, $\beta_2$) in the model, and this subtraction makes the estimator $\hat{\sigma}^2$ unbiased, so that

$$E(\hat{\sigma}^2) = \sigma^2 \qquad (4.6.5)$$

Consequently, before the data are obtained, we have an unbiased estimation procedure for the variance of the error term, $\sigma^2$, at our disposal.

### 4.6.1   ESTIMATING THE VARIANCES AND COVARIANCES OF THE LEAST SQUARES ESTIMATORS

Having an unbiased estimator of the error variance, we can *estimate* the variances of the least squares estimators $b_1$ and $b_2$, and the covariance between them. Replace the unknown error variance $\sigma^2$ in equation 4.2.10 by its estimator to obtain:

$$\text{vâr}(b_1) = \hat{\sigma}^2 \left[ \frac{\Sigma x_t^2}{T\Sigma(x_t - \bar{x})^2} \right], \quad \text{se}(b_1) = \sqrt{\text{vâr}(b_1)}$$

$$\text{vâr}(b_2) = \frac{\hat{\sigma}^2}{\Sigma(x_t - \bar{x})^2}, \quad \text{se}(b_2) = \sqrt{\text{vâr}(b_2)} \qquad (4.6.6)$$

$$\text{côv}(b_1, b_2) = \hat{\sigma}^2 \left[ \frac{-\bar{x}}{\Sigma(x_t - \bar{x})^2} \right]$$

The square roots of the estimated variances, se($b_1$) and se($b_2$), are the *standard errors* of $b_1$ and $b_2$.

## 4.6.2 THE ESTIMATED VARIANCES AND COVARIANCES FOR THE FOOD EXPENDITURE EXAMPLE

Let us apply the results of this section to the food expenditure example. The least squares estimates of the parameters in the food expenditure model are given in Chapter 3.3.2. In order to estimate the variances and covariance of the least squares estimators, we must first compute the least squares residuals and calculate the estimate of the error variance in equation 4.6.4. In Table 4.1 are the least squares residuals for the first five households in Table 3.1.

Using the residuals for all $T = 40$ observations, we estimate the error variance to be

$$\hat{\sigma}^2 = \frac{\Sigma \hat{e}_t^2}{T - 2} = \frac{54311.3315}{38} = 1429.2456$$

The estimated variances, covariances and corresponding standard errors are

$$\text{vâr}(b_1) = \hat{\sigma}^2 \left[ \frac{\Sigma x_t^2}{T\Sigma(x_t - \bar{x})^2} \right] = 1429.2456 \left[ \frac{21020623}{40(1532463)} \right] = 490.1200$$

$$\text{se}(b_1) = \sqrt{\text{vâr}(b_1)} = \sqrt{490.1200} = 22.1387$$

$$\text{vâr}(b_2) = \frac{\hat{\sigma}^2}{\Sigma(x_t - \bar{x})^2} = \frac{1429.2456}{1532463} = 0.0009326$$

$$\text{se}(b_2) = \sqrt{\text{vâr}(b_2)} = \sqrt{0.0009326} = 0.0305$$

**Table 4.1** Least Squares Residuals for Food Expenditure Data

| $y$ | $\hat{y} = b_1 + b_2 x$ | $\hat{e} = y - \hat{y}$ |
|---|---|---|
| 52.25 | 73.9045 | −21.6545 |
| 58.32 | 84.7834 | −26.4634 |
| 81.79 | 95.2902 | −13.5002 |
| 119.90 | 100.7424 | 19.1576 |
| 125.80 | 102.7181 | 23.0819 |

$$\hat{\text{cov}}(b_1, b_2) = \hat{\sigma}^2 \left[ \frac{-\bar{x}}{\Sigma(x_t - \bar{x})^2} \right] = 1429.2456 \left[ \frac{-698}{1532463} \right] = -0.6510$$

In Chapter 5 these estimated variances and covariances are used extensively in the statistical inference procedures of interval estimation and hypothesis testing.

## 4.7 The Least Squares Predictor

The ability to predict values of the dependent variable $y$ is one of the objectives of linear regression analysis. Given the model and assumptions 1–5, we want to predict for a given value of the explanatory variable $x_0$ the value of the dependent variable $y_0$, which is given by

$$y_0 = \beta_1 + \beta_2 x_0 + e_0 \qquad (4.7.1)$$

where $e_0$ is a random error. This possibly normally distributed random error has mean $E(e_0)=0$ and variance $\text{var}(e_0)= \sigma^2$. We also assume that it is uncorrelated with any of the sample observations, so that $\text{cov}(e_0, e_t)=0$.

In equation 4.7.1 we can replace the unknown parameters by their estimators, $b_1$ and $b_2$. Since $y_0$ is not known, the random error $e_0$ cannot be estimated, so we replace it by its expectation, zero. This produces the least squares predictor of $y_0$,

$$\hat{y}_0 = b_1 + b_2 x_0 \qquad (4.7.2)$$

graphed in Figure 4.4. This prediction is given by the point on the least squares fitted line where $x = x_0$.

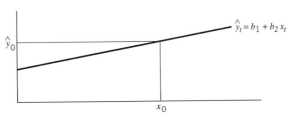

FIGURE **4.4**   A point prediction

How good a prediction procedure is this? Since the least squares estimators $b_1$ and $b_2$ are random variables, then so is $\hat{y}_0 = b_1 + b_2 x_0$. To evaluate the sampling properties of this predictor it is customary to examine the **forecast error**

$$f = \hat{y}_0 - y_0 = b_1 + b_2 x_0 - (\beta_1 + \beta_2 x_0 + e_0)$$

$$= (b_1 - \beta_1) + (b_2 - \beta_2)x_0 - e_0 \qquad (4.7.3)$$

Using the properties of the least squares estimators and the assumptions about $e_0$, the expected value of $f$ is:

$$E(f) = E(\hat{y}_0 - y_0) = E(b_1 - \beta_1) + E(b_2 - \beta_2)x_0 - E(e_0)$$

$$= 0 + 0 - 0 = 0 \tag{4.7.4}$$

which means, on average, the forecast error is zero, and $\hat{y}_0$ is an *unbiased linear predictor* of $y_0$.

Using the expression 4.7.3 for the forecast error, and what we know about the variances and covariances of the least squares estimators, it can be shown that the variance of the forecast error is:

$$\text{var}(f) = \text{var}(\hat{y}_0 - y_0) = \sigma^2 \left[ 1 + \frac{1}{T} + \frac{(x_0 - \bar{x})^2}{\Sigma(x_t - \bar{x})^2} \right] \tag{4.7.5}$$

Notice that the further $x_0$ is from the sample mean $\bar{x}$, the more unreliable the forecast will be, in the sense that the variance of the forecast error is larger.

If the random errors are normally distributed, or if the sample size is large, then the forecast error $f$ is normally distributed with mean zero and variance given by equation 4.7.5.

The forecast error variance is estimated by replacing $\sigma^2$ by its estimator to give

$$\hat{\text{var}}(f) = \hat{\sigma}^2 \left[ 1 + \frac{1}{T} + \frac{(x_0 - \bar{x})^2}{\Sigma(x_t - \bar{x})^2} \right] \tag{4.7.6}$$

The square root of this quantity is the *standard error of the forecast,*

$$\text{se}(f) = \sqrt{\hat{\text{var}}(f)} \tag{4.7.7}$$

which will be used in Chapter 5.3.

### 4.7.1    PREDICTION IN THE FOOD EXPENDITURE MODEL

In equation 3.3.15 we predicted the weekly expenditure on food for a household with $x_0 = \$750$ weekly income. The predicted value was

$$\hat{y}_0 = b_1 + b_2 x_0 = 40.7676 + .1283(750) = 136.98$$

This means we predict that a household with $750 weekly income will spend $136.98 on food per week.

Using our estimate $\hat{\sigma}^2 = 1429.2456$, the estimated variance of the forecast error is

$$\hat{\text{var}}(f) = \hat{\sigma}^2 \left[ 1 + \frac{1}{T} + \frac{(x_0 - \bar{x})^2}{\Sigma(x_t - \bar{x})^2} \right]$$

$$= 1429.2456 \left[ 1 + \frac{1}{40} + \frac{(750 - 698)^2}{1532463} \right] = 1467.4986$$

The standard error of the forecast is then

$$\text{se}(f) = \sqrt{\text{vâr}(f)} = \sqrt{1467.4986} = 38.3079$$

These quantities will be used in Chapter 5 as we attempt to assess the reliability of our prediction.

## *4.8* Summing Up

In this chapter we have constructed a foundation for statistical inference by examining the sampling properties of the least squares estimators and the least squares predictor. *Given assumptions 1–5* of the simple linear regression model, we have learned that:

1.  The least squares estimators $b_1$ and $b_2$, formulas to be used whatever the sample data turn out to be, are random variables with means and variances given in (4.2.10) and (4.4.1).
2.  The statistical properties of the least squares estimation procedures (estimators) can be established prior to the collection of any data.
3.  The least squares estimates from a single sample are numerical values that have no statistical properties. They are widely used because the procedure by which they are obtained has desirable properties.
4.  The least squares estimators are linear estimators. For example, $b_2$ can be written $b_2 = \Sigma w_i y_i$, where the $w_i$ are constants.
5.  The least squares estimators are unbiased, meaning that $E(b_k) = \beta_k$, $k = 1,2$.
6.  The least squares estimators $b_1$ and $b_2$ are the *best linear unbiased estimators* of $\beta_1$ and $\beta_2$.
7.  The least squares estimators are consistent. As the sample size $T \to \infty$ the probability approaches one that the least squares estimate will be "close" to the true parameters, no matter how "close" is defined.
8.  An unbiased estimator of the error variance is $\hat{\sigma}^2 = \dfrac{\Sigma \hat{e}_t^2}{T - 2}$ This estimator can be used to form unbiased estimators of the variances and covariance of the least squares estimators, given in equation 4.6.6.
9.  An unbiased predictor of $y_0$, given by $y_0 = \beta_1 + \beta_2 x_0 + e_0$, is $\hat{y}_0 = b_1 + b_2 x_0$.
10. If the random errors are normally distributed (assumption 6), or if the sample size is large, then it is additionally true that:
    a.  The least squares estimators are normally distributed.
    b.  The forecast error $f$ of the least squares predictor is normally distributed.

## *4.9* Exercises

4.1  Write down your understanding of what is meant by sampling performance of an estimation rule or estimator. Interpret the meaning of "unbiasedness."

4.2    Since we usually have only one sample of data, why should we be interested in the sampling properties of an estimator?

4.3    If the random error $e_t$ is distributed normally with mean zero and variance $\sigma^2$, i.e., $e_t \sim N(0,\sigma^2)$, how are $b_2$, $e_t/\sigma$ and $e_t^2/\sigma^2$ distributed?

4.4    Given the simple linear statistical model $y_t = \beta_1 + x_t\beta_2 + e_t$, and the least squares estimators for $\beta_1$ and $\beta_2$, we can estimate $E[y_t]$, for any value of $x = x_0$ as $\hat{E}(y_0) = b_1 + b_2x_0$.
   (a) Describe the difference between predicting $y_0$, as in Chapter 4.7, and estimating $E(y_0)$.
   (b) Find the expected value and variance of $\hat{E}(y_0) = b_1 + b_2x_0$.

4.5    Discuss the meaning of the following:
   (a) Linear estimator
   (b) Unbiased estimator
   (c) Best linear unbiased estimator
   (d) Gauss–Markov Theorem

4.6    Using the data in Exercise 3.2, calculate the following terms *by hand:*
   (a) $w_t$ given in equation 4.2.2
   (b) $b_2$, using equation 4.2.6
   (c) $\Sigma w_t$
   (d) $\Sigma w_t x_t$
   (e) $\hat{e}_t$
   (f) $\hat{\sigma}^2$
   (g) vâr$(b_2)$
   (h) $\hat{y}_0$ and se$(f)$ for $x_0 = 5$

4.7    Using the Moscow Makkers data in Table 3.3, Exercise 3.6, and your computer software:
   (a) Find the estimated variances and covariance of the least squares estimators.
   (b) Find $\hat{\sigma}^2$.
   (c) Find $\hat{y}_0$ when the hamburger price is $p_0 = 1.50$. What is the corresponding quantity?

4.8    Using the "learning curve" data in Table 3.4, Exercise 3.8, and your computer software:
   (a) Find the estimated variances and covariance of the least squares estimators
   (b) Find $\hat{\sigma}^2$.
   (c) Predict the unit cost of production when cumulative production is $q_0 = 2000$.

4.9    Using the CAPM data discussed in Exercise 3.9, and located in the file "*capm.dat*":
   (a) Find the estimated variances and covariance of the least squares estimators.
   (b) Find $\hat{\sigma}^2$.

4.10   Suppose that $x_t$ is a constant $c$ for all sample observations.
   (a) Compute the denominator of the formula for the least squares estimate of $b_2$ in equation 4.2.6.
   (b) Compare your answer here to your answer in Exercise 3.10.

(c)  Explain, intuitively, why least squares estimation fails in this case. (Hint: See the discussion following equation 4.2.10.)

4.11  Consider Exercise 3.5 and the data in Table 3.2. Use your computer software to:
(a)  Compute the least squares residuals $\hat{e}_t$.
(b)  Compute $\hat{\sigma}^2$.
(c)  Compute vâr$(b_2)$.
(d)  Compute $\hat{y}_0$ and se$(f)$ for $x_0 = 5$.

4.12  The gross income and tax paid by a cross-section of 30 companies in 1988 and 1989 is given in the file "*tax.dat*."
(a)  Use these data to estimate the relationship

$$tax_t = \beta_1 + \beta_2 income_t + e_t$$

for each of the years 1988 and 1989.
(b)  Give interpretations of the two estimates of $\beta_2$.
(c)  Find the average income for each year and predict the tax paid for each average income. Compare the average and marginal tax rates.
(d)*  Consider the estimate for $\beta_2$ for 1989 and the corresponding estimated variance. Pretend that the estimated variance is the same as the true variance var$(b_2)$, and assume that $b_2$ is normally distributed. Find the probability that the sampling error $|b_2 - \beta_2|$ is (*i*) less than .04, and (*ii*) less than .01.
(e)  Pool the observations from the two years of data and use the resulting 40 observations to estimate one tax–income relationship. Compare the estimates for $\beta_1$ and $\beta_2$, and the estimated variances with those from the separate equations. What implicit assumptions are you making when you pool the two sets of observations?

4.13  Show that the least squares estimator $b_1$ is the best linear unbiased estimator of $\beta_1$.

4.14*  Professor E. Z. Stuff has decided that the least squares estimator is too much trouble. Noting that two points determine a line, Dr. Stuff chooses two points from a sample of size $T$ and draws a line between them. The slope of this line he calls the EZ-estimator of $\beta_2$ in the simple regression model. Algebraically, if the two points are $(y_1, x_1)$ and $(y_2, x_2)$, the EZ-estimation rule is:

$$b_{EZ} = \frac{y_2 - y_1}{x_2 - x_1}$$

Assuming that all the assumptions of the simple regression model hold:
(a)  Show that $b_{EZ}$ is a "linear" estimator.
(b)  Show that $b_{EZ}$ is an unbiased estimator.
(c)  Find the variance of $b_{EZ}$.
(d)  Find the probability distribution of $b_{EZ}$.
(e)  Convince Professor E. Z. Stuff that his estimator is not as good as the least squares estimator.

4.15   When discussing the unbiasedness of the least squares predictor $\hat{y}_0$ in Section 4.7 we showed that $E(f) = E(\hat{y}_0 - y_0) = 0$, where $f$ is the forecast error. Why did we define unbiasedness this strange way? What is wrong with saying, as we have in other unbiasedness demonstrations, that $E(\hat{y}_0) = y_0$?

## 4.10   References

For a more complete write-up of the theoretical background for the material in this chapter see:

GRIFFITHS, W. E., R. C. HILL, AND G. G. JUDGE (1993). *Learning and Practicing Econometrics.* New York: John Wiley & Sons, Inc., pp. 208–23.

For another treatment of topics covered in this chapter see:

CANIGLIA, ALAN S. (1992). *Statistics for Econometrics.* New York: HarperCollins, Chapter 10.

GUJARATI, D. N. (1995). *Basic Econometrics, 3rd edition.* New York: McGraw-Hill, Chapter 4.

# Chapter 5

# Inference in the Simple Regression Model: Interval Estimation, Hypothesis Testing, and Prediction

In Chapter 4 we developed the properties of the least squares estimators under the following set of assumptions:

---

**ASSUMPTIONS OF THE SIMPLE LINEAR REGRESSION MODEL**

1. $y_t = \beta_1 + \beta_2 x_t + e_t$
2. $E(e_t) = 0 \Leftrightarrow E(y_t) = \beta_1 + \beta_2 x_t$
3. $\text{var}(e_t) = \sigma^2 = \text{var}(y_t)$
4. $\text{cov}(e_i, e_j) = \text{cov}(y_i, y_j) = 0$
5. $x_t \neq c$ for every observation
6. $e_t \sim N(0, \sigma^2) \Leftrightarrow y_t \sim N[(\beta_1 + \beta_2 x_t), \sigma^2]$ (*optional*)

---

If all these assumptions, including assumption 6 of normality, are correct, then the least squares estimators $b_1$ and $b_2$ are normally distributed random variables and have, from Chapter 4.4, normal distributions with means and variances as follows:

$$b_1 \sim N\left(\beta_1, \frac{\sigma^2 \Sigma x_t^2}{T \Sigma (x_t - \bar{x})^2}\right)$$

$$b_2 \sim N\left(\beta_2, \frac{\sigma^2}{\Sigma (x_t - \bar{x})^2}\right)$$

From Chapter 4.6 we know that the unbiased estimator of the error variance is

$$\hat{\sigma}^2 = \frac{\Sigma \hat{e}_t^2}{T - 2}$$

By replacing the unknown parameter $\sigma^2$ with this estimator we can estimate the variances of the least squares estimators and their covariance.

In Chapter 4 you learned how to calculate *point* estimates of the regression parameters $\beta_1$ and $\beta_2$ using the best, linear unbiased estimation procedure. The estimates represent an *inference* about the regression function $E(y) = \beta_1 + \beta_2 x$ of the population from which the sample of data was drawn. Also in Chapter 4, the least squares predictor of

$$y_0 = \beta_1 + \beta_2 x_0 + e_0$$

was introduced. It allows us to make forecasts about, or *infer* future values of, the dependent variable $y$, for any value of $x$.

In this chapter we introduce the additional tools of statistical inference: **interval estimation**, **interval prediction**, and **hypothesis testing**. Interval estimation and prediction are procedures for creating ranges of values, sometimes called **confidence intervals**, in which the unknown parameters, or the value of $y_0$, are likely to be located. Hypothesis testing procedures are a means of comparing conjectures that we as economists might have about the regression parameters to the information about the parameters contained in a sample of data. Hypothesis tests allow us to say that the data are compatible, or are not compatible, with a particular conjecture, or hypothesis.

The procedures for interval estimation, prediction, and hypothesis testing, depend heavily on assumption 6 of the simple linear regression model, and the resulting normality of the least squares estimators. If assumption 6 is not made, then the sample size must be sufficiently large so that the least squares estimator's distributions are *approximately* normal, in which case the procedures we develop in this chapter are also approximate. In developing the procedures in this chapter we will be using the normal distribution, and distributions related to the normal, namely "Student's" $t$-distribution and the chi-square distribution. You may want to refresh your memory now about these distributions by reviewing Sections 2.6 and 2.7 in Chapter 2.

## *5.1* Interval Estimation

### 5.1.1 THE THEORY

The interval estimation procedures in this chapter involve the $t$-distribution. In the following marked text, which you can skip on the first reading, we develop the key result.

A standard normal random variable that we will use to construct an interval estimator is based on the normal distribution of the least squares estimator. Consider, for example, the normal distribution of $b_2$ the least squares estimator of $\beta_2$, which we denote as

$$b_2 \sim N\left(\beta_2, \frac{\sigma^2}{\Sigma(x_t - \bar{x})^2}\right)$$

A standardized normal random variable is obtained from $b_2$ by subtracting its mean and dividing by its standard deviation:

$$Z = \frac{b_2 - \beta_2}{\sqrt{\text{var}(b_2)}} \sim N(0,1) \qquad (5.1.1)$$

That is, the standardized random variable $Z$ is normally distributed with mean 0 and variance 1.

The second piece of the puzzle involves a chi-square random variable. If assumption 6 holds, then the random error term $e_t$ has a normal distribution, $e_t \sim N(0,\sigma^2)$. Again, we can standardize the random variable by dividing by its standard deviation so that $e_t/\sigma \sim N(0,1)$. The square of a standard normal random variable is a chi-square random variable (see Chapter 2.7.1) with one degree of freedom, so $(e_t/\sigma)^2 \sim \chi^2_{(1)}$. If all the random errors are independent then

$$\sum_t \left(\frac{e_t}{\sigma}\right)^2 = \left(\frac{e_1}{\sigma}\right)^2 + \left(\frac{e_2}{\sigma}\right)^2 + \cdots + \left(\frac{e_T}{\sigma}\right)^2 \sim \chi^2_{(T)} \qquad (5.1.2)$$

Since the true random errors are unobservable we replace them by their sample counterparts, the least squares residuals $\hat{e}_t = y_t - b_1 - b_2 x_t$ to obtain

$$V = \frac{\Sigma_t \hat{e}_t^2}{\sigma^2} = \frac{(T - 2)\hat{\sigma}^2}{\sigma^2} \qquad (5.1.3)$$

The random variable $V$ in equation 5.1.3 does not have a $\chi^2_{(T)}$ distribution because the least squares residuals are *not* independent random variables. All $T$ residuals $\hat{e}_t = y_t - b_1 - b_2 x_t$ depend on the least squares estimators $b_1$ and $b_2$. It can be shown that only $T - 2$ of the least squares residuals are independent in the simple linear regression model. Consequently, the random variable in equation 5.1.3 has a chi-square distribution with $T - 2$ degrees of freedom. That is, when multiplied by the constant $(T - 2)/\sigma^2$ the random variable $\hat{\sigma}^2$ has a *chi-square distribution with $T - 2$ degrees of freedom*,

$$V = \frac{(T - 2)\hat{\sigma}^2}{\sigma^2} \sim \chi^2_{(T-2)}$$

We have *not* established the fact that the chi-square random variable $V$ is statistically independent of the least squares estimators $b_1$ and $b_2$, but it is. Consequently, $V$ and the standard normal random variable $Z$ in equation 5.1.1 are independent. A demonstration of this fact is beyond the scope of this book, which means that it is ugly and you would not want to see it. So, take our word on this.

From the two random variables $V$ and $Z$ we can form a $t$-random variable. Recall that a $t$-random variable is formed by dividing a standard normal random variable, $Z \sim N(0,1)$, by the square root of an *independent* chi-square random variable, $V \sim \chi^2_{(m)}$, that has been divided by its degrees of freedom, $m$. That is, from equation 2.7.3,

$$t = \frac{Z}{\sqrt{V/m}} \sim t_{(m)}$$

The $t$-distribution's shape is completely determined by the degrees of freedom parameter, $m$, and the distribution is symbolized by $t_{(m)}$. Using $Z$ and $V$ from (5.5.1) and (5.5.3), respectively, we have

$$t = \frac{Z}{\sqrt{V/T-2}} = \frac{\dfrac{b_2 - \beta_2}{\sqrt{\dfrac{\sigma^2}{\Sigma(x_t - \bar{x})^2}}}}{\sqrt{\dfrac{(T-2)\hat{\sigma}^2}{\sigma^2} \bigg/ T-2}} = \frac{b_2 - \beta_2}{\sqrt{\dfrac{\hat{\sigma}^2}{\Sigma(x_t - \bar{x})^2}}}$$

$$= \frac{b_2 - \beta_2}{\sqrt{\hat{var}(b_2)}} = \frac{b_2 - \beta_2}{se(b_2)}$$

If assumptions 1–6 of the simple linear regression model hold, then

$$t = \frac{b_k - \beta_k}{se(b_k)} \sim t_{(T-2)}, \quad k = 1,2 \tag{5.1.4}$$

The random variable $t$ has a $t$-distribution with $(T - 2)$ degrees of freedom, which we denote by writing $t \sim t_{(T-2)}$. The random variable $t$ in equation 5.1.4 will be the basis for interval estimation and hypothesis testing in the simple linear regression model. Equation 5.1.4, for $k = 2$, is

$$t = \frac{b_2 - \beta_2}{se(b_2)} \sim t_{(T-2)} \tag{5.1.5}$$

where

$$\hat{var}(b_2) = \frac{\hat{\sigma}^2}{\Sigma(x_t - \bar{x})^2} \quad \text{and} \quad se(b_2) = \sqrt{\hat{var}(b_2)}$$

Using Table 2 at the front of the book, we can find critical values $t_c$ from a $t_{(m)}$ distribution such that

$$P(t \geq t_c) = P(t \leq t_c) = \frac{\alpha}{2}$$

where $\alpha$ is a probability value often taken to be $\alpha = .01$ or $\alpha = .05$. The values $t_c$ and $-t_c$ are depicted in Figure 5.1.

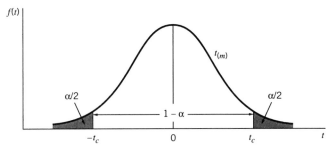

$FIGURE$ **5.1**   Critical values from a $t$-distribution

Each of the shaded "tail" areas contains $\alpha/2$ of the probability, so that $1 - \alpha$ of the probability is contained in the center portion. Consequently, we can make the probability statement

$$P(-t_c \leq t \leq t_c) = 1 - \alpha \qquad (5.1.6)$$

Now, we put all these pieces together to create a procedure for interval estimation. Substitute $t$ from equation 5.1.5 into 5.1.6 to obtain

$$P[-t_c \leq \frac{b_2 - \beta_2}{se(b_2)} \leq t_c] = 1 - \alpha$$

Simplify this expression to obtain

$$P[b_2 - t_c\,se(b_2) \leq \beta_2 \leq b_2 + t_c\,se(b_2)] = 1 - \alpha \qquad (5.1.7)$$

In the interval endpoints, $b_2 - t_c\,se(b_2)$ and $b_2 + t_c\,se(b_2)$, both $b_2$ and $se(b_2)$ are random variables, since their values are not known until a sample of data is drawn. The random endpoints of the interval define an *interval estimator* of $\beta_2$. The probability statement in equation 5.1.7 says that the interval $b_2 \pm t_c\,se(b_2)$, with random endpoints, has probability $1 - \alpha$ of containing the true but unknown parameter $\beta_2$. This interval estimation procedure and its properties are established based on model assumptions 1–6 and may be applied to any sample of data that we might obtain. When $b_2$ and $se(b_2)$ in equation 5.1.7 are *estimated values* (numbers), based on a sample of data, then $b_2 \pm t_c\,se(b_2)$ is called a $(1 - \alpha) \times (100\%)$ *interval estimate* of $\beta_2$, or, equivalently, it is called a $(1 - \alpha) \times (100\%)$ *confidence interval*.

The interpretation of interval *estimators* and interval *estimates* requires a great deal of care. The properties of the *random interval estimator* are based on the notion of repeated sampling. If we were to select *many* random samples of size $T$, compute the least squares estimate $b_2$ and its standard error $se(b_2)$ *for each sample*, and then construct the interval estimate $b_2 + t_c\,se(b_2)$ for each sample, then $(1 - \alpha) \times (100\%)$ of all the intervals constructed *would contain the true parameter* $\beta_2$. This we know before any data are actually collected.

Any *one* interval estimate, based on one sample of data, may or may not contain the true parameter $\beta_2$, and since $\beta_2$ is unknown, we will *never* know if it does or not. When confidence intervals are discussed, remember that our confidence is in the *procedure used to construct the interval estimate;* it is not in any one interval estimate calculated from a sample of data.

### 5.1.2 AN ILLUSTRATION

For the food expenditure data in Table 3.1, where $T = 40$ and the degrees of freedom are $T - 2 = 38$, if we let $\alpha = .05$, equation 5.1.7 becomes

$$P[b_2 - 2.024se(b_2) \le \beta_2 \le b_2 + 2.024se(b_2)] = .95 \qquad (5.1.8)$$

The critical value $t_c = 2.024$, which is appropriate for $\alpha = .05$ and 38 degrees of freedom, does not appear in the $t$ table at the front of the book. However, it can be approximated by interpolating between the values for 30 and 40 degrees of freedom in the $t$ table. Alternatively, it can be computed exactly, as we have done, using SHAZAM, SAS, or some other software package.

To construct an interval estimate for $\beta_2$ we use the least squares estimate $b_2 = .1283$, which has the **standard error**

$$se(b_2) = \sqrt{v\hat{a}r(b_2)} = \sqrt{0.0009326} = 0.0305$$

Substituting these values into equation 5.1.8 we obtain a "95 percent confidence interval estimate" for $\beta_2$:

$$b_2 \pm t_c\, se(b_2) = .1283 \pm 2.024(.0305) = [.0666, .1900]$$

Is $\beta_2$ in the interval [.0666, .1900]? We do not know, and we will never know. What we *do* know is that when the procedure we used is applied to many random samples of data from the same population, then 95 percent of all the interval estimates constructed using this procedure will contain the true parameter. The interval estimation procedure "works" 95 percent of the time. All we can say about the interval estimate based on our one sample is that, given the reliability of the procedure, we would be "surprised" if $\beta_2$ was not in the interval [.0666, .1900]. Since this interval estimate contains no random quantities we *cannot* make probabilistic statements about it such as "There is a .95 probability that $\beta_2$ is in the interval [.0666, .1900]."

What is the usefulness of an interval estimate of $\beta_2$? When reporting regression results we always give a point estimate, such as $b_2 = .1283$. However, the point estimate alone gives no sense of its reliability. Interval estimates incorporate both the point estimate and the standard error of the estimate, which is a measure of the variability of the least squares estimator. If an interval estimate is wide (implying a large standard error), there is not much information in the sample about $\beta_2$. A narrow interval estimate suggests we have learned more about $\beta_2$.

What is "wide" and what is "narrow" depends on the problem at hand. For example, in our model $b_2 = .1283$ is an estimate of how much weekly food expenditure will rise given a $1 increase in weekly income. A prudent supermarket CEO will consider values of $\beta_2$ around .1283 to allow for estimation error. The question is, which values? One answer is provided by the interval estimate [.0666, .1900]. While $\beta_2$ may or may not be in this interval, the CEO knows that the procedure used to obtain the interval estimate "works" 95% of the time. If varying $\beta_2$ within the interval has drastic outcome consequences, then the CEO may conclude that she has insufficient evidence upon which to make a decision, and order a new and larger sample of data.

### 5.1.3  THE REPEATED SAMPLING CONTEXT

To illustrate this point in a slightly different way we present in Table 5.1 least squares estimates of the food expenditure model from ten random samples of size $T=40$ from the same population. Note the variability of the least squares parameter estimates, their standard errors, and the estimated error variance. This variation is due to the simple fact that we obtained 40 *different* households in each sample, and their weekly food expenditure varies randomly.

Using the ten samples of data and the results in Table 5.1 the 95 percent confidence interval estimates for the parameters $\beta_1$ and $\beta_2$ are given in Table 5.2. Sampling variability causes the center of each of the interval estimates to change with the location of the least squares estimates, and it causes the widths of the intervals to change with the standard errors. If we ask the question, "How many of these intervals contain the true parameters, and which ones are they?" we must again answer that we do not know, and we will never know. But since 95 percent of all interval estimates constructed this way contain the true parameter values, we would expect perhaps nine or ten of these intervals to contain the true but unknown parameters.

Note the difference between *point* estimation and *interval* estimation. We have used the least squares estimators (rules) to obtain, from a sample of data, point estimates that are "best guesses" of unknown parameters. The estimated variance $\text{vâr}(b_k)$, for $k = 1$ or 2, and its square root $\sqrt{\text{vâr}(b_k)} = \text{se}(b_k)$, provide information about the *sampling variability* of the least squares estimator from one sample to another. Interval estimators combine point estimation with estimation of sampling variability to provide a range of values in which the unknown parameters might fall. Interval estimates are a convenient way to inform others about the estimated *location* of the unknown parameter and also provide information about the sampling variability of the least squares estimator, through $\text{se}(b_k)$, and the "level of confidence" $1 - \alpha$. When the sampling variability of the least squares estimator is relatively small, then the interval estimates will be relatively narrow, implying that

***Table 5.1***   **Least Squares Estimates from Ten Random Samples**

| $n$ | $b_1$ | $\text{se}(b_1)$ | $b_2$ | $\text{se}(b_2)$ | $\hat{\sigma}^2$ |
|---|---|---|---|---|---|
| 1 | 51.1314 | 27.4260 | 0.1442 | 0.0378 | 2193.4597 |
| 2 | 61.2045 | 24.9177 | 0.1286 | 0.0344 | 1810.5972 |
| 3 | 40.7882 | 17.6670 | 0.1417 | 0.0244 | 910.1835 |
| 4 | 80.1396 | 23.8146 | 0.0886 | 0.0329 | 1653.8324 |
| 5 | 31.0110 | 22.8126 | 0.1669 | 0.0315 | 1517.5837 |
| 6 | 54.3099 | 26.9317 | 0.1086 | 0.0372 | 2115.1085 |
| 7 | 69.6749 | 19.2903 | 0.1003 | 0.0266 | 1085.1312 |
| 8 | 71.1541 | 26.1807 | 0.1009 | 0.0361 | 1998.7880 |
| 9 | 18.8290 | 22.4234 | 0.1758 | 0.0309 | 1466.2541 |
| 10 | 36.1433 | 23.5531 | 0.1626 | 0.0325 | 1617.7087 |

*Table 5.2*  **Interval Estimates from Ten Random Samples**

| $n$ | $b_1 - t_c\text{se}(b_1)$ | $b_1 + t_c\text{se}(b_1)$ | $b_2 - t_c\text{se}(b_2)$ | $b_2 + t_c\text{se}(b_2)$ |
|---|---|---|---|---|
| 1 | −4.3897 | 106.6524 | 0.0676 | 0.2207 |
| 2 | 10.7612 | 111.6479 | 0.0590 | 0.1982 |
| 3 | 5.0233 | 76.5531 | 0.0923 | 0.1910 |
| 4 | 31.9294 | 128.3498 | 0.0221 | 0.1551 |
| 5 | −15.1706 | 77.1926 | 0.1032 | 0.2306 |
| 6 | −0.2105 | 108.8303 | 0.0334 | 0.1838 |
| 7 | 30.6237 | 108.7261 | 0.0464 | 0.1542 |
| 8 | 18.1541 | 124.1542 | 0.0278 | 0.1741 |
| 9 | −26.5649 | 64.2229 | 0.1131 | 0.2384 |
| 10 | −11.5374 | 83.8240 | 0.0968 | 0.2284 |

the least squares estimates are "reliable." On the other hand, if the least squares estimators suffer from large sampling variability, then the interval estimates will be wide, implying that the least squares estimates are "unreliable."

## *5.2* Hypothesis Testing

Interval estimation, or the construction of confidence intervals, is a major technique for making statistical inferences from the data. Another tool of statistical inference is hypothesis testing. Many economic decision problems require some basis for deciding whether or not a parameter is a specified value, or whether it is positive or negative. In the food expenditure example, it makes a good deal of difference for decision purposes whether or not $\beta_2 = 0$. If $\beta_2 = 0$, then income has no effect on the level of household expenditure on food, and there would be no need for supermarket managers to worry about income changes in the planning of new supermarkets.

*Hypothesis testing* procedures compare a conjecture we have about a population to the information contained in a sample of data. More specifically, the conjectures we test concern the parameters of the economic model. Given an economic and statistical model, **hypotheses** are formed about economic behavior. These hypotheses are then represented as conjectures about model parameters.

Hypothesis testing uses the information about a parameter that is contained in a sample of data, namely, its least squares point estimate and its standard error, to draw a conclusion about the conjecture, or hypothesis.

In each and every hypothesis test four ingredients must be present:

---

**COMPONENTS OF HYPOTHESIS TESTS**

1. A *null* hypothesis, $H_0$
2. An *alternative* hypothesis, $H_1$
3. A test *statistic*
4. A *rejection* region

---

We will discuss these components in terms of the food expenditure model, but our comments apply to other models and tests as well.

### 5.2.1 THE NULL HYPOTHESIS

The **null hypothesis,** which is denoted $H_0$ (*H-naught*), specifies a value for a parameter. In the food expenditure model one important null hypothesis is $H_0$: $\beta_2 = 0$. This hypothesis explains the genesis of the term *null* hypothesis, since, if it is true, then income has no (a null) effect on food expenditure. A null hypothesis is the belief we will maintain until we are convinced by the sample evidence that it is not true, in which case we *reject* the null hypothesis.

### 5.2.2 THE ALTERNATIVE HYPOTHESIS

Paired with every null hypothesis is a logical alternative hypothesis, $H_1$, that we will accept if the null hypothesis is rejected. The alternative hypothesis is flexible and depends to some extent on economic theory. For the null hypothesis $H_0$: $\beta_2 = 0$ three possible alternative hypotheses are:

- $H_1$: $\beta_2 \neq 0$. Rejecting the null hypothesis that $\beta_2 = 0$ implies the conclusion that $\beta_2$ takes some other value, and it can be either positive or negative.
- $H_1$: $\beta_2 > 0$. Rejecting the null hypothesis that $\beta_2$ is zero leads to the conclusion that it is positive. Using this alternative *completely* discounts the possibility that $\beta_2 < 0$, based on economic theory, and implies that these values are logically unacceptable alternatives to the null hypothesis. Inequality alternative hypotheses are widely used in economics, since economic theory frequently provides information about the *signs* of relationships between variables. For example, in the food expenditure example we might well use the alternative $H_1$: $\beta_2 > 0$, since economic theory strongly suggests that necessities like food are normal goods, and that food expenditure will rise if income increases.
- $H_1$: $\beta_2 < 0$. Following the previous discussion, use this alternative when the relationship between the variables, if there is one, must be negative.

### 5.2.3 THE TEST STATISTIC

The sample information about the null hypothesis is embodied in the sample value of a **test statistic.** Based on the value of a test statistic, which itself is a random variable, we decide either to reject the null hypothesis or not to reject it. A test statistic has a very special characteristic: its probability distribution must be *completely known when the null hypothesis is true*, and it must have some *other* distribution if the null hypothesis is not true.

As an example, consider in the food expenditure example the null hypothesis $H_0$: $\beta_2 = 0$ and the alternative $H_1$: $\beta_2 \neq 0$. The economically more relevant alternative $H_1$: $\beta_2 > 0$ is introduced in Section 5.2.9.

In equation 5.1.5 we established, under assumptions 1–6 of the simple linear regression model, that

$$t = \frac{b_2 - \beta_2}{se(b_2)} \sim t_{(T-2)} \qquad (5.2.1)$$

*If* the null hypothesis $H_0$: $\beta_2 = 0$ is *true,* then

$$t = \frac{b_2}{se(b_2)} \sim t_{(T-2)} \qquad (5.2.2)$$

but if the null hypothesis is *not true,* then the *t*-statistic in equation 5.2.2 does *not* have a *t*-distribution with $T - 2$ degrees of freedom. You may skip the following explanation on the first reading.

> To examine the distribution of the *t*-statistic in equation 5.2.2 when the null hypothesis is not true, suppose that the true $\beta_2 = 1$. Following the steps in equation 5.1.5, we would find that
>
> $$t = \frac{b_2 - 1}{se(b_2)} \sim t_{(T-2)}$$
>
> If $\beta_2 = 1$, then the test statistic in equation 5.2.2 does not have a *t*-distribution, since, in its formation, the numerator of equation 5.1.5 is *not* standard normal. It is not standard normal because the incorrect value $\beta_2 = 0$ is subtracted from $b_2$.
> If $\beta_2 = 1$ and we *incorrectly* hypothesize that $\beta_2 = 0$, then the numerator of 5.1.5 that is used in forming equation 5.2.2 has the distribution
>
> $$\frac{b_2 - 0}{\sqrt{var(b_2)}} \sim N(1,1)$$
>
> This distribution is *not* standard normal, as required in the formation of a *t* random variable.

### 5.2.4   THE REJECTION REGION

The **rejection region** is the range of values of the test statistic that leads to *rejection* of the null hypothesis. It is possible to construct a rejection region only if we have a test statistic whose distribution is known when the null hypothesis is true. In practice, the rejection region is a set of test statistic values that, *when the null hypothesis is true*, are unlikely and have *low probability* of occurring. If, using a sample of data, a value of the test statistic is obtained that falls in a region of low probability, then it is unlikely that the test statistic has the assumed distribution, and thus it is unlikely that the null hypothesis is true.

To illustrate let us continue to use the food expenditure example. *If* the null hypothesis $H_0$: $\beta_2 = 0$ is *true,* then the test statistic $t = \frac{b_2}{se(b_2)} \sim t_{(T-2)}$. Thus, if the hypothesis is true, then the distribution of $t$ is that shown in Figure 5.1. If the alternative hypothesis $H_1$: $\beta_2 \neq 0$ is true, then values of the test statistic $t$ will tend to be unusually "large" or unusually "small." The terms *large* and *small* are determined by choosing a probability $\alpha$, called the *level of significance of the test,* which provides a meaning for "an unlikely event." The level of significance of the test $\alpha$ is frequently chosen to be .01, .05, or .10. The rejection region is determined by finding critical values $t_c$ such that $P(t \geq t_c) = P(t \leq -t_c) = \alpha/2$. Thus, the rejection region consists of the two "tails" of the $t$-distribution.

When the null hypothesis is true, the probability of obtaining from a sample of data a value of the test statistic that falls in *either* tail area is "small," and, combined, is equal to $\alpha$. Sample values of the test statistic that are in the tail areas are *incompatible with the null hypothesis* and are evidence against the null hypothesis being true. When testing the null hypothesis $H_0$: $\beta_2 = 0$ against the alternative $H_1$: $\beta_2 \neq 0$ we are led to the following rule:

> **Rejection rule for a two-tailed test:** If the value of the test statistic falls in the rejection region, either tail of the $t$-distribution, then we reject the null hypothesis and accept the alternative.

On the other hand, if the null hypothesis $H_0$: $\beta_2 = 0$ is true, then the probability of obtaining a value of the test statistic $t$ in the central *nonrejection* region, $P(-t_c \leq t \leq t_c) = 1 - \alpha$, is high. Sample values of the test statistic in the central nonrejection area are *compatible with the null hypothesis* and are not taken as evidence against the null hypothesis being true. Care must be taken here in interpreting the outcome of a statistical test, however, because one of the basic precepts of hypothesis testing is that finding a sample value of the test statistic in the nonrejection region *does not make the null hypothesis true!* Intuitively, if the true value of $\beta_2$ is near zero, but not equal to it, then the value of the test statistic will still fall in the nonrejection region with high probability. In this case we would not reject the null hypothesis even though it is false. Consequently, when testing the null hypothesis $H_0$: $\beta_2 = 0$ against the alternative $H_1$: $\beta_2 \neq 0$ the rule is:

> If the value of the test statistic falls between the critical values $-t_c$ and $t_c$, in the nonrejection region, then we *do not reject* the null hypothesis.

Avoid saying that "we accept the null hypothesis." This statement implies that we are concluding that the null hypothesis is true, which is not the case at all, based on the preceding discussion. The weaker statements, "We do not reject the null hypothesis," or "We fail to reject the null hypothesis," do not send any misleading message.

The test decision rules are summarized in Figure 5.2.

## 5.2.5  THE FOOD EXPENDITURE EXAMPLE

Let us illustrate the hypothesis testing procedure by testing whether income has an effect (either positive or negative for this illustration) on food expenditure or

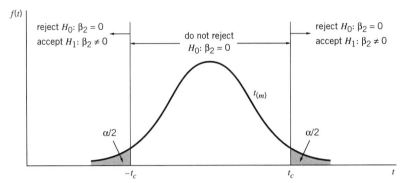

FIGURE 5.2    Rejection region for a test of $H_0$: $\beta_2 = 0$ against $H_1$: $\beta_2 \neq 0$

not. We will carry through the test using, as you should, a standard testing format that summarizes the four test ingredients and the test outcome.

> ### FORMAT FOR TESTING HYPOTHESES
>
> 1. Determine the null and alternative hypotheses.
> 2. Specify the test statistic and its distribution if the null hypothesis is true.
> 3. Select $\alpha$ and determine the rejection region.
> 4. Calculate the sample value of the test statistic.
> 5. State your conclusion.

Apply these steps to our problem.

1. The null hypothesis is $H_0$: $\beta_2 = 0$. The alternative hypothesis is $H_1$: $\beta_2 \neq 0$. If the null hypothesis is true, then there is no economic relationship between weekly household income and weekly household food expenditure, given our economic and statistical model. If the alternative hypothesis is true, then there *is* a relationship between income and food expenditure.

2. The test statistic $t = \dfrac{b_2}{se(b_2)} \sim t_{(T-2)}$ *if the null hypothesis is true.*

3. Let us select $\alpha = .05$. The critical value $t_c$ is 2.024 for a $t$-distribution with $(T-2) = 38$ degrees of freedom. Again, we note this value can be approximated from the $t$ table at the front of the book or computed exactly by using SHAZAM, SAS, or some other software package. Thus, we will reject the null hypothesis in favor of the alternative if $t \geq 2.024$ or $t \leq -2.024$, or, equivalently, if $|t| \geq 2.024$.

4. Using the data in Table 3.1, the least squares estimate of $\beta_2$ is $b_2 = .1283$, with standard error $se(b_2) = 0.0305$. The value of the test statistic is $t = \dfrac{.1283}{.0305} = 4.21$. The value of the $t$-statistic reported by computer software, which carries out the computation with more significant digits, is $t = 4.20$.

5.  Conclusion: Since $t = 4.20 > t_c = 2.024$ we *reject* the null hypothesis and accept the alternative, that there is a relationship between weekly income and weekly food expenditure. This test is sometimes called a "test of significance," since it is a test of whether $b_2$ is *significantly* (in the statistical sense that we have described) different from zero. Consequently, the conclusion is sometimes stated, "The sample indicates a statistically significant relationship between weekly income and weekly food expenditure."

### 5.2.6  TYPE I AND TYPE II ERRORS

Whenever we reject, or do not reject, a null hypothesis, there is a chance that we might be making a mistake. This is unavoidable. In any hypothesis testing situation there are two ways that we can make a correct decision and two ways that we can make an incorrect decision. We make a correct decision if:

- The null hypothesis is *false* and we decide to *reject* it.
- The null hypothesis is *true* and we decide *not* to reject it.

Our decision is incorrect if:

- The null hypothesis is *true* and we decide to *reject* it (a Type I error)
- The null hypothesis is *false* and we decide *not* to reject it (a Type II error)

When we reject the null hypothesis we risk what is called a **Type I error.** The probability of a Type I error is $\alpha$, the **level of significance** of the test. A value of the test statistic in the rejection region, the range of unlikely values for the test statistic where we reject the null hypothesis, occurs with probability $\alpha$ when the null hypothesis is true. Thus, the hypothesis testing procedure we use will *reject* a true hypothesis with probability $\alpha$. The only good news here is that we control the probability of a Type I error by choosing the level of significance of the test. If this type of decision error is a *costly* one, then we should choose the level of significance to be small, perhaps $\alpha = .01$ or .05.

We risk a **Type II error** when we do not reject the null hypothesis. Our testing procedure will lead us to *fail to reject* null hypotheses that are false with a certain probability. The magnitude of the probability of a Type II error is *not* under our control and *cannot* be computed, as it depends on the true but unknown value of the parameter in question. We know these facts about the probability of a Type II error:

- The probability of a Type II error varies inversely with the level of significance of the test, $\alpha$, which is the probability of a Type I error. If you choose to make $\alpha$ smaller, the probability of a Type II error increases.
- The closer the true value of the parameter is to the hypothesized parameter value the larger is the probability of a Type II error. If in the null hypothesis we hypothesize that $\beta_2 = 0$, and if the true (unknown) value of $\beta_2$ is *close* to zero, then the probability of a Type II error is high. Intuitively, the test loses the *power* to discriminate between the true parameter value and the (false) hypothesized value if they are similar in magnitude.

- The larger the sample size $T$, the lower the probability of a Type II error, given a level of Type I error $\alpha$.

- For most types of hypotheses that economists test there is no one best test that can be used in all situations. By "best" test we mean one that has the minimum Type II error for any given level of Type I error, $\alpha$. However, the test based on the $t$-distribution that we have described is a very good test and it is without question the test used most frequently in the situation that we have described.

### 5.2.7   THE $p$-VALUE OF A HYPOTHESIS TEST

When reporting the outcome of statistical hypothesis tests it has become common practice to report the **$p$-value** of a test. In the context of the food expenditure example, when testing the null hypothesis $H_0$: $\beta_2 = 0$ against the alternative hypothesis $H_1$: $\beta_2 \neq 0$, we reject the null hypothesis when the absolute value of the $t$-statistic is greater than or equal to the critical value $t_c$ that corresponds to the level of significance we have chosen. That is, we reject the null hypothesis when $|t| \geq t_c$. The $p$-value of a test is calculated by finding the probability that the $t$-distribution can take a value greater than or equal to the absolute value of the sample value of the test statistic.

Using a $p$-value, we can determine whether to reject a null hypothesis by comparing it to the level of significance $\alpha$. The rule is:

> **Rejection rule for a hypothesis test:** When the **$p$-value** of a hypothesis test is *smaller* than the chosen value of $\alpha$, then the test procedure leads to *rejection* of the null hypothesis.

This rule is very handy. If we have the $p$-value of a test, we can determine the outcome of the test by comparing the $p$-value to the chosen level of significance, $\alpha$, *without* looking up or calculating the critical values ourselves.

In the food expenditure example, the $p$-value for the test of $H_0$: $\beta_2 = 0$ against $H_1$: $\beta_2 \neq 0$ is illustrated in Figure 5.3.

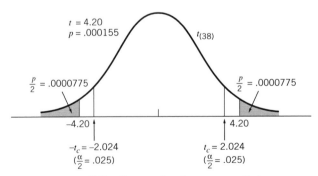

*FIGURE 5.3*   The $p$-value for a two-tailed test

The $p$-value for this hypothesis test is $p = .000155$, which is the area in the tails of the $t_{(38)}$ distribution where $|t| \geq 4.20$. In Figure 5.3 the $p$-value is depicted by the combined shaded tail areas. On the figure we have also marked the $\alpha = .05$ critical values $t_c = \pm 2.024$. The figure makes clear why the rule *reject $H_0$ if $p \leq \alpha$* gives the same result as the $t$-test. When $p \leq \alpha$, the value of the $t$-statistic must fall in the rejection region. The fact that the portion of the $p$-value in the upper tail area is approximately .00008 means that the critical value $t_c$ marking off $\alpha/2 = .025$ must be to the left of $t = 4.20$, and thus the $t$-test will lead to rejection of the null hypothesis.

## 5.2.8    A More General Null Hypothesis

For testing the more general null hypothesis $H_0$: $\beta_2 = c$, where $c$ is any constant, against the alternative $H_1$: $\beta_2 \neq c$ we compute the value of the test statistic

$$t = \frac{b_2 - c}{se(b_2)} \tag{5.2.3}$$

If the null hypothesis is true, then this test statistic has a $t$-distribution with $T - 2$ degrees of freedom. We reject $H_0$: $\beta_2 = c$ if $|t| \geq t_c$, or if the $p$-value is less than the level of significance $\alpha$.

As an example, let us test the null hypothesis that $\beta_2 = .10$ against the alternative that it is not. Following the standard test format, we have:

1.  The null hypothesis is $H_0$: $\beta_2 = .10$. The alternative hypothesis is $H_1$: $\beta_2 \neq .10$

2.  The test statistic $t = \dfrac{b_2 - .10}{se(b_2)} \sim t_{(T-2)}$ *if the null hypothesis is true.*

3.  Let us select $\alpha = .05$. The critical value $t_c$ is 2.024 for a $t$-distribution with $(T-2) = 38$ degrees of freedom. Thus, we will reject the null hypothesis in favor of the alternative if $t \geq 2.024$ or $t \leq -2.024$, or equivalently, if $|t| \geq 2.024$.

4.  Using the data in Table 3.1, the least squares estimate of $\beta_2$ is $b_2 = .1283$, with standard error $se(b_2) = 0.0305$. The value of the test statistic is $t = \dfrac{.1283 - .10}{.0305} = .93$. The computer-generated value is $t = .9263$. To compute the $p$-value we will use this more accurate computation.

5.  Conclusion: Since $t = .9263 < t_c = 2.024$, we *do not reject* the null hypothesis. The sample information we have is *compatible* with the hypothesis that $\beta_2 = .10$. Equivalently, for this test the $p$-value is $p = .3601 > \alpha = .05$, and on this basis we do not reject the null hypothesis.

## 5.2.9    One-Tailed Tests

We have focused so far on testing hypotheses of the form $H_0$: $\beta_k = c$ against the alternative $H_1$: $\beta_k \neq c$. This kind of test is called a two-tailed test, since portions of the rejection region are found in both tails of the test statistic's distribution.

One-tailed tests are used to test $H_0$: $\beta_k = c$ against the alternative $H_1$: $\beta_k > c$, or $H_1$: $\beta_k < c$. The motivation for such alternatives was discussed in Section 5.2.2.

The logic of one-tailed tests is identical to that for the two-tailed tests that we have studied. The test statistic is the same, and is given by equation 5.2.3. What is different is the selection of the rejection region and the computation of the *p*-values. For example, to test $H_0$: $\beta_k = c$ against the alternative $H_1$: $\beta_k > c$ we select the rejection region to be values of the test statistic *t* that support the *alternative* hypothesis and that are *unlikely* if the null hypothesis is true. *Large* values of the *t*-statistic are unlikely if the null hypothesis is true. We define the rejection region to be values of *t* greater than a critical value $t_c$, from a *t*-distribution with $T-2$ degrees of freedom, such that $P(t \geq t_c) = \alpha$, where $\alpha$ is the level of significance of the test and the probability of a Type I error. This critical value is depicted in Figure 5.4.

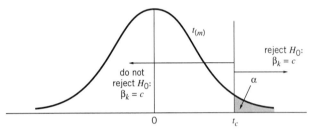

**FIGURE 5.4**    The rejection region for the one-tailed test of $H_0$: $\beta_k = c$ against $H_1$: $\beta_k > c$

The decision rule for this one-tailed test is, "Reject $H_0$: $\beta_k = c$ and accept the alternative $H_1$: $\beta_k > c$ if $t \geq t_c$." If $t < t_c$ then we do not reject the null hypothesis.

Computation of the *p*-value is similarly confined to one tail of the distribution of the test statistic, though its interpretation is exactly as before. For testing $H_0$: $\beta_k = c$ against the alternative $H_1$: $\beta_k > c$, the *p*-value is computed by finding the probability that the test statistic is greater than or equal to the computed sample value of the test statistic.

To illustrate these ideas, let us return to the food expenditure example and test $H_0$: $\beta_2 = 0$ against the alternative $H_1$: $\beta_2 > 0$. This is the relevant "test of significance" for this example, since economic theory rules out negative values of $\beta_2$. Following our standard testing format we have:

1.  The null hypothesis is $H_0$: $\beta_2 = 0$. The alternative hypothesis is $H_1$: $\beta_2 > 0$. If the null hypothesis is true, then there is no economic relationship between weekly household income and weekly household food expenditure, given our economic and statistical model. If the alternative hypothesis is true, then there *is* a positive relationship between income and food expenditure.

2.  The test statistic $t = \dfrac{b_2}{se(b_2)} \sim t_{(T-2)}$ *if the null hypothesis is true.*

3.  For the level of significance $\alpha = .05$ the critical value $t_c$ is 1.686 for a *t*-distribution with $T-2 = 38$ degrees of freedom. Thus, we will reject the null hypothesis in favor of the alternative if $t \geq 1.686$.

4.  Using the data in Table 3.1, the least squares estimate of $\beta_2$ is $b_2 = .1283$, with standard error $se(b_2) = 0.0305$. Exactly as in the two-tailed test, the

value of the test statistic is $t = \dfrac{.1283}{.0305} = 4.21$ The value of the $t$-statistic reported by computer software, which carries out the computation with more significant digits, is $t = 4.20$.

5. Conclusion: Since $t = 4.20 > t_c = 1.686$, we *reject* the null hypothesis and accept the alternative, that there is a positive relationship between weekly income and weekly food expenditure. The $p$-value for this test is $P(t \geq 4.20) = .0000775$, which is far less than the level of significance $\alpha = .05$; thus, we also reject the null hypothesis on this basis. The $p$-value in the one-tailed test is exactly one-half the $p$-value in the two-tailed test. By forming an inequality alternative, we have added the information that negative values of $\beta_2$ are impossible. By adding this "extra" or "nonsample" information we have increased the ability, or power, of the test to discriminate between the null and alternative hypotheses.

### 5.2.10  A COMMENT ON STATING NULL AND ALTERNATIVE HYPOTHESES

We have noted in the previous sections that a statistical test procedure cannot prove the truth of a null hypothesis. When we fail to reject a null hypothesis, all the hypothesis test can establish is that the information in a sample of data is *compatible* with the null hypothesis. On the other hand, a statistical test can lead us to *reject* the null hypothesis, with only a small probability, $\alpha$, of rejecting the null hypothesis when it is actually true. Thus, rejecting a null hypothesis is a stronger conclusion than failing to reject it.

Consequently, the null hypothesis is usually stated in such a way that if our theory is correct then we will reject the null hypothesis. For example, economic theory implies that there should be a positive relationship between income and food expenditure. When using a hypothesis test we would like to establish that there is statistical evidence, based on a sample of data, to support this theory. With this goal we set up the null hypothesis that there is *no* relation between the variables, $H_0: \beta_2 = 0$. In the alternative hypothesis we put the conjecture that we would like to establish, $H_1: \beta_2 > 0$.

Alternatively, suppose the conjecture that we would like to establish is that the marginal propensity to spend on food is greater than .10. To do so, we define the null hypothesis $H_0: \beta_2 = .10$. In the alternative hypothesis we put the conjecture that we would like to establish, $H_1: \beta_2 > .10$. You may view the null hypothesis to be too limited in this case, since it is feasible that $\beta_2 < .10$. The hypothesis testing procedure for testing the null hypothesis that $H_0: \beta_2 \leq .10$ against the alternative hypothesis $H_1: \beta_2 > .10$ is *exactly the same* as testing $H_0: \beta_2 = .10$ against the alternative hypothesis $H_1: \beta_2 > .10$. The test statistic, rejection region, and $p$-value are exactly the same. For a one-tailed test you can form the null hypothesis in either of these ways. What counts is that the alternative hypothesis is properly specified.

Finally, it is important to set up the null and alternative hypotheses *before* you carry out the regression analysis. Failing to do so can lead to errors in formulating the alternative hypothesis. Suppose that we wish to show that $\beta_2 > .10$ and the least squares estimate of $\beta_2$ is $b_2 = .05$. Does that mean we should set up the alternative $\beta_2 < .10$, to be consistent with the estimate? The answer is *no*. The alternative is formed to state the conjecture that we wish to establish, $\beta_2 > .10$.

### 5.2.11   A RELATIONSHIP BETWEEN HYPOTHESIS TESTING AND INTERVAL ESTIMATION

There is an *algebraic* relationship between two-tailed hypothesis tests and confidence interval estimates. Suppose that we are testing the null hypothesis $H_0:\beta_k = c$ against the alternative $H_1:\beta_k \neq c$. If we *fail to reject* the null hypothesis at the $\alpha$ level of significance, then the value $c$ will fall *within* a $(1 - \alpha) \times 100\%$ confidence interval estimate of $\beta_k$. Conversely, if we reject the null hypothesis, then $c$ will fall *outside* the $(1 - \alpha) \times 100\%$ confidence interval estimate of $\beta_k$. This algebraic relationship is true because we fail to reject the null hypothesis when $-t_c \leq t \leq t_c$, or when

$$-t_c \leq \frac{b_k - c}{se(b_k)} \leq t_c$$

which, when rearranged, becomes

$$b_k - t_c\, se(b_k) \leq c \leq b_k + t_c\, se(b_k).$$

The endpoints of this interval are the same as the endpoints of a $(1 - \alpha) \times 100\%$ confidence interval estimate of $\beta_k$. Thus, for any value of $c$ within the interval, we do not reject $H_0$: $\beta_k = c$ against the alternative $H_1$: $\beta_k \neq c$. For any value of $c$ outside the interval we reject $H_0$: $\beta_k = c$ and accept the alternative $H_1$: $\beta_k \neq c$.

This relationship can be handy if you are given only a confidence interval and want to determine what the outcome of a two-tailed test would be. However, you should note two things about this relationship between interval estimation and hypothesis testing:

1.  The relationship is between confidence intervals and *two-tailed* tests. It does not apply to one-tailed tests.
2.  A confidence interval is an *estimation* tool; that is, it is an interval *estimator*. A hypothesis test about one or more parameters is a completely separate form of inference, with the only connection being that the test statistic incorporates the least squares estimator. To test hypotheses you should carry out the steps outlined in Section 5.2.5 and *should not* compute and report an interval estimate. *Keep hypothesis testing and parameter estimation separate at all times!*

## 5.3   Prediction Intervals

In Chapter 4.7 we showed how the least squares estimates could be used as a basis for obtaining *point* predictions. Given the simple linear regression model and assumptions 1–6, let us suppose that we want to predict $y_0$ based on the model

$$y_0 = \beta_1 + \beta_2 x_0 + e_0 \tag{5.3.1}$$

where $e_0 \sim N(0, \sigma^2)$ and is uncorrelated with all of the sample observations; that is $cov(e_0, e_t) = 0$. The least squares predictor of $y_0$ is:

$$\hat{y}_0 = b_1 + b_2 x_0 \qquad (5.3.2)$$

The forecast error is:

$$f = \hat{y}_0 - y_0 = (b_1 - \beta_1) + (b_2 - \beta_2)x_0 - e_0 \qquad (5.3.3)$$

If the random errors are normally distributed, or if the sample size is large, then the forecast error $f$ is normally distributed, $f \sim N(0, \text{var}(f))$, where

$$\text{var}(f) = \text{var}(\hat{y}_0 - y_0) = \sigma^2 \left[ 1 + \frac{1}{T} + \frac{(x_0 - \bar{x})^2}{\Sigma(x_t - \bar{x})^2} \right] \qquad (5.3.4)$$

Consequently, we can construct a standard normal random variable as

$$\frac{f}{\sqrt{\text{var}(f)}} \sim N(0,1) \qquad (5.3.5)$$

If the forecast error variance is estimated by replacing $\sigma^2$ by its estimator $\hat{\sigma}^2$,

$$\text{vâr}(f) = \hat{\sigma}^2 \left[ 1 + \frac{1}{T} + \frac{(x_0 - \bar{x})^2}{\Sigma(x_t - \bar{x})^2} \right] \qquad (5.3.6)$$

then by replacing $\text{var}(f)$ in (5.3.5) by $\text{vâr}(f)$, we obtain a $t$-statistic,

$$\frac{f}{\sqrt{\text{vâr}(f)}} = \frac{f}{\text{se}(f)} \sim t_{(T-2)} \qquad (5.3.7)$$

where the square root of the estimated variance is the *standard error of the forecast,*

$$\text{se}(f) = \sqrt{\text{vâr}(f)} \qquad (5.3.8)$$

Using these results we can construct a prediction interval for $y_0$ just as we constructed confidence intervals for the parameters $\beta_k$. If $t_c$ is a critical value from the $t_{(T-2)}$ distribution such that $P(t \geq t_c) = \alpha/2$, then

$$P(-t_c \leq t \leq t_c) = 1 - \alpha \qquad (5.3.9)$$

Substitute the $t$ random variable from equation 5.3.7 into 5.3.9 to obtain

$$P\left[-t_c \leq \frac{\hat{y}_0 - y_0}{\text{se}(f)} \leq t_c\right] = 1 - \alpha \qquad (5.3.10)$$

and simplify this expression to obtain

$$P[\hat{y}_0 - t_c\,\text{se}(f) \leq y_0 \leq \hat{y}_0 + t_c\,\text{se}(f)] = 1 - \alpha \qquad (5.3.11)$$

A $(1-\alpha) \times 100\%$ confidence interval, or prediction interval, for $y_0$ is

$$\hat{y}_0 \pm t_c\,\text{se}(f) \qquad (5.3.12)$$

Equation 5.3.6 implies that the farther $x_0$ is from the sample mean $\bar{x}$, the larger the variance of the prediction error. The greater the variance, the less reliable the prediction. In other words, our predictions for values of $x_0$ close to the sample mean $\bar{x}$ are more reliable than our predictions for values of $x_0$ far from the sample mean $\bar{x}$. This result is a reasonable one. We would not expect to predict very accurately for an $x$ about which we have little sample information.

The relationship between point and interval predictions for different values of $x_0$ is illustrated in Figure 5.5. A point prediction is always given by the fitted least squares line, $\hat{y}_0 = b_1 + b_2 x_0$. A prediction confidence interval takes the form of two bands around the least squares line. Since the forecast variance increases the farther $x_0$ is from the sample mean of $\bar{x}$, the confidence bands increase in width as $|x_0 - \bar{x}|$ increases.

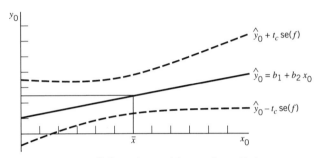

FIGURE **5.5** Point and interval prediction

### 5.3.1 PREDICTION IN THE FOOD EXPENDITURE MODEL

In Chapter 4.7.1 we predicted the weekly expenditure on food for a household with $x_0 = \$750$ weekly income. The point prediction is

$$\hat{y}_0 = b_1 + b_2 x_0 = 40.7676 + .1283(750) = 136.98$$

The estimated variance of the forecast error is

$$\text{vâr}(f) = \hat{\sigma}^2 \left[ 1 + \frac{1}{T} + \frac{(x_0 - \bar{x})^2}{\Sigma(x_t - \bar{x})^2} \right] = 1467.4986$$

The standard error of the forecast is then

$$\text{se}(f) = \sqrt{\text{vâr}(f)} = \sqrt{1467.4986} = 38.3079$$

If we select $1 - \alpha = .95$, then $t_c = 2.024$ and the 95 percent confidence interval for $y_0$ is

$$\hat{y}_0 \pm t_c \, \text{se}(f) = 136.98 \pm 2.024(38.3079)$$

or [59.44 to 214.52]. Our prediction interval thus suggests that a household with $750 weekly income will spend somewhere between $59.44 and $214.52 on food.

Such a wide interval means that our point prediction, \$136.98, is not reliable. We might be able to improve it by measuring the effect that factors other than income might have. Extensions of the model that include other factors will begin in Chapter 7.

## *5.4* **Summing Up**

In this chapter we have explored the tools of statistical inference: confidence intervals, hypothesis tests, and prediction intervals. We have used assumptions 1–6 of the simple regression model. The normal distributions of $y$ and $e$ imply that the least squares estimators $b_1$ and $b_2$ of the regression parameters $\beta_1$ and $\beta_2$ are also normally distributed:

$$b_1 \sim N\left(\beta_1, \frac{\sigma^2 \Sigma x_t^2}{T \Sigma (x_t - \bar{x})^2}\right) \quad b_2 \sim N\left(\beta_2, \frac{\sigma^2}{\Sigma (x_t - \bar{x})^2}\right)$$

In addition we showed that the unbiased estimator of the error variance $\hat{\sigma}^2 = \dfrac{\Sigma \hat{e}_t^2}{T-2}$, when multiplied by a constant, has a *chi-square distribution*:

$$V = \frac{(T-2)\hat{\sigma}^2}{\sigma^2} \sim \chi^2_{(T-2)}$$

Using this information we developed confidence intervals and hypothesis tests. In summary, we showed that

1.  The random variables $t = \dfrac{b_k - \beta_k}{\sqrt{\text{vâr}(b_k)}} = \dfrac{b_k - \beta_k}{\text{se}(b_k)} \sim t_{(T-2)}$

2.  A $(1 - \alpha) \times (100\%)$ confidence interval estimator for the simple regression parameter $\beta_k$ is $P[b_k - t_c \, \text{se}(b_k) \leq \beta_k \leq b_k + t_c \, \text{se}(b_k)] = 1 - \alpha$, where $t_c$ is the critical value from the $t_{(T-2)}$ distribution.

3.  The interpretation of the confidence interval just described is that in a repeated sampling context, intervals constructed this way will contain the true parameter in $(1 - \alpha) \times (100\%)$ of the samples.

4.  The $t$-statistic in (1) can be used as a basis for hypothesis tests about the parameters.

5.  Hypothesis tests always include: (i) A *null* hypothesis, $H_0$; (ii) An *alternative* hypothesis, $H_1$; (iii) A test *statistic*; (iv) A *rejection* region.

6.  To test $H_0$: $\beta_k = c$, where $c$ is any constant, against the alternative $H_1$: $\beta_k \neq c$, the test statistic is $t = \dfrac{b_k - c}{\text{se}(b_k)}$. If the null hypothesis is true, this test statistic has a $t$-distribution with $T-2$ degrees of freedom in the simple regression model, which contains only two parameters. If $t_c$ is the critical value for the $\alpha$ level of significance, we reject $H_0$: $\beta_k = c$ *if* $|t| \geq t_c$.

7.  Rejecting the null hypothesis when it is true is a Type I error, which has probability $\alpha$ (the level of significance of the test) of occurring. Failing to

reject a null hypothesis when it is false is a Type II error, which has a probability of occurring that depends on the true but unknown parameter, and thus cannot be computed.

8. The *p*-value of a test is the smallest level of significance at which the null hypothesis can be rejected. If the *p*-value $\leq \alpha$, then the test procedure will lead to rejection of the null hypothesis.

9. To test $H_0: \beta_k = c$, or $H_0: \beta_k \leq c$, where $c$ is any constant, against the alternative $H_1: \beta_k > c$ the test statistic is $t = \dfrac{b_k - c}{se(b_k)}$. If the null hypothesis is true, this test statistic has a *t*-distribution with $T-2$ degrees of freedom. If $t_c$ is the critical value for the $\alpha$ level of significance, we reject either null hypothesis *if $t \geq t_c$*.

10. There is an algebraic relationship between interval estimation and hypothesis testing. When testing $H_0: \beta_k = c$, where $c$ is any constant, against the alternative $H_1: \beta_k \neq c$, at the $\alpha$ level of significance, the test will fail to reject the hypothesis for values of $c$ within the $(1 - \alpha) \times 100\%$ interval estimate. That is, if $b_k - t_c\, se(b_k) \leq c \leq b_k + t_c\, se(b_k)$, then we will not reject the null hypothesis. If $c$ is not in the interval, then we will reject the null hypothesis and accept the alternative.

11. To predict $y_0 = \beta_1 + \beta_2 x_0 + e_0$ where $e_0 \sim N(0, \sigma^2)$ and $cov(e_0, e_t) = 0$, use the least squares predictor $\hat{y}_0 = b_1 + b_2 x_0$.

12. The forecast error is $f = \hat{y}_0 - y_0$. The forecast error $f$ is normally distributed with mean 0 and estimated variance $\hat{var}(f) = \hat{\sigma}^2\left[1 + \dfrac{1}{T} + \dfrac{(x_0 - \bar{x})^2}{\Sigma(x_t - \bar{x})^2}\right]$. The statistic $\dfrac{f}{\sqrt{\hat{var}(f)}} = \dfrac{f}{se(f)} \sim t_{(T-2)}$.

13. A $(1 - \alpha) \times 100\%$ confidence interval for $y_0$ is $\hat{y}_0 \pm t_c\, se(f)$

## 5.5 Exercises

5.1 Discuss how "repeated sampling theory" relates to interval estimation and hypothesis testing.

5.2 What is the statistical difference between an estimator and an estimate?

5.3 Why are the least squares estimators $b_1$ and $b_2$ considered random variables, and what is the implication of this for interval estimation and hypothesis testing?

5.4 Under what conditions are the least squares estimators $b_1$ and $b_2$ normally distributed random variables?

5.5 Why are we interested in being able to make a normally distributed random variable statement in Exercise 5.4?

5.6 What are the differences between the standard normal and *t*-distributions; what is the difference in the characteristics of these two distributions; and what happens to the *t*-distribution as the sample size increases?

5.7 What is the "level of confidence" of an interval estimator? Explain exactly what it means in a repeated sampling context.

5.8 What is the difference between an interval estimator and an interval estimate? How is an interval estimate interpreted?

5.9   Write down an interval estimator for $\beta_1$ and interpret.

5.10   Write down the test statistic for the null hypothesis $\beta_1 = 0$ against the alternative that $\beta_1 \neq 0$. What is the rejection region? Assume that the test statistic value is in the nonrejection region. What do you conclude?

5.11   Write down the test statistic for the null hypothesis $\beta_1 = 0$ against the alternative that $\beta_1 > 0$. What is the rejection region? Assume that the test statistic value is in the rejection region. What do you conclude?

5.12   What is the *p*-value of a hypothesis test? How is a *p*-value computed in a two-tailed test? In a one-tailed test?

5.13   What is the level of significance of a test?

5.14   What is a Type I error, and how is it related to the level of significance of a test?

5.15   What is a Type II error? How is the probability of a Type II error computed? How is a Type II error related to a Type I error?

5.16   How can a *p*-value be used to test a hypothesis? Explain how this is possible.

5.17   Discuss point and interval prediction. Be sure to discuss the forecast error and the reliability of each type of prediction.

5.18   Using the data for the production function discussed in Exercise 3.5 and the linear regression model and an $\alpha = .05$ level:
   (a) (i) find interval estimates for $\beta_1$ and $\beta_2$ and interpret, (ii) test the hypothesis that $\beta_1 = 0$, against the alternative that it is positive and interpret, (iii) test the hypothesis that $\beta_2 = 0$ against the alternative that it is positive and interpret, (iv) test the hypothesis that the marginal product of the input is 0.35 against the alternative that it is not and interpret.
   (b) Develop point and interval predictors for each input level and construct a figure such as Figure 5.5.
   (c) Compute and compare the estimated forecast error variance for input levels 8 and 16. Discuss the sampling theory interpretation of the variance of the forecast error.

5.19   Using the data for Moscow Makkers (see Exercise 3.6) test the null hypothesis that the elasticity of demand for hamburgers is equal to $-1$ against the alternative that it is not. Construct point and interval predictions for the number of hamburgers that will be sold when the price is $2.

5.20   A life insurance company wishes to examine the relationship between the amount of life insurance held by a family and family income. From a random sample of 20 households, the company collected the data in the file *insur.dat*. The data are in thousands of dollars.
   (a) Estimate a linear relationship between life insurance ($y$) and income ($x$).
   (b) Discuss the relationship you estimated in (a). In particular:
       (i) What is your estimate of the resulting change in the amount of life insurance when income increases by $1,000?
       (ii) What is the standard error of the estimate in (i), and how do you use this standard error for interval estimation and hypothesis testing?
       (iii) One member of the management board claims that for every $1,000 increase in income, the amount of life insurance held will go up by $5,000. Choose an alternative hypothesis and explain your choice. Does your estimated relationship support this claim? Use a 5 percent significance level.

    (iv) Write a short report summarizing your findings about the relationship between income and the amount of life insurance held.

  (c) Test the hypothesis that as income increases the amount of life insurance increases by the same amount. That is, test the hypothesis that the slope of the relationship is 1.

  (d) Predict the amount of life insurance held by a family with an income of $100,000.

5.21 Consider the learning curve data in Exercise 3.8.

  (a) Construct a 95 percent interval estimate for $\beta_2$ and interpret.

  (b) Test at the 5 percent level of significance whether there is no learning against the alternative that there is learning. Formulate the null and alternative hypotheses and discuss your reasoning. Explain your conclusion.

  (c) Write a short report summarizing all your findings (here and in Exercise 3.8) concerning the learning curve in production of titanium dioxide.

5.22 Consider the capital asset pricing model (CAPM) in Exercise 3.9.

  (a) Test at the 5 percent level of significance the hypothesis that Mobil Oil's *beta* value is one against the alternative that it is less than one. What is the economic interpretation of a beta equal to one? Less than one?

  (b) Predict the risk premium for Mobil Oil if the risk premium of the market portfolio is 1 percent, and if it is 10 percent. Construct 95 percent interval estimates of Mobil's risk premium for the same two values of the market's risk premium.

  (c) Test the hypothesis that the intercept term in the CAPM model is zero, against the alternative that it is not. What do you conclude?

  (d) Estimate the model *without* including an intercept and repeat parts (a) and (b).

  (e) Write a short report summarizing what you know about Mobil Oil's stock and its relationship to the stock market as a whole.

## *5.6* References

For other discussions of the concepts discussed in this chapter see:

GRIFFITHS, W. E., R. C. HILL, AND G. G. JUDGE (1993). *Learning and Practicing Econometrics.* New York: John Wiley and Sons, Inc., Chapter 7.

GUJARATI, DAMODAR N. (1995). *Basic Econometrics, Third Edition.* New York: McGraw-Hill, Chapter 5.

KELLER, G., B. WARRACK, AND H. BARTEL (1991). *Statistics for Management and Economics.* Belmont, CA: Duxbury Press, Chapter 7.

MIRER, THAD W. (1995). *Economic Statistics and Econometrics, Third Edition.* Englewood Cliffs, N.J.: Prentice Hall, Chapter 12.

# Chapter 6

# The Simple Linear Regression Model: Reporting the Results and Choosing the Functional Form

In the last three chapters we have considered the simple linear regression model $y_t = \beta_1 + \beta_2 x_t + e_t$ where the random error $e_t \sim N(0,\sigma^2)$. We have developed procedures for estimating the unknown model parameters and for making statistical inferences in the form of point and interval estimates and hypothesis tests. To complete the analysis of the simple linear regression model, in this chapter we will consider

- How to measure the variation in $y_t$, explained by the model
- How to report the results of a regression analysis
- Some alternative functional forms that may be used to represent possible relationships between $y_t$ and $x_t$

## 6.1 The Coefficient of Determination

Two major reasons for analyzing the model

$$y_t = \beta_1 + \beta_2 x_t + e_t \tag{6.1.1}$$

are to explain how the dependent variable ($y_t$) changes as the independent variable ($x_t$) changes, and to predict $y_0$ given an $x_0$. These two objectives come under the broad headings of estimation and prediction. Closely allied with the prediction problem is the desire to use $x_t$ to explain as much of the variation in the dependent variable $y_t$ as possible. In using the statistical model in equation 6.1.1 we introduce the "explanatory" variable $x_t$ in hope that its variation will "explain" the variation in $y_t$.

To develop a measure of the variation in $y_t$ that is explained by the model, we begin by separating $y_t$ into its explainable and unexplainable components. We have assumed that

$$y_t = E(y_t) + e_t \qquad (6.1.2)$$

where $E(y_t) = \beta_1 + \beta_2 x_t$ is the explainable, "systematic" component of $y_t$, and $e_t$ is the random, unsystematic, unexplainable noise component of $y_t$. Although both of these parts are unobservable to us, we can estimate the unknown parameters $\beta_1$ and $\beta_2$ and, analogous to equation 6.1.2, decompose the value of $y_t$ into

$$y_t = \hat{y}_t + \hat{e}_t \qquad (6.1.3)$$

where $\hat{y}_t = b_1 + b_2 x_t$ and $\hat{e}_t = y_t - \hat{y}_t$.

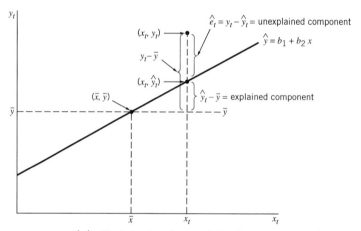

FIGURE **6.1** Explained and unexplained components of $y_t$

In Figure 6.1 the "point of the means" $(\bar{x}, \bar{y})$ is shown, with the least squares fitted line passing through it. This is a characteristic of the least squares fitted line whenever the regression model includes an intercept term. Subtract the sample mean $\bar{y}$ from both sides of the equation to obtain

$$y_t - \bar{y} = (\hat{y}_t - \bar{y}) + \hat{e}_t \qquad (6.1.4)$$

As shown in Figure 6.1, the difference between $y_t$ and its mean value $\bar{y}$ consists of a part that is "explained" by the regression model, $\hat{y}_t - \bar{y}$, and a part that is unexplained, $\hat{e}_t$.

The breakdown in equation 6.1.4 leads to a useful decomposition of the total variability in $y$, within an entire sample, into explained and unexplained parts. There are many ways to measure the "total variation" in a variable. One convenient way is to square the differences between $y_t$ and its mean value $\bar{y}$ and sum over the entire sample. If we square and sum both sides of equation 6.1.4 we obtain

$$\Sigma(y_t - \bar{y})^2 = \Sigma[(\hat{y}_t - \bar{y}) + \hat{e}_t]^2$$

$$= \Sigma(\hat{y}_t - \bar{y})^2 + \Sigma\hat{e}_t^2 + 2\Sigma(\hat{y}_t - \bar{y})\hat{e}_t \qquad (6.1.5)$$

$$= \Sigma(\hat{y}_t - \bar{y})^2 + \Sigma\hat{e}_t^2$$

because as you are asked to show in Exercise 6.1, the cross-product term $\Sigma(\hat{y}_t - \bar{y})\hat{e}_t = 0$ and drops out.

Equation 6.1.5 is a decomposition of the "total sample variation" in $y$ into explained and unexplained components. Specifically, these "sums of squares" are:

1. $\Sigma(y_t - \bar{y})^2$ = total sum of squares = *SST*: a measure of *total variation* in $y$ about its sample mean.
2. $\Sigma(\hat{y}_t - \bar{y})^2$ = explained sum of squares = *SSR*: that part of total variation in $y$ about its sample mean that is explained by the regression.
3. $\Sigma\hat{e}_t^2$ = error sum of squares = *SSE*: that part of total variation in $y$ about its mean that is not explained by the regression.

Thus, equation 6.1.5 becomes

$$SST = SSR + SSE \qquad (6.1.6)$$

This decomposition accompanies virtually every regression analysis. It is usually presented in what is called an **analysis of variance table** with general format of Table 6.1. This table provides a basis for summarizing the decomposition in equation 6.1.5. It gives *SSR*, the variation explained by $x$, *SSE*, the unexplained variation and *SST*, the total variation in $y$. The **degrees of freedom** (*DF*) for these sums of squares are:

1. $df = 1$ for *SSR* (the number of explanatory variables other than the intercept)
2. $df = T - 2$ for *SSE* (the number of observations minus the number of parameters in the model)
3. $df = T - 1$ for *SST* (the number of observations minus 1, which is the number of parameters in a model containing only $\beta_1$)

In the column labeled "Mean Square" are (*i*) the ratio of *SSR* to its degrees of freedom, *SSR*/1, and (*ii*) the ratio of *SSE* to its degrees of freedom, $SSE/(T - 2) = \hat{\sigma}^2$. The "mean square error" is our unbiased estimate of the error variance, which we first developed in Chapter 4.6.

*Table 6.1*  **Analysis of Variance Table**

| Source of Variation | DF | Sum of Squares | Mean Square |
|---|---|---|---|
| Explained | 1 | SSR | SSR/1 |
| Unexplained | $T - 2$ | SSE | $SSE/(T - 2) \ [= \hat{\sigma}^2]$ |
| Total | $T - 1$ | SST | |

One widespread use of the information in the analysis of variance table is to define a measure of the *proportion of variation* in y explained by x within the regression model:

$$R^2 = \frac{SSR}{SST} = 1 - \frac{SSE}{SST} \tag{6.1.7}$$

The measure $R^2$ is called the **coefficient of determination.** The closer $R^2$ is to 1, the better the job we have done in explaining the variation in $y_t$ with $\hat{y}_t = b_1 + b_2 x_t$; and the greater is the predictive ability of our model over all the sample observations.

If $R^2 = 1$, then all the sample data fall exactly on the fitted least squares line, so $SSE = 0$, and the model fits the data "perfectly." If the sample data for y and x are uncorrelated and show no linear association, then the least squares fitted line is "horizontal," and identical to $\bar{y}$, so that $SSR = 0$ and $R^2 = 0$. When $0 < R^2 < 1$, it is interpreted as "the percentage of the variation in y about its mean that is explained by the regression model."

> **REMARK:** $R^2$ is a *descriptive* measure. By itself it does not measure the *quality* of the regression model; this point will be made in Section 6.2.2. It is *not* the objective of regression analysis to find the model with the highest $R^2$. Following a regression strategy focused solely on maximizing $R^2$ is not a good idea.

### 6.1.1  CORRELATION ANALYSIS

In Chapter 2.5 we discussed the *covariance* and *correlation* between two random variables $X$ and $Y$. The correlation coefficient $\rho$ between $X$ and $Y$ is defined in equation 2.5.4 to be:

$$\rho = \frac{\text{cov}(X, Y)}{\sqrt{\text{var}(X)\text{var}(Y)}} \tag{6.1.8}$$

In Chapter 2 we did not discuss *estimating* the correlation coefficient. We will do so now to develop a useful relationship between the sample correlation coefficient and $R^2$.

Given a sample of data pairs $(x_t, y_t)$, $t = 1, \ldots, T$, the sample correlation coefficient is obtained by replacing the covariance and variances in (6.1.8) by their sample analogues:

$$r = \frac{\hat{\text{cov}}(X, Y)}{\sqrt{\hat{\text{var}}(X)\hat{\text{var}}(Y)}} \tag{6.1.9}$$

where

$$\hat{\text{cov}}(X,Y) = \sum_{t=1}^{T}(x_t - \bar{x})(y_t - \bar{y})/(T - 1), \ \hat{\text{var}}(X) = \sum_{t=1}^{T}(x_t - \bar{x})^2/(T - 1) \tag{6.1.10}$$

The sample variance of $Y$ is defined like $\hat{\text{var}}(X)$. So we can write the sample correlation coefficient $r$ as

$$r = \frac{\sum_{t=1}^{T}(x_t - \bar{x})(y_t - \bar{y})}{\sqrt{\sum_{t=1}^{T}(x_t - \bar{x})^2 \sum_{t=1}^{T}(y_t - \bar{y})^2}} \qquad (6.1.11)$$

The sample correlation coefficient $r$ has a value between $-1$ and 1, and it measures the strength of the linear association between observed values of $X$ and $Y$.

### 6.1.2  CORRELATION ANALYSIS AND $R^2$

There are two interesting relationships between $R^2$ and $r$ in the simple linear regression model.

1.  The first is that $r^2 = R^2$. That is, the square of the sample correlation coefficient between the sample data values $x_t$ and $y_t$ is algebraically equal to $R^2$, as you are invited to show in Exercise 6.5. Intuitively, this relationship makes sense: $r^2$ falls between 0 and 1 and measures the strength of the linear association between $x$ and $y$. This interpretation is not far from that of $R^2$: the proportion of variation in $y$ about its mean explained by $x$ in the linear regression model.
2.  It is an interesting fact that $R^2$ can also be computed as the square of the sample correlation coefficient between $y_t$ and $\hat{y}_t = b_1 + b_2 x_t$. As such, it measures the linear association, or goodness of fit, between the sample data and their predicted values. Consequently, $R^2$ is sometimes called a measure of "goodness of fit."

## *6.2* Summarizing Regression Results

In practice regression analyses are carried out using computer software. Various software packages report information in different styles and using slightly different terminology. Some software packages will report more summary information than others. In fact, some regression software will report advanced information that you may not recognize. Skills that you must develop are the ability to read computer output, summarize the information that is presented, and correctly interpret the parts you want.

Furthermore, a report that includes information from a regression analysis usually will not include pages of computer output at the end for the reader to sort through. Instead, regression results are summarized within the text in a form that is convenient for the reader.

In this section we illustrate "typical" computer output and suggest several ways that the information can be summarized and reported. As an example we will use the food expenditure model and data. Compare the computer output in Section 6.2.1 to the output from the software that you are using.

### 6.2.1  COMPUTER OUTPUT

Output from most econometric computer programs contains at least the coefficient estimates, their standard errors, and corresponding $t$-statistics and $p$-values, usually

*Table 6.2* **Computer–Generated Least Squares Results**

| (1)<br>Variable | (2)<br>Coefficient | (3)<br>Standard Error | (4)<br>t-Value | (5)<br>p-Value |
|---|---|---|---|---|
| INTERCEP | 40.7676 | 22.1387 | 1.841 | 0.0734 |
| X | 0.1283 | 0.0305 | 4.201 | 0.0002 |

written in columns as in Table 6.2. Notice that the statistical software does not know the names we have given for the least squares estimates ($b_1$ and $b_2$) and in column (1) substitutes for them the variable names, with INTERCEP being the intercept. The least squares parameter estimates of the intercept and slope parameters are in column (2). The software reports more significant digits than we have in the text, which can mean minor changes in values. In column (3) are the standard errors of the estimates,

$$se(b_1) = \sqrt{\hat{var}(b_1)} = \sqrt{490.12} = 22.1387$$

and

$$se(b_2) = \sqrt{\hat{var}(b_2)} = \sqrt{0.0009326} = 0.0305$$

The $t$-statistics for the null and alternative hypotheses $H_0$: $\beta_1 = 0$ against $H_1$: $\beta_1 \neq 0$ and $H_0$: $\beta_2 = 0$ against $H_1$: $\beta_2 \neq 0$ are given in column (4). These $t$ values are

$$t_1 = \frac{b_1}{se(b_1)} = \frac{40.7676}{22.1387} = 1.84$$

and

$$t_2 = \frac{b_2}{se(b_2)} = \frac{0.1283}{0.0305} = 4.20$$

The $p$-values, in column (5) of Table 6.2, are for the hypotheses $H_0$: $\beta_k = 0$ against $H_1$: $\beta_k \neq 0$, and thus they are computed for these two-tailed tests as $P[|t_{(38)}| > 1.841] = 0.0734$ and $P[|t_{(38)}| > 4.201] = 0.0002$. Given the computer print-out we can compute the one-tailed $p$-value by dividing the reported two-tailed value by 2.

The computer output usually contains the analysis of variance, Table 6.1. For the food expenditure data, the output is shown in Table 6.3. From this table we find that:

*Table 6.3* **Analysis of Variance Table**

| Source | DF | Sum of Squares | Mean Square |
|---|---|---|---|
| Explained | 1 | 25221.2229 | 25221.2229 |
| Unexplained | 38 | 54311.3314 | 1429.2455 |
| Total | 39 | 79532.5544 | |
| | | | $R^2$  0.3171 |

$$SST = \Sigma(y_t - \bar{y})^2 = 79532$$

$$SSR = \Sigma(\hat{y}_t - \bar{y})^2 = 25221$$

$$SSE = \Sigma\hat{e}_t^2 = 54311$$

$$R^2 = \frac{SSR}{SST} = 1 - \frac{SSE}{SST} = 0.317$$

$$SSE/(T - 2) = \hat{\sigma}^2 = 1429.2455$$

Your computer software may include other items in the analysis of variance table, such as an $F$-value. Disregard these items for now, as we will return to them in Chapter 8.

### 6.2.2   REPORTING THE RESULTS OF A REGRESSION ANALYSIS

In a written report Tables 6.2 and 6.3 may appear in appendices, but usually they are not included in the body of any text. One way to summarize the regression results is in the form of a "fitted" regression equation:

$$\hat{y}_t = 40.7676 + 0.1283x_t \qquad R^2 = 0.317$$
$$\quad\,(22.1387) \quad (0.0305) \qquad \text{(s.e.)} \tag{6.2.1}$$

The value $b_1 = 40.7676$ estimates the weekly food expenditure by a household with no income; $b_2 = 0.1283$ implies that given a \$1 increase in weekly income we expect expenditure on food to increase by about \$.13; or, in more reasonable units of measurement, if income increases by \$100 we expect food expenditure to rise by \$12.83. The $R^2 = 0.317$ says that about 32 percent of the variation in food expenditure about its mean is explained by variations in income. The numbers in parentheses underneath the estimated coefficients are the *standard errors* of the least squares estimates. Apart from critical values from the $t$-distribution, equation 6.2.1 contains all the information that is required to construct interval estimates for $\beta_1$ or $\beta_2$ or to test hypotheses about $\beta_1$ or $\beta_2$.

Another conventional way to report results is to replace the standard errors with the $t$-values, given in column (4) of Table 6.2. These values arise when testing $H_0$: $\beta_1 = 0$ against $H_1$: $\beta_1 \neq 0$ and $H_0$: $\beta_2 = 0$ against $H_1$: $\beta_2 \neq 0$. Using these $t$-values we can report the regression results as

$$\hat{y}_t = 40.7676 + 0.1283x_t \qquad R^2 = 0.317$$
$$\quad\,(1.84) \quad\;\; (4.20) \qquad (t) \tag{6.2.2}$$

When reporting the results this way we recognize that the null hypothesis $H_0$: $\beta_2 = 0$ is an important one, since, if $b_2$ is not statistically significantly different from 0, then we cannot conclude that $x$ influences $y$.

Finally, a comment about the $R^2 = 0.317$. This value is interpreted as meaning that the regression model explains 31.7 percent of the variation in $y$ about its mean value, leaving 68.3 percent of the variation unexplained. This $R^2$ value, while sounding "low," is typical in regression studies using **cross-sectional data,** in which a sample of individuals, or other economic units, are observed at the same point in time. Studies using **time-series data,** in which one individual is observed over time, usually have much higher $R^2$ values. The lesson here is that the success of a model cannot be completely judged on the magnitude of its $R^2$. Even if this number is low, the estimated parameters may contain useful information. Thus, attempting to summarize the entire worth of a model by this one number is an error that should be avoided.

### 6.2.3   THE EFFECTS OF SCALING THE DATA

Data we obtain are not always in a convenient form for presentation in a table or use in a regression analysis. When the *scale* of the data is not convenient, it can be altered without changing any of the real underlying relationships between variables. For example, suppose we are interested in the variable $x$ = U.S. total real disposable personal income. In 1989 the value of $x$ = \$2,869,000,000,000 measured in 1982 dollars. That is, 2 trillion, 869 billion dollars. As written the number is very cumbersome. If we were to report such data in a table, it would take up too much space; if we were entering such data into the computer for analysis we would not like typing in all those digits. Thus, it is common practice to report and use data in convenient units of measurement. We might divide the variable $x$ by 1 billion and use instead the scaled variable $x^* = x/1,000,000,000 = $2,869$ billion. This is a much more manageable number, but what, if any, are the effects of scaling the variables in a regression model?

Consider the food expenditure model. The food expenditure data, which we introduced first in Chapter 3, are measured in *dollars* of food expenditure and income per week. Consequently, as in the previous section, we interpret the least squares estimate $b_2 = 0.1283$, as the expected increase in food expenditure, in dollars, given a \$1 increase in weekly income. It may be more convenient to discuss increases in weekly income of \$100. Such a change in the units of measurement is called *scaling the data.* The choice of the scale is made by the investigator so as to make interpretation meaningful and convenient. The choice of the scale does not affect the measurement of the underlying relationship, but it does affect the interpretation of the coefficient estimates and some summary measures. Let us summarize the possibilities:

1.   Changing the scale of $x$: In the linear regression model $y_t = \beta_1 + \beta_2 x_t + e_t$, suppose we change the units of measurement of the explanatory variable $x$ by dividing it by a constant $c$. In order to keep intact the equality of the left- and right-hand sides, the coefficient of $x$ must be multiplied by $c$. That is, $y_t = \beta_1 + \beta_2 x_t + e_t = \beta_1 + (c\beta_2)(x_t / c) + e_t = \beta_1 + \beta_2^* x_t^* + e_t$, where $\beta_2^* = c\beta_2$ and $x_t^* = x_t / c$. For example, if $x_t$ is measured in dollars, and $c = 100$, then $x_t^*$ is measured in hundreds of dollars. Then $\beta_2^*$ measures the expected change in $y$ given a \$100 increase in $x$, and $\beta_2^*$ is 100 times larger than $\beta_2$. The change in interpretation carries over to the estimates as well. Thus, in the food expenditure model $b_2 = 0.1283$ measures the effect of a change in income of \$1 while $100b_2 = $12.83$ measures the effect of a change in income of \$100. When the scale of $x$ is altered, the only other change occurs in the standard error of the regression coefficient, but it changes by

the same multiplicative factor as the coefficient, so that their ratio, the $t$-statistic, is unaffected. All other regression statistics are unchanged.

2.  Changing the scale of $y$: If we change the units of measurement of $y$, but not $x$, then all the coefficients must change in order for the equation to remain valid. That is, $y_t / c = (\beta_1 / c) + (\beta_2 / c)x_t + (e_t / c)$, or $y_t^* = \beta_1^* + \beta_2^* x_t + e_t^*$. In this rescaled model $\beta_2^*$ measures the change we expect in $y^*$ given a 1 unit change in $x$. Because the error term is scaled in this process, the least squares residuals will also be scaled. This will affect the standard errors of the regression coefficients, but it will not affect $t$-statistics or $R^2$.

3.  If the scale of $y$ and the scale of $x$ are changed by the same factor, then there will be no change in the reported regression results for $b_2$, but the estimated intercept and residuals will change; $t$-statistics and $R^2$ are unaffected. The interpretation of the parameters is made relative to the new units of measurement.

In Exercise 6.9 we allow you to explore the effects of rescaling the food expenditure data.

## 6.3 Choosing a Functional Form

In the household food expenditure function the dependent variable, household food expenditure, has been assumed to be a linear function of household income. That is, we represented the economic relationship as $E(y_t) = \beta_1 + \beta_2 x_t$, which implies that there is a linear, straight-line relationship between $E(y)$ and $x$. The statistical model that corresponds to this economic model is

$$y_t = \beta_1 + \beta_2 x_t + e_t \tag{6.3.1}$$

This brings us to our first of many "what if" questions about the model. What if the relationship between $y_t$ and $x_t$ is not linear? Fortunately, all we have done is not lost. One of the neat things about the simple linear regression model is that it is much more flexible than it appears at first glance.

> **REMARK:** The term *linear* in "simple linear regression model" means not a linear relationship between the variables, but a model in which the *parameters* enter in a linear way. That is, the model is "linear in the parameters," but it is not, necessarily, "linear in the *variables*."

By "linear in the parameters" we mean that the *parameters* are not multiplied together, divided, squared, cubed, and so on. The variables, however, can be *transformed* in any convenient way, *as long as the resulting model satisfies assumptions 1–5 of the simple linear regression model.*

The motivation for this discussion is that economic theory does not always imply that there is a linear relationship between the variables. For example, in the food expenditure model we do *not* expect that as household income rises that food expenditures will continue to rise indefinitely at the same constant rate. Instead, as income rises we expect food expenditures to rise, but we expect such expenditures to increase at a decreasing rate. This phrase is used many times in economics classes. What it means graphically is that there is not a straight-line relationship between the two variables, and that it might look something like Figure 6.2. As we will see in the next section, by *transforming* the variables $y$ and $x$ we can represent many "nonlinear-in-the-variables" functions and still use the linear regression model. We first introduced this idea in Chapter 3.3.4 where we used the natural logarithm to transform the variables. You may wish to take a glance back at that section before proceeding.

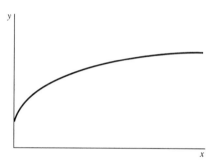

FIGURE **6.2**   A nonlinear relationship between food expenditure and income

Now comes the tricky part. In order to carry out a statistical analysis of a sample of data we must choose an algebraic form that is consistent with economic theory. If we believe that the relationship between $E(y)$ and $x$ looks like Figure 6.2, then specifying a linear relationship between the variables may not produce a satisfactory approximation. In the following section we will present, in a rather straightforward way, some common functional forms, and then apply them.

### 6.3.1   SOME COMMONLY USED FUNCTIONAL FORMS

Choosing an algebraic form for the relationship means choosing *transformations* of the original variables. This is not an easy process, and it requires good analytic geometry skills and some experience. It may not come to you easily. Nevertheless, these skills are an important part of an economist's tool kit. The variable transformations that we begin with are:

1.   The natural logarithm: if $x$ is a variable, then its natural logarithm is $\ln(x)$.
2.   The reciprocal: if $x$ is a variable, then its reciprocal is $1/x$.

Using just these two algebraic transformations, we can represent an amazing variety of "shapes." In Table 6.4 we provide six commonly used statistical models that employ the original variables, $y$ and $x$, their logarithmic transformations, their reciprocal transformations, or some combination. In Figure 6.3 we illustrate the shapes that these models (without the random errors $e_t$) can take. Let us examine each of the functional forms in Table 6.4, the shapes they can take, and some economic implications of their use. In models that are *nonlinear in the variables,* great care must be taken when interpreting the parameter values. They are no

***Table 6.4*** **Some Useful Functional Forms**

| Type | Statistical Model | Slope | Elasticity |
|---|---|---|---|
| 1. Linear | $y_t = \beta_1 + \beta_2 x_t + e_t$ | $\beta_2$ | $\beta_2 \dfrac{x_t}{y_t}$ |
| 2. Reciprocal | $y_t = \beta_1 + \beta_2 \dfrac{1}{x_t} + e_t$ | $-\beta_2 \dfrac{1}{x_t^2}$ | $-\beta_2 \dfrac{1}{x_t y_t}$ |
| 3. Log–Log | $\ln(y_t) = \beta_1 + \beta_2 \ln(x_t) + e_t$ | $\beta_2 \dfrac{y_t}{x_t}$ | $\beta_2$ |
| 4. Log–Linear (Exponential) | $\ln(y_t) = \beta_1 + \beta_2 x_t + e_t$ | $\beta_2 y_t$ | $\beta_2 x_t$ |
| 5. Linear–Log (Semi-log) | $y_t = \beta_1 + \beta_2 \ln(x_t) + e_t$ | $\beta_2 \dfrac{1}{x_t}$ | $\beta_2 \dfrac{1}{y_t}$ |
| 6. Log–Inverse | $\ln(y_t) = \beta_1 - \beta_2 \dfrac{1}{x_t} + e_t$ | $\beta_2 \dfrac{y_t}{x_t^2}$ | $\beta_2 \dfrac{1}{x_t}$ |

longer simply the slope and intercept of a line, as they are in the context of a model written in terms of the original variables.

1.  The model that is *linear in the variables* describes fitting a straight line to the original data, with slope $\beta_2$ and point elasticity $\beta_2 x_t / y_t$. The slope of the relationship is constant, but the elasticity changes at each point.

2.  The reciprocal model takes shapes shown in Figure 6.3(a). As $x$ increases, $y$ approaches the intercept, its asymptote, from above or below depending on the sign of $\beta_2$. The slope of this curve changes, and flattens out, as $x$ increases. The elasticity also changes at each point and is opposite in sign to $\beta_2$. In Figure 6.3(a), when $\beta_2 > 0$, the relationship between $x$ and $y$ is an inverse one and the elasticity is negative: a 1 percent increase in $x$ leads to a reduction in $y$ of $-\beta_2 / (x_t y_t)$ percent.

3.  The log–log model is a very popular one. Its name comes from the fact that the logarithm appears on both sides of the equation. In order to use this model, all values of $y$ and $x$ must be positive. The shapes that this equation can take are shown in Figures 6.3(b) and 6.3(c). Figure 6.3(b) shows cases in which $\beta_2 > 0$, and Figure 6.3(c) shows cases when $\beta_2 < 0$. The slopes of these curves change at every point, but the *elasticity is constant and equal to* $\beta_2$. This **constant elasticity model** is very convenient for economists, since we like to talk about elasticites and are familiar with their meaning. *However, ease of interpretation and convenience are never* sufficient reasons for choosing a functional form. See the following remark.

4.  The log–linear model ("log" on the left-hand-side of the equation and "linear" on the right) can take the shapes shown in Figure 6.3(d). Both its slope and elasticity change at each point and are the same sign as $\beta_2$.

5.  The linear–log model has shapes shown in Figure 6.3(e). It is an increasing or decreasing function, depending on the sign of $\beta_2$.

6.  The log–inverse model ("log" on the left-hand-side of the equation and a reciprocal on the right) has a shape shown in Figure 6.3(f). It has the charac-

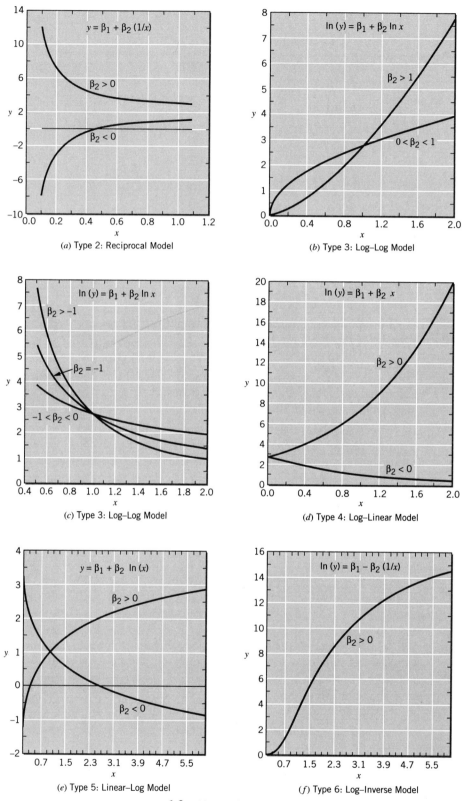

**FIGURE 6.3** Alternative functional forms

teristic that near the origin it increases at an increasing rate (convex) and then, after a point, increases at a decreasing rate (concave).

---

**REMARK:** Given this array of models, some of which have similar shapes, what are some guidelines for choosing a functional form? We must certainly choose a functional form that is sufficiently flexible to "fit" the data. Choosing a satisfactory functional form helps preserve the model assumptions. That is, a major objective of choosing a functional form, or transforming the variables, is to create a model in which the error term has the following properties:

1. $E(e_t) = 0$
2. $\text{var}(e_t) = \sigma^2$
3. $\text{cov}(e_i, e_j) = 0$
4. $e_t \sim N(0, \sigma^2)$

If these assumptions hold, then the least squares estimators have good statistical properties and we can use the procedures for statistical inference that we have developed in Chapters 4 and 5.

---

### 6.3.2 EXAMPLES USING ALTERNATIVE FUNCTIONAL FORMS

In this section we will examine an array of economic examples and possible choices for the functional form.

#### 6.3.2a  The Food Expenditure Model

Suppose that in the food expenditure model we wish to choose a functional form that is consistent with Figure 6.2. From the array of shapes in Figure 6.3 two possible choices that are similar in some aspects to Figure 6.2 are the reciprocal model and the linear–log model. These two functional forms are different ways of modeling the data and lead to estimates of the unknown parameters that have different economic interpretations.

The reciprocal model is

$$y_t = \beta_1 + \beta_2 \frac{1}{x_t} + e_t \qquad (6.3.2)$$

For the food expenditure model, we might assume that $\beta_1 > 0$ and $\beta_2 < 0$. If this is the case, then as income increases, household consumption of food increases at a decreasing rate and reaches an upper bound $\beta_1$. This model is *linear in the parameters* but it is *nonlinear in the variables*. Even so, if the error term $e_t$ satisfies our usual assumptions, then the unknown parameters can be estimated by least squares, and inferences can be made in the usual way.

Another property of the reciprocal model, ignoring the error term, is that when $x < -\beta_2/\beta_1$ the model predicts expenditure on food to be negative. This is unrealistic and implies that this functional form is inappropriate for small values of $x$.

When choosing a functional form, one practical guideline is to consider how the dependent variable changes with the independent variable. In the reciprocal model the slope of the relationship between $y$ and $x$ is

$$\frac{dy}{dx} = -\beta_2 \frac{1}{x_t^2}$$

If the parameter $\beta_2 < 0$, then there is a positive relationship between food expenditure and income, and, as income increases, this "marginal propensity to spend on food" diminishes, as economic theory predicts. Indeed, as $x$ becomes very large the slope approaches zero, which says that as income increases the household expenditure on food stops increasing after some point.

For the food expenditure relationship, an alternative to the reciprocal model is the linear–log model

$$y_t = \beta_1 + \beta_2 \ln(x_t) + e_t \tag{6.3.3}$$

which is shown in Figure 6.3(e). For $\beta_2 > 0$ this function is increasing, but at a decreasing rate. As $x$ increases the slope $\beta_2/x_t$ decreases. Similarly, the greater the amount of food expenditure $y$, the smaller the elasticity, $\beta_2/y_t$. These results are consistent with the idea that at high incomes, and large food expenditures, the effect of an increase in income on food expenditure is small.

### 6.3.2b Some Other Economic Models and Functional Forms
In this section we *briefly* describe some common economic models and functional forms that are used when estimating them.

1.  **Demand models:** statistical models of the relationship between quantity demanded ($y^d$) and price ($x$) are very frequently taken to be linear in the variables, creating a linear demand curve, as so often depicted in textbooks. Alternatively, the log–log form of the model, $\ln(y_t^d) = \beta_1 + \beta_2 \ln(x_t) + e_t$, is very convenient in this situation because of its "constant elasticity" property. Consider Figure 6.3(c), where several log–log models are shown for several values of $\beta_2 < 0$. They are negatively sloped, as is appropriate for demand curves, and the price elasticity of demand is the constant $\beta_2$.

2.  **Supply models:** if $y^s$ is the quantity supplied, then its relationship to price is often assumed to be linear, creating a linear supply curve. Alternatively, the log–log, constant elasticity form, $\ln(y_t^s) = \beta_1 + \beta_2 \ln(x_t) + e_t$, can be used. Economists are *very* interested in supply and demand, and we devote Chapter 13 in its entirety to the these and similar *equilibrium* models.

3.  **Production functions:** another basic economic relationship that can be investigated using the simple linear statistical model is a production function, or total product function, that relates the output of a good produced to the amount of a variable input, such as labor. One of the assumptions of production theory is that diminishing returns hold; the marginal-physical product of the variable input declines as more is used. To permit a decreasing marginal product, the relation between output ($y$) and input ($x$) is often modeled as a log–log model, with $\beta_2 < 1$. This relationship is shown in Figure 6.3(b). It has the property that the marginal product, which is the slope of the total product curve, is diminishing, as required.

4.  **Cost functions:** a family of cost curves, which can be estimated using the simple linear regression model, is based on a "quadratic" total cost curve.

Suppose that you wish to estimate the total cost ($y$) of producing output ($x$); then a potential model is given by

$$y_t = \beta_1 + \beta_2 x_t^2 + e_t \tag{6.3.4}$$

If we wish to estimate the average cost ($y/x$) of producing output $x$ then we might divide both sides of equation 6.3.4 by $x$ and use

$$(y_t/x_t) = \beta_1/x_t + \beta_2 x_t + e_t/x_t \tag{6.3.5}$$

which is consistent with the quadratic total cost curve.

5.  **The Phillips curve:** one important relationship in the macro-literature is the Phillips curve that was suggested by A. W. Phillips in 1958. This important relationship conjectures a systematic relationship between changes in the wage rate and changes in the level of unemployment. If we let $w_t$ be the wage rate in time $t$, then the percentage change in the wage rate is

$$\%\Delta w_t = \frac{w_t - w_{t-1}}{w_{t-1}} \tag{6.3.6}$$

If we assume that $\%\Delta w_t$ is proportional to the excess demand for labor $d_t$, we may write

$$\%\Delta w_t = \gamma d_t \tag{6.3.7}$$

where $\gamma$ is an economic parameter. Since the unemployment rate $u_t$ is inversely related to the excess demand for labor, we could write this using a reciprocal function as

$$d_t = \alpha + \eta \frac{1}{u_t} \tag{6.3.8}$$

where $\alpha$ and $\eta$ are economic parameters. Given equation 6.3.7 we can substitute for $d_t$, and rearrange, to obtain

$$\%\Delta w_t = \gamma\left(\alpha + \eta\frac{1}{u_t}\right)$$

$$= \gamma\alpha + \gamma\eta\frac{1}{u_t}$$

This model is *nonlinear in the parameters* and *nonlinear in the variables*. However, if we represent $y_t = \%\Delta w_t$ and $x_t = 1/u_t$, and $\gamma\alpha = \beta_1$ and $\gamma\eta = \beta_2$, then the simple linear regression model $y_t = \beta_1 + \beta_2 x_t + e_t$ represents the relationship between the rate of change in the wage rate and the unemployment rate.

## *6.4* Summing Up

In this chapter we have focused on describing, reporting, and interpreting regression results. We have also shown that any model that is "linear in the parameters," even if it is "nonlinear in the variables," can be analyzed using least squares regression, as a long as the usual regression assumptions hold. Some specific points of interest are these:

1.  The total variation in the dependent variable $y$ ($SST$) can be broken into variation that is explained by the model ($SSR$) and variation that is unexplained, ($SSE$). That is, $SST = SSR + SSE$.
2.  The coefficient of determination, $R^2 = SSR/SST = 1 - SSE/SST$ is a measure of the goodness of fit, or the explanatory power, of a regression. $0 \leq R^2 \leq 1$ is interpreted as the "percent of the variation in the dependent variable about its mean that is explained by the regression model." $R^2$ is the squared sample correlation between the actual and predicted values of the dependent variable.
3.  An *analysis of variance* table is a format used by statistical regression software. It contains the various sums of squares, degrees of freedom, and mean squares.
4.  Although many economic relationships may be nonlinear in the variables, they can still be analyzed using the simple linear regression model with transformed variables.
5.  It is desirable to choose transformations of the dependent and independent variables, when necessary, so that the assumptions of the simple linear regression model hold. When such transformations are made, the parameters of the model are no longer simply the slope and intercept of a linear relationship between the variables.

## *6.5* Exercises

6.1\*   Show that, if an intercept is present in the regression model, then $\Sigma(\hat{y}_t - \bar{y})\hat{e}_t = 0$

6.2   The Phillips curve that was introduced in Section 6.3 says that the rate of change of money wages is a function of the reciprocal of the unemployment rate. Specifically, let

$$w_t = \text{money wage rate in year } t$$

$$u_t = \text{unemployment rate in year } t$$

$$\%\Delta w_t = \frac{w_t - w_{t-1}}{w_{t-1}} \times 100 = \text{percentage rate of change in the wage rate}$$

The Phillips curve is given by

$$\%\Delta w_t = \beta_1 + \beta_2\frac{1}{u_t} + e_t$$

where it is hypothesized that $\beta_1 < 0$ and $\beta_2 > 0$. Using the aggregate data given in the file *phillips.dat:*
(a) Find least squares estimates for $\beta_1$ and $\beta_2$.
(b) Test whether there is a relationship between $\%\Delta w$ and $(1/u)$.
(c) Draw a graph of the estimated relationship with $u$ on the horizontal axis and $\%\Delta w$ on the vertical axis.
(d) Find an estimate for the "natural rate of unemployment" (the natural rate of unemployment is the rate for which $\%\Delta w = 0$).
(e) Find estimates for $d(\%\Delta w)/du$ when $u = 1$ and when $u = 3$.
(f) When does a change in the unemployment rate have the greatest impact on the rate of change in wages? When does it have the smallest?
(g) What is the economic meaning of $\beta_1$ and what is suggested by its estimate $b_1$?
(h) Find 95 percent interval estimates for $\beta_1$ and $\beta_2$.

6.3* (a) Using the format suggested in Chapter 1.7, write up the research results for Exercise 6.2. Your write-up should include the economic model, the statistical model, the sample observations, the estimation methods, the empirical results, the statistical implications, and the economic implications.
(b) Locate the sources and develop the nominal wage change $\%\Delta w$ and unemployment rate $u$ observations for the period 1974–1983 for the U.S. economy.
(c) Carry through an econometric analysis of the data obtained under (b).

6.4 The catering company Thirst Quenchers has a contract to supply soda at the University of California (Golden Bears) football games. They suspect that the major factor influencing the quantity of soda consumed is the maximum temperature on the day of each game. The last three football seasons have yielded the data in the file *football.dat.*
(a) Estimate a linear equation that relates the quantity of soda sold to the maximum temperature. Construct 95 percent interval estimates for each of the parameters. Comment on the results.
(b) Is there evidence to suggest that the temperature does influence the quantity consumed?
(c) Construct point and 95 percent confidence interval predictions for the amount of soda sold when the maximum temperature is (i) 70° and (ii) 75°.

6.5 Verify numerically using the food expenditure data that:
(a) the square of the sample correlation coefficient between the predicted and actual $y$ values is the coefficient of determination: $r^2 = R^2$.
(b) the square of the sample correlation coefficient between $x$ and $y$ is equal to the coefficient of determination in the simple linear regression model.
(c) Show algebraically that the result in (b) is true.

6.6 Using *only* the computer output in Table 6.2, test the following hypotheses:
(a) $H_0$: $\beta_1 = 0$ vs. $H_1$: $\beta_1 > 0$
(b) $H_0$: $\beta_2 = 0$ vs. $H_1$: $\beta_2 > 0$
(c) Draw a sketch showing the relationship between $p$-values for one- and two-tailed tests.

6.7 Reconsider the learning curve data in Exercise 3.8. Discuss the economic interpretation of the parameters of this model in light of the discussion in Chapter 6.3.

6.8 Use your computer software to graph the relationship between a variable $x > 0$ and its natural logarithm $\ln(x)$.

6.9 Consider the food expenditure data in Table 3.1.
   (a) Using your computer software, create the variables $y_t^* = y_t/100$ and $x_t^* = x_t/100$.
   (b) Estimate the following models and discuss the similarities and differences in the results:
      (i) Regress $y$ on $x$
      (ii) Regress $y$ on $x^*$
      (iii) Regress $y^*$ on $x$
      (iv) Regress $y^*$ on $x^*$

## *6.6* References

BROWN, WILLIAM S. (1991). *Introducing Econometrics.* St. Paul, MN: West Publishing, pages 126–137.

GRIFFITHS, W. E., HILL, R. C., AND G. G. JUDGE (1993). *Learning and Practicing Econometrics.* New York: John Wiley & Sons, Inc., Chapter 8.

GUJARATI, DAMODAR N. (1995). *Basic Econometrics, Third Edition.* New York: McGraw-Hill, Chapter 6.

# *Part II*

# The General Linear Regression Model

In the first six chapters the focus has been on (i) suggesting why econometrics is necessary, (ii) identifying where it fits into the economic scheme of things and (iii) developing a formal basis for learning from a sample of economic data. Building on some of the basic concepts of probability and the conceptual basis provided by economic theory, we specified simple economic and statistical models that could be used for the purposes of estimating unknown parameters, carrying through the process of inference, and drawing economic conclusions.

Given this base, it is now time to leave the simple regression world of Chapters 3 through 6 to enter a slightly more complicated, but more interesting, world in which there are many "what if" questions.

Since many economic variables are interrelated, the first "what if" question we take up is, "What if there is more than one right-hand-side explanatory $x$ variable?" This is an important first-step generalization of our simple regression model because, as we think of such things as demand relations, supply relations, production functions, and consumption functions, having several variables influence the outcome variable $y$ seems reasonable.

For example, from the micro-theory of consumer demand, it seems natural to specify that consumption is a function of the price of the commodity, the prices of substitutes and complements, and the level of income. In a supply relation the supply forthcoming may be a function of current prices, past prices, and even future or expected prices. In a production function, output is not only a function of capital and labor, but possibly many other inputs.

So that you will be able to work with these important real world problems, in Chapter 7 we generalize the statistical model to handle "$K$" right-hand-side explanatory $x$ variables and discuss estimation of the parameters in this larger model. To note the change, we will label this a general or multiple regression model. In Chapter 8, we develop a basis for hypothesis testing and interval estimation, and discuss the use of information not contained in the sample information. Such information is especially useful when the data are collinear and contain relatively little information. In Chapter 9, we extend the multiple regression model to allow for the inclusion of qualitative factors using "dummy" variables. When qualitative factors are included on the right-hand side of the model, they serve to modify the slope and/or intercept of the model. When qualitative factors are on the left-hand side of the model, a new form of estimation is called for, and we briefly describe maximum likelihood estimation.

# Chapter 7

# The Multiple Regression Model: Specification and Estimation

The simple regression model, with one explanatory variable, is useful in a range of situations. However, most problems involve two or more explanatory variables that influence the dependent variable $y$. For example, in a demand equation the quantity demanded of a commodity depends on the price of that commodity, the prices of substitute and complimentary goods, and income. Output in a production function will be a function of more than one input. Aggregate money demand will be a function of aggregate income and the interest rate. Investment will depend on the interest rate and changes in income.

When we turn an economic model with more than one explanatory variable into its corresponding statistical model, we refer to it as a **multiple regression model.** Most of the results we developed for the simple regression model in Chapters 3–6 can be extended naturally to this general case. There are slight changes in the interpretation of the $\beta$ parameters, the degrees of freedom for the $t$-distribution will change, and we will need to modify the assumption concerning the characteristics of the explanatory ($x$) variables.

As an example for introducing and analyzing the multiple regression model, consider a model used to explain total revenue for a fast-food hamburger chain in the San Francisco Bay area. We begin with an outline of this model and the questions that we hope it will answer.

## 7.1 Model Specification and the Data

### 7.1.1 THE ECONOMIC MODEL

Each week the management of a Bay Area Rapid Food hamburger chain must decide how much money should be spent on advertising their products and what specials (lower prices) should be introduced for that week. Of particular interest to management is how total revenue changes as the level of advertising expenditure changes. Does an increase in advertising expenditure lead to an increase in total revenue? If so, is the increase in total revenue sufficient to justify the increased advertising expenditure? Management is also interested in pricing strategy. Will reducing prices lead to an increase or decrease in total revenue? If a reduction in price leads only to a small increase in the quantity sold, total revenue will fall (demand is price inelastic); a price reduction that leads to a large increase in quantity sold will produce an increase in total revenue (demand is price elastic). This economic information is essential for effective management.

The first step is to set up an economic model in which total revenue depends on one or more explanatory variables. We initially hypothesize that total revenue, *tr*, is linearly related to price, *p*, and advertising expenditure, *a*. Thus, the economic model is:

$$tr = \beta_1 + \beta_2 p + \beta_3 a \qquad (7.1.1)$$

where *tr* represents total revenue for a given week, *p* represents price in that week, and *a* is the level of advertising expenditure during that week. Both *tr* and *a* are measured in terms of thousands of dollars.

How we measure price is not so clear, however, since a hamburger outlet sells a number of products: burgers, fries, and shakes, and each product has its own price. What we need for the model in equation 7.1.1 is some kind of average price for all products, and information on how this average price changes from week to week. Let us assume that management has constructed a single weekly price series, *p*, measured in dollars and cents, that describes overall prices.

The remaining items in equation 7.1.1 are the unknown parameters $\beta_1$, $\beta_2$, and $\beta_3$ that describe the dependence of revenue (*tr*) on price (*p*) and advertising (*a*). In the multiple regression model the intercept parameter, $\beta_1$, is the value of the dependent variable when each of the independent, explanatory variables takes the value zero. In many cases this parameter has no clear economic interpretation, but it is almost always included in the regression model. It helps in the overall estimation of the model and in prediction.

The other parameters in the model measure the change in the value of the dependent variable given a unit change in an explanatory variable, *all other variables held constant.* For example, in equation 7.1.1

---

$\beta_2$ = the change in *tr* ($1000) when *p* is increased by one unit ($1), and *a* is held constant

$$= \frac{\Delta tr}{\Delta p}_{(a \text{ held constant})} = \frac{\partial tr}{\partial p}$$

---

The symbol $\partial$ stands for "partial differentiation." Those of you familiar with calculus may have seen this operation. It means that, as the definition states, we calculate the change in one variable, *tr*, when the variable *p* changes, all other factors, *a*, held constant. We will occasionally use this symbol, but you will not be asked to evaluate such derivatives.

The sign of $\beta_2$ could be positive or negative. If an increase in price leads to an increase in revenue, then $\beta_2 > 0$, and the demand for the chain's products is price inelastic. Conversely, a price elastic demand exists if an increase in price leads to a decline in revenue, in which case $\beta_2 < 0$. Thus, knowledge of the *sign* of $\beta_2$ provides information on the price elasticity of demand. The *magnitude* of $\beta_2$ measures the amount of the change in revenue for a given price change.

The parameter $\beta_3$ describes the response of revenue to a change in the level of advertising expenditure. That is,

---

$\beta_3$ = the change in *tr* ($1000) when *a* is increased by one unit ($1000), and *p* is held constant

$$\frac{\Delta tr}{\Delta a}_{(p \text{ held constant})} = \frac{\partial tr}{\partial a}$$

---

We expect the sign of $\beta_3$ to be positive. That is, we expect that an increase in advertising expenditure, unless the ad is offensive, will lead to an increase in total revenue. Whether or not the increase in total revenue is sufficient to justify the added advertising expenditure, and the added cost of producing more hamburgers, is another question. With $\beta_3 < 1$, an increase of $1,000 in advertising expenditure will yield an increase in total revenue that is less than $1,000. For $\beta_3 > 1$, it will be greater. Thus, in terms of the chain's advertising policy, knowledge of $\beta_3$ is very important.

The next step along the road to learning about $\beta_1$, $\beta_2$, and $\beta_3$ is to convert the economic model into a statistical model.

### 7.1.2 THE STATISTICAL MODEL

The economic model (equation 7.1.1) describes the expected behavior of many individual franchises. As such, we should write it as $E(tr) = \beta_1 + \beta_2 p + \beta_3 a$, where $E(tr)$ is the "expected value" of total revenue. Weekly data for total revenue, price, and advertising will not follow a exact linear relationship. Equation 7.1.1 describes not a line as in Chapters 3–6, but a *plane*. The plane intersects the vertical axis at $\beta_1$. The parameters $\beta_2$ and $\beta_3$ measure the slope of the plane in the directions of the "price axis" and the "advertising axis," respectively. Table 7.1 contains 52 weekly observations on total revenue, price and advertising expenditure for a hamburger franchise. If we plot the data we obtain Figure 7.1. These data do not fall exactly on a plane, but instead resemble a "cloud." To allow for a difference between observable total revenue and the expected value of total revenue we add a *random error term, e = tr − E(tr)*. This random error represents all the factors that cause weekly total revenue to differ from its expected value. These factors might include the weather, the behavior of competitors, a new surgeon general's report on the deadly effects of fat intake, and so on. Denoting the *t*'th weekly observation by the subscript *t*, we have

$$tr_t = E(tr_t) + e_t = \beta_1 + \beta_2 p_t + \beta_3 a_t + e_t \qquad (7.1.2)$$

The economic model in equation 7.1.1 describes the average, systematic relationship between the variables *tr*, *p*, and *a*. The expected value $E(tr)$ is the nonrandom, systematic component, to which we add the random error *e* to determine *tr*. Thus,

*Table 7.1* **Weekly Observations on Revenue, Price, and Advertising Expenditure for the Hamburger Chain**

| Week | Revenue (*tr*) $1,000 units | Price (*p*) $ | Advertising (*a*) $1,000 units |
|------|------|------|------|
| 1 | 123.1 | 1.92 | 12.4 |
| 2 | 124.3 | 2.15 | 9.9 |
| 3 | 89.3 | 1.67 | 2.4 |
| 4 | 141.3 | 1.68 | 13.8 |
| 5 | 112.8 | 1.75 | 3.5 |
| 6 | 108.1 | 1.55 | 1.8 |
| 7 | 143.9 | 1.54 | 17.8 |
| 8 | 124.2 | 2.10 | 9.8 |
| 9 | 110.1 | 2.44 | 8.3 |
| 10 | 111.7 | 2.47 | 9.8 |
| 11 | 123.8 | 1.86 | 12.6 |
| 12 | 123.5 | 1.93 | 11.5 |
| 13 | 110.2 | 2.47 | 7.4 |
| 14 | 100.9 | 2.11 | 6.1 |
| 15 | 123.3 | 2.10 | 9.5 |
| 16 | 115.7 | 1.73 | 8.8 |
| 17 | 116.6 | 1.86 | 4.9 |
| 18 | 153.5 | 2.19 | 18.8 |
| 19 | 149.2 | 1.90 | 18.9 |
| 20 | 89.0 | 1.67 | 2.3 |
| 21 | 132.6 | 2.43 | 14.1 |
| 22 | 97.5 | 2.13 | 2.9 |
| 23 | 106.1 | 2.33 | 5.9 |
| 24 | 115.3 | 1.75 | 7.6 |
| 25 | 98.5 | 2.05 | 5.3 |
| 26 | 135.1 | 2.35 | 16.8 |
| 27 | 124.2 | 2.12 | 8.8 |
| 28 | 98.4 | 2.13 | 3.2 |
| 29 | 114.8 | 1.89 | 5.4 |
| 30 | 142.5 | 1.50 | 17.3 |
| 31 | 122.6 | 1.93 | 11.2 |
| 32 | 127.7 | 2.27 | 11.2 |
| 33 | 113.0 | 1.66 | 7.9 |
| 34 | 144.2 | 1.73 | 17.0 |
| 35 | 109.2 | 1.59 | 3.3 |
| 36 | 106.8 | 2.29 | 7.1 |
| 37 | 145.0 | 1.86 | 15.3 |
| 38 | 124.0 | 1.91 | 12.7 |
| 39 | 106.7 | 2.34 | 6.1 |
| 40 | 153.2 | 2.13 | 19.6 |
| 41 | 120.1 | 2.05 | 6.3 |
| 42 | 119.3 | 1.89 | 9.0 |
| 43 | 150.6 | 2.12 | 18.7 |
| 44 | 92.2 | 1.87 | 2.2 |
| 45 | 130.5 | 2.09 | 16.0 |
| 46 | 112.5 | 1.76 | 4.5 |
| 47 | 111.8 | 1.77 | 4.3 |
| 48 | 120.1 | 1.94 | 9.3 |
| 49 | 107.4 | 2.37 | 8.3 |
| 50 | 128.6 | 2.10 | 15.4 |
| 51 | 124.6 | 2.29 | 9.2 |
| 52 | 127.2 | 2.36 | 10.2 |

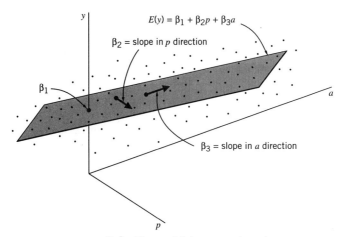

*FIGURE 7.1*  The multiple regression plane

*tr* is a random variable. We do not know what the value of weekly total revenue will be until we observe it.

The introduction of the error term, and assumptions about its probability distribution, turn the economic model into the *statistical* model in equation 7.1.2. The statistical model provides a more realistic description of the relationship between the variables, as well as a framework for developing and assessing estimators of the unknown parameters.

### 7.1.2a   The General Model

Let's digress for a moment and summarize how the concepts developed so far relate to the general case. In a general multiple regression model, a dependent variable $y_t$ is related to a number of *explanatory variables* $x_{t2}, x_{t3}, \ldots, x_{tK}$ through a linear equation that can be written as

$$y_t = \beta_1 + \beta_2 x_{t2} + \beta_3 x_{t3} + \cdots + \beta_K x_{tK} + e_t \qquad (7.1.3)$$

The coefficients $\beta_2, \beta_3, \ldots, \beta_K$ are unknown parameters. The parameter $\beta_k$ measures the effect of a change in the variable $x_{tk}$ upon the expected value of $y_t$, $E(y_t)$, all other variables held constant. The parameter $\beta_1$ is the intercept term. The "variable" to which $\beta_1$ is attached is $x_{t1} = 1$.

The equation for total revenue can be viewed as a special case of equation 7.1.3 where $K = 3$, $y_t = tr_t$, $x_{t1} = 1$, $x_{t2} = p_t$, and $x_{t3} = a_t$. Thus we rewrite equation 7.1.2 as

$$y_t = \beta_1 + \beta_2 x_{t2} + \beta_3 x_{t3} + e_t \qquad (7.1.4)$$

In this chapter we will introduce point and interval estimation in terms of this model with $K = 3$. The results generally will hold for models with more explanatory variables $(K > 3)$.

### 7.1.2b   The Assumptions of the Model

To make the statistical model in equation 7.1.4 complete, assumptions about the probability distribution of the random errors, $e_t$, need to be made. The assumptions that we introduce for $e_t$ are similar to those introduced for the simple regression model in Chapter 3. They are:

1.  $E[e_t] = 0$. Each random error has a probability distribution with zero mean. Some errors will be positive, some will be negative; over a large number of observations they will average out to zero. With this assumption we assert that the average of all the omitted variables, and any other errors made when specifying the model, is zero. Thus, we are asserting that our model is, on average, correct.

2.  $\text{var}(e_t) = \sigma^2$. Each random error has a probability distribution with variance $\sigma^2$. The variance $\sigma^2$ is an unknown parameter and it measures the uncertainty in the statistical model. It is the same for each observation, so that for no observations will the model uncertainty be more, or less, nor is it directly related to any economic variable. Errors with this property are said to be *homoskedastic.*

3.  $\text{cov}(e_t, e_s) = 0$. The covariance between the two random errors corresponding to any two different observations is zero. The size of an error for one observation has no bearing on the likely size of an error for another observation. Thus, any pair of errors is uncorrelated.

4.  We will sometimes further assume that the random errors $e_t$ have normal probability distributions. That is, $e_t \sim N(0, \sigma^2)$.

Because each observation on the dependent variable $y_t$ depends on the random error term $e_t$, each $y_t$ is also a random variable. The statistical properties of $y_t$ follow from those of $e_t$. These properties are

1.  $E(y_t) = \beta_1 + \beta_2 x_{t2} + \beta_3 x_{t3}$. The expected (average) value of $y_t$ depends on the values of the explanatory variables and the unknown parameters. This assumption is equivalent to $E(e_t) = 0$. This assumption says that the average value of $y_t$ changes   for each observation and is given by the *regression function* $E(y_t) = \beta_1 + \beta_2 x_{t2} + \beta_3 x_{t3}$.

2.  $\text{var}(y_t) = \text{var}(e_t) = \sigma^2$. The variance of the probability distribution of $y_t$ does not change with each observation. Some observations on $y_t$ are not more likely to be further from the regression function than others.

3.  $\text{cov}(y_t, y_s) = \text{cov}(e_t, e_s) = 0$. Any two observations on the dependent variable are uncorrelated. For example, if one observation is above $E(y_t)$, a subsequent observation is not more or less likely to be above $E(y_t)$.

4.  We sometimes will assume that the values of $y_t$ are normally distributed about their mean. That is, $y_t \sim N[(\beta_1 + \beta_2 x_{t2} + \beta_3 x_{t3}), \sigma^2]$, which is equivalent to assuming that $e_t \sim N(0, \sigma^2)$.

In addition to the above assumptions about the error term (and hence, about the dependent variable), we make two assumptions about the explanatory variables. The first is that the explanatory variables are not random variables. Thus, we are assuming that the values of the explanatory variables are known to us prior to observing the values of the dependent variable. This assumption is realistic for our hamburger chain where a decision about prices and advertising is made each week and values for these variables are set accordingly. For cases in which this assumption is untenable, our analysis will be conditional upon the values of the explanatory variables in our sample, or, further assumptions must be made.

The second assumption is that any one of the explanatory variables is not an exact linear function of any of the others. This assumption is equivalent to assuming that no variable is redundant. As we will see, if this assumption is violated, a condition called *exact multicollinearity*, the least squares procedure fails.

To summarize then, let us construct a list of the assumptions for the general multiple regression model in equation 7.1.3, much as we have done in the earlier chapters, to which we can refer as needed:

---

**ASSUMPTIONS OF THE MULTIPLE REGRESSION MODEL**

1. $y_t = \beta_1 + \beta_2 x_{t2} + \cdots + \beta_K x_{tK} + e_t, \; t = 1, \ldots, T$
2. $E(y_t) = \beta_1 + \beta_2 x_{t2} + \cdots + \beta_K x_{tK} \Leftrightarrow E(e_t) = 0.$
3. $\mathrm{var}(y_t) = \mathrm{var}(e_t) = \sigma^2.$
4. $\mathrm{cov}(y_t, y_s) = \mathrm{cov}(e_t, e_s) = 0$
5. The values of $x_{tk}$ are not random and are not exact linear functions of the other explanatory variables.
6. $y_t \sim N[(\beta_1 + \beta_2 x_{t2} + \cdots + \beta_K x_{tK}), \sigma^2] \Leftrightarrow e_t \sim N(0, \sigma^2)$

---

# 7.2 Estimating the Parameters of the Multiple Regression Model

In this section we consider the problem of using the least squares principle to estimate the unknown parameters of the multiple regression model. We will discuss estimation in the context of the model in equation 7.1.4, which we repeat here for convenience.

$$y_t = \beta_1 + \beta_2 x_{t2} + \beta_3 x_{t3} + e_t \tag{7.2.1}$$

This model is simpler than the full model, and yet all the results we present carry over to the general case with only minor modifications.

### 7.2.1 LEAST SQUARES ESTIMATION PROCEDURE

To find an estimator or rule for estimating the unknown parameters, we follow the least squares procedure that was first introduced in Chapter 3 for the simple regression model. With the least squares principle we minimize the sum of squared differences between the observed values of $y_t$ and its expected value $E[y_t] = \beta_1 + x_{t2}\beta_2 + x_{t3}\beta_3$. Mathematically, we minimize the sum of squares function $S(\beta_1, \beta_2, \beta_3)$, which is a function of the unknown parameters, given the data,

$$S(\beta_1, \beta_2, \beta_3) = \sum_{t=1}^{T}(y_t - E[y_t])^2 \tag{7.2.2}$$

$$= \sum_{t=1}^{T}(y_t - \beta_1 - \beta_2 x_{t2} - \beta_3 x_{t3})^2$$

Given the sample observations $y_t$, minimizing the sum of squares function is a straightforward exercise in calculus. You can skip the marked text if you want to get straight to the solutions.

To find the least squares estimates $b_1$, $b_2$, and $b_3$ that minimize (7.2.2), we follow the same procedure that was outlined in Chapter 3. As in Chapter 3.3.1, the first step is to partially differentiate (7.2.2) with respect to $\beta_1$, $\beta_2$, $\beta_3$, and to set the first order partial derivatives to zero. This yields

$$\frac{\partial S}{\partial \beta_1} = 2T\beta_1 + 2\beta_2 \Sigma x_{t2} + 2\beta_3 \Sigma x_{t3} - 2\Sigma y_t$$

$$\frac{\partial S}{\partial \beta_2} = 2\beta_1 \Sigma x_{t2} + 2\beta_2 \Sigma x_{t2}^2 + 2\beta_3 \Sigma x_{t2} x_{t3} - 2\Sigma x_{t2} y_t \tag{7.2.3}$$

$$\frac{\partial S}{\partial \beta_3} = 2\beta_1 \Sigma x_{t3} + 2\beta_2 \Sigma x_{t2} x_{t3} + 2\beta_3 \Sigma x_{t3}^2 - 2\Sigma x_{t3} y_t$$

Setting these partial derivatives equal to zero, dividing by 2, and rearranging yields

$$Tb_1 + \Sigma x_{t2} b_2 + \Sigma x_{t3} b_3 = \Sigma y_t$$

$$\Sigma x_{t2} b_1 + \Sigma x_{t2}^2 b_2 + \Sigma x_{t2} x_{t3} b_3 = \Sigma x_{t2} y_t \tag{7.2.4}$$

$$\Sigma x_{t3} b_1 + \Sigma x_{t2} x_{t3} b_2 + \Sigma x_{t3}^2 b_3 = \Sigma x_{t3} y_t$$

The least squares estimates for $b_1$, $b_2$ and $b_3$ are given by the solution of this set of three *simultaneous equations*, known as the *normal equations*. For the model we are considering we will obtain algebraic solutions. For models with more than three parameters the solutions become quite messy without using matrix algebra, and thus we will not show them. Computer software used for multiple regression computations solves systems like (7.2.4) to obtain the least squares estimates.

In order to give expressions for the least squares estimates it is convenient to express each of the variables as deviations from their means. That is, let

$$y_t^* = y_t - \bar{y},\ x_{t2}^* = x_{t2} - \bar{x}_2,\ x_{t3}^* = x_{t3} - \bar{x}_3$$

Then the least squares estimates $b_1$, $b_2$ and $b_3$ are:

$$b_1 = \bar{y} - b_2\bar{x}_2 - b_3\bar{x}_3$$

$$b_2 = \frac{(\Sigma y_t^* x_{t2}^*)(\Sigma x_{t3}^{*2}) - (\Sigma y_t^* x_{t3}^*)(\Sigma x_{t2}^* x_{t3}^*)}{(\Sigma x_{t2}^{*2})(\Sigma x_{t3}^{*2}) - (\Sigma x_{t2}^* x_{t3}^*)^2} \qquad (7.2.5)$$

$$b_3 = \frac{(\Sigma y_t^* x_{t3}^*)(\Sigma x_{t2}^{*2}) - (\Sigma y_t^* x_{t2}^*)(\Sigma x_{t3}^* x_{t2}^*)}{(\Sigma x_{t2}^{*2})(\Sigma x_{t3}^{*2}) - (\Sigma x_{t2}^* x_{t3}^*)^2}$$

These formulas can be used to obtain least squares estimates in the model 7.2.1, whatever the data values are. They are provided as an illustration and are not meant to be memorized. In practice we use computer software to calculate $b_1$, $b_2$, and $b_3$. Looked at as a general way to use sample data, the formulas in equation 7.2.5 are referred to as estimation rules or procedures and are called the *least squares estimators* of the unknown parameters. In general, since their values are not known until the data are observed and the estimates calculated, the *least squares estimators are random variables*. When applied to a specific sample of data, the rules produce the least squares estimates, which are numeric values.

### 7.2.2 LEAST SQUARES ESTIMATES USING HAMBURGER CHAIN DATA

For the data in Table 7.1 for Bay Area Rapid Food, solving equation 7.2.5 results in the following least squares estimates:

$$b_1 = 104.79$$

$$b_2 = -6.642 \qquad (7.2.6)$$

$$b_3 = 2.984$$

The regression function that we are estimating is

$$E[y_t] = \beta_1 + \beta_2 x_{t2} + \beta_3 x_{t3} \qquad (7.2.7)$$

and the fitted regression line is

$$\hat{y}_t = b_1 + b_2 x_{t2} + b_3 x_{t3} \qquad (7.2.8)$$

$$= 104.79 - 6.642 x_{t2} + 2.984 x_{t3}$$

so in terms of the original economic variables found in equation 7.1.1,

$$\hat{tr}_t = 104.79 - 6.642p_t + 2.984a_t \qquad (7.2.9)$$

Based on these results, what can we say?

1.  The negative coefficient of $p_t$ suggests that demand is price elastic, and we estimate that an increase in price of $1 will lead to a fall in weekly revenue of $6,642. Or, stated positively, a reduction in price of $1 will lead to an increase in revenue of $6,642. If such is the case, a strategy of price reduction through the offering of specials would be successful in increasing total revenue.

2.  The coefficient of advertising is positive, and we estimate that an increase in advertising expenditure of $1,000 will lead to an increase in total revenue of $2,984. We can use this information, along with the costs of producing the additional hamburgers, to determine whether an increase in advertising expenditures will increase profit.

3.  The estimated intercept implies that if both price and advertising expenditure were zero the total revenue earned would be $104,790. This is obviously not correct. In this model, as in many others, the intercept is included in the model for mathematical completeness and to improve the model's predictive ability.

The estimated equation can also be used for prediction. Suppose management is interested in predicting total revenue for a price of $2 and an advertising expenditure of $10,000. This prediction is given by

$$\hat{tr}_t = 104.785 - 6.6419(2) + 2.9843(10) \qquad (7.2.10)$$

$$= 121.34$$

Thus, the predicted value of total revenue for the specified values of $p$ and $a$ is approximately $121,340.

---

**REMARK:** A word of caution is in order about interpreting regression results. The negative sign attached to price implies that reducing the price will increase total revenue. If taken literally, why should we not keep reducing the price to zero? Obviously that would not keep increasing total revenue. This makes the following important point: estimated regression models describe the relationship between the economic variables for values *similar* to those found in the sample data. Extrapolating the results to extreme values is generally not a good idea. In general, predicting the value of the dependent variable for values of the explanatory variables far from the sample values invites disaster. Refer to Figure 5.5 and the surrounding discussion.

---

### 7.2.3   ESTIMATION OF THE ERROR VARIANCE $\sigma^2$

There is one remaining parameter to estimate, the variance of the error term, $\sigma^2$. To develop an estimation procedure for $\sigma^2$ we use the least squares residuals, which represent the only sample information we have about the error term values. For this parameter we follow the same steps that were outlined in Section 4.6 of Chapter 4. The least squares residuals for the model in equation 7.2.1 are:

$$\hat{e}_t = y_t - \hat{y}_t = y_t - (b_1 + x_{t2}b_2 + x_{t3}b_3) \tag{7.2.11}$$

One estimator of $\sigma^2$, and the one we will use, is

$$\hat{\sigma}^2 = \frac{\Sigma \hat{e}_t^2}{T - K} \tag{7.2.12}$$

where $K$ is the number of parameters being estimated in the multiple regression model. Note that in Chapter 4, where there was one explanatory variable and two coefficients, $K = 2$.

In the hamburger chain example we have $K = 3$. The estimate for our sample of data in Table 7.1 is

$$\hat{\sigma}^2 = \frac{\Sigma \hat{e}_t^2}{T - K} = \frac{1805.168}{52 - 3} = 36.84 \tag{7.2.13}$$

One major purpose of obtaining this estimate is to enable us to get an estimate of the unknown variances and covariances for the least squares estimators. Let us turn now to the properties of the least squares estimator.

## *7.3* Sampling Properties of the Least Squares Estimator

In a general context, the least squares estimators $(b_1, b_2, b_3)$ in equation 7.2.5 are random variables; they take on different values in different samples and their values are unknown until a sample is collected and their values computed. The sampling properties of a least squares estimator tell us how the estimates vary from sample to sample. They provide a basis for assessing the reliability of the estimates. In Chapter 4 we found that the least squares estimator was unbiased and that there is no other linear unbiased estimator that has a smaller variance, if the model assumptions are correct. This result remains true for the *general* multiple regression model that we are considering in this chapter.

> **THE GAUSS–MARKOV THEOREM:** For the multiple regression model, if assumptions 1-5 listed at the beginning of the chapter hold, then the least squares estimators are the Best Linear Unbiased Estimators (BLUE) of the parameters in a multiple regression model.

If we are able to assume that the errors are *normally distributed,* then $y_t$ will also be a normally distributed random variable. The least squares estimators will also have normal probability distributions, since they are linear functions of $y_t$. If the errors are not normally distributed, then the least squares estimators are approximately normally distributed in large samples, in which $T - K$ is greater than, perhaps, 50. These facts are of great importance for the construction of interval estimates and the testing of hypotheses about the parameters of the regression model.

### 7.3.1 THE VARIANCES AND COVARIANCES OF THE LEAST SQUARES ESTIMATORS

The variances and covariances of the least squares estimators give us information about the reliability of the estimators $b_1$, $b_2$, $b_3$. Since the least squares estimators are unbiased, the smaller their variances the higher is the probability that they will produce estimates "near" the true parameter values. For $K = 3$ we can express the variances and covariances in an algebraic form that provides useful insights into the behavior of the least squares estimator. For example, we can show that:

$$\text{var}(b_2) = \frac{\sigma^2}{(\Sigma x_{t2}^{*2})(1 - r_{23}^2)}$$

$$\text{cov}(b_2, b_3) = \frac{-r_{23}\sigma^2}{(1 - r_{23}^2)\sqrt{\Sigma x_{t2}^{*2}}\sqrt{\Sigma x_{t3}^{*2}}}$$

(7.3.1)

where $r_{23}$ is the sample correlation coefficient (see Chapter 6.1.1) between the $T$ values of $x_{t2}$ and $x_{t3}$,

$$r_{23} = \frac{\Sigma x_{t2}^* x_{t3}^*}{\sqrt{\Sigma x_{t2}^{*2} \Sigma x_{t3}^{*2}}}$$

For the other variances and covariances there are formulas of a similar nature. It is important to understand the factors affecting the variance of $b_2$:

1. The error variance $\sigma^2$ directly affects the variance of the least squares estimators. This is to be expected, since $\sigma^2$ measures the overall uncertainty in the model specification. If $\sigma^2$ is large, then data values may be widely spread about the regression function $E[y_t] = \beta_1 + \beta_2 x_{t2} + \beta_3 x_{t3}$ and there is less information in the data about the parameter values. If $\sigma^2$ is small, then data values are compactly spread about the regression function $E[y_t] = \beta_1 + \beta_2 x_{t2} + \beta_3 x_{t3}$ and there is more information about what the parameter values might be.

2. The sample size $T$ affects the sum in the denominator, which more explicitly is

$$\sum_{t=1}^{T} x_{t2}^{*2} = \sum_{t=1}^{T} (x_{t2} - \bar{x}_2)^2$$

(7.3.2)

The larger is the sample size $T$, the larger is this sum, and thus, the smaller is the variance. More observations yield more precise parameter estimation.

3. The sum of squares in equation 7.3.2 measures the variation in the explanatory variable $x_{t2}$ about its mean. In order to estimate $\beta_2$ precisely, we would like there to be a large amount of variation in $x_{t2}$, just as in the simple regression model. The intuition here is that it is easier to measure $\beta_2$, the

change in $y$ we expect given a change in $x_2$, the more sample variation (change) in the values of $x_2$ that we observe.

4.  In the denominator of var($b_2$) is the term $1-r_{23}^2$, where $r_{23}$ is the correlation between the sample values of $x_{t2}$ and $x_{t3}$. Recall that the correlation coefficient measures the linear association between two variables. If the values of $x_{t2}$ and $x_{t3}$ are correlated then $1-r_{23}^2$ is a fraction that is less than 1. The larger the correlation between $x_{t2}$ and $x_{t3}$ the larger is the variance of the least squares estimator $b_2$. The reason for this fact is that variation in $x_{t2}$ about its mean in equation 7.3.2 adds most to the precision of estimation when it is not connected to variation in the other explanatory variables. "Independent" variables ideally exhibit variation that is "independent" of the variation in other explanatory variables. When the variation in one explanatory variable is connected to variation in another explanatory variable, it is difficult to disentangle their separate effects. In Chapter 8 we discuss "multicollinearity," which is the situation when the independent variables are correlated with one another. Multicollinearity leads to increased variances of the least squares estimators.

These factors affect the variances of the least squares estimators in larger models in the same way.

It is customary to arrange the estimated variances and covariances of the least squares estimators in an array, or matrix, with variances on the diagonal and covariances in the off-diagonal positions. For the $K = 3$ model the arrangement is

$$\text{cov}(b_1, b_2, b_3) = \begin{bmatrix} \text{var}(b_1) & \text{cov}(b_1, b_2) & \text{cov}(b_1, b_3) \\ \text{cov}(b_1, b_2) & \text{var}(b_2) & \text{cov}(b_2, b_3) \\ \text{cov}(b_1, b_3) & \text{cov}(b_2, b_3) & \text{var}(b_3) \end{bmatrix} \qquad (7.3.3)$$

Using the estimate $\hat{\sigma}^2 = 36.84$ found in equation 7.2.12 and our computer software package, the estimated variances and covariances for $b_1, b_2, b_3$, in the Bay Area Rapid Food hamburger chain example are

$$\hat{\text{cov}}(b_1, b_2, b_3) = \begin{bmatrix} 42.026 & -19.863 & -0.16111 \\ -19.863 & 10.184 & -0.05402 \\ -0.16111 & -0.05402 & 0.02787 \end{bmatrix} \qquad (7.3.4)$$

Thus, we have

$$\begin{array}{ll} \hat{\text{var}}(b_1) = 42.026 & \hat{\text{cov}}(b_1, b_2) = -19.863 \\ \hat{\text{var}}(b_2) = 10.184 & \hat{\text{cov}}(b_1, b_3) = -0.16111 \\ \hat{\text{var}}(b_3) = 0.02787 & \hat{\text{cov}}(b_2, b_3) = -0.05402 \end{array}$$

These estimated variances can be used to say something about the range of the least squares estimates if we were to obtain other samples of 52 weeks of data for the burger franchise. For example, the standard error of $b_2$ is given by the square root of 10.184, or approximately se($b_2$) = 3.2. We know that the least squares estimator is unbiased, so its mean value is $E(b_2) = \beta_2$. If $b_2$ is normally distributed, then based on statistical theory we expect 95 percent of the estimates $b_2$, obtained by applying the least squares estimator to other samples, to be within about two standard deviations of the mean $\beta_2$. Given our sample, $2 \times se(b_2) = 6.4$, so we estimate that 95 percent of the $b_2$ values would lie within 6.4 of $\beta_2$. It is in this sense that the estimated variance of $\beta_2$ tells us something about the reliability of the least squares estimates. If the difference between $b_2$ and $\beta_2$ can be large, $b_2$ is not reliable; if the difference between $b_2$ and $\beta_2$ is likely to be small, then $b_2$ is reliable. Whether a particular difference is "large" or "small" will depend on the context of the problem and the use to which the estimates are to be put. In later sections we use the estimated variances and covariances to test hypotheses about the parameters and to construct interval estimates.

### 7.3.2  THE PROPERTIES OF THE LEAST SQUARES ESTIMATORS ASSUMING NORMALLY DISTRIBUTED ERRORS

We have asserted that under assumptions 1–5, listed at the end of Section 7.1.2b, for the multiple regression model,

$$y_t = \beta_1 + \beta_2 x_{t2} + \beta_3 x_{t3} + \cdots + \beta_K x_{tK} + e_t \tag{7.3.5}$$

the least squares estimator $b_k$ is the best linear unbiased estimator of the parameter $\beta_k$. If we add assumption 6, that the random errors $e_t$ have normal probability distributions, then the dependent variable $y_t$ is normally distributed,

$$y_t \sim N[(\beta_1 + \beta_2 x_{t2} + \cdots + \beta_K x_{tK}), \sigma^2] \Leftrightarrow e_t \sim N(0,\sigma^2)$$

Since the least squares estimators are linear functions of dependent variables, it follows that the least squares estimators are normally distributed also,

$$b_k \sim N[\beta_k, \text{var}(b_k)] \tag{7.3.6}$$

That is, each $b_k$ has a normal distribution with mean $\beta_k$ and variance $\text{var}(b_k)$. By subtracting its mean and dividing by the square root of its variance, we can transform the normal random variable $b_k$ into the **standard normal variable** $z$,

$$z = \frac{b_k - \beta_k}{\sqrt{\text{var}(b_k)}} \sim N(0,1), \text{ for } k = 1, 2, \cdots, K \tag{7.3.7}$$

that has mean zero and a variance of one. The variance of $b_k$ depends on the unknown variance of the error term, $\sigma^2$, as illustrated in equation 7.3.1 for the $K = 3$ case. When we replace $\sigma^2$ by its estimator $\hat{\sigma}^2$, from equation 7.2.12, we obtain the estimated $\text{var}(b_k)$, which we denote as $\hat{\text{var}}(b_k)$. When $\text{var}(b_k)$ is replaced by $\hat{\text{var}}(b_k)$ in equation 7.3.7 we obtain a $t$ random variable instead of the normal variable. That is,

$$t = \frac{b_k - \beta_k}{\sqrt{\hat{\text{var}}(b_k)}} \sim t_{(T-K)} \tag{7.3.8}$$

One difference between this result and that in Chapter 5 (see equation 5.1.4) is the degrees of freedom of the $t$ random variable. In Chapter 5, where there were two coefficients to be estimated, the number of degrees of freedom was $(T - 2)$. In this chapter there are $K$ unknown coefficients in the general model and *the number of degrees of freedom for t-statistics is* $(T - K)$.

The square root of the variance estimator $\text{vâr}(b_k)$ is called the standard error of $b_k$, which is written as

$$se(b_k) = \sqrt{\text{vâr}(b_k)} \qquad (7.3.9)$$

Consequently, we will usually express the $t$ random variable as

$$t = \frac{b_k - \beta_k}{se(b_k)} \sim t_{(T-K)} \qquad (7.3.10)$$

We now examine how the result in equation 7.3.10 can be used for interval estimation. The procedures are identical to those described in Chapter 5; only the degrees of freedom change. The discussion will therefore be brief.

## 7.4 Interval Estimation

Interval estimates of unknown parameters are based on the probability statement that

$$P\left(-t_c \le \frac{b_k - \beta_k}{se(b_k)} \le t_c\right) = 1 - \alpha \qquad (7.4.1)$$

Where $t_c$ is the critical value for the $t$-distribution with $(T-K)$ degrees of freedom, such that $P(t \ge t_c) = \alpha/2$. Rearranging equation 7.4.1, we obtain

$$P[b_k - t_c se(b_k) \le \beta_k \le b_k + t_c se(b_k)] = 1 - \alpha \qquad (7.4.2)$$

The interval endpoints,

$$[b_k - t_c se(b_k), \ b_k + t_c se(b_k)] \qquad (7.4.3)$$

define a $100(1 - \alpha)$ percent confidence interval estimator of $\beta_k$. If this interval estimator is used in many samples from the population, then 95 percent of them will contain the true parameter $\beta_k$. This fact we can establish based on the model assumptions alone, before any data are collected. Thus, "pre-data," we have confidence in this *interval estimation procedure (estimator)* when it is used repeatedly.

Returning to the equation used to describe how the hamburger chain's revenue depends on price and advertising expenditure, we have

$$T = 52 \qquad K = 3$$

$$b_1 = 104.79 \quad se(b_1) = \sqrt{\text{vâr}(b_1)} = 6.483$$

$$b_2 = -6.642 \quad se(b_2) = \sqrt{\text{vâr}(b_2)} = 3.191$$

$$b_3 = 2.984 \quad se(b_3) = \sqrt{\text{vâr}(b_3)} = 0.1669$$

We will use this information to construct interval estimates for

$\beta_2$ = the response of revenue to a price change

$\beta_3$ = the response of revenue to a change in advertising expenditure

To construct a 95 percent confidence interval for $\beta_2$, we make use of equation 7.4.3. The degrees of freedom are given by $(T - K) = (52 - 3) = 49$. The critical value $t_c = 2.01$ does not appear in the tabulated values for the $t$-distribution found in Table 2 at the front of the book. However, it can be approximated by interpolating between these values or by using statistical software.

A 95 percent confidence interval for $\beta_2$ based on our particular sample is obtained from equation 7.4.3 by replacing $b_2$ and se($b_2$) by their estimates $b_2 = -6.642$ and se($b_2$) = 3.191. Thus, our 95 percent interval estimate for $\beta_2$ is given by $(-13.06, -0.23)$.

This interval estimate suggests that decreasing price by \$1 will lead to an increase in revenue somewhere between \$230 and \$13,060. This is a wide interval, and it is not very informative. Another way of describing this situation is to say that the point estimate of $b_2 = -6.642$ is not very reliable, as its standard error (which measures sampling variability) is relatively large.

In general, if an interval estimate is uninformative because it is too wide, there is nothing immediate that can be done. A wide confidence interval for the parameter $\beta_2$ arises because the estimated sampling variability of the least squares estimator $b_2$ is large. In the computation of a confidence interval, a large sampling variability is reflected by a large standard error. A narrower interval can only be obtained by reducing the variance of the estimator. Based on the variance expression in equation 7.3.1, one solution is to obtain more and better data, exhibiting more independent variation. This alternative is usually not open to economists, who do not use controlled experiments to obtain data. Alternatively, we might introduce some kind of nonsample information on the coefficients. The question of how to use both sample and nonsample information in the estimation process is taken up in Chapter 8.

Returning to the Bay Area Rapid Food example, we find the 95 percent interval estimate for $\beta_3$, the response of revenue to advertising, as $(2.65, 3.32)$.

This interval is relatively narrow and informative. We estimate that an increase in advertising expenditure of \$1000 leads to an increase in total revenue that is somewhere between \$2,650 and \$3,320.

## 7.5 Summing Up

1. There are many economic models where a dependent variable is a function of a number of explanatory variables. A linear statistical model where there is more than one explanatory variable is called a multiple regression model.

2. A multiple regression model with $(K - 1)$ explanatory variables plus a constant term, and $K$ unknown coefficients, can be written as $y_t = \beta_1 + x_{t2}\beta_2 + x_{t3}\beta_3 + \ldots + x_{tK}\beta_K + e_t$. The parameters $\beta_k$ measure the change in $E(y_t)$ given a one-unit change in $x_{tk}$, all other variables held constant.

3. We continue with the random error assumptions employed earlier, namely that the random errors are uncorrelated and $e_t \sim (0, \sigma^2)$. Also, no exact linear relationships exist between the explanatory variables. It is also sometimes assumed that $e_t \sim N(0, \sigma^2)$.

4. To find estimators for the unknown parameters $\beta_k$, we apply the least squares principle.

5. The least squares estimator $b_k$ of $\beta_k$ is the Best Linear Unbiased Estimator. It has a smaller variance than any other linear unbiased estimator for $\beta_k$. If the random errors are normally distributed, or if the sample size is large, then $b_k$ is also normally distributed.

6. An unbiased estimator of the error variance $\sigma^2$ is given by the sum of squared least squares residuals divided by $(T-K)$. That is, $\hat{\sigma}^2 = \dfrac{\Sigma \hat{e}_t^2}{T-K}$ where $\hat{e}_t = y_t - (b_1 + b_2 x_{t2} + \ldots + b_K x_{tK})$.

7. The variances and covariances of the least squares estimator are arranged into an array called the covariance matrix of the least squares estimator:

$$\text{cov}(b_1, b_2, \cdots, b_K) = \begin{bmatrix} \text{var}(b_1) & \text{cov}(b_1, b_2) & \cdots & \text{cov}(b_1, b_K) \\ \text{cov}(b_1, b_2) & \text{var}(b_2) & & \text{cov}(b_2, b_K) \\ \vdots & & \ddots & \vdots \\ \text{cov}(b_1, b_K) & \text{cov}(b_2, b_K) & \cdots & \text{var}(b_K) \end{bmatrix}$$

8. The factors affecting the magnitude of the variance of $b_k$, and thus the precision of estimation, are $\sigma^2$, $T$, and the amount of independent variation in the variable $x_{tk}$.

9. Interval estimates of individual parameters, and tests concerning them, assuming the errors are normal or the sample is large, are based on $t = \dfrac{b_k - \beta_k}{\text{se}(b_k)} \sim t_{(T-K)}$.

10. A $100(1-\alpha)$ percent interval estimate of $\beta_k$ is $[b_k - t_c \text{se}(b_k), b_k + t_c \text{se}(b_k)]$, where $t_c$ is the upper $\alpha/2$ critical value from a $t_{(T-K)}$ distribution.

## 7.6 Exercises

7.1* Consider the multiple regression model

$$y_t = x_{t1}\beta_1 + x_{t2}\beta_2 + x_{t3}\beta_3 + e_t$$

with the 9 observations on $y_t$, $x_{t1}$, $x_{t2}$ and $x_{t3}$ given in Table 7.2.
(a) Set up the system of equations that must be solved to provide the least squares estimates. (Hint: Consider equations 7.2.4, but make allowance for the fact that there is no "intercept" variable in this model.)
(b) Use a hand calculator to find
  (i) $\sum_t x_{tk}x_{tj}$ and $\sum_t x_{tk}y_t$
  (ii) the least squares estimates $b_1, b_2, b_3$

*Table 7.2*   **Data for Exercise 7.1**

| $y_t$ | $x_{t1}$ | $x_{t2}$ | $x_{t3}$ |
|-------|----------|----------|----------|
| 1     | 1        | 0        | −1       |
| −1    | −1       | 1        | 0        |
| 2     | 1        | 0        | 0        |
| 0     | 0        | 1        | 0        |
| 4     | 1        | 2        | 0        |
| 2     | 0        | 3        | 0        |
| 2     | 0        | 0        | 1        |
| 0     | 1        | −1       | 1        |
| 2     | 0        | 0        | 1        |

(iii) the least squares residuals $\hat{e}_1, \hat{e}_2, \ldots, \hat{e}_9$.

(iv) the variance estimate $\hat{\sigma}^2$.

(c) Use a computer to verify the results you obtained in (b) and to obtain

   (i)   the estimated covariance matrix for $b_1, b_2, b_3$

   (ii)  the standard errors for $b_1, b_2,$ and $b_3$

   (iii) 95 percent and 99 percent interval estimates for $\beta_1, \beta_2$ and $\beta_3$

7.2   Data on per capita consumption of beef, the price of beef, the price of lamb, the price of pork, and per capita disposable income for Australia, for the period 1949–1965, are given in the file *meat.dat*. All prices and income have been deflated, with 1953 as the base year. Consider the log–log demand curve

$$\ln (qb_t) = \beta_1 + \beta_2 \ln (pb_t) + \beta_3 \ln (pl_t) + \beta_4 \ln (pp_t) + \beta_5 \ln (in_t) + e_t$$

where

$qb_t$ is per capita consumption of beef in year $t$ (pounds),

$pb_t$ is the price of beef in year $t$ (pence per pound),

$pl_t$ is the price of lamb in year $t$ (pence per pound),

$pp_t$ is the price of pork in year $t$ (pence per pound), and

$in_t$ is per capita disposable income in year $t$ (Australian currency pounds).

(a) What signs do you expect on each of the coefficients?

(b) Estimate $\beta_1, \beta_2, \beta_3, \beta_4$ and $\beta_5$ using least squares. Interpret the results. Do they seem reasonable?

(c) Compute and interpret the estimated covariance matrix for the least squares estimator and the standard errors.

(d) Compute 95 percent interval estimates for each of the parameters.

7.3   Consider the following total cost function where $y_t$ represents total cost for the $t$-th firm and $x_t$ represents quantity of output.

$$y_t = \beta_1 + \beta_2 x_t + \beta_3 x_t^2 + \beta_4 x_t^3 + e_t$$

Data on a sample of 28 firms in the clothing industry are in the file *clothes.dat*.

(a) Write down the marginal cost function corresponding to the above total cost function. What sign would you expect for $\beta_4$?

(b) Write down the average cost function that corresponds to the above total cost function.

(c) Use the total cost function to find least squares estimates of $\beta_1$, $\beta_2$, $\beta_3$ and $\beta_4$. Graph the total, average and marginal cost functions implied by these estimates.

(d) Compute 95% interval estimates of the parameters.

(e) At what output price is it profitable for firms to produce? How many firms in the sample are producing unprofitable outputs?

(f) Find estimates of $\beta_1$, $\beta_2$, $\beta_3$ and $\beta_4$ by applying least squares to the average cost function you derived in (b). Are the standard errors of the estimates greater or less than those that were obtained in (c) when the total cost function was used? Is it possible to make any conjectures about which set of estimates might be "best?"

7.4 Consider the following aggregate production function for the U.S. manufacturing sector

$$Y_t = f(K_t, L_t, E_t, M_t)$$

where $Y_t$ is gross output in time $t$, $K_t$ is capital, $L_t$ is labor, $E_t$ is energy, and $M_t$ is other intermediate materials. The data underlying these variables are given in index form in the file *manuf.dat*. Assume the statistical model $Y_t = \alpha K_t^{\beta_2} L_t^{\beta_3} E_t^{\beta_4} M_t^{\beta_5} \exp\{e_t\}$ where $e_t \sim N(0, \sigma^2)$.

(a) Estimate the unknown parameters of the production function, and find the corresponding standard errors.

(b) Discuss the economic and statistical implications of these results.

## 7.7 References

GRIFFITHS, W. E., R. C. HILL, AND G. G. JUDGE (1993). *Learning and Practicing Econometrics*. New York: John Wiley and Sons, Chapters 9–10.2.

GUJARATI, DAMODAR (1995). *Basic Econometrics, 3rd Edition*. New York: McGraw-Hill, Inc., pp. 191–200.

MIRER, THAD W. (1995). *Econometric Statistics and Econometrics, 3rd Edition*. Englewood Cliffs, NJ: Prentice Hall, pp. 132–142.

# Chapter 8

# The Multiple Regression Model: Hypothesis Tests and the Use of Nonsample Information

Economists develop and evaluate theories about economic behavior. Hypothesis testing procedures are used to test their theories. We develop and apply $t$-tests of individual hypotheses in this chapter, similar to those in Chapter 5 for the simple regression model. An important new development that we encounter in this chapter is using the $F$-distribution to simultaneously test a null hypothesis consisting of two or more hypotheses about the parameters in the multiple regression model.

The theories that economists develop also sometimes provide *nonsample* information that can be used along with the information in a sample of data to estimate the parameters of a regression model. A procedure that combines these two types of information is called **restricted least squares.** It can be a useful technique when the data are not information-rich, a condition called multicollinearity, and the theoretical information is good. The restricted least squares procedure also plays a useful practical role when testing hypotheses.

In addition to these topics we discuss goodness-of-fit measures for the multiple regression model and the construction of "prediction" intervals.

We use the Bay Area Rapid Food hamburger chain example from Chapter 7 to introduce hypothesis testing concepts. As you recall from Chapter 7.1, we model weekly total revenue ($tr$) of the hamburger chain as a function of a price index of all products sold ($p$) and weekly expenditure on advertising ($a$). The statistical model is

$$tr = \beta_1 + \beta_2 p + \beta_3 a + e$$

or, in general terms,

$$y = \beta_1 + \beta_2 x_2 + \beta_3 x_3 + e$$

In this chapter we adopt assumptions 1–6, including normality, listed at the end of Chapter 7.1.2b. If the errors are not normal, then the results presented in this chapter will hold approximately if the sample is large. The least squares estimates of the total revenue model, based on the data in Table 7.1, are presented in Chapter

7.2.2 and the standard errors are obtained in Chapter 7.3.1. We use this model to illustrate hypothesis tests in Sections 8.1 to 8.4. The model and analysis are extended in Sections 8.5 to 8.6.

## *8.1* One-Tailed Hypothesis Testing for a Single Coefficient

In Section 7.1 we noted that two important considerations for the management of the Bay Area Rapid Food hamburger chain were whether demand was price elastic or inelastic and whether the additional revenue from additional advertising expenditure would cover the costs of the advertising. We now are in a position to state these questions as testable hypotheses, and to ask whether the hypotheses are compatible with the data.

With respect to demand elasticity, we wish to know if:

- $\beta_2 \geq 0$: a decrease in price leads to a decrease in total revenue (demand is price inelastic)
- $\beta_2 < 0$: a decrease in price leads to an increase in total revenue (demand is price elastic)

If we are not prepared to accept that demand is elastic unless there is strong evidence from the data to support this claim, it is appropriate to take the assumption of an inelastic demand as our null hypothesis. Following our standard testing format, developed in Chapter 5.2, and the discussion of one-tailed tests in Chapter 5.2.9, we first state the null and alternative hypotheses:

1. $H_0 : \beta_2 \geq 0$ (demand is unit elastic or inelastic)
2. $H_1 : \beta_2 < 0$ (demand is elastic)
3. To create a test statistic we act as if the null hypothesis were the equality $\beta_2 = 0$. If this null hypothesis is true, then from (7.3.10) the $t$-statistic is $t = \dfrac{b_k}{se(b_k)} \sim t_{(T-K)}$. This result we know prior to the collection of any data. It is based only on the model assumptions.
4. The rejection region consists of values from the $t$-distribution that are unlikely to occur if the null hypothesis is true. If we define "unlikely" in terms of a 5% significance level, we answer this question by finding a critical value $t_c$ such that $P[t_{(T-K)} \leq t_c] = 0.05$. Then, we reject $H_0$ if $t \leq t_c$. Given a sample of $T = 52$ data observations, the degrees of freedom are $T - K = 49$ and the $t$-critical value is $t_c = -1.68$.
5. The value of the test statistic is

$$t = \frac{b_2}{se(b_2)} = \frac{-6.642}{3.191} = -2.08 \tag{8.1.1}$$

Since $t = -2.08 < t_c = -1.68$, we reject $H_0 : \beta_2 \geq 0$ and conclude $H_1 : \beta_2 < 0$ (demand is elastic) is more compatible with the data. The sample evidence supports the proposition that a reduction in price will bring about an increase in total revenue.

An alternative to comparing the computed value $-2.08$ to the critical value $t_c = -1.68$ is to compute the $p$-value that is given by $P[t_{(49)} < -2.08]$ and to reject $H_0$ if this $p$-value is less than 0.05. Using our computer software, we find that $P[t_{(49)} < -2.08] = 0.021$. Since $0.021 < 0.05$, the same conclusion is reached.

The other hypothesis of interest is whether an increase in advertising expenditure will bring an increase in total revenue that is sufficient to cover the increased cost of advertising. This will occur if $\beta_3 > 1$. Setting up the test, we have:

1.   $H_0 : \beta_3 \leq 1$
2.   $H_1 : \beta_3 > 1$
3.   We compute a value for the $t$-statistic as if the null hypothesis were $\beta_3 = 1$. Using equation 7.3.10 we have, if the null hypothesis is true, $t = \dfrac{b_3 - 1}{\mathrm{se}(b_3)} \sim$ $t_{(T-K)}$.
4.   In this case, if the level of significance is $\alpha = .05$, we reject $H_0$ if $t \geq t_c = 1.68$.
5.   The value of the test statistic is:

$$t = \frac{b_3 - \beta_3}{\mathrm{se}(b_3)} = \frac{2.984 - 1}{0.1669} = 11.89$$

Since 11.89 is much greater than 1.68, we do indeed reject $H_0$ and accept the alternative $\beta_3 > 1$ as more compatible with the data. Also, the $p$-value in this case is essentially zero (less than $10^{-12}$). Thus, we have *statistical evidence* that an increase in advertising expenditure will be justified by the increase in revenue. Of course, to totally justify the increase in advertising expenditure, we also need to consider the cost of producing the extra hamburgers that have led to the increase in revenue.

Because both of the foregoing tests are one-sided tests, a critical value from just one side of the $t$-distribution is considered in each case. For testing $\beta_2$, the critical value of $-1.68$ from the left side of the distribution was considered; for $\beta_3$ the critical value of 1.68 from the right side of the distribution was considered. We turn now to examples of two-tailed tests, where critical values from both sides of the $t$-distribution are used.

## 8.2  Testing the Significance of a Single Coefficient

When we set up a multiple regression model, we do so because we believe all the $(K - 1)$ explanatory variables influence the dependent variable $y$. If we are to confirm this belief, we need to examine whether or not it is supported by the data. That is, we need to ask whether the data provide any evidence to suggest that $y$ is related to each of the explanatory variables. If a given explanatory variable, say $x_k$, has no bearing on $y$, then $\beta_k = 0$. Testing this null hypothesis is sometimes called a "test of significance" for the explanatory variable $x_k$. Thus, to find whether the data contain any evidence suggesting $y$ is related to $x_k$ we test the null hypothesis

$$H_0 : \beta_k = 0$$

against the alternative hypothesis

$$H_1 : \beta_k \neq 0$$

To carry out the test we use the test equation 7.3.10, which, if the null hypothesis is true, is

$$t = \frac{b_k}{se(b_k)} \sim t_{(T-K)}$$

For the alternative hypothesis "not equal to" we use a two-tailed test, introduced in Chapter 5.2.3–5.2.4, and reject $H_0$ if the computed $t$-value is greater than or equal to $t_c$ (the critical value from the right side of the distribution), or less than or equal to $-t_c$ (the critical value from the left side of the distribution).

In the Bay Area Rapid Food example we test, following our standard testing format, whether revenue is related to price:

1.  $H_0 : \beta_2 = 0$
2.  $H_1 : \beta_2 \neq 0$

3.  The test statistic, if the null hypothesis is true, is $t = \dfrac{b_2}{se(b_2)} \sim t_{(T-K)}$.

4.  With 49 degrees of freedom and a 5 percent significance level, the critical values that lead to a probability of 0.025 in each tail of the distribution are $t_c = 2.01$ and $-t_c = -2.01$. Thus, we reject the null hypothesis if $t \geq 2.01$ or if $t \leq -2.01$. In shorthand notation, we reject the null hypothesis if $|t| \geq 2.01$.

5.  The computed value of the $t$-statistic is

$$t = \frac{-6.642}{3.191} = -2.08$$

Since $-2.08 < -2.01$, we reject $H_0 : \beta_2 = 0$ and conclude that there is evidence from the data to suggest revenue depends on price. Note that the computed value in this case is identical to that obtained in Section 8.1 when we were testing $H_0 : \beta_2 \leq 0$, but the critical values are different. Also, the $p$-value in this case is given by $P[|t_{(49)}| > 2.08] = 2 \times 0.021 = 0.042$. Using this procedure we reject $H_0$ because $0.042 < 0.05$.

For testing whether revenue is related to advertising expenditure, we have

1.  $H_0 : \beta_3 = 0$
2.  $H_1 : \beta_3 \neq 0$

3.  The test statistic, if the null hypothesis is true, is $t = \dfrac{b_3}{se(b_3)} \sim t_{(T-K)}$.

4.  We reject the null hypothesis if $|t| \geq 2.01$.

5.  The value of the test statistic is

$$t = \frac{2.984}{0.1669} = 17.88$$

Because $17.88 > t_c = 2.01$, the data support the conjecture that revenue is related to advertising expenditure.

More general null hypotheses can be tested using the $t$-statistic, as noted in Chapter 5.2.8. In Section 8.6 of this chapter we extend the use of the $t$-test to a more general context.

## 8.3 Measuring Goodness of Fit and Reporting the Regression Results

### 8.3.1 COEFFICIENT OF DETERMINATION

In Chapter 6, for the simple regression model, we introduced $R^2$ as a measure of the proportion of variation in the dependent variable that is explained by variation in the explanatory variable. In the multiple regression model the same measure is relevant, and the same formulas are valid, but now we talk of the proportion of variation in the dependent variable explained by *all* the explanatory variables in the linear model. The coefficient of determination is

$$R^2 = \frac{SSR}{SST} = \frac{\Sigma(\hat{y}_t - \bar{y})^2}{\Sigma(y_t - \bar{y})^2}$$

$$= 1 - \frac{SSE}{SST} = 1 - \frac{\Sigma\hat{e}_t^2}{\Sigma(y_t - \bar{y})^2}$$

(8.3.1)

where $SSR$ is the variation in $y$ "explained" by the model, $SST$ is the total variation in $y$ about its mean, and $SSE$ is the sum of squared least squares residuals and is the portion of the variation in $y$ that is not explained by the model. The values of these sums of squares appear in the analysis of variance (or ANOVA) table reported by regression software.

For the Bay Area Rapid Food example, the ANOVA table includes the information in Table 8.1.

*Table 8.1*  **Partial ANOVA Table**

| Source | DF | Sum of Squares |
|---|---|---|
| Explained | 2 | 11776.18 |
| Unexplained | 49 | 1805.168 |
| Total | 51 | 13581.35 |

Using these sums of squares, which you are asked to verify in Exercise 8.1, we have

$$R^2 = 1 - \frac{\Sigma \hat{e}_t^2}{\Sigma(y_t - \bar{y})^2} = 1 - \frac{1805.168}{13581.35} = 0.867 \qquad (8.3.2)$$

The interpretation of $R^2$ is that 86.7 percent of the variation in total revenue is explained by the variation in price and by the variation in the level of advertising expenditure. It means that, *in our sample,* only 13.3 percent of the variation in revenue is left unexplained and is due to variation in the error term or to variation in other variables that implicitly form part of the error term.

As mentioned in Chapter 6.1.2, the coefficient of determination is also viewed as a measure of the predictive ability of the model over the sample period, or as a measure of how well the estimated regression fits the data. The value of $R^2$ is equal to the squared sample correlation coefficient between the $\hat{y}_t$ and the $y_t$. Since the sample correlation measures the linear association between two variables, if the $R^2$ is high, that means there is a close association between the values of $y_t$ and the values predicted by the model, $\hat{y}_t$. In this case, the model is said to "fit" the data well. If $R^2$ is low, there is not a close association between the values of $y_t$ and the values predicted by the model, $\hat{y}_t$, and the model does not fit the data well.

One difficulty with $R^2$ is that it can be made large by adding more and more variables, even if the variables added have no economic justification. Algebraically it is a fact that as variables are added the sum of squared errors $SSE$ goes down (it can remain unchanged, but this is rare) and thus, $R^2$ goes up. If the model contains $T - 1$ variables, the $R^2 = 1$. The manipulation of a model just to obtain a high $R^2$ is not wise.

An alternative measure of goodness of fit, called the adjusted $R^2$, and often symbolized as $\bar{R}^2$, is usually reported by regression programs; it is computed as

$$\bar{R}^2 = 1 - \frac{SSE / (T - K)}{SST / (T - 1)}$$

For the Bay Area data the value of this descriptive measure is $\bar{R}^2 = .8617$ This measure does not always go up when a variable is added, because of the degrees of freedom term $T - K$ in the numerator. As the number of variables $K$ increases, $SSE$ goes down, but so does $T - K$. The effect on $\bar{R}^2$ depends on the amount by which $SSE$ falls. While solving one problem, this corrected measure of goodness of fit unfortunately introduces another one. It loses its interpretation; $\bar{R}^2$ is no longer the percent of variation explained. This modified $\bar{R}^2$ is sometimes used and misused as a device for selecting the appropriate set of explanatory variables. This practice should be avoided. Let's concentrate on the unadjusted $R^2$ and think of it as a descriptive device for telling us about the "fit" of the model; it tells us the proportion of variation in the dependent variable explained by the explanatory variables, and the predictive ability of the model over the sample period.

One final note is in order. The intercept parameter $\beta_1$ is the $y$-intercept of the regression "plane," as shown in Figure 7.1. If, for theoretical reasons, you are certain that the regression plane passes through the origin, then $\beta_1 = 0$ and can be omitted from the model. Although this is not a common practice, it does occur, and regression software includes an option that removes the intercept from the model. If the model does not contain an intercept parameter, then the measure $R^2$

given in equation 8.3.1 is no longer appropriate. The reason it is no longer appropriate is that, without an intercept term in the model,

$$\Sigma(y_t - \bar{y})^2 \neq \Sigma(\hat{y}_t - \bar{y})^2 + \Sigma\hat{e}_t^2$$

or

$$SST \neq SSR + SSE$$

Under these circumstances it does not make sense to talk of the proportion of total variation that is explained by the regression. Two alternatives are possible. One is to not report an $R^2$ value if the model does not contain a constant. The other is to measure variation around zero instead of around the sample mean $\bar{y}$ In this latter case we have

$$R_*^2 = 1 - \frac{\Sigma\hat{e}_t^2}{\Sigma y_t^2}$$

### 8.3.2    REPORTING THE REGRESSION RESULTS

A convenient way to report a summary of a multiple regression is to write down the estimated equation, with standard errors of coefficients written in parentheses below the estimated coefficients, and with the $R^2$ value written next to the equation. This approach was adopted for the simple linear model in Chapter 6. Extending this approach to the model estimated in this chapter, a summary of the results can then be reported as

$$\hat{tr}_t = 104.79 - 6.642p_t + 2.984a_t \qquad R^2 = 0.867 \tag{8.3.3}$$
$$\phantom{\hat{tr}_t = } (6.48) \quad (3.191) \quad (0.167) \qquad (s.e.)$$

where the numbers in parentheses are the standard errors of the estimated coefficients.

The usefulness of reporting the results in this way should be clear. From this summary we can read off the estimated effects of changes in the explanatory variables on the dependent variable and we can predict values of the dependent variable for given values of the explanatory variables. For the construction of an interval estimate we need the least squares estimate, its standard error, and a critical value from the $t$-distribution. For a 95 percent confidence interval and at least moderate degrees of freedom, the critical $t$-value is approximately 2. Thus, from the information in equation 8.3.3, an approximate 95 percent confidence interval can be obtained by mentally calculating the points two standard errors either side of the least squares estimate.

Similarly, the $t$-value used to test a null hypothesis of the form $H_0 : \beta_k = 0$ is given by the ratio of the least squares estimate to its standard error that appears underneath. It, too, can be calculated mentally by inspection of equation 8.3.3. If the ratio of an estimate to its standard error is absolutely greater than 2 (approximately), you know that a null hypothesis of the form $H_0 : \beta_k = 0$ would be rejected. Furthermore, as discussed in Chapter 5.2.11, from an interval estimate we can tell whether any hypothesis of the form $H_0 : \beta_k = c$ would be rejected or not in a two-

***Table 8.2*    Summary of Least Squares Results**

| Variable | Coefficient | Standard Error | $t$-value | $p$-value |
|---|---|---|---|---|
| constant | 104.79 | 6.48 | 16.17 | 0.000 |
| price | −6.642 | 3.191 | 2.081 | 0.042 |
| advertising | 2.984 | 0.167 | 17.868 | 0.000 |

tailed test. If $c$ is within the interval, $H_0$ is not rejected, otherwise $H_0$ is rejected. Remembering these quick "inspection techniques" will help you make "on the spot" assessments of reported results.

Sometimes results are reported with $t$-values in parentheses, rather than standard errors. In this case we have

$$\hat{tr} = 104.79 - 6.642p_t + 2.984a_t$$
$$(16.17)\,(-2.081)\,\,(17.868) \qquad\qquad (t) \qquad\qquad (8.3.4)$$

From any estimated equation that has been reported in a conventional way, you should be able to immediately read off, or calculate, point and interval estimates for all the coefficients.

In Table 8.2 the information in Equations 8.3.3 and 8.3.4 is presented in the way that it usually appears on computer output. The format is identical to that given in Table 6.2.

## 8.4 Testing the Significance of the Model

In Section 8.2 we tested whether the dependent variable $y$ is related to a particular explanatory variable $x_k$ using a $t$-test. In this section we extend this idea to a joint test of the relevance of *all* the included explanatory variables. Consider again the general multiple regression model with $(K - 1)$ explanatory variables and $K$ unknown coefficients

$$y_t = \beta_1 + x_{t2}\beta_2 + x_{t3}\beta_3 + \cdots + x_{tK}\beta_K + e_t \qquad\qquad (8.4.1)$$

To examine whether we have a viable explanatory model, we set up the following null and alternative hypotheses

$$H_0 : \beta_2 = 0, \, \beta_3 = 0, \, \cdots, \, \beta_K = 0 \qquad\qquad (8.4.2)$$
$$H_1 : at\ least\ one\ \text{of the } \beta_k \text{ is nonzero}$$

The null hypothesis has $K - 1$ parts, and it is called a joint hypothesis. It states as a conjecture that each and every one of the parameters $\beta_k$, other than the intercept parameter $\beta_1$, is zero. If this null hypothesis is true, none of the explanatory variables influence $y$, and thus our model is of little or no value. If the alternative hypothesis $H_1$ is true, then at least one of the parameters is not zero, and thus, one or more of the explanatory variables should be included in the model. The alternative hypothesis does not indicate, however, which variables those might be. Since we are testing whether or not we have a viable explanatory model, the test for equation

8.4.2 is sometimes referred to as a *test of the overall significance of the regression model.* The *t*-distribution can be used to test a single null hypothesis, but no more. To test the joint null hypothesis $H_0 : \beta_2 = \beta_3 = \cdots = \beta_K = 0$, which actually is $K - 1$ hypotheses, we will use a test based on the *F*-distribution that was introduced in Chapter 2.7.

### 8.4.1   THE *F*-TEST

The test procedure for any set of hypotheses can be based on a comparison of the sum of squared errors from the original, unrestricted multiple regression model to the sum of squared errors from a regression model in which the null hypothesis is assumed to be true. When a null hypothesis is assumed to be true, we in effect place conditions, or constraints, on the values that the parameters can take, and the sum of squared errors increases. The idea of the test is that if these sums of squared errors are substantially different, then the assumption that the joint null hypothesis is true has significantly reduced the ability of the model to fit the data, and thus the data do not support the null hypothesis. If the null hypothesis is true, we expect that the data are compatible with the conditions placed on the parameters. Thus, there would be little change in the sum of squared errors when the null hypothesis is assumed to be true.

Let us call the sum of squared errors in the model that assumes a null hypothesis to be true the *restricted sum of squared errors,* or $SSE_R$, where the subscript "*R*" indicates that the parameters have been restricted or constrained. To make a clear distinction between the restricted sum of squared errors and the sum of squared errors from the original, unrestricted model, we will call the sum of squared errors from the original model, the one whose parameters we are testing, the *unrestricted sum of squared errors,* or $SSE_U$. It is *always* true that $SSE_R - SSE_U \geq 0$. If $J$ denotes the number of hypotheses, then the *F*-test statistic is

$$F = \frac{(SSE_R - SSE_U) / J}{SSE_U / (T - K)} \tag{8.4.3}$$

*If the null hypothesis is true,* then the statistic $F$ follows an *F*-distribution with $J$ numerator degrees of freedom and $T - K$ denominator degrees of freedom. *If the null hypothesis is not true,* then the difference between $SSE_R$ and $SSE_U$ becomes large, implying that the constraints placed on the model by the null hypothesis have a large effect on the ability of the model to fit the data, and the value of $F$ tends to be *large.* Thus, we *reject* the null hypothesis if the value of the *F*-test statistic becomes too large. As usual, we make the judgment about what is too large by comparing the value of $F$ to the critical value $F_c$, which leaves the probability $\alpha$ in the upper tail of the *F*-distribution with $J$ and $T - K$ degrees of freedom. The critical value for the *F*-distribution is depicted in Figure 8.1. Tables of critical values for $\alpha = .01$ and $\alpha = .05$ appear inside the back cover of the book. To summarize, the elements of an *F*-test, which we can establish "pre-data," are:

1.   The null hypothesis $H_0$ consists of one or more ($J$) equality hypotheses. The null hypothesis may *not* include any "greater than or equal to" or "less than or equal to" hypotheses.

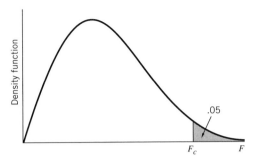

FIGURE **8.1**   The probability density function of an $F$ random variable.

2. The alternative hypothesis states that *one or more* of the equalities in the null hypothesis is not true. The alternative hypothesis may not include any "greater than" or "less than" options.

3. The test statistic is the $F$-statistic in equation 8.4.3.

4. If the null hypothesis is true, $F$ has the $F$-distribution with $J$ numerator degrees of freedom and $T - K$ denominator degrees of freedom. The null hypothesis is *rejected* if $F \geq F_c$, where $F_c$ is the critical value that leaves $\alpha$ percent of the probability in the upper tail of the $F$-distribution.

The $F$-test statistic in equation 8.4.3 is a general one that can be used to test very general sets of joint hypotheses. In the following two sections we show that it can be used to test a single hypothesis and the overall significance of the model, respectively. In Section 8.6.3 we use the $F$-test statistic to test a more general set of joint hypotheses about an extended version of the total revenue model.

### 8.4.2   THE *F*-TEST FOR A SINGLE HYPOTHESIS

To illustrate, we test the hypothesis in the Bay Area Rapid Food hamburger chain example that changes in price have no effect on total revenue against the alternative that price does have an effect. We have tested this hypothesis in Section 8.2 using a $t$-test, and now we will use the $F$-test. The null and alternative hypotheses are: $H_0 : \beta_2 = 0$ and $H_1 : \beta_2 \neq 0$. The original unrestricted model for total revenue is

$$tr_t = \beta_1 + \beta_2 p_t + \beta_3 a_t + e_t$$

The *unrestricted* sum of squared errors comes from this model. From Table 8.1 we see that $SSE_U = 1805.168$. The restricted model, that assumes the null hypothesis is true, is

$$tr_t = \beta_1 + \beta_3 a_t + e_t$$

The *restricted* sum of squared errors comes from estimating this model by least squares; it is $SSE_R = 1964.758$. By imposing the null hypothesis $H_0 : \beta_2 = 0$ on the model the sum of squared errors has increased from 1805.168 to 1964.758. There is a single hypothesis, so $J = 1$ and the $F$-test statistic is:

$$F = \frac{(SSE_R - SSE_U) / J}{SSE_U / (T - K)} = \frac{(1964.758 - 1805.168) / 1}{1805.168 / (52 - 3)}$$

$$= 4.332$$

We compare this value to the critical value from an $F$-distribution with 1 and 49 degrees of freedom. Critical values for the $F$-distribution appear in Tables 3 and 4 inside the back cover of this book, but they are very limited with respect to the degrees of freedom that are reported. With the advent of sophisticated statistical software the problem of finding the critical value has been eliminated, since these packages have functions that calculate the exact critical value for any number of degrees of freedom. For the $F_{(1,49)}$ distribution the $\alpha = .05$ critical value is $F_c = 4.038$. Since $F = 4.332 \geq F_c$ we reject the null hypothesis and conclude that price does have a significant effect on total revenue. The $p$-value for this test is $p = P[F_{(1,49)} \geq 4.332] = .0427$, which is less than $\alpha = .05$, and thus we reject the null hypothesis on this basis as well.

When testing one "equality" null hypothesis against a "not equal to" alternative hypothesis, either a $t$-test or an $F$-test can be used and the outcomes will be identical. The reason for this is that there is an exact relationship between the $t$- and $F$-distributions. The square of a $t$ random variable with $df$ degrees of freedom is an $F$ random variable with distribution $F_{(1, df)}$. When using a $t$-test for $H_0 : \beta_2 = 0$ against $H_1 : \beta_2 \neq 0$, we found that $t = -2.081$, $t_c = 2.01$ and $p = .0427$. The $F$-value that we have calculated is $F = 4.332 = t^2$ and $F_c = (t_c)^2$. Because of this exact relationship, the $p$-values for the two tests are identical, meaning that we will always reach the same conclusion whichever approach we take. There is no equivalence when using a one-tailed $t$-test since the $F$-test is not appropriate when the alternative is an inequality, ">" or "<".

---

**Remark:** When testing a single equality hypothesis it is perfectly correct to use either the $t$- or $F$-test procedure. As we have shown, they are equivalent. In practice, it is customary to test single hypotheses using a $t$-test. The $F$-test is usually reserved for joint hypotheses.

---

### 8.4.3    THE $F$-TEST FOR THE OVERALL SIGNIFICANCE OF THE MODEL

We can use the $F$-test to test the overall significance of a model. The full, unconstrained multiple regression model is

$$y_t = \beta_1 + x_{t2}\beta_2 + x_{t3}\beta_3 + \ldots + x_{tK}\beta_K + e_t$$

If the joint null hypothesis, introduced in equation 8.4.2,

$$H_0 : \beta_2 = 0, \beta_3 = 0, \cdots, \beta_K = 0 \tag{8.4.4}$$

is true, then the restricted model is

$$y_t = \beta_1 + e_t \tag{8.4.5}$$

The least squares estimator of $\beta_1$ in this restricted model is $b_1^* = \dfrac{\Sigma y_t}{T} = \bar{y}$, which is the sample mean of the observations on the dependent variable. The restricted sum of squared errors from the hypothesis (8.4.4) is

$$SSE_R = \Sigma(y_t - b_1^*)^2 = \Sigma(y_t - \bar{y})^2 = SST$$

*In this one case,* in which we are testing the null hypothesis that all the model parameters are zero *except the intercept,* the restricted sum of squared errors is the total sum of squares ($SST$) from the full unconstrained model. The unrestricted sum of squared errors is the sum of squared errors from the unconstrained model, or $SSE_U = SSE$. The number of hypotheses is $J = K - 1$. Thus, to test the overall significance of a model, the $F$-test statistic can be modified as

$$F = \frac{(SST - SSE) / (K - 1)}{SSE / (T - K)} \tag{8.4.6}$$

The calculated value of this test statistic is compared to a critical value from the $F_{(K-1, T-K)}$ distribution. The $F$-test statistic in equation 8.4.6 is used to test the overall significance of a regression model. The outcome of the test is of fundamental importance when carrying out a regression analysis, and it is usually reported by computer software in the ANOVA table, since all the test ingredients, $SST$, $SSE$, $K$, and $T - K$ are summarized there.

To illustrate, we test the overall significance of the regression used to explain Bay Area Rapid Food's total revenue. We want to test whether the coefficients of price and of advertising expenditure are both zero, against the alternative that at least one of the coefficients is not zero. Thus, in the model

$$tr_t = \beta_1 + \beta_2 p_t + \beta_3 a_t + e_t$$

we want to test

$$H_0 : \beta_2 = 0, \beta_3 = 0$$

against the alternative

$$H_1 : \beta_2 \neq 0, \text{ or } \beta_3 \neq 0, \text{ or both are nonzero.}$$

The ingredients for this test, and the test statistic value itself, are reported in the analysis of variance table reported by most regression software. For the Bay Area Rapid Food data, the complete ANOVA table is shown in Table 8.3. From Table 8.1 we know that $SSE_R = SST = 13581.35$ and $SSE_U = SSE = 1805.168$. In Table 8.3 the values of *mean square* are the ratios of the sums of squares values to the degrees of freedom, DF. In turn, the ratio of the mean squares is the $F$-value for

*Table 8.3*    **Analysis of Variance Table**

| Source | DF | Sum of Squares | Mean Square | $F$-Value | $p$-value |
|---|---|---|---|---|---|
| Explained | 2 | 11776.18 | 5888.09 | 159.828 | 0.0001 |
| Unexplained | 49 | 1805.168 | 36.84 | | |
| Total | 51 | 13581.35 | | | |

the test of overall significance of the model. For the Bay Area hamburger data this calculation is

$$F = \frac{(SST - SSE) / (K - 1)}{SSE / (T - K)} = \frac{(13581.35 - 1805.168) / 2}{1805.168 / (52 - 3)} = \frac{5888.09}{36.84} = 159.83$$

The 5 percent critical value for the $F$-statistic with (2, 49) degrees of freedom is $F_c = 3.187$. Since $159.83 > 3.187$, we reject $H_0$ and conclude that the estimated relationship is a significant one. Instead of looking up the critical value, we could have made our conclusion based on the $p$-value, which is calculated by most software, and is reported in Table 8.3. Our sample of data suggests that price or advertising expenditure or both have an influence on total revenue. Note that this conclusion is consistent with conclusions reached using separate $t$-tests for testing the significance of price and the significance of advertising expenditure in Section 8.2.

*Note: The material in the following Section is difficult and can be skipped without loss of continuity.*

### 8.4.4    THE RELATIONSHIP BETWEEN JOINT AND INDIVIDUAL TESTS

We conclude this section by asking the question: Why use the $F$-distribution to perform a simultaneous test of $H_0 : \beta_2 = 0, \beta_3 = 0$? Why not just use separate $t$-tests on each of the null hypotheses $H_0 : \beta_2 = 0$ and $H_0 : \beta_3 = 0$? The answer relates to the correlation between the least squares estimators. The $F$-test that tests both hypotheses simultaneously makes allowance for the fact that the least squares estimators $b_2$ and $b_3$ are correlated. It is a test for whether the *pair* of values $\beta_2 = 0$ and $\beta_3 = 0$ are consistent with the data. When separate $t$-tests are performed, the possibility that $\beta_2 = 0$ is not considered when testing $H_0 : \beta_3 = 0$, and vice versa. It is not a pair of values being tested with $t$-tests, but a conjecture about a single parameter at a time. Each $t$-test is treated in isolation from the other, no allowance is made for the correlation between $b_2$ and $b_3$. As a consequence, the joint $F$-test at a 5 percent significance level is not equivalent to separate $t$-tests that each use a 5 percent significance level. Conflicting results can occur. For example, it is possible for individual $t$-tests to fail to conclude that coefficients are significantly different from zero, while the $F$-test implies that the coefficients are *jointly* significant. This situation frequently arises when the data are multicollinear, as described in Section 8.8.

## *8.5* **An Extended Model**

We have hypothesized so far in this chapter that total revenue at the Bay Area Rapid Food franchise is explained by product price and advertising expenditures,

$$tr_t = \beta_1 + \beta_2 p_t + \beta_3 a_t + e_t \tag{8.5.1}$$

One aspect of this model that is worth questioning is whether the *linear* relationship between revenue, price, and advertising expenditure is a good approximation to reality. This linear model implies that increasing advertising expenditure will continue to increase total revenue at the same rate, irrespective of the existing level of revenue and advertising expenditure. That is, the coefficient $\beta_3$, that measures the response of $E(tr)$ to a change in $a$, is constant; it does not depend on $a$. However, as the level of advertising expenditure increases, we would expect diminishing returns to set in. That is, the increase in revenue that results from an advertising expenditure increase of \$1,000 is likely to decline as the total amount spent on advertising grows. One way of allowing for diminishing returns to advertising is to include the squared value of advertising, $a^2$, into the model as another explanatory variable, so

$$tr_t = \beta_1 + \beta_2 p_t + \beta_3 a_t + \beta_4 a_t^2 + e_t \tag{8.5.2}$$

Adding the term $\beta_4 a_t^2$ to our original specification yields a model in which the response of expected revenue to advertising depends on the level of advertising. The response of $E(tr)$ to $a$ is

$$\frac{\Delta E(tr_t)}{\Delta a_t}\bigg|_{(p \text{ held constant})} = \frac{\partial E(tr_t)}{\partial a_t} = \beta_3 + 2\beta_4 a_t \tag{8.5.3}$$

When $a_t$ increases by one unit (\$1,000), and $p_t$ is held constant, $E(tr_t)$ increases by $(\beta_3 + 2\beta_4 a_t) \times \$1,000$. To determine the anticipated signs for $\beta_3$ and $\beta_4$ we note that we would expect the response of revenue to advertising to be positive when $a_t = 0$. That is, we expect that $\beta_3 > 0$. Also, to achieve diminishing returns the response must decline as $a_t$ increases. That is, we expect $\beta_4 < 0$.

Having proposed an extended model that might be more realistic, our next step is to estimate it. For estimation purposes, the squared value of advertising is "just another variable." That is, we can write equation 8.5.2 as

$$y_t = \beta_1 + \beta_2 x_{t2} + \beta_3 x_{t3} + \beta_4 x_{t4} + e_t \tag{8.5.4}$$

where

$$y_t = tr_t, \ x_{t2} = p_t, \ x_{t3} = a_t, \ x_{t4} = a_t^2$$

The least squares estimates, using the data in Table 7.1, are

$$\hat{tr}_t = 104.81 - 6.582 p_t + 2.948 a_t + 0.0017 a_t^2$$
$$\quad (6.58) \ \ (3.459) \quad (0.786) \quad (0.0361) \qquad\qquad (\text{s.e.}) \tag{8.5.5}$$

What can we say about the addition of $a_t^2$ to the equation? The first thing to notice is that its coefficient is positive, not negative, as was expected. Second, its $t$-value for the hypothesis $H_0 : \beta_4 = 0$ is $t = 0.0017/0.0361 = 0.048$. This very low value indicates that $b_4$ is not significantly different from zero. If $\beta_4$ is zero, there are no diminishing returns to advertising, which is counter to our belief in the phenomenon of diminishing returns. Thus, we conclude that $\beta_4$ has been estimated imprecisely and its standard error is too large.

When economic parameters are estimated imprecisely, one solution is to obtain more and better data. Recall that the variances of the least squares estimators are reduced by increasing the number of sample observations. Consequently, another 26 weeks of data were collected. These data are presented in Table 8.4. The ranges of $p_t$ and $a_t$ are wider in this data set, and greater variation in the explanatory variables leads to a reduction in the variances of the least squares estimators, and may help us achieve more precise least squares estimates. This fact, coupled with the fact that we now have a total of 78 observations, rather than 52, gives us a chance of obtaining a more precise estimate of $\beta_4$, and the other parameters as well. Combining the additional data in Table 8.4 with the previous data in Table 7.1 yields the following least squares estimated equation:

$$\hat{tr}_t = 110.46 - 10.198p_t + 3.361a_t - 0.0268a_t^2 \tag{8.5.6}$$
$$\quad (3.74) \quad (1.582) \quad (0.422) \quad (0.0159) \qquad \text{(s.e.)}$$

A comparison of the standard errors in this equation with those in (8.5.5) indicates that the inclusion of the additional 26 observations has greatly improved the precision of our estimates. In particular, the estimated coefficient of $a_t^2$ now has the expected sign. Its $t$-value of $t = -0.0268/0.0159 = -1.68$ implies that $b_4$ is significantly different from zero, using a one-tailed test and $\alpha = .05$. The 78 data points we have are compatible with the assumption of diminishing returns to advertising expenditures.

**Table 8.4**   **An Additional 26 Weeks of Data on tr, p, and a**

| Week | tr | p | a | Week | tr | p | a |
|------|------|------|------|------|------|------|------|
| 53 | 129.9 | 2.87 | 16.0 | 66 | 108.6 | 1.61 | 4.8 |
| 54 | 101.5 | 2.05 | 4.0 | 67 | 158.8 | 2.66 | 27.7 |
| 55 | 136.3 | 2.55 | 19.6 | 68 | 147.2 | 1.74 | 20.6 |
| 56 | 97.6 | 3.49 | 10.2 | 69 | 146.3 | 3.21 | 25.4 |
| 57 | 118.9 | 3.45 | 17.5 | 70 | 121.2 | 1.50 | 10.2 |
| 58 | 130.5 | 3.45 | 18.3 | 71 | 107.0 | 1.78 | 4.9 |
| 59 | 128.5 | 2.58 | 18.2 | 72 | 121.2 | 2.43 | 12.1 |
| 60 | 138.3 | 2.87 | 22.1 | 73 | 125.4 | 2.04 | 12.3 |
| 61 | 103.6 | 1.76 | 4.1 | 74 | 141.9 | 2.99 | 19.7 |
| 62 | 151.8 | 2.97 | 24.9 | 75 | 120.0 | 2.83 | 14.3 |
| 63 | 128.5 | 2.77 | 14.7 | 76 | 101.9 | 2.47 | 4.8 |
| 64 | 128.5 | 2.64 | 18.6 | 77 | 130.4 | 2.04 | 11.6 |
| 65 | 143.7 | 1.50 | 20.9 | 78 | 139.9 | 1.87 | 19.8 |

## 8.6  Testing Some Economic Hypotheses

Using the expanded model for Bay Area Rapid Food total revenue in equation 8.5.2 and the $T = 78$ observations in Tables 7.1 and 8.4, we can test some interesting economic hypotheses and illustrate the use of $t$- and $F$-tests in economic analysis.

### 8.6.1  THE SIGNIFICANCE OF ADVERTISING

In the context of our expanded model

$$tr_t = \beta_1 + \beta_2 p_t + \beta_3 a_t + \beta_4 a_t^2 + e_t \qquad (8.6.1)$$

how would we test whether advertising has an effect on total revenue? If either $\beta_3$ or $\beta_4$ are not zero, then advertising has an effect on revenue. Based on one-tailed $t$-tests we can conclude that individually, $\beta_3$ and $\beta_4$, are not zero, and are of the correct sign. But the question we are now asking involves both $\beta_3$ and $\beta_4$, and thus a joint test is appropriate. The joint test will use the $F$-statistic in equation 8.4.3 to test $H_0 : \beta_3 = 0, \beta_4 = 0$. We will compare the unrestricted model in equation 8.6.1 to the restricted model, which assumes the null hypothesis is true. The restricted model is

$$tr_t = \beta_1 + \beta_2 p_t + e_t \qquad (8.6.2)$$

The elements of the test are:

1. The joint null hypothesis $H_0 : \beta_3 = 0, \beta_4 = 0$.
2. The alternative hypothesis $H_1 : \beta_3 \neq 0$, or $\beta_4 \neq 0$, or both are nonzero.
3. The test statistic is $F = \dfrac{(SSE_R - SSE_U)\,/\,J}{SSE_U\,/\,(T - K)}$ where $J = 2$, $T = 78$ and $K = 4$. $SSE_U = 2592.301$ is the sum of squared errors from (8.6.1). $SSE_R = 20907.331$ is the sum of squared errors from (8.6.2)
4. If the joint null hypothesis is true, then $F \sim F_{(J, T-K)}$. The critical value $F_c$ comes from the $F_{(2,74)}$ distribution, and for the $\alpha = .05$ level of significance it is 3.120.
5. The value of the $F$-statistic is $F = 261.41 > F_c$ and we reject the null hypothesis that both $\beta_3 = 0$ and $\beta_4 = 0$ and conclude that at least one of them is not zero, implying that advertising has a significant effect on total revenue.

### 8.6.2  THE OPTIMAL LEVEL OF ADVERTISING

Economic theory tells us that we should undertake all those actions for which the marginal benefit is greater than the marginal cost. This optimizing principle applies to the Bay Area Rapid Food franchise as it attempts to choose the optimal level of advertising expenditure. From equation 8.5.3, the marginal benefit from another unit of advertising is the increase in total revenue:

$$\frac{\Delta E(tr_t)}{\Delta a_t}\Big|_{(p \text{ held constant})} = \beta_3 + 2\beta_4 a_t$$

The marginal cost of another unit of advertising is the cost of the advertising plus the cost of preparing additional products sold due to effective advertising. If we ignore the latter costs, advertising expenditures should be increased to the point where the marginal benefit of \$1 of advertising falls to \$1, or where

$$\beta_3 + 2\beta_4 a_t = 1$$

Using the least squares estimates for $\beta_3$ and $\beta_4$ in equation 8.5.6 we can *estimate* the optimal level of advertising from

$$3.361 + 2(-.0268)\hat{a}_t = 1$$

Solving, we obtain $\hat{a}_t = 44.0485$, which implies that the optimal weekly advertising expenditure is \$44,048.50.

Suppose that the franchise management, based on experience in other cities, thinks that \$44,048.50 is too high, and that the optimal level of advertising is actually about \$40,000. We can easily test this conjecture using either a $t$- or $F$-test. The null hypothesis we wish to test is $H_0 : \beta_3 + 2\beta_4(40) = 1$ against the alternative that $H_1 : \beta_3 + 2\beta_4(40) \neq 1$. The test statistic is

$$t = \frac{(b_3 + 80b_4) - 1}{\text{se}(b_3 + 80b_4)}$$

which has a $t_{(74)}$ distribution if the null hypothesis is true. The only tricky part of this test is calculating the denominator of the $t$-statistic. Using the properties of variance developed in Chapter 2.5.2,

$$\hat{\text{var}}(b_3 + 80b_4) = \hat{\text{var}}(b_3) + 80^2 \, \hat{\text{var}}(b_4) + 2(80)\hat{\text{cov}}(b_3, b_4) = .76366$$

where the estimated variances and covariance are provided by your statistical software. Then, the calculated value of the $t$-statistic is

$$t = \frac{1.221 - 1}{\sqrt{.76366}} = .252$$

The critical value for this two-tailed test comes from the $t_{(74)}$ distribution. At the $\alpha = .05$ level of significance $t_c = 1.993$, and thus we cannot reject the null hypothesis that the optimal level of advertising is \$40,000 per week.

Alternatively, using an $F$-test, the test statistic is $F = \dfrac{(SSE_R - SSE_U) / J}{SSE_U / (T - K)}$ where $J = 1$, $T = 78$ and $K = 4$. $SSE_U = 2592.301$ is the sum of squared errors from the full, unrestricted model in (8.6.1). $SSE_R$ is the sum of squared errors from the restricted model, in which it is assumed that the null hypothesis is true. The restricted model is

$$tr_t = \beta_1 + \beta_2 p_t + (1 - 80\beta_4)a_t + \beta_4 a_t^2 + e_t$$

Rearranging this equation by collecting terms, to put it in a form that is convenient for estimation, we have

$$(tr_t - a_t) = \beta_1 + \beta_2 p_t + \beta_4(a_t^2 - 80a_t) + e_t$$

Estimating this model by least squares yields the restricted sum of squared errors $SSE_R = 2594.533$. The calculated value of the $F$-statistic is

$$F = \frac{(2594.533 - 2592.301) / 1}{2592.302 / 74}$$
$$= .0637$$

The value $F = .0637$ is $t^2 = (.252)^2$, obeying the relationship between $t$- and $F$-random variables that we mentioned previously. The critical value $F_c$ comes from the $F_{(1,74)}$ distribution. For $\alpha = .05$ the critical value is $F_c = 3.970$.

> **Remark**: While it is frequently convenient to compute an $F$-value by using the restricted and unrestricted sums of squares, it is often more convenient to use the power of modern statistical software. Most statistical software packages have TEST statements of some sort that automatically compute the $F$-value when provided the null hypotheses. You should check out the commands necessary to carry out such tests using your software.

### 8.6.3    THE OPTIMAL LEVEL OF ADVERTISING AND PRICE

If weekly advertising is the optimal $40,000, suppose that management believes that at a price of $p = \$2$, the weekly total revenue is expected to be $175,000. That is, in the context of our model,

$$E(tr_t) = \beta_1 + \beta_2 p_t + \beta_3 a_t + \beta_4 a_t^2$$
$$= \beta_1 + \beta_2(2) + \beta_3(40) + \beta_4(40)^2$$
$$= 175$$

Are these two conjectures compatible with the evidence contained in the sample of data? We now formulate the two joint hypotheses

$$H_0 : \beta_3 + 2\beta_4(40) = 1, \qquad \beta_1 + 2\beta_2 + 40\beta_3 + 1600\beta_4 = 175$$

The alternative is that at least one of these hypotheses is not true. Because there are $J = 2$ hypotheses to test jointly, we will use an $F$-test. Constructing the restricted model will now require substituting both of these hypotheses into our extended model, which is left as an exercise. The test statistic is $F = \dfrac{(SSE_R - SSE_U) / J}{SSE_U / (T - K)}$, where $J = 2$. The computed value of the $F$-statistic is $F = 1.75$. The critical value for the test comes from the $F_{(2,74)}$ distribution and is $F_c = 3.120$. Since $F < F_c$, we do not reject the null hypothesis, and conclude that the sample data are compatible with the hypotheses that the optimal level of advertising is $40,000 per week and that if the price is $2 the total revenue will be, on average, $175,000 per week.

## 8.7 The Use of Nonsample Information

In many estimation and inference problems we have information over and above the information contained in the sample observations. This nonsample information may come from many places, such as economic principles or experience. When it is available it seems intuitive that we should find a way to use it. If the nonsample information is correct, and if we combine it with the sample information, the precision with which we can estimate the parameters will be improved.

To illustrate how we might go about combining sample and nonsample information, consider a model designed to explain the demand for beer. From the theory of consumer choice in microeconomics, we know that the demand for a good will depend on the price of that good, on the prices of other goods, particularly substitutes and complements, and on income. In the case of beer, it is reasonable to relate the quantity demanded ($q$) to the price of beer ($p_B$), the price of other liquor ($p_L$), the price of all other remaining goods and services ($p_R$), and income ($m$). We write this relationship as

$$q = f(p_B, p_L, p_R, m) \tag{8.7.1}$$

Using *ln* to denote the natural logarithm, we assume the log–log functional form is appropriate for this demand relationship

$$\ln(q) = \beta_1 + \beta_2 \ln(p_B) + \beta_3 \ln(p_L) + \beta_4 \ln(p_R) + \beta_5 \ln(m) \tag{8.7.2}$$

This model is a convenient one because it precludes infeasible negative prices, quantities, and income, and because the coefficients $\beta_2$, $\beta_3$, $\beta_4$, and $\beta_5$ are elasticities.

A relevant piece of nonsample information can be derived by noting that, if all prices and income go up by the same proportion, we would expect there to be no change in quantity demanded. For example, a doubling of all prices and income should not change the quantity of beer consumed. This assumption is that economic agents do not suffer from "money illusion." Let us impose this assumption on our demand model and see what happens. Having all prices and income change by the same proportion is equivalent to multiplying each price and income by a constant. Denoting this constant by $\lambda$, and multiplying each of the variables in (8.7.2) by $\lambda$, yields

$$\ln(q) = \beta_1 + \beta_2 \ln(\lambda p_B) + \beta_3 \ln(\lambda p_L) + \beta_4 \ln(\lambda p_R) + \beta_5 \ln(\lambda m)$$

$$= \beta_1 + \beta_2 \ln(p_B) + \beta_3 \ln(p_L) + \beta_4 \ln(p_R) + \beta_5 \ln(m) \tag{8.7.3}$$

$$+ (\beta_2 + \beta_3 + \beta_4 + \beta_5)\ln(\lambda)$$

Comparing equation 8.7.2 with 8.7.3 shows that multiplying each price and income by $\lambda$ will give a change in $\ln(q)$ equal to $(\beta_2 + \beta_3 + \beta_4 + \beta_5)\ln(\lambda)$. Thus, for there to be no change in $\ln(q)$ when all prices and income go up by the same proportion, it must be true that

$$\beta_2 + \beta_3 + \beta_4 + \beta_5 = 0 \qquad (8.7.4)$$

Thus, we can say something about how quantity demanded should not change when prices and income change by the same proportion, and this information can be written in terms of a specific restriction on the parameters of the demand model. We call such a restriction nonsample information. If we believe that this nonsample information makes sense, and hence that the parameter restriction in (8.7.4) holds, then it seems desirable to be able to obtain estimates that obey this restriction.

To obtain estimates that obey equation 8.7.4, begin with the multiple regression model

$$\ln(q_t) = \beta_1 + \beta_2 \ln(p_{Bt}) + \beta_3 \ln(p_{Lt}) + \beta_4 \ln(p_{Rt}) + \beta_5 \ln(m_t) + e_t \quad (8.7.5)$$

and a sample of data consisting of thirty years of annual data on beer consumption collected from a randomly selected household. These data appear in Table 8.5.

To introduce the nonsample information, we solve the parameter restriction $\beta_2 + \beta_3 + \beta_4 + \beta_5 = 0$ for one of the $\beta_k$s. It is not important mathematically which we solve for, but for reasons explained shortly we solve for $\beta_4$:

$$\beta_4 = -\beta_2 - \beta_3 - \beta_5 \qquad (8.7.6)$$

Substituting this expression into the original model in equation 8.7.5 gives

$$\ln(q_t) = \beta_1 + \beta_2 \ln(p_{Bt}) + \beta_3 \ln(p_{Lt}) + (-\beta_2 - \beta_3 - \beta_5)\ln(p_{Rt}) + \beta_5 \ln(m_t) + e_t$$

$$= \beta_1 + \beta_2(\ln(p_{Bt}) - \ln(p_{Rt})) + \beta_3(\ln(p_{Lt}) - \ln(p_{Rt})) + \beta_5(\ln(m_t) - \ln(p_{Rt}))$$

$$+ e_t = \beta_1 + \beta_2 \ln\left(\frac{p_{Bt}}{p_{Rt}}\right) + \beta_3 \ln\left(\frac{p_{Lt}}{p_{Rt}}\right) + \beta_5 \ln\left(\frac{m_t}{p_{Rt}}\right) + e_t \qquad (8.7.7)$$

We have used the parameter restriction to eliminate the parameter $\beta_4$ and in so doing, and in using the properties of logarithms, we have constructed the new variables $\ln(p_{Bt}/p_{Rt})$, $\ln(p_{Lt}/p_{Rt})$, and $\ln(m_t/p_{Rt})$. The last line in equation 8.7.7 is our "restricted" model. To get least squares estimates that satisfy the parameter restriction, called "restricted least squares estimates," we apply the least squares estimation procedure directly to the restricted model in equation 8.7.7. The estimated equation is

$$\ln \hat{q}_t = -4.798 - 1.2994 \ln\left(\frac{p_{Bt}}{p_{Rt}}\right) + 0.1868 \ln\left(\frac{p_{Lt}}{p_{Rt}}\right) + 0.9458 \ln\left(\frac{m_t}{p_{Rt}}\right) \qquad (8.7.8)$$

$$(3.714) \quad (0.166) \qquad\qquad (0.284) \qquad\qquad\qquad (0.427)$$

*Table 8.5*  **Price, Quantity and Income Data for Beer Demand Model**

| $q$ (liters) | $p_B$ ($) | $p_L$ ($) | $p_R$ ($) | $m$ ($) |
|---|---|---|---|---|
| 81.7 | 1.78 | 6.95 | 1.11 | 25088 |
| 56.9 | 2.27 | 7.32 | 0.67 | 26561 |
| 64.1 | 2.21 | 6.96 | 0.83 | 25510 |
| 65.4 | 2.15 | 7.18 | 0.75 | 27158 |
| 64.1 | 2.26 | 7.46 | 1.06 | 27162 |
| 58.1 | 2.49 | 7.47 | 1.10 | 27583 |
| 61.7 | 2.52 | 7.88 | 1.09 | 28235 |
| 65.3 | 2.46 | 7.88 | 1.18 | 29413 |
| 57.8 | 2.54 | 7.97 | 0.88 | 28713 |
| 63.5 | 2.72 | 7.96 | 1.30 | 30000 |
| 65.9 | 2.60 | 8.09 | 1.17 | 30533 |
| 48.3 | 2.87 | 8.24 | 0.94 | 30373 |
| 55.6 | 3.00 | 7.96 | 0.91 | 31107 |
| 47.9 | 3.23 | 8.34 | 1.10 | 31126 |
| 57.0 | 3.11 | 8.10 | 1.50 | 32506 |
| 51.6 | 3.11 | 8.43 | 1.17 | 32408 |
| 54.2 | 3.09 | 8.72 | 1.18 | 33423 |
| 51.7 | 3.34 | 8.87 | 1.37 | 33904 |
| 55.9 | 3.31 | 8.82 | 1.52 | 34528 |
| 52.1 | 3.42 | 8.59 | 1.15 | 36019 |
| 52.5 | 3.61 | 8.83 | 1.39 | 34807 |
| 44.3 | 3.55 | 8.86 | 1.60 | 35943 |
| 57.7 | 3.72 | 8.97 | 1.73 | 37323 |
| 51.6 | 3.72 | 9.13 | 1.35 | 36682 |
| 53.8 | 3.70 | 8.98 | 1.37 | 38054 |
| 50.0 | 3.81 | 9.25 | 1.41 | 36707 |
| 46.3 | 3.86 | 9.33 | 1.62 | 38411 |
| 46.8 | 3.99 | 9.47 | 1.69 | 38823 |
| 51.7 | 3.89 | 9.49 | 1.71 | 38361 |
| 49.9 | 4.07 | 9.52 | 1.69 | 41593 |

Let the restricted least squares estimates in equation 8.7.8 be denoted as $b_k^*$. In equation 8.7.8 we have estimates of $\beta_1$, $\beta_2$, $\beta_3$, and $\beta_5$. To obtain an estimate of $\beta_4$ we use the restriction 8.7.6

$$b_4^* = -b_2^* - b_3^* - b_5^*$$

$$= -(-1.2994) - 0.1868 - 0.9458$$

$$= 0.1668$$

By using the restriction *within* the model, we have ensured that the estimates obey the constraint, so that $b_2^* + b_3^* + b_4^* + b_5^* = 0$.

> **Remark:** While it is always possible to obtain restricted estimates by substituting the constraints into the model, it may become messy if there are a number of restrictions or if the restrictions involve several parameters. Most statistical software packages have RESTRICT statements of some sort that automatically compute the restricted least squares estimates when provided the constraints. You should check out the commands available in your software.

What are the properties of this "restricted" least squares estimation procedure? First, the restricted least squares estimator is biased, and $E(b_k^*) \neq \beta_k$, *unless* the constraints we impose are *exactly* true. This result makes an important point about econometrics. A *good economist* will obtain more reliable parameter estimates than a poor one, because a good economist will introduce better nonsample information. This is true at the time of model specification and later, when constraints might be applied to the model. *Good economic theory* is a very important ingredient in empirical research.

The second property of the restricted least squares estimator is that its variance is smaller than the variance of the least squares estimator, *whether the constraints imposed are true or not.* By combining nonsample information with the sample information, we reduce the variation in the estimation procedure caused by random sampling. The reduction in variance obtained by imposing restrictions on the parameters is not at odds with the Gauss–Markov Theorem. The Gauss–Markov result, that the least squares estimator is the best linear unbiased estimator, applies to linear and unbiased estimators that use data alone, with no constraints on the parameters. By incorporating the additional information with the data, we usually give up unbiasedness in return for reduced variances.

## *8.8* Collinear Economic Variables

Most economic data that are used for estimating economic relationships are nonexperimental. Indeed, in most cases they are simply "collected" for administrative or other purposes. Consequently, the data are not the result of a planned experiment in which an experimental design is specified for the explanatory variables. In controlled experiments, such as discussed in Chapter 1, the right-hand-side variables in the statistical model can be assigned values in such a way that their individual effects can be identified and estimated with precision. When data are the result of an uncontrolled experiment, many of the economic variables may move together in systematic ways. Such variables are said to be **collinear,** and the problem is labeled **collinearity,** or **multicollinearity** when several variables are involved. In this case there is no guarantee that the data will be "rich in information," nor that it will be possible to isolate the economic relationship or parameters of interest.

As an example, consider the problem faced by Bay Area Rapid Food marketing executives when trying to estimate the increase in the total revenue attributable to advertising that appears in newspapers *and* the increase in total revenue attributable to coupon advertising. Suppose it has been common practice to coordinate these two advertising devices, so that at the same time advertising appears in the newspapers there are flyers distributed containing coupons for price reductions on hamburgers. If variables measuring the expenditures on these two forms of advertising appear on the right-hand side of a total revenue equation like equation 7.1.2, then the data on these variables will show a systematic, positive relationship; intuitively, it will be difficult for such data to reveal the separate effects of the two types of ads. Because the two types of advertising expenditure move together, it may be difficult to sort out their separate effects on total revenue.

As a second example, consider a production relationship explaining output over time as a function of the amounts of various quantities of inputs employed. There are certain factors of production (inputs), such as labor and capital, that are used in *relatively fixed proportions*. As production increases, the amounts of two, or more, such inputs reflect proportionate increases. Proportionate relationships between variables are the very sort of systematic relationships that epitomize "collinearity." Any effort to measure the individual or separate effects (marginal products) of various mixes of inputs from such data will be difficult.

We should also note at this point that it is not just *relationships between variables* in a sample of data that make it difficult to isolate the separate effects of individual explanatory variables in an economic or statistical model. A related problem exists when the values of an explanatory variable do not vary or change much within the sample of data. When an explanatory variable exhibits little variation, then it is difficult to isolate its impact. In Chapter 7.3.1, equation 7.3.2, we noted that the more variation in an explanatory variable, the more precisely its coefficient can be estimated. Lack of variation is the other side of the coin, and it leads to estimator imprecision. This problem also falls within the context of "collinearity."

### 8.8.1   THE STATISTICAL CONSEQUENCES OF COLLINEARITY

The consequences of collinear relationships among explanatory variables in a statistical model may be summarized as follows:

1.  Whenever there are one or more *exact* linear relationships among the explanatory variables, then *the condition of exact collinearity, or exact multicollinearity, exists. In this case, the least squares estimator is not defined.* We *cannot* obtain estimates of the $\beta_k$'s using the least squares principle. This is indicated in equation 7.3.1. If there is an exact linear relationship between $x_{t2}$ and $x_{t3}$, for example, then the correlation between them is $r_{23} = \pm 1$, and the variance of $b_2$ is undefined, since 0 appears in the denominator. The same is true of the covariance and the formulas for $b_2$ and $b_3$.

2.  When *nearly* exact linear dependencies among the explanatory variables exist, some of the variances, standard errors, and covariances of the least squares estimators may be large. We have noted the effect on estimator variance of a high correlation between two explanatory variables in Chapter 7.3.1. Large standard errors for the least squares estimators imply high sampling variability, estimated coefficients that are unstable to small changes in the sample or model specification, interval estimates that are wide, and relatively imprecise information provided by the sample data about the unknown parameters.

3.  When estimator standard errors are large, it is likely that the usual $t$-tests will lead to the conclusion that parameter estimates are not significantly different from zero. This outcome occurs despite possibly high $R^2$ or $F$-values indicating "significant" explanatory power of the model as a whole. The

problem is that *collinear variables do not provide enough information to estimate their separate effects,* even though economic theory may indicate their importance in the relationship.

4. Estimators may be very sensitive to the addition or deletion of a few observations, or the deletion of an apparently insignificant variable.

5. Despite the difficulties in isolating the effects of individual variables from such a sample, accurate forecasts may still be possible if the nature of the collinear relationship remains the same within the new (future) sample observations. For example, in an aggregate production function where the inputs labor and capital are nearly collinear, accurate forecasts of output may be possible for a particular ratio of inputs but not for various mixes of inputs.

### 8.8.2 IDENTIFYING AND MITIGATING COLLINEARITY

One simple way to detect collinear relationships is to use sample correlation coefficients between pairs of explanatory variables. These sample correlations are descriptive measures of linear association. A commonly used rule of thumb is that a correlation coefficient between two explanatory variables greater than 0.8 or 0.9 in absolute value indicates a strong linear association and a potentially harmful collinear relationship. The problem with examining only pairwise correlations is that the multicollinearity relationships may involve more than two of the explanatory variables, which may or may not be detected by examining pairwise correlations.

A second simple and effective procedure for identifying the presence of collinearity is to estimate so-called "auxiliary regressions." In these least squares regressions the left-hand-side variable is *one* of the explanatory variables, and the right-hand-side variables are all the remaining explanatory variables. For example, the auxiliary regression for $x_{t2}$ is

$$x_{t2} = a_1 x_{t1} + a_3 x_{t3} + \cdots + a_K x_{tK} + error$$

If the $R^2$ from this artificial model is high, above .80, the implication is that a large portion of the variation in $x_{t2}$ is explained by variation in the other explanatory variables. In Chapter 7.3.1 we made the point that it is variation in a variable that is *not* associated with any other explanatory variable that is valuable in improving the precision of the least squares estimator $b_2$. If the $R^2$ from the auxiliary regressions is not high, then the variation in $x_{t2}$ is not explained by the other explanatory variables, and the estimator $b_2$'s precision is not affected by this problem.

The multicollinearity problem is that the data do not contain enough "information" about the individual effects of explanatory variables to permit us to estimate all the parameters of the statistical model precisely. Consequently, one solution is to obtain more information and include it in the analysis.

One form the new information can take is more, and better, sample data. Unfortunately, in economics, this is not always possible. Cross-sectional data are expensive to obtain, and, with time series data, one must wait for the data to appear. Alternatively, if new data are obtained via the same nonexperimental process as the original sample of data, then the new observations may suffer the same collinear relationships and provide little in the way of new, independent information. Under these circumstances the new data will help little to improve the precision of the least squares estimates.

We may add structure to the problem by introducing, as we did in Section 8.7, *nonsample* information in the form of restrictions on the parameters. This nonsample information may then be combined with the sample information to provide restricted least squares estimates. The good news is that using nonsample information in the form of linear constraints on the parameter values reduces estimator sampling variability. The bad news is that the resulting restricted estimator is *biased* unless the restrictions are *exactly* true. Thus, is it important to use good nonsample information, so that the reduced sampling variability is not bought at a price of large estimator biases.

## 8.9 Prediction

The prediction problem for a linear statistical model with one explanatory variable was covered in depth in Chapter 4. The results in these sections extend naturally to the more general model that has more than one explanatory variable. Let us summarize these results.

Consider a linear statistical model with an intercept term and two explanatory variables $x_2$, $x_3$. That is

$$y_t = \beta_1 + x_{t2}\beta_2 + x_{t3}\beta_3 + e_t \qquad (8.9.1)$$

where the $e_t$ are uncorrelated random variables with mean 0 and variance $\sigma^2$. Given a set of values for the explanatory variables, $(1 \quad x_{02} \quad x_{03})$ the prediction problem is to predict the value of the dependent variable $y_0$, which is given by

$$y_0 = \beta_1 + x_{02}\beta_2 + x_{03}\beta_3 + e_0 \qquad (8.9.2)$$

Note that in this prediction problem we are assuming that the parameter values determining $y_0$ are the same as those in equation 8.9.1 describing the original sample of data. Furthermore, the random error $e_0$ we assume to be uncorrelated with each of the sample errors $e_t$ and to have the same mean, 0, and variance, $\sigma^2$. Under these assumptions, the best linear unbiased predictor of $y_0$ is given by

$$\hat{y}_0 = b_1 + x_{02}b_2 + x_{03}b_3 \qquad (8.9.3)$$

where the $b_k$'s are the least squares estimators. This predictor is unbiased in the sense that the average value of the forecast error is zero. That is, if $f = (y_0 - \hat{y}_0)$ is the forecast error, then $E(f) = 0$. The predictor is best in that for any other linear and unbiased predictor of $y_0$, the variance of the forecast error is larger than $\text{var}(f) = \text{var}(y_0 - \hat{y}_0)$.

The variance of forecast error $\text{var}(y_0 - \hat{y}_0)$ contains two components. One component results from the fact that we can be in error because $b_1$, $b_2$, $b_3$ are estimates of the true parameters, and the other component results because $e_0$ is random. An expression for $\text{var}(y_0 - \hat{y}_0)$ is obtained by computing

$$
\begin{aligned}
\text{var}(f) &= \text{var}[(\beta_1 + \beta_2 x_{02} + \beta_3 x_{03} + e_0) - (b_1 + b_2 x_{02} + b_3 x_{03})] \\
&= \text{var}(e_0 - b_1 - b_2 x_{02} - b_3 x_{03}) \\
&= \text{var}(e_0) + \text{var}(b_1) + x_{02}^2\,\text{var}(b_2) + x_{03}^2\,\text{var}(b_3) + 2x_{02}\,\text{cov}(b_1, b_2) \\
&\quad + 2x_{03}\,\text{cov}(b_1, b_3) + 2x_{02}x_{03}\,\text{cov}(b_2, b_3).
\end{aligned}
$$

To obtain var($f$) we have used the facts that the unknown parameters and the values of the explanatory variables are constants, and that $e_0$ is uncorrelated with the sample data, and thus is uncorrelated with the least squares estimators $b_k$. Then var($e_0$) $= \sigma^2$ and the remaining variances and covariances of the least squares estimators are obtained using the rule for calculating the variance of a weighted sum in equation 2.5.8. Each of these terms involves $\sigma^2$, which we replace with its estimator $\hat{\sigma}^2$ to obtain the estimated variance of the forecast error vâr($f$). The square root of this quantity is the standard error of the forecast, se($f$) $= \sqrt{\text{vâr}(f)}$.

If the random errors $e_t$ and $e_0$ are normally distributed, or if the sample is large, then

$$\frac{f}{se(f)} = \frac{y_0 - \hat{y}_0}{\sqrt{\text{vâr}(y_0 - \hat{y}_0)}} \sim t_{(T-K)} \qquad (8.9.5)$$

Following the steps we have used many times, a $100(1 - \alpha)$ percent interval predictor for $y_0$ is $\hat{y}_0 \pm t_c se(f)$, where $t_c$ is a critical value from the $t_{(T-K)}$ distribution.

Thus, we have shown that the methods for prediction in the model with $K = 3$ are straightforward extensions of the results from the simple linear regression model. If $K > 3$, the methods extend similarly.

## *8.10* **Summary**

1. Tests of hypotheses about individual parameters can be carried out by using a $t$-test statistic. When testing the null hypothesis $H_0 : \beta_k = c$ against one of the alternatives $H_1 : \beta_k \neq c$, $H_1 : \beta_k > c$, or $H_1 : \beta_k < c$, the appropriate test statistic is $t = \dfrac{b_k - c}{se(b_k)}$. This statistic has a $t$-distribution with $T - K$ degrees of freedom if the null hypothesis is true. The rejection region depends on the type of alternative hypothesis. If the constant $c = 0$, then the test is called a *test of significance*.

2. The proportion of variation in the dependent variable explained by the estimated function is given by the coefficient of determination $R^2 = 1 - \dfrac{\Sigma\hat{e}_t^2}{\Sigma(y_t - \bar{y})^2} = 1 - \dfrac{SSE}{SST} = \dfrac{SSR}{SST}$

3. To test a set of $J$ joint hypotheses use the $F$-statistic $F = \dfrac{(SSE_R - SSE_U) / J}{SSE_U / (T - K)}$, where $SSE_U$ is the sum of squared least squares residuals from the original, unrestricted model; $SSE_R$ is the sum of squared residuals from the restricted model in which the joint hypotheses are assumed to be true. The null hypothesis is rejected if $F \geq F_c$ where $F_c$ is the critical value from an $F_{(J,T-K)}$ distribution.

4. The "overall test of model significance" is an $F$-test of the $K - 1$ joint null hypotheses $H_0 : \beta_2 = 0, \beta_3 = 0, \cdots , \beta_K = 0$ against the alternative that at least one $\beta_k$ is not zero. In this case the $F$-statistic is simplified, and is $F = \dfrac{(SST - SSE) / (K - 1)}{SSE / (T - K)}$, where $SST$ is the total sum of squares and $SSE$

is the sum of squared residuals from the original, unrestricted model. This $F$-statistic is usually reported by statistical software in an analysis of variance (ANOVA) table that accompanies each regression.

5. The restricted least squares estimator combines sample and nonsample information. It imposes exact linear constraints upon the parameters. This estimator is biased, unless the constraints are exactly true, but it has smaller variance than the least squares estimator.

6. Multicollinearity exists when there are one or more near exact linear relations among the explanatory variables. This condition causes the least squares estimator to have inflated variances, resulting in imprecise and unreliable estimates. Countermeasures include using more and better data, and/or using nonsample information via restricted least squares.

7. In order to predict a value of the dependent variable, $y_0 = \beta_1 + x_{02}\beta_2 + x_{03}\beta_3 + \cdots + x_{0K}\beta_K + e_0$, the best linear unbiased predictor is $\hat{y}_0 = b_1 + x_{02}b_2 + x_{03}b_3 + \cdots + x_{0K}b_K$ where the $b_k$s are the least squares estimators. A prediction interval is $\hat{y}_0 \pm t_c \text{se}(f)$, where $\text{se}(f)$ is the standard error of the forecast.

## 8.11 Exercises

8.1 Use the data in Table 7.1 to:
   (a) Obtain least squares estimates for the model of total revenue in equation 7.1.2.
   (b) Verify the sums of squares in Table 8.1 and the calculation of $R^2$ in equation 8.3.2.
   (c) Verify that $R^2$ is the squared sample correlation between $y_t$ and $\hat{y}_t$.
   (d) Obtain the adjusted $R^2$ value, $\overline{R}^2$
   (e) Verify the value of the $t$-statistic in equation 8.1.1.

8.2 Write up the results relating to the estimation of the total revenue model in equation 7.1.2 based on the data in Table 7.1. The report should be complete, beginning with the economic model and including a discussion of the results and all standard tests.

8.3 Using the combined data in Tables 7.1 and 8.4
   (a) Obtain the results reported in equation (8.5.6).
   (b) Estimate the model in (8.6.2) and obtain from it the sum of squared errors used in the test of the significance of advertising.
   (c) Use your software's "TEST" statement to carry out the tests described in Sections 8.6.1, 8.6.2 and 8.6.3.
   (d) Obtain the restricted model for the test described in Section 8.6.3 and use it to calculate the restricted sum of squared errors, $SSE_R$.
   (e) Obtain a 95 percent prediction interval for total revenue if $p = 2$ and $a = 20$.
   (f) Is there any evidence of multicollinearity present in the data?
   (g) Write a report summarizing all your findings.

8.4 In Exercise 7.4 the model

$$Y_t = \alpha K_t^{\beta_2} L_t^{\beta_3} E_t^{\beta_4} M_t^{\beta_5} \exp\{e_t\}$$

was estimated using the data in the file *manuf.dat*. Using the data and results from Exercise 7.4, test the following hypotheses
(a) $H_0 : \beta_2 = 0$ against $H_1 : \beta_2 \neq 0$
(b) $H_0 : \beta_2 = 0, \beta_3 = 0$ against $H_1 : \beta_2 \neq 0$ and / or $\beta_3 \neq 0$
(c) $H_0 : \beta_2 = 0, \beta_4 = 0$ against $H_1 : \beta_2 \neq 0$ and / or $\beta_4 \neq 0$
(d) $H_0 : \beta_2 = 0, \beta_3 = 0, \beta_4 = 0$ against $H_1 : \beta_2 \neq 0$ and / or $\beta_3 \neq 0$ and / or $\beta_4 \neq 0$
(e) $H_0 : \beta_2 + \beta_3 + \beta_4 + \beta_5 = 1$ against the alternative $H_1 : \beta_2 + \beta_3 + \beta_4 + \beta_5 \neq 1$
(f) Analyze the impact of collinearity on this model.

8.5 Consider the model

$$y_t = \beta_1 + x_{t2}\beta_2 + x_{t3}\beta_3 + e_t$$

and suppose that application of least squares to 20 observations on these variables yields the following results:

$$\begin{bmatrix} b_1 \\ b_2 \\ b_3 \end{bmatrix} = \begin{bmatrix} 0.96587 \\ 0.69914 \\ 1.7769 \end{bmatrix} \quad \hat{cov}\begin{bmatrix} b_1 \\ b_2 \\ b_3 \end{bmatrix} = \begin{bmatrix} 0.21812 & 0.019195 & -0.050301 \\ 0.019195 & 0.048526 & -0.031223 \\ -0.050301 & -0.031223 & 0.037120 \end{bmatrix}$$

$$\hat{\sigma}^2 = 2.5193 \qquad R^2 = 0.9466$$

(a) Find the total variation, unexplained variation, and explained variation for this model.
(b) Find 95 percent interval estimates for $\beta_2$ and $\beta_3$.
(c) Use a $t$-test to test the hypothesis $H_0 : \beta_2 \geq 1$ against the alternative $H_1 : \beta_2 < 1$.
(d) Use your answers in part (a) to test the joint hypothesis $H_0 : \beta_2 = 0, \beta_3 = 0$.

8.6 Consider Exercise 7.3 where the cubic cost function

$$y_t = \beta_1 + \beta_2 x_t + \beta_3 x_t^2 + \beta_4 x_t^3 + e_t$$

was estimated.
(a) Find 95 percent interval estimates for the parameters $\beta_2$, $\beta_3$, and $\beta_4$.
(b) Test whether the data suggest that a linear function will suffice.
(c) Test whether the data suggest that a quadratic function will suffice.
(d) What parameter restrictions imply a linear average cost function? Test these restrictions.
(e) Estimate a log-linear cost function of the form $\ln y_t = \alpha_1 + \alpha_2 \ln x_t + e_t$.

Do you think this is preferable to the cubic? Is the log–linear cost function reasonable from an economic standpoint?

8.7 Suppose that, from a sample of 63 observations, the least squares estimates and the corresponding estimated covariance matrix are given by

$$\begin{bmatrix} b_1 \\ b_2 \\ b_3 \end{bmatrix} = \begin{bmatrix} 2 \\ 3 \\ -1 \end{bmatrix} \quad \hat{cov}\begin{bmatrix} b_1 \\ b_2 \\ b_3 \end{bmatrix} = \begin{bmatrix} 3 & -2 & 3 \\ -2 & 4 & 0 \\ 1 & 0 & 3 \end{bmatrix}$$

Test each of the following hypotheses and state the conclusion:
(a) $\beta_2 = 0$
(b) $\beta_1 + 2\beta_2 = 5$
(c) $\beta_1 - \beta_2 + \beta_3 = 4$

8.8   Use the sample data for beer consumption in Table 8.5 to:
   (a) Compute the coefficients of the demand relation using only sample information. Compare and contrast these results to the restricted coefficient results given in Section 8.7.
   (b) Examine the presence of multicollinearity.
   (c) Use equation 8.7.7 to construct a 95 percent prediction interval for $q$ when $p_B = 3.00$, $p_L = 10$, $p_R = 2.00$ and $m = 50,000$. (Hint: construct the interval for $\ln(q)$ and then take antilogs.)
   (d) Repeat part (c) using the unconstrained model from part (a).

8.9   Consider production functions of the form $Q = f(L, K)$ where $Q$ is the output measure and $L$ and $K$ are labor and capital inputs respectively. A popular functional form is the Cobb–Douglas equation

$$\ln(Q) = \beta_1 + \beta_2 \ln(L) + \beta_3 \ln(K) + e_t.$$

   (a) Use the data in the file *cobb.dat* to estimate the Cobb–Douglas production function. Is there evidence of multicollinearity?
   (b) Re-estimate the model with the restriction of constant returns to scale, i.e., $\beta_2 + \beta_3 = 1$, and comment on the results.

## *8.12* References

GRIFFITHS, W. E., R. C. HILL, AND G. G. JUDGE (1993). *Learning and Practicing Econometrics.* New York: John Wiley and Sons, Chapters 9–11 and 13.

GUJARATI, DAMODAR (1995). *Basic Econometrics, 3rd Edition.* New York: McGraw-Hill, Chapters 7.8, 8, 10.

STUDENMUND, A. H. (1992). *Using Econometrics: A Practical Guide, 2nd Edition.* New York: HarperCollins, Chapters 5 and 8.

# *Chapter* 9

# Extensions of the Multiple Regression Model

## *9.1* Introduction

In chapters 7 and 8 we discussed the multiple regression model

$$y_t = \beta_1 + \beta_2 x_{t2} + \beta_3 x_{t3} + \cdots + \beta_K x_{tK} + e_t \tag{9.1.1}$$

and the assumptions of the model, which are

---

**ASSUMPTIONS OF THE MULTIPLE REGRESSION MODEL**

1. $y_t = \beta_1 + \beta_2 x_{t2} + \cdots + \beta_K x_{tK} + e_t, \; t = 1, \ldots, T$
2. $E(y_t) = \beta_1 + \beta_2 x_{t2} + \cdots + \beta_K x_{tK} \Leftrightarrow E(e_t) = 0$
3. $\mathrm{var}(y_t) = \mathrm{var}(e_t) = \sigma^2$
4. $\mathrm{cov}(y_t, y_s) = \mathrm{cov}(e_t, e_s) = 0$
5. The values of $x_{tk}$ are not random and are not exact linear functions of the other explanatory variables
6. $y_t \sim N(\beta_1 + \beta_2 x_{t2} + \cdots + \beta_K x_{tK}, \sigma^2) \Leftrightarrow e_t \sim N(0, \sigma^2)$

---

Assumption 1 defines the statistical model that we assume is appropriate for *all T* of the observations in our sample. One part of the assertion is that the parameters of the model, $\beta_k$, are the same for each and every observation. Recall that

$\beta_k$ = the change in $E(y_t)$ when $x_{tk}$ is increased by one unit, and all other variables are held constant

$$= \frac{\Delta E(y_t)}{\Delta x_{tk}} \text{ (other variables held constant)} = \frac{\partial E(y_t)}{\partial x_{tk}}$$

That is, assumption 1 implies that for each of the observations $t = 1, \ldots, T$ the effect of a one-unit change in $x_{tk}$ on $E(y_t)$ is exactly the same. If this assumption does not hold, and if the parameters are not the same for all the observations, then the meaning of the least squares estimates of the parameters in equation 9.1.1 is not clear.

In this chapter we consider several procedures for extending the multiple regression model of chapter 8 to situations in which the regression parameters are different for some or all of the observations in a sample. First, we use **dummy variables,** which are explanatory variables that take one of two values, usually 0 or 1. These simple variables are a very powerful tool for capturing qualitative characteristics of individuals, such as gender, race, and geographic region of residence. In general, we use dummy variables to describe any event that has only two possible outcomes. We will use dummy variables to account for such features in our model. As a second tool for capturing parameter variation, we make use of **interaction variables.** These are variables formed by multiplying two or more explanatory variables together. When using either dummy variables or interaction variables, some changes in model interpretation are required. We will discuss each of these scenarios.

We end the chapter with a discussion of an entirely different type of model, in which a qualitative characteristic is on the *left-hand* side of an equation. That is, we have a **qualitative dependent variable.** The statistical methods required for such a situation are different from those we have considered so far. We will provide a brief introduction to these interesting models and methods.

## *9.2* The Use of Intercept Dummy Variables

Dummy variables allow us to construct models in which some or all model parameters, including the intercept, change for some of the observations in the sample. In this section we examine how to modify the regression model so that we can identify changes in the intercept parameter.

To make matters specific, let us consider the classic problem of estimating the relationship between U.S. consumption and income during the period 1929–1970. Let $C_t$ denote the real per capita personal consumption in year $t$ and $Y_t$ denote real per capita disposable income in year $t$. Initially we may specify the regression model as

$$C_t = \beta_1 + \beta_2 Y_t + e_t \quad t = 1929, \ldots, 1970 \qquad (9.2.1)$$

A moment's reflection will indicate a difficulty with this specification. During part of this period the world was waging war, and we know that personal consumption expenditures were drastically reduced during the years of confrontation; the relationship between consumption and income was altered during these years. Perhaps either $\beta_1$ or $\beta_2$, or both, changed during the sample period. If such changes are ignored, then we violate model assumption 1. To account for the change, and to recognize the fact that some years of the sample period were war years, we must develop a way to incorporate such nonquantitative, or *qualitative,* factors into an economic model.

One way to capture qualitative characteristics within economic models is to use dummy variables. These are often called *binary* or *dichotomous* variables as they take just two values, usually 1 or 0, to indicate the presence or absence of a characteristic. That is, a dummy variable $D$ is

$$D = \begin{cases} 1 & \text{if characteristic is present} \\ 0 & \text{if characteristic is not present} \end{cases} \qquad (9.2.2)$$

To incorporate this idea into the consumption model, let us define the war period for the United States as 1941–1946 and construct the dummy variable $D$ as

$$D_t = \begin{cases} 1 & \text{if } t = 1941, \ldots, 1946 \\ 0 & \text{otherwise} \end{cases} \qquad (9.2.3)$$

Thus, the dummy variable $D$ is 1 during the war period and 0 during nonwar years. If we add this variable to the regression model (equation 9.2.1), along with $\delta$, a new parameter, we obtain

$$C_t = \beta_1 + \delta D_t + \beta_2 Y_t + e_t \quad t = 1929, \ldots, 1970 \qquad (9.2.4)$$

The effect of the inclusion of a dummy variable $D_t$ into the regression model is best seen by examining the regression function, $E(C_t)$, during the war and nonwar years. If the model in equation 9.2.4 is correctly specified, then $E(e_t) = 0$ and

$$E(C_t) = \begin{cases} (\beta_1 + \delta) + \beta_2 Y_t & \text{when } D_t = 1 \\ \beta_1 + \beta_2 Y_t & \text{when } D_t = 0 \end{cases} \qquad (9.2.5)$$

We see that by adding the term $\delta D_t$ to the model, the value of the intercept parameter is different for the war and nonwar years. During the war years, when $D_t = 1$, the intercept of the regression function is $(\beta_1 + \delta)$. During the nonwar years the regression function intercept is simply $\beta_1$. This difference is depicted in Figure 9.1.

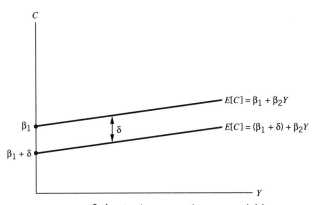

**FIGURE 9.1**   An intercept dummy variable

Adding the dummy variable $D_t$ to the regression model creates a *parallel shift* in the relationship by the amount $\delta$. In the context of the consumption model, the interpretation of the parameter $\delta$ is that it is the change in autonomous consumption during the war years. A dummy variable like $D_t$ that is incorporated into a regression model *to capture a shift in the intercept as the result of some qualitative factor* is called an **intercept dummy variable.** In this consumption function example we expect the level of consumption to decline, and anticipate that $\delta$ will be negative.

The least squares estimator's properties are not affected by the fact that one of the explanatory variables consists only of zeros and ones. $D_t$ is treated as any other explanatory variable. We can construct an interval estimate for $\delta$ or we can test the significance of its least squares estimate. Such a test is a statistical test of whether the war had a "significant effect" on autonomous consumption. If $\delta = 0$, then the war years have no effect on the amount of autonomous consumption.

To further illustrate these ideas, let us examine the sample of data. Table 9.1 contains data on U.S. per capita consumption and disposable income in 1958 dollars.

Using these data we estimate the model in equation 9.2.4 by least squares and obtain the following results:

$$\hat{C}_t = 101.36 - 204.95D_t + .86Y_t \qquad (9.2.6)$$
$$(3.98) \quad (-10.91) \quad (58.73)$$

where $t$-statistics are shown in parentheses. Note that, as anticipated, the estimated value of the parameter $\delta$ is negative. Based on the reported $t$-statistic, we reject the null hypothesis that the war years had no effect on autonomous consumption, $H_0: \delta = 0$, in favor of the alternative $H_1: \delta < 0$ at the .01 level of significance. The

**Table 9.1**   **U.S. Real Per Capita Income and Consumption**

| Year | C | Y | Year | C | Y |
|---|---|---|---|---|---|
| 1929 | 1145 | 1236 | 1950 | 1520 | 1646 |
| 1930 | 1059 | 1128 | 1951 | 1509 | 1657 |
| 1931 | 1016 | 1077 | 1952 | 1525 | 1678 |
| 1932 | 919 | 921 | 1953 | 1572 | 1726 |
| 1933 | 897 | 893 | 1954 | 1575 | 1714 |
| 1934 | 934 | 952 | 1955 | 1659 | 1795 |
| 1935 | 985 | 1035 | 1956 | 1673 | 1839 |
| 1936 | 1080 | 1158 | 1957 | 1683 | 1844 |
| 1937 | 1110 | 1187 | 1958 | 1666 | 1831 |
| 1938 | 1097 | 1105 | 1959 | 1735 | 1881 |
| 1939 | 1131 | 1190 | 1960 | 1749 | 1883 |
| 1940 | 1178 | 1259 | 1961 | 1755 | 1909 |
| 1941 | 1240 | 1427 | 1962 | 1813 | 1968 |
| 1942 | 1197 | 1582 | 1963 | 1865 | 2013 |
| 1943 | 1213 | 1629 | 1964 | 1945 | 2123 |
| 1944 | 1238 | 1673 | 1965 | 2044 | 2235 |
| 1945 | 1308 | 1642 | 1966 | 2123 | 2331 |
| 1946 | 1439 | 1606 | 1967 | 2160 | 2398 |
| 1947 | 1431 | 1513 | 1968 | 2248 | 2480 |
| 1948 | 1438 | 1567 | 1969 | 2301 | 2517 |
| 1949 | 1451 | 1547 | 1970 | 2323 | 2579 |

fitted regression lines for the war and nonwar years, and the data scatter, are shown in Figure 9.2.

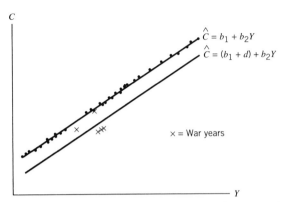

FIGURE **9.2**    The estimated consumption function for the war and nonwar years

The data points for the war years are indicated and are clearly "below" the fitted regression for the nonwar years. We conclude that during the war years the level of consumption spending dropped in a significant way. That is, there was a *structural change* in the economy during the war period that manifested itself, in one way, by a change in the relationship between disposable income and consumption. This is one example of the use of intercept dummy variables. Other examples are discussed in section 9.4.

## 9.3 Slope Dummy Variables

Instead of assuming that the effect of the war caused a change in the intercept of the consumption relationship in equation 9.2.1, let us assume that the change was in the slope of the relationship. We can allow for a change in a slope by including in the model an additional explanatory variable that is equal to the *product* of a dummy variable and a continuous variable. In our model the slope of the relationship is the marginal propensity to consume. If we assume it is one value during the war period and another value during peace, we may specify

$$C_t = \beta_1 + \beta_2 Y_t + \gamma(Y_t D_t) + e_t, \quad t = 1929, \dots, 1970 \qquad (9.3.1)$$

The new variable $(Y_t D_t)$ is the product of income and the dummy variable and is called an **interaction variable,** as it captures the interaction effect of war and income on consumption. Alternatively, it can be called a **slope dummy variable** because it allows for a change in the slope of the relationship. The interaction variable takes a value equal to income during the war period, when $D_t = 1$, and zero during nonwar years, when $D_t = 0$. Despite its unusual nature it is treated just as any other explanatory variable in a regression model. The effect of the inclusion of the interaction variable into the economic model is best seen by examining the regression function during the war and nonwar years.

$$E(C_t) = \beta_1 + \beta_2 Y_t + \gamma(Y_t D_t) = \begin{cases} \beta_1 + (\beta_2 + \gamma)Y_t & \text{when } D_t = 1 \\ \beta_1 + \beta_2 Y_t & \text{when } D_t = 0 \end{cases} \quad (9.3.2)$$

During the war years the slope of the consumption function is $(\beta_2 + \gamma)$; it is $\beta_2$ in peacetime. We would anticipate that $\gamma$, the difference between the war and nonwar marginal propensities to consume, is negative. This situation is depicted in Figure 9.3a.

Another way to see the effect of including an interaction variable is to use calculus. The partial derivative of expected consumption with respect to income, which gives the slope of the relation, is

$$\frac{\partial E(C_t)}{\partial Y_t} = \begin{cases} \beta_2 + \gamma & \text{when } D_t = 1 \\ \beta_2 & \text{when } D_t = 0 \end{cases}$$

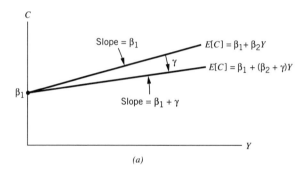

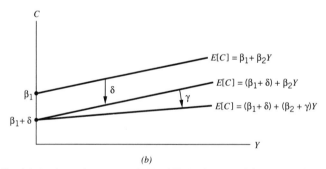

FIGURE **9.3**    (a) A slope dummy variable (b) A slope and intercept dummy variable

If the assumptions of the regression model hold for equation 9.3.1, then the least squares estimators have their usual good properties, as discussed in chapter 7.3. A test of the hypothesis that the marginal propensity to consume did not change during the war period can be carried out by testing the null hypothesis $H_0: \gamma = 0$ against the alternative $H_1: \gamma \neq 0$. In this case, we might test $H_0: \gamma \geq 0$ against $H_1: \gamma < 0$, since we expect the effect to be negative.

If we assume that the war affected *both* the intercept (autonomous consumption) and the slope (the marginal propensity to consume), then both effects may be incorporated into a single model. The resulting regression model is

$$C_t = \beta_1 + \delta D_t + \beta_2 Y_t + \gamma(Y_t D_t) + e_t, \quad t = 1929, \ldots, 1970 \qquad (9.3.3)$$

In this case the regression functions for the war and nonwar years are

$$E(C_t) = \begin{cases} (\beta_1 + \delta) + (\beta_2 + \gamma)Y_t & \text{when } D_t = 1 \\ \beta_1 + \beta_2 Y_t & \text{when } D_t = 0 \end{cases} \qquad (9.3.4)$$

In Figure 9.3$b$ we depict the consumption relations assuming that $\delta < 0$ and $\gamma < 0$.

## 9.4 Some Additional Examples

There are countless situations in which dummy variables are used to capture changes in either intercepts or slopes, or both. Consider the following brief descriptions of problems, some of which reappear in the exercises, in which dummy variables are used:

1. Suppose we wish to study the determinants of wages ($W$) for individuals in a certain profession. Explanatory factors that should be considered are experience ($EXP$), measures of performance ($OUTPUT$), measures of qualifications ($QUAL$), and so on. Also, the gender of the individual might affect his or her wage. To allow for this possibility we can create a dummy variable $D$ that takes the value 1 for male employees and 0 for female employees. If we include $D$ as an intercept dummy variable, we have

$$W = \beta_1 + \delta D + \beta_2 EXP + \beta_3 OUTPUT + \beta_4 QUAL + e \quad (9.4.1)$$

   The parameter $\delta$ measures the difference in wages between male and female employees *after* accounting for experience, performance, and qualifications. A *positive* $\delta$ may indicate wage discrimination, since it implies that males earn more than females with the same characteristics.

2. Modifying example 1, suppose we examine the starting salaries ($SAL$) of economics majors upon graduation. As explanatory variables we might consider qualifications ($GPA$), a dummy variable for gender ($D = 1$ for males), and a dummy variable ($METRICS$) that is 1 for students who completed a course in econometrics and 0 otherwise. The resulting regression model is:

$$SAL = \beta_1 + \delta_1 D + \delta_2 METRICS + \beta_2 GPA + e \qquad (9.4.2)$$

   The coefficient $\delta_1$ measures potential discrimination. The coefficient $\delta_2$ measures the effect on starting salary of taking econometrics, after controlling for gender and grade point average. It is a *large positive number*. That should make you happy! This example makes the point that more than one dummy variable can be used in an equation.

3. Real estate economists study the factors that determine the value of houses ($PRICE$). The major explanatory factors are the size of the home ($SIZE$), the size of the lot ($LOT$), and the age of the home ($AGE$). In addition, however, homes have many qualitative characteristics that contribute to their

value. For example, some homes have swimming pools. We might consider a dummy variable *POOL,* that takes the value 1 if the home has a pool and 0 otherwise. The coefficient of *POOL* measures the additional home value provided by this amenity. Some homes are located in desirable neighborhoods. To capture any neighborhood effect we can use a dummy variable *HOOD* that equals 1 for desirable locations and 0 otherwise. The resulting model is

$$PRICE = \beta_1 + \beta_2 SIZE + \beta_3 LOT + \beta_4 AGE \\ + \delta_1 POOL + \delta_2 HOOD + e \tag{9.4.3}$$

If we believed that the value of a square foot of housing might be different in more desirable neighborhoods, we could include the slope dummy, interaction variable $(SIZE \times HOOD)$ into the model, so that

$$PRICE = \beta_1 + \beta_2 SIZE + \beta_3 LOT + \beta_4 AGE \\ + \delta_1 POOL + \delta_2 HOOD + \gamma(HOOD \times SIZE) + e \tag{9.4.4}$$

In this case the relationship between house price and the size of the house changes, depending on the type of neighborhood. The regression function $E(PRICE)$ is

$$E(PRICE) = \begin{cases} \beta_1 + \beta_2 SIZE + \beta_3 LOT + \beta_4 AGE & POOL = 0, HOOD = 0 \\ (\beta_1 + \delta_1) + \beta_2 SIZE + \beta_3 LOT + \beta_4 AGE & POOL = 1, HOOD = 0 \\ (\beta_1 + \delta_2) + (\beta_2 + \gamma)SIZE + \beta_3 LOT + \beta_4 AGE & POOL = 0, HOOD = 1 \\ (\beta_1 + \delta_1 + \delta_2) + (\beta_2 + \gamma)SIZE + \beta_3 LOT + \beta_4 AGE & POOL = 1, HOOD = 1 \end{cases}$$

In the desirable neighborhood an increase in the size of the house by one unit increases the expected price by $(\beta_2 + \gamma)$; in the less desirable neighborhood the effect of an increase in size on expected price is $\beta_2$. Another way to see this is to use calculus. The change in expected price given a change in size, all other things held constant, is

$$\frac{\partial E(PRICE)}{\partial(SIZE)} = \beta_2 + \gamma \, HOOD = \begin{cases} \beta_2 + \gamma & HOOD = 1 \\ \beta_2 & HOOD = 0 \end{cases}$$

To illustrate, suppose we obtain a sample of data, estimate the model 9.4.4, and obtain the estimates: $b_2 = 50.25$ (for $\beta_2$) and $\hat{\gamma} = 12.75$. These estimates imply that

$$\frac{\partial E(\hat{PRICE})}{\partial(SIZE)} = 50.25 + 12.75 \, HOOD = \begin{cases} 63.00 & HOOD = 1 \\ 50.25 & HOOD = 0 \end{cases}$$

That is, in a desirable neighborhood the price of an additional square foot of house area is \$63.00, while in other neighborhoods the value of an additional square foot of area is only \$50.25. Other qualitative characteristics of this sort are the presence or absence of fireplaces, garages, carports, and so on.

4.  Marketing researchers study the factors that contribute to sales of a product. Suppose we are interested in explaining the weekly sales of Pasta Magic, a

particular brand of spaghetti sauce, in a large supermarket. The weekly sales ($QMAGIC$) are a function of the shelf price ($PMAGIC$) and the shelf price of its major competitor, Chef Rufino's Gourmet Pasta ($PCHEF$). Also, sales are a function of advertising, a feature of particular interest to the marketing experts. For example, if the store constructs a special display for Pasta Magic, then sales might go up. We might construct a dummy variable $DISPLAY$ that equals 1 if a display appears during the week and 0 otherwise. Similarly, if the newspaper contains an advertisement for Pasta Magic we could construct a dummy variable $AD$ equaling 1 if an advertisement appeared during the week and 0 otherwise. Our model in this case would be:

$$QMAGIC = \beta_1 + \beta_2 PMAGIC + \beta_3 PCHEF \\ + \delta_1 DISPLAY + \delta_2 AD + e \qquad (9.4.5)$$

The coefficient $\delta_1$ measures the effect on sales of the store display and $\delta_2$ measures the effect of the newspaper ad. Executives of the Pasta Magic company are keenly interested in the signs and magnitudes of these coefficients, for it helps them determine how much to spend on advertising their product, and where to spend it.

5.  Dummy variables can be used to capture regional effects. In the United States there may be substantial behavioral differences between states in the north, south, east, and west. As an example, the economists at the National Pancake Foundation, whose motto is "a batter life through pancakes," suspect a different relationship between the state per capita consumption of pancakes ($CAKES$) and state per capita income ($INCOME$) within different regions of the country. We create dummy variables $N$ (1 if state is northern; 0 otherwise), $S$ (1 if southern; 0 otherwise), $E$ (1 if eastern; 0 otherwise), and $W$ (1 if western; 0 otherwise). To capture regional effects we will use intercept dummy variables, but if the country is divided into just these four regions, we must avoid including *all four* of the intercept dummy variables. The reason is that, for each and every observation, $N + S + E + W = 1$. The "variable" associated with the intercept parameter takes the value 1 for all observations. If we include all four dummy variables, then there is an exact relationship between them and the intercept variable, violating assumption 5 of the multiple regression model. The least squares estimates cannot be obtained when this assumption is violated. Consequently, we omit one of the dummy variables, with the omitted region serving as the basis for comparison. It is for the same reason that separate dummy variables for both males ($D$) and females ($F = 1 - D$) are not included in the wage equation in the first example. If we omit the eastern dummy variable $E$, the regression model is:

$$CAKES = \beta_1 + \delta_1 N + \delta_2 S + \delta_3 W + \beta_2 INCOME + e \qquad (9.4.6)$$

The regression functions, $E(CAKES)$, for the different regions are:

$$E(CAKES) = \begin{cases} \beta_1 + \beta_2 INCOME & EASTERN\ STATE \\ \beta_1 + \delta_1 + \beta_2 INCOME & NORTHERN\ STATE \\ \beta_1 + \delta_2 + \beta_2 INCOME & SOUTHERN\ STATE \\ \beta_1 + \delta_3 + \beta_2 INCOME & WESTERN\ STATE \end{cases}$$

The parameter $\beta_1$ is the intercept of the relationship in the eastern region, and it represents "autonomous" consumption of pancakes and includes any eastern regional effect. The parameter $\delta_1$ measures the *difference* in the intercepts between the northern and eastern regions, and thus, it measures the effect of a state being in the northern region, relative to the eastern region. If $\delta_1 > 0$, for example, then there is a larger autonomous consumption of pancakes in the northern region than in the eastern region. Similarly, $\delta_2$ measures the effect of a state being southern, relative to eastern, and $\delta_3$ measures the western regional effect. Which region is omitted does not matter mathematically. The interpretation of the regional dummies is always with respect to the omitted region.

## 9.5 Testing for the Existence of Qualitative Effects

If the regression model assumptions hold, and the errors $e$ are normally distributed (assumption 6), or if the errors are not normal but the sample is large, then the testing procedures outlined in chapter 8, sections 8.1 and 8.2, may be used to test for the presence of qualitative effects.

### 9.5.1 TESTING FOR A SINGLE QUALITATIVE EFFECT

Tests for the presence of a single qualitative effect can be based on the $t$-distribution. For example, in the consumption model from section 9.2,

$$C_t = \beta_1 + \delta D_t + \beta_2 Y_t + e_t \quad t = 1929, \ldots, 1970 \tag{9.2.4}$$

let $d$ be the least squares estimator of $\delta$. Then,

$$t = \frac{d - \delta}{\text{se}(d)} \sim t_{(T-K)} \tag{9.5.1}$$

To test the null hypothesis $H_0$: $\delta = c$, where $c$ is any constant, against the alternative $H_1$: $\delta \neq c$, we use the test statistic

$$t = \frac{d - c}{\text{se}(d)} \tag{9.5.2}$$

The test statistic $t$ in (9.5.2) has a $t$-distribution with $T - K$ degrees of freedom if the null hypothesis is true. We reject the null hypothesis if $|t| \geq t_c$, where $t_c$ is the critical value (for a two-tailed test) corresponding to the chosen level of significance $\alpha$.

In a test of significance we choose $c = 0$. If $\delta = 0$, then there is no difference in the regression functions, equation 9.2.5, for the war and nonwar years. Testing whether the war had an effect on autonomous consumption, as in equation 9.2.4, we have, in our standard testing format,

1. $H_0$: $\delta = 0$
2. $H_1$: $\delta \neq 0$

3.  The test statistic, if the null hypothesis is true, is

$$t = \frac{d}{se(d)} \sim t_{(T-K)}$$

4.  At the $\alpha = .01$ level of significance we reject the null hypothesis if $|t| \geq 2.708$

5.  The value of the test statistic is

$$t = \frac{d - c}{se(d)} = \frac{-204.95}{18.79} = -10.91$$

Because $-10.91 < -t_c = -2.708$, we reject the null hypothesis and conclude that the war did have an impact upon autonomous consumption.

In this example the relevant null and alternative hypotheses might be $H_0$: $\delta \geq 0$ and $H_1$: $\delta < 0$. For this one-tailed test, we compare the calculated value of $t$ to the critical value $-t_c = -2.4258$ for an $\alpha = 0.01$ level of significance. We reject this null hypothesis and conclude that the war had a *negative* effect on autonomous consumption.

### 9.5.2  TESTING JOINTLY FOR THE PRESENCE OF SEVERAL QUALITATIVE EFFECTS

If a model has more than one dummy variable, representing several qualitative characteristics, the significance of each, apart from the others, can be tested using the *t*-test outlined in the previous section. It is often of interest, however, to test the *joint* significance of *all* the qualitative factors. Consider the following examples:

1.  The regression model in equation 9.4.6 contains dummy variables that allow regional differences. In addition to testing the significance of the individual regional effects using *t*-tests, we can test for the presence of *any* regional effects by testing the joint null hypothesis $H_0$: $\delta_1 = 0$, $\delta_2 = 0$, $\delta_3 = 0$ against the alternative $H_1$: at least one $\delta_i \neq 0$. If the null hypothesis is true, then there are no regional effects, and the regression functions in equation 9.4.7 are all identical and equal to $E(CAKES) = \beta_1 + \beta_2 INCOME$, implying that there are no regional differences in behavior when it comes to pancake consumption.

    The *F*-test procedure is described in chapter 8, section 8.4. The test statistic for a joint hypothesis is

$$F = \frac{(SSE_R - SSE_U)/J}{SSE_U/(T - K)} \tag{9.5.3}$$

where $SSE_R$ is the sum of squared least squares residuals from the "restricted" model in which the null hypothesis is assumed to be true, $SSE_U$ is the sum of squared residuals from the original, "unrestricted," model, $J$ is the number of joint hypotheses, and $(T - K)$ is the number of degrees of freedom in the unrestricted model. If the null hypothesis is true, then the test statistic $F$ has an $F$-distribution with $J$ numerator degrees of freedom and $(T - K)$ denominator degrees of freedom, $F_{(J, T-K)}$. We reject the null hypothesis if $F \geq F_c$, where $F_c$ is the critical value, illustrated in Figure 8.1, for the level of significance $\alpha$.

To test the $J = 3$ joint null hypotheses $H_0$: $\delta_1 = 0$, $\delta_2 = 0$, $\delta_3 = 0$, we obtain the unrestricted sum of squared errors $SSE_U$ by estimating equation 9.4.6. The restricted sum of squares $SSE_R$ is obtained by estimating the restricted model

$$CAKES = \beta_1 + \beta_2 INCOME + e \qquad (9.5.4)$$

2. As the second example, the real estate model, in section 9.4 we introduced both intercept ($HOOD$) and slope dummy variables ($HOOD \times SIZE$) to capture a neighborhood effect in equation 9.4.4. In this model we can test whether there is a neighborhood effect on the intercept by testing $H_0$: $\delta_2 = 0$ against $H_1$: $\delta_2 \neq 0$. We can test whether there is a neighborhood effect on the slope by testing $H_0$: $\gamma = 0$ against $H_1$: $\gamma \neq 0$. Each of these are $t$-tests of a single hypothesis. To test for *any* neighborhood effect, on either the intercept or slope, we test the $J = 2$ joint null hypotheses $H_0$: $\delta_2 = 0$, $\gamma = 0$ against $H_1$: $\delta_2 \neq 0$ and/or $\gamma \neq 0$. The unrestricted model is the original equation 9.4.4. The restricted model, which assumes the joint null hypothesis is true, is

$$PRICE = \beta_1 + \beta_2 SIZE + \beta_3 LOT + \beta_4 AGE + \delta_1 POOL + e \quad (9.5.5)$$

For the $F$-test the restricted sum of squared errors, $SSE_R$, is obtained by estimating equation 9.5.5.

## 9.6 Testing the Equivalence of Two Regressions Using Dummy Variables

So far we have considered the possibility that a qualitative factor affects the intercept, or a slope, or both, within a regression equation. We now extend the effects of the qualitative factor to the intercept and *all* slopes in a regression equation. As a first example let us return to the first example in section 9.4, the wage equation, which we rewrite here with one minor notational change:

$$W = \beta_1 + \delta_1 D + \beta_2 EXP + \beta_3 OUTPUT + \beta_4 QUAL + e \qquad (9.6.1)$$

The intercept dummy variable $D$ (1 for men; 0 for women) allows for a parallel shift in the wage equation for women relative to men. But what if discrimination affects not only the intercept, but also changes rewards for experience, output, and qualifications? To allow for all these possibilities we add slope dummy variables for each of these explanatory variables:

$$W = \beta_1 + \delta_1 D + \beta_2 EXP + \delta_2 (D \times EXP) + \beta_3 OUTPUT \qquad (9.6.2)$$
$$+ \delta_3 (D \times OUTPUT) + \beta_4 QUAL + \delta_4 (D \times QUAL) + e$$

The regression functions $E(W)$, from equation 9.6.2, for men and women are

$E(W) =$
$$\begin{cases} (\beta_1 + \delta_1) + (\beta_2 + \delta_2)EXP + (\beta_3 + \delta_3)OUTPUT + (\beta_4 + \delta_4)QUAL & \text{if } D = 1 \\ \beta_1 + \beta_2EXP + \beta_3OUTPUT + \beta_4QUAL & \text{if } D = 0 \end{cases}$$
$$(9.6.3)$$

Not only are the intercepts of these regression equations different, but also the effects of *all* the other explanatory variables are different for men and women. Estimating equation 9.6.2 is equivalent to estimating two entirely separate wage equations, one for men and one for women.

We can test whether there are any differences in the wage equations for men and women by testing the $J = 4$ joint hypotheses $H_0$: $\delta_1 = 0$, $\delta_2 = 0$, $\delta_3 = 0$, $\delta_4 = 0$ against the alternative $H_1$: at least one of the $\delta_i \neq 0$. If the null hypothesis is true, then the regression functions $E(W)$ for men and women are identical, implying that there is no difference in how men and women are rewarded, and thus no gender discrimination. If the null hypothesis is *not* true, then there is a difference in how men and women are rewarded, and the parameters in their wage equations are not identical.

Testing the equivalence of regression equations is sometimes called a **Chow test,** after the econometrician Gregory Chow, who studied some aspects of this type of testing. One important use of the test is to determine if data from two or more sources can be "pooled" together for the purposes of a regression analysis. As an example, let us consider the investment behavior of two large corporations, General Electric and Westinghouse. These firms compete against each other and produce many of the same types of products. We might wonder if they have similar investment strategies. In Table 9.2 are investment data for the years 1935 to 1954 (this is a famous data set) for these two corporations. The variables, for each firm, in 1947 dollars, are

$INV$ = gross investment in plant and equipment

$V$ = value of the firm = value of common and preferred stock

$K$ = stock of capital

A simple investment function is

$$INV_t = \beta_1 + \beta_2V_t + \beta_3K_t + e_t \qquad (9.6.4)$$

If we combine the data for both firms we have $T = 40$ observations with which to estimate the parameters of the investment function. But combining the two sources of data is valid only if the regression parameters *and* the variances of the error terms are the *same* for both corporations. If these parameters are not the same, and we combine the data sets anyway, it is equivalent to *restricting* the investment functions of the two firms to be identical when they are not, and the least squares estimators of the parameters in the restricted model (equation 9.6.4) are biased and inconsistent. Estimating the restricted model by least squares provides the *restricted* sum of squared errors, $SSE_R$, that we will use in the formation of an $F$-test statistic.

*Table 9.2*   **Time Series Data on real *INV*, *V* and *K***

| Year | General Electric | | | Westinghouse | | |
|---|---|---|---|---|---|---|
| | INV | V | K | INV | V | K |
| 1 | 33.1 | 1170.6 | 97.8 | 12.93 | 191.5 | 1.8 |
| 2 | 45.0 | 2015.8 | 104.4 | 25.90 | 516.0 | 0.8 |
| 3 | 77.2 | 2803.3 | 118.0 | 35.05 | 729.0 | 7.4 |
| 4 | 44.6 | 2039.7 | 156.2 | 22.89 | 560.4 | 18.1 |
| 5 | 48.1 | 2256.2 | 172.6 | 18.84 | 519.9 | 23.5 |
| 6 | 74.4 | 2132.2 | 186.6 | 28.57 | 628.5 | 26.5 |
| 7 | 113.0 | 1834.1 | 220.9 | 48.51 | 537.1 | 36.2 |
| 8 | 91.9 | 1588.0 | 287.8 | 43.34 | 561.2 | 60.8 |
| 9 | 61.3 | 1749.4 | 319.9 | 37.02 | 617.2 | 84.4 |
| 10 | 56.8 | 1687.2 | 321.3 | 37.81 | 626.7 | 91.2 |
| 11 | 93.6 | 2007.7 | 319.6 | 39.27 | 737.2 | 92.4 |
| 12 | 159.9 | 2208.3 | 346.0 | 53.46 | 760.5 | 86.0 |
| 13 | 147.2 | 1656.7 | 456.4 | 55.56 | 581.4 | 111.1 |
| 14 | 146.3 | 1604.4 | 543.4 | 49.56 | 662.3 | 130.6 |
| 15 | 98.3 | 1431.8 | 618.3 | 32.04 | 583.8 | 141.8 |
| 16 | 93.5 | 1610.5 | 647.4 | 32.24 | 635.2 | 136.7 |
| 17 | 135.2 | 1819.4 | 671.3 | 54.38 | 723.8 | 129.7 |
| 18 | 157.3 | 2079.7 | 726.1 | 71.78 | 864.1 | 145.5 |
| 19 | 179.5 | 2371.6 | 800.3 | 90.08 | 1193.5 | 174.8 |
| 20 | 189.6 | 2759.9 | 888.9 | 68.60 | 1188.9 | 213.5 |

Using the Chow test we can test whether or not the investment functions for the two firms are identical. To do so, let $D$ be a dummy variable that is 1 for the 20 Westinghouse observations, and 0 otherwise. We then include an intercept dummy variable and a complete set of slope dummy variables

$$INV_t = \beta_1 + \delta_1 D_t + \beta_2 V_t + \delta_2(D_t V_t) + \beta_3 K_t + \delta_3(D_t K_t) + e_t \quad (9.6.5)$$

This is an *unrestricted* model. From the least squares estimation of this model we will obtain the unrestricted sum of squared errors, $SSE_U$, that we will use in the construction of an $F$-statistic shown in equation 8.4.3.

We test the equivalence of the investment regression functions for the two firms by testing the $J = 3$ joint null hypotheses $H_0$: $\delta_1 = 0$, $\delta_2 = 0$, $\delta_3 = 0$ against the alternative $H_1$: at least one $\delta_i \neq 0$. Let us use the data in Table 9.2 to carry out this test. The estimated restricted and unrestricted models, with $t$-statistics in parentheses, and their sums of squared residuals are as follows.

Restricted (one relation for all observations):

$$\hat{INV} = 17.8720 + 0.0152V + 0.1436K$$
$$(2.544) \quad (2.452) \quad (7.719) \quad\quad (9.6.6)$$

$$SSE_R = 16563.00$$

Unrestricted:

$$I\hat{N}V = -9.9563 + 9.4469D + 0.0266V + 0.0263(D \times V) + 0.1517K - 0.0593(D \times K)$$
$$\quad\; (0.421) \quad (0.328) \quad (2.265) \quad (0.767) \qquad\qquad (7.837) \quad (-0.507) \qquad\qquad (9.6.7)$$

$SSE_U = 14989.82$

Constructing the $F$-statistic, which we developed in chapter 8.4, we have

$$F = \frac{(SSE_R - SSE_U)/J}{SSE_U/(T - K)} = \frac{(16563.00 - 14989.82)/3}{14989.82/(40 - 6)} = 1.1894 \qquad (9.6.8)$$

The $\alpha = .05$ critical value $F_c = 2.8826$ comes from the $F_{(3,34)}$ distribution. Since $F < F_c$, we cannot reject the null hypothesis that the investment functions for General Electric and Westinghouse are identical. In this case the joint $F$-test and the individual $t$-tests of the dummy variable and slope dummy variables reach the same conclusion. *However, remember that the t- and F-tests have different purposes and their outcomes will not always match in this way.*

It is interesting that for the Chow test we can calculate $SSE_U$, the unrestricted sum of squared errors, another way, which is frequently used in practice. Instead of estimating the model (equation 9.6.5) to obtain $SSE_U$, we can estimate the simpler model in equation 9.6.4 twice. Using the $T = 20$ General Electric observations, estimate equation 9.6.4 by least squares; call the sum of squared residuals from this estimation $SSE_1$. Then, using the $T = 20$ Westinghouse observations, estimate equation 9.6.4 by least squares; call the sum of squared residuals from this estimation $SSE_2$. The unrestricted sum of squared residuals $SSE_U$ from equation 9.6.5 is identical to the sum $SSE_1 + SSE_2$. You are invited to demonstrate this for this investment example in Exercise 9.10. The advantage of this approach to the Chow test is that it does not require the construction of the dummy and interaction variables.

## 9.7 Interaction Variables

Using a slope dummy variable, which is the product of a dummy variable and a continuous explanatory variable, we can allow the slope of the regression model to be different for a set of observations corresponding to a particular qualitative factor. Using interaction variables, formed by the product of two continuous variables, we can model relationships in which the slope of the regression model is *continuously* changing. In this section we consider two such cases, interaction variables, that are the product of a variable by itself, producing a polynomial term, and interaction variables that are the product of two different variables.

### 9.7.1 POLYNOMIAL TERMS IN A REGRESSION MODEL

In microeconomics you studied "cost" curves and "product" curves that describe a firm. Total cost and total product curves are mirror images of each other, taking the standard "cubic" shapes shown in Figure 9.4.

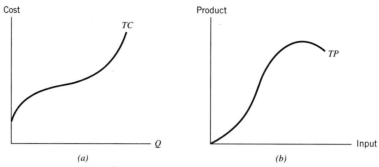

FIGURE **9.4**   (*a*) Total cost curve and (*b*) total product curve

Average and marginal cost curves, and their mirror images, average and marginal product curves, take quadratic shapes, usually represented as shown in Figure 9.5.

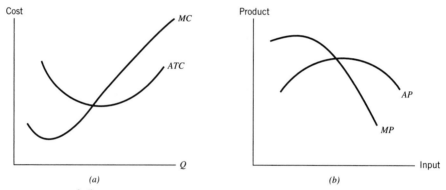

FIGURE **9.5**   Average and marginal (*a*) cost curves and (*b*) product curves

The slopes of these relationships are not constant and cannot be represented by regression models that are "linear in the variables." However, these shapes are easily represented by polynomials, that are a special case of interaction variables in which variables are multiplied by themselves. For example, if we consider the average cost relationship in Figure 9.5a, a suitable regression model is:

$$AC = \beta_1 + \beta_2 Q + \beta_3 Q^2 + e \tag{9.7.1}$$

This quadratic function can take the "U" shape we associate with average cost functions. For the total cost curve in Figure 9.4a a cubic polynomial is in order:

$$TC = \alpha_1 + \alpha_2 Q + \alpha_2 Q^2 + \alpha_4 Q^3 + e \tag{9.7.2}$$

These functional forms, which represent nonlinear shapes, *are still linear regression models, since the parameters enter in a linear way.* The variables $Q^2$ and $Q^3$ are explanatory variables that are treated no differently from any others. This is the same situation we encountered in chapter 6, in which alternative functional forms for regression models were considered. The parameters in equations 9.7.1 and 9.7.2 can still be estimated by least squares.

A difference in these models, also true for the models discussed in chapter 6.3, is in the interpretation of the parameters. The parameters of these models are not themselves slopes. The slope of the average cost curve (equation 9.7.1) is

$$\frac{dE(AC)}{dQ} = \beta_2 + 2\beta_3 Q \qquad (9.7.3)$$

The slope of the average cost curve changes for every value of $Q$ and depends on the parameters $\beta_2$ and $\beta_3$. For this U-shaped curve we expect $\beta_2 < 0$ and $\beta_3 > 0$.

The slope of the total cost curve (equation 9.7.2), which is the marginal cost, is

$$\frac{dE(TC)}{dQ} = \alpha_2 + 2\alpha_3 Q + 3\alpha_4 Q^2 \qquad (9.7.4)$$

The slope is a quadratic function of $Q$, involving the parameters $\alpha_2$, $\alpha_3$, and $\alpha_4$. For a U-shaped marginal cost curve $\alpha_2 > 0$, $\alpha_3 < 0$, and $\alpha_4 > 0$.

Using polynomial terms is an easy and flexible way to capture nonlinear relationships between variables. Their inclusion does not complicate least squares estimation, with one exception, which is explored in Exercise 9.4. As we have shown, however, care must be taken when interpreting the parameters of models containing polynomial terms.

### 9.7.2   INTERACTIONS BETWEEN TWO CONTINUOUS VARIABLES

When the product of two continuous variables is included in a regression model, the effect is to alter the relationship between each of them and the dependent variable. We will consider a "life-cycle" model to illustrate this idea. Suppose we are economists for Gutbusters Pizza, and we wish to study the effect of income and age on an individual's expenditure on pizza. For that purpose we take a random sample of forty individuals, age 18 and older, and record their annual expenditure on pizza (*PIZZA*), their income (*Y*) and age (*AGE*). These data are given in Table 9.3.

As an initial model, let us consider

$$PIZZA = \beta_1 + \beta_2 AGE + \beta_3 Y + e \qquad (9.7.5)$$

The implications of this specification are:

1. $\dfrac{\partial E\,(PIZZA)}{\partial AGE} = \beta_2$    For a *given level of income,* the expected expenditure on pizza changes by the amount $\beta_2$ with an additional year of age. What would you expect here? Based on our casual observation of college students, who appear to consume massive quantities of pizza, we expect the sign of $\beta_2$ to be negative. With the effects of income removed, we expect that as a person ages his or her pizza expenditure will fall.

2. $\dfrac{\partial E(PIZZA)}{\partial Y} = \beta_3$    For individuals of a *given age,* an increase in income of \$1 increases expected expenditures on pizza by $\beta_3$. Since pizza is probably

*Table 9.3*  **Pizza Expenditure Data**

| PIZZA | Y | AGE |
|-------:|-------:|-------:|
| 109 | 15000 | 25 |
| 0 | 30000 | 45 |
| 0 | 12000 | 20 |
| 108 | 20000 | 28 |
| 220 | 15000 | 25 |
| 189 | 30000 | 35 |
| 64 | 12000 | 40 |
| 262 | 12000 | 22 |
| 64 | 28000 | 30 |
| 35 | 22000 | 21 |
| 94 | 44000 | 40 |
| 71 | 10000 | 21 |
| 403 | 222000 | 45 |
| 41 | 32000 | 36 |
| 10 | 45000 | 36 |
| 110 | 55000 | 40 |
| 239 | 29000 | 23 |
| 63 | 39000 | 32 |
| 0 | 70000 | 52 |
| 106 | 55000 | 30 |
| 0 | 90000 | 45 |
| 141 | 6000 | 32 |
| 299 | 18000 | 20 |
| 148 | 55000 | 55 |
| 424 | 10000 | 18 |
| 242 | 23000 | 30 |
| 119 | 35000 | 45 |
| 338 | 38000 | 40 |
| 135 | 45000 | 50 |
| 590 | 85000 | 32 |
| 324 | 22000 | 30 |
| 87 | 25000 | 51 |
| 395 | 29000 | 22 |
| 513 | 132000 | 40 |
| 56 | 35000 | 30 |
| 400 | 80000 | 36 |
| 384 | 55000 | 27 |
| 262 | 30000 | 24 |
| 336 | 27000 | 21 |
| 281 | 80000 | 45 |

a normal good, we expect the sign of $\beta_3$ to be positive. The parameter $\beta_3$ might be called the marginal propensity to spend on pizza.

These are the implications of the model in equation 9.7.5. However, is it reasonable to expect that, *regardless* of the age of the individual, an increase in income by \$1 should lead to an increase in pizza expenditure by $\beta_3$ dollars? Probably not. It would seem more reasonable to assume that as a person grows older, their marginal propensity to spend on pizza declines. That is, as a person ages, less of each extra dollar is expected to be spent on pizza. This is a case in which *the effect of income depends on the age of the individual.* That is, the effect of one variable is modified by another. One way of accounting for such interactions is to include an interaction variable that is the product of the two variables involved. Since $AGE$ and $Y$ are the variables that interact, we will add the variable $(AGE \times Y)$ to the regression model. The result is

$$PIZZA = \beta_1 + \beta_2 AGE + \beta_3 Y + \beta_4(AGE \times Y) + e \qquad (9.7.6)$$

Just as in the cases when we interacted a continuous variable with a dummy variable, and when we interacted a continuous variable with itself, when the product of two continuous variables is included in a model, the interpretation of the parameters requires care. The effects of $Y$ and $AGE$ are:

1. $\dfrac{\partial E(PIZZA)}{\partial AGE} = \beta_2 + \beta_4 Y$     The effect of $AGE$ now depends on income.

   As a person ages, pizza expenditure is expected to fall, and, because $\beta_4$ is expected to be negative, the greater the income, the greater will be the fall attributable to a change in age.

2. $\dfrac{\partial E(PIZZA)}{\partial Y} = \beta_3 + \beta_4 AGE$     The effect of a change in income on ex-

   pected pizza expenditure, which is the marginal propensity to spend on pizza, now depends on $AGE$. If our logic concerning the effect of aging is correct, then $\beta_4$ should be negative. Then, as $AGE$ increases, the value of the partial derivative declines.

Estimates of equations 9.7.5 and 9.7.6, with *t*-statistics in parentheses, are:

$$PI\hat{Z}ZA = 342.8848 - 7.5756AGE + 0.0024Y \qquad (9.7.8)$$
$$(4.740) \qquad (-3.270) \qquad (3.947)$$

$$PI\hat{Z}ZA = 161.4654 - 2.9774AGE + 0.0091Y - 0.00016(Y \times AGE) \quad (9.7.9)$$
$$(1.338) \qquad (-0.888) \qquad (2.473) \qquad (-1.847)$$

In equation 9.7.8 the signs of the estimated parameters are as we anticipated. Both $AGE$ and income ($Y$) have significant coefficients, based on their *t*-statistics. In equation 9.7.9 the product ($Y \times AGE$) enters the equation. Its estimated coefficient is negative and significant at the $\alpha = .05$ level using a one-tailed test. The signs of other coefficients remain the same, but $AGE$, by itself, no longer appears to be a significant explanatory factor. This suggests that $AGE$ affects pizza expenditure through its interaction with income—that is, it affects the marginal propensity to spend on pizza.

Using the estimates in equation 9.7.9 let us estimate the marginal effect of age on pizza expenditure for two individuals; one with $25,000 income and one with $90,000 income.

$$\frac{\partial E(PI\hat{Z}ZA)}{\partial AGE} = b_2 + b_4 Y = -2.9774 - 0.00016Y$$

$$= \begin{cases} -6.9774 & \text{for } Y = \$25,000 \\ -17.3774 & \text{for } Y = \$90,000 \end{cases}$$

That is, we expect that an individual with $25,000 income will reduce expenditure on pizza by $6.98 per year, while the individual with $90,000 income will reduce pizza expenditures by $17.38 per year, all other factors held constant. In Exercise 9.11 you are invited to evaluate more marginal effects of income and age for this model.

As a final note, in sections 9.2 through 9.7 we have examined the use of interaction variables between dummy variables and continuous variables and between two continuous variables. You encountered squared variables earlier in the book; in our discussion of cost curve functional forms in chapter 6.3.2b, and in the extended model of Bay Area Rapid Food total revenues, in equation 8.5.2. You may want to look at these examples again, now with fresh insights, given what you have learned in this chapter.

*The following section contains relatively advanced material and can be skipped without loss of continuity.*

## 9.8  Dummy Dependent Variables

Many of the choices that individuals and firms make are "either–or" in nature. For example, a high school graduate decides to attend college or not. A worker decides to drive to work or get there another way. A household decides to purchase a house or to rent. A firm decides to advertise its product on the Internet or it decides against such advertising. As economists we are interested in explaining why particular choices are made, and what factors enter into the decision process. We also want to know *how much* each factor affects the outcome. Such questions lead us to the problem of constructing a statistical model of discrete, either-or, choices. Following previous sections, choices such as those just listed can be represented by a dummy variable that takes the value 1 if one outcome is chosen, and takes the value 0 otherwise. Unlike previous sections, the dummy variable describing a choice is now the *dependent* variable rather than an independent variable. This fact affects our choice of a statistical model.

### 9.8.1  THE LINEAR PROBABILITY MODEL

We will illustrate *discrete choice models* using an important problem from transportation economics: How can we explain an individual's choice between driving (private transportation) and taking the bus (public transportation) when commuting to work, assuming, for simplicity, that these are the only two alternatives? Represent an individual's choice by the dummy variable

$$y = \begin{cases} 1 & \text{individual drives to work} \\ 0 & \text{individual takes bus to work} \end{cases} \tag{9.8.1}$$

If we collect a random sample of workers who commute to work, then the outcome $y$ will be unknown to us until the sample is drawn. Thus, $y$ is a random variable.

In chapter 2, example 2.1, we described the probability function for such dichotomous random variables by

$$f(y) = p^y(1 - p)^{1-y}, \ y = 0, 1 \tag{9.8.2}$$

where $p$ is the probability that $y$ takes the value 1. This discrete random variable
has expected value $E(y) = p$.

What factors might affect the probability that an individual chooses one transportation mode over the other? One factor will certainly be how long it takes to get
to work one way or the other. Define the explanatory variable

$$x = (\text{commuting time by bus} - \text{commuting time by car})$$

There are other factors that affect the decision, but let us focus on this single
explanatory variable. *A priori* we expect that as $x$ increases, an individual would
be more inclined to drive. That is, we expect a positive relationship between $x$ and
$p$, the probability that an individual will drive to work.

In regression analysis we break the dependent variable into fixed and random
parts. If we do this for the random variable $y$, we have

$$y = E(y) + e = p + e \tag{9.8.3}$$

We then relate the fixed, systematic portion of $y$ to explanatory variables that we
believe help explain its expected value. In this transportation model we explain
$E(y) = p$ by $x$. Assuming that the relationship is linear,

$$E(y) = p = \beta_1 + \beta_2 x \tag{9.8.4}$$

The linear regression model, called the *linear probability model,* that explains the
choice variable $y$ is

$$y = E(y) + e = \beta_1 + \beta_2 x + e \tag{9.8.5}$$

This model is flawed and now rarely applied in practice. One problem with the
linear probability model is that the error term is *heteroskedastic;* the variance of
the error term $e$ varies from one observation to another. The reason for this is
discussed in Griffiths, et al. (1993, p. 739). How we deal with heteroskedastic errors
is the topic of the next chapter. The other problem with the linear probability
model is more serious. If we estimate the parameters of equation 9.8.5 by least
squares, we will obtain the fitted model explaining the systematic portion of $y$,
which is $p$, the probability that an individual chooses to drive to work. That is,

$$\hat{p} = b_1 + b_2 x \tag{9.8.6}$$

When using this model to predict behavior, by substituting alternative values of $x$,
we can easily obtain values of $\hat{p}$ that are less than 0 or greater than 1. Values like
these do not make sense as probabilities, and we are left in a difficult situation.
The problem lies in the fact that in the linear probability model (equation 9.8.4)

we implicitly assume that increases in $x$ have a constant effect on the probability of choosing to drive,

$$\frac{dp}{dx} = \beta_2 \qquad (9.8.7)$$

That is, as $x$ increases, the probability of driving continues to increase at a constant rate. However, since $0 \leq p \leq 1$, a constant rate of increase is impossible. To overcome this problem we consider the nonlinear *probit* model.

### 9.8.2 THE PROBIT MODEL OF DISCRETE CHOICE

To keep the choice probability $p$ within the interval $[0,1]$, a nonlinear S-shaped relationship between $x$ and $p$ can be used. Figure 9.6(a) illustrates such a curve.

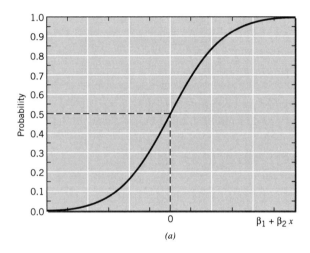

*(a)*

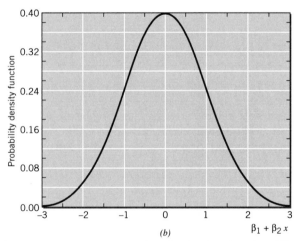

*(b)*

**FIGURE *9.6*** (*a*) Standard normal cumulative distribution function (*b*) Standard normal probability density function

As $x$ increases, the probability curve rises rapidly at first, and then begins to increase at a decreasing rate. The change in probability given a one-unit change in $x$ is given by the *slope* of this curve; it is not constant, as in the linear probability model.

A functional relationship that is used to represent such a curve is the probit function. The probit function is related to the standard normal probability distribution. If $Z$ is a standard normal random variable, then its probability density function is

$$f(z) = \frac{1}{\sqrt{2\pi}} e^{-.5z^2}$$

The probit function is

$$F(z) = P[Z \leq z] = \int_{-\infty}^{z} \frac{1}{\sqrt{2\pi}} e^{-.5u^2} du \qquad (9.8.8)$$

If you are not familiar with integral calculus, ignore the last expression in equation 9.8.8. This mathematical expression is the probability that a standard normal random variable falls to the left of point $z$. In geometric terms it is the area under the standard normal probability density function to the left of $z$.

The probit statistical model expresses the probability $p$ that $y$ takes the value 1 to be

$$p = P[Z \leq \beta_1 + \beta_2 x] = F(\beta_1 + \beta_2 x) \qquad (9.8.9)$$

where $F$ is the probit function. The probit model is said to be *nonlinear* because (9.8.9) is a nonlinear function of $\beta_1$ and $\beta_2$. If $\beta_1$ and $\beta_2$ were known, we could use (9.8.9) to find the probability that an individual will drive to work. However, since these parameters are not known, we will undertake the task of estimating them.

### 9.8.3  ESTIMATION OF THE PROBIT MODEL

To estimate this nonlinear model we take a slightly different approach than the least squares principle. Suppose we randomly select three individuals and observe that the first two drive to work and the third takes the bus; $y_1 = 1$, $y_2 = 1$ and $y_3 = 0$. Furthermore suppose that the values of $x$, the extra minutes it takes commuting by bus, for these individuals are $x_1 = 15$, $x_2 = 20$ and $x_3 = 5$. What is the joint probability of observing $y_1 = 1$, $y_2 = 1$, and $y_3 = 0$? The probability function for $y$ is given by equation 9.8.2, which we now combine with the probit model (equation 9.8.9) to obtain

$$f(y_i) = [F(\beta_1 + \beta_2 x_i)]^{y_i} [1 - F(\beta_1 + \beta_2 x_i)]^{1-y_i}, \; y_i = 0, 1 \qquad (9.8.10)$$

If the three individuals are independently drawn, then the joint probability density function for $y_1$, $y_2$, and $y_3$ is the product of the marginal density functions:

$$f(y_1, y_2, y_3) = f(y_1)f(y_2)f(y_3)$$

Consequently, the probability of observing $y_1 = 1$, $y_2 = 1$, and $y_3 = 0$ is

$$P[y_1 = 1, y_2 = 1, y_3 = 0] = f(1,1,0) = f(1)f(1)f(0)$$

Substituting in equation 9.8.10, and the values of $x_i$, we have

$$
\begin{aligned}
P[y_1 = 1, y_2 = 1, y_3 = 0] = \\
F[\beta_1 + \beta_2(15)] \cdot F[\beta_1 + \beta_2(20)] \cdot \{1 - F[\beta_1 + \beta_2(5)]\} \quad (9.8.11)
\end{aligned}
$$

In statistics, the function (9.8.11), which gives us the probability of observing the sample data, is called the *likelihood function.* Intuitively it makes sense to choose as estimates for $\beta_1$ and $\beta_2$ the values $b_1$ and $b_2$ that *maximize the probability, or likelihood,* of observing the sample. Unfortunately, there are no formulas that give us the values for $b_1$ and $b_2$ as there are in least squares estimation of the linear regression model. Consequently, we must use the computer and techniques from numerical analysis to obtain $b_1$ and $b_2$. On the surface, this appears to be a daunting task, because $F(z)$ from equation 9.8.8 is such an ugly function. As it turns out, however, using a computer to maximize equation 9.8.11 is a relatively easy process. We will spare you the details.

What is most interesting about this *maximum likelihood* estimation procedure is that, although its properties in small samples are not known, we can show that in *large samples,* the maximum likelihood estimator is normally distributed, consistent, and *best,* in the sense that no competing estimator has smaller variances.

Econometric software packages have the maximum likelihood estimation procedure built in for the probit model, and thus, it is not difficult to estimate the parameters $\beta_1$ and $\beta_2$ in practice. However, in order for the maximum likelihood estimation procedure to be reliable, large samples are required. Our expression in equation 9.8.11 was limited to three observations for illustration only, and maximum likelihood estimation should not be carried out with such a small amount of data. In section 9.8.5 we give an empirical example based on a larger sample.

### 9.8.4   INTERPRETATION OF THE PROBIT MODEL

The probit model is represented by equation 9.8.9. In this model we can examine the effect of a one-unit change in $x$ on the probability that $y = 1$ by considering the derivative,

$$\frac{dp}{dx} = \frac{dF(t)}{dt} \cdot \frac{dt}{dx} = f(\beta_1 + \beta_2 x)\beta_2 \quad (9.8.12)$$

where $t = \beta_1 + \beta_2 x$ and $f(\beta_1 + \beta_2 x)$ is the standard normal probability density function evaluated at $\beta_1 + \beta_2 x$. To obtain this result we have used the *chain rule* of differentiation. We estimate this effect by replacing the unknown parameters by their estimates $b_1$ and $b_2$.

In Figure 9.6 we show the probit function $F(z)$ and the standard normal probability density function $f(z)$ just below it.

The expression in equation 9.8.12 shows the effect of an increase in $x$ on $p$. The effect depends on the slope of the probit function, which is given by $f(\beta_1 + \beta_2 x)$ and the magnitude of the parameter $\beta_2$. Equation 9.8.12 has the following implications:

1. Since $f(\beta_1 + \beta_2 x)$ is a probability density function, its value is always *positive*. Consequently the sign of $dp/dx$ is determined by the sign of $\beta_2$. In the transportation problem we expect $\beta_2$ to be positive so that $dp/dx > 0$; as $x$ increases, we expect $p$ to increase.

2. As $x$ changes, the value of the function $f(\beta_1 + \beta_2 x)$ changes. The standard normal probability density function reaches its maximum when $z = 0$, or when $\beta_1 + \beta_2 x = 0$. In this case $p = F(0) = 0.5$, and an individual is equally likely to choose car or bus transportation. It makes sense that in this case the effect of a change in $x$ has its greatest effect, since the individual is "on the borderline" between car and bus transportation. The slope of the probit function $p = F(z)$ is at its maximum when $z = 0$, the borderline case.

3. On the other hand, if $\beta_1 + \beta_2 x$ is large, say near 3, then the probability that the individual chooses to drive is very large and close to 1. In this case, a change in $x$ will have relatively little effect, since $f(\beta_1 + \beta_2 x)$ will be nearly 0. The same is true if $\beta_1 + \beta_2 x$ is a large negative value, say, near $-3$. These results are consistent with the notion that if an individual is "set" in his or her ways, with $p$ near 0 or 1, the effect of a small change in commuting time will be negligible.

   The results of a probit model can also be used to predict an individual's choice. The ability to predict discrete outcomes is very important in many applications. For example, banks prior to approving loans predict the probability that an applicant will default. If the probability of default is high, the loan is either not approved, or additional conditions, such as extra collateral or a higher interest rate, will be imposed.

   In order to predict the probability that an individual chooses the alternative $y = 1$, we may use the probability model $p = F(\beta_1 + \beta_2 x)$. If we obtain estimates $b_1$ and $b_2$ of the unknown parameters, then we estimate the probability $p$ to be

$$\hat{p} = F(b_1 + b_2 x) \qquad (9.8.13)$$

By comparing to a threshold value, like 0.5, we can predict choice using the rule

$$\hat{y} = \begin{cases} 1 & \hat{p} > 0.5 \\ 0 & \hat{p} \le 0.5 \end{cases}$$

### 9.8.5  AN EXAMPLE

As a basis for bringing these models and methods to life, data from Ben-Akiva and Lerman (1985) on automobile and public transportation travel times and the alternative chosen for $T = 21$ individuals are given in Table 9.4. In this table the variable $x_i =$ (bus time $-$ auto time) and the dependent variable $y_i = 1$ if automobile transportation is chosen.

Using the data in Table 9.4, and a numerical optimization program for the probit model (such programs are available in most econometric packages), the maximum likelihood estimates of the parameters are

$$b_1 + b_2 x_i = -0.0644 + 0.0299 x_i$$
$$(-.161) \quad (2.915)$$

where the values in parentheses below the parameter estimates are $t$-values, which are based on estimated standard errors that are valid in large samples. The negative sign of $b_1$ implies that individuals, given that commuting times via bus and auto are equal so $x = 0$, have a bias against driving to work, relative to public transportation, although the estimated coefficient is not statistically significant. The positive sign of $b_2$ indicates that an increase in public transportation travel time increases the probability that an individual will choose to drive to work, and this coefficient is statistically significant.

Based on the positive sign on the estimated coefficient $b_2$ we infer that an increase in public transportation time relative to auto travel increases the probability of auto travel. Suppose that we wish to make a judgment about the magnitude of the effect of increased public transportation time, given that travel via public transportation currently takes 20 minutes longer than auto travel. Using equation 9.8.12,

$$\frac{d\hat{p}}{dx} = f(b_1 + b_2 x)b_2 = f(-0.0644 + 0.0299 \times 20)(0.0299)$$

$$= f(.5355)(0.0299) = 0.3456 \times 0.0299 = 0.0104$$

For the probit probability model, an incremental (one-minute) increase in the travel time via public transportation increases the probability of travel via auto by

**Table 9.4    Data for Transportation Example**

| Auto Time | Bus Time | $x$ | $y$ |
|---|---|---|---|
| 52.9 | 4.4 | −48.5 | 0 |
| 4.1 | 28.5 | 24.4 | 0 |
| 4.1 | 86.9 | 82.8 | 1 |
| 56.2 | 31.6 | −24.6 | 0 |
| 51.8 | 20.2 | −31.6 | 0 |
| 0.2 | 91.2 | 91.0 | 1 |
| 27.6 | 79.7 | 52.1 | 1 |
| 89.9 | 2.2 | −87.7 | 0 |
| 41.5 | 24.5 | −17.0 | 0 |
| 95.0 | 43.5 | −51.5 | 0 |
| 99.1 | 8.4 | −90.7 | 0 |
| 18.5 | 84.0 | 65.5 | 1 |
| 82.0 | 38.0 | −44.0 | 1 |
| 8.6 | 1.6 | −7.0 | 0 |
| 22.5 | 74.1 | 51.6 | 1 |
| 51.4 | 83.8 | 32.4 | 1 |
| 81.0 | 19.2 | −61.8 | 0 |
| 51.0 | 85.0 | 34.0 | 1 |
| 62.2 | 90.1 | 27.9 | 1 |
| 95.1 | 22.2 | −72.9 | 0 |
| 41.6 | 91.5 | 49.9 | 1 |

approximately 0.01, given that taking the bus already requires 20 minutes more travel time than driving.

The estimated parameters of the probit model can also be used to "predict" the behavior of an individual who must choose between auto and public transportation to travel to work. If an individual is faced with the situation that it takes 30 minutes longer to take public transportation than to drive to work, then the estimated probability that auto transportation will be selected is calculated using equation 9.8.13.

$$\hat{p} = F(b_1 + b_2 x) = F(-0.0644 + 0.0299 \times 30) = .798$$

Since the estimated probability that the individual will choose to drive to work is 0.798, which is greater than 0.5, we "predict" that when public transportation takes 30 minutes longer than driving to work, the individual will choose to drive.

### 9.8.6 CONCLUDING REMARKS ABOUT DISCRETE CHOICE MODELS

The list of economic models in which probit statistical models may be useful is a long one. These statistical models are useful in *any* economic setting in which an agent must choose one of two alternatives. Examples include the following:

1.  An economic model explaining why some states in the United States ratified the Equal Rights Amendment and others did not.
2.  An economic model explaining why some individuals take a second, or third, job and engage in "moonlighting."
3.  An economic model of why some legislators in the U.S. House of Representatives vote for a particular bill and others do not.
4.  An economic model of why the federal government awards development grants to some large cities and not others.
5.  An economic model explaining why some loan applications are accepted and others are not at a large metropolitan bank.
6.  An economic model explaining why some individuals vote "yes" for increased spending in a school board election and others vote "no."
7.  An economic model explaining why some female college students decide to study engineering and others do not.

This list illustrates the great variety of circumstances in which a probit model of discrete choice may be used. In each case an economic decision maker chooses between two mutually exclusive outcomes.

We have not gone into technical detail concerning the properties of the maximum likelihood estimator of the probit model, nor have we considered the wide range of hypothesis testing procedures that can be used in such models. For an introductory discussion of these issues consult Griffiths, et al. (1993, Chapter 23).

Probit is one model for binary qualitative choice. Another model, called *logit,* is also frequently used. In fact, the two models are very similar. The difference between them is that while probit is based on the normal distribution, logit is based on the *logistic* distribution. That is, instead of the probit function in equation 9.8.8, logit is based on the logistic cumulative distribution function

$$F(z) = P[Z \le z] = \frac{1}{1 + \exp(-z)}$$

A brief discussion of the logit model can be found in Griffiths, et al. (1993, pp. 751–752.)

In addition to either-or type choices, between two alternatives, economists are also interested in choices among more than two alternatives. As examples, consider the following:

1. Given that you are going to purchase a fast-food pizza, which of the many alternatives will you choose, and why?
2. Given that you are going to a mall for a shopping spree, which mall will you go to, and why?
3. If you are going to enroll in the business school at your university, will you major in economics, marketing, management, or finance?

Models for choices among several alternatives are called *multinomial choice models*. There are probit and logit versions of these models. The estimation of such models is, in principle, similar to estimation of the probit model for binary choice that we have examined. Discussion of multinomial choice models appears in references that are technically more difficult than this book. A good presentation of this and other qualitative choice models can be found in Greene (1990, Chapter 21.)

## *9.9* Summing Up

In this chapter we have considered linear regression models whose parameters may not be the same for all observations in a sample.

1. Using a regression model that assumes fixed coefficients, when the parameters actually vary over individuals, time, or space, is an example of model misspecification.
2. Dummy variables may be incorporated into the regression model to permit parameters to differ for groups of observations with distinct qualitative characteristics, such as gender, race, or occupation.
3. The inclusion of a dummy variable creates a parallel shift in the regression function by altering the intercept for some observations.
4. When dummy variables are interacted with continuous variables, the result is a change in the slope of the regression function for some observations.
5. Interactions between continuous variables serve to modify the slope of the regression function for each value of the continuous variables.

In section 9.8 we discussed the probit model, which is designed for situations in which the dependent variable only takes two values. The probit model is estimated using the maximum likelihood principle.

## *9.10* Exercises

9.1   Use the data in Table 9.1 to estimate the model given in equation 9.2.1. Examine the least squares residuals. Can you identify the war period?

9.2 Use the data in Table 9.1 to do the following:
(a) Estimate the model in equation 9.2.4.
(b) Define a dummy variable $H = 1 - D$. Re-estimate the model in 9.2.4 with $H$ replacing $D$.
(c) Compare the results of the models including $D$ and $H$. Are they consistent with one another?
(d) Estimate equation 9.2.4 but include *both* $H$ and $D$. See how your computer software responds. What is the problem?

9.3 Use the data in Table 9.1 to:
(a) Estimate the model in equation 9.3.1. Test the significance of $\gamma$ at the 5 percent level of significance. Comment on your results.
(b) Estimate the model in equation 9.3.3. Test the joint significance of $\delta$ and $\gamma$ at the 5 percent level of significance. What do you conclude?

9.4 In section 9.7.2 the effect of income on pizza expenditure was permitted to vary by the age of the individual. Before proceeding with this exercise, divide the income data series in Table 9.3 by 1000.
(a) Estimate the regression model in which pizza expenditure depends *only* on income, $Y$.
(b) Estimate the model in equation 9.7.5. Comment on the signs and significance of the parameters, and on the effect of scaling the income variable.
(c) Estimate the model in equation 9.7.6. Comment on the signs and significance of the parameters. Is there a significant interaction effect between age and income? What is the effect of scaling income?
(d) In equation 9.7.6 test the hypothesis that age does not affect pizza expenditure. That is, test the joint null hypothesis $H_0$: $\beta_2 = 0$, $\beta_4 = 0$. What do you conclude?
(e) Construct point estimates and 95 percent interval estimates of the marginal propensity to spend on pizza for individuals of age 20, 30, 40, and 50. Comment on these estimates.
(f) Modify equation 9.7.6 to permit a "life-cycle" effect in which the marginal effect of income on pizza expenditure increases with age, up to a point, and then falls. Do so by adding the term $(AGE^2 \times Y)$ to the model. What sign do you anticipate on this term? Estimate the model and test the significance of the coefficient for this variable.
(g) Check the model used in part (f) for multicollinearity. Add the term $(AGE^3 \times Y)$ to the model in (f) and check the resulting model for multicollinearity.

9.5 A more complete version of Table 9.3 is contained in the file *pizza.dat*. It includes additional information about the forty individuals used in the pizza expenditure example. The dummy variable $S = 1$ for females; 0 otherwise. The variables $E_1$, $E_2$, and $E_3$ are dummy variables indicating level of educational attainment. $E_1 = 1$ for individuals whose highest degree is a high school diploma. $E_2 = 1$ for individuals whose highest degree is a college diploma. $E_3 = 1$ if individuals have a graduate degree. If $E_1$, $E_2$, and $E_3$ are all 0 the individual did not complete high school.
(a) Begin with the model in equation 9.7.6. Include gender ($S$) as an explanatory variable and estimate the resulting model. What is the effect of including this dummy variable? Is gender a relevant explanatory variable?
(b) Begin with the model in equation 9.7.6. Include the dummy variables $E_1$, $E_2$, and $E_3$ as explanatory variables and estimate the resulting model. What

is the effect of including these dummy variables? Is level of educational attainment a significant explanatory variable?

(c) Consider equation 9.7.6. Test the hypothesis that separate regression equations for males and females are identical, against the alternative that they are not. Use the 5 percent level of significance and discuss the consequences of your findings.

9.6*  Data on the weekly sales of a major brand of canned tuna by a supermarket chain in a large midwestern U.S. city during a recent calendar year are contained in the file *tuna.dat*. The variables are

$SAL1$     = unit sales of brand no. 1 canned tuna
$APR1$     = price per can of brand no. 1 canned tuna
$APR2,3$  = price per can of brands nos. 2 and 3 of canned tuna
$Disp$      = a dummy variable that takes the value 1 if there is a store display for brand no. 1 during the week but no newspaper ad; 0 otherwise
$DispAd$ = a dummy variable that takes the value 1 if there is a store display *and* a newspaper ad during the week; 0 otherwise

(a)  Estimate, by least squares, the log–linear model

$$\ln(SAL1) = \beta_1 + \beta_2 APR1 + \beta_3 APR2 + \beta_4 APR3 + \beta_5 Disp + \beta_6 DispAd + e$$

(b)  Discuss and interpret the estimates of $\beta_2$, $\beta_3$, and $\beta_4$.

(c)  Are the signs and *relative* magnitudes of the estimates of $\beta_5$ and $\beta_6$ consistent with economic logic? (*Note:* To interpret the dummy variables within this log–linear equation, you may wish to consult "Estimation with Correctly Interpreted Dummy Variables in Semilogarithmic Equations," by Peter Kennedy, *American Economic Review*, 71, 1981, p. 801.)

(d)  Test, at the $\alpha = .05$ level of significance, each of the following hypotheses:

(i)   $H_0: \beta_5 = 0$, $H_1: \beta_5 \neq 0$
(ii)  $H_0: \beta_6 = 0$, $H_1: \beta_6 \neq 0$
(iii) $H_0: \beta_5 = 0$, $\beta_6 = 0$; $H_1: \beta_5$ or $\beta_6 \neq 0$
(iv) $H_0: \beta_6 \leq \beta_5$, $H_1: \beta_6 > \beta_5$

Discuss the relevance of these hypothesis tests for the supermarket chain's executives.

9.7*  Use the data in Table 9.4 and your computer software to obtain maximum likelihood estimates of the probit model for the auto/public transportation example.

9.8*  Within the context of the auto/public transportation example, what is the probability of choosing to drive to work, and what is the effect of an incremental increase in public transportation travel time on the probability of auto travel, under the following circumstances?

(a) It takes exactly the same amount of time to travel to work via car and public transportation.
(b) The auto takes 15 minutes less.
(c) The auto takes 60 minutes less.

9.9*  Data from William Greene's *Econometric Analysis, 2nd Edition* (1990, p. 672) on the voting outcome, by state, in the 1976 U. S. presidential election are contained in the file *vote.dat.* The outcome variable *y* takes the value of 1 if the popular vote favored the Democratic candidate (Jimmy Carter) and 0 if the vote favored the Republican candidate (Gerald Ford). The other variables are

*Income* = 1975 median income

*School* = median number of years of school completed by persons 18 years of age or older

*Urban* = percentage of population living in an urban area

*Region* = 1 for Northeast, 2 for southeast, 3 for midwest and Middle South, 4 for West and Mountain regions.

(a) Estimate a probit model for the vote outcome using the explanatory variables *Income, School, Urban,* and dummy variables for the Midwest and West. Discuss the fitted model.
(b) Calculate the effect on the probability of the state voting Democratic, given an increase in income of $1,000, in the states of Louisiana, Oklahoma, and California.
(c) What is the estimated probability that Oregon would favor the Democratic candidate?

9.10 Show that the unrestricted sum of squared residuals given in equation 9.6.7 can be obtained by adding together the sums of squared least squares residuals obtained by estimating equation 9.6.4 twice; once using the General Electric data and once using the Westinghouse data.

9.11 Use the data in Table 9.3 to do the following:
(a) Estimate the model 9.7.6 and compare your results to those in equation 9.7.9.
(b) Calculate the marginal effect $\partial E(PIZZA)/\partial Y$ for an individual of average age and income and test the statistical significance of the estimate.
(c) Calculate a 95 percent interval estimate for the marginal effect in (b).
(d) Calculate the marginal effect $\partial E(PIZZA)/\partial AGE$ for an individual of average age and income and test the statistical significance of the estimate.
(e) Calculate a 95 percent interval estimate for the marginal effect in (d).
(f) Write a report to the president of Gutbusters summarizing your findings.

## *9.11* References

There are many text books with more examples of dummy variable use. Three are

GRIFFITHS, W. E., R. C. HILL, AND G. G. JUDGE (1993). *Learning and Practicing Econometrics.* New York: John Wiley and Sons, Chapter 12.

GUJARATI, D. N. (1995). *Basic Econometrics,* (3d ed.). New York: McGraw-Hill, Inc., Chapter 15.

JOHNSTON, J. (1984). *Econometric Methods,* (3d ed.). New York: McGraw-Hill, Inc., Chapter 6.3.

KENNEDY, P. (1981). "Estimation with Correctly Interpreted Dummy Variables in Semi-logarithmic Equations," *American Economic Review, 71,* p. 801.

KENNEDY, P. (1992). *A Guide to Econometrics,* (3d ed.). Cambridge, Mass: MIT Press, Chapter 14.

References for the models of qualitative choice discussed in Section 9.8 are

BEN-AKIVA AND LERMAN (1985). *Discrete Choice Analysis.* Cambridge, Mass.: MIT Press.

GREENE, WILLIAM (1990). *Econometric Analysis,* (2d ed.). New York: MacMillan.

# Part III

# Violations of Basic Assumptions

In both the simple and multiple regression models we made important assumptions about the distribution of $y_t$ and the random error term $e_t$. We assumed that $e_t$ was a random variable with zero mean, $E(e_t) = 0$, that its variance is constant over all the sample observations, $\text{var}(e_t) = \sigma^2$, and that the errors corresponding to different observations were uncorrelated, $\text{cov}(e_t, e_s) = 0$.

Now we address two more "what if" questions. What if the error variance is not constant over all observations? What if the different errors are correlated? We need to ask whether and when such violations of the basic error assumptions are likely to occur. What type of data are likely to lead to heteroskedasticity (different error variances)? What type of data are likely to lead to autocorrelation (correlated errors)? What are the consequences for least squares estimation? How do we detect the presence of autocorrelation or heteroskedasticity? How do we build an alternative model and an alternative set of assumptions when these violations exist? Does a new estimation procedure have to be developed?

These questions are answered in the next two chapters.

# Chapter 10

# Heteroskedasticity

## 10.1 The Nature of Heteroskedasticity

In chapter 3 we introduced the linear model

$$y = \beta_1 + \beta_2 x \tag{10.1.1}$$

to explain household expenditure on food ($y$) as a function of household income ($x$). In this function $\beta_1$ and $\beta_2$ are unknown parameters that convey information about the expenditure function. The response parameter $\beta_2$ describes how household food expenditure changes when household income increases by one unit. The intercept parameter $\beta_1$ measures expenditure on food for a zero income level. Knowledge of these parameters aids planning by institutions such as government agencies or food retail chains.

We begin this section by asking whether a function such as $y = \beta_1 + \beta_2 x$ is better at explaining expenditure on food for low-income households than it is for high-income households. If you were to guess food expenditure for a low-income household and food expenditure for a high-income household, which guess do you think would be easier? Low-income households do not have the option of extravagant food tastes; comparatively, they have few choices, and are almost forced to spend a particular portion of their income on food. High-income households, on the other hand, could have simple food tastes or extravagant food tastes. They might dine on caviar or spaghetti, while their low-income counterparts have to take the spaghetti. Thus, income is less important as an explanatory variable for food expenditure of high-income families. It is harder to guess their food expenditure.

This type of effect can be captured by a statistical model that exhibits heteroskedasticity. To discover how, and what we mean by heteroskedasticity, let us return to the statistical model for the food expenditure–income relationship that we analyzed in chapters 3 through 6. Given $T = 40$ cross-sectional household observations on food expenditure and income, the statistical model specified in chapter 3 was given by

$$y_t = \beta_1 + \beta_2 x_t + e_t \tag{10.1.2}$$

where $y_t$ represents weekly food expenditure for the $t$-th household, $x_t$ represents weekly household income for the $t$-th household, and $\beta_1$ and $\beta_2$ are unknown parameters to estimate. We assumed the $e_t$ were uncorrelated random error terms with mean zero and constant variance $\sigma^2$. That is,

$$E(e_t) = 0 \qquad \text{var}(e_t) = \sigma^2 \qquad \text{cov}(e_i, e_j) = 0 \qquad (10.1.3)$$

Using the least squares procedure and the data in Table 3.1 we found estimates $b_1 = 40.768$ and $b_2 = 0.1283$ for the unknown parameters $\beta_1$ and $\beta_2$. Including the standard errors for $b_1$ and $b_2$, the estimated mean function was

$$\hat{y}_t = 40.768 + 0.1283 \, x_t \qquad (10.1.4)$$
$$(22.139) \quad (0.0305)$$

A graph of this estimated function, along with all the observed expenditure-income points $(y_t, x_t)$, appears in Figure 10.1. Notice that, as income $(x_t)$ grows, the observed data points $(y_t, x_t)$ have a tendency to deviate more and more from the estimated mean function. The points are scattered further away from the line as $x_t$ gets larger. Another way of describing this feature is to say that the least squares residuals, defined by

$$\hat{e}_t = y_t - b_1 - b_2 x_t \qquad (10.1.5)$$

increase in absolute value as income grows.

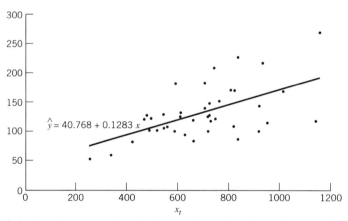

**FIGURE 10.1** Least squares estimated expenditure function and observed data points

The observable least squares residuals $(\hat{e}_t)$ are proxies for the unobservable errors $(e_t)$ that are given by

$$e_t = y_t - \beta_1 - \beta_2 x_t \qquad (10.1.6)$$

Thus, the information in Figure 10.1 suggests that the unobservable errors also increase in absolute value as income $(x_t)$ increases. That is, the variation of food expenditure $y_t$ around mean food expenditure $E(y_t)$ increases as income $x_t$ increases. This observation is consistent with the hypothesis that we posed earlier, namely, that the mean food expenditure function is better at explaining food expenditure for low-income (spaghetti-eating) households than it is for high-income households who might be spaghetti eaters or caviar eaters.

Is this type of behavior consistent with the assumptions of our model? The parameter that controls the spread of $y_t$ around the mean function, and measures the uncertainty in the regression model, is the variance $\sigma^2$. If the scatter of $y_t$ around the mean function increases as $x_t$ increases, then the uncertainty about $y_t$ increases as $x_t$ increases, and we have evidence to suggest that the variance is not constant. Instead, we should be looking for a way to model a variance $\sigma^2$ that increases as $x_t$ increases.

Thus, we are questioning the constant variance assumption, which we have written as

$$\text{var}(y_t) = \text{var}(e_t) = \sigma^2 \qquad (10.1.7)$$

The most general way to relax this assumption is to simply add a subscript $t$ to $\sigma^2$, recognizing that the variance can be different for different observations. We then have

$$\text{var}(y_t) = \text{var}(e_t) = \sigma_t^2 \qquad (10.1.8)$$

In this case, when the variances for all observations are not the same, we say that **heteroskedasticity** exists. Alternatively, we say the random variable $y_t$ and the random error $e_t$ are *heteroskedastic.* Conversely, if equation 10.1.7 holds we say that **homoskedasticity** exists, and $y_t$ and $e_t$ are *homoskedastic.*

The heteroskedastic assumption is illustrated in Figure 10.2. At $x_1$, the probability density function $f(y_1|x_1)$ is such that $y_1$ will be close to $E(y_1)$ with high probability. When we move to $x_2$, the probability density function $f(y_2|x_2)$ is more spread out; we are less certain about where $y_2$ might fall. When homoskedasticity exists, the probability density function for the errors does not change as $x$ changes, as we illustrated in Figure 3.3.

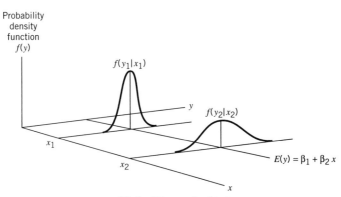

FIGURE **10.2**   Heteroskedastic errors

The existence of different variances, or heteroskedasticity, is often encountered when using **cross-sectional data.** The term *cross-sectional data* refers to having data on a number of economic units such as firms or households, *at a given point in time.* The household data on income and food expenditure fall into this category. Other possible examples include data on costs, outputs, and inputs for a number of firms, and data on quantities purchased and prices for some commodity, or commodities, in a number of retail establishments. Cross-sectional data invariably involve observations on economic units of varying sizes. For example, data on households will involve households with varying numbers of household members and different levels of household income. With data on a number of firms, we might measure the size of the firm by the quantity of output it produces. Frequently, the larger the firm, or the larger the household, the more difficult it is to explain the variation in some outcome variable $y_t$ by the variation in a set of explanatory variables. Larger firms and households are likely to be more diverse and flexible with respect to the way in which values for $y_t$ are determined. What this means for the linear regression model is that, as the size of the economic unit becomes larger, there is more uncertainty associated with the outcomes $y_t$. For our linear regression model to describe a data-generation process with this property, the variance of the error term has to be larger, the larger the size of the economic unit.

Heteroskedasticity is not a property that is necessarily restricted to cross-sectional data. With *time-series data,* where we have data *over time on one economic unit,* such as a firm, a household, or even a whole economy, it is possible that the error variance will change. This would be true if there was an external shock or change in circumstances that created more or less uncertainty about y. An example that fits into this category is the supply response example that we consider in section 10.4.

Given that we have a model that exhibits heteroskedasticity, we need to ask about the consequences on least squares estimation of the violation of one of our assumptions. Is there a better estimator that we can use? Also, how might we detect whether or not heteroskedasticity exists? It is to these questions that we now turn.

## *10.2* The Consequences of Heteroskedasticity for the Least Squares Estimator

If we have a linear regression model with heteroskedasticity (the assumption $\text{var}(e_t) = \sigma^2$ is violated), and we use the least squares estimator to estimate the unknown coefficients, then:

1.  The least squares estimator is still a linear and unbiased estimator, but it is no longer the best linear unbiased estimator (B.L.U.E.).
2.  The standard errors usually computed for the least squares estimator are incorrect. Confidence intervals and hypothesis tests that use these standard errors may be misleading.

We will explore these issues. We do so in the context of the simple linear regression model, with only one explanatory variable. However, the results generalize to the more general multiple regression model that was introduced in chapter 8. If you do not wish to participate in our exciting exploration, please skip the marked text down to the kangaroo.

We consider the model

$$y_t = \beta_1 + \beta_2 x_t + e_t \tag{10.2.1}$$

where

$$E(e_t) = 0, \quad \text{var}(e_t) = \sigma_t^2, \quad \text{cov}(e_i, e_j) = 0, \quad (i \neq j)$$

Note the heteroskedastic assumption $\text{var}(e_t) = \sigma_t^2$. In chapter 4, equation 4.2.1, we wrote the least squares estimator for $\beta_2$ as

$$b_2 = \beta_2 + \Sigma w_t e_t \tag{10.2.2}$$

where

$$w_t = \frac{x_t - \bar{x}}{\Sigma (x_t - \bar{x})^2} \tag{10.2.3}$$

This expression is a useful one for exploring the properties of least squares estimation under heteroskedasticity. The first property that we establish is that of unbiasedness. This property was derived under homoskedasticity in equation 4.2.3 of chapter 4. This proof still holds because the only error term assumption that it used, $E(e_t) = 0$, still holds. We reproduce it here for completeness.

$$E(b_2) = E(\beta_2) + E(\Sigma w_t e_t)$$
$$= \beta_2 + \Sigma w_t E(e_t) = \beta_2 \tag{10.2.4}$$

The next result is that the least squares estimator is no longer best. That is, although it is still unbiased, it is no longer *the* best linear unbiased estimator. The way we tackle this question is to derive an alternative estimator that *is* the best linear unbiased estimator. This new estimator is considered in sections 10.3 and 10.4.

To show that the usual formulas for the least squares standard errors are incorrect under heteroskedasticity, we return to the derivation of $\text{var}(b_2)$ in equation 4.2.11. From that equation, and using equation 10.2.2, we have

$$\text{var}(b_2) = \text{var}(\beta_2) + \text{var}(\Sigma w_t e_t)$$

$$= \text{var}(\Sigma w_t e_t)$$

$$= \Sigma w_t^2 \, \text{var}(e_t) + \underset{i \neq j}{\Sigma \Sigma} w_i w_j \, \text{cov}(e_i, e_j)$$

$$= \Sigma w_t^2 \sigma_t^2$$

$$= \frac{\Sigma [(x_t - \bar{x})^2 \sigma_t^2]}{[\Sigma (x_t - \bar{x})^2]^2} \tag{10.2.5}$$

In an earlier proof, where the variances were all the same ($\sigma_i^2 = \sigma^2$), we were able to write the next-to-last line as $\sigma^2 \Sigma w_i^2$. Now, the situation is more complex; the point to note from the last line in equation 10.2.5 is that

$$\text{var}(b_2) \neq \frac{\sigma^2}{\Sigma(x_t - \bar{x})^2} \qquad (10.2.6)$$

Thus, if we use the least squares estimation procedure and ignore heteroskedasticity when it is present, we will be using an estimate of equation 10.2.6 to obtain the standard error for $b_2$, when in fact we should be using an estimate of equation 10.2.5. Using incorrect standard errors means that interval estimates and hypothesis tests will no longer be valid. Note that standard computer software for least squares regression will compute the estimated variance for $b_2$ based on equation 10.2.6, unless told otherwise.

### 10.2.1  WHITE'S APPROXIMATE ESTIMATOR FOR THE VARIANCE OF THE LEAST SQUARES ESTIMATOR

Given that the conventional least squares standard errors are incorrect under heteroskedasticity, we ask whether there is a way of computing correct standard errors. Getting suitable standard errors for the least squares estimator overcomes one of its adverse consequences. Getting a better estimator, with lower variance, is considered in subsequent sections.

Halbert White, an econometrician, has suggested an estimator for the variances and covariances of the least squares coefficient estimators when heteroskedasticity exists. In the context of the simple regression model, his estimator for var($b_2$) is obtained by replacing $\sigma_i^2$ by the squares of the least squares residuals $\hat{e}_i^2$, in equation 10.2.5. Large variances are likely to lead to large values of the squared residuals. Because the squared residuals are used to approximate the variances, White's estimator is strictly appropriate only in large samples.

> **REMARK:** Most regression software packages include an option for calculating standard errors using White's estimator. Check out the options provided by your software.

If we apply White's estimator to the food expenditure–income data, we obtain

$$\text{vâr}(b_1) = 561.89, \qquad \text{vâr}(b_2) = 0.0014569$$

Taking the square roots of these quantities yields the standard errors, so that we could write our estimated equation as

$$\begin{aligned}
\hat{y}_t = \quad &40.768 \quad + \quad 0.1283 \; x_t \\
&(23.704) \quad (0.0382) \; (\text{White}) \\
&(22.139) \quad (0.0305) \; (\text{incorrect})
\end{aligned}$$

In this case, ignoring heteroskedasticity and using incorrect standard errors tends to overstate the precision of estimation; we tend to get confidence intervals that are narrower than they should be. Specifically, following equation 5.1.7 of chapter 5, we can construct two corresponding 95 percent confidence intervals for $\beta_2$.

White:    $b_2 \pm t_c \text{se}(b_2) = 0.1283 \pm 2.024(0.0382) = [0.051, 0.206]$

Incorrect:    $b_2 \pm t_c \text{se}(b_2) = 0.1283 \pm 2.024(0.0305) = [0.067, 0.190]$

If we ignore heteroskedasticity, we estimate that $\beta_2$ lies between 0.067 and 0.190. However, recognizing the existence of heteroskedasticity means recognizing that our information is less precise, and we estimate that $\beta_2$ lies between 0.051 and 0.206.

White's estimator for the standard errors helps overcome the problem of drawing incorrect inferences from least squares estimates in the presence of heteroskedasticity. However, if we can get a better estimator than least squares, then it makes more sense to use this better estimator and its corresponding standard errors. What *is* a "better estimator" will depend on how we model the heteroskedasticity. That is, it will depend on what further assumptions we make about the $\sigma_t^2$. In the next two sections we consider two examples with two different heteroskedastic structures.

## *10.3* Proportional Heteroskedasticity

In this section we return to the example where weekly food expenditure ($y_t$) is related to weekly income ($x_t$) through the equation

$$y_t = \beta_1 + \beta_2 x_t + e_t \tag{10.3.1}$$

Following the discussion in section 10.1, we make the following statistical assumptions:

$$E(e_t) = 0, \quad \text{var}(e_t) = \sigma_t^2, \quad \text{cov}(e_i, e_j) = 0, \quad (i \neq j)$$

By itself, the assumption $\text{var}(e_t) = \sigma_t^2$ is not adequate for developing a better procedure for estimating $\beta_1$ and $\beta_2$. We would need to estimate $T$ different variances $(\sigma_1^2, \sigma_2^2, \ldots, \sigma_T^2)$ plus $\beta_1$ and $\beta_2$, with only $T$ sample observations; it is not possible to consistently estimate $T$ or more parameters. We overcome this problem by making a further assumption about the $\sigma_t^2$. Our earlier inspection of the least squares residuals suggested that the error variance increases as income increases. A reasonable model for such a variance relationship is

$$\text{var}(e_t) = \sigma_t^2 = \sigma^2 x_t \tag{10.3.2}$$

That is, we assume that the variance of the $t$-th error term $\sigma_t^2$ is given by a positive unknown constant parameter $\sigma^2$ multiplied by the positive income variable $x_t$. As explained earlier, in economic terms this assumption implies that for low levels of income ($x_t$), food expenditure ($y_t$) will be clustered close to the mean function $E(y_t) = \beta_1 + \beta_2 x_t$. Expenditure on food for low-income households will be largely explained by the level of income. At high levels of income, food expenditures can deviate more from the mean function. This means that there are likely to be many other factors, such as specific tastes and preferences, that reside in the error term, and that lead to a greater variation in food expenditure for high-income households. Thus, the assumption of heteroskedastic errors in equation 10.3.2 is a reasonable one for the expenditure model. In any given practical setting it is important to think not only about whether the residuals from the data exhibit heteroskedasticity, but also about whether such heteroskedasticity is a likely phenomenon from an economic standpoint.

Under heteroskedasticity the least squares estimator is not the best linear unbiased estimator. One way of overcoming this dilemma is *to change or transform our statistical model into one with homoskedastic errors.* Leaving the basic structure of the model intact, it is possible to turn the heteroskedastic error model into a homoskedastic error model. Once this transformation has been carried out, application of least squares to the transformed model gives a best linear unbiased estimator.

To demonstrate these facts, we begin by dividing both sides of equation 10.3.1 by $\sqrt{x_t}$:

$$\frac{y_t}{\sqrt{x_t}} = \beta_1\left(\frac{1}{\sqrt{x_t}}\right) + \beta_2\left(\frac{x_t}{\sqrt{x_t}}\right) + \frac{e_t}{\sqrt{x_t}} \tag{10.3.3}$$

Now, define the following *transformed variables*

$$y_t^* = \frac{y_t}{\sqrt{x_t}} \qquad x_{t1}^* = \frac{1}{\sqrt{x_t}} \qquad x_{t2}^* = \frac{x_t}{\sqrt{x_t}} = \sqrt{x_t} \qquad e_t^* = \frac{e_t}{\sqrt{x_t}} \tag{10.3.4}$$

so that equation 10.3.3 can be rewritten as

$$y_t^* = \beta_1 x_{t1}^* + \beta_2 x_{t2}^* + e_t^* \tag{10.3.5}$$

The beauty of this transformed model is that the new transformed error term $e_t^*$ is homoskedastic. The proof of this result is:

$$\text{var}(e_t^*) = \text{var}\left(\frac{e_t}{\sqrt{x_t}}\right) = \frac{1}{x_t}\text{var}(e_t) = \frac{1}{x_t}\sigma^2 x_t = \sigma^2 \tag{10.3.6}$$

Also, the transformed error term will retain the properties of zero mean, $E(e_t^*) = 0$, and zero correlation between different observations, $\text{cov}(e_i^*, e_j^*) = 0$ for $i \neq j$. As a consequence, we can apply least squares to the transformed variables, $y_t^*$, $x_{t1}^*$, and $x_{t2}^*$, to obtain the best linear unbiased estimator for $\beta_1$ and $\beta_2$. Note that these transformed variables are all observable; it is a straightforward matter to compute "the observations" on these variables. Also, the transformed model is linear in the unknown parameters $\beta_1$ and $\beta_2$. These are the original parameters that we are interested in estimating. They have not been affected by the transformation. In short, the transformed model is a linear statistical model to which we can apply least squares estimation. The transformed model satisfies the conditions of the Gauss–Markov Theorem, and the least squares estimators defined in terms of the transformed variables are B.L.U.E.

To summarize, to obtain the best linear unbiased estimator for a model with heteroskedasticity of the type specified in equation 10.3.2:

1. Calculate the transformed variables given in equation 10.3.4.
2. Use least squares to estimate the transformed model given in 10.3.5.

The estimator obtained in this way is called a generalized least squares estimator.

One way of viewing the generalized least squares estimator is as a *weighted least squares estimator*. Recall that the least squares estimator is those values of $\beta_1$ and $\beta_2$ that minimize the sum of squared errors. In this case, we are minimizing the sum of squared transformed errors that are given by

$$\sum_{t=1}^{T} e_t^{*2} = \sum_{t=1}^{T} \frac{e_t^2}{x_t}$$

The squared errors are *weighted* by the reciprocal of $x_t$. When $x_t$ is small, the data contain more information about the regression function and the observations are weighted heavily. When $x_t$ is large, the data contain less information and the observations are weighted lightly. In this way we take advantage of the heteroskedasticity to improve parameter estimation.

> **REMARK:** In the transformed model $x_{t1}^* \neq 1$. That is, the variable associated with the intercept parameter is no longer equal to one. Since least squares software usually automatically inserts a "1" for the intercept, when dealing with transformed variables you will need to learn how to turn this option off. If you use a "weighted" or "generalized" least squares option on your software, the computer will do both the transforming and the estimating. In this case suppressing the constant will not be necessary.

Applying the generalized (weighted) least squares procedure to our household expenditure data yields the following estimates:

$$\hat{y}_t = \underset{(17.986)}{31.924} + \underset{(0.0270)}{0.1410} \, x_t \qquad (10.3.7)$$

That is, we estimate the intercept term as $\hat{\beta}_1 = 31.924$ and the slope coefficient that shows the response of food expenditure to a change in income as $\hat{\beta}_2 = 0.1410$. These estimates are somewhat different from the least squares estimates $b_1 = 40.768$ and $b_2 = 0.1283$ that did not allow for the existence of heteroskedasticity. It is important to recognize that the interpretations for $\beta_1$ and $\beta_2$ are the same in the transformed model (equation 10.3.5) as they are in the untransformed model (equation 10.3.1). *Transformation of the variables should be regarded as a device for converting a heteroskedastic error model into a homoskedastic error model, not as something that changes the meaning of the coefficients.*

The standard errors in equation 10.3.8, namely $se(\hat{\beta}_1) = 17.986$ and $se(\hat{\beta}_2) = 0.0270$, are both lower than their least squares counterparts that were calculated from White's estimator, namely $se(b_1) = 23.704$ and $se(b_2) = 0.0382$. Since generalized least squares is a better estimation procedure than least squares, we do expect the generalized least squares standard errors to be lower.

> **REMARK:** Remember that standard errors are square roots of *estimated* variances; in a single sample the relative magnitudes of variances may not always be reflected by their corresponding variance estimates. Thus, lower standard errors do not *always* mean better estimation.

The smaller standard errors have the advantage of producing narrower, more informative confidence intervals. For example, using the generalized least squares results, a 95 percent confidence interval for $\beta_2$ is given by

$$\hat{\beta}_2 \pm t_c \text{se}(\hat{\beta}_2) = 0.1410 \pm 2.024(0.0270) = [0.086, 0.196]$$

The least squares confidence interval computed using White's standard errors was [0.051, 0.206].

The food expenditure example is an example of how heteroskedasticity can arise in a cross-sectional sample of observations. The next section looks at another form of heteroskedasticity that has arisen in the context of time-series data.

## *10.4* A Sample with a Heteroskedastic Partition

### 10.4.1  ECONOMIC AND STATISTICAL MODEL

Consider modeling the supply of wheat in a particular wheat-growing area in Australia. In the supply function the quantity of wheat supplied will typically depend on the production technology of the firm, on the price of wheat or expectations about the price of wheat, and on weather conditions. We can depict this supply function as

$$\text{Quantity} = f(\text{Price, Technology, Weather}) \qquad (10.4.1)$$

Information on the response of quantity supplied to price is important for government policy purposes. If the government is to pay a guaranteed price to wheat growers, or to support the price in any other way, it needs an idea of the wheat supply that a given price will bring forth; a large proportion of this wheat needs to be sold on the international market.

To estimate how the quantity supplied responds to price and other variables, we move from the economic model in equation 10.4.1 to a statistical model that we can estimate. If we have a sample of time-series data, aggregated over all farms, there will be price variation from year to year, variation that can be used to estimate the response of quantity to price. Also, production technology will improve over time, meaning that a greater supply can become profitable at the same level of output price. Finally, a large part of the year-to-year variation in supply could be attributable to weather conditions.

The data we have available from the Australian wheat-growing district consist of 26 years of aggregate time-series data on quantity supplied and price. Because there is no obvious index of production technology, some kind of proxy needs to be used for this variable. We use a simple linear time-trend—a variable that takes the value 1 in year 1, 2 in year 2, and so on, up to 26 in year 26. An obvious weather variable is also unavailable; thus, in our statistical model, weather effects will form part of the random error term. Using these considerations, we specify the linear supply function

$$q_t = \beta_1 + \beta_2 p_t + \beta_3 t + e_t \qquad t = 1, 2, \ldots, 26 \qquad (10.4.2)$$

where

$q_t$   is the quantity of wheat produced in year $t$,

$p_t$   is the price of wheat guaranteed for year $t$,

$t = 1, 2, \ldots, 26$ is a trend variable introduced to capture changes in production technology, and

$e_t$   is a random error term that includes, among other things, the influence of weather.

As before, $\beta_1$, $\beta_2$, and $\beta_3$ are unknown parameters that we wish to estimate. The data on $q$, $p$, and $t$ are given in Table 10.1.

To complete the statistical model in equation 10.4.2, some statistical assumptions for the random error term $e_t$ are needed. One possibility is to assume the $e_t$ are independent identically distributed random variables with zero mean and constant variance. This assumption is in line with those made in earlier chapters. In this case, however, we have additional information that makes an alternative assumption more realistic. We know that, after the thirteenth year, new wheat varieties whose yields are less susceptible to variations in weather conditions were introduced. These new varieties do not have an average yield that is higher than that of the old varieties, but the variance of their yields is lower because yield is less dependent on weather conditions. Since the weather effect is a major component of the random error term $e_t$, we can model the reduced weather effect of the last thirteen years by assuming the error variance in those years is different from the error variance in the first thirteen years. Thus, we assume that

*Table 10.1*   **Data on Quantity, Price, and Trend for an Australian Wheat Growing District**

| q | p | t | q | p | t |
|---|---|---|---|---|---|
| 197.6 | 1.47 | 1 | 240.0 | 2.42 | 14 |
| 140.1 | 1.30 | 2 | 236.1 | 2.45 | 15 |
| 162.3 | 1.59 | 3 | 234.5 | 2.44 | 16 |
| 166.5 | 1.44 | 4 | 239.0 | 2.26 | 17 |
| 159.5 | 1.89 | 5 | 258.4 | 2.50 | 18 |
| 195.6 | 1.49 | 6 | 247.9 | 2.41 | 19 |
| 207.0 | 1.94 | 7 | 272.2 | 2.83 | 20 |
| 218.4 | 1.52 | 8 | 266.2 | 2.79 | 21 |
| 239.0 | 2.15 | 9 | 284.1 | 3.17 | 22 |
| 208.2 | 2.09 | 10 | 283.4 | 2.83 | 23 |
| 253.4 | 1.74 | 11 | 277.4 | 2.69 | 24 |
| 278.7 | 2.51 | 12 | 301.0 | 3.65 | 25 |
| 221.1 | 2.14 | 13 | 281.4 | 3.36 | 26 |

$$E(e_t) = 0 \qquad t = 1, 2, \ldots, 26$$

$$\text{var}(e_t) = \sigma_1^2 \qquad t = 1, 2, \ldots, 13$$

$$\text{var}(e_t) = \sigma_2^2 \qquad t = 14, 15, \ldots, 26 \tag{10.4.3}$$

$$\text{cov}(e_i, e_j) = 0 \qquad i \neq j$$

From the above argument, we expect that $\sigma_2^2 < \sigma_1^2$

Since the error variance in equation 10.4.3 is not constant for all observations, this model describes another form of heteroskedasticity. It is a form that partitions the sample into two subsets, one subset where the error variance is $\sigma_1^2$ and one where the error variance is $\sigma_2^2$.

## 10.4.2   GENERALIZED LEAST SQUARES THROUGH MODEL TRANSFORMATION

Given the heteroskedastic error model with two variances, one for each subset of thirteen years, we consider transforming the model so that the variance of the transformed error term is constant over the whole sample. This approach was followed for the household expenditure example; it made it possible to obtain a best linear unbiased estimator by applying least squares to the transformed model.

With this idea in mind, we write the model corresponding to the two subsets of observations as

$$q_t = \beta_1 + \beta_2 p_t + \beta_3 t + e_t \qquad \text{var}(e_t) = \sigma_1^2 \qquad \text{for } t = 1, 2, \ldots, 13$$

$$q_t = \beta_1 + \beta_2 p_t + \beta_3 t + e_t \qquad \text{var}(e_t) = \sigma_2^2 \qquad \text{for } t = 14, 15, \ldots, 26 \tag{10.4.4}$$

Dividing each variable by $\sigma_1$ for the first 13 observations and by $\sigma_2$ for the last 13 observations yields

$$\frac{q_t}{\sigma_1} = \beta_1 \left(\frac{1}{\sigma_1}\right) + \beta_2 \left(\frac{p_t}{\sigma_1}\right) + \beta_3 \left(\frac{t}{\sigma_1}\right) + \frac{e_t}{\sigma_1} \qquad \text{for } t = 1, 2, \ldots, 13$$

$$\frac{q_t}{\sigma_2} = \beta_1 \left(\frac{1}{\sigma_2}\right) + \beta_2 \left(\frac{p_t}{\sigma_2}\right) + \beta_3 \left(\frac{t}{\sigma_2}\right) + \frac{e_t}{\sigma_2} \qquad \text{for } t = 14, 15, \ldots, 26 \tag{10.4.5}$$

This transformation yields transformed error terms that have the same variance for all observations. Specifically, the transformed error variances are all equal to *one* because

$$\text{var}\left(\frac{e_t}{\sigma_1}\right) = \frac{1}{\sigma_1^2}\text{var}(e_t) = \frac{\sigma_1^2}{\sigma_1^2} = 1 \qquad \text{for } t = 1, 2, \ldots, 13$$

$$\text{var}\left(\frac{e_t}{\sigma_2}\right) = \frac{1}{\sigma_2^2}\text{var}(e_t) = \frac{\sigma_2^2}{\sigma_2^2} = 1 \qquad \text{for } t = 14, 15, \ldots, 26$$

Providing $\sigma_1$ and $\sigma_2$ are known, the transformed model in equation 10.4.5 provides a set of new transformed variables to which we can apply the least squares principle to obtain the best linear unbiased estimator for $(\beta_1, \beta_2, \beta_3)$. The transformed variables are

$$\left(\frac{q_t}{\sigma_i}\right), \quad \left(\frac{1}{\sigma_i}\right), \quad \left(\frac{p_t}{\sigma_i}\right), \quad \text{and} \left(\frac{t}{\sigma_i}\right) \tag{10.4.6}$$

where $\sigma_i$ is either $\sigma_1$ or $\sigma_2$, depending on which half of the observations are being considered. Like before, the complete process of transforming variables, then applying least squares to the transformed variables, is called *generalized least squares*.

### 10.4.3    IMPLEMENTING GENERALIZED LEAST SQUARES

An important difference between this generalized least squares estimator and the one we used for the earlier heteroskedastic error model is that the transformed variables in equation 10.4.6 depend on the unknown variance parameters $\sigma_1^2$ and $\sigma_2^2$. Thus, as they stand, the transformed variables cannot be calculated. To overcome this difficulty, we use estimates of $\sigma_1^2$ and $\sigma_2^2$ and transform the variables as if the estimates were the true variances.

What is a reasonable way to estimate $\sigma_1^2$ and $\sigma_2^2$? Since $\sigma_1^2$ is the error variance from the first half of the sample and $\sigma_2^2$ is the error variance from the second half of the sample, it makes sense to split the sample into two, applying least squares to the first half to estimate $\sigma_1^2$ and applying least squares to the second half to estimate $\sigma_2^2$. Substituting these estimates for the true values causes no difficulties in large samples.

If we follow this strategy for the wheat supply example we obtain

$$\hat{\sigma}_1^2 = 641.64, \qquad \hat{\sigma}_2^2 = 57.76 \tag{10.4.7}$$

Using these estimates to calculate observations on the transformed variables in equation 10.4.6, and then applying least squares to the complete sample defined in equation 10.4.5, yields the estimated equation:

$$\hat{q}_t = 138.1 + 21.72p_t + 3.283t \tag{10.4.8}$$
$$\quad\; (12.7) \quad (8.81) \quad (0.812)$$

These estimates suggest that an increase in price of 1 unit will bring about an increase in supply of 21.72 units. The coefficient of the trend variable suggests that, each year, technological advances mean that an additional 3.283 units will be supplied, given constant prices. The standard errors are sufficiently small to make the estimated coefficients significantly different from zero. However, the 95 percent confidence intervals for $\beta_2$ and $\beta_3$, derived using these standard errors, are relatively wide.

$$\hat{\beta}_2 \pm t_c \text{se}(\hat{\beta}_2) = 21.72 \pm 2.069(8.81) = [3.5, 39.9]$$

$$\hat{\beta}_3 \pm t_c \text{se}(\hat{\beta}_3) = 3.283 \pm 2.069(0.812) = [1.60, 4.96]$$

> **REMARK:** A word of warning about calculating the standard errors is necessary. As demonstrated after equation 10.4.5, the transformed errors in equation 10.4.5 have a variance equal to one. However, when you transform your variables using $\hat{\sigma}_1$ and $\hat{\sigma}_2$, and apply least squares to the transformed variables for the complete sample, your computer program will automatically *estimate* a variance for the transformed errors. This estimate will not be *exactly* equal to one. The standard errors in equation 10.4.8 were calculated by forcing the computer to use *one* as the variance of the transformed errors. Most software packages will have options that let you do this, but it is not a crucial flaw if your package does not; the variance estimate will usually be close to one anyway.

## *10.5* Detecting Heteroskedasticity

In the earlier sections of this chapter we studied two heteroskedastic models, each with a different form of heteroskedasticity. In each case we used the nature of the economic problem and data to argue why heteroskedasticity of a particular form might be present. We then pursued the question of estimation in the presence of heteroskedasticity. A common question is: How do I know if heteroskedasticity is likely to be a problem for my model and my set of data? Is there a way of detecting heteroskedasticity so that I know whether to use generalized least squares techniques? We will consider two ways of investigating these questions. One is the use of residual plots. The second is a statistical test known as the Goldfeld–Quandt test.

### 10.5.1 RESIDUAL PLOTS

One way of investigating the existence of heteroskedasticity is to estimate your model using least squares and to plot the least squares residuals. If the errors are homoskedastic, there should be no patterns of any sort in the residuals. If the errors are heteroskedastic, they may tend to exhibit greater variation in some systematic way. For example, for the household expenditure data, we suspected that the variance may increase as income increased. In Figure 10.1 we plotted the estimated least squares function and the residuals and discovered that the absolute values of the residuals did indeed tend to increase as income increased. This method of investigating heteroskedasticity can be followed for any simple regression.

When we have more than one explanatory variable, the estimated least squares function is not so easily depicted on a diagram. However, what we can do is plot the least squares residuals against each explanatory variable, against time, or against $\hat{y}_t$, to see if those residuals vary in a systematic way relative to the specified variable. In the wheat-supply example, since we suspect that the variance may have decreased over time, it makes sense to plot the least squares residuals against time. We do so in Figure 10.3.

Note that, after year 13, there is dramatic drop in the variation of the least squares residuals. This observation lends support to our belief that the variance has decreased.

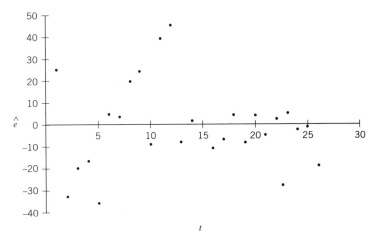

FIGURE **10.3**   Least squares residuals plotted against time

## 10.5.2   THE GOLDFELD–QUANDT TEST

To introduce the **Goldfeld–Quandt test** for heteroskedasticity, we return to the wheat-supply example and the two variance estimates $\hat{\sigma}_1^2 = 641.64$ and $\hat{\sigma}_2^2 = 57.76$. These estimates certainly suggest that the introduction of the new varieties has reduced the error variance. However, with a formal test we can establish whether the difference in estimates could be attributable to chance, or whether there is statistical evidence to support the hypothesis that $\sigma_2^2 < \sigma_1^2$. If the variances are equal, then combining both subsets of observations, and applying least squares to the combined data set will yield the B.L.U.E. for the coefficients. If the variances are not equal, we need to follow our generalized least squares procedure.

We begin by setting up the null and alternative hypotheses

$$H_0: \sigma_1^2 = \sigma_2^2$$

$$H_1: \sigma_2^2 < \sigma_1^2$$

(10.5.1)

Providing we make the additional assumption that the equation errors are normally distributed, Goldfeld and Quandt have noted that, when $H_0$ is true,

$$GQ = \frac{\hat{\sigma}_1^2}{\hat{\sigma}_2^2} \sim F_{[T_1 - K_1, \, T_2 - K_2]}$$

(10.5.2)

That is, under $H_0$, the ratio of the two variance estimators follows an $F$ distribution with $[(T_1 - K_1), (T_2 - K_2)]$ degrees of freedom (see Exercise 10.10). Here, $T_1$, $T_2$, $K_1$, and $K_2$ refer to the number of observations and number of coefficients in each of the subsets of observations. Thus, $(T_1 - K_1)$ is the degrees of freedom for the first subset and $(T_2 - K_2)$ is the degrees of freedom for the second subset. It is important that $\hat{\sigma}_2^2$ and $\hat{\sigma}_1^2$ are independent random variables, as will be guaranteed when they are estimates from two separate least squares regressions. If $GQ$ is sufficiently large, $H_0$ is rejected in favor of $H_1$.

In our example we have

$$GQ = \frac{641.64}{57.76} = 11.11$$

Also, $T_1 = T_2 = 13$ and $K_1 = K_2 = 3$; thus, if $H_0$ is true, 11.11 is an observed value from an $F$-distribution with (10, 10) degrees of freedom. The corresponding 5 percent critical value is $F_c = 2.98$. Since $GQ = 11.11 > F_c = 2.98$, we reject $H_0$ and conclude that the observed difference between $\hat{\sigma}_1^2$ and $\hat{\sigma}_2^2$ could not reasonably be attributable to chance. There is evidence to suggest the new varieties have reduced the variance in the supply of wheat.

The Goldfeld–Quandt test is also useful for detecting other forms of heteroskedasticity. In the example on household food expenditure we postulated that

$$\sigma_t^2 = \sigma^2 x_t \qquad (10.5.3)$$

If there is no heteroskedasticity, $\sigma_t^2 = \sigma^2$, and separate least squares estimation on two halves of the data will yield independent variance estimates $\hat{\sigma}_1^2$ and $\hat{\sigma}_2^2$; the ratio of these estimates will follow an $F$-distribution. If the null hypothesis is not true, but instead equation 10.5.3 holds, then $GQ = \hat{\sigma}_1^2/\hat{\sigma}_2^2$ will tend to be large if $\hat{\sigma}_1^2$ is estimated from that half of the sample where $x_t$ is large, and $\hat{\sigma}_2^2$ is estimated from that half of the sample where $x_t$ is small. Thus, to employ the Goldfeld–Quandt test where the suspected form of heteroskedasticity is like that in equation 10.5.3, we:

1. Sort the observations on all variables according to the magnitude of $x_t$, from the largest value of $x_t$ to the smallest value of $x_t$.
2. Split the sample in half, or approximate halves, and find $\hat{\sigma}_1^2$ and $\hat{\sigma}_2^2$ from each half of the data. (With sufficient data, it is good to leave out some central observations to improve the power of the test.)
3. Compute $GQ = \hat{\sigma}_1^2/\hat{\sigma}_2^2$ and carry out the test.

Following this procedure for the household expenditure data, with a partition of 20 observations in each subset of data, we find $\hat{\sigma}_1^2 = 2285.9$ and $\hat{\sigma}_2^2 = 682.46$. Hence, the value of the Goldfeld–Quandt statistic is

$$GQ = \frac{2285.9}{682.46} = 3.35$$

The 5 percent critical value for (18, 18) degrees of freedom is $F_c = 2.22$. Thus, because $GQ = 3.35 > F_c = 2.22$, we reject $H_0$ and conclude that heteroskedasticity does exist, and that the error variance does depend on the level of income.

Both of the Goldfeld–Quandt tests that we have performed in this section are one-sided tests; the alternative hypothesis suggested which sample partition will have the larger variance. If we suspect that two sample partitions could have different variances, but we do not know which variance is potentially larger, then a two-sided test with alternative hypothesis $H_1$: $\sigma_1^2 \neq \sigma_2^2$ is more appropriate. To perform a two-sided test at the 5 percent significance level we put the larger variance estimate in the numerator and use a critical value $F_c$ such that $P[F > F_c] = 0.025$.

 *The following section contains relatively advanced material and can be skipped without loss of continuity.*

## *10.6* A More General Heteroskedastic Error Model

The food-expenditure and wheat-supply models are both heteroskedastic examples where the error variance depends on only one factor. In the food-expenditure model the variance was dependent on income. In the wheat-supply model the variance was dependent on an observational subset. In these and other models, it might be more reasonable for the variance to depend on two or more factors. For example, the variance of household food expenditure might depend on the number of people in the household, as well as on income. The variance of the error in a firm cost function might depend on the output of the firm and the location of the firm. To accommodate such possibilities, consider the variance specification

$$\sigma_t^2 = \sigma^2 \exp\{\alpha_1 z_{t1} + \alpha_2 z_{t2}\} \tag{10.6.1}$$

The variables $z_{t1}$ and $z_{t2}$ are any observable variables on which we believe the variance could depend. They may include some or all of the explanatory variables $x_{tk}$. The unknown parameters are $\sigma^2$, $\alpha_1$, and $\alpha_2$. The exponential function $\exp\{ . \}$ is a convenient one for a variance specification because it ensures $\sigma_t^2$ will be positive whatever the values of $\alpha_1$, $\alpha_2$, $z_{t1}$, and $z_{t2}$.

Suppose we wish to test a null hypothesis of homoskedasticity against the alternative in equation 10.6.1. The relevant hypotheses are

$$H_0: \alpha_1 = 0, \alpha_2 = 0 \quad \text{and} \quad H_1: \alpha_1 \neq 0 \text{ and/or } \alpha_2 \neq 0$$

Note that when $H_0$ is true, equation 10.6.1 reduces to $\sigma_t^2 = \sigma^2$.

Because it is impossible to order the observations according to *both $z_{t1}$ and $z_{t2}$*, the Goldfeld–Quandt test is not suitable. To obtain an alternative test, we begin by taking logarithms of equation 10.6.1 to obtain

$$\ln(\sigma_t^2) = \ln(\sigma^2) + \alpha_1 z_{t1} + \alpha_2 z_{t2}$$

$$= \alpha_0 + \alpha_1 z_{t1} + \alpha_2 z_{t2}$$

where $\alpha_0 = \ln(\sigma^2)$. Next, we replace $\sigma_t^2$ by the squared least squares residuals to get the equation

$$\ln(\hat{e}_t^2) = \alpha_0 + \alpha_1 z_{t1} + \alpha_t z_{t2} + v_t \tag{10.6.2}$$

where $v_t$ is an error term introduced to allow for the fact that we are using $\hat{e}_t^2$ as a proxy for $\sigma_t^2$.

Equation 10.6.2 is like a regression equation. It has a dependent variable $\ln(\hat{e}_t^2)$, explanatory variables $z_{t1}$ and $z_{t2}$, and unknown coefficients $(\alpha_0, \alpha_1, \alpha_2)$. Within this regression framework we can test $H_0$: $\alpha_1 = \alpha_2 = 0$ using the overall $F$-test developed in chapter 8. The statistic for that test was

$$F = \frac{(SSE_R - SSE_U)/J}{SSE_U/(T - K)} \tag{10.6.3}$$

where $SSE_U$ comes from equation 10.6.2 and $SSE_R$ comes from this model estimated without $z_{t1}$ and $z_{t2}$. We reject $H_0$ if $F > F_c$, where $F_c$ is the critical value from an $F$-distribution with $(J, T - K)$ degrees of freedom. In the model specified in equation 10.6.1, $J = 2$.

> **REMARK:** In many software packages this test is referred to as the Harvey test; it can be computed in a slightly modified form as a $\chi_{(J)}^2$ test. Its modified form arises because a large sample is needed for its validity and, in large samples, approximately equivalent representations of the same test statistic exist. Specifically, $\chi_{(J)}^2 = J \cdot F_{(J, T-K)}$.

What if $H_0$: $\alpha_1 = \alpha_2 = 0$ is rejected? Acceptance of the alternative hypothesis implies the existence of heteroskedasticity of the kind in equation 10.6.1, and the need for generalized least squares estimation. We need a transformation that can be applied to the original equation to eliminate the heteroskedasticity. The appropriate transformation is to multiply through by

$$\frac{1}{\sqrt{\exp\{\hat{\alpha}_1 z_{t1} + \hat{\alpha}_2 z_{t2}\}}} \tag{10.6.4}$$

where $\hat{\alpha}_1$ and $\hat{\alpha}_2$ are the least squares estimates from equation 10.6.2. You should prove that this transformation gives a transformed error term with constant variance $\sigma^2$.

To conclude this section, we note that the variance specification in equation 10.6.1 is more flexible than it appears at first. For example, suppose there is only one variable $z_t$ that influences the variance:

$$\sigma_t^2 = \sigma^2 \exp\{\alpha z_t\} \tag{10.6.5}$$

Now, let $z_t = \ln(x_t)$, so that

$$\sigma_t^2 = \sigma^2 \exp\{\alpha \ln(x_t)\} = \sigma^2 \exp\{\ln(x_t^\alpha)\} = \sigma^2 x_t^\alpha$$

The variance specification that we used for the food expenditure example is a special case of this one where $\alpha = 1$.

For a second example, consider again equation 10.6.5. Let $z_t$ be a dummy variable that is equal to 1 for the first half of the sample and 0 for the second half. Then, the variance specification for the wheat-supply example can be written as equation 10.6.5, where

$$\sigma_1^2 = \sigma^2 e^\alpha \qquad \text{for} \qquad t = 1, 2, \ldots, 13.$$

$$\sigma_2^2 = \sigma^2 \qquad \text{for} \qquad t = 14, 15, \ldots, 26.$$

For experience with the model outlined in this section, see Exercises 10.8 and 10.9.

## *10.7* Summing Up

1.  When the economic data generation process is such that error variance for a regression model is not constant for all observations, we say the errors are *heteroskedastic.* The heteroskedastic error assumption is often a reasonable one for cross-sectional data where the sample involves a number of firms or households. In such cases the error variance could be related to variables such as household income or firm output. Heteroskedastic errors can also arise with aggregate time-series data, and a natural basis for partitioning the sample of data may exist.

2.  The two examples we studied fit into these categories. In the food-expenditure model the error variance was related to household income, as

$$\text{var}(e_t) = \sigma^2 x_t \qquad (10.7.1)$$

    In the wheat-supply example the error variance assumption was

$$\text{var}(e_t) = \sigma_1^2 \qquad t = 1, 2, \ldots, T_1$$
$$\text{var}(e_t) = \sigma_2^2 \qquad t = T_1 + 1, \ldots, T_1 + T_2 \qquad (10.7.2)$$

    Under both these specifications the generalized least squares estimator is the best linear unbiased estimator.

3.  One way to compute the generalized least squares estimator is to transform the model so that it has a new transformed error term that is homoskedastic, and to then apply least squares to the transformed model. For the error specification in equation 10.7.1, the food-expenditure model is transformed by dividing the $t$-th observation by $\sqrt{x_t}$. For the error specification in equation 10.7.2, the $t$-th observation in the wheat-supply model is divided by $\sigma_1$ if it is one of the first $T_1$ observations, and by $\sigma_2$ if it is one of the last $T_2$ observations.

4.  In the wheat-supply model, where the variables are transformed using the standard deviations $\sigma_1$ and $\sigma_2$, there is the added complication of $\sigma_1$ and $\sigma_2$ being unknown. We transform the variables using the estimates $\hat{\sigma}_1$ and $\hat{\sigma}_2$ in place of $\sigma_1$ and $\sigma_2$, and then apply least squares to the resulting transformed variables. This procedure is valid in large samples.

5.  If we ignore or are unaware of heteroskedasticity, and the least squares estimator is used instead of the generalized least squares estimator, we will be using an estimator that is not B.L.U.E. Also, unless we use White's estimator, we will compute incorrect standard errors, making interval estimates and hypothesis tests invalid.

6.  To test for heteroskedasticity the Goldfeld–Quandt statistic

$$GQ = \frac{\hat{\sigma}_1^2}{\hat{\sigma}_2^2} \sim F_{[T_1 - K_1, \, T_2 - K_2]}$$

can be employed. Here we assume the observations have been ordered according to potentially decreasing variance magnitudes and that $\hat{\sigma}_2^2$ and $\hat{\sigma}_1^2$ are independent variance estimates from two subsamples. Plotting least squares residuals is also a good way of detecting heteroskedasticity.

7.  A convenient, more general heteroskedastic variance specification is

$$\sigma_t^2 = \sigma^2 \exp\{\alpha_1 z_{t1} + \alpha_2 z_{t2}\} \qquad (10.7.3)$$

Both the food-expenditure and wheat-supply models can fit within this specification. The parameters $\alpha_1$ and $\alpha_2$ can be estimated by applying least squares to the equation

$$\ln(\hat{e}_t^2) = \alpha_0 + \alpha_1 z_{t1} + \alpha_2 z_{t2} + v_t$$

To test for homoskedasticity against the alternative specification in equation 10.7.3, the $F$-test that uses restricted and unrestricted sums of squared errors can be used to test $H_0$: $\alpha_1 = \alpha_2 = 0$. If $H_0$ is rejected, the model can be transformed by multiplying the original equation by $1/\sqrt{\exp\{\hat{\alpha}_1 z_{t1} + \hat{\alpha}_2 z_{t2}\}}$, before the application of least squares.

## *10.8* Exercises

10.1  Reconsider the household expenditure model that appears in the text, and the data for which appear in Table 3.1. That is, we have the model

$$y_t = \beta_1 + \beta_2 x_t + e_t$$

where $y_t$ is food expenditure for the $t$-th household and $x_t$ is income. Find generalized least squares estimates for $\beta_1$ and $\beta_2$ under the assumptions
(a) $\mathrm{var}(e_t) = \sigma^2 \sqrt{x_t}$
(b) $\mathrm{var}(e_t) = \sigma^2 x_t$
(c) $\mathrm{var}(e_t) = \sigma^2 x_t^2$
(d) $\mathrm{var}(e_t) = \sigma^2 \ln(x_t)$

Comment on the sensitivity of the estimates and their standard errors to the heteroskedastic specification. For each case, use the Goldfeld–Quandt test and the residuals from the transformed model to test to see whether heteroskedasticity has been eliminated. (Use a two-tailed test and a 10 percent significance level.)

10.2  In the file *pubexp.dat* there are data on public expenditure on education ($EE$), gross domestic product ($GDP$), and population ($P$) for thirty-four countries in the year 1980. These data are taken from Dougherty, C. (1992), *Introduction to Econometrics,* Oxford University Press. It is hypothesized that per capital expenditure on education is linearly related to per capita *GDP*. That is,

$$y_t = \beta_1 + \beta_2 x_t + e_t \tag{10.8.1}$$

where $\quad y_t = \left(\dfrac{EE_t}{P_t}\right) \quad$ and $\quad x_t = \left(\dfrac{GDP_t}{P_t}\right)$

It is suspected that $e_t$ may be heteroskedastic with a variance related to $x_t$.

(a) Why might the suspicion about heteroskedasticity be reasonable?

(b) Estimate equation 10.8.1 using least squares; plot the least squares function and the residuals. Is there any evidence of heteroskedasticity?

(c) Test for the existence of heteroskedasticity using the Goldfeld–Quandt test.

(d) Use White's formula for least squares variance estimates to find some alternative standard errors for the least squares estimates obtained in part (b). Use these standard errors and those obtained in part (b) to construct two alternative 95 percent confidence intervals for $\beta_2$. What can you say about the confidence interval that ignores the heteroskedasticity?

(e) Re-estimate the equation under the assumption that $\mathrm{var}(e_t) = \sigma^2 x_t$. Report the results. Construct a 95 percent confidence interval for $\beta_2$. Comment on its width relative to that of the confidence intervals found in part (d).

10.3    In section 9.6 of chapter 9, firm investment (*INV*) was related to value of the firm (*V*) and the firm's capital stock (*K*) through the equation

$$INV_t = \beta_1 + \beta_2 V_t + \beta_3 K_t + e_t \tag{10.8.2}$$

Table 9.2 contains data on these variables for two firms, General Electric and Westinghouse. You wish to examine whether the error variances for the two firms could be the same.

(a) Set up and estimate two investment equations, one for General Electric and one for Westinghouse. Test, at the 10 percent significance level, the null hypothesis of equal error variances against the alternative that the error variances are different.

(b) Assuming the error variances are different, but the coefficients are the same for each firm, pool the data from both firms and estimate the responses of investment to capital stock and value, using

 (i) generalized least squares, and

 (ii) least squares with White's variance estimator.

Compare the two sets of estimates and their standard errors.

10.4*   This question is a continuation of Exercise 10.3. You wish to test whether the assumption of equal coefficients for each of the two firms is a reasonable one. One way to carry out this test is to set up the model with a dummy variable attached to each of the explanatory variables:

$$INV_t = \beta_1 + \delta_1 D_t + \beta_2 V_t + \delta_2 V_t D_t + \beta_3 K_t + \delta_3 K_t D_t + e_t \tag{10.8.3}$$
$$t = 1, 2, \ldots, 40$$

where $D_t = 0$ for the General Electric observations and $D_t = 1$ for the Westinghouse observations. You wish to test the hypothesis $H_0: \delta_1 = \delta_2 = \delta_3 = 0$. This hypothesis was tested in section 9.6, assuming the error variances for General Electric and Westinghouse were the same. If this assumption is not true, the test result from that Section may be misleading.

(a) Carry out the test by estimating equation 10.8.3 using generalized least squares. How does your result compare with that in section 9.6?

(b) In chapters 8 and 9, you learned that hypotheses such as $H_0: \delta_1 = \delta_2 = \delta_3 = 0$ can be tested using an $F$-statistic calculated from restricted and unrestricted sums of squares; the formula is

$$F = \frac{(SSE_R - SSE_U)/J}{SSE_U/(T - K)}$$

(i) For the the case where equation 10.8.3 is estimated using least squares, verify that $SSE_U = SSE_W + SSE_{GE}$ where $SSE_W$ and $SSE_{GE}$ are the sums of squared errors from separate estimation of the General Electric and Westinghouse equations.

(ii) For the case where equation 10.8.3 is estimated using generalized least squares, use the result in (i) to explain why

$$SSE_U = T - K = 34$$

Prove that the $F$-statistic becomes

$$F = (SSE_R - 34)/3 \qquad (10.8.4)$$

(iii) Verify that equation 10.8.4 gives the same answer as that obtained by your computer in part (a).

10.5   Consider the following cost function. Assume that $\text{var}(e_{1t}) = \sigma^2 Q_{1t}$. Data are in the file *cloth.dat*.

$$C_{1t} = \beta_1 + \beta_2 Q_{1t} + \beta_3 Q_{1t}^2 + \beta_4 Q_{1t}^3 + e_{1t}$$

(a) Find generalized least squares estimates of $\beta_1$, $\beta_2$, $\beta_3$ and $\beta_4$.
(b) Test the hypothesis $\beta_1 = \beta_4 = 0$.
(c) What can you say about the nature of the average cost function if the hypothesis in (b) is true?
(d) Under what assumption about the error term would it be more appropriate to estimate the average cost function than the total cost function?

10.6*   In the file *cloth.dat* there are 28 time-series observations on total cost ($C$) and output ($Q$) for two clothing manufacturing firms. It is hypothesized that both firms' cost functions are cubic and can be written as:

$$\text{firm 1: } C_{1t} = \beta_1 + \beta_2 Q_{1t} + \beta_3 Q_{1t}^2 + \beta_4 Q_{1t}^3 + e_{1t}$$

$$\text{firm 2: } C_{2t} = \gamma_1 + \gamma_2 Q_{2t} + \gamma_3 Q_{2t}^2 + \gamma_4 Q_{2t}^3 + e_{2t}$$

where

$$E(e_{1t}) = E(e_{2t}) = 0, \quad \text{var}(e_{1t}) = \sigma_1^2, \quad \text{var}(e_{2t}) = \sigma_2^2$$

and $e_{1t}$ and $e_{2t}$ are independent of each other and over time.

(a) Estimate each function using least squares. Report and comment on the results. Do the estimated coefficients have the expected signs?

(b) Test the hypothesis that $H_0$: $\sigma_1^2 = \sigma_2^2$ against the alternative that $H_1$: $\sigma_1^2 \neq \sigma_2^2$. Use a 10 percent significance level and note that this is a two-tailed test.

(c) Estimate both equations jointly, assuming that $\beta_1 = \gamma_1$, $\beta_2 = \gamma_2$, $\beta_3 = \gamma_3$, and $\beta_4 = \gamma_4$. Report and comment on the results.

(d) Test the hypothesis

$$H_0\colon \beta_1 = \gamma_1, \beta_2 = \gamma_2, \beta_3 = \gamma_3, \beta_4 = \gamma_4$$

against

$H_1$: at least one of the equalities in $H_0$ does not hold.

Comment on the test outcome. (*Hint:* Look over Exercise 10.4(c).)

10.7  The file *foodus.dat* contains observations on food expenditure ($y_t$), income ($x_t$), and number of persons in each household ($n_t$) from a random sample of 38 households in a large U.S. city. Food expenditure and income are measured in terms of thousands of dollars. Consider the statistical model

$$y_t = \beta_1 + \beta_2 x_t + \beta_3 n_t + e_t \tag{10.8.5}$$

where the $e_t$ are independent normal random errors with zero mean.

(a) Estimate equation 10.8.5 using least squares. Report and comment on the results.

(b) Plot the least squares residuals from (a) against (i) income $x$, and (ii) number of persons $n$. Do these plots suggest anything about the existence of heteroskedasticity?

(c) Use a Goldfeld–Quandt test to test for heteroskedasticity with the observations ordered (i) according to decreasing values of $x_t$ and (ii) according to decreasing values of $n_t$. Comment on the outcomes.

(d) Based on results from using White's variance estimator, do you think the usual least squares results over- or underestimate the reliability of estimation of $\beta_2$ and $\beta_3$?

(e) Find generalized least squares estimates of equation 10.8.5 under the assumption that

$$\text{var}(e_t) = \sigma_t^2 = \sigma^2 \exp\{0.055x_t + 0.12n_t\}$$

Compare the estimates with those obtained using least squares. Does allowing for heteroskedasticity appear to have improved the precision of estimation?

10.8* Reconsider the variance specification given in Exercise 10.7(e).
(a) Show where the estimates $\hat{\alpha}_1 = 0.055$ and $\hat{\alpha}_2 = 0.12$ come from.
(b) Use a 5 percent significance level to test $H_0$: $\alpha_1 = \alpha_2 = 0$ against the alternative $H_1$: $\alpha_1 \neq 0$ and/or $\alpha_2 \neq 0$.

10.9* Reconsider the wheat-supply example given in section 10.4. Let $\sigma_t^2 = \sigma^2 \exp\{\alpha z_t\}$ where $z_t$ is a dummy variable that takes the value 1 for the first 13 observations and the value 0 for the last 13.
(a) Estimate $\alpha$.
(b) Test $H_0$: $\alpha = 0$ against $H_1$: $\alpha \neq 0$ using a 5 percent significance level.
(c) Find generalized least squares estimates of $\beta_1$, $\beta_2$, and $\beta_3$ using the transformation $1/\sqrt{\exp\{\hat{\alpha} z_t\}}$.
(d) How do your results from (a), (b) and (c) compare with the results in the body of the chapter.

10.10* Consider two regression models with error variances $\sigma_1^2$ and $\sigma_2^2$ and corresponding estimators $\hat{\sigma}_1^2$ and $\hat{\sigma}_2^2$. Suppose the first has $T_1$ observations and $K_1$ coefficients and the second $T_2$ observations and $K_2$ coefficients. Given that

$$V_1 = \frac{(T_1 - K_1)\hat{\sigma}_1^2}{\sigma_1^2} \sim \chi^2_{(T_1-K_1)}, \quad V_2 = \frac{(T_2 - K_2)\hat{\sigma}_2^2}{\sigma_2^2} \sim \chi^2_{(T_2-K_2)}$$

use the result in equation 2.7.4 to prove that when $\sigma_1^2 = \sigma_2^2$,

$$GQ = \frac{\hat{\sigma}_1^2}{\hat{\sigma}_2^2} \sim F_{(T_1-K_1, \, T_2-K_2)}$$

## *10.9* References

Other treatments of heteroskedasticity can be found in

DORAN, H. E. (1989). *Applied Regression Analysis in Econometrics,* New York: Marcel Dekker, Chapter 8.

DOUGHERTY, C. (1992). *Introduction to Econometrics,* Oxford University Press.

GUJARATI, D. N. (1995). *Basic Econometrics* (3d ed.). New York: McGraw Hill, Chapter 11.

KENNEDY, P. (1992). *A Guide to Econometrics* (3d ed.). Cambridge, MA: MIT Press, Chapter 8.

MADDALA, G. S. (1992). *Introduction to Econometrics* (2d ed.). New York: Macmillan, Chapter 5.

# Chapter 11

# Autocorrelation

## 11.1 The Nature of the Problem

In chapters 3 through 9 we assumed that the errors $(e_t)$ in the linear regression model were *uncorrelated* random variables with mean zero and a constant variance $\sigma^2$. The constant variance assumption, which implies the error variance is the same for each observation, was relaxed in chapter 10. Now, it is time to relax the other main assumption about the error terms, the assumption that they are uncorrelated.

Cross-sectional data are often generated by way of a random sample of a number of economic units such as households or firms. The randomness of the sample implies that the error terms for different observations (households or firms) will be uncorrelated. However, when we have time-series data, where the observations follow a natural ordering through time, there is always a possibility that successive errors will be correlated with each other. To see how such correlation might arise, suppose that we have an equation that relates the aggregate demand for money in the economy to a number of explanatory variables. Any policy shock that occurs will have an impact on money demanded through the error term. Also, a shock usually takes several periods to work through the system. This means that, in any one period, the current error term contains not only the effects of current shocks but also the carryover from previous shocks. This carryover will be related to, or *correlated with,* the effects of the earlier shocks. When circumstances such as these lead to error terms that are correlated, we say that **autocorrelation** exists. The possibility of autocorrelation should always be entertained when we are dealing with time-series data. How we check for autocorrelation and how to take the appropriate course of action when it exists are the subjects of this chapter.

Before we turn to a specific example to illustrate the nature of the autocorrelation problem and how to solve it, it is useful to be more explicit about which assumption we are relaxing. Suppose we have a linear regression model with two explanatory variables. That is,

$$y_t = \beta_1 + \beta_2 x_{t2} + \beta_3 x_{t3} + e_t \qquad (11.1.1)$$

The error term assumptions utilized in chapters 3 through 9 are

$$E(e_t) = 0, \qquad \text{var}(e_t) = \sigma^2 \qquad (11.1.2a)$$

$$\text{cov}(e_t, e_s) = 0 \quad \text{for } t \neq s \qquad (11.1.2b)$$

Of interest now is relaxing the zero covariance assumption in equation 11.1.2b. When equation 11.1.2b does not hold, we say that the random errors $e_t$ are autocorrelated.

### 11.1.1    AN AREA RESPONSE MODEL FOR SUGAR CANE

One way of modeling supply response for an agricultural crop is to specify a model in which area planted (acres) depends on price. When the price of the crop's output is high, farmers plant more of that crop than when its price is low. Letting $A$ denote area planted, and $P$ denote output price, and assuming a log–log (constant elasticity) functional form, an area response model of this type can be written as

$$\ln(A) = \beta_1 + \beta_2 \ln(P) \tag{11.1.3}$$

As an example of a situation where autocorrelated errors exist, we use the model in equation 11.1.3 to explain the area of sugar cane planted in a region of Bangladesh, a country in the southern part of Asia. Information on the area elasticity $\beta_2$ is useful for government planning. It is important to know whether existing sugar processing mills are likely to be able to handle predicted output, whether there is likely to be excess milling capacity, and whether a pricing policy linking production, processing, and consumption is desirable.

Data comprising 34 annual observations on area and price are given in Table 11.1. After we specify a statistical model corresponding to equation 11.1.3, our task is to use these data to estimate the parameters $\beta_1$ and $\beta_2$. The statistical model is obtained by using the subscript $t$ to describe area and price in year $t$, and adding a random error term $e_t$. Thus, we have

*Table 11.1*    **Data for Area Response for Sugar Cane in Bangladesh**

| Area | Price of Sugar Cane | Area | Price of Sugar Cane |
|------|---------------------|------|---------------------|
| 29   | 0.075258            | 91   | 0.205394            |
| 71   | 0.114894            | 121  | 0.267396            |
| 42   | 0.101075            | 162  | 0.230411            |
| 90   | 0.110309            | 143  | 0.368771            |
| 72   | 0.109562            | 138  | 0.285076            |
| 57   | 0.132486            | 230  | 0.360332            |
| 44   | 0.141783            | 128  | 0.322976            |
| 61   | 0.209559            | 87   | 0.301266            |
| 60   | 0.188259            | 124  | 0.287834            |
| 70   | 0.195946            | 97   | 0.401437            |
| 88   | 0.226087            | 152  | 0.404692            |
| 80   | 0.145585            | 197  | 0.353188            |
| 125  | 0.194030            | 220  | 0.410233            |
| 232  | 0.270362            | 171  | 0.360418            |
| 125  | 0.235821            | 208  | 0.463087            |
| 99   | 0.220826            | 237  | 0.401582            |
| 250  | 0.380952            | 235  | 0.391660            |

$$\ln(A_t) = \beta_1 + \beta_2 \ln(P_t) + e_t \qquad (11.1.4)$$

In line with our earlier notation, we can write this equation as

$$y_t = \beta_1 + \beta_2 x_t + e_t \qquad (11.1.5)$$

where

$$y_t = \ln(A_t) \quad \text{and} \quad x_t = \ln(P_t) \qquad (11.1.6)$$

### 11.1.1a   Least Squares Estimation

Given our previous experience with least squares estimation, our first natural strategy to estimate equation 11.1.5 is to apply the least squares rule. In so doing, we are assuming, initially at least, that the statistical assumptions in equations 11.1.2a and 11.1.2b hold; there is no heteroskedasticity or autocorrelation. Application of least squares yields the following estimated equation.

$$\begin{aligned} \hat{y}_t = \; & 6.111 \; + \; 0.971 \, x_t \qquad R^2 = 0.706 \\ & (0.169) \quad\; (0.111) \qquad \text{(std. errors)} \end{aligned} \qquad (11.1.7)$$

The results indicate that both coefficients are significantly different from 0, and suggest that the elasticity of area response to price is approximately 1.

Suppose now that we wish to investigate whether autocorrelation might be a problem. After all, we have time-series data, and we have been warned that such a problem may exist. It is likely that farmers' decisions about area of sugar cane planted will depend on their perceptions about future prices, and about government policies on prices and the establishment of processing mills. Since variables for these perceptions are not explicitly included in the model, their effect on area planted will be felt through the error term $e_t$. Also, if perceptions change slowly over time, or at least not in a completely random manner, the $e_t$ will be correlated over time.

Later in the chapter we introduce a specific test, called the Durbin–Watson test, that we can use to test for the existence of autocorrelation. For the time being, let us examine the least squares residuals ($\hat{e}_t$) to see if they can tell us anything about the nature of autocorrelation. The $\hat{e}_t$ are likely to have characteristics that are similar to those of the errors ($e_t$) and they could give us an indication of what to expect when the assumption $\text{cov}(e_t, e_s) = 0$ is violated.

The least squares residuals appear in Table 11.2 and are plotted against time in Figure 11.1.

From both the table and the figure we can see that there is a tendency for negative residuals to follow negative residuals and for positive residuals to follow positive residuals. There is a long run of negative residuals from observation 6 to observation 11, followed by a run of positive residuals from observation 12 to observation 15. Similarly, the residuals from observation 24 to observation 28 are all negative, while those from observation 29 to observation 34 are all positive (except for a small negative value at observation 32). This kind of behavior is consistent with an assumption of positive correlation between successive residuals. With uncorrelated errors, we would not expect to see any particular pattern. If the

***Table 11.2***    **Least Squares Residuals for the Sugar Cane Example**

| Time | $\hat{e}_t$ | Time | $\hat{e}_t$ | Time | $\hat{e}_t$ | Time | $\hat{e}_t$ |
|---|---|---|---|---|---|---|---|
| 1 | −0.233 | 10 | −0.281 | 19 | −0.035 | 27 | −0.651 |
| 2 | 0.251 | 11 | −0.191 | 20 | 0.401 | 28 | −0.209 |
| 3 | −0.149 | 12 | 0.141 | 21 | −0.180 | 29 | 0.182 |
| 4 | 0.528 | 13 | 0.308 | 22 | 0.034 | 30 | 0.147 |
| 5 | 0.312 | 14 | 0.605 | 23 | 0.317 | 31 | 0.021 |
| 6 | −0.106 | 15 | 0.119 | 24 | −0.162 | 32 | −0.027 |
| 7 | −0.431 | 16 | −0.050 | 25 | −0.481 | 33 | 0.242 |
| 8 | −0.484 | 17 | 0.347 | 26 | −0.082 | 34 | 0.258 |
| 9 | −0.396 | 18 | −0.064 | | | | |

errors are negatively autocorrelated, we would expect the residuals to show a tendency to oscillate in sign.

When attempting to detect autocorrelation, we can examine the least squares residuals as we have done for the sugar cane example. However, any conclusions from such an examination will be subjective, because we will need to decide "how long" a long run of residuals with the same sign needs to be before we conclude it is caused by autocorrelation. An objective assessment can be carried out using the Durbin–Watson test, which is considered later in the chapter. Our next task is to suggest a way of modeling autocorrelation.

## 11.2 First-Order Autoregressive Errors

Given the likely existence of correlated errors, the next question is: How should we take this correlation into account when constructing a statistical model? If the assumption $\text{cov}(e_t, e_s) = 0$ is no longer valid, what alternative assumption can we use to replace it? Is there some way to describe how the $e_t$ are correlated? If we

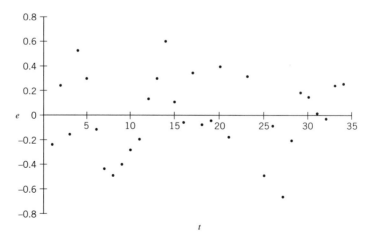

***FIGURE 11.1***    Least squares residuals plotted against time

are going to allow for autocorrelation when estimating $\beta_1$ and $\beta_2$, then we need some way to represent it. There are a number of models that can be used to represent correlated errors. By far the most common is what is known as a first-order autoregressive model or, more simply, an AR(1) model. In this model $e_t$ depends on its lagged value $e_{t-1}$ plus another random component that is uncorrelated over time and has zero mean and constant variance. That is,

$$e_t = \rho e_{t-1} + v_t \qquad (11.2.1)$$

where $\rho$ (rho) is a parameter that determines the correlation properties of $e_t$, and the $v_t$ are uncorrelated random variables with a constant variance $\sigma_v^2$. Thus, $v_t$ has the statistical properties that we assumed about $e_t$ in the earlier chapters.

$$E(v_t) = 0 \,, \text{var}(v_t) = \sigma_v^2 \,, \text{cov}(v_t, v_s) = 0 \quad t \neq s \qquad (11.2.2)$$

The rationale for the autoregressive model in equation 11.2.1 is a simple one. It is that the random component $e_t$ in time period $t$ is composed of two parts: (i) $\rho e_{t-1}$ is a carryover from the random error in the previous period, due to the inertia in economic systems, with the magnitude of the parameter $\rho$ determining how much carryover there is, and (ii) $v_t$ is a "new" shock to the level of the economic variable. In our example, the "carryover" might be farmers' perceptions of government policies on pricing and the establishment of mills. A new shock could be the announcement of a new policy or information on sugar cane shortages or excesses. The autoregressive model asserts that shocks to an economic variable do not work themselves out in one period. The parameter $\rho$ in equation 11.2.1 is the autoregressive parameter that determines how quickly the effect of a shock dissipates. The larger the magnitude of $\rho$, the greater the carryover from one period to another and the more slowly the shock spreads over time.

### 11.2.1 STATISTICAL PROPERTIES OF AN AR(1) ERROR

Our next task is to examine the implications of the AR(1) error model in equations 11.2.1 and 11.2.2 for the statistical properties (mean, variance, and correlations) of the $e_t$. For the $e_t$ to have properties that do not change from year to year, we assume that $\rho$ is less than one in absolute value. That is,

$$-1 < \rho < 1 \qquad (11.2.3)$$

If we did not make this assumption, then, through the relationship $e_t = \rho e_{t-1} + v_t$, the $e_t$ would tend to become larger and larger through time, eventually becoming infinite, which is not consistent with our experience.

It can be shown that the mean, variance and the covariances of the $e_t$ are:

1.                          $$E(e_t) = 0 \qquad (11.2.4)$$

When the equation errors follow an AR(1) model, they continue to have a zero mean.

2.
$$\text{var}(e_t) = \sigma_e^2 = \frac{\sigma_v^2}{1 - \rho^2}$$

(11.2.5)

This equation describes the relationship between the variance ($\sigma_e^2$) of the original equation error $e_t$ and the variance ($\sigma_v^2$) of the uncorrelated homoskedastic error $v_t$. Because $\sigma_e^2$ does not change over time, the error $e_t$ is also homoskedastic.

3.
$$\text{cov}(e_t, e_{t-k}) = \sigma_e^2 \rho^k \quad k > 0$$

(11.2.6)

This equation is our replacement for the zero-correlation assumption $\text{cov}(e_t, e_s) = 0$. The symbol $k$ is used to represent the time between errors. The expression says that the covariance between two errors that are $k$ periods apart depends on the variance $\sigma_e^2$, and on the parameter $\rho$ raised to the power $k$.

To describe the correlation behavior implied by the covariance in equation 11.2.6, we use equation 2.5.4 from chapter 2. In terms of our quantities of interest, this equation yields

$$\text{corr}(e_t, e_{t-k}) = \frac{\text{cov}(e_t, e_{t-k})}{\sqrt{\text{var}(e_t)\,\text{var}(e_{t-k})}}$$

(11.2.7)

$$= \frac{\sigma_e^2 \rho^k}{\sqrt{\sigma_e^2 \sigma_e^2}} = \rho^k$$

An interpretation or definition of the unknown parameter $\rho$ can be obtained by setting $k = 1$. Specifically,

$$\text{corr}(e_t, e_{t-1}) = \rho$$

(11.2.8)

Thus, $\rho$ represents the correlation between two errors that are one period apart; it is sometimes called the autocorrelation coefficient.

Also from equation 11.2.7, we can consider the sequence of correlations between errors as those errors become further apart in time. Considering one period apart, two periods apart, three periods apart, and so on, we obtain the sequence

$$\rho, \rho^2, \rho^3, \ldots\ldots$$

Since $-1 < \rho < 1$, the values in this sequence are declining. The greatest correlation between errors is for those that are one period apart; as the errors become further apart, the correlation between them becomes smaller and smaller. This characteristic of an AR(1) error model is one that seems reasonable for many economic phenomena.

## *11.3* Consequences for the Least Squares Estimator

Given the existence of autocorrelated errors, we need to ask about the consequences for least squares estimation. If we have an equation whose errors exhibit autocorrelation, but we ignore it, or are simply unaware of it, what kind of impact does it have on the properties of least squares estimates? The consequences are essentially the same as those of heteroskedasticity.

1.  The least squares estimator is still a linear unbiased estimator, but it is no longer best.
2.  The formulas for the standard errors usually computed for the least squares estimator are no longer correct, and hence, confidence intervals and hypothesis tests that use these standard errors may be misleading.

We can illustrate these facts using results from chapter 4. If you would prefer to avoid this illustration, do the kangaroo trick; skip the marked text.

In Chapter 4, for the simple regression model $y_t = \beta_1 + \beta_2 x_t + e_t$, we wrote the least squares estimator for $\beta_2$ as

$$b_2 = \beta_2 + \Sigma w_t e_t \tag{11.3.1}$$

where

$$w_t = \frac{(x_t - \bar{x})}{\Sigma(x_t - \bar{x})^2} \tag{11.3.2}$$

We can prove $b_2$ is still an unbiased estimator for $\beta_2$ under autocorrelation by showing that

$$E(b_2) = \beta_2 + \Sigma w_t E(e_t) = \beta_2 \tag{11.3.3}$$

For the variance of $b_2$ we have

$$\text{var}(b_2) = \Sigma w_t^2 \, \text{var}(e_t) + \underset{i \neq j}{\Sigma\Sigma} \, w_i w_j \, \text{cov}(e_i, e_j)$$

$$= \sigma_e^2 \Sigma w_t^2 + \sigma_e^2 \underset{i \neq j}{\Sigma\Sigma} \, w_i w_j \rho^k \quad (\text{where } k = |i - j|) \tag{11.3.4}$$

$$= \frac{\sigma_e^2}{\Sigma(x_t - \bar{x})^2}\left(1 + \frac{1}{\Sigma(x_t - \bar{x})^2}\underset{i \neq j}{\Sigma\Sigma}(x_i - \bar{x})(x_j - \bar{x})\rho^k\right)$$

When we were proving that $\text{var}(b_2) = \sigma_e^2/\Sigma(x_t - \bar{x})^2$ in the absence of autocorrelation, the terms $\text{cov}(e_i, e_j)$ were all zero. This simplification no longer holds, however. From equation 11.3.4 we see that the variance of the least squares estimator for $\beta_2$ under autocorrelation is equal to the variance of the least squares estimator in the absence of autocorrelation, multiplied by another factor that depends on the explanatory variable and $\rho$. Thus, ignoring autocorrelation can lead to a misleading estimate of $\text{var}(b_2)$; this has consequences for interval estimates and hypothesis tests.

To give an idea of how least squares standard errors can lead to incorrect interval estimates, we return to least squares estimation of the sugar cane example. Given estimates for $\rho$ and $\sigma_e^2$, it is possible to use a computer to calculate an estimate for var($b_2$) from equation 11.3.4. A similar estimate for var($b_1$) can also be obtained. How to estimate $\rho$ and $\sigma_e^2$, in a manner that is consistent with the autocorrelation assumptions in equations 11.2.4 to 11.2.6, is covered later in this chapter. Suppose, for the moment, that we have such estimates, and that we have used them to estimate var($b_1$) and var($b_2$). The square roots of these quantities we can call *correct* standard errors, while those we calculated with our least squares estimates and reported in equation 11.1.7 we call *incorrect*. The two sets of standard errors, along with the estimated equation, are:

$$\hat{y}_t = 6.111 + 0.971\, x_t$$
$$(0.169) \quad (0.111) \text{ "incorrect" se}$$
$$(0.226) \quad (0.146) \text{ "correct" se}$$

Note that the correct standard errors are larger than the incorrect ones. If we ignored the autocorrelation, we would tend to overstate the reliability of the least squares estimates. The confidence intervals would be narrower than they should be. For example, using $t_c = 2.037$, we find the following 95 percent confidence intervals for $\beta_2$:

$$(0.715, 1.227) \qquad \text{(incorrect)}$$
$$(0.634, 1.308) \qquad \text{(correct)}$$

If we are unaware of the autocorrelation, we estimate that the elasticity of area response lies between 0.715 and 1.227. In reality, the reliability of least squares estimation is such that the interval estimate should be from 0.634 to 1.308. Although autocorrelation can lead to either overstatement or understatement of the reliability of the least squares estimates, understatement of reliability, as illustrated in this example, is the most common occurrence.

## *11.4* Generalized Least Squares Estimation for the AR(1) Model

In practice, after autocorrelation has been diagnosed, it is *not* common to stick with our least squares estimates and to simply look for better estimates of the standard errors. We did follow this strategy in the previous section. However, our purpose there was to illustrate the dangers of using least-squares standard errors, not to describe what is common practice. The more usual strategy is to employ a better estimation procedure, namely, generalized least squares. Generalized least squares tends to give us narrower, more informative, confidence intervals than the "correct" ones from least squares.

In chapter 10 we discovered that the generalized least squares estimator for a heteroskedastic error model can be computed by transforming the model so that it has a new, uncorrelated homoskedastic error term, and by applying least squares to the transformed model. We can pursue this same kind of approach when autocorrelation exists.

### 11.4.1   A Transformation

Our objective is to transform the model in equation 11.1.5

$$y_t = \beta_1 + \beta_2 x_t + e_t \tag{11.4.1}$$

so that the autocorrelated error $e_t$ is replaced by the uncorrelated error $v_t$, without altering the basic structure of the model. The relationship between $e_t$ and $v_t$ is given by

$$e_t = \rho e_{t-1} + v_t \tag{11.4.2}$$

and the properties of $e_t$ and $v_t$ were outlined in equations 11.2.2 through 11.2.6. Substituting equation 11.4.2 into 11.4.1 yields

$$y_t = \beta_1 + \beta_2 x_t + \rho e_{t-1} + v_t \tag{11.4.3}$$

We have eliminated $e_t$ from the equation, but it still contains $e_{t-1}$. To substitute out $e_{t-1}$, we note that equation 11.4.1 holds for every single observation. In particular, in terms of the previous period we can write

$$e_{t-1} = y_{t-1} - \beta_1 - \beta_2 x_{t-1} \tag{11.4.4}$$

Multiplying equation 11.4.4 by $\rho$ yields

$$\rho e_{t-1} = \rho y_{t-1} - \rho \beta_1 - \rho \beta_2 x_{t-1} \tag{11.4.5}$$

Substituting equation 11.4.5 into equation 11.4.3 yields

$$y_t = \beta_1 + \beta_2 x_t + \rho y_{t-1} - \rho \beta_1 - \rho \beta_2 x_{t-1} + v_t$$

or, after rearranging,

$$y_t - \rho y_{t-1} = \beta_1(1 - \rho) + \beta_2(x_t - \rho x_{t-1}) + v_t \tag{11.4.6}$$

This is the transformed equation that we seek. The transformed dependent variable is

$$y_t^* = y_t - \rho y_{t-1} \qquad t = 2,3, \ldots, T \tag{11.4.7a}$$

The transformed explanatory variable is

$$x_{t2}^* = x_t - \rho x_{t-1} \qquad t = 2,3, \ldots, T \tag{11.4.7b}$$

and the new constant term is

$$x_{t1}^* = 1 - \rho \qquad t = 2,3, \ldots, T. \tag{11.4.7c}$$

Making these substitutions we have

$$y_t^* = x_{t1}^* \beta_1 + x_{t2}^* \beta_2 + v_t \qquad (11.4.8)$$

Thus, we have formed a new statistical model with transformed variables $y_t^*$, $x_{t1}^*$, and $x_{t2}^*$ and, *importantly*, with an error term that is *not* the correlated $e_t$, but the uncorrelated $v_t$ that we have assumed to be distributed $(0, \sigma_v^2)$. We would expect application of least squares to equation 11.4.8 to yield a best linear unbiased estimator for $\beta_1$ and $\beta_2$.

There are two additional problems that we need to solve, however:

1. Because lagged values of $y_t$ and $x_t$ had to be formed, only $(T - 1)$ new observations were created by the transformation in equation 11.4.7. We have values $(y_t^*, x_{t1}^*, x_{t2}^*)$ for $t = 2, 3, \ldots, T$. But, we have no $(y_1^*, x_{11}^*, x_{12}^*)$.
2. The value of the autoregressive parameter $\rho$ is not known. Since $y_t^*$, $x_{t1}^*$ and $x_{t2}^*$ depend on $\rho$, we cannot compute these transformed observations without estimating $\rho$.

### 11.4.1a Transforming the First Observation

One way of tackling the problem of having $(T - 1)$ instead of $T$ transformed observations is to ignore it, and to proceed with estimation on the basis of the $(T - 1)$ observations. If $T$ is large, this strategy might be a reasonable one. However, the resulting estimator is not the best linear unbiased generalized least squares estimator. To get the generalized least squares estimator we need to transform the first observation so that its transformed error has the same variance as the errors $(v_2, v_3, \ldots, v_T)$.

The first observation in the regression model is

$$y_1 = \beta_1 + x_1 \beta_2 + e_1 \qquad (11.4.9)$$

with error variance $\text{var}(e_1) = \sigma_e^2 = \sigma_v^2/(1 - \rho^2)$. The transformation that yields an error variance of $\sigma_v^2$ is multiplication by $\sqrt{1 - \rho^2}$. The result is

$$\sqrt{1 - \rho^2} y_1 = \sqrt{1 - \rho^2} \beta_1 + \sqrt{1 - \rho^2} x_1 \beta_2 + \sqrt{1 - \rho^2} e_1 \qquad (11.4.10)$$

or

$$y_1^* = x_{11}^* \beta_1 + x_{12}^* \beta_2 + e_1^* \qquad (11.4.11a)$$

where

$$
\begin{aligned}
y_1^* &= \sqrt{1 - \rho^2} y_1 & x_{11}^* &= \sqrt{1 - \rho^2} \\
x_{12}^* &= \sqrt{1 - \rho^2} x_1 & e_1^* &= \sqrt{1 - \rho^2} e_1
\end{aligned} \qquad (11.4.11b)
$$

To confirm that the variance of $e_1^*$ is the same as that of the errors $(v_2, v_3, \ldots, v_T)$, note that

$$\text{var}(e_1^*) = (1 - \rho^2)\,\text{var}(e_1) = (1 - \rho^2)\frac{\sigma_v^2}{1 - \rho^2} = \sigma_v^2$$

To be able to use the first transformed observation in (11.4.11$b$), we also require that $e_1^*$ be uncorrelated with $(v_2, v_3, \ldots, v_T)$. This result will hold because each of the $v_t$ does not depend on any past values for $e_t$.

---

**REMARK:** We can summarize these results by saying that, *providing $\rho$ is known*, we can find the best linear unbiased estimator for $\beta_1$ and $\beta_2$ by applying least squares to the transformed model

$$y_t^* = \beta_1 x_{t1}^* + \beta_2 x_{t2}^* + v_t \tag{11.4.12}$$

where the transformed variables are defined by

$$y_1^* = \sqrt{1 - \rho^2}\,y_1, \quad x_{11}^* = \sqrt{1 - \rho^2}, \quad x_{12}^* = \sqrt{1 - \rho^2}\,x_1$$

for the first observation, and

$$y_t^* = y_t - \rho y_{t-1}, \quad x_{t1}^* = 1 - \rho, \quad x_{t2}^* = x_t - \rho x_{t-1}$$

for the remaining $t = 2, 3, \ldots, T$ observations.

---

All the procedures you have learned for testing hypotheses and constructing interval estimates hold, providing you use transformed variables rather than original variables to do your calculations. One caveat to this statement is that the interpretation of $R^2$ no longer holds in the usual way and its use should probably be avoided in econometric models with correlated errors. When you study econometrics at a more advanced level you will learn alternative ways of calculating summary goodness-of-fit statistics for this and similar models.

## 11.5 Implementing Generalized Least Squares

The remaining problem is the fact that the transformed variables $y_t^*$, $x_{t1}^*$, and $x_{t2}^*$ cannot be calculated without knowledge of the parameter $\rho$. We overcome this problem by using instead an estimate of $\rho$. As a method for estimating $\rho$ consider the equation

$$e_t = \rho e_{t-1} + v_t \tag{11.5.1}$$

If the $e_t$ values were observable, we could treat this equation as a linear regression model and estimate $\rho$ by least squares. However, the $e_t$ are not observable because they depend on the unknown parameters $\beta_1$ and $\beta_2$ through the equation

$$e_t = y_t - \beta_1 - \beta_2 x_t \tag{11.5.2}$$

As an approximation to the $e_t$ we use instead the least squares residuals

$$\hat{e}_t = y_t - b_1 - b_2 x_t \tag{11.5.3}$$

where $b_1$ and $b_2$ are the least squares estimates from the untransformed model. Substituting the $\hat{e}_t$ for the $e_t$ in equation 11.5.1 is justified, providing that the sample size $T$ is large. Making this substitution yields the model

$$\hat{e}_t = \rho \hat{e}_{t-1} + \hat{v}_t \tag{11.5.4}$$

The least squares estimator of $\rho$ from equation 11.5.4 has good statistical properties if the sample size $T$ is large; it is given by

$$\hat{\rho} = \frac{\sum_{t=2}^{T} \hat{e}_t \hat{e}_{t-1}}{\sum_{t=2}^{T} \hat{e}_{t-1}^2} \tag{11.5.5}$$

Thus, in practice, the transformed data that are defined below equation 11.4.12 are computed using the estimated value of $\hat{\rho}$ from equation 11.5.5. In line with the heteroskedastic error model of section 10.4, the estimator for $\beta_1$ and $\beta_2$ that uses $\hat{\rho}$ instead of the true value $\rho$ has good properties if the sample size is large. If the sample is not large, then great care must be taken when making claims about the results of hypothesis tests and interval estimations, so as not to overstate the importance of the results obtained.


### 11.5.1  THE SUGAR CANE EXAMPLE REVISITED

In sections 11.1 and 11.3 we obtained least squares estimates of the coefficients in the sugar-cane area response model. We saw how the least squares residuals tend to exhibit autocorrelation and how misleading interval estimates can arise from using incorrect least squares standard errors. We are now in a position to use the least squares residuals that were displayed in Figure 11.1 and Table 11.2 to estimate $\rho$ and to use this estimate in a generalized least squares estimator for $\beta_1$ and $\beta_2$. Specifically, we obtain

$$\hat{\rho} = \frac{\sum_{t=2}^{T} \hat{e}_t \hat{e}_{t-1}}{\sum_{t=2}^{T} \hat{e}_{t-1}^2} = 0.342 \tag{11.5.6}$$

The next step toward finding generalized least squares estimates is to transform the data as shown below equation 11.4.12. To illustrate, we give the first 4 observations in Table 11.3.

*Table 11.3*    **The First Four Transformed and Untransformed Observations**

|   | $x^*_{t1}$ | $x_t$ | $x^*_{t2}$ | $y_t$ | $y^*_t$ |
|---|---|---|---|---|---|
| 1 | 0.93970 | −2.5868 | −2.4308 | 3.3673 | 3.1642 |
| 2 | 0.65799 | −2.1637 | −1.2790 | 4.2627 | 3.1110 |
| 3 | 0.65799 | −2.2919 | −1.5519 | 3.7377 | 2.2798 |
| 4 | 0.65799 | −2.2045 | −1.4206 | 4.4998 | 3.2215 |

As examples, note that

$$y^*_1 = \sqrt{1 - \hat{\rho}^2}\, y_1$$

$$= \sqrt{1 - 0.342^2}(3.3673)$$

$$= 3.1642$$

and

$$x^*_{32} = x_{32} - \hat{\rho} x_{22}$$

$$= -2.2919 - (0.342)(-2.1637)$$

$$= -1.5519$$

You are encouraged to verify some of the other entries. Computations such as these are usually done automatically on the computer, but nevertheless, it is instructive to understand their nature.

Applying least squares to all transformed observations yields the generalized least squares estimated model

$$\ln(\hat{A}_t) = 6.164 + 1.007\ln(P_t) \tag{11.5.7}$$
$$(0.213)\quad(0.137)$$

Comparing these estimates with the least squares ones—$b_1 = 6.111$, $b_2 = 0.971$—we see that there has been little change in the estimates for $\beta_1$ and $\beta_2$. There is also not a great deal of variation in the standard errors. In Table 11.4 those from equation 11.5.7 are given alongside those we obtained in section 11.3.

*Table 11.4*    **Different Standard Errors**

|   | Standard Errors for Estimators | |
|---|---|---|
|   | $\beta_1$ | $\beta_2$ |
| GLS | 0.213 | 0.137 |
| incorrect LS | 0.169 | 0.111 |
| correct LS | 0.226 | 0.146 |

> **REMARK:** Software packages automatically estimate ρ, transform the variables, and obtain generalized least squares estimates, without you having to do each step separately. Also, we have considered just one of a number of alternative methods for estimating ρ. Your software package is likely to have options for some of these alternative methods.

## *11.6* Testing for Autocorrelation

So far in this chapter we have described the nature of an autocorrelated error term, and how to estimate the parameters $\beta_1$ and $\beta_2$ in the presence of an autocorrelated error. We have not yet indicated how to detect the presence of autocorrelation. Clearly, such detection is vital. If autocorrelation does not exist, then there is no need to estimate ρ and to then proceed with estimating $\beta_1$ and $\beta_2$ using transformed data; least squares applied to the original data will be adequate. On the other hand, if autocorrelation is present, we need to implement the procedures we have described in this chapter. In section 11.1 we illustrated how positively autocorrelated least squares residuals tend to appear in runs of positive and runs of negative values. Thus, looking for runs in the least squares residuals gives some indication of whether autocorrelation is likely to be a problem. We do, however, need a more objective procedure than "just looking." Thus, we consider the **Durbin–Watson test,** named after its inventors, Durbin and Watson, way back in 1950. Although this is an old test, it is by far the most important one for detecting AR(1) errors.

To introduce this test, consider again the linear regression model

$$y_t = \beta_1 + \beta_2 x_t + e_t \tag{11.6.1}$$

where the errors may follow the first-order autoregressive model

$$e_t = \rho e_{t-1} + v_t \tag{11.6.2}$$

It is assumed that the $v_t$ are independent random errors with distribution $N(0, \sigma_v^2)$. The assumption of *normally* distributed random errors is needed to derive the probability distribution of the test statistic used in the Durbin–Watson test.

Note that if $\rho = 0$, then $e_t = v_t$, and so the errors in equation 11.6.1 will not be autocorrelated. Thus, for a null hypothesis of no autocorrelation, we can use $H_0$: $\rho = 0$. For an alternative hypothesis we could use $H_1$: $\rho > 0$ or $H_1$: $\rho < 0$ or $H_1$: $\rho \neq 0$. We will choose $H_1$: $\rho > 0$; in most empirical applications in economics, positive autocorrelation is the most likely form that autocorrelation will take. Thus, we consider testing

$$H_0\text{: } \rho = 0 \text{ against } H_1\text{: } \rho > 0 \tag{11.6.3}$$

To test the null hypothesis it seems natural to compute $\hat{\rho}$ and to investigate whether this estimate is significantly greater than zero. However, derivation of the exact probability distribution of $\hat{\rho}$ is difficult. As an alternative, Durbin and Watson chose a different but closely related statistic whose probability distribution can be derived. Their statistic is

$$d = \frac{\sum\limits_{t=2}^{T}(\hat{e}_t - \hat{e}_{t-1})^2}{\sum\limits_{t=1}^{T}\hat{e}_t^2} \qquad (11.6.4)$$

where the $\hat{e}_t$ are the least squares residuals $\hat{e}_t = y_t - b_1 - b_2 x_t$. To see why $d$ is closely related to $\hat{\rho}$, and is a reasonable statistic for testing for autocorrelation, we expand equation 11.6.4 as

$$d = \frac{\sum\limits_{t=2}^{T}\hat{e}_t^2 + \sum\limits_{t=2}^{T}\hat{e}_{t-1}^2 - 2\sum\limits_{t=2}^{T}\hat{e}_t\hat{e}_{t-1}}{\sum\limits_{t=1}^{T}\hat{e}_t^2}$$

$$= \frac{\sum\limits_{t=2}^{T}\hat{e}_t^2}{\sum\limits_{t=1}^{T}\hat{e}_t^2} + \frac{\sum\limits_{t=2}^{T}\hat{e}_{t-1}^2}{\sum\limits_{t=1}^{T}\hat{e}_t^2} - 2\frac{\sum\limits_{t=2}^{T}\hat{e}_t\hat{e}_{t-1}}{\sum\limits_{t=1}^{T}\hat{e}_t^2} \qquad (11.6.5)$$

$$\approx 1 + 1 - 2\hat{\rho}$$

The last line in equation 11.6.5 holds only approximately. The first two terms differ from one through the exclusion of $\hat{e}_1^2$ and $\hat{e}_T^2$ from the first and second numerator summations, respectively. The last term differs from $2\hat{\rho}$ through the inclusion of $\hat{e}_T^2$ in the denominator summation. Thus, we have

$$d \approx 2(1 - \hat{\rho}) \qquad (11.6.6)$$

If the estimated value of $\rho$ is $\hat{\rho} = 0$, then the Durbin–Watson statistic $d \approx 2$, which is taken as an indication that the model errors are not autocorrelated. If the estimate of $\rho$ happened to be $\hat{\rho} = 1$ then $d \approx 0$, and thus a low value for the Durbin–Watson statistic implies that the model errors are correlated, and $\rho > 0$.

The question we need to answer is: How close to zero does the value of the test statistic have to be before we conclude that the errors are correlated? In other words, what is a critical value $d_c$ such that we reject $H_0$ when $d \le d_c$?

Following section 5.2 of chapter 5, determination of a critical value and a rejection region for the test requires knowledge of the probability distribution of the test statistic under the assumption that the null hypothesis, $H_0$: $\rho = 0$, is true. If a 5 percent significance level is required, knowledge of the probability distribution $f(d)$ under $H_0$ allows us to find $d_c$ such that $P(d \le d_c) = 0.05$. Then, as illustrated in Figure 11.2, we reject $H_0$ if $d \le d_c$ and fail to reject $H_0$ if $d > d_c$. Alternatively, we can state the test procedure in terms of the $p$-value of the test. For this one-tail test, the $p$-value is given by the area under $f(d)$ to the left of the calculated value of $d$. Thus, if the $p$-value is less than or equal to 0.05, it follows that $d \le d_c$, and $H_0$ is rejected. If the $p$-value is greater than 0.05, then $d > d_c$, and $H_0$ is accepted. (If this use of the $p$-value is not clear, it would be a good idea to review section 5.2.)

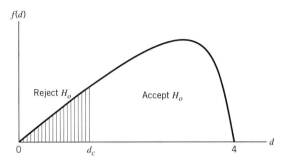

$FIGURE$ $\textbf{11.2}$   Testing for positive autocorrelation

In any event, whether the test result is found by comparing $d$ with $d_c$, or by computing the $p$-value, the probability distribution $f(d)$ is required. A difficulty associated with $f(d)$, and one that we have not previously encountered when using other test statistics, is that this probability distribution depends on the values of the explanatory variables. Different sets of explanatory variables lead to different distributions for $d$. Because $f(d)$ depends on the values of the explanatory variables, the critical value $d_c$ for any given problem will also depend on the values of the explanatory variables. This property means that it is impossible to tabulate critical values that can be used for every possible problem. With other test statistics, such as $t$, $F$ and $\chi^2$, the tabulated critical values are relevant for all models.

Fortunately, this problem can be overcome using modern-day computing software, that can compute the Durbin–Watson $p$-value for any problem being considered. So, instead of comparing the calculated $d$ value with some tabulated values of $d_c$, we get our computer to calculate the $p$-value of the test. If this $p$-value is less than the specified significance level, $H_0$: $\rho = 0$ is rejected and we conclude that autocorrelation does exist.

In the sugar cane area response model the calculated value for the Durbin–Watson statistic is $d = 1.291$. Is this value sufficiently close to zero (or sufficiently less than 2), to reject $H_0$ and conclude that autocorrelation exists? Using computer software we find that

$$p\text{-value} = P(d \leq 1.291) = 0.0098$$

This value is much less than a conventional 0.05 significance level; we conclude, therefore, that the equation's error is positively autocorrelated.

**REMARK:** When Durbin and Watson developed their test, they did not have the luxury of modern-day computing. They partially solved the problem of having no general critical values by deriving some "critical bounds." These bounds are such that $H_0$: $\rho = 0$ is rejected if $d \leq d_L$ where $d_L$ is a lower bound, and $H_0$ is not rejected if $d > d_U$ where $d_U$ is an upper bound. For $d_L < d \leq d_U$, the test was regarded as inconclusive. See Griffiths, et al. (1993, Chapter 16.5.3) for a discussion of the bounds test and relevant tables.

## *11.7* Prediction With AR(1) Errors

In chapters 4 (section 4.7) and 8 (section 8.9) we considered the problem of forecasting or predicting a future observation $y_0$ that we assumed is generated from the linear regression model

$$y_0 = \beta_1 + x_0\beta_2 + e_0 \qquad (11.7.1)$$

where $x_0$ is a given future value of an explanatory variable and $e_0$ is a future error term. Equation 11.7.1 can be extended to include more than one explanatory variable, as was illustrated in section 8.9. We discovered that, when the errors are uncorrelated, the best linear unbiased predictor for $y_0$ is the least squares predictor

$$\hat{y}_0 = b_1 + b_2x_0 \qquad (11.7.2)$$

There are two important differences between this forecasting problem and the forecasting problem that involves a linear model with AR(1) errors. The first difference relates to the best way to estimate $\beta_1$ and $\beta_2$. When the errors are autocorrelated, the generalized least squares estimators, denoted by $\hat{\beta}_1$ and $\hat{\beta}_2$, are more precise than their least squares counterparts $b_1$ and $b_2$. A better predictor is obtained, therefore, if we replace $b_1$ and $b_2$ by $\hat{\beta}_1$ and $\hat{\beta}_2$.

The second difference between the prediction problem in chapters 4 and 8 and that for the AR(1) error model relates to the best forecast for the future error $e_0$. When $e_0$ is uncorrelated with past errors, as was assumed in chapters 4 and 8, the best forecast of $e_0$ is its mean value of zero. When $e_0$ is correlated with past errors, as it is in the AR(1) error model, we can use information contained in the past errors to improve upon zero as a forecast for $e_0$. For example, if the last error $e_T$ is positive, then it is likely that the next error $e_{T+1}$ will also be positive.

To see how an improvement can be made, note that, when we are predicting one period into the future, the model with an AR(1) error can be written as

$$
\begin{aligned}
y_{T+1} &= \beta_1 + \beta_2x_{T+1} + e_{T+1} \\
&= \beta_1 + \beta_2x_{T+1} + \rho e_T + v_{T+1}
\end{aligned}
\qquad (11.7.3)
$$

where we have used $e_{T+1} = \rho e_T + v_{T+1}$. Equation 11.7.3 has three distinct components:

1.  Given the explanatory variable $x_{T+1}$, the best linear unbiased predictor for $\beta_1 + \beta_2x_{T+1}$ is $\hat{\beta}_1 + \hat{\beta}_2x_{T+1}$ where $(\hat{\beta}_1, \hat{\beta}_2)$ are generalized least squares estimates.

2.  To predict the component $\rho e_T$, we need estimates for both $\rho$ and $e_T$. For $\rho$ we can use the estimator $\hat{\rho}$ specified in equation 11.5.5. To estimate $e_T$ we use the generalized least squares residual, defined as

$$\tilde{e}_T = y_T - \hat{\beta}_1 - \hat{\beta}_2x_T \qquad (11.7.4)$$

3.  The best forecast of the third component $v_{T+1}$ is zero because this component is uncorrelated with past values $v_1, v_2, \ldots, v_T$.

Collecting all these results, *our predictor for $y_{T+1}$ is given by*

$$\hat{y}_{T+1} = \hat{\beta}_1 + \hat{\beta}_2 x_{T+1} + \hat{\rho}\tilde{e}_T \qquad (11.7.5)$$

A comparison of equations 11.7.5 and 11.7.3 shows that we are using $\hat{\rho}\tilde{e}_T$ to predict the future error $e_{T+1}$. That is, we are using information on the $t$-th error $e_T$, and our knowledge that $e_T$ and $e_{T+1}$ are correlated, to improve on zero as a predictor for $e_{T+1}$.

What about predicting more than one period into the future? For $h$ periods ahead, it can be shown that the best predictor is

$$\hat{y}_{T+h} = \hat{\beta}_1 + \hat{\beta}_2 x_{T+h} + \hat{\rho}^h \tilde{e}_T \qquad (11.7.6)$$

Assuming $|\hat{\rho}| < 1$, the influence of the term $\hat{\rho}^h \tilde{e}_T$ diminishes the further we go into the future (the larger $h$ becomes).

In the Bangladesh sugar cane example

$$\hat{\beta}_1 = 6.1641, \quad \hat{\beta}_2 = 1.0066, \quad \hat{\rho} = 0.342$$

and

$$\tilde{e}_T = y_T - \hat{\beta}_1 - \hat{\beta}_2 x_T$$

$$= \ln(A_T) - \hat{\beta}_1 - \hat{\beta}_2 \ln(P_T)$$

$$= 5.4596 - 6.1641 - 1.0066(-0.9374)$$

$$= 0.239$$

To predict $y_{T+1}$ and $y_{T+2}$ for a sugar cane price of 0.4, in both periods $(T + 1)$ and $(T + 2)$, we have

$$\hat{y}_{T+1} = \hat{\beta}_1 + \hat{\beta}_2 x_{T+1} + \hat{\rho}\tilde{e}_T$$

$$= 6.1641 + 1.0066 \ln(0.4) + (0.342)(0.239)$$

$$= 5.3235$$

$$\hat{y}_{T+2} = \hat{\beta}_1 + \hat{\beta}_2 x_{T+2} + \hat{\rho}^2 \tilde{e}_T$$

$$= 6.1641 + 1.0066 \ln(0.4) + (0.342)^2(0.239)$$

$$= 5.2697$$

Note that these predictions are for the logarithm of area; they correspond to areas of 205 and 194, respectively.

## *11.8* Summing Up

1.  When the economic data generation process is such that the errors in a linear regression model are correlated, we say that autocorrelation exists. The existence of autocorrelated errors is always a real possibility and is worth investigating when we have a sample of time-series observations.

2.  If a model possesses autocorrelated errors, but we ignore or are unaware of the correlation and, hence, use the least squares estimator, we will be using an estimator that has a larger variance than the generalized least squares estimator. We will also be using standard errors that are not a proper reflection of the precision of the least squares estimates.

3.  There are many time-series models that can be used to model autocorrelated errors. For a review of alternatives see Ramanathan (1995, Chapter 9). The most common, and the one considered in this chapter, is the first-order autoregressive model

$$e_t = \rho e_{t-1} + v_t \tag{11.8.1}$$

where the $v_t$ are independent identically distributed errors. If $-1 < \rho < 1$, then

$$E(e_t) = 0, \qquad \text{var}(e_t) = \frac{\sigma_v^2}{1 - \rho^2}, \qquad \text{corr}(e_t, e_{t-k}) = \rho^k \tag{11.8.2}$$

4.  To detect the presence of autocorrelated errors of the form given in (11.8.1) we use the Durbin–Watson test to test the null hypothesis $\rho = 0$ against the alternative that $\rho > 0$. Because of the impossibility of producing Durbin–Watson critical values relevant for all possible problems, we utilize computer software that can automatically compute the relevant $p$-value for the test.

5.  If $\rho > 0$, a generalized least squares estimation technique is called for. The first step toward finding generalized least squares estimates is to estimate $\rho$ from the least squares residuals as

$$\hat{\rho} = \sum_{t=2}^{T} \hat{e}_t \hat{e}_{t-1} \bigg/ \sum_{t=2}^{T} \hat{e}_{t-1}^2$$

Then, using the dependent variable $y_t$ as an example, the observations are transformed as

$$y_t^* = y_t - \hat{\rho} y_{t-1}, \quad t = 2, 3, \ldots, T$$

$$y_1^* = \sqrt{1 - \hat{\rho}^2} y_1 \tag{11.8.3}$$

The generalized least squares estimator is equivalent to least squares applied to the transformed observations.

6.  A future observation, $h$ periods ahead, is defined as

$$y_{T+h} = \beta_1 + \beta_2 x_{T+h} + e_{T+h} \tag{11.8.4}$$

To predict $y_{T+h}$, when the errors follow an AR(1) process, we use the predictor

$$\hat{y}_{T+h} = \hat{\beta}_1 + \hat{\beta}_2 x_{T+h} + \hat{\rho}^h \tilde{e}_T \tag{11.8.5}$$

where $\tilde{e}_T$ is the most recent generalized least squares residual.

7. It should be emphasized that the range of economic models where autocorrelated errors might exist is much broader than our example might suggest. Routine checking for the presence of autocorrelated errors is advisable in all economic models that utilize time-series data.

## 11.9 Exercises

11.1  Consider the investment function

$$I_t = \beta_1 + \beta_2 Y_t + \beta_3 R_t + e_t$$

where $I_t$ = investment in year $t$

$Y_t$ = GNP in year $t$

$R_t$ = interest rate in year $t$

Thirty observations on $I$, $Y$, and $R$ are given in the file *inv.dat*. Use these data to answer the following questions.

(a) Find least squares estimates of $\beta_1$, $\beta_2$ and $\beta_3$ and report the results in the usual way. Comment on the implied statistical reliability of the results. Do the estimates for $\beta_2$ and $\beta_3$ have the expected signs?
(b) Plot the least squares residuals. Do they suggest the existence of autocorrelation?
(c) Use the Durbin–Watson test to test for positive autocorrelation.
(d) Re-estimate the model after correcting for autocorrelation. Report the results. Note any differences between these results and those obtained in part (a). Suggest how the results obtained in part (a) could be misleading.
(e) Predict next year's level of investment given that next year's values for $Y$ and $R$ are $Y = 36$ and $R = 14$. How does this forecast compare with the one that would be obtained if autocorrelation is ignored?

11.2*  Consider the AR(1) error model

$$e_t = \rho e_{t-1} + v_t$$

where $E(v_t) = 0$, $\text{var}(v_t) = \sigma_v^2$ and $E(v_t v_s) = 0$ for $t \neq s$. Given that $\text{var}(e_t) = \text{var}(e_{t-1}) = \sigma_e^2$, prove that

$$\sigma_e^2 = \frac{\sigma_v^2}{1 - \rho^2}$$

Show that

$$E(e_t e_{t-1}) = \sigma_e^2 \rho \text{ and } E(e_t e_{t-2}) = \sigma_e^2 \rho^2$$

11.3  To investigate the relationship between job vacancies ($JV$) and the unemployment rate ($U$), a researcher sets up the model

$$\ln(JV_t) = \beta_1 + \beta_2 \ln(U_t) + e_t$$

and assumes that the $e_t$ are independent $N(0, \sigma_e^2)$ random variables.
(a) Use the data in the file *vacan.dat* to find least squares estimates for $\beta_1$ and $\beta_2$. Construct a 95 percent confidence interval for $\beta_2$.
(b) Find the value of the Durbin–Watson statistic. In light of this value, what can you say about the original assumptions for the error $e_t$, what can you say about the confidence interval for $\beta_2$ found in (a)?
(c) Re-estimate the model assuming the errors follow an AR(1) error model. Find a new 95 percent confidence interval for $\beta_2$ and comment on the results, particularly in relation to your answers for part (a).

11.4*  Data for a monopolist's total revenue ($tr$), total cost ($tc$), and output ($q$), for 48 consecutive months, appear in the file *monop.dat*. Suppose that the monopolist's economic models for total revenue and total cost are given respectively by

$$tr = \beta_1 q + \beta_2 q^2$$

$$tc = \alpha_1 + \alpha_2 q + \alpha_3 q^2$$

(a) Show that marginal cost and marginal revenue are given by

$$mc = \alpha_2 + 2\alpha_3 q \qquad mr = \beta_1 + 2\beta_2 q$$

(b) Show that the profit maximizing quantity which equates marginal revenue and marginal cost is

$$q^* = \frac{\alpha_2 - \beta_1}{2(\beta_2 - \alpha_3)}$$

(c) Use the least squares estimator to estimate the total revenue and total cost functions. For what statistical models are these estimates appropriate? What do the least squares estimates suggest is the profit maximizing level of output?
(d) After rounding the optimizing output to an integer, use that output to predict total revenue, total cost, and profit for the next three months. (Continue to assume the least squares statistical assumptions are appropriate.)
(e) Separately test the errors for each of the functions to see if these errors might be autocorrelated.
(f) Where autocorrelation has been suggested by the tests in part (e), find generalized least squares estimates of the relevant function(s).

(g) What is the profit-maximizing level of output suggested by the results in part (f)?

(h) Given the output level found in part (g), and the autocorrelation assumption, predict total revenue, total cost, and hence, profit for the next three months. Compare the predictions with those from part (d).

11.5  Consider the learning curve data and model given in Exercise 3.8 and file *learn.dat*. The model is

$$\ln(u_t) = \beta_1 + \beta_2 \ln(q_t) + e_t$$

(a) Test a null hypothesis of no autocorrelation in the $e_t$ against an alternative of positive autocorrelation at a 1 percent level of significance.

(b) Compare 95 percent confidence intervals for $\beta_2$ obtained using:
   (i)  least squares estimates and standard errors, and
   (ii) generalized least squares estimates and standard errors after correcting for autocorrelation.
   What does this comparison suggest?

(c) Suppose that cumulative production in year 1971 is 3800. Under the following conditions, do you expect cost per unit in 1971 to be more or less than it was in 1970?
   (i)  If the errors are not autocorrelated
   (ii) If the errors are autocorrelated

11.6  The file *icecr.dat* contains observations on variables potentially relevant for modeling the demand for ice cream. This example is taken from a classic paper on autocorrelation by Hildreth and Lu (1960). Each observation represents a four-week period during the years 1951–53. The variables are:
   $Q$: per capita consumption of ice cream in pints
   $P$: price per pint in dollars
   $I$: weekly family income in dollars
   $F$: mean temperature in Fahrenheit
(a) Use least squares to estimate the model

$$Q_t = \beta_1 + \beta_2 P_t + \beta_3 I_t + \beta_4 F_t + e_t$$

(b) Are there any coefficient estimates that are not significantly different from zero? Do you think the corresponding variable(s) is (are) not relevant for explaining ice cream demand?

(c) Is there any evidence of autocorrelated errors? Check for runs of positive and negative least squares residuals, as well as the Durbin–Watson *p*-value.

(d) Estimate the model after transforming the variables to correct for autocorrelation.

(e) Do your estimates from part (d) change your answer to part (b)?

11.7*  Reconsider Exercise 11.6:
(a) Compute the Durbin–Watson *p*-value for the residuals from the transformed model estimated in 11.6(d). Does there still seem to be an autocorrelation problem?

(b) Get your computer software to estimate the equation assuming the errors follow what is called a "second order" autoregressive model. Comment on the coefficient estimates.

# *11.10* References

Other treatments of autocorrelation can be found in

DORAN, H. E. (1989). *Applied Regression Analysis in Econometrics.* New York: Marcel Dekker, Chapter 8.

GRIFFITHS, W. E., R. C. HILL, AND G. G. JUDGE (1993). *Learning and Practicing Econometrics,* New York: John Wiley and Sons, Inc.

GUJARATI, D. N. (1995). *Basic Econometrics* (3d ed.). New York: McGraw-Hill, Chapter 12.

HILDRETH, C. AND J. Y. LU (1960). "Demand Relations with Autocorrelated Disturbances," *Technical Bulletin 276,* Michigan State University.

KENNEDY, P. (1992). *A Guide to Econometrics,* (3d ed.). Cambridge, MA: MIT Press.

LARDARO, L. (1993). *Applied Econometrics,* New York: HarperCollins, Chapter 11.

MADDALA, G. S. (1989). *Introduction to Econometrics,* New York: Macmillan, Chapter 6.

PINDYCK, R. S., AND D. L. RUBINFELD (1991). *Econometric Models and Economic Forecasts* (3d ed.). New York: McGraw-Hill, Chapter 6.

RAMANATHAN, R. (1995). *Introductory Econometrics with Applications* (3d ed.). New York: Harcourt, Brace and Jovanovich, Chapter 11.

# *Part IV*

# Topics in Econometrics

The field of econometrics is vast. What has been covered in the first three parts of this book can be regarded as the basic foundations upon which further study can be built. The direction that you take next is largely one of personal preference. The remaining chapters, which come under the heading of Topics in Econometrics, are designed to give an introduction to a variety of possible directions. These chapters do not build on each other, so they can be studied in any order.

In chapter 12 we discuss two models that can be used when we are fortunate enough to have data that vary over time and space. For example, we may have annual data on a hundred households over a ten-year period. Special models and techniques can be applied to such data. In chapter 13 the simultaneous nature of many economic relationships is recognized. For example, supply and demand curves simultaneously determine quantity and price. Macroeconomic relationships simultaneously determine consumption expenditures and national income. The existence of this simultaneity requires special estimation techniques.

How to estimate models that are nonlinear in the parameters, such as constant elasticity of substitution production functions, is covered in chapter 14. The implications of including lagged variables into a regression model and the resulting dynamic effects are the subjects of chapter 15. In chapter 16 an introduction to time-series models is given. Time-series models are popular techniques for forecasting and modeling macroeconomic relationships. Possible sources of economic data that can be utilized for econometric projects or research investigations are described in chapter 17.

# Chapter *12*

# Pooling Time-Series and Cross-Sectional Data

When investigating the behavior of economic units such as households, firms, or even nations, we often have observations on a number of such units for a number of time periods. For example, if we are studying the economic behavior of electric utility firms, we may observe costs, inputs, and outputs for a number of firms across the United States. These observations could be made every year for a number of years. On the aggregate level, if we are studying the international usage of oil and coal, we may observe usage and the corresponding explanatory variables for a number of countries, in each quarter or each year, for a number of years. In these examples an investigator will possess a time-series of data on a cross-section of economic units. The problem is how to specify a statistical model that will capture individual differences in behavior so that we may combine, or **pool,** all the data (information) for estimation and inference purposes. In this chapter we consider three models for pooling time-series and cross-sectional data. They are (i) the seemingly unrelated regressions model, (ii) a dummy variable model, and (iii) an error components model. The same economic example will be carried through the chapter to illustrate all three models. Before turning to these models we introduce the economic example, and a general equation for pooling data.

## *12.1* An Economic Model

Investment demand is the purchase of durable goods by both households and firms. In terms of total spending, investment spending is the volatile component. Therefore, understanding what determines investment is crucial to understanding the sources of fluctuations in aggregate demand. In addition, a firm's net fixed investment, which is the flow of additions to capital stock or replacements for worn out capital, is important because it determines the future value of the capital stock and thus affects future labor productivity and aggregate supply.

There are several interesting and elaborate theories that seek to describe the determinants of the investment process for the firm. Most of these theories evolve to the conclusion that perceived profit opportunities (expected profits or present discounted value of future earnings) and desired capital stock are two important determinants of a firm's fixed business investment. Unfortunately, neither of these variables are directly observable. Therefore, in formulating our economic model, we use observable proxies for these variables instead.

In terms of expected profits, one alternative is to identify the present discounted value of future earnings as the market value of the firms securities. The price of a firm's stock represents and contains information about these expected profits. Consequently, the stock market value of the firm at the beginning of the year, denoted by $V_t$, may be used as a proxy for expected profits.

In terms of desired capital stock, expectations play a definite role. To catch these expectational effects, one possibility is to use a model that recognizes that actual capital stock in any period is the sum of a large number of past desired capital stocks. Thus, we use the beginning of the year actual capital stock $K_t$ as a proxy for permanent desired capital stock.

Focusing on these explanatory variables, an economic model for describing gross firm investment for the $i$-th firm in the $t$-th time period may be expressed as

$$INV_{it} = f(V_{it}, K_{it}) \tag{12.1.1}$$

Let $y_{it} = INV_{it}$ denote values for the dependent variable and $x_{2it} = V_{it}$ and $x_{3it} = K_{it}$ denote values for the explanatory variables. A very flexible linear statistical model that corresponds to equation 12.1.1 is

$$y_{it} = \beta_{1it} + \beta_{2it}x_{2it} + \beta_{3it}x_{3it} + e_{it} \tag{12.1.2}$$

In this general model the intercepts and response parameters are permitted to differ for each firm in each time period. The model cannot be estimated in its current form, as there are more unknown parameters than data points. However, there are many types of simplifying assumptions that can be made to make the model operational. One of the challenges of econometrics is to specify a statistical model that is consistent with how the data are generated. The three models that we outline in this chapter can be viewed as special cases of the general model in equation 12.1.2.

## 12.2 Seemingly Unrelated Regressions

The simplification of equation 12.1.2 that yields what is called the **seemingly unrelated regressions (SUR)** model is

$$\beta_{1it} = \beta_{1i} \qquad \beta_{2it} = \beta_{2i} \qquad \beta_{3it} = \beta_{3i} \tag{12.2.1}$$

That is, the parameters of the investment function differ across firms (note that the "$i$" subscript remains) but are constant across time. This assumption means that the model in equation 12.1.2 becomes

$$y_{it} = \beta_{1i} + \beta_{2i}x_{2it} + \beta_{3i}x_{3it} + e_{it} \tag{12.2.2}$$

The data we use to illustrate the SUR model are given in Table 9.2; they consist of 20 time-series observations on investment, stock market value, and capital stock for two firms, General Electric ($G$) and Westinghouse ($W$). Thus, in terms of the subscripts in equation 12.2.2, $i = G$ and $W$, and $t = 1,2,\ldots,20$. The investment functions for these two firms were considered in chapters 9 (section 9.6) and 10

(Exercises 10.3 and 10.4); further aspects of the functions are explored now, and are related to the earlier specifications.

## 12.2.1  ESTIMATING SEPARATE EQUATIONS

Corresponding to the model in equation 12.2.2, we can specify two regression models, one for General Electric and one for Westinghouse.

$$INV_{Gt} = \beta_{1G} + \beta_{2G}V_{Gt} + \beta_{3G}K_{Gt} + e_{Gt} \tag{12.2.3a}$$

$$INV_{Wt} = \beta_{1W} + \beta_{2W}V_{Wt} + \beta_{3W}K_{Wt} + e_{Wt} \tag{12.2.3b}$$

For the moment we make the usual least squares assumptions about the errors.

$$E(e_{Gt}) = 0 \quad \text{var}(e_{Gt}) = \sigma_G^2 \quad \text{cov}(e_{Gt}, e_{Gs}) = 0 \tag{12.2.4a}$$

$$E(e_{Wt}) = 0 \quad \text{var}(e_{Wt}) = \sigma_W^2 \quad \text{cov}(e_{Wt}, e_{Ws}) = 0 \tag{12.2.4b}$$

Assumption 12.2.4a says that the errors in the first investment function (i) have zero mean, (ii) are homoskedastic with constant variance $\sigma_G^2$, and (iii) are not correlated over time; autocorrelation does not exist. A similar set of assumptions is made in 12.2.4b for the second investment function. Note, however, that the two functions do have different error variances $\sigma_G^2$ and $\sigma_W^2$.

So far, the assumptions in 12.2.4 are precisely those for which least squares is the best linear unbiased estimator for the unknown coefficients. We are able to confidently apply least squares separately to each equation, knowing we have chosen the appropriate estimator. However, when we follow this strategy, we are saying: Given the information we have on General Electric, what is the best estimator of the General Electric equation? And, given the information on Westinghouse, what is the best estimator for the Westinghouse equation? We are treating the two equations separately. We are not asking whether we might have information on General Electric that could be utilized to obtain a better estimator of the Westinghouse equation; or vice versa. For information on one equation to improve estimation of the other, we need some kind of link between the two equations. Let us investigate some possible linkages.

One way of linking the two equations was explored in section 9.6 of chapter 9. In that chapter the two equations were combined using a dummy variable to give the model

$$INV_t = \beta_{1G} + \delta_1 D_t + \beta_{2G}V_t + \delta_2 D_t V_t + \beta_{3G}K_t + \delta_3 D_t K_t + e_t \tag{12.2.5}$$

where $D_t$ is a dummy variable equal to 1 for the Westinghouse observations and 0 for the General Electric observations. You should think of equation 12.2.5 as representing the pooled set of 40 observations. Because we have combined the 20 General Electric observations with the 20 Westinghouse observations, we have dropped the $G$ and $W$ subscripts from the variables.

Equation 12.2.5 is just another way of writing 12.2.3. You should satisfy yourself that this is so by seeing what happens when $D = 1$ and what happens when $D = 0$. You will find that they are identical specifications with the following relationships between the parameters

$$\beta_{1W} = \beta_{1G} + \delta_1 \qquad \beta_{2W} = \beta_{2G} + \delta_2 \qquad \beta_{3W} = \beta_{3G} + \delta_3$$

A natural question to ask is: What happens if we apply least squares to equation 12.2.5, utilizing all 40 observations? How would this estimation differ from applying least squares twice, once to the 20 observations for Westinghouse and once to the 20 observations for General Electric? The answer is that the estimates of the $\beta$s turn out to be exactly the same. The new model treats all the coefficients in exactly the same way. However, the standard errors from the two procedures will be different. If we estimate the pooled dummy variable model by least squares, we are implicitly assuming that the error variance for $e_t$ is constant over all 40 observations. When estimating separate equations for General Electric and Westinghouse, we are recognizing that one set of 20 values of $e_t$ has variance $\sigma_G^2$ and the other set of 20 values of $e_t$ has variance $\sigma_W^2$; correspondingly, we get different variance *estimates* for each equation.

What happens, then, if we recognize the existence of heteroskedasticity ($\sigma_G^2 \neq \sigma_W^2$), and apply generalized least squares to the pooled dummy-variable model? In this case all the results, both coefficient estimates and standard errors, will be exactly the same as those obtained from separate least squares estimation of the two equations (see Exercise 10.4(a)). In other words, if we recognize that $\sigma_G^2 \neq \sigma_W^2$, estimation by linking the two equations with the dummy variable model is not any more precise than separate least squares estimation. We need to look for an additional link.

## 12.2.2  JOINT ESTIMATION OF THE EQUATIONS

An assumption that lets us utilize a joint estimation procedure that is better than separate least squares estimation is

$$\text{cov}(e_{Gt}, e_{Wt}) = \sigma_{GW} \qquad (12.2.6)$$

This assumption says that the error terms in the two equations, at the same point in time, are correlated. This kind of correlation is often called **contemporaneous correlation.** To understand why $e_{Gt}$ and $e_{Wt}$ might be correlated, recall that these errors contain the influence on investment of factors that have been omitted from the equations. Such factors might include capacity utilization, current and past interest rates, liquidity, and the general state of the economy. Since the two firms are similar in many respects, it is likely that the effects of the omitted factors on investment by General Electric will be similar to their effect on investment by Westinghouse. If so, then $e_{Gt}$ and $e_{Wt}$ will be capturing similar effects and will be correlated. Adding the contemporaneous correlation assumption (equation 12.2.6) has the effect of introducing additional information that is not included when we carry out separate least squares estimation of the two equations.

What are the implications of equation 12.2.6 for the error term $e_t$ in the pooled dummy variable model in equation 12.2.5? It means that all 40 errors will not be uncorrelated. The General Electric errors are not correlated with each other, and the Westinghouse errors are not correlated with each other, but equation 12.2.6 implies that the first Westinghouse error will be correlated with the first General Electric error, the second Westinghouse error will be correlated with the second General Electric error, and so on. This information cannot be utilized when the equations are estimated separately. However, it can be utilized to produce better estimates when the equations are jointly estimated as they are in the dummy variable model.

To improve the precision of the dummy variable model estimates, the errors must be transformed so that they all have the same variance and are uncorrelated. In particular, we need the transformed Westinghouse errors to be uncorrelated with the transformed General Electric errors. The variables are correspondingly transformed. This transformation is too complicated to present here, but it is automatically carried out by your computer software, usually using some kind of "seemingly unrelated regression" command. The steps that your software follows are: (i) Estimate the equations separately using least squares; (ii) Use the least squares residuals from step (i) to estimate $\sigma_G^2$, $\sigma_W^2$ and $\sigma_{GW}$; (iii) Use the estimates from step (ii) to estimate the two equations jointly within a generalized least squares framework. For details, see Griffiths et al. (1993, Ch.17).

Estimates of the coefficients of the two investment functions are presented in Table 12.1. Standard errors are in parentheses. Two sets of estimates are given, those obtained from separate least squares estimation of the two equations and those obtained using the joint seemingly unrelated regression (SUR) technique. Since the SUR technique utilizes the information on the correlation between the error terms, it is more precise than least squares. This fact is supported by the lower standard errors of the SUR estimates. You should be cautious, however, when making judgments about precision on the basis of standard errors. Standard errors are themselves estimates; it is possible for a standard error for SUR to be greater than a corresponding least squares standard error even when SUR is a better estimator than least squares. From an economic standpoint our estimated coefficients for the capital stock and value variables have the expected positive signs. Also, all are significantly different from zero except for the coefficient of capital stock in the Westinghouse equation. This coefficient has a low $t$-value, and hence, is estimated with limited precision.

Equations that exhibit contemporaneous correlation were called "seemingly unrelated" by Zellner (1962); the equations seem to be unrelated, but the additional information provided by the correlation between the equation errors means that joint generalized least squares estimation is better than single-equation least squares.

*Table 12.1*   **Least Squares and Seemingly Unrelated Regression Estimates for Two Investment Functions**

| Variable | General Electric | | Westinghouse | |
|---|---|---|---|---|
| | LS | SUR | LS | SUR |
| constant | −9.956 | −27.719 | −0.509 | −1.252 |
| | (31.374) | (27.033) | (8.015) | (6.956) |
| V | 0.0265 | 0.0383 | 0.0529 | 0.0576 |
| | (0.0156) | (0.0133) | (0.0157) | (0.0134) |
| K | 0.1517 | 0.1390 | 0.0924 | 0.0640 |
| | (0.0257) | (0.0230) | (0.0561) | (0.0489) |

### 12.2.3   SEPARATE OR JOINT ESTIMATION

Is it always better to estimate two or more equations jointly? Or are there circumstances when it is just as good to estimate each equation separately?

There are two situations where separate least squares estimation is just as good as the SUR technique. The first of these cases is where the errors are not correlated. If the errors are not correlated, there is nothing linking the two equations, and separate estimation cannot be improved upon.

The second situation is less obvious. Indeed, some advanced algebra is needed to prove that least squares and SUR give *identical* estimates when the same explanatory variables appear in each equation. By the "same explanatory variables," we mean more than variables with similar definitions, like the value and capital stock variables for General Electric and Westinghouse. We mean the same variables with the same observations on those variables. For example, suppose we are interested in estimating demand equations for beef, chicken, and pork. Since these commodities are all substitute meats, it is reasonable to specify the quantity demanded for each of the meats as a function of the price of beef, the price of chicken, and the price of pork, as well as income. The same variables with the same observations appear in all three equations. Even if the errors of these equations are correlated, as is quite likely, the use of SUR will not yield an improvement over separate estimation.

If the explanatory variables in each equation are different, then a test to see if the correlation between the errors is significantly different from zero is of interest. If a null hypothesis of zero correlation is not rejected, then there is no evidence to suggest that SUR will improve on separate least squares estimation. To carry out such a test we compute the squared correlation

$$r_{GW}^2 = \frac{\hat{\sigma}_{GW}^2}{\hat{\sigma}_G^2 \hat{\sigma}_W^2} = \frac{(176.45)^2}{(660.83)(88.662)} = (0.729)^2 = .53139$$

The variance estimates $\hat{\sigma}_G^2$ and $\hat{\sigma}_W^2$ are the usual ones from separate least squares estimation, except that $T = 20$ rather than $T - K = 17$ has, for large-sample approximation reasons, been used as the divisor in the formulas. The estimated covariance is computed from

$$\hat{\sigma}_{GW} = \frac{1}{T} \sum_{t=1}^{20} \hat{e}_{Gt} \hat{e}_{Wt}$$

To check the statistical significance of $r_{GW}^2$, we test the null hypothesis $H_0$: $\sigma_{GW} = 0$. If $\sigma_{GW} = 0$, then $\lambda = Tr_{GW}^2$ is a test statistic that is distributed as a $\chi_{(1)}^2$ random variable in large samples. The 5 percent critical value of a chi-square distribution with one degree of freedom is 3.84. The value of the test statistic from our data is $\lambda = 10.628$. Hence, we reject the null hypothesis of no correlation between the $e_{Gt}$ and $e_{Wt}$.

If we are testing for the existence of correlated errors for more than two equations, the relevant test statistic is equal to $T$ times the sum of squares of all the correlations; the probability distribution under $H_0$ is a chi-square distribution with degrees of freedom equal to the number of correlations. For example, with three equations, denoted by subscripts "1," "2," and "3," the null hypothesis is

$$H_0:\ \sigma_{12} = \sigma_{13} = \sigma_{23} = 0$$

and the $\chi^2_{(3)}$ test statistic is

$$\lambda = T(r^2_{12} + r^2_{13} + r^2_{23})$$

There are many economic problems where we have cause to consider a system of equations. The investment function example was one; estimation of demand functions, like the meat functions we alluded to in this section, is another. Further examples are given in the exercises.

## 12.3 A Dummy Variable Specification

To introduce the dummy variable model as a method for pooling time-series and cross-sectional data, we return to equation 12.1.2, which is

$$y_{it} = \beta_{1it} + \beta_{2it}x_{2it} + \beta_{3it}x_{3it} + e_{it} \tag{12.3.1}$$

Both the dummy variable model to be described in this section and the error components model considered in the next section assume that

$$\beta_{1it} = \beta_{1i} \qquad \beta_{2it} = \beta_2 \qquad \beta_{3it} = \beta_3 \tag{12.3.2}$$

This model of parameter variation specifies that *only the intercept parameter varies,* not the response parameters; and the intercept varies only across firms and not over time. Also, we will assume that the errors $e_{it}$ are independent and distributed $N(0, \sigma^2_e)$ for all individuals and in all time periods. Given this assumption, and equation 12.3.2, it follows that *all behavioral differences between individual firms and over time are captured by the intercept.* The resulting statistical model is

$$y_{it} = \beta_{1i} + \beta_2 x_{2it} + \beta_3 x_{3it} + e_{it} \tag{12.3.3}$$

The feature that distinguishes the dummy variable model from the error components model is the way in which the varying intercept $\beta_{1i}$ is treated. The dummy variable model treats it as a fixed, unknown parameter. We make inferences only about the firms on which we have data. The error components model views the firms on which we have data as a random sample from a larger population of firms. The intercepts are treated as random drawings from the population distribution of firm intercepts. Inferences are made about the population of firms. Further details about this distinction can be found in Judge et al. (1988, p. 489). Also, in much of the literature the dummy variable model is called a **fixed effects model,** and the error components model bears the name **random effects model.**

The example we use for introducing the dummy variable and error components frameworks is the same investment behavior example that we used for the section on SUR. However, instead of using only two firms, we extend our data set to include ten firms. These data are given in Table 12.2 and are taken from a book by Vinod and Ullah (1981). They comprise $T = 20$ time-series observations on $N = 10$ firms.

### 12.3.1   THE MODEL

To introduce the dummy variable version of equation 12.3.3, we define dummy variables of the following type

$$D_{1i} = \begin{cases} 1 & i = 1 \\ 0 & \text{otherwise} \end{cases} \quad D_{2i} = \begin{cases} 1 & i = 2 \\ 0 & \text{otherwise} \end{cases} \quad D_{3i} = \begin{cases} 1 & i = 3 \\ 0 & \text{otherwise} \end{cases}, \text{ etc}$$

Under these definitions equation 12.3.3 becomes

$$y_{it} = \beta_{11}D_{1i} + \beta_{12}D_{2i} + \cdots + \beta_{1,10}D_{10i} + \beta_2 x_{2it} + \beta_3 x_{3it} + e_{it} \qquad (12.3.4)$$

Compared to the model setups in chapter 9 and in the SUR specification, the dummy variables in equation 12.3.4 are introduced in a slightly different way. In this equation there are ten dummy variables, one for each firm, and no constant term; the coefficients $\beta_{1i}$ are equal to the firm intercepts. To make equation 12.3.4 consistent with our earlier treatments, we would need to specify a constant and nine dummy variables; each dummy variable coefficient would be equal to the difference between the intercept for its firm and the intercept for the base firm for which we did not specify a dummy variable. The specification in equation 12.3.4 is more convenient for our current discussion. However, you should recognize that the two alternatives are just different ways of looking at the same model.

Given that the error terms $e_{it}$ are independent and $N(0, \sigma_e^2)$ for all observations, the best linear unbiased estimator of equation 12.3.4 is the least squares estimator. The results from this estimation (coefficients, standard errors, and $t$ values) appear in Table 12.3. The response parameters for value ($x_2$) and capital stock ($x_3$) have small standard errors, implying that their influence on investment has been accurately estimated. The firm intercepts vary considerably, and some of them have large $t$-values, suggesting that the assumption of differing intercepts for different firms is appropriate. To confirm this fact, we can test the following hypothesis.

$$H_0: \beta_{11} = \beta_{12} = \cdots = \beta_{1N}$$

$$(12.3.5)$$

$$H_1: \text{the } \beta_{1i} \text{ are not all equal}$$

These $(N - 1)$ joint null hypotheses may be tested using the usual $F$-test statistic.

$$F = \frac{(SSE_R - SSE_U)/J}{SSE_U/(NT - K)}$$

$$= \frac{(1749127 - 522855)/9}{522855/(200 - 12)}$$

$$= 48.99$$

*Table 12.2*  Data on Investment *INV*, Expected Profits *V*, and Desired Capital Stock *K* for 10 Firms and 20 Years

| INV | V | K | INV | V | K | INV | V | K |
|---|---|---|---|---|---|---|---|---|
| General Motors | | | Atlantic Richfield | | | Westinghouse | | |
| 317.60 | 3078.50 | 2.80 | 39.68 | 157.70 | 183.20 | 12.93 | 191.50 | 1.8 |
| 391.80 | 4661.70 | 52.60 | 50.73 | 167.90 | 204.00 | 25.90 | 516.00 | 0.8 |
| 410.60 | 5387.10 | 156.90 | 74.24 | 192.90 | 236.00 | 35.05 | 729.00 | 7.4 |
| 257.70 | 2792.20 | 209.20 | 53.51 | 156.70 | 291.70 | 22.89 | 560.40 | 18.1 |
| 330.80 | 4313.20 | 203.40 | 42.65 | 191.40 | 323.10 | 18.84 | 519.90 | 23.5 |
| 461.20 | 4643.90 | 207.20 | 46.48 | 185.50 | 344.00 | 28.57 | 628.50 | 26.5 |
| 512.00 | 4551.20 | 255.20 | 61.40 | 199.60 | 367.70 | 48.51 | 537.10 | 36.2 |
| 448.00 | 3244.10 | 303.70 | 39.67 | 189.50 | 407.20 | 43.34 | 561.20 | 60.8 |
| 499.60 | 4053.70 | 264.10 | 62.24 | 151.20 | 426.60 | 37.02 | 617.20 | 84.4 |
| 547.50 | 4379.30 | 201.60 | 52.32 | 187.70 | 470.00 | 37.81 | 626.70 | 91.2 |
| 561.20 | 4840.90 | 265.00 | 63.21 | 214.70 | 499.20 | 39.27 | 737.20 | 92.4 |
| 688.10 | 4900.90 | 402.20 | 59.37 | 232.90 | 534.60 | 53.46 | 760.50 | 86.0 |
| 568.90 | 3526.50 | 761.50 | 58.02 | 249.00 | 566.60 | 55.56 | 581.40 | 111.1 |
| 529.20 | 3254.70 | 922.40 | 70.34 | 224.50 | 595.30 | 49.56 | 662.30 | 130.6 |
| 555.10 | 3700.20 | 1020.10 | 67.42 | 237.30 | 631.40 | 32.04 | 583.80 | 141.8 |
| 642.90 | 3755.60 | 1099.00 | 55.74 | 240.10 | 662.30 | 32.24 | 635.20 | 136.7 |
| 755.90 | 4833.00 | 1207.70 | 80.30 | 327.30 | 683.90 | 54.38 | 723.80 | 129.7 |
| 891.20 | 4924.90 | 1430.50 | 85.40 | 359.40 | 729.30 | 71.78 | 864.10 | 145.5 |
| 1304.40 | 6241.70 | 1777.30 | 81.90 | 398.40 | 774.30 | 90.08 | 1193.50 | 174.8 |
| 1486.70 | 5593.60 | 2226.30 | 81.43 | 365.70 | 804.90 | 68.60 | 1188.90 | 213.5 |
| US Steel | | | IBM | | | Goodyear | | |
| 209.90 | 1362.40 | 53.80 | 20.36 | 197.00 | 6.50 | 26.63 | 290.60 | 162.0 |
| 355.30 | 1807.10 | 50.50 | 25.98 | 210.30 | 15.80 | 23.39 | 291.10 | 174.0 |
| 469.90 | 2676.30 | 118.10 | 25.94 | 223.10 | 27.70 | 30.65 | 335.00 | 183.0 |
| 262.30 | 1801.90 | 260.20 | 27.53 | 216.70 | 39.20 | 20.89 | 246.00 | 198.0 |
| 230.40 | 1957.30 | 312.70 | 24.60 | 286.40 | 48.60 | 28.78 | 356.20 | 208.0 |
| 361.60 | 2202.90 | 254.20 | 28.54 | 298.00 | 52.50 | 26.93 | 289.80 | 223.0 |
| 472.80 | 2380.50 | 261.40 | 43.41 | 276.90 | 61.50 | 32.08 | 268.20 | 234.0 |
| 445.60 | 2168.60 | 298.70 | 42.81 | 272.60 | 80.50 | 32.21 | 213.30 | 248.0 |
| 361.60 | 1985.10 | 301.80 | 27.84 | 287.40 | 94.40 | 35.69 | 348.20 | 274.0 |
| 288.20 | 1813.90 | 279.10 | 32.60 | 330.30 | 92.60 | 62.47 | 374.20 | 282.0 |
| 258.70 | 1850.20 | 213.80 | 39.03 | 324.40 | 92.30 | 52.32 | 387.20 | 316.0 |
| 420.30 | 2067.70 | 232.60 | 50.17 | 401.90 | 94.20 | 56.95 | 347.40 | 302.0 |
| 420.50 | 1796.70 | 264.80 | 51.85 | 407.40 | 111.40 | 54.32 | 291.90 | 333.0 |
| 494.50 | 1625.80 | 306.90 | 64.03 | 409.20 | 127.40 | 40.53 | 297.20 | 359.0 |
| 405.10 | 1667.00 | 351.10 | 68.16 | 482.20 | 149.30 | 32.54 | 276.90 | 370.0 |
| 418.80 | 1677.40 | 357.80 | 77.34 | 673.80 | 164.40 | 43.48 | 274.60 | 376.0 |
| 588.20 | 2289.50 | 342.10 | 95.30 | 676.90 | 177.20 | 56.49 | 339.90 | 391.0 |
| 645.20 | 2159.40 | 444.20 | 99.49 | 702.00 | 200.00 | 65.98 | 474.80 | 414.0 |
| 641.00 | 2031.30 | 623.60 | 127.52 | 793.50 | 211.50 | 66.11 | 496.00 | 443.0 |
| 459.30 | 2115.50 | 669.70 | 135.72 | 927.30 | 238.70 | 49.34 | 474.50 | 468.0 |
| General Electric | | | Union Oil | | | Diamond Match | | |
| 33.10 | 1170.60 | 97.80 | 24.43 | 138.00 | 100.20 | 2.54 | 70.91 | 4.50 |
| 45.00 | 2015.80 | 104.40 | 23.21 | 200.10 | 125.00 | 2.00 | 87.94 | 4.71 |
| 77.20 | 2803.30 | 118.00 | 32.78 | 210.10 | 142.40 | 2.19 | 82.20 | 4.57 |
| 44.60 | 2039.70 | 156.20 | 32.54 | 161.20 | 165.10 | 1.99 | 58.72 | 4.56 |

(continues)

***Table 12.2*** *(Continued)*

| General Electric | | | Union Oil | | | Diamond Match | | |
|---|---|---|---|---|---|---|---|---|
| 48.10 | 2256.20 | 172.60 | 26.65 | 161.70 | 194.80 | 2.03 | 80.54 | 4.38 |
| 74.40 | 2132.20 | 186.60 | 33.71 | 145.10 | 222.90 | 1.81 | 86.47 | 4.21 |
| 113.00 | 1834.10 | 220.90 | 43.50 | 110.60 | 252.10 | 2.14 | 77.68 | 4.12 |
| 91.90 | 1588.00 | 287.80 | 34.46 | 98.10 | 276.30 | 1.86 | 62.16 | 3.83 |
| 61.30 | 1749.40 | 319.90 | 44.28 | 108.80 | 300.30 | 0.93 | 62.24 | 3.58 |
| 56.80 | 1687.20 | 321.30 | 70.80 | 118.20 | 318.20 | 1.18 | 61.82 | 3.41 |
| 93.60 | 2007.70 | 319.60 | 44.12 | 126.50 | 336.20 | 1.36 | 65.85 | 3.31 |
| 159.90 | 2208.30 | 346.00 | 48.98 | 156.70 | 351.20 | 2.24 | 69.54 | 3.23 |
| 147.20 | 1656.70 | 456.40 | 48.51 | 119.40 | 373.60 | 3.81 | 64.97 | 3.90 |
| 146.30 | 1604.40 | 543.40 | 50.00 | 129.10 | 389.40 | 5.66 | 68.00 | 5.38 |
| 98.30 | 1431.80 | 618.30 | 50.59 | 134.80 | 406.70 | 4.21 | 71.24 | 7.39 |
| 93.50 | 1610.50 | 647.40 | 42.53 | 140.80 | 429.50 | 3.42 | 69.05 | 8.74 |
| 135.20 | 1819.40 | 671.30 | 64.77 | 179.00 | 450.60 | 4.67 | 83.04 | 9.07 |
| 157.30 | 2079.70 | 726.10 | 72.68 | 178.10 | 466.90 | 6.00 | 74.42 | 9.93 |
| 179.50 | 2371.60 | 800.30 | 73.86 | 186.80 | 486.20 | 6.53 | 63.51 | 11.68 |
| 189.60 | 2759.90 | 888.90 | 89.51 | 192.70 | 511.30 | 5.12 | 58.12 | 14.33 |

| Chrysler | | |
|---|---|---|
| 40.29 | 417.50 | 10.50 |
| 72.76 | 837.80 | 10.20 |
| 66.26 | 883.90 | 34.70 |
| 51.60 | 437.90 | 51.80 |
| 52.41 | 679.70 | 64.30 |
| 69.41 | 727.80 | 67.10 |
| 68.35 | 643.60 | 75.20 |
| 46.80 | 410.90 | 71.40 |
| 47.40 | 588.40 | 67.10 |
| 59.57 | 698.40 | 60.50 |
| 88.78 | 846.40 | 54.60 |
| 74.12 | 893.80 | 84.80 |
| 62.68 | 579.00 | 96.80 |
| 89.36 | 694.60 | 110.20 |
| 78.98 | 590.30 | 147.40 |
| 100.66 | 693.50 | 163.20 |
| 160.62 | 809.00 | 203.50 |
| 145.00 | 727.00 | 290.60 |
| 174.93 | 1001.50 | 346.10 |
| 172.49 | 703.20 | 414.90 |

If the null hypothesis is true, then $F \sim F_{9,188}$. The value of the test statistic $F = 48.99$ yields a $p$-value of less than .0001; we reject the null hypothesis that the intercept parameters for all firms are equal.

## 12.4  An Error Components Model

In an error components framework, we continue to model differences in firm investment behavior by permitting each firm to have a different intercept parameter.

*Table 12.3*  **Dummy Variable Results**

| Variable | Parameter Estimate | Standard Error | t-Statistic |
|---|---|---|---|
| $D_1$ | −69.14 | 49.68 | −1.39 |
| $D_2$ | 100.86 | 24.91 | 4.05 |
| $D_3$ | −235.12 | 24.42 | −9.63 |
| $D_4$ | −27.63 | 14.07 | −1.96 |
| $D_5$ | −115.32 | 14.16 | −8.14 |
| $D_6$ | −23.07 | 12.66 | −1.82 |
| $D_7$ | −66.68 | 12.84 | −5.19 |
| $D_8$ | −57.36 | 13.99 | −4.10 |
| $D_9$ | −87.28 | 12.89 | −6.77 |
| $D_{10}$ | −6.55 | 11.82 | −0.55 |
| $x_2$ | 0.1098 | 0.0119 | 9.26 |
| $x_3$ | 0.3106 | 0.0174 | 17.88 |

However, we assume the intercepts are random variables; this alternative model is useful *if the individual firms (or cross-sectional units) appearing in the sample are randomly chosen and taken to be "representative" of a larger population of firms.* Returning to equation 12.3.3

$$y_{it} = \beta_{1i} + \beta_2 x_{2it} + \beta_3 x_{3it} + e_{it} \qquad (12.4.1)$$

we take $\beta_{1i}$ to be *random* and modeled as

$$\beta_{1i} = \overline{\beta}_1 + \mu_i \qquad i = 1, \ldots, N \qquad (12.4.2)$$

$\overline{\beta}_1$ is an unknown parameter that represents the **population mean intercept,** and $\mu_i$ is an unobservable random error that accounts for individual differences in firm behavior. We assume that the $\mu_i$ are independent of each other and $e_{it}$, and that

$$E(\mu_i) = 0 \quad \text{var}(\mu_i) = \sigma_\mu^2$$

Consequently, $E(\beta_{1i}) = \overline{\beta}_1$ and $\text{var}(\beta_{1i}) = \sigma_\mu^2$

Substituting equation 12.4.2 into 12.4.1 yields

$$y_{it} = (\overline{\beta}_1 + \mu_i) + \beta_2 x_{2it} + \beta_3 x_{3it} + e_{it}$$

$$= \overline{\beta}_1 + \beta_2 x_{2it} + \beta_3 x_{3it} + (e_{it} + \mu_i) \qquad (12.4.3)$$

$$= \overline{\beta}_1 + \beta_2 x_{2it} + \beta_3 x_{3it} + v_{it}$$

where $v_{it} = e_{it} + \mu_i$. The phrase *error components* comes from the fact that the error term $v_{it} = (e_{it} + \mu_i)$ consists of two components: the overall error $e_{it}$ and the individual specific error $\mu_i$. The error $\mu_i$ reflects individual differences; it varies across individuals, but is constant across time.

The choice of estimation technique depends on the properties of the new error $v_{it}$. It can be shown that the following are true.

$E(v_{it}) = 0$          ($v_{it}$ has zero mean)          (12.4.4a)

$\text{var}(v_{it}) = \sigma_\mu^2 + \sigma_e^2$          ($v_{it}$ is homoskedastic)          (12.4.4b)

$\text{cov}(v_{it}, v_{is}) = \sigma_\mu^2 \ (t \neq s)$      (the errors from the same firm in      (12.4.4c)
different time periods are correlated)

$\text{cov}(v_{it}, v_{js}) = 0 \ (i \neq j)$      (errors from different firms are always      (12.4.4d)
uncorrelated)

The nonzero correlation in equation 12.4.4c means that least squares is not the optimal technique. The generalized least squares estimator, which uses a transformed model, with appropriately transformed error term, is a better estimator. Also, it yields standard errors that are appropriate for interval estimation and hypothesis testing.

     These tasks are performed automatically using appropriate econometric software. If we do so for the investment function that utilizes the 20 time-series observations on ten firms, we obtain the following generalized least squares estimated equation

$$\hat{y}_{it} = -57.873 + 0.1095 \ x_{2it} + 0.3087 \ x_{3it} \qquad (12.4.5)$$
$$(28.875) \quad (0.0105) \qquad (0.0172)$$

In this case the response parameters for the value and capital stock variables, and their standard errors, are virtually identical to those obtained from the dummy variable model. It makes little difference which model is specified. Such is not always the case, however. A test for checking out whether the randomness assumption required by the error components model is a reasonable one is available. For details, see Judge et al. (1988, p. 489).

## 12.5 Summing Up

1. Many models and corresponding estimation techniques can be used to pool time-series and cross-sectional data. These models differ according to their assumptions about the constancy of coefficients and the various error terms.

2. The seemingly unrelated regression model is one possible model. It is a model where two or more equations have errors that are correlated at the same point in time. Such correlation is called contemporaneous correlation.

3. It is better to use generalized least squares to jointly estimate a set of seemingly unrelated regressions than to estimate each equation separately using least squares, providing contemporaneous correlation does exist *and* the explanatory variables in each equation are not identical.

4. A chi-square test can be used to test for contemporaneously correlated errors.

5. Dummy variable and error components models are other alternatives for pooling time-series and cross-sectional data. The dummy variable model can be estimated using least squares. The error components model is relevant when the cross-sectional units are randomly sampled from some population. For estimation it requires generalized least squares.

## *12.6* Exercises

12.1   Consider the following three demand equations

$$\ln q_{1t} = \beta_{11} + \beta_{12} \ln p_{1t} + \beta_{13} \ln y_t + e_{1t}$$

$$\ln q_{2t} = \beta_{21} + \beta_{22} \ln p_{2t} + \beta_{23} \ln y_t + e_{2t} \qquad (12.6.1)$$

$$\ln q_{3t} = \beta_{31} + \beta_{32} \ln p_{3t} + \beta_{33} \ln y_t + e_{3t}$$

where $q_{it}$ is the quantity consumed of the $i$-th commodity, $i = 1, 2, 3$, in the $t$-th time period, $t = 1, 2, \ldots, 30$, $p_{it}$ is the price of the $i$-th commodity in time $t$, and $y_t$ is disposable income in period $t$. The commodities are meat ($i = 1$), fruits and vegetables ($i = 2$), and cereals and bakery products ($i = 3$). Prices and income are in real terms, and all data are in index form. They can be found in the file *demand.dat*.
(a) Estimate each equation by least squares and test whether the equation errors for each time period are correlated. Report the estimates and their standard errors. Do the elasticities have the expected signs?
(b) Estimate the system jointly using the SUR estimator. Report the estimates and their standard errors. Do they differ much from your results in part (a)?
(c) Test the null hypothesis that all income elasticity's are equal to unity. (Consult your software to see how such a test is implemented.)

12.2*  Consider the two-equation investment model that utilizes the General Electric/Westinghouse data. Namely,

$$INV_{Gt} = \beta_{1G} + \beta_{2G}V_{Gt} + \beta_{3G}K_{Gt} + e_{Gt}$$

$$INV_{Wt} = \beta_{1W} + \beta_{2W}V_{Wt} + \beta_{3W}K_{Wt} + e_{Wt}$$

In section 9.6, the equality of the coefficients of these functions was tested under the assumption of equal error variances and no error correlation. In Exercise 10.4, the same hypothesis was tested assuming $e_{Gt}$ and $e_{Wt}$ had different variances, but remained uncorrelated. Test the equality of the coefficients under the assumptions of this chapter—that is, using different error variances and contemporaneous correlation. Discuss the test outcomes under the different assumptions.

12.3   The U.S. Secretary of Agriculture asks one of his economists to provide him with a basis for determining cattle inventories in the Midwest, Southwest, and West regions. Let $i = 1, 2, 3$ denote the three regions. The economist hypothesizes that in each region cattle numbers at the end of the year ($c_{it}$) depend on average price during the year ($p_{it}$), rainfall during the year ($r_{it}$), and cattle numbers at the end of the previous year ($c_{it-1}$). Because growing conditions are quite different in the three regions, he wants to try three separate equations, one for each region, that he writes as

$$c_{1t} = \beta_{11} + \beta_{12}p_{1t} + \beta_{13}r_{1t} + \beta_{14}c_{1,t-1} + e_{1t}$$

$$c_{2t} = \beta_{21} + \beta_{22}p_{2t} + \beta_{23}r_{2t} + \beta_{24}c_{2,t-1} + e_{2t}$$

$$c_{3t} = \beta_{31} + \beta_{32}p_{3t} + \beta_{33}r_{3t} + \beta_{34}c_{3,t-1} + e_{3t}$$

(a) What signs would you expect on the various coefficients? Why?
(b) Under what assumptions about the $e_{it}$ should the three equations be estimated jointly, as a set, rather than individually?
(c) Use the data that appear in the file *cattle.dat* to find separate least squares estimates for each equation, and the corresponding standard errors.
(d) Test for the existence of contemporaneous correlation between the $e_i$.
(e) Estimate the three equations jointly using the seemingly unrelated regression technique. Compare these results with those obtained in (c) in terms of reliability and economic feasibility.

12.4*  Consider the production function

$$Q_t = f(K_t, L_t)$$

where $Q_t$ is output, $K_t$ is capital, and $L_t$ is labor, all for the $t$-th firm. Suppose the function $f(\cdot)$ is a CES or constant elasticity of substitution production function. The elasticity of substitution, which we denote by $\omega$, measures the degree to which capital and labor are substituted when the factor price ratio changes. Let $P_t$ be the price of output, $R_t$ be the price of capital, and $W_t$ the price of labor. If the function $f(\cdot)$ is a CES production function, then the conditions for profit maximization, with errors attached, are

$$\ln\left(\frac{Q_t}{L_t}\right) = \gamma_1 + \omega \ln\left(\frac{W_t}{P_t}\right) + e_{1t} \qquad \text{where } e_{1t} \sim N(0,\sigma_1^2)$$

$$\ln\left(\frac{Q_t}{K_t}\right) = \gamma_2 + \omega \ln\left(\frac{R_t}{P_t}\right) + e_{2t} \qquad \text{where } e_{2t} \sim N(0,\sigma_2^2)$$

Since these equations are linear in $\gamma_1$, $\gamma_2$, and $\omega$, some version(s) of least squares can be used to estimate these parameters. Data on twenty firms appear in the file *cespro.dat*.

(a) Find separate least squares estimates of each of the first-order conditions. Compare the two estimates of the elasticity of substitution.
(b) Test for contemporaneous correlation between $e_{1t}$ and $e_{2t}$.
(c) Estimate the two equations using generalized least squares, allowing for the existence of contemporaneous correlation.
(d) Repeat part (c), but impose a restriction so that only one estimate of the elasticity of substitution is obtained. (Consult your software to see how to impose such a restriction.) Comment on the results.
(e) Compare the standard errors obtained in parts (a), (c), and (d). Do they reflect the efficiency gains that you would expect?
(f) If $\omega = 1$, the CES production function becomes a Cobb–Douglas production function. Use the results in (d) to test whether a Cobb–Douglas production function is adequate.

12.5  This exercise illustrates the transformation that is necessary to produce generalized least squares estimates for the error components model. It utilizes the data on the investment example that appears in Table 12.2.

(a) Compute the sample means for *INV*, *V*, and *K* for each of the firms. (We can denote these means as $(\bar{y}_i, \bar{x}_{2i}, \bar{x}_{3i})$, $i = 1, 2, \ldots, 10$.)

(b) Show that the error variance estimate from regressing $\bar{y}_i$ on $\bar{x}_{2i}$ and $\bar{x}_{3i}$ is

$$\hat{\sigma}_*^2 = 7218.2329$$

(c) Show that the error variance estimate from the dummy variable model is

$$\hat{\sigma}_e^2 = 2781.1445$$

(d) Show that

$$\alpha = 1 - \sqrt{\frac{\hat{\sigma}_e^2}{T\hat{\sigma}_*^2}} = 0.8612$$

(e) Show that the results in equation 12.4.5 are obtained from least squares applied to the regression model

$$y_{it}^* = \bar{\beta}_1 x_{1it}^* + \beta_2 x_{2it}^* + \beta_3 x_{3it}^* + v_{it}^*$$

where the transformed variables are given by

$$y_{it}^* = y_{it} - \alpha \bar{y}_i \qquad x_{1it}^* = 1 - \alpha$$

$$x_{2it}^* = x_{2it} - \alpha \bar{x}_{2i} \qquad x_{3it}^* = x_{3it} - \alpha \bar{x}_{3i}$$

12.6  The file *liquor.dat* contains observations on annual expenditure on liquor (*L*) and annual income (*X*), (both in thousands of dollars) for forty randomly selected households for three consecutive years. Consider the model

$$L_{it} = \beta_{1i} + \beta_2 X_{it} + e_{it}$$

where $i = 1, 2, \ldots, 40$ refers to household and $t = 1, 2, 3$ refers to year; the $e_{it}$ are assumed to be uncorrelated with $e_{it} \sim N(0, \sigma_e^2)$.

(a) Compare the alternative estimates for $\beta_2$, and their corresponding standard errors, that are obtained under the following circumstances:

(i)   The different household intercepts are modeled using dummy variables.

(ii)  Only average data are available, averaged over the three years.

(iii) The $\beta_{1i}$ are random drawings with mean $\bar{\beta}_1$ and variance $\sigma_\mu^2$.

Comment on the estimates and their relative precision.

(b) Test the hypothesis that all household intercepts are equal.

## *12.7* References

A more complete discussion of all the topics in this chapter can be found in:

GRIFFITHS, W. E., R. C. HILL, AND G. G. JUDGE (1993). *Learning and Practicing Econometrics.* John Wiley and Sons.

JUDGE, G. G., R. C. HILL, W. E. GRIFFITHS, H. LÜTKEPOHL, AND T.-C. LEE (1988). *Introduction to the Theory and Practice of Econometrics* (2d ed.). John Wiley and Sons.

Also, specialist books on the topics are available. For example:

SRIVASTAVA, V. K., AND D. E. A. GILES (1987). *Seemingly Unrelated Regression Equations Models: Estimation and Inference.* New York: Marcel Dekker.

HSIAO, C. (1986). *Analysis of Panel Data.* Cambridge, Mass.: Cambridge University Press.

BALTAGI, B. (1995). *Econometric Analysis of Panel Data.* John Wiley and Sons.

The classic reference on seemingly unrelated regressions is

ZELLNER, A. (1962). "An Efficient Method of Estimating Seemingly Unrelated Regressions and Tests of Aggregation Bias." *Journal of the American Statistical Association,* 57, 348–368.

The investment data can be found in:

VINOD, H. D., AND A. ULLAH (1981). *Recent Advances in Regression Methods.* New York: Marcel Dekker.

# Chapter *13*

# Simultaneous Equations Models

## 13.1 Introduction

For most of us, our first encounter with economic models comes through studying **supply and demand models,** in which the market price and quantity of goods sold are *jointly determined* by the equilibrium of supply and demand. The first macroeconomic model most people study is the **Keynesian–Cross model** in which national income and aggregate consumption are jointly determined by the equilibrium between income, consumption, and investment. In this chapter we consider econometric models for data that are jointly determined by two or more economic relations, as in the supply and demand and Keynesian–Cross examples. These **simultaneous equations models** differ from those we have considered in previous chapters because in each model there are two or more dependent variables, rather than just one.

Simultaneous equations models also differ from most of the econometric models we have considered so far because they consist of a *set of equations*. For example, price and quantity are determined by the interaction of two equations, one for supply and one for demand. Simultaneous equations models, which contain more than one dependent variable and more than one equation, require special statistical treatment. The least squares estimation procedure is *not* appropriate in these models, so we must develop new ways to obtain reliable estimates of economic parameters. We will begin this chapter by illustrating the problem with least squares estimation in this context.

## 13.2 A Macroeconomic Model

Consider a simple Keynesian model in which we assume that:

- Consumption expenditures, $c$, are a function of income, $y$.
- Aggregate expenditure is the sum of consumption expenditures and investment, $i$.
- Investment expenditures $i$ are assumed to be planned by firms and are assumed to be independent of income.

The economic model is represented by two equations: the consumption function

$$c = \beta_1 + \beta_2 y \qquad (13.2.1)$$

and the income "identity"

$$y = c + i \qquad (13.2.2)$$

In this model the levels of consumption and income are jointly determined. Graphing equations 13.2.1 and 13.2.2, and a 45-degree line, produces the familiar Keynesian–Cross diagram illustrated in Figure 13.1.

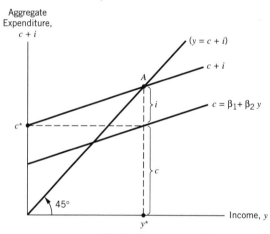

**FIGURE *13.1*   A macro model**

In this diagram, equilibrium occurs at the intersection of the 45-degree line, tracing out the values where $y = c + i$, and the consumption plus income function, $c + i = (\beta_1 + i) + \beta_2 y$, located at point $A$ on Figure 13.1. The corresponding equilibrium value of income is $y^*$ and the equilibrium value of consumption is $c^*$. These two values are the solutions of the equations 13.2.1 and 13.2.2.

The point we wish to make very clear is that it takes *two* equations to describe the macroeconomic equilibrium. The two equilibrium values, for income and consumption, $y^*$ and $c^*$ respectively, are determined at the same time. In this model the variables $y$ and $c$ are called **endogenous variables** because their values are determined within the system we have created. The investment variable $i$ has a value that is given to us. Variables like that, determined outside this system, are called **exogenous variables.**

### 13.2.1   A SIMULTANEOUS EQUATIONS STATISTICAL MODEL

The macroeconomic model consists of two equations that work together. It is reasonable to suppose that the econometric model should also have two equations that work together. To form the econometric model we add a time subscript $t = 1, \ldots, T$ to the variables to reflect the fact that they will be observed over time, and we add an error term $e_t$ to the consumption function. The statistical model is

$$c_t = \beta_1 + \beta_2 y_t + e_t \qquad (13.2.3)$$

$$y_t = c_t + i \qquad (13.2.4)$$

The consumption function (13.2.3) is called a **behavioral equation** because it describes the behavior of the economy. Equation 13.2.4 is an *identity* that defines income to be the sum of its components. *Identity equations* have no error term, since they are exact, and they contain no unknown parameters. Taken together, the equations are called a **structural model** since they describe the structure of the economy. Taken together, they are also called a **simultaneous equations** model, since they jointly, or simultaneously, determine the values of the two endogenous variables $c$ and $y$.

The statistical characteristics of this model are quite different from those that we have previously considered. The value of the exogenous variable $i_t$ is determined outside the model; it is considered to be a fixed constant, not a random variable. Because of the structure of the model, the endogenous variables $c_t$ and $y_t$ are *both random variables*. The random error term $e_t$ is added to the consumption function for the usual reasons, and we assume that $E(e_t) = 0$, $\text{var}(e_t) = \sigma_e^2$, and $\text{cov}(e_t, e_s) = 0$ for $t \neq s$. Equation 13.2.3 shows that if $e_t$ is random, then $c_t$ must also be random. In equation 13.2.4 the value of $y_t$ is the sum of $i_t$, which is a fixed constant, and $c_t$, which is random. Consequently, $y_t$ must also be random.

To emphasize the difference between the simultaneous equations model and the regression model let us use an "influence diagram" that is a graphical representation of relationships between model components. In the previous chapters we have modeled the relationship between consumption and income as diagrammed in Figure 13.2.

FIGURE **13.2** Influence diagram for a regression model

In this diagram the circles represent random variables and the squares represent fixed, exogenous, quantities. In regression analysis the direction of the influence is one-way: from the explanatory variable and the error term to the dependent variable. In the simultaneous world the influence diagram looks like Figure 13.3.

FIGURE **13.3** Influence diagram for a simultaneous equations model

There is a two-way influence between consumption $c_t$ and income $y_t$ because they are *jointly determined*. The error term $e_t$ directly affects $c_t$ and, thus, indirectly affects $y_t$, suggesting that $e_t$ and $y_t$ are correlated. Investment is a fixed, exogenous, variable that affects both $c_t$ and $y_t$, but there is no feedback to $i_t$.

The fact that $y_t$ is random means that on the right-hand side of the consumption function (equation 13.2.3) we have an explanatory variable that is random. This is contrary to the assumption of "fixed explanatory variables" that we usually make in regression model analysis. Furthermore, as we have suggested, $y_t$ and $e_t$ are correlated, which, as we will see, has a devastating impact on our usual least squares estimation procedure for $\beta_1$ and $\beta_2$.

## 13.2.2   THE REDUCED FORM EQUATIONS

The two structural equations 13.2.3 and 13.2.4 can be solved to express the endogenous variables $c$ and $y$ as functions of the exogenous variable $i$. This reformulation of the model is called the *reduced form* of the structural equations system. The reduced form is important in its own right, and it also helps us understand the structural equation system. To find the reduced form we solve equations 13.2.3 and 13.2.4 simultaneously for $y_t$ and $c_t$. In order to find the reduced form equations, there must be as many structural equations as there are endogenous variables.

As a first step, substitute $y_t$ from equation 13.2.4 into 13.2.3 to obtain

$$c_t = \beta_1 + \beta_2(c_t + i_t) + e_t$$

$$= \frac{\beta_1}{1 - \beta_2} + \frac{\beta_2}{1 - \beta_2} i_t + \frac{1}{1 - \beta_2} e_t \qquad (13.2.5)$$

$$= \pi_{11} + \pi_{21} i_t + v_t$$

where

$$\pi_{11} = \frac{\beta_1}{1 - \beta_2} \qquad \pi_{21} = \frac{\beta_2}{1 - \beta_2}$$

are the reduced form parameters and

$$v_t = \frac{1}{1 - \beta_2} e_t$$

is the reduced form error term. From the assumptions we have made about the random error $e_t$, namely that $E(e_t) = 0$, $\text{var}(e_t) = \sigma_e^2$, and $\text{cov}(e_t, e_s) = 0$, we find the properties of $v_t$ to be

$$E(v_t) = 0 \quad \text{var}(v_t) = \frac{\sigma_e^2}{(1 - \beta_2)^2} = \sigma_v^2 \quad \text{cov}(v_t, v_s) = 0$$

The reduced form equation

$$c_t = \pi_{11} + \pi_{21} i_t + v_t \qquad (13.2.6)$$

is like the regression models we have considered in previous chapters. On the right-hand side the explanatory variable $i_t$ is exogenous and is assumed to be a fixed constant. The error term $v_t$ has the usual properties. Consequently, we know we can use the least squares estimation procedure to obtain estimates of the unknown reduced form intercept $\pi_{11}$ and slope $\pi_{21}$ parameters.

To find the reduced form equation for $y_t$, take the expression for $c_t$ from equation 13.2.5 and substitute it into the identity (equation 13.2.4) and simplify to obtain

$$y_t = \left( \frac{\beta_1}{1 - \beta_2} + \frac{\beta_2}{1 - \beta_2} i_t + \frac{1}{1 - \beta_2} e_t \right) + i_t$$

$$= \frac{\beta_1}{1 - \beta_2} + \frac{1}{1 - \beta_2} i_t + \frac{1}{1 - \beta_2} e_t \qquad (13.2.7)$$

$$= \pi_{12} + \pi_{22} i_t + v_t$$

The reduced form parameters are

$$\pi_{12} = \frac{\beta_1}{1 - \beta_2} \qquad \pi_{22} = \frac{1}{1 - \beta_2}$$

The reduced form equation for $y_t$,

$$y_t = \pi_{12} + \pi_{22} i_t + v_t \qquad (13.2.8)$$

is also a typical regression equation that can be estimated by least squares.

If we estimate equations 13.2.6 and 13.2.8 by least squares, we obtain the fitted equations

$$\hat{c}_t = \hat{\pi}_{11} + \hat{\pi}_{21} i_t \qquad (13.2.9)$$

$$\hat{y}_t = \hat{\pi}_{12} + \hat{\pi}_{22} i_t \qquad (13.2.10)$$

The value of these estimated reduced form equations is twofold. First, the reduced form parameters

$$\pi_{21} = \frac{\beta_2}{1 - \beta_2} \quad \text{and} \quad \pi_{22} = \frac{1}{1 - \beta_2}$$

are *investment multipliers* that tell us the effect of a change in investment upon the equilibrium values of consumption and income, respectively. These numbers are very useful for analysis of an economy. By estimating the reduced form equations we are estimating these multipliers. Second, the fitted equations 13.2.9 and 13.2.10 can be used to *predict* the values of consumption and income for different levels of investment. Economists in both the public and private sector are constantly engaged in predicting the behavior of the economy. By estimating the reduced form equations we have a device for making such predictions.

### 13.2.3  THE FAILURE OF LEAST SQUARES ESTIMATION IN SIMULTANEOUS EQUATIONS MODELS

In this section we explain why the least squares estimator should not be used to estimate the consumption equation (13.2.3) in the simultaneous equations model given by the two equations

$$c_t = \beta_1 + \beta_2 y_t + e_t$$

$$y_t = c_t + i_t$$

In the consumption equation, the random explanatory variable on the right-hand side of the equation is *correlated* with the error term $e_t$. The existence of this correlation can be seen in both intuitive and algebraic ways. Intuitively, suppose there is a small change, or blip, in the error term $e_t$, say $\Delta e_t$. Let us trace the effect of this change through the system in Figure 13.4.

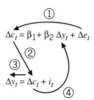

FIGURE *13.4* The effect of a blip in the error term in a simultaneous equations system

1. The blip in the error term of equation 13.2.3 is directly transmitted to the left-hand side of the equation, producing the change $\Delta c_t$.
2. Since consumption also appears in the income identity, $\Delta c_t$ appears there too.
3. Then, using this identity, the change in $c_t$ causes the change in $y_t$ ($\Delta y_t$) on the left-hand side of equation 13.2.4.
4. $\Delta y_t$ then feeds back into the right-hand side of equation 13.2.3.

Thus, every time there is a change in $e_t$ there is an associated change in $y_t$ in the same direction. This connection between the two random variables is a *positive* correlation.

The failure of ordinary least squares estimation for the consumption equation can be explained as follows: Ordinary least squares estimation of the relation between $c_t$ and $y_t$ gives "credit" to income for the effect of changes in the disturbances. This occurs because we do not observe the change in the disturbance, but only the change in $y_t$ resulting from its correlation with the disturbance. The least squares estimator of $\beta_2$ will *overstate* the true parameter value in this model. In large samples, the least squares estimator will tend to be positively biased. This bias persists even when the sample size is large, and thus the least squares estimator is inconsistent. Referring back to Figure 4.3, this means that the probability distribution of the least squares estimator will "collapse" about a point that is not the true parameter value.

The intuitive argument will now be verified algebraically. The demonstration can be skipped if you wish to move ahead quickly. The results are summarized as follows:

> The least squares estimator of parameters in a structural simultaneous equation is biased and inconsistent because of the correlation between the random error and the endogenous variables on the right-hand side of the equation.

Let us calculate the covariance between $y_t$ and $e_t$. Using the definition of covariance, and substituting the reduced form equation 13.2.8 for $y_t$, we have

$$\text{cov}(y_t, e_t) = E[y_t - E(y_t)][e_t - E(e_t)] = E(y_t e_t) \quad [\text{since } E(e_t) = 0]$$

$$= E[(\pi_{12} + \pi_{22} i_t + v_t) e_t] = E(\pi_{12} e_t) + E(\pi_{22} i_t e_t) + E(v_t e_t)$$

$$= \pi_{12} E(e_t) + \pi_{22} i_t E(e_t) + E(v_t e_t) \tag{13.2.11}$$

$$= E\left[\left(\frac{1}{1 - \beta_2} e_t\right) e_t\right] = \left(\frac{1}{1 - \beta_2}\right) E(e_t^2) = \left(\frac{1}{1 - \beta_2}\right) \sigma_e^2 > 0$$

The covariance between $y_t$ and $e_t$ is positive in this model because we know that $0 < \beta_2 < 1$ and $\sigma_e^2 > 0$.

Now let us consider least squares estimation of $\beta_2$ in the consumption equation. From chapter 4.2, equation 4.2.8, we can write the least squares estimator of $\beta_2$ in deviation from the mean form as

$$b_2 = \frac{\Sigma(y_t - \bar{y})(c_t - \bar{c})}{\Sigma(y_t - \bar{y})^2}$$

$$= \beta_2 + \Sigma w_t e_t$$

where

$$w_t = \frac{y_t - \bar{y}}{\Sigma(y_t - \bar{y})^2}$$

The expected value of $b_2$ is

$$E(b_2) = E(\beta_2 + \Sigma w_t e_t) = E(\beta_2) + \Sigma E(w_t e_t)$$

$$= \beta_2 + \Sigma E(w_t e_t) \neq \beta_2 \quad [\text{since } E(w_t e_t) \neq 0]$$

The expectation $E(w_t e_t)$ is *not* zero, as it was in chapter 4, since $w_t$ depends on $y_t$, and $y_t$ is correlated with $e_t$. The expectation $E(w_t e_t)$ is not zero, but its exact value is unknown, because it is the expectation of a ratio of random variables, which cannot be determined. However, it can be shown that in large samples the term $E(w_t e_t)$ converges to a positive constant. Thus, the least squares estimator of $\beta_2$ is positively biased in the consumption equation, as our intuitive argument suggested. To summarize, the least squares estimator of $\beta_2$ is biased, and the bias does not disappear no matter how large the sample.

In chapter 4 the term $w_t$ was a constant, but now it is a random variable, since $y_t$ is random. A rule about expected values that we have not encountered before states that the expected value of a product of two random variables is the product of their expected values only if the random variables are *statistically independent*. If $w_t$ and $e_t$ *were* independent, then

$$E(b_2) = \beta_2 + \Sigma E(w_t)E(e_t) = \beta_2$$

and the least squares estimator would be unbiased. It is not the fact that $y_t$ is random that causes the problem for least squares. The problem for least squares estimation occurs because $y_t$ is *random and correlated* with the error term.

In chapter 4.5 we discussed a very reassuring property of the least squares estimator. If assumptions 1 through 5 listed at the beginning of chapter 4 hold, then the least squares estimator is *consistent*. This means that in a large sample, the least squares estimator has a high probability of giving us an estimate near the true parameter value, as shown in Figure 4.3. An estimator is consistent if two conditions hold: (1) the estimator is unbiased, or, if it is biased, then the bias disappears in large samples; and (2) the variance of the estimator goes to zero as the sample size $T$ goes to infinity. The least squares estimator for $\beta_2$ in this structural equation is *inconsistent* since it is biased and the bias *does not disappear* even in large samples. The fact that the least squares estimator is inconsistent leads us to search for another estimator to use in simultaneous equations models.

### 13.2.4 CONSISTENT ESTIMATION OF THE PARAMETERS OF THE CONSUMPTION FUNCTION

Given that the least squares principle cannot be used to obtain consistent estimators for the parameters in the consumption function, how can we proceed? Is it possible to obtain consistent estimators for the slope and intercept of the consumption function via some other procedure? In this simple model it is easy to see that the answer is "yes."

The key to consistent estimation of the structural parameters lies in the fact that the reduced form equations 13.2.6 and 13.2.7 can be consistently estimated by least squares. This is so because they have error terms with zero means, constant variances, and zero covariances. Furthermore, the variable on their right-hand side, investment, is an exogenous variable. It is determined outside the system we are considering and is not correlated with the error terms in the reduced form equations.

Using the reduced form parameters $\pi_{21} = \beta_2/(1 - \beta_2)$, $\pi_{12} = \beta_1/(1 - \beta_2)$, and $\pi_{22} = 1/(1 - \beta_2)$ we can determine the intercept and slope of the consumption function as

$$\beta_1 = \frac{\pi_{12}}{\pi_{22}} \quad \text{and} \quad \beta_2 = \frac{\pi_{21}}{\pi_{22}}$$

If we replace the true reduced form parameters by their estimated values we have estimates of the structural parameters

$$\hat{\beta}_1 = \frac{\hat{\pi}_{12}}{\hat{\pi}_{22}} \quad \text{and} \quad \hat{\beta}_2 = \frac{\hat{\pi}_{21}}{\hat{\pi}_{22}}$$

This indirect way of obtaining structural parameter estimates is a consistent estimation procedure, but it is unsatisfactory in larger, more realistic models, and we will not use it further. Our point here is that the consistently estimated reduced form equations can lead to consistently estimated structural parameter estimates. In the following section we present a slightly larger model and outline a general estimation procedure for structural equations within a simultaneous equations model.

## *13.3* A Supply and Demand Model

Supply and demand *jointly* determine the market price of a good and the amount of it that is sold. Graphically, you recall that market equilibrium occurs at the intersection of the supply and demand curves, as shown in Figure 13.5.

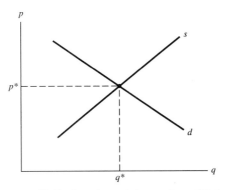

FIGURE *13.5*  Supply and demand equilibrium

An econometric model that explains market price and quantity should consist of two equations, one for supply and one for demand. It will be a simultaneous equations model, since both equations work together to determine price and quantity. A very simple model might look like the following.

$$\text{Demand: } q = \alpha_1 p + \alpha_2 y + e_d$$

$$\text{(13.3.1)}$$

$$\text{Supply: } \quad q = \beta_1 p + e_s$$

In this model we assume that the quantity demanded ($q$) is a function of price ($p$) and income ($y$), plus an error term $e_d$. Quantity supplied is taken to be only a function of price. We have omitted the intercepts to make the algebra easier. In this model price and quantity ($p$, $q$) are the endogenous variables. Income ($y$) is exogenous, since its value is not determined within this system.

Let us again emphasize the difference between simultaneous equations models and regression models using influence diagrams. Modeling supply and demand as separate regressions implies the influence diagrams in Figure 13.6. All the influence is directed from the quantities on the right-hand side of the equation to the left-hand side. In this case there is no equilibrating mechanism that will lead quantity demanded, $q_d$, to equal quantity supplied, $q_s$, at a market-clearing price. For price to adjust to the market-clearing equilibrium, there must be an influence running from $p$ to $q$ *and* from $q$ to $p$.

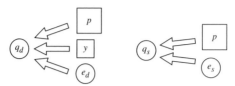

FIGURE **13.6**   Influence diagrams for two regression models

Recognizing that price $p$ and quantity $q$ are jointly determined, and that there is feedback between them, suggests the influence diagram in Figure 13.7.

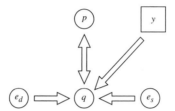

FIGURE **13.7**   Influence diagram for a simultaneous equations model

In the simultaneous equations model we see the feedback between $p$ and $q$ because they are jointly determined. The random error terms $e_d$ and $e_s$ affect both $p$ and $q$, suggesting a correlation between each of the endogenous variables *and* each of the random error terms. Income, $y$, is a fixed, exogenous, variable that affects the endogenous variables, but *not* vice versa. The correlation between the random errors and the endogenous variable $p$ causes the least squares estimator to be biased and inconsistent.

We assume that the random errors have the usual properties

$$E(e_d) = 0 \quad \text{var}(e_d) = \sigma_d^2$$

$$E(e_s) = 0 \quad \text{var}(e_s) = \sigma_s^2 \tag{13.3.2}$$

$$\text{cov}(e_d, e_s) = 0$$

Following the same procedure used in the macroeconomic example in section 13.2, we find the reduced form equations

$$p = \frac{\alpha_2}{\beta_1 - \alpha_1} y + \frac{e_d - e_s}{\beta_1 - \alpha_1} = \pi_1 y + v_1$$

$$q = \frac{\beta_1 \alpha_2}{\beta_1 - \alpha_1} y + \frac{\beta_1 e_d - \alpha_1 e_s}{\beta_1 - \alpha_1} = \pi_2 y + v_2 \tag{13.3.3}$$

The reduced form parameters $\pi_1$ and $\pi_2$ can be consistently estimated by least squares. How might we estimate the structural parameters $\alpha_1$, $\alpha_2$, and $\beta_1$?

### 13.3.1    THE IDENTIFICATION PROBLEM

In the supply and demand model given by equation 13.3.1 the parameters of the demand equation, $\alpha_1$ and $\alpha_2$, cannot be consistently estimated by *any* estimation method. The slope of the supply equation, $\beta_1$, can be consistently estimated. How are we able to make such statements? The answer is quite intuitive and it can be illustrated graphically. What happens when income $y$ changes? The demand curve shifts and a new equilibrium price and quantity are created. In Figure 13.8 we show the demand curves $d_1$, $d_2$, and $d_3$ and equilibria, at points $a$, $b$, and $c$, for three levels of income.

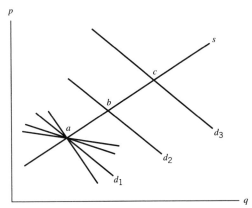

FIGURE *13.8*    The effect of changing income

As income changes, data on price and quantity will be observed around the intersections of supply and demand. The random errors $e_d$ and $e_s$ cause small shifts in the supply and demand curves, creating equilibrium observations on price and quantity that are scattered about the intersections at points $a$, $b$, and $c$.

The data values will trace out the *supply curve,* suggesting that we can fit a line through them to estimate the slope $\beta_1$. The data values fall along the supply curve because income is present in the demand curve and absent from the supply curve. As income changes, the demand curve shifts but the supply curve remains fixed, resulting in observations along the supply curve.

There are *no* data values falling along any of the demand curves, and there is no way to estimate their slope. Any one of an infinite number of demand curves passing through the equilibrium points could be correct. Given the data, there is no way to distinguish the true demand curve from all the rest. We have drawn a few demand curves through the equilibrium point $a$, each of which could have generated the data we observe.

The problem lies with the model that we are using. There is no variable in the supply equation that will shift it relative to the demand curve. If we were to add a variable to the supply curve, say $w$, then each time $w$ changed the supply curve would shift and the demand curve would stay fixed. The shifting of supply relative to a fixed demand curve (since $w$ is *absent* from the demand equation) would create equilibrium observations along the demand curve, making it possible to estimate the slope of the demand curve and the effect of income on demand.

It is the *absence* of variables from an equation that makes it possible to estimate its parameters. A general rule, called a **condition for identification** of an equation, is this:

> **A NECESSARY CONDITION FOR IDENTIFICATION:** In a system of $M$ simultaneous equations, which jointly determine the values of $M$ endogenous variables, at least $M - 1$ variables must be absent from an equation for estimation of its parameters to be possible. If $M - 1$ variables or more are omitted from an equation, then the equation is said to be *identified,* and its parameters can be estimated consistently. If less than $M - 1$ variables are omitted from an equation, then it is said to be *unidentified,* and its parameters cannot be consistently estimated.

In the supply and demand model (equation 13.3.1) there are $M = 2$ equations and there are a total of three variables: $p,$ $q,$ and $y.$ In the demand equation none of the variables are omitted; thus, it is unidentified and its parameters cannot be estimated consistently. In the supply equation $M - 1 = 1$ and one variable, income, is omitted; thus, the supply curve is identified and its parameter can be estimated.

The identification condition must be checked *before* trying to estimate an equation. If an equation is not identified, then changing the model must be considered before it is estimated. However, changing the model should not be done in a haphazard way; no important variable should be omitted from an equation just to identify it. The structure of a simultaneous equations model should reflect your understanding of how equilibrium is achieved and should be consistent with economic theory. Creating a false model is not a good solution to the identification problem.

One additional point needs to be made. The preceding identification condition is called *necessary* because if it does not hold, then an equation is not identified. Unfortunately, it is possible for the necessary condition to be satisfied and yet have an equation that is not identified. To catch misfits like this, there is a *necessary and sufficient* condition. It is studied in more advanced econometric courses. The brave and curious reader can see Judge et al. (1988, pp. 623–26) or Gujarati (1995, pp. 666–69.) The necessary and sufficient condition is seldom needed in a carefully constructed model, and for our purposes the necessary condition is adequate.

### 13.3.2 A Two-Stage Least Squares Estimation Procedure for the Supply Equation

In this section we describe the most widely used method for estimating the parameters in an identified structural equation. It is called **two-stage least squares** (often abbreviated as $2SLS$) because it is based on two least squares regressions. We will explain how it works by considering the supply equation in equation 13.3.1,

$$q = \beta_1 p + e_s \tag{13.3.4}$$

We cannot apply least squares to estimate $\beta_1$ in this equation because the endogenous variable $p$ on the right-hand side of the equation is random, and it is correlated with the error term $e_s$ (see Exercise 13.1).

The variable $p$ is composed of a systematic part, which is its expected value $E(p)$, and a random part, which is the reduced form random error $v_1$. Furthermore, drawing on equation 13.3.3, we get

$$p = E(p) + v_1 = \pi_1 y + v_1 \qquad (13.3.5)$$

In the supply equation 13.3.4 the portion of $p$ that causes problems for the least squares estimator is $v_1$, the random part. It is $v_1$ that causes $p$ to be correlated with the error term $e_s$. Suppose we replace $p$ in equation 13.3.4 the expression in equation 13.3.5 to obtain

$$\begin{aligned} q &= \beta_1[E(p) + v_1] + e_s \\ &= \beta_1 E(p) + (\beta_1 v_1 + e_s) \\ &= \beta_1 E(p) + e_* \end{aligned} \qquad (13.3.6)$$

In equation 13.3.6 the explanatory variable on the right-hand side is $E(p)$. It is not a random variable and it is not correlated with the error term $e_*$. We could apply least squares to equation 13.3.6 to consistently estimate $\beta_1$.

Of course, we cannot use the variable $E(p) = \pi_1 y$ in place of $p$, since we do not know the value of $\pi_1$. However, we can *estimate* $\pi_1$ using $\hat{\pi}_1$ from the reduced form equation for $p$. Then, a consistent estimator for $E(p)$ is

$$\hat{p} = \hat{\pi}_1 y$$

Using $\hat{p}$ as a replacement for $E(p)$ in equation 13.3.6 we obtain

$$q = \beta_1 \hat{p} + \hat{e}_* \qquad (13.3.7)$$

In large samples, $\hat{p}$ and the random error $\hat{e}_*$ are uncorrelated, and consequently, the parameter $\beta_1$ can be consistently estimated by applying least squares to equation 13.3.7.

The two stages of this method are

1. Least squares estimation of the reduced form equation for $p$ and the calculation of its predicted value, $\hat{p}$

2. Least squares estimation of the structural equation in which the right-hand side endogenous variable $p$ is replaced by its predicted value $\hat{p}$

### 13.3.3 THE GENERAL TWO-STAGE LEAST SQUARES ESTIMATION PROCEDURE

The two-stage least squares estimation procedure can be used to estimate the parameters of any identified equation within a simultaneous equations system. In a system of $M$ simultaneous equations, let the endogenous variables be $y_1, y_2, \ldots, y_M$. Let there be $K$ exogenous variables, $x_1, x_2, \ldots, x_K$. Suppose the first structural equation within this system is

$$y_1 = \alpha_2 y_2 + \alpha_3 y_3 + \beta_1 x_1 + \beta_2 x_2 + e_1 \qquad (13.3.8)$$

If this equation is identified, then its parameters can be estimated in the two steps:

1.  Estimate the parameters of the reduced form equations

$$y_2 = \pi_{12} x_1 + \pi_{22} x_2 + \cdots + \pi_{K2} x_K + v_2$$

$$y_3 = \pi_{13} x_1 + \pi_{23} x_2 + \cdots + \pi_{K3} x_K + v_3$$

by least squares and obtain the predicted values

$$\hat{y}_2 = \hat{\pi}_{12} x_1 + \hat{\pi}_{22} x_2 + \cdots + \hat{\pi}_{K2} x_K \qquad (13.3.9)$$

$$\hat{y}_3 = \hat{\pi}_{13} x_1 + \hat{\pi}_{23} x_2 + \cdots + \hat{\pi}_{K3} x_K$$

2.  Replace the endogenous variables, $y_2$ and $y_3$ on the right-hand side of the structural equation 13.3.8 by their predicted values from 13.3.9:

$$y_1 = \alpha_2 \hat{y}_2 + \alpha_3 \hat{y}_3 + \beta_1 x_1 + \beta_2 x_2 + e_1^*$$

Estimate the parameters of this equation by least squares.

### 13.3.4   THE PROPERTIES OF THE TWO-STAGE LEAST SQUARES ESTIMATOR

We have described how to obtain estimates for structural equation parameters in identified equations. As for the properties of the two-stage least squares estimator, we will say the following:

*   The 2*SLS* estimator is a biased estimator, but it is consistent.
*   In large samples the 2*SLS* estimator is approximately normally distributed.
*   The variances and covariances of the 2*SLS* estimator are unknown in small samples, but for large samples we have expressions that we can use as approximations. These formulas are built into econometric software packages, which report standard errors and *t*-values just like an ordinary least squares regression program.
*   If you obtain 2*SLS* estimates by applying two least squares regressions using ordinary least squares regression software, the standard errors and *t*-values reported in the *second* regression are *not* correct for the 2*SLS* estimator. Always use specialized 2*SLS* software when obtaining estimates of structural equations.

Further discussion of the properties of the 2*SLS* estimator can be found in Chapter 19 of *Learning and Practicing Econometrics* by Griffiths, Hill, and Judge (1993), Gujarati (1995, chapters 18–20) and Judge et al. (1988, chapters 14–15). These references are given in order of increasing difficulty.

## *13.4* **An Example of Two-Stage Least Squares Estimation**

Truffles are a gourmet delight. They are edible fungi that grow below the ground. In France they are often located by collectors who use pigs to sniff out the truffles and "point" to them. Actually, the pigs dig frantically for the truffles because pigs—as well as the French—have an insatiable taste for them, and they must be restrained from "pigging out" on them. Let us consider a supply and demand model for truffles:

$$\text{demand: } q_t = \alpha_1 + \alpha_2 p_t + \alpha_3 ps_t + \alpha_4 di_t + e_t^d \qquad (13.4.1)$$

$$\text{supply: } q_t = \beta_1 + \beta_2 p_t + \beta_3 pf_t + e_t^s \qquad (13.4.2)$$

In this demand equation $q$ is the quantity of truffles traded in a particular French market at time $t$, $p$ is the market price of truffles, $ps$ is the market price of a substitute for real truffles (another fungus much less highly prized), and $di$ is per capita disposable income. The supply equation contains the market price and quantity supplied. Also, it includes $pf$, the price of a factor of production, which in this case is the hourly rental price of truffle pigs used in the search process. In this model we assume that $p$ and $q$ are endogenous variables. The exogenous variables are $ps$, $di$, $pf$, and the intercept variable.

### 13.4.1   IDENTIFICATION

Before thinking about estimation, let us check the identification of each equation. The rule for identifying an equation is that in a system of $M$ equations at least $M - 1$ variables must be omitted from each equation in order for it to be identified. In the demand equation the variable $pf$ is not included and thus the necessary $M - 1 = 1$ variable is omitted. In the supply equation both $ps$ and $di$ are absent— more than enough to satisfy the identification condition. Note, too, that the variables that are omitted are different for each equation, ensuring that each contains at least one *shift* variable not present in the other. We conclude that each equation in this system is identified and can thus be estimated by two-stage least squares.

   Why are the variables omitted from their respective equations? Because economic theory says that the price of a factor of production should affect supply but not demand—and the price of substitute goods and income should affect demand and not supply. The specifications we used are based on the microeconomic theory of supply and demand.

### 13.4.2   THE REDUCED FORM EQUATIONS

The reduced form equations express each endogenous variable, $p$ and $q$, in terms of the exogenous variables $ps$, $di$, $pf$, and the intercept variable, plus an error term.

$$q_t = \pi_{11} + \pi_{21} ps_t + \pi_{31} di_t + \pi_{41} pf_t + v_{t1}$$

$$p_t = \pi_{12} + \pi_{22} ps_t + \pi_{32} di_t + \pi_{42} pf_t + v_{t2}$$

We can estimate these equations by least squares since the right-hand-side variables are exogenous and uncorrelated with the random errors $v_{t1}$ and $v_{t2}$. Data for each of the endogenous and exogenous variables are given in Table 13.1. The price $p$ is measured in dollars per ounce, $q$ is measured in ounces, $ps$ is measured in dollars per pound, $di$ is in thousands of dollars, and $pf$ is the hourly rental rate for a truffle-finding pig. The results of the least squares estimations of the reduced form equations for $q$ and $p$ are reported in Tables 13.2a and 13.2b, respectively. In Table 13.2a we see that the estimated coefficients are statistically significant, and thus, we conclude that the exogenous variables affect the quantity of truffles traded, $q$, in this reduced form equation. The $R^2 = .697$ and the overall $F$-statistic is 19.973, which has a $p$-value of less than .0001. In Table 13.2b the estimated coefficients are statistically significant, indicating that the exogenous variables have an effect on market price $p$. The $R^2 = .889$, implying a good fit of the reduced form equation to the data. The overall $F$-statistic value is 69.189, which has a $p$-value of less than .0001, indicating that the model has statistically significant explanatory power. The reduced form equations are used to obtain $\hat{p}_t$, which will be used in place of $p_t$ on the right-

*Table 13.1* **Truffle Supply and Demand Data**

| OBS | $p$ | $q$ | $ps$ | $di$ | $pf$ |
|-----|------|------|------|------|------|
| 1 | 9.88 | 19.89 | 19.97 | 21.03 | 10.52 |
| 2 | 13.41 | 13.04 | 18.04 | 20.43 | 19.67 |
| 3 | 11.57 | 19.61 | 22.36 | 18.70 | 13.74 |
| 4 | 13.81 | 17.13 | 20.87 | 15.25 | 17.95 |
| 5 | 17.79 | 22.55 | 19.79 | 27.09 | 13.71 |
| 6 | 12.84 | 6.37 | 15.98 | 24.89 | 24.95 |
| 7 | 18.11 | 15.02 | 17.94 | 22.94 | 24.17 |
| 8 | 13.52 | 10.22 | 17.09 | 21.96 | 23.61 |
| 9 | 22.45 | 23.64 | 22.72 | 38.85 | 19.52 |
| 10 | 16.55 | 16.12 | 15.74 | 31.69 | 20.03 |
| 11 | 19.39 | 24.55 | 24.64 | 26.23 | 15.38 |
| 12 | 22.29 | 18.92 | 23.70 | 30.07 | 22.98 |
| 13 | 16.65 | 11.94 | 15.93 | 33.67 | 25.76 |
| 14 | 21.65 | 18.93 | 23.34 | 32.90 | 25.17 |
| 15 | 17.56 | 12.60 | 15.21 | 37.46 | 25.82 |
| 16 | 20.40 | 20.49 | 26.04 | 35.18 | 19.31 |
| 17 | 26.85 | 22.94 | 22.95 | 43.81 | 26.02 |
| 18 | 29.98 | 21.08 | 27.10 | 41.21 | 29.65 |
| 19 | 23.59 | 16.68 | 23.65 | 38.20 | 27.45 |
| 20 | 19.11 | 17.61 | 20.06 | 43.98 | 18.00 |
| 21 | 15.41 | 16.62 | 26.38 | 37.64 | 18.87 |
| 22 | 25.81 | 20.99 | 24.28 | 45.24 | 24.58 |
| 23 | 27.67 | 24.53 | 26.64 | 48.15 | 25.25 |
| 24 | 23.57 | 19.67 | 22.65 | 36.70 | 24.24 |
| 25 | 22.25 | 23.29 | 19.68 | 43.92 | 22.63 |
| 26 | 25.60 | 16.64 | 23.82 | 46.03 | 27.35 |
| 27 | 27.90 | 20.81 | 28.98 | 46.32 | 27.80 |
| 28 | 27.00 | 14.95 | 18.52 | 48.94 | 30.34 |
| 29 | 29.48 | 26.27 | 28.16 | 51.25 | 24.12 |
| 30 | 35.15 | 20.65 | 28.43 | 48.36 | 34.01 |

### Table 13.2a    Reduced Form Equation for Quantity of Truffles ($q$)

| Variable | Estimate | Std. Error | $t$-value | $p$-value |
|----------|----------|------------|-----------|-----------|
| Const | 7.895 | 3.019 | 2.615 | 0.0147 |
| PS | 0.656 | 0.133 | 4.947 | 0.0001 |
| DI | 0.217 | 0.065 | 3.323 | 0.0026 |
| PF | −0.507 | 0.113 | −4.491 | 0.0001 |

### Table 13.2b    Reduced Form Equation for Price of Truffles ($p$)

| Variable | Estimate | Std. Error | $t$-value | $p$-value |
|----------|----------|------------|-----------|-----------|
| Const | −10.837 | 2.478 | −4.374 | 0.0002 |
| PS | 0.569 | 0.109 | 5.229 | 0.0001 |
| DI | 0.253 | 0.054 | 4.736 | 0.0001 |
| PF | 0.451 | 0.093 | 4.872 | 0.0001 |

hand side of the supply and demand equations in the second stage of two-stage least squares.

$$\hat{p}_t = \hat{\pi}_{12} + \hat{\pi}_{22}ps_t + \hat{\pi}_{32}di_t + \hat{\pi}_{42}pf_t$$

$$= -10.837 + .569ps_t + .253di_t + .451pf_t$$

The *2SLS* results are given in Tables 13.3a and 13.3b.

### Table 13.3a    2SLS Estimates for Truffle Demand ($q_d$)

| Variable | Estimate | Std. Error | $t$-value | $p$-value |
|----------|----------|------------|-----------|-----------|
| Const | −4.279 | 5.161 | −0.829 | 0.4145 |
| P | −1.123 | 0.460 | −2.441 | 0.0217 |
| PS | 1.296 | 0.331 | 3.919 | 0.0006 |
| DI | 0.501 | 0.213 | 2.359 | 0.0261 |

### Table 13.3b    2SLS Estimates for Truffle Supply ($q_s$)

| Variable | Estimate | Std. Error | $t$-value | $p$-value |
|----------|----------|------------|-----------|-----------|
| Const | 20.033 | 1.160 | 17.264 | 0.0001 |
| P | 1.014 | 0.071 | 14.297 | 0.0001 |
| PF | −1.001 | 0.078 | −12.784 | 0.0001 |

The estimated demand curve results are in Table 13.3a. Note that the coefficient of price is negative, indicating that as the market price rises the quantity demanded of truffles declines, as predicted by the law of demand. The standard errors that are reported are obtained from *2SLS* software. They and the *t*-values are valid in large samples. The *p*-value indicates that the estimated slope of the demand curve is significantly different from zero. Increases in the price of the substitutes for truffles increase the demand for truffles, which is a characteristic of substitute goods. Finally, the effect of income is positive, indicating that truffles are a normal good. All of these variables have statistically significant coefficients, and thus have an effect on the quantity demanded.

The supply equation results appear in Table 13.3b. As anticipated, increases in the price of truffles increase the quantity supplied, and increases in the rental rate for truffle-seeking pigs, which is an increase in the cost of a factor of production, reduce supply. Both of these variables have statistically significant coefficient estimates.

## *13.5* Summing Up

1.  In this chapter we have considered statistical models that consist of several equations. The equations describe an economic system in which several endogenous variables are jointly determined. The system must have as many equations as endogenous variables.

2.  In a simultaneous equations model, the values of endogenous variables are jointly determined within the system. Also present in the system will be exogenous variables whose values are determined by forces external to the system, and random error terms. The distinguishing feature of exogenous variables is that they are not correlated with the random errors, at least in large samples.

3.  In an equation within a simultaneous equations model the endogenous variables are correlated with the random errors. When endogenous variables appear on the right-hand side of an equation, then the least squares estimator of the parameters of that equation are biased and inconsistent.

4.  A system of simultaneous equations can be "solved" to obtain reduced form equations for the endogenous variables. That is, the endogenous variables can be expressed as functions of exogenous variables and random error terms. These equations can be estimated by least squares, since the right-hand-side variables are not correlated with the error term. These reduced form equations are valuable as a basis for predicting values of the endogenous variables given values of the exogenous variables. Also, the coefficients of the reduced form equations can be interpreted as "multipliers" in macroeconomic models.

5.  In order to estimate the parameters of an equation within a simultaneous system the equation must be identified. Intuitively, identification requires that one or more variables that appear in other equations must be omitted from the equation of interest. They must be omitted so that the other equations can *shift* relative to the equation in question, creating observed data points along it. The necessary condition for identification is that in a system of $M$ equations, at least $M - 1$ variables must be omitted.

6.  The *two-stage least squares* estimation procedure can be used to estimate an equation within a system of simultaneous equations. In the first stage the reduced form equations are estimated by least squares, and the estimated equations are used to obtain predicted values of the endogenous variables. In the second stage the endogenous variables on the right-hand side of an equation are replaced by their predicted values, and the resulting equation is estimated by least squares.

## *13.6* **Exercises**

13.1* Find the covariance between $p$ and the error term $e_s$ in the supply equation 13.3.4, $q = \beta_1 p + e_s$.

13.2  Derive the reduced form equations 13.3.3.

13.3  Can you suggest a method for using the reduced form equations 13.3.3 to obtain an estimate of the slope of the supply function $q = \beta_1 p + e_s$? (*Hint:* look at the expressions for $\pi_1$ and $\pi_2$.)

13.4  Derive the reduced form equations from the demand and supply equations in equations 13.4.1 and 13.4.2 and use your computer software for least squares regression analysis and the data in Table 13.1 to obtain the estimated reduced form equations in Table 13.2.

13.5  Use your computer software for simultaneous equations and the data in Table 13.1 to obtain *2SLS* estimates of the system in equations 13.4.1 and 13.4.2. Compare your results to those in Table 13.3.

13.6  Estimate equations 13.4.1 and 13.4.2 by least squares regression, ignoring the fact that they form a simultaneous system. Use the data in Table 13.1. Compare your results to those in Table 13.3. Do the signs of the least squares estimates agree with economic reasoning?

13.7  In the data file *keynes.dat* are observations on U.S. consumption expenditures ($c$), disposable income ($y$) and investment and government expenditures ($i$) for the years 1955–86 in billions of 1982 dollars. Use these data to:
    (a) Estimate the reduced form equations 13.2.6 and 13.2.8.
    (b) Obtain predicted values of the endogenous variables as in equations 13.2.9 and 13.2.10.
    (c) Replace $y$ on the right-hand side of 13.2.3 by its predicted value from part (b) and apply least squares to the resulting equation to estimate the parameters $\beta_1$ and $\beta_2$. Compare these estimates to those obtained by using *2SLS* software.

13.8  Assume the following simultaneous equations model for the U.S. economy:

$$c_t = \alpha_1 + \alpha_2 y_t + e_{t1}$$

$$i_t = \beta_1 + \beta_2 r_t + e_{t2}$$

$$y_t = c_t + i_t + g_t$$

where $c$ is private consumption expenditure, $i$ is private investment expenditure, $y$ is gross national product, $r$ is a weighted average of interest rates, and $g$ is government expenditure. In this model $c$, $i$, and $y$ are endogenous. Data for these variables are contained in the file *keynes-2.dat.*

(a) Briefly explain the signs you expect for the unknown parameters.
(b) Derive the reduced form equations.
(c) Estimate the reduced form equations by least squares. Use the estimated reduced form equations to predict the values of the endogenous variables if $r = 15.0$ and $g = 20.0$.
(d) Check the identification of each equation.
(e) Obtain *2SLS* estimates of the unknown parameters for the identified equations and comment on their signs and statistical significance.

13.9    Assume the following simultaneous equations model for the U.S. economy:

$$c_t = \alpha_1 + \alpha_2 y_t + \alpha_3 c_{t-1} + e_{t1}$$

$$i_t = \beta_1 + \beta_2 r_t + \beta_3 y_t + e_{t2}$$

$$y_t = c_t + i_t + g_t$$

where $c$ is private consumption expenditure, $i$ is private investment expenditure, $y$ is gross national product, $r$ is a weighted average of interest rates, and $g$ is government expenditure. In this model $c$, $i$, and $y$ are endogenous. The lagged endogenous variable $c_{t-1}$ is treated as if it were exogenous. Data for these variables are contained in the file *keynes-2.dat.*

(a) Briefly explain the signs you expect for the unknown parameters.
(b) Derive the reduced form equations.
(c) Estimate the reduced form equations by least squares. Use the estimated reduced form equations to predict the values of the endogenous variables in the next period, given $r = 15.0$ and $g = 20.0$.
(d) Check the identification of each equation.
(e) Obtain *2SLS* estimates of the unknown parameters for the identified equations and comment on their signs and statistical significance.

## *13.7* References

GRIFFITHS, W. E., R. C. HILL, G. G. JUDGE (1993). *Learning and Practicing Econometrics.* New York: John Wiley and Sons, Chapters 18 and 19.

GUJARATI, D. (1995). *Basic Econometrics, Third Edition.* New York: McGraw-Hill, Chapters 18, 19, and 20.

JUDGE, G. G., W. E. GRIFFITHS, R. C. HILL, H. LÜTKEPOHL, AND T. C. LEE (1988). *Introduction to the Theory and Practice of Econometrics,* (2d ed.). New York: John Wiley and Sons, Inc.

MIRER, T. (1995). *Economic Statistics and Econometrics* (3d ed.). Englewood Cliffs, NJ: Prentice Hall, Chapter 17.

Ramanathan, R. (1995). *Introductory Econometrics with Applications* (3d ed.). Fort Worth, Tx: The Dryden Press, Chapter 13.

# Chapter 14

# Nonlinear Least Squares

Throughout this book we have been concerned with estimating economic relationships that can be written as a *linear* function of a set of unknown parameters. Nonlinear functions that we have considered have been nonlinear functions of the *explanatory variables,* not nonlinear functions of the *unknown parameters.* For example, the Cobb–Douglas production function that relates output ($Y$) to labor ($L$) and capital ($K$) can be written as

$$Y = \alpha L^\beta K^\gamma$$

At first glance this function appears to be nonlinear and difficult to estimate using least squares. However, taking logarithms yields

$$\ln(Y) = \delta + \beta \ln(L) + \gamma \ln(K)$$

where $\delta = \ln(\alpha)$. This function is nonlinear in the variables $Y$, $L$, and $K$, but it is linear in the parameters $\delta$, $\beta$, and $\gamma$, and can be readily estimated using least squares.

It is not always possible to transform a seemingly nonlinear model into one that is linear in the parameters. However, we can still proceed with estimation using a technique known as **nonlinear least squares.** In this chapter we introduce three examples that are nonlinear in the parameters and explain how nonlinear least squares can be used to estimate them.

## *14.1* A Simple Nonlinear Model

To introduce nonlinear least squares we consider the following artificial example

$$y_t = \beta x_{t1} + \beta^2 x_{t2} + e_t \tag{14.1.1}$$

where $y_t$ is a dependent variable, $x_{t1}$ and $x_{t2}$ are explanatory variables, $\beta$ is an unknown parameter that we wish to estimate, and the $e_t$ are uncorrelated random errors with mean zero and variance $\sigma_e^2$. This example differs from the conventional linear model because the coefficient of $x_{t2}$ is equal to the square of the coefficient of $x_{t1}$.

How can $\beta$ be estimated? Think back to chapter 3. What did we do when we had a simple linear regression equation with two unknown parameters $\beta_1$ and $\beta_2$? We set up a sum of squared errors function that, in the context of equation 14.1.1, is

$$S(\beta) = \sum_{t=1}^{T} e_t^2 = \sum_{t=1}^{T} (y_t - \beta x_{t1} - \beta^2 x_{t2})^2 \qquad (14.1.2)$$

Then we asked what values of the unknown parameters make $\sum_{t=1}^{T} e_t^2$ a minimum. We searched for the bottom of the bowl in Figure 3.8. We found that we could derive *algebraic expressions* for the minimizing values $b_1$ and $b_2$. We called these algebraic expressions the *least squares estimators*.

When we have a nonlinear function like equation 14.1.1, we *cannot* derive an algebraic expression for the parameter $\beta$ that minimizes equation 14.1.2. However, for a given set of data, we can ask the computer to look for the parameter value that take us to the bottom of the bowl. Many software algorithms can be used to find *numerically* the value that minimizes $\sum e_t^2$. This value is called a **nonlinear least squares estimate.** It is also impossible to get algebraic expressions for standard errors, but it *is* possible for the computer to calculate a numerical standard error that assesses the reliability of a parameter estimate on the basis of whether the bottom of the bowl is flat or spiked. Estimates and standard errors computed in this way have good properties in large samples.

As an example, consider the data on $y_t$, $x_{t1}$, and $x_{t2}$ in Table 14.1. The sum of squared errors function in equation 14.1.2 is graphed in Figure 14.1. Because we have only one unknown parameter, we have a two-dimensional curve, not a "bowl." It is clear that the minimizing value for $\beta$ lies between 1.0 and 1.5. Using nonlinear least squares software, we find that the nonlinear least squares estimate and its standard error are

*Table 14.1*   **Data for Simple Example**

| $y_t$ | $x_{1t}$ | $x_{2t}$ |
|---|---|---|
| 3.284 | .286 | .645 |
| 3.149 | .973 | .585 |
| 2.877 | .384 | .310 |
| −.467 | .276 | .058 |
| 1.211 | .973 | .455 |
| 1.389 | .543 | .779 |
| 1.145 | .957 | .259 |
| 2.321 | .948 | .202 |
| .998 | .543 | .028 |
| .379 | .797 | .099 |
| 1.106 | .936 | .142 |
| .428 | .889 | .296 |
| .011 | .006 | .175 |
| 1.179 | .828 | .180 |
| 1.858 | .399 | .842 |
| .388 | .617 | .039 |
| .651 | .939 | .103 |
| .593 | .784 | .620 |
| .046 | .072 | .158 |
| 1.152 | .889 | .704 |

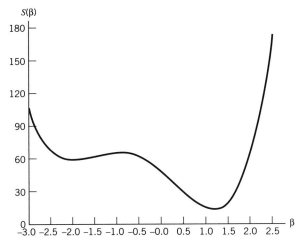

FIGURE **14.1**   Sum of squares function for single-parameter example

$$b = 1.1612, \quad se(b) = 0.129$$

Be warned that different software can yield slightly different approximate standard errors. However, the nonlinear least squares estimate should be the same for all packages.

## 14.2  The CES Production Function

A common production function specification that is used in economics is the **constant elasticity of substitution (CES) production function.** It can be written as

$$Y = \alpha[\delta L^{-\rho} + (1 - \delta)K^{-\rho}]^{-\eta/\rho} \qquad (14.2.1)$$

where output $(Y)$ is related to two inputs, labor $(L)$ and capital $(K)$. The unknown parameters in this function are the efficiency parameter $(\alpha > 0)$, the returns to scale parameter $(\eta > 0)$, the substitution parameter $(\rho > -1)$, and the distribution parameter $(0 < \delta < 1)$ that relates the share of output to the two inputs. It can be shown that as $\rho \to 0$, the CES production function reduces to the simpler Cobb–Douglas production function. One of the disadvantages of the Cobb–Douglas function is that its elasticity of substitution, which measures how capital can substitute for labor and vice versa, is always equal to 1. The elasticity of substitution for the CES production function is given by

$$ES = \frac{1}{1 + \rho} \qquad (14.2.2)$$

In this case the elasticity of substitution depends on $\rho$; it does not have to be equal to 1, but can be estimated empirically from data on the industry of interest.

Estimation of the unknown parameters in equation 14.2.1 looks daunting. This relationship is certainly not a linear function of the unknown parameters. Taking logarithms yields

$$\ln(Y) = \beta - \frac{\eta}{\rho}\ln[\delta L^{-\rho} + (1 - \delta)K^{-\rho}] \qquad (14.2.3)$$

where $\beta = \ln(\alpha)$. The nonlinearity problem remains. Converting this equation to a statistical model by adding an error term $e_t$ and including a "$t$"subscript to denote the $t$-th observation yields

$$\ln(Y_t) = \beta - \frac{\eta}{\rho}\ln[\delta L_t^{-\rho} + (1 - \delta)K_t^{-\rho}] + e_t \qquad (14.2.4)$$

Suppose we assume the $e_t$ are uncorrelated random errors with $e_t \sim (0, \sigma^2)$. How can we estimate the unknown parameters $\beta$, $\eta$, $\rho$, and $\delta$? We follow the same strategy as for the previous example, and set up the sum of squared errors function

$$S(\beta, \eta, \rho, \delta) = \sum_{t=1}^{T} e_t^2 = \sum_{t=1}^{T} \left\{ \ln(Y_t) - \beta + \frac{\eta}{\rho}\ln[\delta L_t^{-\rho} + (1 - \delta)K_t^{-\rho}] \right\}^2 \quad (14.2.5)$$

Because there are four parameters involved, it is harder to find the minimum of this function. Nevertheless, nonlinear least squares software can do it. Using the data in Table 14.2, we find the following estimates.

$$\hat{\beta} = 0.1245 \qquad \hat{\eta} = 1.0126 \qquad \hat{\rho} = 3.0109 \qquad \hat{\delta} = 0.3367$$

$$\text{se}(\hat{\beta}) = 0.0692 \qquad \text{se}(\hat{\eta}) = 0.0459 \qquad \text{se}(\hat{\rho}) = 2.0165 \qquad \text{se}(\hat{\delta}) = 0.0988$$

$$\hat{\sigma}^2 = 0.0587$$

The estimate of $\eta$ is close to unity, suggesting that the industry may be operating at constant returns to scale. From the estimate of $\rho$, an estimate of the elasticity of substitution can be found as

$$E\hat{S} = \frac{1}{1 + \hat{\rho}} = \frac{1}{1 + 3.0109} = 0.249$$

This value is quite a bit different from unity, suggesting that the Cobb–Douglas production function would not be an adequate specification. However, when we take into account the uncertainty associated with estimation of $\rho$, as reflected by its standard error, we find that $\hat{\rho}$ is not significantly different from zero. Specifically, for testing $H_0: \rho = 0$ against the alternative $H_1: \rho \neq 0$, we compute

$$t = \frac{3.0109}{2.0165} = 1.493$$

Using a 5 percent significance level, we compare this value with the critical value 2.06 from the $t_{(26)}$ distribution. Since $-2.06 < 1.493 < 2.06$, we do not have sufficient

*Table 14.2*   **Data for CES Production Function Example**

| $L_t$ | $K_t$ | $Y_t$ |
|-------|-------|-------|
| .228 | .802 | .256918 |
| .258 | .249 | .183599 |
| .821 | .771 | 1.212883 |
| .767 | .511 | .522568 |
| .495 | .758 | .847894 |
| .487 | .425 | .763379 |
| .678 | .452 | .623130 |
| .748 | .817 | 1.031485 |
| .727 | .845 | .569498 |
| .695 | .958 | .882497 |
| .458 | .084 | .108827 |
| .981 | .021 | .026437 |
| .002 | .295 | .003750 |
| .429 | .277 | .461626 |
| .231 | .546 | .268474 |
| .664 | .129 | .186747 |
| .631 | .017 | .020671 |
| .059 | .906 | .100159 |
| .811 | .223 | .252334 |
| .758 | .145 | .103312 |
| .050 | .161 | .078945 |
| .823 | .006 | .005799 |
| .483 | .836 | .723250 |
| .682 | .521 | .776468 |
| .116 | .930 | .216536 |
| .440 | .495 | .541182 |
| .456 | .185 | .316320 |
| .342 | .092 | .123811 |
| .358 | .485 | .386354 |
| .162 | .934 | .279431 |

evidence to reject $H_0$. There is not sufficient evidence from the data to suggest that the Cobb–Douglas function is inadequate.

Other tests of hypotheses for other coefficients can be performed in a similar manner. For example, to test a hypothesis about $\eta$, we use the approximate result that

$$\frac{\hat{\eta} - \eta}{\text{se}(\hat{\eta})} \sim t_{(26)}$$

## 14.3  An AR(1) Error Model

As a third example of nonlinear least squares, we return to chapter 11 and the topic of autocorrelation. In that chapter, the logarithm of sugar cane area in Bangladesh ($y_t$) was related to the logarithm of the relative price of sugar cane ($x_t$). The equation specified was

$$y_t = \beta_1 + \beta_2 x_t + e_t \qquad (14.3.1)$$

where $e_t$ followed the first-order autoregressive model

$$e_t = \rho e_{t-1} + v_t \qquad (14.3.2)$$

with the errors $v_t$ assumed uncorrelated and $v_t \sim (0, \sigma_v^2)$. For the purpose of estimation, we derived equation 11.4.6, which, again, is

$$y_t - \rho y_{t-1} = \beta_1(1 - \rho) + \beta_2(x_t - \rho x_{t-1}) + v_t \qquad (14.3.3)$$

This equation was useful because, for a known $\rho$, it is a linear function of the unknown parameters $\beta_1$ and $\beta_2$. Specifically, we wrote

$$y_t^* = \beta_1 x_{t1}^* + \beta_2 x_{t2}^* + v_t \qquad (14.3.4)$$

where $y_t^*$, $x_{t1}^*$, and $x_{t2}^*$ are transformed variables whose values we can compute, providing we know $\rho$. The problem of an unknown $\rho$ was overcome by using least squares residuals to estimate it.

To see how nonlinear least squares could be used as an alternative estimation technique, note that equation 14.3.3 can be written as

$$y_t = \beta_1(1 - \rho) + \rho y_{t-1} + \beta_2 x_t - \beta_2 \rho x_{t-1} + v_t \qquad (14.3.5)$$

We can view this equation as a nonlinear function of the *three parameters,* $\beta_1$, $\beta_2$, and $\rho$. Thus, instead of estimating the parameters in two stages, once to get $\rho$ and once to get $\beta_1$ and $\beta_2$, we can use nonlinear least squares to estimate $\beta_1$, $\beta_2$, and $\rho$ simultaneously. The estimates we get, alongside those obtained in chapter 11 using generalized least squares, are given in Table 14.3. The entries in this table show both techniques yielding similar estimates; the greatest percentage difference is between the estimates for the response parameter $\beta_2$.

### 14.3.1  CHECKING THE DYNAMIC SPECIFICATION

Equation 14.3.5 can be viewed as a special case of the more general specification

*Table 14.3*  **Alternative Estimates and Standard Errors for the Sugar Cane Response Example**

| Technique | $\beta_1$ | $\beta_2$ | $\rho$ |
|---|---|---|---|
| GLS | 6.164 | 1.007 | 0.342 |
|  | (0.213) | (0.137) | (0.161) |
| Nonlinear LS | 6.089 | 0.944 | 0.339 |
|  | (0.229) | (0.154) | (0.164) |

$$y_t = \alpha_1 + \alpha_2 y_{t-1} + \alpha_3 x_t + \alpha_4 x_{t-1} + v_t \qquad (14.3.6)$$

Notice that this equation has the same variables as equation 14.3.5. In both cases, the dependent variable $y_t$ is a linear function of $y_{t-1}$, $x_t$, and $x_{t-1}$. However, in equation 14.3.6, $y_t$ is also a *linear* function of $\alpha_1$, $\alpha_2$, $\alpha_3$, and $\alpha_4$. This equation can be estimated using (linear) least squares. The fact that equation 14.3.6 contains four unknown parameters when equation 14.3.5 contains only three unknown parameters suggests that equation 14.3.5 is a restricted version of 14.3.6. Such is indeed the case. We can get 14.3.5 from 14.3.6 by imposing the restriction

$$\alpha_2\alpha_3 + \alpha_4 = 0 \qquad (14.3.7)$$

Is this restriction appropriate? If not, perhaps we should be modeling the sugar cane response using the more general dynamic model in equation 14.3.6, rather than the AR(1) error model in equation 14.3.5.

Although equation 14.3.7 is a nonlinear restriction, we can still test it using the *F*-test that is based on restricted and unrestricted sums of squared errors. However, this test does now only have a large sample justification. The value of the test statistic for our data is

$$F = \frac{(SSE_R - SSE_U)/J}{SSE_U/(T - K)}$$

$$= \frac{(2.6419 - 2.6321)/1}{2.6321/(33 - 4)}$$

$$= 0.1087$$

This very low value is not significant at any conventional significance level. Hence, we conclude that there is no evidence to suggest that the more general dynamic model is an improvement over the AR(1) error model.

## 14.4 Summing Up

Models that are nonlinear in the parameters can be estimated using least squares. However, they require numerical algorithms to find estimates that minimize the least squares function. In contrast to (linear) least squares, algebraic formula are not available. Three examples were given in this chapter. More can be found in the exercises.

## 14.5 Exercises

14.1 (a) Use nonlinear least squares with the observations on $K$, $L$, and $Q$ in the file *cespro.dat* to directly estimate the CES production function

$$\ln(Q_t) = \beta - \frac{\eta}{\rho}\ln[\delta L_t^{-\rho} + (1 - \delta)K_t^{-\rho}] + e_t$$

Report estimates and standard errors and comment.
(b) Test the hypothesis that the elasticity of substitution equals unity by
   (i) testing $H_0$: $\rho = 0$ against $H_1$: $\rho \neq 0$ with a $t$ test.
   (ii) estimating the Cobb–Douglas function

$$\ln(Q_t) = \beta + \alpha_1 \ln(L_t) + \alpha_2 \ln(K_t) + v_t$$

and using an $F$-test that compares restricted and unrestricted sums of squared errors.

14.2*  Consider the following equation, where the quantity of wool demanded, $q$, depends on the price of wool, $p$, and the price of synthetics, $s$:

$$q_t = \beta_1 + \frac{\beta_2(p_t^\lambda - 1)}{\lambda} + \frac{\beta_3(s_t^\lambda - 1)}{\lambda} + e_t \qquad (14.5.1)$$

where $\beta_1$, $\beta_2$, $\beta_3$, and $\lambda$ are unknown parameters and $e_t$ is an independent, identically distributed random error with mean zero and variance $\sigma^2$.
(a) Find, in terms of the unknown parameters, the elasticity of demand for wool with respect to
   (i) its own price
   (ii) the price of synthetics
(b) Show that equation 14.5.1 is a linear function of $p$ and $s$ if $\lambda = 1$.
(c) Use the 45 observations given in the file *wool.dat* and nonlinear least squares to estimate the unknown parameters. Find corresponding elasticity estimates at the means of the sample data. Comment.
(d) Test the hypothesis $\lambda = 1$. What is the relevance of this test?
(e) Test the hypothesis that $\beta_2 = -\beta_3$.

14.3   Consider the following consumption function where consumption $c_t$ depends on income $y_t$ through the model:

$$c_t = \beta_1 + \beta_2 y_t + e_t$$
$$e_t = \theta_1 e_{t-1} + \theta_2 e_{t-2} + v_t$$

where the $v_t$ are independent identically distributed random errors with mean 0 and variance $\sigma_v^2$. The error $e_t$ is known as a second-order autoregressive error (or AR(2) error).
(a) Show that the model can also be written as

$$c_t = \beta_1(1 - \theta_1 - \theta_2) + \theta_1 c_{t-1} + \theta_2 c_{t-2} + \beta_2 y_t - \beta_2\theta_1 y_{t-1} - \beta_2\theta_2 y_{t-2} + v_t.$$

(b) Use the 38 observations that appear in the file *con2.dat* and nonlinear least squares to estimate $\beta_1$, $\beta_2$, $\theta_1$, and $\theta_2$.
(c) Test the hypothesis that the marginal propensity to consume equals 0.85 against the alternative that it does not.
(d) Test whether an AR(1) error model would have been adequate.

(e) Use linear least squares to estimate the $\pi$s in the equation

$$c_t = \pi_1 + \pi_2 c_{t-1} + \pi_3 c_{t-2} + \pi_4 y_t + \pi_5 y_{t-1} + \pi_6 y_{t-2} + e_t$$

What restrictions on the $\pi$ parameters will give a model that is equivalent to that in part (a)? Use an $F$-test to test the validity of these restrictions.

## *14.6* References

A more complete, but advanced, discussion of nonlinear least squares can be found in:

GRIFFITHS, W. E., R. C. HILL, AND G. G. JUDGE (1993). *Learning and Practicing Econometrics*. New York: John Wiley and Sons, Chapter 22.

JUDGE, G. G., R. C. HILL, W. E. GRIFFITHS, H. LÜTKEPOHL, AND T. C. LEE (1988). *Introduction to the Theory and Practice of Econometrics* (2d ed.). New York: John Wiley and Sons, Inc., Chapter 12.

A specialist book on nonlinear least squares is:

GALLANT, A. R. (1987). *Nonlinear Statistical Models*. New York: John Wiley and Sons, Inc.

A less advanced reference is:

PINDYCK, R. S., AND D. L. RUBINFELD (1991). *Econometric Models and Economic Forecasts* (3d ed.). New York: McGraw-Hill, Inc., Chapter 9.

# Chapter *15*

# Distributed Lag Models

## *15.1* Introduction

The consequences of economic decisions can last a long time. When the income tax is increased, consumers have less disposable income, reducing their expenditures on goods and services, which reduces profits of suppliers, which reduces the demand for productive inputs, which reduces the profits of the input suppliers, and so on. The effect of the tax increase ripples through the economy. These effects do not occur instantaneously but are spread, or *distributed*, over future time periods. As shown in Figure 15.1, economic actions or decisions taken at one point in time, *t*, affect the economy at time *t*, but also at times $t + 1$, $t + 2$, and so on.

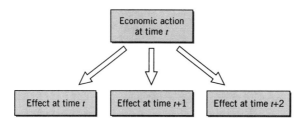

FIGURE *15.1*   The distributed lag effect

Monetary and fiscal policy changes, for example, may take six to eight months to have a noticeable effect; then it may take twelve to eighteen months for the policy effects to work through the economy. Algebraically, we can represent this lag effect by saying that a change in a policy variable $x_t$ has an effect on economic outcomes $y_t$, $y_{t+1}$, $y_{t+2}$, .... If we turn this around slightly, then we can say that $y_t$ is affected by the values of $x_t$, $x_{t-1}$, $x_{t-2}$, ..., or

$$y_t = f(x_t, x_{t-1}, x_{t-2}, \ldots) \tag{15.1.1}$$

Policymakers are, of course, aware of the lagged effects of their actions. In order to make policy changes they must be concerned with the *timing* of the changes and the length of time it takes for the major effects to take place. In order to make policy, they must know *how much* of the policy change will take place at the time of the change, *how much* will take place one month after the change, *how much* will take place two months after the change, and so on. We are back, again, to the problem of using an economic model and economic data to learn about the workings of the economy.

In this chapter we will consider econometric models based on economic models like equation 15.1.1. Such models are said to be *dynamic* since they describe the evolving economy and its reactions over time. One immediate question with models like this is how far back in time we must go, or the *length* of the distributed lag. **Infinite distributed lag models** portray the effects as lasting, essentially, forever. Such models arise from economic theory and have the practical advantage of avoiding the question of how long the lag effect might be. In **finite distributed lag models** we assume that the effect of a change in a (policy) variable $x_t$ affects economic outcomes $y_t$ only for a certain, fixed, period of time. We begin by considering the finite lag model.

## *15.2* Finite Distributed Lag Models

### 15.2.1  AN ECONOMIC MODEL

Quarterly capital expenditures by manufacturing firms arise from appropriations decisions in prior periods. The appropriations decisions themselves are based on projections of the profitability of alternative investment projects, and comparison of the marginal efficiency of investments to the cost of capital funds. Once an investment project is decided on, funds for it are *appropriated*, or approved for expenditure. The actual expenditures arising from any appropriation decision are observed over subsequent quarters as plans are finalized, materials and labor are engaged in the project, and construction is carried out. Thus, if $x_t$ is the amount of capital appropriations observed at a particular time, we can be sure that the effects of that decision, in the form of capital expenditures $y_t$, will be "distributed" over periods $t$, $t + 1$, $t + 2$, and so on until the projects are completed. Furthermore, since a certain amount of "start-up" time is required for any investment project, we would not be surprised to see the major effects of the appropriation decision delayed for several quarters. Furthermore, as the work on the investment projects draws to a close, we expect to observe the expenditures related to the appropriation $x_t$ declining.

Since capital appropriations at time $t$, designated by $x_t$, affect capital expenditures in the current and future periods ($y_t$, $y_{t+1}$, . . .), until the appropriated projects are completed, we may say equivalently that current expenditures $y_t$ are a function of current and past appropriations $x_t$, $x_{t-1}$, . . . . Furthermore, let us assert that after $n$ quarters, where $n$ is the lag length, the effect of any appropriation decision on capital expenditure is exhausted. We can represent this economic model as

$$y_t = f(x_t, x_{t-1}, x_{t-2}, \ldots, x_{t-n}) \tag{15.2.1}$$

Current capital expenditures $y_t$ depend on current capital appropriations, $x_t$, as well as the appropriations in the previous $n$ periods, $x_{t-1}, x_{t-2}, \ldots, x_{t-n}$. This distributed lag model is *finite* as the duration of the effects is a finite period of time, namely $n$ periods. We now must convert this economic model into a statistical one so that we can give it empirical content.

### 15.2.2 THE STATISTICAL MODEL

In order to convert equation 15.2.1 into a statistical model we must choose a functional form, add an error term, and make assumptions about the properties of the error term. As a first approximation let us assume that the functional form is linear, so that the finite lag model, with an additive error term, is

$$y_t = \alpha + \beta_0 x_t + \beta_1 x_{t-1} + \beta_2 x_{t-2} + \cdots + \beta_n x_{t-n} + e_t \quad t = n + 1, \ldots, T \quad (15.2.2)$$

where we assume that $E(e_t) = 0$, $\text{var}(e_t) = \sigma^2$, and $\text{cov}(e_t, e_s) = 0$. Note that if we have $T$ observations on the pairs $(y_t, x_t)$ then only $T - n$ *complete* observations are available for estimation, since $n$ observations are "lost" in creating $x_{t-1}$, $x_{t-2}, \ldots, x_{t-n}$.

In this finite distributed lag the parameter $\alpha$ is the intercept and the parameter $\beta_i$ is called a **distributed lag weight** to reflect the fact that it measures the effect of changes in past appropriations, $\Delta x_{t-i}$, on expected current expenditures, $\Delta E(y_t)$, all other things held constant. That is,

$$\frac{\partial E(y_t)}{\partial x_{t-i}} = \beta_i \quad (15.2.3)$$

Equation 15.2.2 can be estimated by least squares if the error term $e_t$ has the usual desirable properties. However, multicollinearity is often a serious problem in such models. Recall from chapter 8 that multicollinearity is a problem caused by explanatory variables that are correlated with one another. In equation 15.2.2 the variables $x_t$ and $x_{t-1}$, and other pairs of lagged $x$'s as well, are likely to be closely related when using time-series data. If $x_t$ follows a pattern over time, then $x_{t-1}$ will follow a similar pattern, thus causing $x_t$ and $x_{t-1}$ to be correlated. The consequence of multicollinearity is imprecise least squares estimation, leading to wide interval estimates, coefficients that are statistically insignificant, estimated coefficients that may have incorrect signs, and results that are very sensitive to changes in model specification or the sample period. These consequences mean that the least squares estimates may be unreliable. Since the pattern of lag weights will often be used for policy analysis, this imprecision may have adverse social consequences. Imposing a tax cut at the *wrong* time in the business cycle can do much harm.

### 15.2.3 AN EMPIRICAL ILLUSTRATION

To give an empirical illustration of this type of model, consider the data in Table 15.1 on quarterly capital expenditures and appropriations for U.S. manufacturing firms. We assume that $n = 8$ periods are required to exhaust the expenditure effects of a capital appropriation in manufacturing. The basis for this choice is investigated in Exercise 15.7, since the lag length $n$ is actually an unknown constant. The least squares parameter estimates for the finite lag model 15.2.2 are given in Table 15.2. The $R^2$ for the estimated relation is 0.99 and the overall $F$-test value is 1174.8. The statistical model "fits" the data well, and the $F$-test of the joint hypotheses that all distributed lag weights $\beta_i = 0$, $i = 0, \ldots, 8$, is rejected at the $\alpha = .01$ level of significance. Examining the estimated parameter estimates themselves, we notice several disquieting facts. First, only the lag weights $b_2$, $b_3$, $b_4$, and $b_8$ are statistically

**Table 15.1** Quarterly Capital Expenditures ($y_t$) and Appropriations ($x_t$) for U.S. Manufacturing Firms

| t | y | x | t | y | x |
|---|---|---|---|---|---|
| 1 | 2072 | 1767 | 45 | 3136 | 4123 |
| 2 | 2077 | 2061 | 46 | 3299 | 4656 |
| 3 | 2078 | 2289 | 47 | 3514 | 4906 |
| 4 | 2043 | 2047 | 48 | 3815 | 4344 |
| 5 | 2062 | 1856 | 49 | 4040 | 5080 |
| 6 | 2067 | 1842 | 50 | 4274 | 5539 |
| 7 | 1964 | 1866 | 51 | 4565 | 5583 |
| 8 | 1981 | 2279 | 52 | 4838 | 6147 |
| 9 | 1914 | 2688 | 53 | 5222 | 6545 |
| 10 | 1991 | 3264 | 54 | 5406 | 6770 |
| 11 | 2129 | 3896 | 55 | 5705 | 5955 |
| 12 | 2309 | 4014 | 56 | 5871 | 6015 |
| 13 | 2614 | 4041 | 57 | 5953 | 6029 |
| 14 | 2896 | 3710 | 58 | 5868 | 5975 |
| 15 | 3058 | 3383 | 59 | 5573 | 5894 |
| 16 | 3309 | 3431 | 60 | 5672 | 5951 |
| 17 | 3446 | 3613 | 61 | 5543 | 5952 |
| 18 | 3466 | 3205 | 62 | 5526 | 5723 |
| 19 | 3435 | 2426 | 63 | 5750 | 6351 |
| 20 | 3183 | 2330 | 64 | 5761 | 6636 |
| 21 | 2697 | 1954 | 65 | 5943 | 6799 |
| 22 | 2338 | 1936 | 66 | 6212 | 7753 |
| 23 | 2140 | 2201 | 67 | 6631 | 7595 |
| 24 | 2012 | 2233 | 68 | 6828 | 7436 |
| 25 | 2071 | 2690 | 69 | 6645 | 6679 |
| 26 | 2192 | 2940 | 70 | 6703 | 6475 |
| 27 | 2240 | 3127 | 71 | 6659 | 6319 |
| 28 | 2421 | 3131 | 72 | 6337 | 5860 |
| 29 | 2639 | 2872 | 73 | 6165 | 5705 |
| 30 | 2733 | 2515 | 74 | 5875 | 5521 |
| 31 | 2721 | 2271 | 75 | 5798 | 5920 |
| 32 | 2640 | 2711 | 76 | 5921 | 5937 |
| 33 | 2513 | 2394 | 77 | 5772 | 6570 |
| 34 | 2448 | 2457 | 78 | 5874 | 7087 |
| 35 | 2429 | 2720 | 79 | 5872 | 7206 |
| 36 | 2516 | 2703 | 80 | 6159 | 8431 |
| 37 | 2534 | 2992 | 81 | 6583 | 9718 |
| 38 | 2494 | 2516 | 82 | 6961 | 10921 |
| 39 | 2596 | 2817 | 83 | 7449 | 11672 |
| 40 | 2572 | 3153 | 84 | 8093 | 12199 |
| 41 | 2601 | 2756 | 85 | 9013 | 12865 |
| 42 | 2648 | 3269 | 86 | 9752 | 14985 |
| 43 | 2840 | 3657 | 87 | 10704 | 16378 |
| 44 | 2937 | 3941 | 88 | 11597 | 12680 |

*Table 15.2*    **Least Squares Estimates for the Unrestricted Finite Distributed Lag Model**

| Variable | Estimate | Std. Error | t-value | p-value |
|---|---|---|---|---|
| *const.* | 33.414 | 53.709 | 0.622 | 0.5359 |
| $x_t$ | 0.038 | 0.035 | 1.107 | 0.2721 |
| $x_{t-1}$ | 0.067 | 0.069 | 0.981 | 0.3300 |
| $x_{t-2}$ | 0.181 | 0.089 | 2.028 | 0.0463 |
| $x_{t-3}$ | 0.194 | 0.093 | 2.101 | 0.0392 |
| $x_{t-4}$ | 0.170 | 0.093 | 1.824 | 0.0723 |
| $x_{t-5}$ | 0.052 | 0.092 | 0.571 | 0.5701 |
| $x_{t-6}$ | 0.052 | 0.094 | 0.559 | 0.5780 |
| $x_{t-7}$ | 0.056 | 0.094 | 0.597 | 0.5526 |
| $x_{t-8}$ | 0.127 | 0.060 | 2.124 | 0.0372 |

significantly different from zero based on individual *t*-tests, reflecting the fact that the estimates' standard errors are large relative to the estimated coefficients. Second, the estimated lag weights $b_7$ and $b_8$ are *larger* than the estimated lag weights for lags of five and six periods. This does not agree with our anticipation that the lag effects of appropriations should decrease with time and in the most distant periods should be small and approaching zero.

These characteristics are symptomatic of multicollinearity in the data. The simple correlations among the current and lagged values of capital appropriations are large (see Exercise 15.9). Consequently, a high level of *linear* dependence is indicated among the explanatory variables. Thus, we conclude that the least squares estimates in Table 15.2 are subject to great sampling variability and are unreliable, owing to the limited independent information provided by each explanatory variable $x_{t-i}$.

In chapter 8 we noted that one way to combat the ill-effects of multicollinearity is to use restricted least squares. By placing restrictions on the model parameters we reduce the variances of the estimator. In the context of distributed lag models we often have an idea of the pattern of the time effects, which we can translate into parameter restrictions. We will illustrate this idea with two examples of restricted lag weights.

## 15.2.4   THE ARITHMETIC LAG

A very early version of a polynomial lag was proposed by Irving Fisher (1937). He specified that the lag weights decline *linearly*. He did so by placing restrictions on the distributed lag weights of the form

$$\beta_0 = (n + 1)\gamma$$

$$\beta_1 = n\gamma$$

$$\beta_2 = (n - 1)\gamma \tag{15.2.4}$$

$$\vdots$$

$$\beta_n = \gamma$$

where $\gamma > 0$ is a positive constant. In this scheme the effect of a change in $x_{t-i}$ declines *linearly*. The arithmetic distributed lag is depicted in Figure 15.2.

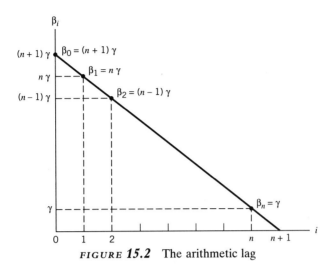

FIGURE **15.2**   The arithmetic lag

Note that the effect of a change in $x_t$ in the current period is $\beta_0 = (n + 1)\gamma$, and then the effect declines by the amount $\gamma$ in each period. In the $(n + 1)$ period the effect has disappeared.

To estimate the arithmetic lag we substitute equation 15.2.4 into the finite lag model 15.2.2 and simplify. This is exactly the strategy we used in chapter 8.7 when introducing nonsample information, as we are now, into the regression model. For illustration purposes, suppose that the lag length has been found to be $n = 4$ periods. Then the finite lag model is

$$y_t = \alpha + \beta_0 x_t + \beta_1 x_{t-1} + \beta_2 x_{t-2} + \beta_3 x_{t-3} + \beta_4 x_{t-4} + e_t, \quad t = 5, \ldots, T \qquad (15.2.5)$$

Substituting equation 15.2.4 with $n = 4$ into 15.2.5 we have

$$y_t = \alpha + (5\gamma)x_t + (4\gamma)x_{t-1} + (3\gamma)x_{t-2} + (2\gamma)x_{t-3} + \gamma x_{t-4} + e_t$$

$$= \alpha + \gamma[5x_t + 4x_{t-1} + 3x_{t-2} + 2x_{t-3} + x_{t-4}] + e_t \qquad (15.2.6)$$

$$= \alpha + \gamma z_t + e_t$$

where $z_t$ is the constructed variable

$$z_t = [5x_t + 4x_{t-1} + 3x_{t-2} + 2x_{t-3} + x_{t-4}]$$

By using the constraints in equation 15.2.4 we have expressed $(n + 1) = 5$ distributed lag weights in terms of one unknown, $\gamma$. The disappearance of $n = 4$ parameters from the model signifies that we have, in effect, imposed $J = n = 4$ parameter restrictions on the finite lag model 15.2.2. After the arithmetic lag restrictions have been imposed, the resulting model (equation 15.2.6) can be estimated using least squares. Correlation between variables is no longer a problem since we have "eliminated" all but one explanatory variable.

Obtaining the least squares estimate of $\gamma$, say $\hat{\gamma}$, we can estimate the distributed lag weights as

$$\hat{\beta}_i = (n + 1 - i)\hat{\gamma}, \quad i = 0, \ldots, n$$

These estimated lag weights will decline in a linear fashion by construction.

Several questions might have occurred to you. First, the arithmetic lag declines from the initial period, and this might not always describe the time pattern of effects. We might want to build some flexibility into the model. Second, we still must address the question of how the lag length $n$ is selected. Both of these issues are addressed in subsequent sections.

Third, you recall from chapter 8 that imposing restrictions on a regression model leads to an estimator with *smaller* variance than the least squares estimator of the original unrestricted model. However, unless the constraints we impose are *true*, the resulting restricted estimator is biased. To protect against imposing constraints that are too incompatible with the data, we can test the restrictions in equation 15.2.4 using an *F*-test described in chapter 8.4. The restricted sum of squared errors, $SSE_R$, will come from least squares estimation of equation 15.2.6, the unrestricted sum of squared errors, $SSE_U$, comes from least squares estimation of equation 15.2.2, and, as we indicated, there are $J = n$ parameter restrictions/hypotheses.

What are the degrees of freedom in the unrestricted model? If we have a total of $T$ time-series observations on $y_t$ and $x_t$, we will have only $T - n$ observations with which to estimate the parameters in the unrestricted model (equation 15.2.2). In this model there are $(n + 2)$ parameters to estimate, and consequently, there are $df = [(T - n) - (n + 2)]$ degrees of freedom in the unrestricted model. Note that the $T - n$ observations we use to estimate equation 15.2.2 must also be used to estimate the restricted model 15.2.6.

### 15.2.5  POLYNOMIAL DISTRIBUTED LAGS

Shirley Almon (1965) recognized that the arithmetic lag is a special case of a polynomial lag. To increase the flexibility of the finite lag, while still imposing some shape to the lag distribution to reduce the effects of multicollinearity, Almon suggested that we constrain the distributed lag weights to fall on a polynomial, probably of a low order. That is, suppose we select a second-order polynomial to represent the pattern of lag weights. Then the effect of a change in $x_{t-i}$ on $E(y_t)$ is

$$\frac{\partial E(y_t)}{\partial x_{t-i}} = \beta_i = \gamma_0 + \gamma_1 i + \gamma_2 i^2, \quad i = 0, \ldots, n \tag{15.2.7}$$

An example of this quadratic polynomial lag is depicted in Figure 15.3. The polynomial lag in Figure 15.3 depicts a situation that commonly arises when modeling the effects of monetary and fiscal policy. At time $t$ the effect of a change in a policy variable is

$$\frac{\partial E(y_t)}{\partial x_t} = \beta_0 = \gamma_0$$

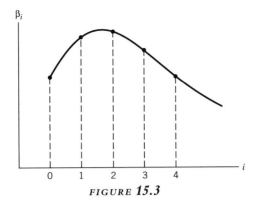

FIGURE **15.3**

The immediate impact might well be less than the impact after several quarters, or months. After reaching its maximum, the policy effect diminishes for the remainder of the finite lag.

For illustrative purposes, again suppose that the lag length is $n = 4$ periods. Then the relations in equation 15.2.7 are

$$\beta_0 = \gamma_0$$

$$\beta_1 = \gamma_0 + \gamma_1 + \gamma_2$$

$$\beta_2 = \gamma_0 + 2\gamma_1 + 4\gamma_2 \qquad (15.2.8)$$

$$\beta_3 = \gamma_0 + 3\gamma_1 + 9\gamma_2$$

$$\beta_4 = \gamma_0 + 4\gamma_1 + 16\gamma_2$$

In order to estimate the parameters describing the polynomial lag, $\gamma_0$, $\gamma_1$, and $\gamma_2$, we substitute equation 15.2.8 into the finite lag model (equation 15.2.5) to obtain

$$y_t = \alpha + \gamma_0 x_t + (\gamma_0 + \gamma_1 + \gamma_2)x_{t-1} + (\gamma_0 + 2\gamma_1 + 4\gamma_2)x_{t-2}$$

$$+ (\gamma_0 + 3\gamma_1 + 9\gamma_2)x_{t-3} + (\gamma_0 + 4\gamma_1 + 16\gamma_2)x_{t-4} + e_t \qquad (15.2.9)$$

$$= \alpha + \gamma_0 z_{t0} + \gamma_1 z_{t1} + \gamma_2 z_{t2} + e_t$$

In this equation we have defined the constructed variables $z_{tk}$ as

$$z_{t0} = x_t + x_{t-1} + x_{t-2} + x_{t-3} + x_{t-4}$$

$$z_{t1} = x_{t-1} + 2x_{t-2} + 3x_{t-3} + 4x_{t-4}$$

$$z_{t2} = x_{t-1} + 4x_{t-2} + 9x_{t-3} + 16x_{t-4}$$

Once these variables are created the polynomial coefficients are estimated by applying least squares to equation 15.2.9. If we denote the estimated values of $\gamma_k$ by $\hat{\gamma}_k$, then we can obtain the estimated lag weights as

$$\hat{\beta}_i = \hat{\gamma}_0 + \hat{\gamma}_1 i + \hat{\gamma}_2 i^2, \quad i = 0, \ldots, n \qquad (15.2.10)$$

Whatever the degree of the polynomial, the general procedure is an extension of what we have described for the quadratic polynomial.

Equation 15.2.9 is a restricted model. We have replaced $(n + 1) = 5$ distributed lag weights with three polynomial coefficients. This implies that in constraining the distributed lag weights to a polynomial of degree 2, we have imposed $J = (n + 1) - 3 = 2$ parameter restrictions. Just as in the arithmetic lag, we may wish to check the compatibility of the quadratic polynomial lag model with the data by performing an *F*-test, comparing the sum of squared errors from the restricted model in equation 15.2.9 to the sum of squared errors from the unrestricted model, equation 15.2.2.

More flexible polynomial models have been applied in many situations. In Shirley Almon's original work she found that a fourth-order polynomial fits the lagged relationship between corporations' expenditures on capital goods and the actual appropriation for those expenditures. We will illustrate using the quadratic model in equation 15.2.7, with a lag length of $n = 8$ periods. In Table 15.3 are the estimated polynomial coefficients from such a model.

*Table 15.3*   **Estimated (Almon) Polynomial Coefficients**

| Parameter | Estimates | *t*-value | *p*-value |
|---|---|---|---|
| $\alpha$ | 51.573 | 0.970 | 0.3351 |
| $\gamma_0$ | 0.067 | 4.411 | 0.0001 |
| $\gamma_1$ | 0.038 | 2.984 | 0.0038 |
| $\gamma_2$ | −0.005 | −3.156 | 0.0023 |

In Table 15.4 we present the distributed lag weights calculated using equation 15.2.10. The reported standard errors are based on the fact that the estimated distributed lag weights are combinations of the estimates in Table 15.3. Since the estimated weights in Table 15.4 are linear combinations of the estimated polynomial coefficients in Table 15.3, as shown in equation 15.2.10, their estimated variances are calculated using equation 2.5.8, from chapter 2. Constraining the distributed lag weights to fall on a polynomial of degree two has drastically affected their values as compared to the unconstrained values in Table 15.2. Also, note that the standard errors of the estimated coefficients are much smaller than those in the unconstrained model, indicating more precise parameter estimation.

*Table 15.4*    **Estimated (Almon) Distributed Lag Weights from Polynomial of Degree Two**

| Parameter | Estimate | Std. Error | *t*-value | *p*-value |
|-----------|----------|------------|-----------|-----------|
| $\beta_0$ | 0.067 | 0.015 | 4.41 | 0.0001 |
| $\beta_1$ | 0.100 | 0.005 | 19.60 | 0.0001 |
| $\beta_2$ | 0.123 | 0.005 | 22.74 | 0.0001 |
| $\beta_3$ | 0.136 | 0.009 | 14.40 | 0.0001 |
| $\beta_4$ | 0.138 | 0.011 | 12.86 | 0.0001 |
| $\beta_5$ | 0.130 | 0.009 | 14.31 | 0.0001 |
| $\beta_6$ | 0.112 | 0.005 | 20.92 | 0.0001 |
| $\beta_7$ | 0.083 | 0.007 | 11.32 | 0.0001 |
| $\beta_8$ | 0.044 | 0.018 | 2.47 | 0.0156 |

> **REMARK:**   Recall that imposing restrictions on parameters leads to bias unless the restrictions are true. In this case we do not really believe that the distributed lag weights fall exactly on a polynomial of degree 2. However, if this assumption approximates reality, then the constrained estimator will exhibit a small amount of bias. Our objective is to trade a large reduction in sampling variance for the introduction of some bias, increasing the probability of obtaining estimates *close* to the true values.

In Figure 15.4 we plot the unrestricted estimates of lag weights and the restricted estimates. Note that the restricted estimates display the increasing-then-decreasing "humped" shape that economic reasoning led us to expect. The effect of a change in capital appropriations $x_t$ at time $t$ leads to an increase in capital expenditures in the current period, $y_t$, by a relatively small amount. However, the expenditures arising from the appropriation decision increase during the next four quarters, before the effect begins to taper off.

### 15.2.6   SELECTION OF THE LENGTH OF THE FINITE LAG

Numerous procedures have been suggested for selecting the length $n$ of a finite distributed lag. None of the proposed methods is entirely satisfactory. The issue is an important one, however, because fitting a polynomial lag model in which the lag length is either over- or understated may lead to biases in the estimation of the lag weights, even if an appropriate polynomial degree has been selected. We offer two suggestions that are based on "goodness-of-fit" criteria. Begin by selecting a lag length $N$ that is the *maximum* that you are willing to consider. The unrestricted finite lag model is then

$$y_t = \alpha + \beta_0 x_t + \beta_1 x_{t-1} + \beta_2 x_{t-2} + \beta_3 x_{t-3} + \cdots + \beta_N x_{t-N} + e_t$$

We wish to assess the goodness of fit for lag lengths $n \leq N$. The usual measures of goodness-of-fit, $R^2$ and $\overline{R}^2$, have been found not to be useful for this task.

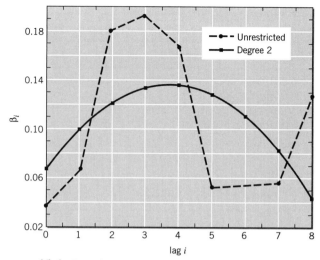

FIGURE **15.4** Restricted and unrestricted distributed lag weights

Two goodness-of-fit measures that are more appropriate are Akaike's *AIC* criterion

$$AIC = \ln\frac{SSE_n}{T - N} + \frac{2(n + 2)}{T - N}$$

and Schwarz's *SC* criterion

$$SC = \ln\frac{SSE_n}{T - N} + \frac{(n + 2)\ln(T - N)}{T - N}$$

These values are routinely computed by some software packages. A discussion of these criteria can be found in Judge et al. (1988, chapter 20.4). For each of these measures we seek that lag length $n^*$ that minimizes the criterion used. Since adding more lagged variables reduces *SSE*, the second part of each of the criteria is a *penalty function* for adding additional lags. These measures weigh reductions in sum of squared errors obtained by adding additional lags against the penalty imposed by each. They are useful for comparing lag lengths of alternative models estimated using the same number of observations.

## 15.3 The Geometric Lag

An *infinite distributed lag model* in its most general form is:

$$y_t = \alpha + \beta_0 x_t + \beta_1 x_{t-1} + \beta_2 x_{t-2} + \beta_3 x_{t-3} + \cdots + e_t$$

$$= \alpha + \sum_{i=0}^{\infty} \beta_i x_{t-i} + e_t \tag{15.3.1}$$

In this model, $y_t$ is taken to be a function of $x_t$ and *all* its previous values. There may also be other explanatory variables on the right-hand side of the equation.

The model in equation 15.3.1 is a general one, and as it stands it is impossible to estimate, since there are an infinite number of parameters. Consequently, models have been developed that are *parsimonious,* and that reduce the number of parameters to estimate. The cost of reducing the number of parameters is that these models must assume particular patterns for the parameters $\beta_i$, which are called *distributed lag weights.*

One popular model is the **geometric lag,** in which the lag weights are positive and decline geometrically. That is

$$\beta_i = \beta\phi^i, \quad |\phi| < 1 \tag{15.3.2}$$

The parameter $\beta$ is a scaling factor and the parameter $\phi$ is less than 1 in absolute value. The pattern of lag weights $\beta_i$ is shown in Figure 15.5.

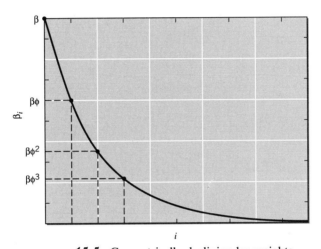

FIGURE **15.5**  Geometrically declining lag weights

The lag weights $\beta_i = \beta\phi^i$ decline towards zero as $i$ gets larger. The most recent past is more heavily weighted than the more distant past, and, although the weights never reach zero, beyond a point they become negligible.

Substituting equation 15.3.2 into 15.3.1, we obtain,

$$y_t = \alpha + \beta_0 x_t + \beta_1 x_{t-1} + \beta_2 x_{t-2} + \beta_3 x_{t-3} + \cdots + e_t$$
$$= \alpha + \beta(x_t + \phi x_{t-1} + \phi^2 x_{t-2} + \phi^3 x_{t-3} + \cdots) + e_t \tag{15.3.3}$$

which is the **infinite geometric distributed lag model.** In this model there are three parameters—$\alpha$, an intercept parameter; $\beta$, a scale factor; and $\phi$, which controls the rate at which the weights decline.

In equation 15.3.3 the effect of a one-unit change in $x_{t-i}$ on $E(y_t)$ is

$$\frac{\partial E(y_t)}{\partial x_{t-i}} = \beta_i = \beta\phi^i \tag{15.3.4}$$

This equation says that the change in the average value of $y$ in period $t$ given a change in $x$ in period $t - i$, all other factors held constant, is $\beta_i = \beta\phi^i$. The change in $E(y_t)$ given a unit change in $x_t$, is $\beta$; it is called an **impact multiplier,** since it measures the change in the current period. If the change in period $t$ is sustained for another period, then the combined effect $\beta + \beta\phi$ is felt in period $t + 1$. If the change is sustained for three periods, the effect on $E(y_{t+2})$ is $\beta + \beta\phi + \beta\phi^2$. These sums are called **interim multipliers** and are the effect of sustained changes in $x_t$. If the change is sustained permanently, then the total effect, or the **long-run multiplier,** is

$$\beta(1 + \phi + \phi^2 + \phi^3 + \cdots) = \frac{\beta}{1 - \phi}$$

## 15.4 The Koyck Transformation

How shall we estimate the geometric lag model represented by equation 15.3.3? As it stands, it appears to be an ugly task, since the model has an infinite number of terms, and the parameters $\beta$ and $\phi$ are multiplied together, making the model *nonlinear in the parameters.* One way around these difficulties (though not a magic bullet, as it turns out) is to use the very clever **Koyck transformation,** in deference to L. M. Koyck (1954), who developed it.

To apply the Koyck transformation, lag equation 15.3.3 one period, multiply by $\phi$, and subtract that result from the equation 15.3.3. We obtain

$$
\begin{aligned}
y_t - \phi y_{t-1} &= [\alpha + \beta(x_t + \phi x_{t-1} + \phi^2 x_{t-2} + \phi^3 x_{t-3} + \cdots) + e_t] \\
&\quad - \phi[\alpha + \beta(x_{t-1} + \phi x_{t-2} + \phi^3 x_{t-3} + \phi^3 x_{t-4} + \cdots) + e_{t-1}] \\
&= \alpha(1 - \phi) + \beta x_t + (e_t - \phi e_{t-1})
\end{aligned}
\tag{15.4.1}
$$

Solving for $y_t$ we obtain the Koyck form of the geometric lag,

$$
\begin{aligned}
y_t &= \alpha(1 - \phi) + \phi y_{t-1} + \beta x_t + (e_t - \phi e_{t-1}) \\
&= \beta_1 + \beta_2 y_{t-1} + \beta_3 x_t + v_t
\end{aligned}
\tag{15.4.2}
$$

where $\beta_1 = \alpha(1 - \phi)$, $\beta_2 = \phi$, $\beta_3 = \beta$ and the random error $v_t = (e_t - \phi e_{t-1})$.

### 15.4.1   LEAST SQUARES ESTIMATION OF THE KOYCK MODEL

The last line of equation 15.4.2 looks like a multiple regression model, with two special characteristics. The first is that one of the explanatory variables is the *lagged dependent variable,* $y_{t-1}$. The second is that the error term $v_t$ depends on $e_t$ and on $e_{t-1}$. The consequence of these characteristics is that the least squares estimator of the parameters is biased, and the bias does not disappear even in large samples, making the least squares estimator *inconsistent.* Consequently, in equation 15.4.2 we should *not* use the least squares estimator to obtain estimates of $\beta_1$, $\beta_2$, and $\beta_3$.

To see the source of the inconsistency, note that $y_{t-1}$ and the error term $v_t$ must be *correlated,* since equation 15.3.3 shows that $y_{t-1}$ depends directly on $e_{t-1}$.

> When a right-hand-side explanatory variable is correlated with the error term, the least squares estimator is biased and inconsistent.

This same problem occurred in chapter 13 when we discussed the estimation of simultaneous equations models. The reasoning behind this fact is discussed in chapter 13.2.3.

In the context of the lagged dependent variable model 15.4.2, what if we did not know whether the error term was correlated with the lagged dependent variable? If it is not, then we can use least squares estimation; if it is, we should not use least squares estimation. The key question is whether $v_t$ is serially correlated, since if it is then it is also correlated with $y_{t-1}$. A test for the presence of autocorrelation in the lagged dependent variable model has been proposed by Durbin (1970). It should be used when there is a lagged dependent variable on the right-hand side of an equation, since in this case the usual Durbin–Watson test (see chapter 11.6) is biased toward finding no autocorrelation. The new test is valid in large samples and is based on the $h$-statistic, obtained from least squares estimation results of equation 15.4.2. The $h$-statistic is

$$h = \left(1 - \frac{d}{2}\right) \sqrt{\frac{T - 1}{1 - (T - 1)[\mathrm{se}(b_2)]^2}}$$

where $d$ is the usual Durbin–Watson test statistic for AR(1) errors, $T$ is the sample size, and $\mathrm{se}(b_2)$ is the conventional least squares standard error for $b_2$, which is the estimated coefficient of the lagged dependent variable, $y_{t-1}$. In large samples the $h$-statistic has a standard normal distribution if $v_t$ is not autocorrelated. If $|h| \geq 1.96$, we reject the null hypothesis of no autocorrelation in favor of the alternative that there is positive autocorrelation.

The $h$-test fails if $[\mathrm{se}(b_2)]^2 > 1/(T - 1)$, since the term under the square root becomes negative. In this case there is an alternative test. Estimate equation 15.4.2 by least squares and compute the least squares residuals, $\hat{e}_t$. Then, regress those residuals on the right-hand-side variables, $y_{t-1}$ and $x_t$, and $\hat{e}_{t-1}$. Test the significance of the coefficient on $\hat{e}_{t-1}$ using the usual $t$-test. If the coefficient is significant, then reject the null hypothesis of no autocorrelation. This alternative test is also useful in some other general circumstances. See Ramanathan (1995, chapter 10.3) for further discussion of both the $h$-test and the alternative test.

## 15.4.2   TWO-STAGE LEAST SQUARES ESTIMATION OF THE KOYCK LAG

We can estimate the parameters in equation 15.4.2 consistently using two-stage least squares, just as we did in chapter 13 in the context of simultaneous equations. The "problem" variable in equation 15.4.2 is $y_{t-1}$ since it is the one correlated with the error term $v_t$. The two-stage least squares procedure *replaces* $y_{t-1}$ with $\hat{y}_{t-1} = a_0 + a_1 x_{t-1}$, where the coefficients $a_0$ and $a_1$ are obtained by a simple least squares regression of $y_{t-1}$ on $x_{t-1}$. The predicted value $\hat{y}_{t-1}$ of $y_{t-1}$ is *uncorrelated* with $v_t$ in large samples, and thus, the least squares estimator in the model

$$y_t = \beta_1 + \beta_2 \hat{y}_{t-1} + \beta_3 x_t + error$$

is consistent, and in large samples it is normally distributed. Using the consistent estimates of $\beta_1$, $\beta_2$, and $\beta_3$ we can derive consistent estimates of $\alpha$, $\beta$, and $\phi$.

Let us remind you that using least squares regression software twice to carry out 2SLS will yield the correct parameter estimates, but it will not produce proper standard errors or t-values. Use a program designed for two-stage least squares estimation. Such programs are commonly included in econometric software packages.

It is also possible to estimate geometric lags in a completely different way, taking into account the nonlinear (in the parameters) form of equation 15.4.2. See chapter 14 on *nonlinear* least squares for a discussion of this approach.

## *15.5* An Infinite Distributed Lag Based on the Adaptive Expectations Hypothesis

Certain assumptions about economic behavior lead to geometric lag models. One such model is the **adaptive expectations model.** A famous application of the model of adaptive expectations is to the demand for money. The demand for money $y_t$ at any point in time depends on the interest rate $x_t$. However, most individuals and firms do not adjust their demand for money from day to day according to fluctuations in the interest rate. Rather, they base their demand on expectations about what the interest rate will "normally" be. If the expected, or anticipated, interest rate is $x_t^*$, then we might write the demand for money as

$$y_t = \alpha + \beta x_t^* + e_t \qquad (15.5.1)$$

This model cannot be estimated because the anticipated interest rate $x_t^*$ is not observable.

### 15.5.1   ADAPTIVE EXPECTATIONS

How do we form expectations about the future? Expectations are formed on the basis of past experience. The adaptive expectations model asserts that the anticipated value, here the interest rate $x_t^*$, depends on past values of the interest rate that we have observed, with a built-in correction based on the errors in our previous anticipation. That is, the model states that the change in expectations from one period to the next is a fraction $0 < \lambda < 1$ of the difference between last period's expectation $x_{t-1}^*$ and the value $x_{t-1}$ that actually occurred:

$$x_t^* - x_{t-1}^* = \lambda(x_{t-1} - x_{t-1}^*) \qquad (15.5.2)$$

Rearranging equation 15.5.2 we have

$$x_t^* = \lambda x_{t-1} + (1 - \lambda)x_{t-1}^* \qquad (15.5.3)$$

To incorporate this model of expectations, lag equation 15.5.1 one period, and multiply by $(1 - \lambda)$ to obtain

$$(1 - \lambda)y_{t-1} = (1 - \lambda)\alpha + (1 - \lambda)\beta x_{t-1}^* + (1 - \lambda)e_{t-1} \qquad (15.5.4)$$

Subtract equation 15.5.4 from 15.5.1 and rearrange, to obtain

$$y_t = \alpha\lambda + (1 - \lambda)y_{t-1} + \beta[x_t^* - (1 - \lambda)x_{t-1}^*] + e_t - (1 - \lambda)e_{t-1} \quad (15.5.5)$$

Now replace $x_t^*$ on the right-hand side of 15.5.5 with equation 15.5.3 to *finally* (economists do a lot of algebra, don't they?) obtain:

$$y_t = \alpha\lambda + (1 - \lambda)y_{t-1} + \beta\lambda x_{t-1} + e_t - (1 - \lambda)e_{t-1} \quad (15.5.6)$$

This is identical to equation 15.4.2 with $\phi$ replaced by $(1 - \lambda)$, and thus we can set the parameters $\beta_1 = \alpha\lambda$, $\beta_2 = (1 - \lambda)$, and $\beta_3 = \beta\lambda$. Also, in equation 15.5.6 we have $x_{t-1}$ on the right-hand side instead of $x_t$, which appears in 15.4.2. The parameters can be estimated by two-stage least squares as just described, as we illustrate in the next section.

In addition to money demand, many other economic theories require the econometrician to make some assumptions about how expectations are formed. Arguments similar to those previously given can be applied, for example, to situations like the following:

1. How much wheat is planted by a farmer in any one season? The answer will depend on the price the farmer *anticipates* receiving at the end of the growing season. The adaptive expectations model implies that predictions about prices will be based on previous prices, with the most recent historical prices receiving the most weight.

2. The permanent income hypothesis suggests that consumption patterns are set not by current income, but by the expected *normal* level of income. How can the level of permanent income be measured? One way is to use adaptive expectations and assume that permanent income is a weighted average of current and all past incomes, as we now will illustrate.

### 15.5.2    AN EXAMPLE OF THE ADAPTIVE EXPECTATIONS MODEL

Consider the consumption function

$$c_t = \alpha + \beta y_t^* + e_t$$

where $c_t$ is measured consumption, $y_t^*$ is "normal" real income, and $e_t$ is a random disturbance. We assume that "normal" income is unobservable, but that it satisfies the adaptive expectations hypothesis equation 15.5.2 so that

$$y_t^* - y_{t-1}^* = \lambda(y_{t-1} - y_{t-1}^*)$$

Using equation 15.5.6 we have

$$c_t = \alpha\lambda + (1 - \lambda)c_{t-1} + \beta\lambda y_{t-1} + e_t - (1 - \lambda)e_{t-1}$$
$$(15.5.9)$$
$$= \beta_1 + \beta_2 c_{t-1} + \beta_3 y_{t-1} + v_t$$

where $\beta_1 = \lambda\alpha$, $\beta_2 = 1 - \lambda$, $\beta_3 = \beta\lambda$, and the random error $v_t = e_t - (1 - \lambda)e_{t-1}$.

To estimate this model we first replace $c_{t-1}$ by $\hat{c}_{t-1} = a_0 + a_1 y_{t-1} + a_2 y_{t-2}$, where the coefficients $a_0$, $a_1$ and $a_2$ are obtained by a simple least squares regression of $c_{t-1}$ on $y_{t-1}$ and $y_{t-2}$, which are the lagged values of the exogenous variable on the right-hand side of this equation. Then we estimate by least squares the model

$$c_t = \beta_1 + \beta_2 \hat{c}_{t-1} + \beta_3 y_{t-1} + error \qquad (15.5.10)$$

To illustrate we use data on consumption and income in Table 15.5. These data, in billions of 1954 dollars, span the period 1947.I–1960.IV, where I–IV are the first through fourth quarter, and are taken from a famous paper by Griliches et al. (1962, pp. 499–500). The two-stage least squares estimates of the parameters in equation 15.5.10 are given in Table 15.6. The standard errors we report are obtained using software designed to implement two-stage least squares and thus, they are correctly calculated. The estimates themselves are not directly of interest to us, but we can use them to solve for $\alpha$, $\beta$, and $\lambda$. Specifically,

$$\hat{\lambda} = 1 - \hat{\beta}_2 = 1 - .927 = .073$$

$$\hat{\beta} = \hat{\beta}_3 / \hat{\lambda} = .070/.073 = .959$$

$$\hat{\alpha} = \hat{\beta}_1 / \hat{\lambda} = 1.339/.073 = 18.342$$

The estimated value of the adjustment parameter $\lambda$ implies that we adjust our expectations about our normal income by approximately 7 percent of the difference between last year's income and the amount we expected last year. Furthermore, we estimate that $\beta$, the marginal propensity to consume out of normal income, is .96, implying that we spend, on average, $ .96 of each additional dollar of income.

*Table 15.5*  **Consumption and Income Data**

| | **Consumption** | | | | **Income** | | | |
|------|-------|-------|-------|-------|-------|-------|-------|-------|
| Year | **I** | **II** | **III** | **IV** | **I** | **II** | **III** | **IV** |
| 1947 | 192.5 | 196.1 | 196.9 | 197.0 | 202.3 | 197.1 | 202.9 | 202.2 |
| 1948 | 198.1 | 199.0 | 199.4 | 200.6 | 203.5 | 211.7 | 215.3 | 215.1 |
| 1949 | 199.9 | 203.6 | 204.8 | 209.0 | 212.9 | 213.9 | 214.0 | 214.9 |
| 1950 | 210.7 | 214.2 | 225.6 | 217.0 | 228.0 | 227.3 | 232.0 | 236.1 |
| 1951 | 223.3 | 214.5 | 217.5 | 219.8 | 230.9 | 236.3 | 239.1 | 240.8 |
| 1952 | 220.0 | 227.7 | 223.8 | 230.2 | 231.1 | 240.9 | 245.8 | 248.8 |
| 1953 | 234.0 | 236.2 | 236.0 | 234.1 | 253.3 | 256.1 | 255.9 | 255.9 |
| 1954 | 233.4 | 236.4 | 239.0 | 243.2 | 254.4 | 254.8 | 257.0 | 260.9 |
| 1955 | 248.7 | 253.7 | 259.9 | 261.8 | 263.0 | 271.5 | 276.5 | 281.4 |
| 1956 | 263.2 | 263.7 | 263.4 | 266.9 | 282.0 | 286.2 | 287.7 | 291.0 |
| 1957 | 268.9 | 270.4 | 273.4 | 272.1 | 291.1 | 294.6 | 296.1 | 293.3 |
| 1958 | 268.9 | 270.9 | 274.4 | 278.7 | 291.3 | 292.6 | 299.9 | 302.1 |
| 1959 | 283.8 | 289.7 | 290.8 | 292.8 | 305.9 | 312.5 | 311.3 | 313.2 |
| 1960 | 295.4 | 299.5 | 298.6 | 299.6 | 315.4 | 320.3 | 321.0 | 320.1 |

*Table 15.6*   **Estimates of Koyck Lag Model**

| Parameter | Estimate | Std. Error | $t$-Value | $p$-Value |
|-----------|----------|------------|-----------|-----------|
| $\beta_1$ | 1.339 | 8.347 | 0.160 | 0.873 |
| $\beta_2$ | 0.927 | 0.476 | 1.947 | 0.057 |
| $\beta_3$ | 0.070 | 0.415 | 0.169 | 0.867 |

## 15.6 An Infinite Distributed Lag Based on the Partial Adjustment Hypothesis

Another economic model that gives rise to a geometric lag is the **partial adjustment model.** It arises in situations such as the following. Suppose a firm is concerned about managing its level of inventories. A firm that does not have the optimal amount of inventory on hand faces two costs: the foregone profit from having too much or too little inventory and the cost of adjusting the current level of inventory to the optimal one. The adjustment may require obtaining new storage facilities, or finding a buyer for the current excess. To minimize costs the adjustment to the optimal level of inventories should be gradual. That is, suppose $y_t^*$ is the optimal level of inventories at time $t$. If $y_t$ is the actual level of inventories, then a possible adjustment is

$$y_t - y_{t-1} = \gamma(y_t^* - y_{t-1}) \tag{15.6.1}$$

where $0 < \gamma < 1$ is an adjustment coefficient. Equation 15.6.1 indicates that the change in inventories from period $t - 1$ to period $t$ is a *fraction* of the difference between the actual inventory level $y_{t-1}$ and the optimal inventory level $y_t^*$.

Suppose the optimal level of inventories is a function of the level of sales, $x_t$,

$$y_t^* = \alpha + \beta x_t + e_t \tag{15.6.2}$$

This relationship cannot be estimated, since $y_t^*$ is unobservable. However, we can use the partial adjustment relationship by substituting equation 15.6.2 into 15.6.1 to obtain

$$y_t - y_{t-1} = \gamma(y_t^* - y_{t-1}) = \gamma(\alpha + \beta x_t + e_t - y_{t-1})$$
$$= \gamma\alpha + \gamma\beta x_t - \gamma y_{t-1} + \gamma e_t \tag{15.6.3}$$

Solving equation 15.6.3 for $y_t$ we have

$$y_t = \gamma\alpha + (1 - \gamma)y_{t-1} + \gamma\beta x_t + \gamma e_t$$
$$= \beta_1 + \beta_2 y_{t-1} + \beta_3 x_t + v_t \tag{15.6.4}$$

The partial adjustment model leads to a lagged dependent variable model similar to equation 15.4.2. The significant difference here is that the error term $v_t$ does not involve $e_{t-1}$ and it is not correlated with the lagged dependent variable $y_{t-1}$ on the right-side of the equation. Thus, the least squares procedure can be used to consistently estimate the parameters of 15.6.4.

Another important application of the partial adjustment model is to the study of investment behavior. If the optimal level of the capital stock $y_t^*$ is a function of firm output, then the partial adjustment hypothesis equation 15.6.1 implies that the change in the capital stock between periods $t - 1$ and $t$ is proportional to the difference between the desired level of capital stock and the level in period $t - 1$. Equation 15.6.4 then relates the amount of capital at time $t$ to the level of output and the level of capital in period $t - 1$. For this particular application, the model in equation 15.6.4 is often modified by lagging it one period and subtracting the result from that equation. The change in the level of the capital stock $(y_t - y_{t-1})$ is investment in period $t$, $inv_t$. The model then becomes

$$
\begin{aligned}
y_t - y_{t-1} = inv_t &= [\gamma\alpha + (1 - \gamma)y_{t-1} + \gamma\beta x_t + \gamma e_t] \\
&\quad - [\gamma\alpha + (1 - \gamma)y_{t-2} + \gamma\beta x_{t-1} + \gamma e_{t-1}] \\
&= (1 - \gamma)(y_{t-1} - y_{t-2}) + \gamma\beta(x_t - x_{t-1}) + \gamma(e_t - e_{t-1}) \quad (15.6.5) \\
&= (1 - \gamma)inv_{t-1} + \gamma\beta(x_t - x_{t-1}) + \gamma(e_t - e_{t-1})
\end{aligned}
$$

Or, adding an intercept,

$$ inv_t = \beta_1 + \beta_2 inv_{t-1} + \beta_3(x_t - x_{t-1}) + v_t \quad (15.6.6) $$

This model of investment is called the **flexible accelerator model.** It relates the *level* of investment to the level of investment in the previous period and the *change* in the level of output.

Note, however, that the last simplification has produced a model in which the error term $v_t$ is correlated with the lagged value of investment on the right-hand side of the equation. Thus, we should not estimate equation 15.6.6 by least squares, but we can estimate it using *2SLS*.

## 15.7 Summing Up

In this chapter we modeled dynamic economic relationships of the form $y_t = f(x_t, x_{t-1}, x_{t-2}, \ldots)$. In these models the effect of a change in $x_t$ persists into future periods. We considered several models:

1.  In the finite distributed lag model $y_t = \alpha + \sum_{i=0}^{n} \beta_i x_{t-i} + e_t$, the effect of a change in $x$ on $y$ lasts only $n$ periods. In this model we must choose the length of the lag, $n$. Usually least squares estimation is plagued by multicollinearity. Consequently, restrictions are often placed on the parameters $\beta_i$ such that they fall on a polynomial of a low degree. Such models are called Almon distributed

lags, and they provide more precise parameter estimates than least squares. However, the Almon estimator is subject to bias.

2.  The general infinite lag model is $y_t = \alpha + \sum_{i=0}^{\infty} \beta_i x_{t-i} + e_t$. The parameters of this model cannot be estimated unless additional structure is imposed.

3.  The geometric infinite distributed lag model incorporates the assumption that the lag weights decline geometrically, $\beta_i = \beta \phi^i$, $|\phi| < 1$.

4.  The geometric lag model is estimated by applying the Koyck transformation (section 15.4) to obtain $y_t = \beta_1 + \beta_2 y_{t-1} + \beta_3 x_t + v_t$. The least squares estimator of this model is biased and inconsistent due to the correlation between the lagged dependent variable and the error term. However, the two-stage least squares estimator is consistent. In the first stage the lagged variable $y_{t-1}$ is regressed against $x_{t-1}$ and the predicted value $\hat{y}_{t-1}$ is obtained. In the second stage $\hat{y}_{t-1}$ is substituted into the Koyck model and least squares is applied to the resulting model.

5.  In the adaptive expectations model a dependent variable is taken to be a function of an unobservable variable, $y_t = \alpha + \beta x_t^* + e_t$. Adaptive expectations imply that $x_t^* = \lambda x_{t-1} + (1 - \lambda)x_{t-1}^*$. Applying the Koyck transformation, we obtain $y_t = \beta_1 + \beta_2 y_{t-1} + \beta_3 x_{t-1} + v_t$. Least squares estimation is again inconsistent. In the first stage of two-stage least squares, we regress $y_{t-1}$ on $x_{t-2}$. The predicted value $\hat{y}_{t-1}$ of $y_{t-1}$ is then substituted into the Koyck model and least squares is applied.

6.  In the partial adjustment model $y_t^* = \alpha + \beta x_t + e_t$, and the dependent variable $y_t^*$ is unobservable. We assume the adjustment process $y_t - y_{t-1} = \gamma(y_t^* - y_{t-1})$. Applying the Koyck transformation we obtain $y_t = \beta_1 + \beta_2 y_{t-1} + \beta_3 x_t + v_t$. This lagged dependent variable model *can* be estimated by least squares, because the error term is not correlated with any variable on the right-hand side of the equation.

## *15.8* Exercises

15.1  Consider the consumption example in section 15.5.2. Using the data in Table 15.5 and your two-stage least squares software, obtain the estimates for the Koyck Model reported in Table 15.6.

15.2  Verify the results in Table 15.6. First, obtain the estimated values $a_0$ and $a_1$ by a simple least squares regression of $c_{t-1}$ on $y_{t-2}$. Construct $\hat{c}_{t-1} = a_0 + a_1 y_{t-2}$. Then estimate by least squares the model 15.5.10.

15.3  Using the data in Table 15.5, estimate model 15.5.10. Modify the procedure described in the text in the following way. In the first stage of two-stage least squares, estimate by least squares the model $c_{t-1} = a_0 + a_1 y_{t-2} + a_2 y_{t-3} + error$. Construct $\hat{c}_{t-1} = a_0 + a_1 y_{t-2} + a_2 y_{t-3}$ using the estimated values of $a_0$, $a_1$ and $a_2$ from the first stage. Compare these results to those in Table 15.6.

15.4  In the file *adaptive.dat* are quarterly data on real per capita consumption and real per capita disposable income from 1947.I to 1980.IV. Use these data on consumption and income to estimate the adaptive expectations model in section 15.5.2. Compare the results to those in Table 15.6.

15.5 Equation 15.6.4 is a lagged dependent variable model based on the partial adjustment hypothesis. Lag this equation repeatedly and replace the lagged dependent variable on the right-hand side to produce a geometric lag model. Compare the resulting model to equation 15.3.3.

15.6 Consider the consumption data in Table 15.5. Assume that a finite distributed lag model has been specified, such that $c_t = \alpha + \sum_{i=0}^{n} \beta_i y_{t-i} + e_t$ with $n = 12$.

    (a) Estimate the unrestricted finite distributed lag model.

    (b) Estimate the finite lag imposing an arithmetic lag. Carry out an $F$-test of the imposed restrictions. See the last paragraph of section 15.2.4 for a discussion in the context of arithmetic lags.

    (c) Estimate the finite lag imposing an Almon polynomial distributed lag of order 3. Carry out an $F$-test of the imposed restrictions.

    (d) Discuss the estimates obtained in parts (a) through (c).

15.7 In section 15.2.5 we assumed that the length $n$ of the finite lag was 8 periods. If the maximum length of the lag we are willing to consider is $N = 12$ periods, evaluate the information criteria $AIC$ and $SC$ for lags of lengths $n = 6, 7, \ldots,$ 12 using the data in Table 15.1. What lag length minimizes these criteria?

15.8 In Exercise 15.6 we assumed that the length $n$ of the finite lag was 12 periods. If the maximum length of the lag we are willing to consider is $N = 18$ periods, evaluate the information criteria $AIC$ and $SC$ for lags of lengths $n = 8,$ 9, $\cdots$, 18. What lag length minimizes these criteria?

15.9 The least squares estimates for the finite lag model discussed in section 15.2.2 are contained in Table 15.2. Calculate the simple correlations among the current and lagged capital appropriations variables $x_t, x_{t-1}, \ldots, x_{t-8}$. Based on these correlations, does multicollinearity appear to be a severe problem in this model?

## *15.9* References

ALMON, S. (1965). "The Distributed Lag Between Capital Appropriations and Expectations." *Econometrica, 33,* 178–196.

DURBIN, J. (1970). "Testing for Serial Correlation in Least-Squares Regression When Some of the Regressors Are Lagged Dependent Variables." *Econometrica,* 38, 410–421.

FISHER, I. (1957). "Note on a Short-Cut Method for Calculating Distributed Lags," *Bulletin de L'Institut International de Statistique, 29,* pp. 323–328.

GRIFFITHS, W. E., R. C. HILL, AND G. G. JUDGE (1993). *Learning and Practicing Econometrics.* New York: John Wiley and Sons, Chapter 21.

GRILICHES, Z., G. S. MADDALA, R. LUCAS, AND N. WALLACE (1962). "Notes on Estimated Aggregate Quarterly Consumption Functions." *Econometrica,* 30, 491–500.

GUJARATI, D. (1995). *Basic Econometrics* (3d ed.). New York: McGraw-Hill, Chapter 17.

KOYCK, L. M. (1954). *Distributed Lags and Investment Analysis,* Amsterdam: North-Holland.

MIRER, THAD W. (1995). *Economic Statistics and Econometrics* (3d ed.). Englewood Cliffs, NJ: Prentice Hall, pp. 345–356.

PINDYCK, ROBERT S., AND D. L. RUBINFELD (1991). *Econometric Models and Economic Forecasts* (3d ed.). New York: McGraw-Hill, pp. 204–215.

RAMANATHAN, RAMU (1995). *Introductory Econometrics with Applications* (3d ed.). Fort Worth, TX: The Dryden Press.

# Chapter 16

# Time–Series Analysis

One objective of analyzing economic data is to predict or forecast the future values of economic variables. The econometric model building approach we have used in the preceding chapters for obtaining forecasts is to: (1) formulate an economic model that explains the behavior of a variable of interest; (2) construct a statistical model that is thought to be consistent with the data; (3) use a sample of data, and an appropriate estimation procedure, to estimate the unknown parameters of the statistical model; and (4) use the estimated model to forecast the variable of interest.

In this chapter we focus on a different technique that may be useful in short-term forecasting situations. Instead of building an economic and statistical model that relates the values of an economic variable to a set of explanatory variables, the *time-series approach* that we discuss in this chapter relates current values of an economic variable to its past values, possibly past values of other variables that we also wish to forecast, and the values of current and past random errors. Models that relate the current value of a variable *only* to past values of itself and current and past errors are called **univariate time-series models.** Models within this class that are discussed in this chapter are autoregressive processes, moving-average processes, and autoregressive integrated moving-average processes. Models where past values of a number of variables are used to explain movements in the current values of all these variables jointly are called **multivariate time-series models.** Vector autoregressions, which we discuss later in this chapter, belong to this class of models. With time-series models, the emphasis is on making use of the information in the past values of a variable for forecasting its future values. These methods offer the possibility of making accurate forecasts, even when the underlying economic model is unknown. A particular time-series model can be chosen from information provided by the data, rather than from information provided by both theory and data, as is the case with conventional econometric models. We will not describe in depth all the techniques of time-series analysis—we could easily spend an entire semester on this topic. (You might investigate course offerings in your department to see if a time-series or economic forecasting course is offered.)

## *16.1* Autoregressive Processes

One example of a univariate time-series model where a random variable is related to past values of itself and random errors is an autoregressive model or process. The most elementary form of an autoregressive model is the following model of order 1:

$$y_t = \delta + \theta_1 y_{t-1} + e_t, \qquad t = 1, 2, \ldots, T \qquad (16.1.1)$$

In this model $\delta$ is an intercept parameter, $\theta_1$ is an unknown parameter that is assumed to take a value between $-1$ and $1$, and $e_t$ is an uncorrelated random error with mean zero and constant variance $\sigma_e^2$. Equation 16.1.1 is an autoregressive time-series model of the *first* order since $y_t$ depends only on its value in the previous period, $y_{t-1}$, plus a random error $e_t$. This specification is denoted as an AR(1) time series model, or AR(1) *process.*

This is not the first time we have encountered the first-order autoregressive process. In chapter 11 we dealt with the problem of autocorrelation in the context of the linear regression model. In that chapter it was the unobservable random error that was assumed to follow an AR(1) process, and the zero mean of the error term meant that there was no intercept parameter. Now, it is the observable variable $y_t$ that is assumed to follow an AR(1) process, and we allow for the possibility of a nonzero mean through the parameter $\delta$.

More general versions of AR processes exist. Specifically, $y_t$ may not only depend on $y_{t-1}$, but also on $y_{t-2}$, $y_{t-3}$, and so on. To allow for these more general dependencies, we introduce the statistical model of an autoregressive process of order $p$, which we denote AR($p$), and write as

$$y_t = \delta + \theta_1 y_{t-1} + \theta_2 y_{t-2} + \cdots + \theta_p y_{t-p} + e_t \qquad (16.1.2)$$

where $\delta$ is an intercept parameter that is related to the mean of $y_t$, the $\theta_i$s are the unknown autoregressive parameters, and the errors $e_t$ are assumed to be uncorrelated random variables with mean zero and variance $\sigma_e^2$.

The parameters $\delta$ and $\theta_1, \theta_2, \ldots, \theta_p$ in an AR model can be estimated using least squares. Having explanatory variables that are lagged values of the left-hand-side variable means that least squares is no longer the best linear unbiased estimator; but it does have good properties in large samples, including consistency.

As an example of an AR(2) process we use data on U.S. quarterly unemployment rates (seasonally adjusted) from first quarter 1948 through first quarter 1978. There are 121 observations. They are stored in the file *unempl.dat* and are taken from Cryer (1986). Using these data, the least squares estimated AR(2) model, with standard errors in parentheses, is

$$\hat{y}_t = \underset{(0.1267)}{0.5051} + \underset{(0.0707)}{1.5537}\, y_{t-1} - \underset{(0.0708)}{0.6515}\, y_{t-2} \qquad (16.1.3)$$

The unemployment rate is positively related to the rate in the previous quarter and negatively related to the rate two quarters ago. All coefficient estimates are significantly different from zero.

A natural question at this point in time is: Why choose $p = 2$ as the order of the AR lag used to model the unemployment data? There are several methods for assessing the appropriate order; books on time-series analysis go into these methods in detail. One such device is the **partial autocorrelation function.** The partial autocorrelation function is the sequence of correlations between ($y_t$ and $y_{t-1}$), ($y_t$ and $y_{t-2}$), ($y_t$ and $y_{t-3}$), and so on, *given that the effects of earlier lags on $y_t$ are held constant.* For example, the partial autocorrelation between $y_t$ and $y_{t-2}$ has the effect of $y_{t-1}$ on $y_t$ "subtracted out" or held constant; the partial correlation between $y_t$ and $y_{t-3}$ has the effects of $y_{t-1}$ and $y_{t-2}$ on $y_t$ held constant. The partial autocorrelation function for the first twelve lags of the unemployment data series is depicted diagrammatically in Figure 16.1. Note that partial autocorrelations at lags 1 and 2 are relatively large, going well beyond the bounds given by the "+" signs; the partial autocorrelations beyond lag 2 are relatively small. The "+" signs represent statistical significance bounds; autocorrelations larger than these bounds are significantly different from zero. Thus, the unemployment data have significant partial autocorrelations at lags 1 and 2, but no significant partial autocorrelations beyond lag 2. These results suggest that an AR(2) model is appropriate. In general, this modeling strategy says to choose the highest lag with a significant partial autocorrelation as the order of the AR model. Other strategies are to choose the order that minimizes Akaike's $AIC$ criterion or the one that minimizes Schwarz's $SC$ criterion. These criteria were discussed in chapter 15.

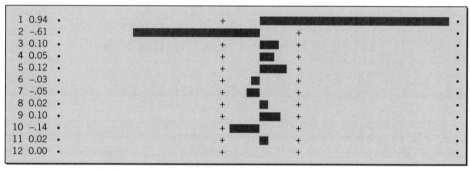

FIGURE **16.1** Partial autocorrelation function for unemployment data

How do we use the estimated AR model for forecasting? Using $t = 1, 2, \ldots, T$ to denote observations for the unemployment data model, the last two observations in the series are

$$y_{T-1} = 6.63 \qquad y_T = 6.20$$

Using these values, forecasts for the unemployment rate in the next three quarters are computed as follows.

$$\hat{y}_{T+1} = \hat{\delta} + \hat{\theta}_1 y_T + \hat{\theta}_2 y_{T-1}$$

$$= 0.5051 + (1.5537)(6.2) - (0.6515)(6.63)$$

$$= 5.8186$$

$$\hat{y}_{T+2} = \hat{\delta} + \hat{\theta}_1 \hat{y}_{T+1} + \theta_2 y_T$$

$$= (0.5051) + (1.5537)(5.8186) - (0.6515)(6.2)$$

$$= 5.5062$$

$$\hat{y}_{T+3} = \hat{\delta} + \hat{\theta}_1 \hat{y}_{T+2} + \hat{\theta}_2 \hat{y}_{T+1}$$

$$= (0.5051) + (1.5537)(5.5062) - (0.6515)(5.8186)$$

$$= 5.2693$$

For predicting one period ahead, we use actual values on the right-hand side. After that, we must start using the predictions from the earlier periods. AR(2) models are often used to describe cyclical behavior. The preceding predictions suggest that we are in the downward phase of an unemployment cycle.

## *16.2* Moving-Average Processes

In autoregressive processes the current value of a time series $y_t$ is expressed as a linear function of a finite number of lags of itself, $y_{t-1}, y_{t-2}, \ldots, y_{t-p}$. There is another class of models or processes known as *moving-average processes* where $y_t$ is written as a linear function of a finite number of lags of uncorrelated errors. Specifically, a moving-average model of order $q$, denoted by MA($q$), is written as

$$y_t = \mu + e_t + \alpha_1 e_{t-1} + \alpha_2 e_{t-2} + \cdots + \alpha_q e_{t-q} \qquad (16.2.1)$$

where the $e_t$ are uncorrelated, unobservable random errors with zero mean and constant variance $\sigma_e^2$. The constants $\mu, \alpha_1, \alpha_2, \ldots, \alpha_q$ are unknown constants that describe the relationship.

If an MA process is being used to model a data series, its parameters can be estimated using nonlinear least squares. For example, the parameters $\mu$ and $\alpha_1$ in the MA(1) process

$$y_t = \mu + e_t + \alpha_1 e_{t-1} \qquad (16.2.2)$$

can be estimated by minimizing

$$S(\mu, \alpha_1) = \sum_{t=1}^{T} e_t^2 = \sum_{t=1}^{T} (y_t - \mu - \alpha_1 e_{t-1})^2 \qquad (16.2.3)$$

At first glance, minimization of equation 16.2.3 appears to be a linear least squares problem. However, nonlinearities arise because there is a feedback from $e_{t-1}$ to $e_t$ when equation 16.2.3 is being computed. Fortunately, special computer programs that will obtain nonlinear least squares estimates of the moving-average parameters are available.

To illustrate a moving-average process, we use first differences of data on daily closing prices of IBM common stock. We use 180 observations taken from Box and Jenkins (1976). They are stored in the file *ibm.dat*. Let $z_0, z_1, z_2, \ldots, z_{179}$ be the daily closing prices. The first differences are defined as

$$y_t = z_t - z_{t-1}, \quad t = 1, 2, \ldots, 179 \qquad (16.2.4)$$

Taking differences like we have done in equation 16.2.4 is a common procedure for converting a *nonstationary* series to a *stationary* one. More will be said on this point in the next section.

The $y_t$ can be modeled as an MA(1) process; the nonlinear least squares estimated equation is

$$\hat{y}_t = 0.5460 + e_t + 0.2742\ e_{t-1} \qquad (16.2.5)$$
$$(0.4923) \qquad (0.0722)$$

The coefficient of $e_{t-1}$ is significantly different from zero, but the intercept estimate is not. Modeling $y_t$ with a zero intercept (and hence a zero mean) might be adequate.

In the previous section we discovered that the order of an AR process can be assessed by examining the partial autocorrelation function of the data series. The order of an MA process can be chosen in a similar way, but this time we examine what is called the **autocorrelation function,** not the partial autocorrelation function. The autocorrelation function is a similar concept. It gives the sequence of correlations between ($y_t$ and $y_{t-1}$), ($y_t$ and $y_{t-2}$), ($y_t$ and $y_{t-3}$), and so on, *without* holding the effects of intermediate lags constant. The autocorrelation function for the differenced IBM data, for the first twelve lags, is depicted in Figure 16.2. The largest lag with a significant autocorrelation is lag 1, suggesting that a lag order of $q = 1$ is appropriate for an MA model.

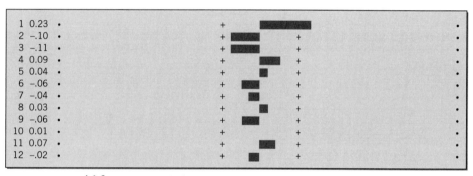

```
 1 0.23  ·              +        ████████████     ·
 2 -.10  ·              +    ████        +         ·
 3 -.11  ·              +    ████        +         ·
 4 0.09  ·              +      ██        +         ·
 5 0.04  ·              +       █        +         ·
 6 -.06  ·              +     ███        +         ·
 7 -.04  ·              +      ██        +         ·
 8 0.03  ·              +       █        +         ·
 9 -.06  ·              +     ███        +         ·
10 0.01  ·              +                +         ·
11 0.07  ·              +        ██      +         ·
12 -.02  ·              +      █         +         ·
```

*FIGURE 16.2*   Autocorrelation function of differenced IBM stock price data

To illustrate how this model can be used to forecast the stock price, we first must recognize that it is $z_{T+1}$, $z_{T+2}$, ... that are of direct interest, not the differences $y_{T+1}$, $y_{T+2}$, .... Substituting equation 16.2.4 into equation 16.2.5 gives

$$\hat{z}_t - z_{t-1} = 0.5460 + e_t + 0.2742\ e_{t-1}$$

The equation on which we base forecasts is

$$\hat{z}_t = z_{t-1} + 0.5460 + 0.2742\ e_{t-1} \qquad (16.2.6)$$

We have omitted $e_t$; since $e_t$ is not correlated with anything that has happened in the past, the best forecast of its value is its mean zero. The last value in the data series is $z_T = 558$ and the last (nonlinear) least squares residual is $\hat{e}_T = 0.38007$. Using this information and equation 16.2.6, we can forecast the next two days beyond the sample period.

$$\hat{z}_{T+1} = z_T + 0.5460 + 0.2742\,\hat{e}_T$$

$$= 558 + 0.5460 + (0.2742)(0.38007)$$

$$= 558.7$$

$$\hat{z}_{T+2} = \hat{z}_{T+1} + 0.5460 + 0.2742\,\hat{e}_{T+1}$$

$$= 558.7 + 0.5460 + (0.2742)0$$

$$= 559.2$$

After forecasting for the first period, the error term makes no contribution. Our best guess for $\hat{e}_{T+1}$, $\hat{e}_{T+2}$, etc. is zero.

### 16.2.1 AUTOREGRESSIVE MOVING-AVERAGE PROCESSES

A more general class of models known as autoregressive moving-average (ARMA) models can be created by combining the autoregressive and moving-average components of the previous two models. For example, an ARMA(1,2) model, with one autoregressive lag and two moving-average lags, can be written as

$$y_t = \delta + \theta_1 y_{t-1} + e_t + \alpha_1 e_{t-1} + \alpha_2 e_{t-2} \tag{16.2.7}$$

Software packages that estimate models of this type, and that use the estimated model for forecasting, are available.

## *16.3* Integrated Nonstationary Processes

For a data series to be adequately modeled using an AR, an MA, or an ARMA model, it must be *stationary*. A stationary time series is one whose mean, variance, and autocorrelation function do not change over time. This condition is violated by data that tend to trend upward or downward over time. Since trending data are very common in economics, we frequently encounter what are called *nonstationary* data series. Fortunately, many nonstationary time series can be transformed to stationary time series by differencing them one or more times. Such time series are called **integrated nonstationary processes.** The number of times $d$ that an integrated process must be differenced to be stationary is said to be the *order* of the integrated process. Because the IBM price data were stationary after differencing once, this series is integrated of order 1. We often say simply that the IBM data is I(1).

The autocorrelation function provides evidence of a nonstationary series. Typically, such series exhibit large significant autocorrelations for many lags. See, for example, the autocorrelation function for the *original* IBM series depicted in Figure 16.3.

**Unit root tests** provide another basis for assessing whether a time series is nonstationary and integrated of a particular order. To illustrate how they work, consider the process used to model the IBM data, namely

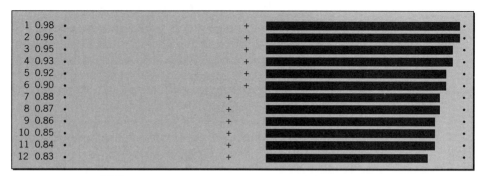

| 1 | 0.98 |
| 2 | 0.96 |
| 3 | 0.95 |
| 4 | 0.93 |
| 5 | 0.92 |
| 6 | 0.90 |
| 7 | 0.88 |
| 8 | 0.87 |
| 9 | 0.86 |
| 10 | 0.85 |
| 11 | 0.84 |
| 12 | 0.83 |

*FIGURE* **16.3**  Autocorrelation function of original IBM stock price data

$$y_t = z_t - z_{t-1} = \mu + e_t + \alpha_1 e_{t-1} \qquad (16.3.1)$$

This model can also be written as

$$z_t = \theta_1 z_{t-1} + \mu + e_t + \alpha_1 e_{t-1} \qquad (16.3.2)$$

where $\theta_1 = 1$. Having $\theta_1 = 1$ is what we call a **unit root,** so named because it is the root of a polynomial. Also, it is the fact that $\theta_1 = 1$ that makes $z_t$ a nonstationary I(1) series. If $-1 < \theta_1 < 1$, equation 16.3.2 describes a stationary time-series process that has a first-order AR component and a first-order MA component. In other words, it is an ARMA(1,1) model. Thus, to assess whether $z_t$ is a nonstationary I(1) series, we can test $H_0$: $\theta_1 = 1$ against the alternative $H_1$: $-1 < \theta_1 < 1$. Tests for this purpose are called unit root tests.

It is convenient to subtract $z_{t-1}$ from both sides of equation 16.3.2 to obtain

$$z_t - z_{t-1} = (\theta_1 - 1)z_{t-1} + \mu + e_t + \alpha_1 e_{t-1}$$

$$\Delta z_t = \theta_1^* z_{t-1} + \mu + e_t + \alpha_1 e_{t-1} \qquad (16.3.3)$$

where $\Delta z_t = z_t - z_{t-1}$ and $\theta_1^* = \theta_1 - 1$. Unit root tests are usually performed in terms of $\theta_1^*$ with the null and alternative hypotheses:

$$H_0: \theta_1^* = 0 \qquad H_1: \theta_1^* < 0 \qquad (16.3.4)$$

This test is implemented by special computer programs. The precise way in which it is carried out depends on how additional terms in the model (such as $\alpha_1 e_{t-1}$) are treated in the estimation process. It also depends on whether the model includes a deterministic trend, and on which of two test statistics are chosen. Named after their inventors, the alternative test statistics are the Dickey–Fuller test and the Phillips–Perron test. With the IBM data, no deterministic trend, and two additional lag terms (see Griffiths, Hill and Judge (1993), p. 699), the value of the Dickey–Fuller test statistic is $-1.80$; the 10 percent critical value is $-2.57$. Thus, we fail to reject $H_0$. The estimate of $\theta_1^*$ is not significantly negative. We proceed under the assumption that a unit root does exist and therefore differencing the data is appropriate.

## *16.4* Autoregressive Integrated Moving–Average Models

In the preceding sections we introduced autoregressive (AR) models, moving-average (MA) models, and nonstationary integrated (I) time series. A general model that includes all these components is an **autoregressive integrated moving-average model** of order $(p, d, q)$. Given that $y_t$ is the data series obtained by differencing the original model $d$ times, an ARIMA $(p, d, q)$ model can be written as

$$y_t = \delta + \theta_1 y_{t-1} + \cdots + \theta_p y_{t-p} + e_t + \alpha_1 e_{t-1} + \cdots + \alpha_q e_{t-q} \qquad (16.4.1)$$

In terms of this notation, the AR(2) model we used for the unemployment data series would be written as ARIMA(2,0,0); the differenced MA(1) model used for the IBM data becomes ARIMA(0,1,1).

We have described how the partial autocorrelation function can be used to "identify" the order $p$ of an AR process, how the autocorrelation function can be used to identify the order $q$ of an MA process, and how to identify a nonstationary integrated process. In practice we must also choose between AR and MA processes, and possibly a combined ARMA process. Such choices are usually made on the basis of autocorrelation and partial autocorrelation functions, as well as post-estimation diagnostic checking. In general, the Box–Jenkins approach to model-building and forecasting can be described as one with the following four steps:

1. *Identification.* Appropriate values for $p$, $d$, and $q$ are found by examining various autocorrelations and partial autocorrelations, which are summarized in numerical or graphical forms called **correlograms.**

2. *Estimation.* Having selected appropriate values for $p$, $d$, and $q$, the model parameters are estimated, usually using least squares or nonlinear least squares.

3. *Diagnostic Checking.* Does the estimated model fit the data well? If it does, and if the calculated residuals exhibit no autocorrelation, then all is well and good. If the estimated residuals are not uncorrelated with constant variance, then we need to go back to the drawing board and choose new values of $p$, $d$, and $q$. This process of identification, estimation, and checking continues until a satisfactory model is selected.

4. *Forecasting.* Once we have a model with which we are happy, we can use it to forecast future values of $y_t$. The Box–Jenkins methodology is most useful for *short-term* forecasting.

## *16.5* Vector Autoregressive (VAR) Models

A **vector autoregressive model,** or VAR for short, is a time-series model used to forecast values of two or more economic variables. It is an extension of the AR model in section 16.1 that considers only one economic variable at a time. Furthermore, it is related to simultaneous equations models in that the variables are considered to be endogenous and jointly determined. Unlike simultaneous equations models, however, the VAR model uses only past regularities and patterns in historical data as a basis for forecasting. No structural model is built. Because no simultaneous equations model is needed, VAR models provide a convenient basis for forecasting within subregions of the country or at the state level. For example, the Federal Reserve Banks in the United States have constructed VAR models to forecast outcomes in the regions that they serve (Anderson, 1979) or in a particular state (Fomby and Hirschberg, 1989). They can do this without building a simultaneous equations model of their region and trying to integrate it into a national model.

Suppose $x_t$ and $y_t$ are economic variables whose values we wish to forecast. A VAR model for these variables is given by these equations.

$$y_t = \theta_0 + \theta_1 y_{t-1} + \cdots + \theta_p y_{t-p} + \phi_1 x_{t-1} + \phi_2 x_{t-2} + \cdots + \phi_p x_{t-p} + e_t$$
$$x_t = \delta_0 + \delta_1 y_{t-1} + \cdots + \delta_p y_{t-p} + \alpha_1 x_{t-1} + \alpha_2 x_{t-2} + \cdots + \alpha_p x_{t-p} + u_t$$

(16.5.1)

In this model, the current value of a variable $y_t$, is explained by lagged values of itself *and lagged values of the variable x,* plus a random error $e_t$. Thus, the AR($p$) model in equation 16.1.2 has been extended by adding $p$ lags of the variable $x$. Note that the current value of $y_t$ does *not* depend directly on the current value $x_t$, and thus, the two-equation model 16.5.1 is not a simultaneous equations model. The random disturbance $e_t$ is assumed to have zero mean, constant variance $\sigma_e^2$, and to be serially uncorrelated.

Similarly, the value of $x_t$ is explained by its own lagged values, the lagged values of $y_t$ and the random disturbance $u_t$. The random disturbance $u_t$ is assumed to have mean zero, constant variance $\sigma_u^2$, and to be serially uncorrelated. Each of the variables $x_t$ and $y_t$ is explained by its lagged values, but no other economic variables are involved. Thus, the VAR model captures the historical patterns of each variable and its relationship to the other.

One interesting additional assumption of this model involves the relationship between the random errors $e_t$ and $u_t$. These random errors include economic shocks to $x_t$ and $y_t$ from factors outside the two-equation system. These shocks might arise from changes in government policies, national and international events, and random factors not in the model. Since many of the same shocks may be included in both $e_t$ and $u_t$, it is possible that these two random errors are *correlated*. As we discovered when discussing seemingly unrelated regressions in chapter 12, such correlation is called *contemporaneous correlation*. The two equations in 16.5.1 can be viewed as a seemingly unrelated regression system where the same explanatory variables appear in each equation. Having identical explanatory variables means that joint estimation is not better than separate least squares estimation of each equation. Both techniques yield the same answers. Thus, *the parameters of the VAR model can be consistently estimated by least squares, one equation at a time.*

The VAR model specified in equation 16.5.1 is called a two-dimensional vector autoregressive model of order $p$; it is denoted by VAR($p$). It is called two-dimensional because it contains two variables and two equations; its dimension can be increased by adding more variables and more equations. It is of order $p$ because it contains lags up to order $p$. One problem of model specification is selecting the length of lag. As for univariate time-series models and distributed lag models, a variety of criteria are used, including the *AIC* and *SC* criteria. No one method has been found to be *best,* and there is a possibility of a misspecification when using any method.

As an example of a two-dimensional VAR model, we consider U.S. quarterly data on real per capita disposable income (*DI*) and *nondurable* consumption (*NC*) stored in the file *macrovar.dat.* There are 136 observations beginning with the first quarter in 1947 and ending with the fourth quarter of 1980. An examination of the *DI* and *NC* series along the lines suggested in earlier sections of this chapter reveals that both can be regarded as nonstationary I(1) time series. Before proceeding with estimation, we take first differences

$$y_t = DI_t - DI_{t-1} \qquad x_t = NC_t - NC_{t-1}$$

so that the resulting series ($y_t$, $x_t$) will be stationary. The least squares estimated first-order VAR, with standard errors in parentheses, is

$$\hat{y}_t = \begin{matrix} 34.58 \\ (7.25) \end{matrix} - \begin{matrix} 0.1577 \ y_{t-1} \\ (0.0877) \end{matrix} + \begin{matrix} 1.330 \ x_{t-1} \\ (0.2863) \end{matrix}$$

$$\hat{x}_t = \begin{matrix} 4.799 \\ (2.310) \end{matrix} + \begin{matrix} 0.0565 \ y_{t-1} \\ (0.0279) \end{matrix} + \begin{matrix} 0.0498 \ x_{t-1} \\ (0.0912) \end{matrix}$$

With the exception of the standard error of the coefficient of $x_{t-1}$ in the second equation, all standard errors are relatively small, indicating estimates that are moderately precise. Experimenting with longer lags than 1 did not appear to improve the model. The way in which the equations can be used for forecasting is a straightforward extension of the univariate forecasting methodology that was described in the earlier sections.

Unlike the univariate AR model, in the VAR case the presence of I(1) variables does not always mean the model should be estimated with variables expressed in terms of first differences. This matter is taken up in the next section.

## *16.6* Nonstationary Series and Cointegration

Let us return to the file *macrovar.dat* that contains quarterly observations on real per capita consumption *C*, nondurable consumption *NC*, and disposable income *DI*. In the previous section we estimated a VAR model involving nondurable consumption and income. Suppose, now, that we are interested in the relationship between (total) consumption and income, and that we set up the regression equation

$$C_t = \beta_1 + \beta_2 DI_t + \varepsilon_t \tag{16.6.1}$$

Suppose, also, that our investigations reveal that $C_t$ and $DI_t$ are both nonstationary I(1) series. It is reasonable to expect that $\varepsilon_t = C_t - \beta_1 - \beta_2 DI_t$ will also be I(1). If so, is it suitable to proceed with least squares estimation of the consumption function? The answer is no. If $\varepsilon_t$ is I(1), it cannot be a serially uncorrelated random error with constant variance; it will be autocorrelated and its variance will change over time. Specifically, $\varepsilon_t$ being I(1) implies that we can write

$$\varepsilon_t = \varepsilon_{t-1} + \upsilon_t \tag{16.6.2}$$

where $\upsilon_t$ is a stationary, not necessarily serially uncorrelated, random error. Also, we can view equation 16.6.2 as having an AR component with a unit root. That is,

$$\varepsilon_t = \theta_1 \varepsilon_{t-1} + \upsilon_t \tag{16.6.3}$$

where $\theta_1 = 1$.

These properties of $\varepsilon_t$ mean that least squares is not a suitable estimation technique. Granger and Newbold have shown that, under these circumstances, least squares is likely to produce an apparently highly significant relationship between $C_t$ and $DI_t$, even when $\beta_2 = 0$. They called such instances **spurious regressions.** Although spurious regressions are a potential problem, the nature of the error term in equation 16.6.3 is such that they should be detected by a low Durbin–Watson statistic.

The fact that $C_t$ and $DI_t$ are I(1) does not always imply that the error $\varepsilon_t$ is also I(1). In fact, it is possible that the error be stationary or I(0). If so, we say that $C_t$ and $DI_t$ are *cointegrated.* Cointegration implies that $C_t$ and $DI_t$ have similar stochastic trends; they exhibit a *long-term equilibrium* relationship that is defined by $C_t = \beta_1 + \beta_2 DI_t$ and $\varepsilon_t$ represents a short-term deviation from that equilibrium relationship. If $C_t$ and $DI_t$ are cointegrated, least squares estimation of the consumption function yields consistent estimates of $\beta_1$ and $\beta_2$.

How do we detect whether $C_t$ and $DI_t$ are cointegrated? One way is to estimate equation 16.6.1 by least squares, get the residuals $\hat{\varepsilon}_t$ and test to see if $\hat{\varepsilon}_t$ has a unit root, like the procedure followed in section 16.3. Specifically, we can write

$$\hat{\varepsilon}_t = \theta_1 \hat{\varepsilon}_{t-1} + \hat{\upsilon}_t$$

$$\Delta\hat{\varepsilon}_t = \hat{\varepsilon}_t - \hat{\varepsilon}_{t-1} = (\theta_1 - 1)\hat{\varepsilon}_{t-1} + \hat{\upsilon}_t \tag{16.6.4}$$

$$\Delta\hat{\varepsilon}_t = \theta_1^* \hat{\varepsilon}_{t-1} + \hat{\upsilon}_t$$

We test $H_0$: $\theta_1^* = 0$ against the alternative $H_1$: $\theta_1^* < 0$. Rejection of $H_0$ implies $C_t$ and $DI_t$ are cointegrated. Special computer programs perform this test; the precise outcome can depend on how possible autocorrelation in $\hat{\upsilon}_t$ is modeled. It is conventional to model it with additional right-hand-side variables of the form $\Delta\hat{\varepsilon}_{t-j}$, $j = 1, 2, \ldots, n$ where $n$ is some number. Using a Dickey–Fuller test and $n = 1, 2, 3$, or 4, we find that $H_0$: $\theta_1^* = 0$ is rejected. We conclude, therefore, that $C_t$ and $DI_t$ are cointegrated.

### 16.6.1    AN ERROR CORRECTION MODEL

The existence of cointegration has implications for VAR modeling. In section 16.5, when constructing a VAR(1) model relating nondurable consumption and income, we assumed that the I(1) nature of the variables made it appropriate to set up a VAR model in first differences. However, if cointegration is present, there is a better specification. To illustrate, suppose that we set up the following VAR(1) model for $C_t$ and $DI_t$, expressed in terms of the *original* (not differenced) series.

$$C_t = \theta_0 + \theta_1 C_{t-1} + \phi_1 DI_{t-1} + e_t$$

$$DI_t = \delta_0 + \delta_1 C_{t-1} + \alpha_1 DI_{t-1} + u_t$$

(16.6.5)

Subtracting $C_{t-1}$ from the first equation and $DI_{t-1}$ from the second equation yields the following pair of equations.

$$\Delta C_t = C_t - C_{t-1} = \theta_0 + (\theta_1 - 1)C_{t-1} + \phi_1 DI_{t-1} + e_t$$

$$\Delta DI_t = DI_t - DI_{t-1} = \delta_0 + \delta_1 C_{t-1} + (\alpha_1 - 1)DI_{t-1} + u_t$$

(16.6.6)

Examining "the roots" of a two-equation, two-variable system like this one is not as simple as with a univariate AR(1) model. However, it can be shown that if $DI_t$ and $C_t$ are both I(1), and they are cointegrated, then the coefficients in equation 16.6.6 must satisfy the following restriction:

$$\theta_1 = 1 + \frac{\phi_1 \delta_1}{\alpha_1 - 1}$$

(16.6.7)

Substituting this equation into 16.6.6 yields

$$\Delta C_t = \theta_0 + \frac{\phi_1 \delta_1}{\alpha_1 - 1} C_{t-1} + \phi_1 DI_{t-1} + e_t$$

Note that we can now write the pair of equations as

$$\Delta C_t = \theta_0 + \frac{\phi_1 \delta_1}{\alpha_1 - 1}\left[ C_{t-1} - \frac{(1 - \alpha_1)}{\delta_1} DI_{t-1} \right] + e_t$$

$$\Delta DI_t = \delta_0 + \delta_1 \left[ C_{t-1} - \frac{(1 - \alpha_1)}{\delta_1} DI_{t-1} \right] + u_t$$

and when we set

$$\beta_2 = \frac{1 - \alpha_2}{\delta_1} \qquad \gamma_1 = \frac{\phi_1 \delta_1}{\alpha_1 - 1}, \qquad \gamma_2 = \delta_1$$

$$\theta_0^* = \theta_0 + \gamma_1 \beta_1 \qquad\qquad \delta_0^* = \delta_0 + \gamma_2 \beta_1$$

the equations become

$$\Delta C_t = \theta_0^* + \gamma_1(C_{t-1} - \beta_1 - \beta_2 DI_{t-1}) + e_t$$

$$\Delta DI_t = \delta_0^* + \gamma_2(C_{t-1} - \beta_1 - \beta_2 DI_{t-1}) + u_t$$

(16.6.8)

This representation of a VAR is known as an **error correction model.** It says that the changes in $C$ and $DI$ from period $t - 1$ to period $t$ both depend on the quantity

$$\varepsilon_{t-1} = C_{t-1} - \beta_1 - \beta_2 DI_{t-1}$$

Interestingly, this quantity represents the deviation $\varepsilon$, in period $t - 1$, from the long-run equilibrium path $C = \beta_1 + \beta_2 DI$. Thus, changes in $C$ and $DI$ (or *corrections* to $C$ and $DI$) depend on the magnitude of the departure of the system from its long-run equilibrium in the previous period. The shocks $e$ and $u$ lead to short-term departures from the cointegrating equilibrium path; then, there is a tendency to correct back toward the equilibrium.

Notice that the quantities on both sides of the equations in 16.6.8 will be stationary I(0) variables. The left sides, $\Delta C_t$ and $\Delta DI_t$, are I(0) because $C_t$ and $DI_t$ are I(1). The right side, $C_{t-1} - \beta_1 - \beta_2 DI_{t-1}$, is I(0) because $C$ and $DI$ are cointegrated. Another point to notice is that if cointegrated I(1) variables are being used in VAR model specification, setting up a model solely in terms of first differences and lags of first differences is a misspecification. The correct specification is one that includes an error correction mechanism.

One way to estimate the error correction model in 16.6.8 is to use least squares to estimate the cointegrating relationship between $C$ and $DI$, and to then use the lagged residuals from this estimation as the right-hand side variable in both equations. Following this strategy, we obtain

$$\hat{C}_t = 325.97 + 0.8616 \, DI_t$$

and

$$\Delta\hat{C}_t = 31.187 - 0.0541\hat{\varepsilon}_{t-1}$$

$$\Delta\hat{D}I_t = 36.412 + 0.3047\hat{\varepsilon}_{t-1}$$

where

$$\hat{\varepsilon}_{t-1} = C_{t-1} - 325.97 - 0.8616 \, DI_{t-1}$$

Notice that the signs of the coefficients of $\hat{\varepsilon}_{t-1}$ make sense. If $\hat{\varepsilon}_{t-1}$ is positive, then, relative to the long-run equilibrium, $C_{t-1}$ is too large and $DI_{t-1}$ is too small. Consequently, the adjustment $\Delta C_t$ is negative and the adjustment $\Delta DI_t$ is positive. The relative magnitudes of the coefficients of $\hat{\varepsilon}_{t-1}$ indicate that most of the adjustment is in $DI$, with a relatively minor adjustment to $C$.

## *16.7* Summing Up

Time-series analysis is a vast area of study. Many fat books have been written just on this subject. In this chapter the surface has barely been scratched. However, we have introduced a number of important concepts. Attempting Exercise 16.1 will help you consolidate those concepts. The main points brought out in this chapter are:

1. The class of autoregressive integrated moving average (ARIMA) models is useful for short-term forecasting.

2. To choose a particular model from the ARIMA class it is customary to examine the autocorrelation and partial autocorrelation functions of a data series.

3. The partial autocorrelation function is particularly useful for selecting the order on an AR model; the autocorrelation function is particularly useful for selecting the order of an MA model.

4. Least squares can be used to estimate AR models, but nonlinear least squares is required for MA and ARMA models. However, estimation is not usually a major concern; suitable software is available.

5. Trending data possess a property called nonstationarity. Nonstationary data series are often converted to stationary series by differencing. We call such series integrated. Nonstationary integrated series can be identified through their autocorrelations and by using unit root tests.

6. One way of jointly modeling two or more time-series variables is through a vector autoregressive (VAR) model.

7. If variables within a VAR model are cointegrated, that model can be written as an error correction model where changes in variables depend on deviations from a long-term equilibrium that is defined by the cointegrating relationship.

8. If two variables are integrated, but not cointegrated, estimating a relationship between them could lead to a spurious regression.

## *16.8* Exercises

16.1 Define the following terms:
   (a) autoregressive process
   (b) moving-average process
   (c) autoregressive moving-average process
   (d) autocorrelation function
   (e) partial autocorrelation function
   (f) integration
   (g) cointegration
   (h) spurious regression
   (i) vector autoregressive model
   (j) unit root
   (k) error correction model
   (l) stationary time series
   (m) first difference

16.2 In the file *bond.dat* there are 102 monthly observations on AA railroad bond yields for the period January 1968 to June 1976. (They are taken from Cryer (1986).)
   (a) Use the autocorrelation function and/or a unit root test to demonstrate that the series is nonstationary.
   (b) Use the partial autocorrelation function of the first differences of the series to demonstrate that an AR(1) model applied to first differences is appropriate.
   (c) Use least squares to estimate the model suggested in part (b) and use this estimated model to forecast the railroad bond yields for three months beyond the period of the sample data.

16.3   In the file *oil.dat* are 88 annual observations on the price of oil (in 1967 constant dollars) for the period 1883–1970. These data are from Pindyck and Rubinfeld (1991, p. 463).

   (a) Use a unit root test to demonstrate the series is stationary.
   (b) Fit an ARIMA(1,0,4) model to the data. Comment on the significance of the estimates. Are there any restrictions you might put on the coefficients of this model?
   (c) Use the model estimated in part (b) to forecast the price of oil for the years 1971–74.

16.4   Use the estimated VAR model given in section 16.5 to forecast nondurable consumption and disposable income for the next two quarters beyond the sample period.

16.5   Test whether the nondurable consumption and disposable income series that are in the file *macrovar.dat* are cointegrated.

16.6   Use the error correction model estimated in section 16.6.1 to forecast consumption and disposable income for the next two quarters beyond the sample period.

16.7*  In the file *texas.dat* there are 57 quarterly observations on the real price of oil (*RPO*), Texas nonagricultural employment (*TXNAG*), and nonagricultural employment in the rest of the United States (*USNAG*). The data cover the first quarter of 1974 through the first quarter of 1988 and were used in a study by Fomby and Hirschberg (1989). Let $x_t = \ln(RPO_t/RPO_{t-1})$, $y_t = \ln(TXNAG_t/TXNAG_{t-1})$, and $z_t = \ln(USNAG_t/USNAG_{t-1})$.

   (a) Test *RPO*, *TXNAG*, and *USNAG* for unit roots, and for the existence of a cointegrating relationship between these three variables. Comment.
   (b) Test $x_t$, $y_t$, and $z_t$ for the existence of unit roots.
   (c) Using $x_t$, $y_t$, and $z_t$, estimate a three-dimensional VAR(2) model. Does employment in Texas or in the United States appear to influence the price of oil? Is employment in Texas dependent on (i) the oil price, or (ii) the U.S. level of employment?
   (d) Use the model estimated in part (c) to forecast *RPO, TXNAG,* and *USNAG* for the fourth quarter of 1988.

## *16.9* References

More details on time-series models can be found in:

GRIFFITHS, W. E., R. C. HILL, AND G.G. JUDGE (1993). *Learning and Practicing Econometrics,* New York: John Wiley and Sons, Chapters 20, 21.

JUDGE, G. G., R. C. HILL, W. E. GRIFFITHS, H. LÜTKEPOHL, AND T.C. LEE (1988). *Introduction to the Theory and Practice of Econometrics.* New York: John Wiley and Sons, Inc., Chapters 16, 18.

PINDYCK, R. S., AND D. L. RUBINFELD (1991). *Econometric Models and Economic Forecasts* (3d ed.). New York: McGraw-Hill, Chapters 15–19.

Specialist time series books are:

BOX, G. E. P. AND G. M. JENKINS (1976). *Time Series Analysis: Forecasting and Control (Rev. ed.).* San Francisco: Holden-Day.

CRYER, J. D. (1986). *Time Series Analysis,* Boston: Duxbury Press.

ENDERS, W. (1995). *Applied Econometric Time Series,* New York: John Wiley and Sons, Inc.

Two applications of VAR models are:

ANDERSON, P. A. (1979, Summer). "Help for the Regional Economic Forecaster: Vector Autoregression." *Federal Reserve Bank of Minneapolis Quarterly Review,* pp. 2–7.

FOMBY, T. B., AND J. G. HIRSCHBERG (1989, January). "Texas in Transition: Dependence on Oil and the National Economy," *Federal Reserve Bank of Dallas Economic Review,* pp. 11–28.

# Chapter 17

# Economic Data Sources, Guidelines for Choosing a Research Project, and the Writing of a Research Report

In the preceding chapters we emphasized (1) the formulation of an econometric model from an economic model; (2) estimation of the econometric model by an appropriate procedure; (3) interpretation of the estimates; and (4) inferences, in the form of interval estimates, hypothesis tests, and predictions. In this chapter we recognize that the model, the method, and the data are all interdependent links in an econometric research project. In particular, we discuss different types of economic data and their sources, the selection of a suitable topic for a research project, and the essential components of a research report.

## *17.1* Sources and Characteristics of Economic Data

There are three primary methods for obtaining data used in econometric analyses.

1. Experimental data are generated from controlled experiments. This ideal situation is described in Figure 1.1. In this setting, the values of explanatory variables are assigned by the researcher to ensure sufficient independent variation so that their effects on the economic outcome can be estimated precisely. Examples include the experimental data coming from agricultural experiments (such as measuring corn output using alternative levels of fertilizer inputs) and public policy experiments (such as income maintenance and the peak load pricing of electricity).

2. Nonexperimental data differ from experimental data in that there is no one at the controls. These economic data are generated from an experiment carried on by society and are recorded, usually by a government agency, for administrative or planning purposes. These observational data are sometimes called passively generated data since society, and not the researcher, defines the settings of the explanatory variables. This sample information includes

data such as daily, monthly, and annual prices; outputs of final, intermediate, and primary commodities; the level of unemployment; total and per capita disposable income; and gross and net private investment.

3. Survey data are collected through an interview process. In surveys no explanatory variables are assigned values. The survey is designed to collect information on particular variables of interest, such as level of income for a particular individual or household, level of education, number of members of a household, and the level of durable purchases.

Each of these data generation methods provides sample information that permits us to describe economic activity. It also is a basis for investigating the relationships between economic variables. Let's look at each method for obtaining data in a little more detail.

### 17.1.1 NONEXPERIMENTAL DATA

Most economic data are collected for administrative rather than research purposes. However, these data, over which the econometrician exercises no control, form the basis for a large proportion of applied econometric research. The data may be collected in two ways:

*time-series form*—data collected over discrete intervals of time (for example, the annual price of wheat in the United States from 1880 to 1997 or the daily stock price of General Electric from 1980 to 1997)

*cross-sectional form*—data collected over sample units in a particular time period (for example, income by counties in California during 1997)

These data may be collected at various levels of aggregation:

*micro*—data collected on individual economic-decision-making units such as individuals, households, or firms

*macro*—data resulting from a pooling or aggregating over individuals, households, or firms at the local, state, or national levels

The data collected may also represent a flow or a stock:

*flow*—outcome measures over a period of time, such as the consumption of gasoline during the last quarter of 1997

*stock*—outcome measured at a particular point in time, such as the quantity of crude oil held by Chevron in its U.S. storage tanks April 1, 1997, or the asset value of the Wells Fargo Bank on July 1, 1997

The data collected may be quantitative or qualitative:

*quantitative*—outcomes such as prices or income that may be expressed as numbers or some transformation of them, such as real prices or per capita income

*qualitative*—outcomes that are of an "either-or" situation (for example, a consumer either did or did not make a purchase of a particular good, or a person either is or is not married); such qualitative outcomes were discussed in chapter 9 and represented by dummy variables

### 17.1.1a.  Data Published in Text Form

There are several books that list and serve as a guide to the various sources of economic and business data: Daniels (1976) and Johnson (1993) are two examples. Also, see chapter 3 in Intriligator, Bodkin, and Hsiao (1996) and *Hidden Treasures!: Census Bureau Data and Where to Find It!* (1990).

At the international level, macro data are published by agencies such as the International Monetary Fund (IMF), the European Economic Community (OECD), the United Nations (UN), and the Food and Agriculture Organization (FAO). Some examples of publications by these agencies include:

*International Financial Statistics* (IMF, monthly)

*Basic Statistics of the Community* (OECD, annual)

*Consumer Price Indices in the European Community* (OECD, annual)

*World Statistics* (UN, annual)

*Yearbook of National Accounts Statistics* (UN, annual)

*FAO Trade Yearbook* (annual)

The major sources of U.S. economic data are the Bureau of Economic Analysis (BEA), the Bureau of the Census (BC), the Bureau of Labor Statistics (BLS), the Federal Reserve (FR), and the Statistical Reporting Service of the Department of Agriculture (USDA). Some examples of publications by these U.S. agencies include:

*Survey of Current Business* (BEA, monthly)

*Handbook of Basic Economic Statistics* (Bureau of Economic Statistics, Inc., monthly)

*Monthly Labor Review* (BLS, monthly)

*Federal Reserve Bulletin* (FR, monthly)

*Statistical Abstract of the US* (BC, annual)

*Economic Report of the President* (annual)

*Agricultural Statistics* (USDA, annual)

*Agricultural Situation Reports* (USDA, monthly)

*Economic Indicators* (Council of Economic Advisors, monthly)

A table from the 1996 *Economic Report of the President* is typical of how economic data are usually presented. It is reproduced in Table 17.1. Hoel, Clarkson, and Miller (1983) go into considerable detail concerning how the main economic statistical series are compiled and discuss some of their strengths and weaknesses.

Data reported at the national level are often also available at the state, SMSA, county, and census tract levels. Some of these sources include:

*State and Metropolitan Area Data Book* (Commerce and BC, annual)

*CPI Detailed Report* (BLS, annual)

*Census of Population and Housing* (Commerce, BC, annual)

*County & City Data Book* (Commerce, BC, annual)

*Table 17.1* Total and per capita disposable personal income and personal consumption expenditures in current and real dollars, 1959–95 [Quarterly data at seasonally adjusted annual rates, except as noted]

| | Disposable personal income | | | | Personal consumption expenditures | | | | Gross domestic product per capita (dollars) | | Population (thousands)[1] |
|---|---|---|---|---|---|---|---|---|---|---|---|
| | Total (billions of dollars) | | Per capita (dollars) | | Total (billions of dollars) | | Per capita (dollars) | | | | |
| Year of quarter | Current dollars | Chained (1992) dollars | Current dollars | Chained (1992) dollars | Current dollars | Chained (1992) dollars | Current dollars | Chained (1992) dollars | Current dollars | Chained (1992) dollars | |
| 1959 . . . . . . | 349.0 | 1,530.1 | 1,971 | 8,641 | 318.1 | 1,394.6 | 1,796 | 7,876 | 2,865 | 12,494 | 177,073 |
| 1960 . . . . . . | 362.9 | 1,565.4 | 2,008 | 8,660 | 332.2 | 1,432.6 | 1,838 | 7,926 | 2,913 | 12,512 | 180,760 |
| 1961 . . . . . . | 378.8 | 1,615.8 | 2,062 | 8,794 | 342.6 | 1,461.5 | 1,865 | 7,954 | 2,965 | 12,571 | 183,742 |
| 1962 . . . . . . | 401.3 | 1,693.7 | 2,151 | 9,077 | 363.4 | 1,533.8 | 1,948 | 8,220 | 3,136 | 13,125 | 186,590 |
| 1963 . . . . . . | 421.1 | 1,755.5 | 2,225 | 9,274 | 383.0 | 1,596.6 | 2,023 | 8,434 | 3,261 | 13,492 | 189,300 |
| 1964 . . . . . . | 457.6 | 1,881.9 | 2,384 | 9,805 | 411.4 | 1,692.3 | 2,144 | 8,817 | 3,455 | 14,083 | 191,927 |
| 1965 . . . . . . | 493.9 | 2,000.2 | 2,541 | 10,292 | 444.3 | 1,799.1 | 2,286 | 9,257 | 3,700 | 14,792 | 194,347 |
| 1966 . . . . . . | 533.7 | 2,106.6 | 2,715 | 10,715 | 481.9 | 1,902.0 | 2,451 | 9,674 | 4,007 | 15,565 | 196,599 |
| 1967 . . . . . . | 571.9 | 2,198.4 | 2,877 | 11,061 | 509.5 | 1,958.6 | 2,563 | 9,854 | 4,194 | 15,800 | 198,752 |
| 1968 . . . . . . | 621.4 | 2,298.2 | 3,096 | 11,448 | 559.8 | 2,070.2 | 2,789 | 10,313 | 4,536 | 16,382 | 200,745 |
| 1969 . . . . . . | 668.4 | 2,373.6 | 3,297 | 11,708 | 604.7 | 2,147.5 | 2,982 | 10,593 | 4,845 | 16,712 | 202,736 |
| 1970 . . . . . . | 727.1 | 2,465.6 | 3,545 | 12,022 | 648.1 | 2,197.8 | 3,160 | 10,717 | 5,050 | 16,520 | 205,089 |
| 1971 . . . . . . | 790.2 | 2,564.0 | 3,805 | 12,246 | 702.5 | 2,279.5 | 3,383 | 10,975 | 5,419 | 16,853 | 207,692 |
| 1972 . . . . . . | 855.3 | 2,680.8 | 4,074 | 12,770 | 770.7 | 2,415.9 | 3,671 | 11,508 | 5,894 | 17,579 | 209,924 |
| 1973 . . . . . . | 965.0 | 2,869.4 | 4,553 | 13,539 | 851.6 | 2,532.6 | 4,018 | 11,950 | 6,524 | 18,412 | 211,939 |
| 1974 . . . . . . | 1,054.2 | 2,847.0 | 4,928 | 13,310 | 931.2 | 2,514.7 | 4,353 | 11,756 | 6,998 | 18,178 | 213,898 |
| 1975 . . . . . . | 1,159.2 | 2,895.0 | 5,367 | 13,404 | 1,029.1 | 2,570.0 | 4,765 | 11,899 | 7,550 | 17,896 | 215,981 |
| 1976 . . . . . . | 1,273.0 | 3,008.0 | 5,837 | 13,793 | 1,148.8 | 2,714.3 | 5,268 | 12,446 | 8,341 | 18,713 | 218,086 |
| 1977 . . . . . . | 1,401.4 | 3,105.1 | 6,362 | 14,095 | 1,277.1 | 2,829.8 | 5,797 | 12,846 | 9,201 | 19,426 | 220,289 |
| 1978 . . . . . . | 1,580.1 | 3,264.2 | 7,097 | 14,662 | 1,428.8 | 2,951.6 | 6,418 | 13,258 | 10,292 | 20,185 | 222,629 |
| 1979 . . . . . . | 1,769.5 | 3,353.9 | 7,861 | 14,899 | 1,593.5 | 3,020.2 | 7,079 | 13,417 | 11,361 | 20,541 | 225,106 |
| 1980 . . . . . . | 1,973.3 | 3,373.3 | 8,665 | 14,813 | 1,760.4 | 3,009.7 | 7,730 | 13,216 | 12,226 | 20,252 | 227,726 |
| 1981 . . . . . . | 2,200.2 | 3,452.3 | 9,566 | 15,009 | 1,941.3 | 3,046.4 | 8,440 | 13,245 | 13,547 | 20,542 | 230,008 |
| 1982 . . . . . . | 2,347.3 | 3,483.0 | 10,108 | 14,999 | 2,076.8 | 3,081.5 | 8,943 | 13,270 | 13,961 | 19,911 | 232,218 |
| 1983 . . . . . . | 2,522.4 | 3,579.2 | 10,764 | 15,277 | 2,283.4 | 3,240.6 | 9,744 | 13,829 | 14,988 | 20,527 | 234,332 |
| 1984 . . . . . . | 2,810.0 | 3,841.9 | 11,887 | 16,252 | 2,492.3 | 3,407.6 | 10,543 | 14,415 | 16,508 | 21,736 | 236,394 |
| 1985 . . . . . . | 3,002.0 | 3,958.6 | 12,587 | 16,597 | 2,704.8 | 3,566.5 | 11,341 | 14,954 | 17,529 | 22,345 | 238,506 |
| 1986 . . . . . . | 3,187.6 | 4,087.0 | 13,244 | 16,981 | 2,892.7 | 3,708.7 | 12,019 | 15,409 | 18,374 | 22,810 | 240,682 |
| 1987 . . . . . . | 3,363.1 | 4,154.1 | 13,849 | 17,106 | 3,094.5 | 3,822.3 | 12,743 | 15,740 | 19,323 | 23,260 | 242,842 |
| 1988 . . . . . . | 3,640.8 | 4,318.1 | 14,857 | 17,621 | 3,349.7 | 3,972.7 | 13,669 | 16,211 | 20,605 | 23,924 | 245,061 |
| 1989 . . . . . . | 3,894.5 | 4,403.7 | 15,742 | 17,801 | 3,594.8 | 4,064.6 | 15,531 | 16,430 | 21,984 | 24,497 | 247,387 |
| 1990 . . . . . . | 4,166.8 | 4,484.6 | 16,670 | 17,942 | 3,839.3 | 4,132.2 | 15,360 | 16,532 | 22,979 | 24,559 | 249,956 |
| 1991 . . . . . . | 4,343.7 | 4,486.4 | 17,191 | 17,755 | 3,975.1 | 4,105.8 | 15,732 | 16,249 | 23,416 | 24,058 | 262,680 |
| 1992 . . . . . . | 4,613.7 | 4,613.7 | 18,062 | 18,062 | 4,219.8 | 4,219.8 | 16,520 | 16,520 | 24,447 | 24,447 | 255,432 |
| 1993 . . . . . . | 4,789.3 | 4,666.2 | 18,552 | 18,075 | 4,454.1 | 4,339.7 | 17,263 | 16,810 | 25,373 | 24,728 | 258,159 |
| 1994 . . . . . . | 5,018.8 | 4,775.6 | 19,253 | 18,320 | 4,698.7 | 4,471.1 | 18,025 | 17,152 | 26,589 | 25,335 | 260,681 |
| 1990: I. . . . . | 4,074.8 | 4,475.5 | 16,369 | 17,979 | 3,759.2 | 4,128.9 | 15,102 | 16,587 | 22,739 | 24,722 | 248,928 |
| II. . . . | 4,143.3 | 4,494.3 | 16,602 | 18,008 | 3,811.8 | 4,134.7 | 15,274 | 16,568 | 23,044 | 27,741 | 249,564 |
| III . . . | 4,207.6 | 4,499.7 | 16,810 | 17,977 | 3,879.2 | 4,148.5 | 15,498 | 16,574 | 23,102 | 24,551 | 250,299 |
| IV . . . | 4,241.5 | 4,468.8 | 16,896 | 17,802 | 3,907.0 | 4,116.4 | 15,564 | 16,398 | 23,031 | 24,224 | 251,031 |
| 1991: I. . . . . | 4,263.3 | 4,452.7 | 16,941 | 17,694 | 3,910.7 | 4,084.5 | 15,540 | 16,231 | 23,136 | 24,033 | 251,650 |
| II. . . . | 4,329.6 | 4,492.6 | 17,161 | 17,807 | 3,961.0 | 4,110.0 | 15,700 | 16,291 | 23,355 | 24,075 | 252,295 |
| III . . . | 4,365.6 | 4,494.2 | 17,263 | 17,761 | 4,001.6 | 4,119.5 | 15,815 | 16,280 | 23,515 | 24,065 | 253,033 |
| IV . . . | 4,416.4 | 4,506.3 | 17,405 | 17,759 | 4,027.1 | 4,109.1 | 15,871 | 16,194 | 23,655 | 24,058 | 253,743 |
| 1992: I. . . . . | 4,515.2 | 4,565.6 | 17,753 | 17,951 | 4,127.6 | 4,173.8 | 16,229 | 16,410 | 24,070 | 24,280 | 254,338 |
| II. . . . | 4,585.1 | 4,599.8 | 17,979 | 18,036 | 4,183.0 | 4,196.4 | 16,402 | 16,454 | 24,316 | 24,366 | 255,032 |
| III . . . | 4,613.9 | 4,600.6 | 18,036 | 17,984 | 4,238.9 | 4,226.7 | 16,570 | 16,522 | 24,516 | 24,474 | 255,815 |
| IV . . . | 4,740.5 | 4,688.7 | 18,478 | 18,277 | 4,329.6 | 4,282.3 | 16,877 | 16,692 | 24,881 | 24,664 | 256,543 |

*(continues)*

***Table 17.1***   *(Continued)*

| Year of quarter | Disposable personal income | | | | Personal consumption expenditures | | | | Gross domestic product per capita (dollars) | | Population (thousands)[1] |
| | Total (billions of dollars) | | Per capita (dollars) | | Total (billions of dollars) | | Per capita (dollars) | | | | |
| | Current dollars | Chained (1992) dollars | Current dollars | Chained (1992) dollars | Current dollars | Chained (1992) dollars | Current dollars | Chained (1992) dollars | Current dollars | Chained (1992) dollars | |
|---|---|---|---|---|---|---|---|---|---|---|---|
| 1993: I..... | 4,686.3 | 4,602.8 | 18,223 | 17,899 | 4,367.8 | 4,290.0 | 16,985 | 16,682 | 25,054 | 24,604 | 257,155 |
| II.... | 4,771.6 | 4,657.6 | 18,510 | 18,068 | 4,424.7 | 4,319.0 | 17,164 | 16,754 | 25,227 | 24,647 | 257,787 |
| III ... | 4,804.1 | 4,674.0 | 18,585 | 18,081 | 4,481.0 | 4,359.7 | 17,335 | 16,865 | 25,421 | 24,721 | 258,501 |
| IV ... | 4,895.3 | 4,730.4 | 18,887 | 18,251 | 4,543.0 | 4,390.0 | 17,528 | 16,937 | 25,787 | 24,939 | 259,192 |
| 1994: I..... | 4,856.9 | 4,666.4 | 18,699 | 17,966 | 4,599.2 | 4,418.8 | 17,707 | 17,013 | 26,076 | 25,043 | 259,738 |
| II.... | 5,002.2 | 4,779.8 | 19,215 | 18,361 | 4,665.1 | 4,457.7 | 17,920 | 17,123 | 26,448 | 25,282 | 260,327 |
| III ... | 5,070.4 | 4,804.2 | 19,427 | 18,407 | 4,734.4 | 4,485.8 | 18,139 | 17,187 | 26,772 | 25,438 | 261,004 |
| IV ... | 5,145.7 | 4,852.0 | 19,666 | 18,544 | 4,796.0 | 4,522.3 | 18,330 | 17,283 | 27,059 | 25,573 | 261,653 |
| 1995: I..... | 5,225.5 | 4,895.5 | 19,931 | 18,672 | 4,836.3 | 4,530.9 | 18,447 | 17,282 | 27,263 | 25,561 | 262,181 |
| II.... | 5,260.4 | 4,896.1 | 20,021 | 18,634 | 4,908.7 | 4,568.8 | 18,682 | 17,388 | 27,389 | 25,536 | 262,748 |
| III ... | 5,330.6 | 4,939.8 | 20,238 | 18,754 | 4,965.1 | 4,601.1 | 18,850 | 17,468 | 27,704 | 25,677 | 263,395 |

[1]Population of the United States including Armed Forces overseas; includes Alaska and Hawaii beginning 1960. Annual data are averages of quarterly data. Quarterly data are averages for the period.
*Source:* Department of Commerce (Bureau of Economic Analysis and Bureau of the Census), in 1996 *Economic Report of the President,* Table 13-27.

Although public agencies are a major source of economic data, some private firms are also major players. For example, Standard and Poor (e.g., *Analyst's Handbook*), Dow Jones, Forbes, and Moody (e.g., *Handbook of Common Stocks*) offer a vast array of micro-oriented data. Much of this type of data is available on tapes such as Compustat.

**17.1.1b.   Data on Electronic Media**
Some data can be obtained on computer tapes, diskettes, or on CD-ROM formats. A primary example is Data Resources, Incorporated's (DRI's) Citibase data. Citibase contains detailed data that are easily retrieved. There are data on:

- Financial series, including the money supply, interest rates, exchange rates, credit and the stock market
- Business formation, investment, and consumer sentiment
- Construction of housing
- Manufacturing, including measures of the business cycle, and domestic and foreign trade
- Prices, including producer and consumer price indexes
- Industrial production
- Capacity and productivity
- Population
- Labor statistics, including surveys of households and business establishments, and unemployment indicators

- National income and product accounts in great detail
- Forecasts and projections
- Business cycle indicators
- Energy consumption, petroleum production, prices, and costs
- International data series, including trade statistics

Other sources of easily usable data are on the Internet, as described in the next section.

### 17.1.1c.    Data Sources on the Internet

As you probably know, the Internet is an ever-expanding global web of information on virtually every subject. It is too vast an undertaking to describe every location that contains material of interest to economists. So we will describe two "gateways" to the wealth of material and give you some other World Wide Web addresses that you might also explore. The only way to truly appreciate this resource is to sit in front of your computer and browse, remembering to note interesting sites as you go. As a word of warning, web sites appear, disappear, or move daily. Thus, the addresses we provide are subject to change. Also, web sites that we give not only contain data sources, but also much other information that is of interest to economists. Thus, when you visit a particular site, you will have to do at least a little searching to find the data.

All economists should become familiar with *Resources for Economists on the Internet* by Bill Goffe. This is a massive document that can be obtained from numerous sites. One is

*http://econwpa.wustl.edu/EconFAQ/EconFAQ.html*

At this site you may see the entire table of contents or search through the index for specific items. You will also find a list of sites where the entire guide can be obtained via *ftp* or *e-mail*. An abbreviated table of contents is shown in Table 17.2.

Other interesting sites containing links to many pages of interests to economists and many data sources are in Table 17.3. This information just scratches the surface. We recommend that you visit these web sites and spend some time looking around. Many interesting sites are given in Simkens et al. (1997).

### 17.1.2    DATA FROM SURVEYS

A large amount of micro-oriented data is obtained from surveys. For example, each month the Bureau of Labor Statistics analyzes and publishes statistics on the labor force, employment, unemployment, and persons not in the labor force, classified by a variety of demographic, social, and economic characteristics. These data come from a monthly survey conducted by the Bureau of the Census for the Bureau of Labor Statistics using a sample of 60,000 or more households that are representative of the noninstitutional population of the United States.

The above example is a national large-scale survey. However, survey techniques are useful any time information is needed about a group or population, such as consumers or firms. The objective is to examine only a few observations, as we did

*Table 17.2*  Abbreviated Table of Contents to Bill Goffe's *Resources for Economists on the Internet*. Data Sources in Bold Print.

- WHERE TO OBTAIN THIS GUIDE
- INTRODUCTION
- **SHORTCUT TO ALL RESOURCES**
- **MACRO AND REGIONAL DATA**
- **OTHER U.S. DATA**
- **WORLD AND NON-U.S. DATA**
- **FINANCE AND FINANCIAL MARKETS**
- ECONOMIC CONSULTING AND FORECASTING SERVICES
- **DATA ARCHIVES**
- WORKING PAPERS
- BIBLIOGRAPHICAL SERVICES
- INTERNET STYLE "PAPERS"
- NEWSLETTERS
- WORKING PAPER, PUBLICATION, AND REPORT NOTIFICATION SERVICES
- INFORMATION ABOUT MEETINGS
- WEBEC-ECONOMICS JOURNALS ON THE INTERNET
- INFORMATION ABOUT JOURNALS
- **JOURNAL DATA AND PROGRAM ARCHIVES**
- ON-LINE JOURNALS
- PUBLISHERS
- ELECTRONIC NEWSPAPERS AND OTHER NEWS MEDIA
- ECONOMIC SOCIETIES AND ASSOCIATIONS
- ACADEMIC RESEARCH ORGANIZATIONS AND INSTITUTES
- NON-ACADEMIC RESEARCH AND POLICY ORGANIZATIONS
- SINGLE SUBJECT SITES
- MULTIPLE SUBJECT ECONOMIC SITES
- DIRECTORIES TO COLLEGES AND UNIVERSITIES
- DIRECTORIES TO BUSINESS SCHOOLS
- DIRECTORIES TO ECONOMICS DEPARTMENTS
- ECONOMICS DEPARTMENTS WITH PHD PROGRAMS
- DIRECTORIES TO ECONOMISTS' HOME PAGES
- UNIVERSITY AND RESEARCH LIBRARY ONLINE CATALOGS
- PROGRAM LIBRARIES
- EDUCATIONAL SERVICES
- EDUCATIONAL SERVICES—COURSES
- USENET NEWSGROUPS
- MAILING LISTS

*(continues)*

*Table 17.2*    *(Continued)*

- COMMERCIAL ABSTRACT AND ANNOUNCEMENT SERVICES
- INFORMATION ABOUT THE ECONOMICS PROFESSION
- INFORMATION ABOUT THE FINANCE PROFESSION
- WORD PROCESSING
- ECONOMICS-RELATED COMPUTER PROGRAMS FOR THE INTERNET
- CONTACTS AND INFORMATION ON STATISTICAL AND COMPUTATIONAL SOFTWARE
- USEFUL SOFTWARE FOR THE INTERNET
- USEFUL RESOURCES ABOUT THE INTERNET
- NEAT STUFF

in chapters 3 and 4, and extend the finding to the whole group. In this process there are four major elements: (1) identifying the population of interest; (2) designing the survey, determining the sample size, and selecting the sample; (3) collecting the information; and (4) reducing the data, making estimates, and making inferences about the population. Many universities have survey laboratories whose mission is to carry through these data creation and analysis steps. Many private firms also perform the same function, and much of these data are in the public domain.

*Table 17.3*    **Useful and Interesting Internet Addresses**

1. *http://seamonkey.ed.asu.edu/~behrens/teach/WWW_data.html* "Dr. B's Wide World of Web Data," a gateway to many types of data from a variety of fields

2. *http://www.sims.berkeley.edu/~hal/pages/interesting.html* Professor Hal Varian's list of interesting places, from which you can link to information on jobs in economics, addresses, research materials, financial economics, government sites, and many other items

3. *http://www.stls.frb.org* This is the site for the Federal Reserve Bank of St. Louis, which provides links to each of the Federal Reserve Banks and has a user-friendly database called FRED

4. *http://www.bls.gov* The Bureau of Labor Statistics

5. *http://nber.harvard.edu* National Bureau of Economic Research

6. *http://www.inform.umd.edu:8080/EdRes/Topic/Economics/EconData/.www/eca.html* University of Maryland

7. *http://www.bog.frb.fed.us* The Board of Governors for the U.S. Federal Reserve System

8. *http://www.webcom.com/~yardeni/economic.html* Dr. Ed Yardeni's Economics Network linking to extensive financial data

### 17.1.3 CONTROLLED EXPERIMENTAL DATA

One major problem faced by economists is how to obtain data that may be used to measure or predict the effect of changes in policy variables on the behavior of economic units. In this context, where appropriate data are not available, social experimentation in a controlled setting offers an attractive alternative. Through this process one seeks to generate data that may be used to measure the effects of changes in policy or instrument variables by applying "treatments" to human populations under conditions of controlled experimentation. If a fundamental policy change is being considered, in many cases the way to obtain information on the effect of the policy is to put the policy into effect on a limited scale and see what happens. In the past this approach has been used for the following types of policy questions:

1. How will labor force participation be influenced by a guaranteed minimum income? To measure the work behavior of families receiving income supports (negative income tax), experiments were conducted in New Jersey and North Carolina.

2. What is the effect of a national program of cash housing allowances on the recipients of the allowances, on other households, on the market for housing and on housing intermediaries? The experimental housing allowance program sought to measure the effect of such a cash allowance program on the demand and supply of housing. Experiments were conducted in Pennsylvania, Arizona, Wisconsin, and Indiana.

3. How will the use of medical care change if a small fraction of the people in a given area have their medical costs reduced for a period of three to five years? A health insurance experiment sought to provide information that would be useful in estimating the sensitivity of different income groups to price changes in the face of a fixed total supply of health services. Six thousand families in each of four sites were involved in the experiment.

4. How does the price of electricity affect its usage and availability? During the 1970s and 1980s, national concern about the cost and availability of energy focused public attention on the pricing of electricity. The treatment of peak-load-pricing, where higher rates are charged during hours and seasons of higher demand, was advocated as a way of lowering the overall social cost of energy. No satisfactory database existed that would permit one to forecast the changes in load (demand) curves that would result from using various peak-load rate structures. Toward this end, rate-structure experiments were set up in Los Angeles and other areas to generate a database on the daily pattern of electricity use by residential customers through systematic experimentation with a variety of peak-load tariffs. The objective was to provide information on the central policy questions concerning the peak-load pricing of electricity in the United States.

The above examples should be sufficient to indicate that social experiments offer unique opportunities for generating databases that may be used for estimating response at the micro level to alternative economic policies. Social experimentation is a useful addition to the economist–econometrician's set of tools. Each experiment carries with it a unique set of problems, and much remains to be learned on how to best exploit this technique. Such experimental data are very valuable to research economists, but are also very expensive to obtain, and thus are rarely available.

### 17.1.4  SOME CHARACTERISTICS OF ECONOMIC DATA

Economic relations are seldom free of shocks or disturbances and economic data are seldom free of specification and/or measurement error. In an econometric model we can usually be quite precise as to the definition of our variables and in regard to such things as their timing and degree of aggregation. Unfortunately, there is seldom consistency between the theoretical models and the economic data that are used in an empirical analysis.

With passively generated, nonexperimental data we must be content with whatever experimental design society decided to use. Out of this set of data we are then restricted to whatever information the statistical agency decided to collect. Since the experimental design was not specified by the researcher, some of the variables of interest may not vary over a range that will let us identify their impact in the relation of interest. In other cases the variables (for example, prices) may move together over time in a collinear way, and again, we may not be able to separate out their individual impacts. Some data may contain large measurement errors. For example, in one theory of the consumption function, the consumption data ($c$) that are usually available are viewed as made up of permanent ($c_P$) and transitory ($c_T$) components, that is, $c = c_P + c_T$. What is desired as a basis for estimating the consumption function are data in the form of $c_P$. Permanent consumption $c_P$ is, however, unobservable. There are ways around this problem, but still we add noise into our applied estimation and inference procedures. These and many other things concerning the data rear their ugly heads as we go from the theoretical model to the empirical counterpart.

As we have noted, much of the passively generated data are collected for administrative rather than research purposes. Thus, for any particular research problem there may be considerable labor involved in transforming the data to a form that is usable for the problem at hand. It is impossible to overemphasize the importance of knowing how the data have been measured and of making sure they are conformable over space, time, and individuals. If data for a cross-country study are collected from national sources they may need to be standardized. Alternatively, international agencies such as IMF and the World Bank use their own procedures for standardizing and cleaning data. Thus, before pushing the computer button the researcher should be aware of how data may have been transformed or modified.

Even when the data are collected by the researcher, using the survey or controlled experiment routes, they may not be consistent with the specifications in the theoretical model. The survey or experimental design may have been inappropriate, the questionnaire may not have been correctly designed, the interviewer may not have recorded the actual response, or the experimenter may not have measured the outcome without error or held relevant factors constant.

All these things happen in the data search phase of an econometric analysis. How to handle these pitfalls requires a good deal of creativity, patience, and experience. Just as you must be explicit in terms of the assumptions made in your economic and statistical models, you must also be explicit in terms of the data that you have used and any transformation that you have made. Several applied econometric journals now require that the data used in an econometric analysis be made available so that others may replicate and extend the results. For example, many applied econometrics books include a disk containing the data for the problems analyzed.

# *17.2* Selecting a Topic for an Economics Project

Economics research is *fun!* A research project is an opportunity to investigate a topic in which you are interested. However, before you begin the actual research and writing of a report, it is a good idea to give some quality thinking time to the selection of a *good* topic. Then, once you have an idea formulated, it is wise to write an abstract of the project, summarizing what you know and what you hope to learn. These two steps are the focus of this section.

## 17.2.1 CHOOSING A TOPIC

Choosing a good research topic is essential if you are to successfully complete a class project. A starting point is the question, "What am I interested in?" If you are interested in a particular topic, then that will add to the pleasure of research effort. However, even if you begin working on a topic that is not totally fascinating to you, remember that "inspiration is 99 percent perspiration." This means that as you begin researching one topic, other questions will occur to you. These new questions may put a new light on the original topic, or they may represent new paths to follow that are more interesting to you.

By the time you have completed several semesters of economics classes, you will find yourself enjoying some areas more than others. For each of us, specialized areas such as industrial organization, public finance, resource economics, monetary economics, environmental economics, and international trade hold a different appeal. If you are generally interested in one of these areas, but do not have a specific idea of where to start in the selection of a topic, speak with your instructor. He or she will be able to suggest some ideas that will give you a start, and can cite some published research for you to read, or can suggest specific professional journals that carry applied research articles on a general area. Also, books by Intriligator et al. (1996), Berndt (1991), and Lott and Ray (1991) summarize empirical research in a number of areas. A perusal of these sources might give you an idea. If you find an area or topic in which you are interested, consult the *Journal of Economic Literature* for a list of related journal articles. The *JEL* has a classification scheme that makes isolating particular areas of study an easy task.

Once you have tentatively identified a problem that you wish to work on, the next issues are pragmatic ones. During one semester you will not be able to collect your own data to use in a project. Thus, you must find out whether suitable data are available for the problem you have identified. Once again, your instructor may be of help in this regard.

We have so far identified two aspects of a good research topic: the topic should be of interest to you and data that are relevant to the topic should be readily available. The third aspect of a good project is again a pragmatic one: you should be able to finish in the time remaining in your semester. This requires not only the availability of the data, but also implies that you are familiar with the theoretical econometric procedures that are appropriate for analyzing the data and that you can implement them on the computer, or learn the procedure in a reasonable amount of time.

### 17.2.2    WRITING AN ABSTRACT

After you have selected a specific topic, it is a good idea to write up a brief abstract. Writing the abstract will help you focus your thoughts about what you really want to do, and you can show it to your instructor for preliminary approval and comments. The abstract should be short, usually no more than five hundred words, and should include:

1.  A concise statement of the problem
2.  Comments on the information that is available with one or two key references
3.  A description of the research design that includes:
    (a)  the economic model
    (b)  the statistical model
    (c)  data sources
    (d)  estimation, hypothesis testing and prediction procedures; and
4.  The contribution of the research

## *17.3*  A Format for Writing a Research Report

Economics research reports have a standard format in which the various steps of the research project are discussed and the results are interpreted. The following outline is typical:

1.  ***Statement of the problem.*** The place to start your report is with a summary of the questions you have investigated, why they are important and who should be interested in the results. Identify the contents of each section of the report.

2.  ***Review of the literature.*** Briefly summarize the relevant literature in the research area you have chosen, so that you may make clear how your work extends our knowledge.

3.  ***The economic model.*** Specify the general economic model that you used, define the economic variables. State the model's assumptions and identify hypotheses you wish to test.

4.  ***The statistical model.*** Identify the statistical model that corresponds to the economic model. Make sure you include a discussion of the variables in the model, the functional form, the error assumptions and any other assumptions that you make.

5.  ***The data.*** Describe the data you used, the source of the data, and any reservations you have about their appropriateness within the economic and statistical models.

6.  ***The estimation and inference procedures.*** Describe the estimation methods you used and why they were chosen. Identify hypothesis testing procedures and their use.

7. *The empirical results and conclusions.* Report the parameter estimates, their interpretation, and values of test statistics. Comment on their statistical significance, their relation to previous estimates, and their economic implications.

8. *Possible extensions and limitations of the study.* Your research will raise questions about the economic model, data, and estimation techniques. What future research is suggested by your findings, and how might you go about it?

9. *Acknowledgments.* It is appropriate to recognize those who have commented on and contributed to your research. This may include your instructor, a librarian who helped you find data, and a fellow student who read and commented on your paper, for example.

10. *References.* An alphabetical list of the literature you cite in your study, as well as references to the data sources you used.

## *17.4* Exercises

17.1  Check out in your library the *Economic Report of the President* for 1996 and become acquainted with the aggregate income, employment, and production data and their sources that are reported therein. Note how these data are used in the narrative portion of the report.

17.2  Locate the *Survey of Current Business* in your library and describe its contents.

17.3  Visit the web site of the Federal Reserve Bank of St. Louis, whose address is shown in Table 17.3. Download data on the prime interest rate and graph it against time.

17.4  Suppose you were interested in household food consumption and its relation to income and number in the household. Design a survey that could be used for obtaining data that could be used for estimation and hypothesis testing. If you obtained this information over the various food groups, what type of statistical model would you use in your statistical analysis?

17.5  Suppose you are the economist for a retail food chain and you want to devise an advertising and pricing policy for canned tuna. How would you go about designing an experiment that would generate data that could be used for your statistical analysis?

17.6  Locate one of the Internet data sources described in section 17.1.1c and download data on two variables that you think should be related.
(a) What relationship do you think should hold between the variables, and why?
(b) Use the data to estimate this relationship. Do the estimates agree with your expectations? If not, why not?
(c) How would you rate the statistical quality of your estimated equation?
(d) Is there any evidence of heteroskedasticity or autocorrelation?
(e) Is there any way in which you might be able to improve your model? Discuss possible improvements from both an economic and a statistical perspective.

## *17.5*  References

BERNDT, E. R. (1991). *The Practice of Econometrics.* Reading, MA: Addison Wesley.

DANIELS, L. M. (1976). *Business Information Sources.* Berkeley: University of California Press.

*Hidden Treasures!: Census Bureau Data and Where to Find It!* (1990). Washington, DC: U.S. Department of Commerce, Bureau of the Census.

HOEL, A. A., K. W. CLARKSON, AND R. M. MILLER (1983). *Economic Sourcebook of Government Statistics.* Lexington, MA: Lexington Books (D. C. Heath and Company).

INTRILIGATOR, M., R. G. BODKIN, AND C. HSIAO (1996). *Economic Models, Techniques and Applications* (2d ed.). Upper Saddle River, NJ: Prentice Hall.

JOHNSON, D. B. (1993). *Finding and Using Economic Information: A Guide to Sources and Interpretation.* Mountain View, CA: Mayfield Publishing Co.

LOTT, W., AND S. C. RAY (1992). *Applied Econometrics: Problems with Data Sets.* Fort Worth, TX: The Dryden Press.

SIMKINS, S., J. BARBOUR, AND A. STULL (1997). *Surfing for Success in Economics: A Student's Guide to the INTERNET.* Upper Saddle River, NJ: Prentice Hall.

# Index

Adaptive expectations model, 322–325
AIC criterion, 318, 338
Akaike's AIC criterion, 318, 338
Almon, Shirley, 314–317
Almon distributed lags, 314–317, 326, 327
Alternative hypothesis, 94, 95
Analysis of variance (ANOVA) table, 113, 154
AR models, 303–333
AR(1) model
   generalized least squares estimation, 244–247
   nonlinear least squares, 303–305
   overview, 241
   prediction, 253, 254
   statistical properties of AR(1) error, 241, 242
Arithmetic lag, 312–314
Assumptions
   multiple regression model, 136, 137
   simple linear regression model, 66
Autocorrelation, 237–259
   AR(1) model, 240–242
   cross-sectional data, and, 237
   detecting, 250–252
   Durbin-Watson test, 250–252
   generalized least squares estimation, 244–250
   least squares estimator, 242–244
   overview of problem, 237–240
   prediction, 253, 254
   time-series data, and, 237
Autocorrelation function, 334
Autoregressive integrated moving-average (ARIMA) models, 337
Autoregressive moving-average (ARMA) models, 335
Autoregressive processes, 330–333. See also AR(1) model
Auxiliary regressions, 173

Behavioral equation, 281
Best linear unbiased estimator (B.L.U.E.), 75, 216

Binary variables, 180
Box-Jenkins approach to model-building, 337

Chi-square distribution, 33, 34
Chow test, 191, 193
Citibase, 350
Cobb-Douglas production function, 299, 301–303
Coefficient of determination, 111–115, 154–156
Cointegration, 340
Collinearity. See Multicollinearity
Condition for identification, 289, 290
Conditional probability density functions, 22, 23
Confidence interval, 88, 104, 146. See also Interval estimation
Consistency, 78
Constant elasticity model, 121
Constant elasticity of substitution (CES) production function, 301–303
Contemporaneous correlation, 266, 338
Continuous random variable, 12
Controlled experiment, 5, 6, 10, 11
Correlation, 27
Correlation analysis, 114, 115
Correlograms, 337
Cost functions, 124, 125
Covariance, 25–27
Cross-sectional data
   autocorrelation, and, 237
   coefficient of determination, 117, 118
   heteroskedasticity, and, 215, 216
   pooling. See Pooling of data

Data. See Economic data, Examples (data)
Degrees of freedom, 33, 34, 113
Demand models, 124. See also Simultaneous equations model
Dependent variable, 48, 50
Dichotomous variables, 180
Dickey-Fuller test, 336

Discrete choice models, 198–205
Discrete random variable, 12
Distributed lag models, 308–329
  adaptive expectations model, 322–325
  finite lag models. *See* Finite distributed
    lag models
  geometric lags, 318–320
  infinite lag models, 309, 318, 325
  Koyck transformation, 320–322
  partial adjustment model, 325, 326
Distributed lag weights, 310, 319
Double summation, 16, 17
Dummy dependent variables, 198–206
Dummy variable model, 269–272
Dummy variables, 12, 180
Durbin-Watson test, 250–252, 321

Econometric model, 45, 48
Econometrics, 6, 60
Economic data
  experimental data, 346, 354, 355
  nonexperimental data. *See*
    Nonexperimental data
  survey data, 347, 351, 353, 355
Economic model, 45
*Economic Report of the President,* 348–350
Elasticities, 58
Endogenous variables, 280
Equation, 14
Equivalence of regression equations,
    190–193
Error components model, 272–274
Error correction model, 340–342
Error variance
  linear regression model, 78–81
  multiple regression model, 140–142
Estimation rules/procedures, 139
Estimators/estimates, distinguished, 56
Exact multicollinearity, 137. *See also*
    Multicollinearity
Examples (data)
  beer demand model, 170
  capital expenditures (manufacturing
    firms), 311
  dummy variable model, 271, 272
  food expenditure/income example, 51
  hamburger chain, 134
  pizza expenditure, 196
  sugar cane example, 238
  transportation example, 204
  truffle supply and demand, 294
  U.S. per capita income/consumption, 182
  wheat-supply model, 223
Exogenous variables, 280, 296

Expected value
  functions of random variables, 18
  least squares estimators, 68–70
  random variable, 17
  weighted sum, 28, 29
Experimental data, 10, 11, 346, 354, 355
Explanatory (x) variables, 129, 131

*F*-distribution, 35, 36
*f*-test, 157–162
Finite distributed lag models
  arithmetic lag, 312–314
  economic model, 309
  empirical illustration, 310–312
  length of lag, 317, 318
  multicollinearity, 310, 312
  polynomial distributed lags, 314–317
  statistical model, 310
First difference, 333, 339
First-order autoregressive model, 241. *See
    also* AR(1) error model
Fisher, Irving, 312
Fitted regression equation, 117
Fitted regression line, 57
Flexible accelerator model, 326
Forecast error, 81
Forecasting. *See* Prediction, Time-series
    analysis
Format for learning, 8
Functional forms, 119–125

Gauss-Markov Theorem, 74–77, 141
General infinite lag model, 318, 327
General linear regression model. *See*
    Multiple regression model
Generalized least squares estimation
  autocorrelation, and, 244–250
  heteroskedasticity, and, 221–225
  seemingly unrelated regressions, 267
Geometric lag, 318–320
Goldfeld-Quandt test, 227–229
Goodness-of-fit
  coefficient of determination, 115,
    154–156
  lag lengths, 317, 318

*h*-statistic, 321
Harvey test, 230
Heteroskedasticity, 47, 199, 213–236
  cross-sectional data, and, 215, 216
  detecting, 226–229
  example (wheat-supply model), 222–225
  general heteroskedastic error model,
    229–231

generalized least squares estimation, 221–225
  Goldfeld-Quandt test, 227–229
  least squares estimator, and, 216–219
  nature of, 213–216
  proportional, 219–222
  residual plots, 226, 227
  time-series data, nad, 216
Homoskedasticity, 47, 136, 215
Hypothesis testing, 88, 93, 94
  alternative hypothesis, 94, 95, 103
  components, 94
  format for testing hypotheses, 97, 98
  interval estimation, and, 103, 104
  more general null hypothesis, 100, 101
  multiple regression models. *See* Hypothesis tests—multiple regression models
  null hypothesis, 94, 100, 102, 103
  one-tailed tests, 101, 102
  *p*-value, 99, 100
  rejection region, 96
  test decision rules, 96, 97
  test statistic, 95
  type I/II errors, 98, 99
Hypothesis tests—multiple regression models, 150
  coefficient of determination, 154–156
  extended model, 163, 164
  *f*-test, 157–162
  goodness of fit, 154–156
  one-tailed testing—single coefficient, 151, 152
  reporting results, 156, 157
  *t*-test, 152–154
  testing economic hypotheses, 165–167
  testing significance of model, 157–162
  testing significance of single coefficient, 152–154

Identity equations, 281
Impact multiplier, 319
Independent random variables, 23–25
Infinite geometric distributed lag model, 319
Infinite lag models, 309, 318, 325
Influence diagram, 281, 288
Inspection techniques, 156, 157
Integrated nonstationary processes, 335, 336
Interaction variables, 180, 183, 193
Intercept dummy variable, 181
Intercept parameter, 45
Interim multiplier, 320

Internet, 351–353
Interval estimation
  multiple regression model, 145, 146
  simple linear regression model, 88–93, 103
Interval prediction, 88, 104–106

Joint hypothesis, 157
Joint probability density functions, 20–22
*Journal of Economic Literature,* 356

Keynesian-Cross model, 279, 280
Koyck transformation, 320–322

Lagged dependent variable, 320
Lagged effects. *See* Distributed lag models
Learning, format for, 8
Least squares estimates, 56
Least squares estimators, 56
  adaptive expectations model, and, 327
  autocorrelation, and, 242–244
  consistency, 78
  estimation of error variance, 78–81, 140, 141
  expected values, 68–70
  Gauss-Markov Theorem, 74–77, 141
  heteroskedasticity, and, 216–219
  Koyck model, and, 320, 321
  partial adjustment model, and, 326
  probability distribution, 77, 78
  random variables, as, 66, 67
  sampling properties, 67–74, 141–145
  simultaneous equations models, and, 283–286
  unbiased estimators, as, 69, 83
Least squares predictor, 81–83
Least squares principle, 52–56. *See also* Least squares estimators
Least squares residuals, 53
Level of significance, 98
Likelihood function, 202
Linear combinations, 74
Linear estimators, 74, 83
Linear in the parameters, 119
Linear-log model, 121
Linear model, 121
Linear probability model, 198–200
Log-inverse model, 121, 122
Log-linear model, 121, 122
Log-log model, 121, 122
Logit model, 205, 206
Long-run multiplier, 320

Macroeconomic model, 279, 280. *See also* Simultaneous equations model

Marginal probability density functions, 22
Mathematical expectation, 17–19
Maximum likelihood estimation procedure, 202
Mean, 17. *See also* Expected value
Minimization problem, 54, 55
Moving-average (MA) processes, 333–335
Multicollinearity, 171–174, 310, 312
Multinomial choice models, 206
Multiple regression model
   assumptions, 136, 137
   collinear economic variables, 171–174
   discrete choice models, 198–205
   dummy dependant variables, 198–206
   dummy variables, 180–188
   economic model, 131–133
   estimating parameters, 137–145
   estimation of error variance, 140, 141
   hypothesis tests. *See* Hypothesis
      tests—multiple regression models
   interactive variables, 193–198
   intercept dummy variables, 180–183
   interval estimation, 145, 146
   least squares estimation procedure, 137–140
   linear probability model, 198–200
   nonsample information, and, 168–171
   polynomial terms, 193–195
   prediction, 174, 175
   probit models, 200–206
   slope dummy variables, 183–185
   statistical model, 133–135
   testing equivalence, 190–193
   testing for qualitative effects, 188–190
Multivariate time-series models, 330

Natural logarithm, 59
95 percent confidence interval, 146
Noise, 6
Nonexperimental data, 11, 346, 347, 355
   collection methods, 347
   electronic media, 350, 351
   flow/stock, 347
   Internet, 351–353
   levels of aggregation, 347
   quantitative/qualitative, 347, 348
   texts, 348–350
Nonlinear in the variables, 120, 123, 125, 320
Nonlinear least squares, 299–307
   AR(1) error model, 303–305
   CES production function, 301–303
   simple nonlinear model, 299–301
Nonlinear least squares estimate, 300

Nonsample information, 168
Nonstationary data series, 335, 339, 340
Normal distribution, 30–33
Normal equations, 55, 138
Null hypothesis, 94

$(1 - \alpha) \times (100\%)$ confidence interval, 91
One-tailed tests, 101
Order of the integrated process, 335
Overall test of model significance, 161, 162, 175

*p*-value, 99, 100
Parameters, 3
Partial adjustment model, 325, 326
Partial autocorrelation function, 331, 332
Passively generated data, 346. *See also* Nonexperimental data
Phillips curve, 125
Phillips-Perron test, 336
Polynomial distributed lags, 314–317
Polynomial terms, 193–195
Pooling of data, 263–278
   dummy variable model, 269–272
   economic model, 263, 264
   error components model, 272–274
   seemingly unrelated regressions, 264–269
Population mean intercept, 273
Prediction, 58
   autocorrelation, 253, 254
   linear statistical model, 81–83
   multiple regression model, 174, 175
Prediction intervals, 104–106
Probability, 10–40
   chi-square distribution, 33, 34
   conditional probability density functions, 22, 23
   controlled experiments, 10, 11
   covariance/correlation, 25–28
   expected values, 15–20
   *f*-distribution, 35, 36
   independent random variables, 23–25
   joint probability density functions, 20–22
   marginal probability density functions, 22
   normal distribution, 30–33
   probability distribution, 13–15
   random variables, 10–12
   *t*-distribution, 34, 35
   uncontrolled experiments, 11
   weighted sums, 28–30
Probability density function, 13
Probability distribution, 13
Probability function, 13
Probit model, 200–206

Production functions, 124. *See also*
    Nonlinear least squares

Qualitative choice models, 206
Qualitative dependent variable, 180
Qualitative effects, 188–190

Random error, 4, 48–51
Random variables, 10, 11
Reciprocal model, 121, 122
Reduced form equations, 282, 283, 293–295
Regression model, 43. *See also* Simple
    linear regression model, Multiple
    regression model
Regression parameters, 45
Rejection region, 96
Repeated sampling, 91
Reporting results
    multiple regression model, 156, 157
    simple linear regression model, 115–119
Research project/report, 346–359
    abstract, 357
    choosing a topic, 356
    economic data.*See* Economic data
    format, 357, 358
Residual plots, 226, 227
*Resources for Economists on the Internet*,
    351–353
RESTRICT statements, 171
Restricted least squares estimates, 150, 169
Restricted sum of squared errors ($SSE_R$),
    158

Sample, 6
Sample correlation coefficient, 114, 115
Sampling precision, 71
Sampling properties, 68
Sampling variance, 71
Sampling variation, 6, 11
SC criterion, 318, 338
Scaling the data, 118, 119
Scatter diagram, 52
Schwarz's SC criterion, 318, 338
Seemingly unrelated regressions (SUR)
    model, 264–269
Simple linear regression model
    assumptions, 66
    econometric model, 46–51
    economic model, 43–46
    estimating parameters, 51–60
    functional forms, 119–125
    inference. *See* Statistical inference
    least squares principle, 52–56
    reporting results (computer output),
        115–119

Simple regression function, 45
Simultaneous equations models, 279–298
    consistent estimation of structural
        parameters, 286, 287
    endogenous variables, 280, 296
    identification problem, 289, 290, 293, 296
    least squares estimation, 283–286
    reduced form equations, 282, 283,
        293–295
    regression model, contrasted, 281
    supply and demand model, 287–292
    two-stage least squares estimation,
        290–296
Slope dummy variable, 183
Slope parameter, 45, 46
Sources of data. *See* Economic data
Spurious regressions, 340, 343
Standard deviation, 20
Standard error, 92
Standard error of the forecast, 82, 105
Standard normal probability density
    function, 32, 33
Standard normal random variable, 31, 32,
    144
Stationary time series, 335
Statistical inference, 7, 87–110
    hypothesis testing. *See* Hypothesis testing
    interval estimation, 88–93
    prediction intervals, 104–106
Statistical model, 4, 46, 66
Structural model, 281
Sufficiently large, 77, 78
Summation, rule of, 15–17
Summing out, 22
Supply models, 124. *See also* Simultaneous
    equations model
Survey data, 347, 351, 353, 355

*t*-distribution, 34, 35
*t*-test, 152–154
Test of significance, 98, 102, 153, 175
Test statistic, 95
Time-series analysis, 330–345
    autoregressive integrated moving-average
        models, 337
    autoregressive moving-average models,
        335
    autoregressive processes, 330–333
    error correction model, 340–342
    integrated nonstationary processes, 335,
        336
    moving-average processes, 333–335
    nonstationary series, 339, 340
    vector autoregressive models, 337–339

Time-series data
  autocorrelation, and, 237
  coefficient of determination, 117, 118
  heteroskedasticity, and, 216
  pooling. *See* Pooling of data
Total variation, 112, 113
Two-stage least squares (2SLS)
  adaptive expectations model, 323, 324
  example (truffles), 293–296
  Kocyk lag, 321, 322
  overview, 290–292
  partial adjustment model, 326
  2SLS estimator, 292
Type I error, 98
Type II error, 98, 99

Unbiased estimator, 69
Uncontrolled experiments, 7, 11, 171

Uniform random variable, 15
Unit root, 336
Unit root tests, 335, 336
Univariate time-series models, 330
Unrestricted sum of squared errors ($SSE_U$), 158

Variance
  least squares estimators, 71–74, 79, 80
  random variable, 19
  weighted sum, 29, 30
Vector autoregressive (VAR) models, 337–339

Weighted least squares estimator, 221
Weighted sums, 28–30
White's estimator, 218, 219

Zero covariance, 27

## Table 3  Right-Tail Critical Values for the F-Distribution

| $\nu_2 \backslash \nu_1$ | 1 | 2 | 3 | 4 | 5 | 6 | 7 | 8 | 9 | 10 | 12 | 15 | 20 | 24 | 30 | 40 | 60 | 120 | $\infty$ |
|---|---|---|---|---|---|---|---|---|---|---|---|---|---|---|---|---|---|---|---|
| | | | | | | | | | Upper 5% Points | | | | | | | | | | |
| 1 | 161.45 | 199.50 | 215.71 | 224.58 | 230.16 | 233.99 | 236.77 | 238.88 | 240.54 | 241.88 | 243.91 | 245.95 | 248.01 | 249.05 | 250.10 | 251.14 | 252.20 | 253.25 | 254.31 |
| 2 | 18.51 | 19.00 | 19.16 | 19.25 | 19.30 | 19.33 | 19.35 | 19.37 | 19.38 | 19.40 | 19.41 | 19.43 | 19.45 | 19.45 | 19.46 | 19.47 | 19.48 | 19.49 | 19.50 |
| 3 | 10.13 | 9.55 | 9.28 | 9.12 | 9.01 | 8.94 | 8.89 | 8.85 | 8.81 | 8.79 | 8.74 | 8.70 | 8.66 | 8.64 | 8.62 | 8.59 | 8.57 | 8.55 | 8.53 |
| 4 | 7.71 | 6.94 | 6.59 | 6.39 | 6.26 | 6.16 | 6.09 | 6.04 | 6.00 | 5.96 | 5.91 | 5.86 | 5.80 | 5.77 | 5.75 | 5.72 | 5.69 | 5.66 | 5.63 |
| 5 | 6.61 | 5.79 | 5.41 | 5.19 | 5.05 | 4.95 | 4.88 | 4.82 | 4.77 | 4.74 | 4.68 | 4.62 | 4.56 | 4.53 | 4.50 | 4.46 | 4.43 | 4.40 | 4.37 |
| 6 | 5.99 | 5.14 | 4.76 | 4.53 | 4.39 | 4.28 | 4.21 | 4.15 | 4.10 | 4.06 | 4.00 | 3.94 | 3.87 | 3.84 | 3.81 | 3.77 | 3.74 | 3.70 | 3.67 |
| 7 | 5.59 | 4.74 | 4.35 | 4.12 | 3.97 | 3.87 | 3.79 | 3.73 | 3.68 | 3.64 | 3.57 | 3.51 | 3.44 | 3.41 | 3.38 | 3.34 | 3.30 | 3.27 | 3.23 |
| 8 | 5.32 | 4.46 | 4.07 | 3.84 | 3.69 | 3.58 | 3.50 | 3.44 | 3.39 | 3.35 | 3.28 | 3.22 | 3.15 | 3.12 | 3.08 | 3.04 | 3.01 | 2.97 | 2.93 |
| 9 | 5.12 | 4.26 | 3.86 | 3.63 | 3.48 | 3.37 | 3.29 | 3.23 | 3.18 | 3.14 | 3.07 | 3.01 | 2.94 | 2.90 | 2.86 | 2.83 | 2.79 | 2.75 | 2.71 |
| 10 | 4.96 | 4.10 | 3.71 | 3.48 | 3.33 | 3.22 | 3.14 | 3.07 | 3.02 | 2.98 | 2.91 | 2.85 | 2.77 | 2.74 | 2.70 | 2.66 | 2.62 | 2.58 | 2.54 |
| 11 | 4.84 | 3.98 | 3.59 | 3.36 | 3.20 | 3.09 | 3.01 | 2.95 | 2.90 | 2.85 | 2.79 | 2.72 | 2.65 | 2.61 | 2.57 | 2.53 | 2.49 | 2.45 | 2.40 |
| 12 | 4.75 | 3.89 | 3.49 | 3.26 | 3.11 | 3.00 | 2.91 | 2.85 | 2.80 | 2.75 | 2.69 | 2.62 | 2.54 | 2.51 | 2.47 | 2.43 | 2.38 | 2.34 | 2.30 |
| 13 | 4.67 | 3.81 | 3.41 | 3.18 | 3.03 | 2.92 | 2.83 | 2.77 | 2.71 | 2.67 | 2.60 | 2.53 | 2.46 | 2.42 | 2.38 | 2.34 | 2.30 | 2.25 | 2.21 |
| 14 | 4.60 | 3.74 | 3.34 | 3.11 | 2.96 | 2.85 | 2.76 | 2.70 | 2.65 | 2.60 | 2.53 | 2.46 | 2.39 | 2.35 | 2.31 | 2.27 | 2.22 | 2.18 | 2.13 |
| 15 | 4.54 | 3.68 | 3.29 | 3.06 | 2.90 | 2.79 | 2.71 | 2.64 | 2.59 | 2.54 | 2.48 | 2.40 | 2.33 | 2.29 | 2.25 | 2.20 | 2.16 | 2.11 | 2.07 |
| 16 | 4.49 | 3.63 | 3.24 | 3.01 | 2.85 | 2.74 | 2.66 | 2.59 | 2.54 | 2.49 | 2.42 | 2.35 | 2.28 | 2.24 | 2.19 | 2.15 | 2.11 | 2.06 | 2.01 |
| 17 | 4.45 | 3.59 | 3.20 | 2.96 | 2.81 | 2.70 | 2.61 | 2.55 | 2.49 | 2.45 | 2.38 | 2.31 | 2.23 | 2.19 | 2.15 | 2.10 | 2.06 | 2.01 | 1.96 |
| 18 | 4.41 | 3.55 | 3.16 | 2.93 | 2.77 | 2.66 | 2.58 | 2.51 | 2.46 | 2.41 | 2.34 | 2.27 | 2.19 | 2.15 | 2.11 | 2.06 | 2.02 | 1.97 | 1.92 |
| 19 | 4.38 | 3.52 | 3.13 | 2.90 | 2.74 | 2.63 | 2.54 | 2.48 | 2.42 | 2.38 | 2.31 | 2.23 | 2.16 | 2.11 | 2.07 | 2.03 | 1.98 | 1.93 | 1.88 |
| 20 | 4.35 | 3.49 | 3.10 | 2.87 | 2.71 | 2.60 | 2.51 | 2.45 | 2.39 | 2.35 | 2.28 | 2.20 | 2.12 | 2.08 | 2.04 | 1.99 | 1.95 | 1.90 | 1.84 |
| 21 | 4.32 | 3.47 | 3.07 | 2.84 | 2.68 | 2.57 | 2.49 | 2.42 | 2.37 | 2.32 | 2.25 | 2.18 | 2.10 | 2.05 | 2.01 | 1.96 | 1.92 | 1.87 | 1.81 |
| 22 | 4.30 | 3.44 | 3.05 | 2.82 | 2.66 | 2.55 | 2.46 | 2.40 | 2.34 | 2.30 | 2.23 | 2.15 | 2.07 | 2.03 | 1.98 | 1.94 | 1.89 | 1.84 | 1.78 |
| 23 | 4.28 | 3.42 | 3.03 | 2.80 | 2.64 | 2.53 | 2.44 | 2.37 | 2.32 | 2.27 | 2.20 | 2.13 | 2.05 | 2.01 | 1.96 | 1.91 | 1.86 | 1.81 | 1.76 |
| 24 | 4.26 | 3.40 | 3.01 | 2.78 | 2.62 | 2.51 | 2.42 | 2.36 | 2.30 | 2.25 | 2.18 | 2.11 | 2.03 | 1.98 | 1.94 | 1.89 | 1.84 | 1.79 | 1.73 |
| 25 | 4.24 | 3.39 | 2.99 | 2.76 | 2.60 | 2.49 | 2.40 | 2.34 | 2.28 | 2.24 | 2.16 | 2.09 | 2.01 | 1.96 | 1.92 | 1.87 | 1.82 | 1.77 | 1.71 |
| 26 | 4.23 | 3.37 | 2.98 | 2.74 | 2.59 | 2.47 | 2.39 | 2.32 | 2.27 | 2.22 | 2.15 | 2.07 | 1.99 | 1.95 | 1.90 | 1.85 | 1.80 | 1.75 | 1.69 |
| 27 | 4.21 | 3.35 | 2.96 | 2.73 | 2.57 | 2.46 | 2.37 | 2.31 | 2.25 | 2.20 | 2.13 | 2.06 | 1.97 | 1.93 | 1.88 | 1.84 | 1.79 | 1.73 | 1.67 |
| 28 | 4.20 | 3.34 | 2.95 | 2.71 | 2.56 | 2.45 | 2.36 | 2.29 | 2.24 | 2.19 | 2.12 | 2.04 | 1.96 | 1.91 | 1.87 | 1.82 | 1.77 | 1.71 | 1.65 |
| 29 | 4.18 | 3.33 | 2.93 | 2.70 | 2.55 | 2.43 | 2.35 | 2.28 | 2.22 | 2.18 | 2.10 | 2.03 | 1.94 | 1.90 | 1.85 | 1.81 | 1.75 | 1.70 | 1.64 |
| 30 | 4.17 | 3.32 | 2.92 | 2.69 | 2.53 | 2.42 | 2.33 | 2.27 | 2.21 | 2.16 | 2.09 | 2.01 | 1.93 | 1.89 | 1.84 | 1.79 | 1.74 | 1.68 | 1.62 |
| 40 | 4.08 | 3.23 | 2.84 | 2.61 | 2.45 | 2.34 | 2.25 | 2.18 | 2.12 | 2.08 | 2.00 | 1.92 | 1.84 | 1.79 | 1.74 | 1.69 | 1.64 | 1.58 | 1.51 |
| 60 | 4.00 | 3.15 | 2.76 | 2.53 | 2.37 | 2.25 | 2.17 | 2.10 | 2.04 | 1.99 | 1.92 | 1.84 | 1.75 | 1.70 | 1.65 | 1.59 | 1.53 | 1.47 | 1.39 |
| 120 | 3.92 | 3.07 | 2.68 | 2.45 | 2.29 | 2.18 | 2.09 | 2.02 | 1.96 | 1.91 | 1.83 | 1.75 | 1.66 | 1.61 | 1.55 | 1.50 | 1.43 | 1.35 | 1.25 |
| $\infty$ | 3.84 | 3.00 | 2.60 | 2.37 | 2.21 | 2.10 | 2.01 | 1.94 | 1.88 | 1.83 | 1.75 | 1.67 | 1.57 | 1.52 | 1.46 | 1.39 | 1.32 | 1.22 | 1.00 |

Source: This table was generated using the SAS® function FINV. $\nu_1$ = numerator degrees of freedom; $\nu_2$ = denominator degrees of freedom